OXFORD IB DIPLOMA PROGRAMME

HISTORY OF THE AMERICAS 1880–1981

COURSE COMPANION

Alexis Mamaux
David M. Smith
Mark Rogers

Yvonne Berliner
Shannon Leggett
Matt Borgmann

OXFORD
UNIVERSITY PRESS

OXFORD
UNIVERSITY PRESS

Great Clarendon Street, Oxford, OX2 6DP, United Kingdom

Oxford University Press is a department of the University of Oxford. It furthers the University's objective of excellence in research, scholarship, and education by publishing worldwide. Oxford is a registered trade mark of Oxford University Press in the UK and in certain other countries

© Oxford University Press 2015

The moral rights of the authors have been asserted

First published in 2015

British Library Cataloguing in Publication Data
Data available

978-0-19-831023-5

1 3 5 7 9 10 8 6 4 2

Paper used in the production of this book is a natural, recyclable product made from wood grown in sustainable forests.
The manufacturing process conforms to the environmental regulations of the country of origin.

Printed in the UK by Bell and Bain Ltd, Glasgow

Acknowledgements

The publishers would like to thank the following for permissions to use their photographs:

p11: World History Archive/Alamy; **p13:** Archive Pics/Alamy; **p16(T):** Corbis; **p16(B):** Archive Image/Alamy; **p21:** ClassicStock/Alamy; **p22:** Glasshouse Images/Alamy; **p25(L):** Fotosearch/Getty Images; **p25(R):** Corbis; **p28:** PF-(bygone1)/Alamy; **p31:** GL Archive/Alamy; **p33:** Niday Picture Library/Alamy; **p35:** Heritage Image Partnership Ltd/Alamy; **p38:** SOTK2011/Alamy; **p48:** INTERFOTO/Alamy; **p49:** The Art Archive/Alamy; **p57:** Robert Hunt Collection/Mary Evans; **p72:** DeAgostini/Getty Images; **p75:** Private Collection/The Stapleton Collection/Bridgeman Images; **p78:** Prisma Archivo/Alamy; **p79:** Historic Collection/Alamy; **p80:** Pictorial Press Ltd/Alamy; **p81(T):** Underwood & Underwood/Corbis; **p81(B):** Pharcide/Mary Evans; **p82:** Private Collection/The Stapleton Collection/Bridgeman Images; **p83:** Corbis; **p84:** Underwood & Underwood/Corbis; **p87:** Private Collection/Peter Newark American Pictures/Bridgeman Images; **p93:** Private Collection/The Stapleton Collection/Bridgeman Images; **p97(T):** World History Archive/Alamy; **p97(B):** World History Archive/Alamy; **p98:** Keystone-France/Gamma-Keystone via Getty Images; **p107:** Keystone-France/Gamma-Keystone via Getty Images; **p109:** Private Collection/Peter Newark American Pictures/Bridgeman Images; **p112:** Maurizio Biso/Shutterstock; **p113(T):** Orozco, Jose Clemente (1883-1949)/Private Collection/Index/Bridgeman Images; **p113(B):** EDU Vision/Alamy; **p122:** Sean Sprague/Alamy; **p126:** Lordprice Collection/Alamy; **p130:** The Art Archive/Alamy; **p131:** The Art Archive/Alamy; **p133:** Bettmann/Corbis; **p134:** Bryan Mullennix/Tetra Images/Corbis; **p138:** Corbis; **p141:** Corbis; **p145:** Fotosearch/Getty Images; **p152:** Arch Dale/Winnipeg Free Press; **p156:** Glenbow Archives/M-1753-4; **p161(L):** Regina Public Library; **p161(R):** Regina Public Library; **p164:** The Print Collector/Alamy; **p168:** Bettmann/Corbis; **p170:** Keystone-France/Gamma-Keystone/Getty Images; **p175:** John Phillips/The LIFE Picture Collection/Getty Images; **p176:** Gonzalo Azumendi/Getty Images; **p180:** Archive Holdings Inc./Alamy; **p181:** Photo Inc/Getty Images; **p183(L):** Andre Jenny/Alamy; **p183(R):** Efrain Padro/Alamy; **p192:** Underwood & Underwood/Corbis; **p197:** Hulton-Deutsch Collection/Corbis; **p207(R):** The Art Archive/Alamy; **p210:** Bettmann/Corbis; **p212:** Jacobs, Leonebel/Library of Congress; **p214(T):** David Pollack/Corbis; **p214(B):** Bettmann/Corbis; **p217:** Corbis; **p218:** Bettmann/Corbis; **p229:** Library and Archives Canada; **p219(T):** Marie Hansen/Time Life Pictures/Getty Images; **p219(B):** Everett Collection/REX; **p226:** Jack Long/National Film Board of Canada/Photothèque/Library and Archives Canada; **p231:** Corbis; **p233(T):** Louie Psihoyos/Corbis; **p233(B):** Museum of Flight/Corbis; **p239:** Bettmann/Corbis; **p245:** Corbis; **p247:** RIA Novosti/Alamy; **p248:** Gerard SIOEN/Gamma-Rapho/Getty Images; **p249:** F1online digitale Bildagentur GmbH/Alamy; **p250:** STF/AFP/Getty Images; **p251:** RIA Novosti; **p255:** Associated Newspapers Ltd/Solo Syndication/British Cartoon Archive; **p256:** AFP/Getty Images; **p258:** Bettmann/Corbis; **p262:** Wikipedia/Argentina Railways; **p264:** Popperfoto/Getty Images; **p266:** Charles Allmon/National Geographic/Getty Images; **p273(R):** STF/AFP/Getty Images; **p273(L):** AFP/Getty Images; **p275:** El Mercurio newspaper; **p276(T):** Horacio Villalobos/Corbis; **p276(B):** Horacio Villalobos/Corbis; **p277:** National Historical Museum; **p278:** Rodrigo Arangua/AFP/Getty Images; **p280:** epa european pressphoto agency b.v/Alamy; **p286:** Bernard Bisson/Sygma/Corbis; **p295:** Corbis; **p299:** Found Image Press/Corbis; **p304:** Corbis; **p305:** Estate of Stanley Tretick LLC/Corbis; **p307:** Underwood & Underwood/Corbis; **p311(T):** Bettmann/Corbis; **p311(B):** Bettmann/Corbis; **p319:** Bettmann/Corbis; **p326:** Owen Franken/Corbis; **p329:** Bettmann/Corbis; **p334:** Wayne State University; **p337:** The Carter Center; **p344:** Design Pics Inc/Alamy; **p346:** Keystone Pictures USA/Alamy; **p353:** Glenbow Archives/M-8000-591; **p355:** Simon Fraser University; **p365:** William J. Smith/AP Images; **p369(R):** AFP/Getty Images; **p369(L):** The Kobal Collection; **p371:** Getty Images; **p383(TL):** Hulton-Deutsch Collection/Corbis; **p383(TR):** Corbis; **p383(B):** Corbis; **p390(R):** Paul Schutzer/The LIFE Picture Collection/Getty Images; **p390(L):** Frank Scherschel/The LIFE Picture Collection/Getty Images; **p390(C):** Bettmann/Corbis; **p394:** DOD/AP Images; **p395:** Bettmann/Corbis; **p397:** CBS Photo Archive/Getty Images; **p398:** John Filo/Getty Images; **p400:** Torstar Syndication Services; **p401:** Bettmann/Corbis; **p406(L):** Bettmann/Corbis; **p406(R):** Beth Wald/Getty Images; **p409:** Owen Franken/Corbis; **p411(T):** Jon Hicks/Corbis; **p411(B):** Bettmann/Corbis; **p416(L):** Bettmann/Corbis; **p416(R):** Bettmann/Corbis; **p418:** Bettmann/

Corbis; **p434:** Everett Collection Inc/Alamy; **p438:** Marcel Montoya/Cultural Foundation Jorge González Camarena; **p440:** Martin Alipaz/EPA; **p444:** Everett Collection Inc/Alamy; **p446:** Reprinted by arrangement with The Heirs to the Estate of Martin Luther King Jr., c/o Writers House as agent for the proprietor New York, NY.; **p447:** Everett Collection Inc/Alamy; **p448:** Everett Collection Inc/Alamy; **p450:** Everett Collection Inc/Alamy; **p455:** Everett Collection Inc/Alamy; **p457:** Everett Collection Inc/Alamy; **p459:** Everett Collection Inc/Alamy; **p462(T):** Everett Collection/Superstock; **p462(B):** Everett Collection/Superstock; **p465:** Everett Collection Inc/Alamy; **p471:** JP Laffont/Sygma/Corbis; Case Study_CH08_p3: Frank Fife/AFP/Getty Images; **p477:** Bettmann/Corbis; **p484:** Everett Collection Inc/Alamy; **p485:** Don Kechely/ UC Berkeley/University Archives; **p487:** INTERFOTO/Alamy; **p489:** Dick Darrell/GetStock; **p493:** Bettmann/Corbis; **p494:** Michael Nicholson/Corbis.

Cover illustration by Karolis Strautniekas, Folio Illustration Agency.

Artwork by QBS Learning and OUP.

The authors and publisher are grateful for permission to reprint the following copyright material:

From "A Declaration of First Nations" (as posted at http://www.afn.ca/index.php/en/about-afn/a-declaration-of-first-nations). Reprinted with permission of the Assembly of First Nations.

From a document issued by Social Credit League of Alberta in 1935. Reprinted with permission of the Social Credit Party of Alberta.

From http://articles.baltimoresun.com/2000-12-19/news/0012190382_1_electoral-college-democratic-electors-popular-vote. Republished with permission from The Baltimore Sun. All rights reserved.

Bill Albert and Paul Henderson: *South America and the First World War: The Impact of the War on Brazil, Argentina, Peru and Chile* 1988. Reprinted with permission of Cambridge University Press.

Jonathan Bernstein: 'Nixon's smoking-gun tape and the presidency', June 22, 2012, The Washington Post. Reprinted by permission of PARS International Corp on behalf of The Washington Post.

Adam Fairclough: 'Historians and the Civil Rights Movement', *Journal of American Studies*, Volume 24 No. 3 (1990). Reprinted by permission of Cambridge University Press on behalf of the British Association for American Studies.

J F Kennedy: Remarks upon signing the Housing Act, 30 June 1961 from The American Presidency Project on http://www.presidency.ucsb.edu/ws/?pid=8216. Reproduced by permission.

Extract from the International Labour Organization (ILO) UN Convention 169, ILO Publications. Reprinted with permission of ILO Publications.

Philip A Klinker with Rogers M Smith. *The Unsteady March: The Rise and Decline of Racial Equality in America* (1999). Chicago, IL, USA. The University of Chicago Press Ltd., London © 1999 by The University of Chicago. All rights reserved. Reprinted with permission.

Steven F Lawson and Charles Payne: *Debating the Civil Rights Movement, 1945-1968* (*Debating Twentieth-Century America*), 2nd revised edition, 14 March 2006, Rowman and Littlefield Publishers. Reprinted with permission.

Roberta Lexier: "The Backdrop Against Which Everything Happened": English-Canadian Student Movements and Off-Campus Movements for Change," in *History of Intellectual Culture*, 2007, Volume 7, No. 1. Reproduced by permission of Professor Paul Stortz, University of Calgary.

Martin Luther King, Jr: 'I Have a Dream' (March on Washington 28 August 1963). Reprinted by arrangement with The Heirs to the Estate of Martin Luther King, Jr., c/o Writer's House as agent for the proprietor New York, NY © 1963 Dr. Martin Luther King, Jr., © renewed 1991 Coretta Scott King.

Martin Luther King, Jr: speech made 5 December 1955. Reprinted by arrangement with The Heirs to the Estate of Martin Luther King, Jr., c/o Writer's House as agent for the proprietor New York, NY © 1955 Dr Martin Luther King, Jr., © renewed 1983 Coretta Scott King.

Martin Luther King, Jr: Letter from Birmingham Jail dated 16 April 1963. Reprinted by arrangement with The Heirs to the Estate of Martin Luther King Jr., c/o Writer's House as agent for the proprietor New York, NY © 1963 Dr. Martin Luther King, Jr., © renewed 1991 Coretta Scott King.

Nancy Mitchell: The DANGER OF DREAMS: GERMAN AND AMERICAN IMPERIALISM IN LATIN AMERICA. Copyright © 1999 by the University of North Carolina Press. Used by permission of the publisher. www.uncpress.unc.edu.

Chester J Pach, Jr: "Dwight Eisenhower: Domestic Affairs," on American President. Charlottesville, Virginia: Miller Center at the University of Virginia, 2014. Reprinted with permission.

Excerpt from the 'Manifesto of the Front de liberation du Québec', 1970 from http://faculty.marianopolis.edu/c.Belanger/quebechistory/docs/october/manifest.htm

Table with dates of women's suffrage http://faculty.chass.ncsu.edu/slatta/hi216/documents/suff.pdf. Reprinted by permission of Professor Richard W. Slatta from North Carolina State University.

Chart showing the percentage of indigenous populations in 11 Latin American countries from http://celade.cepal.org/redatam/PRYESP/SISPPI/ Accessed 12 August 2014. Reprinted by permission of Fabiana Delpopolo.

John Saywell: *Quebec 70 A Documentary Narrative*, University of Toronto Press. (Originally published in the 'Canadian Annual Review', 1970). Reproduced by permission of CBC, Canada.

John Womack Jr: Extract from *Zapta and the Mexican Revolution* copyright © 1968 by John Womack Jr. Used by permission of alfred A. Knopf, an imprint of the Knopf Doubeday Publishing Group, a division of Penguin Random House LLC. All rights reserved.

Course Companion definition

The IB Diploma Programme Course Companions are resource materials designed to support students throughout their two-year Diploma Programme course of study in a particular subject. They will help students gain an understanding of what is expected from the study of an IB Diploma Programme subject while presenting content in a way that illustrates the purpose and aims of the IB. They reflect the philosophy and approach of the IB and encourage a deep understanding of each subject by making connections to wider issues and providing opportunities for critical thinking.

The books mirror the IB philosophy of viewing the curriculum in terms of a whole-course approach; the use of a wide range of resources, international mindedness, the IB learner profile and the IB Diploma Programme core requirements, theory of knowledge, the extended essay, and creativity, activity, service (CAS).

Each book can be used in conjunction with other materials and indeed, students of the IB are required and encouraged to draw conclusions from a variety of resources. Suggestions for additional and further reading are given in each book and suggestions for how to extend research are provided.

In addition, the Course Companions provide advice and guidance on the specific course assessment requirements and on academic honesty protocol. They are distinctive and authoritative without being prescriptive.

IB mission statement

The International Baccalaureate aims to develop inquiring, knowledgable and caring young people who help to create a better and more peaceful world through intercultural understanding and respect.

To this end the IB works with schools, governments and international organizations to develop challenging programmes of international education and rigorous assessment.

These programmes encourage students across the world to become active, compassionate, and lifelong learners who understand that other people, with their differences, can also be right.

The IB learner Profile

The aim of all IB programmes is to develop internationally minded people who, recognizing their common humanity and shared guardianship of the planet, help to create a better and more peaceful world. IB learners strive to be:

Inquirers They develop their natural curiosity. They acquire the skills necessary to conduct inquiry and research and show independence in learning. They actively enjoy learning and this love of learning will be sustained throughout their lives.

Knowledgable They explore concepts, ideas, and issues that have local and global significance. In so doing, they acquire in-depth knowledge and develop understanding across a broad and balanced range of disciplines.

Thinkers They exercise initiative in applying thinking skills critically and creatively to recognize and approach complex problems, and make reasoned, ethical decisions.

Communicators They understand and express ideas and information confidently and creatively in more than one language and in a variety of modes of communication. They work effectively and willingly in collaboration with others.

Principled They act with integrity and honesty, with a strong sense of fairness, justice, and respect for the dignity of the individual, groups, and communities. They take responsibility for their own actions and the consequences that accompany them.

Open-minded They understand and appreciate their own cultures and personal histories, and are open to the perspectives, values, and traditions of other individuals and communities. They are accustomed to seeking and evaluating a range of points of view, and are willing to grow from the experience.

Caring They show empathy, compassion, and respect towards the needs and feelings of others. They have a personal commitment to service, and act to make a positive difference to the lives of others and to the environment.

Risk-takers They approach unfamiliar situations and uncertainty with courage and forethought, and have the independence of spirit to explore new roles, ideas, and strategies. They are brave and articulate in defending their beliefs.

Balanced They understand the importance of intellectual, physical, and emotional balance to achieve personal well-being for themselves and others.

Reflective They give thoughtful consideration to their own learning and experience. They are able to assess and understand their strengths and limitations in order to support their learning and personal development.

A note on academic honesty

It is of vital importance to acknowledge and appropriately credit the owners of information when that information is used in your work. After all, owners of ideas (intellectual property) have property rights. To have an authentic piece of work, it must be based on your individual and original ideas with the work of others fully acknowledged. Therefore, all assignments, written or oral, completed for assessment must use your own language and expression. Where sources are used or referred to, whether in the form of direct quotation or paraphrase, such sources must be appropriately acknowledged.

How do I acknowledge the work of others?

The way that you acknowledge that you have used the ideas of other people is through the use of footnotes and bibliographies.

Footnotes (placed at the bottom of a page) or endnotes (placed at the end of a document) are to be provided when you quote or paraphrase from another document, or closely summarize the information provided in another document. You do not need to provide a footnote for information that is part of a 'body of knowledge'. That is, definitions do not need to be footnoted as they are part of the assumed knowledge.

Bibliographies should include a formal list of the resources that you used in your work. The listing should include all resources, including books, magazines, newspaper articles, Internet-based resources, CDs and works of art. 'Formal' means that you should use one of the several accepted forms of presentation. You must provide full information as to how a reader or viewer of your work can find the same information. A bibliography is compulsory in the extended essay.

What constitutes misconduct?

Misconduct is behaviour that results in, or may result in, you or any student gaining an unfair advantage in one or more assessment component. Misconduct includes plagiarism and collusion.

Plagiarism is defined as the representation of the ideas or work of another person as your own. The following are some of the ways to avoid plagiarism:

- Words and ideas of another person used to support one's arguments must be acknowledged.

- Passages that are quoted verbatim must be enclosed within quotation marks and acknowledged.

- CD-ROMs, email messages, web sites on the Internet, and any other electronic media must be treated in the same way as books and journals.

- The sources of all photographs, maps, illustrations, computer programs, data, graphs, audio-visual, and similar material must be acknowledged if they are not your own work.

- Works of art, whether music, film, dance, theatre arts, or visual arts, and where the creative use of a part of a work takes place, must be acknowledged.

Collusion is defined as supporting misconduct by another student. This includes:

- allowing your work to be copied or submitted for assessment by another student

- duplicating work for different assessment components and/or diploma requirements.

Other forms of misconduct include any action that gives you an unfair advantage or affects the results of another student. Examples include, taking unauthorized material into an examination room, misconduct during an examination, and falsifying a CAS record.

Contents

For additional resources related to this title, please visit
www.oxfordsecondary.com/ibhistory-resources.

Coverage of the IB History HL exam

All of the HL options have 18 sections. Chronologically, all options run from 750 to 2005 AD. This is a very long time span and it would be difficult to cover all the material in sufficient depth for the content-based study that is expected. While your teacher might cover a lot of the material from the *History of the Americas* option it is important to know precisely what you need to know to be prepared for the exam and fulfill the course requirements. This book covers 8 of the 18 sections, focusing on the time period 1880–1981, but for complete preparation you must study **THREE** sections in their entirety.

If you examine the course outline for the Americas option in the History guide, you will see that each section has bulleted information that you are required to know. All of the examination questions will come from these bullet points, and the material is, to a large extent, prescriptive.

In certain cases, you will be able to choose a particular country as a case study, but you still must cover all of the information in the bullet points. For example, in Topic 12: Great Depression and the Americas, you must choose one country in Latin America and study the impact of the Great Depression of that country. You may select any Latin American country but you still must cover the information in that bullet point, "political instability and challenges to democracy; economic and social challenges".

Preparing for the IB History HL exam

In many schools the HL option is taught in the first year of the IB program so be sure to give yourself enough time to review material you haven't considered in nearly a year. If your school gives you the opportunity to take mock exams, use those as a benchmark so that you know what you understand well, and where you need to go back and review material. This textbook will provide you with details directly linked to the bullet points in each section so be sure to go back to the chapters that cover the sections you will be preparing for the exam.

As you work through the book make sure you develop strategies to help you learn and retain the information and understanding you have acquired. These may include timelines (chronology is important), spider diagrams, cue cards or whatever method suits your individual learning style. It is better to consolidate knowledge and understanding as you go along as this will make revision for the examination easier.

The structure of the Paper 3 History of the Americas exam

Beginning in May 2017 the Paper 3 exam will have 36 questions: two questions from each of the 18 sections. You may answer *any three* of these questions – two may come from one section or each could come from a different section.

This exam is specific to History of the Americas. Knowledge of other regions is only relevant where it applies to its relationship to countries in the Americas.

<u>Example</u>

Section 13: The Second World War in the Americas, 1933–1945

Examine the participation of two countries in the Americas in the Second World War.

In this question you could discuss particular battles in Italy as they relate to Brazilian, Canadian or US participation, but you could not use Italy's participation in the war as an example.

The content needed for appropriate responses comes directly from the bullet points in each section, so if you have detailed knowledge of all the bullet points you will be able to answer both questions from that section. In some instances you will be able to choose which country you use in your response, but in other instances, the country will be prescribed.

<u>Example</u>

Section 14: Political developments in Latin America, 1945–1980

Discuss the political, economic and social causes of the Cuban revolution.

Examine the reasons for the rise of a military dictatorship in one country in the Americas between 1945 and 1980.

Preparing for Paper 3 essay questions

1. Make sure you understand what the **command** terms used in essay questions are asking you to do and learn how to 'unpack' an essay question. The Skills Section at the end of Chapter 1 provides you with advice on how to do this.

   Understanding the focus of a question is vital as this is one of the skills and examiner looks for. There are usually two or three **focus words** in a question. The focus words are identified in italics in the examples below:

   <u>Example</u>

   Examine the *causes* of *the Quiet Revolution* in Quebec in the 1960s

   This question is asking you to explain why there was a period of vast social change in the Canadian province of Quebec. The question also explicitly provides the time-frame parameters. You will need to keep the essay in this frame (1960–70).

2. Provide a clear, well-structured essay

   Effective essays generally consist of three elements

   - **Introduction**
     A paragraph that demonstrates that you understand the **focus** of the question. It could contain an outline of the factors that need to be considered before and answer can be reached. It may also contain an indication of your line of argument or thesis in response to the question.

   - **Main body**
     Several paragraphs that focus on one of the factors outlines in your introduction. These paragraphs should be a combination of specific knowledge relevant to the question and analytical comment on that knowledge which links to the focus of the question.

   - **Conclusion**
     This should be clearly linked to the focus of the question, and summarize your line of argument with reference to each of the key factors considered in the main body of the essay.

These sections are covered in detail in Chapters 2, 5 and 8. Even if you haven't studied these sections, the skills sections provide you with advice and examples.

3. **Familiarize yourself with the grading rubric**

   All IB history essays are marked on a 15-point scale which rewards you in a holistic manner. This means that essays are graded in its entirety, not in parts, and it is up to the examiner to determine which markband is the best fit. Examiners are instructed to mark your work positively, so they will reward you for what you have included and done well – not what you have left out. In History there are an infinite number of approaches to any given question, so it would be impossible for you to cover every possible view. However, you should be as thorough, detailed and analytical as you can manage in the time constraints.

For more information on markbands and their analysis, please visit www.oxfordsecondary.com/ib-history-resources.

Managing your time

A wise teacher tells her students to consider each of the examinations as a race in which Paper 1 is a sprint, Paper 2 is a 10K and Paper 3 is a marathon. If you start off too quickly in Paper 3 you could burn out early and push to finish as quickly as possible rather than using all the time allocated to you to write the best answers that you are capable of.

You have 2.5 hours to write three essays, which equates to 50 minutes per essay. Even though you may be in a hurry to write as much as possible, that is not necessarily the best strategy. There are certain key ways in which slowing down can be very helpful:

- Slow down so that your writing is legible. While examiners will do their best to read what you wrote, if it cannot be read then it might as well not be there.

- Rather than starting essays immediately when you are allowed to begin writing, take the time to develop a plan to structure your essay.

- Listing facts and dates that you are worried you might forget can also be useful, as can writing down different historical perspectives. However, do not feel the need to use every piece of evidence you write down.

- If your mind starts to wander, it might be worth it to take a brief mental break before you keep going.

- Reviewing your essays once you have completed them is also very helpful. If you have finished your essays and have some time left, reading through your work gives you one last opportunity to add material that you forgot or delete irrelevancies.

Final thoughts

With the IB, you are not competing against other students, so work together. Develop a wiki or a document that everyone in your class can view, augment and discuss. Social media can be used in this circumstance.

IB History HL is a journey that lasts nearly two years; be sure to enjoy it!

1 THE EMERGENCE OF THE AMERICAS IN GLOBAL AFFAIRS, 1880–1929

Global context

The last decades of the 19th century were a period of national consolidation, modernization, expansion and national awaking for states around the world. The political reality of Europe, along with its map, had been radically altered after a long period of relative stability following the Napoleonic Wars. New entities such as the German Empire and the nation state of Italy now existed. In the wake of these new creations, France had suffered its fourth revolution in a century, resulting in yet another French republic. Industrialization was sweeping the European continent, leaving some countries behind while catapulting others into wealth and modernity. These new circumstances would start a period of growing competition between European powers – competition for resources, colonies, influence and wealth.

This same period found China fighting a rearguard action against Western domination. Russia gnawed away at its northern frontiers, France fought for concessions in Indochina and Britain continued to gain influence in the interior. The Imperial Chinese government responded with half-hearted reform, while the Chinese street would eventually respond with violence during the Boxer Rebellion. Such imperial expansion was gaining in both breadth and depth throughout other parts of Asia, as were nationalist responses. The Indian National Congress was founded in 1885, eight years after Queen Victoria added Empress of India to her list of titles.

In the Americas, Canada too was consolidating after the confederation project of 1867. Between 1870 and 1905, Canada would add five new provinces and two territories, stretching this new dominion from sea to sea. A transcontinental railway project stood as an important engineering and economic feat, tying the immense new country together. Meanwhile in the south, the last decades of the 19th century were years of war, modernization and economic expansion for the countries of Latin America. Paraguay went to war against Argentina, Bolivia and Uruguay, while coups and civil wars wracked other Latin American countries. Later, the War of the Pacific would pit Chile against Bolivia and Peru, while slavery was being swept from the continent and Brazil inaugurated a long period of democratically elected governments.

Timeline

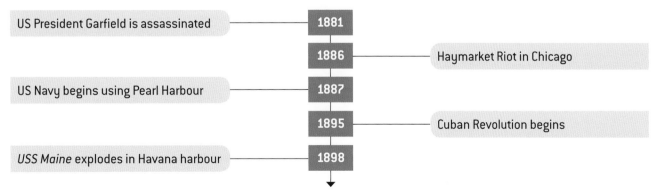

US President Garfield is assassinated	1881	
	1886	Haymarket Riot in Chicago
US Navy begins using Pearl Harbour	1887	
	1895	Cuban Revolution begins
USS Maine explodes in Havana harbour	1898	

	1899 Spanish–American War starts
1899 Treaty of Paris ending the Spanish Civil War ratified by US Congress	
	1901 US President McKinley assassinated
1904 US construction of the Panama Canal begins	
	1904 Roosevelt Corollary used in Santo Domingo
1914 Canada is at war with Germany by virtue of Great Britain's declaration of war	
	1914 The Panama Canal opens
1914 US Navy occupies Veracruz	
	1915 US President Wilson orders US forces into the Dominican Republic
1915 *Lusitania* sunk by German U-Boat	
	1915 Canadian Expeditionary Force arrives in France
1915 Canadian troops gassed at the Second Battle of Ypres	
	1917 Zimmerman Telegraph
1917 Canadian troops win Battle of Vimy Ridge	
	1917 United States declares war on Germany
1917 Canadians participate in Battle of Passchendaele	
	1917 Military Service Act establishes conscription in Canada
1917 Wartime Elections Act grants the vote to women relatives of soldiers in Canada	
	1917 Brazil declares war on Germany
1918 Nicaragua declares war on Germany	
	1918 Guatemala declares war on Germany
1919 Red Scare in United States	
	1919 "Tragic Week" in Argentina
1919 Winnipeg General Strike	
	1920 US Congress votes against ratification of the Treaty of Versailles

3

Conceptual understanding

Key questions

→ Why did the USA embark on a period of territorial expansion in the years 1880–1900?

→ To what extent was this expansion consistent with prior US foreign policy?

→ To what extent was there domestic opposition to this expansion?

Key concepts

→ Change

→ Continuity

→ Causation

Background

The most deadly war in US history came to an end in the spring of 1865. By the time General Robert Lee had surrendered the Army of Northern Virginia to General Grant at Appattomax and the remaining Confederate armies had laid down their arms, over 620 000 Americans had died. What lay ahead was the difficult process of reconstruction, deciding how to bring the secessionist southern states back into the union in a meaningful and productive way. At the same time, the northern economy had to adjust to a decline in industrial demand that would accompany the peace. Banking, railways and other industrial interests had all expanded during the war. In an effort to maintain this growth, government land grants, subsidies and loans flowed to the private sector, most notably to the railway industry. When Ulysses S Grant took office as the 18th President of the United States in 1869, he brought with him an aggressive period of reconstruction that would sweep over the south and last into the 1870s. Industrial interests became political interests, and accusations of political corruption were common.

The 1870s, however, were also a period of economic dislocation and depression. The rapid industrial expansion of the war years and the early reconstruction period had caused an expansion of the money supply, inducing the Grant administration into a restrictive **monetary policy** as a countermeasure. When Jay Cooke & Company, an important Philadelphia banking firm, collapsed in September 1873, the subsequent panic led to a cascade of bank failures, plunging the USA into what became known as the Long Depression. Grant's monetary policy exacerbated matters, restricting access to capital that could stimulate the stagnating economy. Unemployment and low wages spread across the country, and with it labour strife, culminating in the Great Railway Strikes of 1877 that further paralyzed US commerce, revealing deep class divisions in American society.

monetary policy
Government policy that controls the supply of money in the economy.

In 1879 the USA emerged from the Long Depression into yet another period of rapid and immense economic expansion. As capital became more available, industrial enterprises consumed natural and human resources with a voracious appetite. A new wave of immigration brought labour from southern Europe and Asia to feed this appetite. New supplies of coal, iron and oil were discovered and exploited. Electricity powered more and more of the country. The efficiency of agriculture, mining, textile manufacture and steel production dramatically improved, creating new wealth across the country. **Infrastructure** networks multiplied throughout the land, led by another wave of railway construction, moving raw materials, finished goods and even consumers across all regions of the USA. New business models and financial vehicles accelerated the already dizzying pace of expansion. Terms such as **horizontal and vertical integration** began to appear, and monopolies, trusts and corporations became powerful archetypes of business organization. Money, legislation and land from state and federal governments lubricated the entire process and iconic businessmen such as Rockefeller, Morgan, Carnegie and Mellon arose as commanding figures in American society.

Some dislocation must necessarily accompany such expansion. Rapid urbanization created poor living conditions in areas of many US, Canadian and Latin American cities. Workers toiled under poor working conditions, long hours, low wages and no job security. In response, workers began to organize into unions large and small, local and national. With this organization came conflict with those whose profits depended on the status quo. Strikes, demonstrations and riots dotted this period in all major industries from mining to railways to the steel industry. New political alternatives such as socialism, Marxism and anarchism surfaced in response to worker exploitation.

It is against this backdrop of rapid economic and social change that the USA embarked on an increasingly expansionist foreign policy both within the Americas and around the world. This expansion corresponds to a period when all countries of the region emerged onto the international stage. Although it coincided with another wave of European imperialism and shared many motives and elements with it, it was also distinct in its manifestation. It is to this expansion that we now turn.

Ideological reasons for expansion

Monroe Doctrine

By the 1820s, the Spanish and Portuguese empires in the Americas had been replaced by nascent and largely unstable independent states, the legitimacy of which the USA unilaterally recognized in 1822. The **Monroe Doctrine**, however, was as much a product of the situation in Europe as it was of the situation in Latin America. In the years following the Congress of Vienna, which rebuilt Europe in the wake of the Napoleonic Wars, Russia emerged as a dominant continental force, a European power with definite interests on the North American continent. Ideologically, much of the system set up at Vienna and after was designed to disempower nationalist independence movements of the very kind that had been recently triumphant in Latin America. In such a context, it was easy to conceive of situations in which European powers might feel the need to intervene in the western hemisphere.

---

infrastructure
Elements of the economy that assist in the production and distribution of raw materials, goods and labour. Infrastructure generally includes railroads, telegraphs, roadways, ports and canals.

horizontal integration
Exists when a single company owns or controls a number of firms in the same stage of the production process.

vertical integration
Exists when a number of steps in the production of a single product are owned or controlled by a single company.

Monroe Doctrine
The doctrine stated that the United States would view any attempt by European countries to interfere in the political affairs of Western Hemisphere countries as an act of aggression justifying an US response.

Presidents of the USA, 1880–1929		
President	**Political Party**	**Years**
Rutherford B Hayes	Republican	1877–81
James Garfield	Republican	1881
Chester Arthur	Republican	1881–85
Grover Cleveland	Democratic	1885–89
Benjamin Harrison	Republican	1889–93
Grover Cleveland	Democratic	1893–97
William McKinley	Republican	1897–1901
Theodore Roosevelt	Republican	1901–09
William Taft	Republican	1909–13
Woodrow Wilson	Democratic	1913–21
Warren Harding	Republican	1921–23
Calvin Coolidge	Republican	1923–29
Herbert Hoover	Republican	1929–33

With this in mind, President Monroe (1817–25), with his Secretary of State, John Quincy Adams sent a note to Congress outlining what would later become known as the Monroe Doctrine. This doctrine would raise its head throughout the rest of the century, in Mexico, Venezuela and Cuba. Early in the 20th century, President Theodore Roosevelt would expand on the doctrine with what became known as the Roosevelt Corollary, with which he added to the essentially defensive nature of Monroe's original idea the view that the USA had the right to intervene to manage independent states in the western hemisphere.

Manifest Destiny in the post-reconstruction period

First coined in the 1840s as a justification for the **annexation** of Texas, 'Manifest Destiny' came to mean different things to different people throughout the rest of the 19th century. At its simplest it was the belief that it was the inevitable mission of the USA to expand beyond its 1840s boundaries and to eventually stretch from the Atlantic to the Pacific. The popularizer of the phrase, John L Sullivan, took as its evidence the population growth to that point (1845) and used terms such as 'natural law', 'natural flow of events' and 'the spontaneous working of principles'. It fit well with other emerging and often equally malleable ideas, such as American exceptionalism and continentalism. With such a broad concept it is not hard to understand that it could be moulded to any number of specific worldviews – geographic, racial, economic, religious, practical or social Darwinian. Although the convulsions of the civil war meant that notions of Manifest Destiny were consumed with more pressing internal issues, it would re-emerge in the post-reconstruction period when the United States began again to look beyond its borders.

annexation
The process of attaching territory to an existing country, nation or state to which it had not hitherto belonged.

5

Expansion as moral duty

We can see two broad impulses to American expansion that developed in the second half of the 19th century. The first has sometimes been broadly characterized as a moral justification and motive for an expanded USA. From 1859, this argument drew increasing energy from the spread of Darwin's powerful idea. Although Charles Darwin had really only discussed the idea of evolution by means of natural selection of animals in his *Origin of Species* (1859), it did not take long for thinkers from all over Europe and North America to apply this concept to all manner of social constructions, from business to human society. Emblematic of the growing popularity of a Darwinian approach to social issues was the growing influence of the British philosopher Herbert Spencer. Spencer, who coined the phrase 'survival of the fittest', conceived of society as evolving from a state of undifferentiated homogeneity to one of highly differentiated heterogeneity, as exemplified in the modern industrial state driven by relatively unfettered individualism. This became a popular notion with the growing class of US industrialists a number of who sponsored Spencer's tour of the USA in 1882, notable among them was the steel magnate Andrew Carnegie. Spencer seemed to hold out a philosophical, if not scientific, justification for the continued growth of the USA's industrial economy based on unrestrained self-interest and therefore the expansion of the USA itself.

The ideas of Spencer and Darwin and later Francis Galton – the father of the eugenics movement – spread around the world. As Jürgen Buchenau has pointed out, Latin American leaders who read these philosophers developed a view of society as something that evolved from simple to complex, following the European model. These philosophers developed a view of society as evolving from simple to complex, following the European model. Buchenau goes on to argue that this is reflected in the high levels of European migration to Latin America at the end of the 19th century. This migration was encouraged by these leaders as a way of increasing the influence of European values and institutions on 'evolving' countries.

In Canada, one of Spencer's chief advocates was historian and journalist Goldwin Smith. Spencer's ideas led Smith to the conclusion that the new country of Canada was not economically developed enough to be viable in the context of the late 19th century. To Smith, the only logical solution was to join Canada and the USA. Spencer and Darwin found an American voice in the historian John Fiske. Fiske's writings and lectures in the 1880s emphasized the evolutionary superiority of the Anglo-Saxon race, as evidenced in its population growth, geographical influence and economic strength. He envisioned a day when the world would resemble the USA in institutions, language and religion. Although he stopped short of calling for anything like a crusade of annexation and military expansion, he certainly helped develop an intellectual foundation in which any such expansion could be seen as 'natural'.

ATL Research skills

So influential were the ideas of Herbert Spencer and Francis Galton that many of their ideas found their way into legislation and the press throughout the Americas. Examples included eugenics legislation in Canada and immigration policies throughout the region. Conduct some research and complete the following table.

Country	Social Darwinian idea	Example
Uruguay		
Argentina		
Brazil		
Canada		
USA		

The clergyman Josiah Strong gave Fiske's position a more racial and religious tone. In his book *Our Country: Its Possible Future and Its Present Crisis* (1885), he posited the Anglo-Saxon race, especially as it had developed in the USA, as destined to dominate the globe. In many ways he saw such domination by what he believed to be a superior race as a duty. According to Strong, the combination of liberal democracy and Christianity as expressed in the USA was the chief means by which the world would progress and the vehicle of this progress was to be imperialist expansion – US expansion.

John Burgess, a political scientist from Columbia University, argued in *Political Science and Comparative Constitutional Law* (1890) that it was the Teutonic races that had the greatest innate ability to create the modern nation state and those who resisted the progress towards such states were justly subjugated. Again, the concept of duty rings throughout this work. Among the most notable of Burgess's students was one who would have the power to act directly on the foreign policy implications of Burgess's ideas – Theodore Roosevelt.

Of course these sentiments were not confined to the USA. European powers were busy parcelling out portions of Africa and other territories throughout this period and they too looked to racist theories for justification. At the same time Canada more than doubled its territory inaugurating a period of assimilation and subjugation of the First Nations people that would last a century. Notions of the superiority of the 'white races' and its attendant responsibilities appear in the arguments of German, French and British imperialists throughout this period. Perhaps one of the most famous of these justifications came not in a scholarly work, but rather in a popular poem by Rudyard Kipling that leant its title to many a rationalization for imperial expansion at the time. Although published in 1899 and directed at the Philippines annexation debate, 'The White Man's Burden' expressed what many had been arguing in various forms for the previous two decades.

Class discussion

How Christian was the USA at the end of the 19th century? What other religious traditions existed in the USA at this time? To what extent should government policy reflect religious ideas?

Expansion as practical necessity

While vague notions of duty, destiny and race inspired the imperial visions of some Americans, others were more practical in their outlook. This realist approach to American expansion took as its starting point the rapid population, economic and geographic expansion of the USA in the second half of the century and then looked to what it would take to protect this and ensure further growth. Such concerns naturally revolved around military and economic might. Foremost among these 'realists' was Alfred Thayer Mahan. Mahan was the President of the United States Naval War College; his lectures, magazine articles and books such as *Influence of Sea Power on History, 1660–1783* (1890) popularized the thesis that it was maritime trade and the tools of this trade – ships, both merchant and military – that brought national greatness. To Mahan it further meant that secure supplies of coal for these ships would be readily available at ports around the world. It also meant control of any advantageous waterways, natural and man-made. In this he was primarily looking to any future canal cutting across the Isthmus of Panama and to islands that could potentially protect the approaches to such a waterway. Mahan's thesis found avid readers around the world, perhaps most notably in Berlin. His book was an important influence on Kaiser Wilhelm's decision to embark on a major naval building programme that would have such far-reaching consequences. Closer to home Mahan's work also found an audience in the likes of Theodore Roosevelt and Henry Cabot Lodge.

Economic reasons for expansion

There was a growing economic imperative to national expansion at the end of the 19th century. But even those who saw in expansion a more divine or moral mission, men such as the Protestant clergyman and author Josiah Strong, saw the expansion of the Anglo-Saxon race as inextricably linked to the expansion of its institutions and economic system.

The leaders of domestic economic expansion in the 1880s also sought markets beyond North America. Despite the fact that a great deal of European capital was still flowing into the USA, American oil and steel companies sought new markets and resources around the globe, and in so doing came into competition with other economic powers such as the United Kingdom and Germany. Other American companies such as Dupont, Colt and Singer explored foreign markets for their manufactured goods. The depression that hit the world after 1873 meant that businesses, regardless of nationality, had to work that much harder to maintain profits. The move to the gold standard by most industrializing powers by the 1870s also placed downward pressure on prices until new gold deposits were discovered at the end of the century. On the other hand, the convertibility that the **gold standard** provided greased the wheels of international trade by making most currencies easily exchangeable. Although the USA had a massive domestic market, importing far less than it consumed, there was a growing sense by the 1890s that the US economy was destined to produce more than could be consumed by existing markets, domestic and foreign. The United States, therefore, had to expand its markets.

Class discussion

What role did a powerful navy play in the building of other empires such as the British Empire, the Russian Empire, the Austrian Empire and the Chinese Empire? How has that changed in the 21st century?

---

gold standard

A monetary policy in which currency is readily convertible to gold. The gold standard requires that a country's supply of currency be tied to its supply of gold.

 Research skills

US economic expansion, 1865–1898	
Wheat	256%
Corn	222%
Sugar	460%
Coal	800%
Steel rails	523%

Source: Kennedy, Paul. 1988. *Rise and Fall of the Great Powers: Economic and Military Conflict from 1500 to 2000*. London: Fontana Press. P. 312

Research economic growth in two other countries in the region, then answer the following questions:

1 How do these numbers compare to those in the USA?

2 What are some reasons for the differences?

3 Who was consuming these goods?

4 Were they exported or consumed within the country?

5 What are the implications for export-reliant versus import-reliant economies?

Another depression gripped the USA in 1893 bringing with it a sense of social and economic dislocation, the solution to which seemed to some to be the expansion of the USA itself. The historian Richard Hofstadter contends that the depression affected the country like never before. It was radicalizing the working class and this seemed to pose a dangerous threat to what the middle class perceived as the established economic order. With the republic now stretched from sea to sea, there appeared no obvious opportunities to funnel this discontent into North American expansion, as had been the case in the past. Despite the depression, the flow of immigrants continued unabated, as did the growth of urban centres. To Hofstadter, one of the prime expressions of this mood was national self-assertion and aggression.

Source skills

The gold standard

Research the issue of the gold standard at the end of the 19th century.

1 How was coinage minted in the USA prior to the 1890s?

2 Describe how the gold standard worked in the international economic system of the 1890s.

3 Which countries in the world benefited from the gold standard? Which countries were put at a disadvantage by the gold standard? Why was this?

4 What are the advantages and disadvantages of a country adopting the gold standard as a basis for its monetary system?

5 How was this issue resolved in the USA?

Read the following excerpt from a speech by William Jennings Bryan delivered in 1896. Bryan was the Democratic presidential nominee and a supporter of the free coinage of silver.

We say to you that you have made the definition of a business man too limited in its application. The man who is employed for wages is as much a business man as his employer; the attorney in a country town is as much a business man as the corporation counsel in a great metropolis; the merchant at the cross-roads store is as much a business man as the merchant of New York; the farmer who goes forth in the morning and toils all day—who begins in the spring and toils all summer—and who by the application of brain and muscle to the natural resources of the country creates wealth, is as much a business man as the man who goes upon the board of trade and bets upon the price of grain; the miners who go down a thousand feet into the earth, or climb two thousand feet upon the cliffs, and bring forth from their hiding places the precious metals to be poured into the channels of trade are as much business men as the few financial magnates who, in a back room, corner the money of the world. We come to speak for this broader class of business men.

It is the issue of 1776 over again. Our ancestors, when but three millions in number, had the courage to declare their political independence of every other nation; shall we, their descendants, when we have grown to seventy millions, declare that we are less independent than our forefathers? No, my friends, that will never be the verdict of our people. Therefore, we care not upon what lines the battle is fought. If they say bimetallism is good, but that we cannot have it until other nations help us, we reply that, instead of having a gold standard because England has, we will restore bimetallism, and then let England have bimetallism because the United States has it. If they dare to come out in the open field and defend the gold standard as a good thing, we will fight them to the uttermost. Having behind us the producing

masses of this nation and the world, supported by the commercial interests, the laboring interests, and the toilers everywhere, we will answer their demand for a gold standard by saying to them: "You shall not press down upon the brow of labor this crown of thorns; you shall not crucify mankind upon a cross of gold."

Questions

1 Bryan supports bimetallism as being advantageous to the majority of US workers. To what degree do you agree with him? How does the gold standard help or hurt the working classes?

2 What does this speech tell us about political divisions in the USA at the turn of the century?

3 Draft a response to Bryan from the perspective of a supporter of the gold standard.

Political reasons for expansion

In some cases of late 19th-century expansion, US policy and official action seemed hard-pressed to keep pace with the actions of US citizens and officials abroad. In the case of the Samoan Islands, US merchant ships had used the island increasingly as a coaling station for Pacific trade, a trade that had quickened since the transcontinental railroad opened up the Pacific coast to the goods of the American interior. The strategic importance of the islands was not lost on the Navy, which contemplated a naval base at Pago Pago in the 1870s. Despite Congress's rejection of a formal treaty with Samoa at that time, US commercial interests continued in the islands and by the end of the decade a treaty established a formal relationship between the Samoans and the USA. Britain and Germany, also recognizing the importance of the islands, were not about to allow the US a free hand, and after some tense encounters agreed to a three-way **protectorate** over the islands. The threat posed by Germany and Britain elicited a great deal of posturing and aggressive language from politicians and newspapers across the United States. By 1899 this arrangement morphed into a two-way split of the islands between Germany and the USA.

Just as the Samoan Islands were an important mid-ocean link between the Americas and the South Pacific, the Hawaiian Islands grew into an important way station in the growing China trade. Missionaries, merchants and sailors settled in the islands throughout the middle of the century. As the non-native population increased, stories of the islands' commercial potential reached the USA and sugar plantations soon followed, providing some evidence for Josiah Strong's claim in 1885 that 'commerce follows the missionary'. The military was not far behind commerce. To the growing US Navy, Pearl Harbor in the islands seemed to provide an easily

protectorate
A protectorate is a territory that is nominally independent but under the official diplomatic or military protection of another country.

defended natural harbour from which it could protect America's growing trans-Pacific trade.

Hawaii's sugar trade with the USA provided at once a reason and a method by which the US could exert more influence on the islands. In 1875 the USA dropped all tariffs on Hawaiian sugar and guaranteed Hawaii against any third party influence in the islands' affairs, thus making the Hawaiian Islands a protectorate of the US in all but name. By 1887 the US Navy had the use of Pearl Harbor.

The American commercial presence in the islands grew steadily. Fruit and sugar plantations made up the bulk of these enterprises, with the USA as their sole market. When a Representative from Ohio named William McKinley introduced a tariff bill that was passed into law in 1890, Hawaiian sugar interests fell through the cracks. While the McKinley tariff, as it became known, drastically increased the tariffs on foreign-produced goods, it also paid subsidies to American sugar producers. All at once, Hawaiian sugar was subject to the tariffs, but ineligible for the subsidy.

Fearing economic ruin, US citizens in the islands took matters into their own hands and overthrew the young Hawaiian queen Liliuokalani early in 1893. Those involved immediately petitioned the USA government for annexation – to bring them within the McKinley tariff wall. The request caught the government and the voting public in the US by surprise. Now they had to confront the reality of the theories of Strong, Burgess, Fiske and Mahan. Did the USA really want to be an imperial power?

The immediate answer to this question was ... not right now. The new President, Grover Cleveland, may have been moderately in favour of annexation; he was enough of a politician to understand that the people of the USA and the politicians who represented them, and upon whom he would depend to pass legislation, were split on the issue. He sent a fact-finding mission to the islands and found that the so-called 'revolution' was engineered by US business interests in the islands and had little native support. Nevertheless, the provisional government in Hawaii put in place would not be dissuaded, and Cleveland was in the unenviable position of having to depose the revolutionaries with force or to find some sort of intermediate status for Hawaii. He chose the latter. It proved only a temporary reprieve for the anti-annexationists. By the time William McKinley was in office in 1897 the global context had changed considerably and by joint resolution of Congress the US annexed Hawaii in 1898.

Venezuela

The Monroe Doctrine would again emerge as a vital American policy in the mid-1890s when a boundary dispute re-erupted between the United Kingdom and Venezuela. Gold had been discovered in the border region between Venezuela and British Guiana and this raised the stakes considerably. The relative merits of the gold standard and the free coinage of silver had been building as an important issue for some years. Cleveland and other supporters of the gold standard saw in this discovery a possible source of new gold that could take some of the fight out of the free silver agitators.

▲ Liliuokalani, Queen of Hawaii (1838–1917)

ATL Thinking skills

For each of the following groups, write a paragraph taking and defending a position on the annexation of the Hawaiian Islands in 1893.

- Josiah Strong
- Alfred Mahan
- A San Francisco merchant
- A US naval officer
- A US clergyman
- The British Ambassador to the United States of America
- A US sugar producer

ATL Thinking skills

War over the Venezuelan boundary dispute seemed a definite possibility in December 1895. Evaluate the case for and against war in both the United Kingdom and the USA. To what extent do you think that war was a real possibility throughout this crisis?

jingoism

An expression of extreme national sentiment. It can also manifest itself in an aggressive foreign policy.

Cleveland, on the whole a conservative when it came to matters of foreign policy, was torn between those in Congress, the state legislatures and the press, who called for a strong response to what was perceived as high-handed British interference in the US sphere of influence, and his own beliefs on foreign policy. After studying the somewhat limited information available to him, Cleveland came to the conclusion that the former was indeed the better case and advocated for arbitration of the dispute by a third party, sending a note saying as much to the British Foreign Ministry. In a letter drafted by his aggressive Secretary of State Richard Olney, Cleveland reasserted the Monroe Doctrine as he interpreted it applying to the Venezuelan situation. The note also made veiled threats of more aggressive action should the British not heed the US demand for arbitration. The reply from Lord Salisbury was straightforward: Britain would not submit the matter to arbitration and the Monroe Doctrine did not apply, nor was it a recognized element of international law. When Cleveland's response to the British rebuff came before Congress in December 1895 its aggressive tone and language startled the British and energized **jingoists** in Congress and the press. After a period of negotiation, the US and Britain agreed on an arbitration treaty and eventually the terms of the arbitration itself. On the surface, the aggressive sabre rattling of Cleveland and Olney seemed to bear fruit. Cleveland had reclaimed for himself and the Democratic Party the status of defender of US interests from their Republican Party critics such as Theodore Roosevelt. Further, the Monroe Doctrine seemed to be alive and well as the century drew to a close.

ATL Thinking and social skills

Research possible responses of the Venezuelan government to the British and US positions on the border dispute. Discuss possible outcomes for each response. Use the following table to help you.

Response	Possible US reaction	Possible British reaction

1.2 The Spanish–American War

Conceptual understanding

Key questions

→ To what extent did domestic issues in the USA cause the Spanish–American War?

→ How did the Spanish–American War affect hemispheric relations in the years after 1898?

Key concepts

→ Causation

→ Consequence

Causes of the Spanish–American War: The Cuban Revolution

The Spanish–American War started as a revolution by Cuban nationalists on behalf of a population oppressed by a colonial power. Indeed it was not the first time the Cubans had tried to shake off their Spanish overlords. In the 1870s, Cuban revolutionaries had waged a 10-year struggle for independence. Although there was considerable sympathy in the USA for the plight of the revolutionaries, and not a small amount of provocation from Spain, the US government remained neutral.

In 1895, the Cubans rose up against the Spanish colonial administration, which seemed just as determined to retain the island colony as it had been two decades earlier. The most influential Cuban nationalist in 1895 was the poet and writer José Martí. Martí called for an insurrection, and in February of that year Cuban guerrillas began attacking government installations and troops. In response, General Valeriano Weyler led some 150 000 Spanish troops across the Atlantic to quell the rising. What ensued was a war, the ferocity of which startled many. As in many such wars, civilians bore much of the suffering. In order to deprive the guerrillas of food and support, Weyler ordered rural populations into camps without adequate food or sanitation and in which thousands died.

▲ William Randolph Hearst, magnate of the Yellow Press

The USA took a keen interest in this war for a number of reasons. The United States had invested some $50 million in Cuba, and the revolution was threatening this investment and damaging business interests. But this was not enough to explain the growing popular outrage in the US at the Spanish actions in Cuba. By 1895, there were an estimated 20 000 Cubans living in the USA and a number of them set up a committee to agitate in favour of independence, lobby the American government to recognize the revolutionary government organized by the rebels, and raise funds to fight the war. Centred in New York, this committee attempted to gain the support of organized

Yellow Press

Originally a group of sensationalist newspapers in the United States at the end of the 19th century. Each newspaper tried to outsell its rivals by printing ever-more shocking stories. The atrocities, real and imagined, during the Cuban Revolution, supplied a great deal of material for the Yellow Press.

Class discussion

How does the press decide what gets reported? How does this affect the work of the historian? What does this tell us about the relationship of the past to the present and the extent to which the past is knowable?

labour, springing from the support of the cigar makers' union. The committee also fed sensational news stories to newspapers across the country. The infamous '**Yellow Press**' of William Randolph Hearst and Joseph Pulitzer capitalized on these stories, eventually sending their own correspondents to supply the lurid copy. Mass meetings and demonstrations were held in major cities such as Chicago, New York, Kansas City and Philadelphia. When the issue reached the floor of Congress, many of the ideological arguments for expansion reemerged. Some argued that a free Cuba would mean expanded markets for American business. Others invoked the Monroe Doctrine in support of the rebels. A friendly Cuba could help the US Navy protect the eastern approaches to the much-heralded canal to be cut across the Isthmus of Panama in the same way that Hawaii could protect its western approaches. Despite this initial furore, interest in the plight of the revolutionaries did not hold the popular American imagination for long and President Cleveland steadfastly refused to intervene. Even during the 1896 election campaign, there was little talk of Cuba. The war, however, was hurting some American interests more than others. By 1897, the revolution in Cuba had significantly affected the sugar market in the USA. Likewise, tobacco imports from the embattled island were shrinking, driving prices higher.

ATL Communication and thinking skills

Choose a current event in your country that has two or more clearly identifiable and opposing positions. Write a newspaper article or draw a cartoon, keeping as strictly as possible to the established facts of the event, before preparing a newspaper article or a political cartoon in the style of the Yellow Press with the opposing point of view. There are examples from the Spanish–American War at the PBS site on its series *The Crucible of Empire*.

Use the following table to help you:

Event?	Position?	Facts to emphasize?	Facts to ignore?	Symbols?	Audience?

1 How much did the three articles/cartoons differ from each other? Were there facts/ideas that appeared in all three accounts?

2 Analyse the language or symbols used in each of the accounts. To what extent are these used to evoke emotion or appeal to reason?

3 How is the choice of audience important to the writing/drawing of these articles/cartoons?

4 What is the value and limitation for the historian of using Yellow Press articles in understanding the past?

The US diplomatic response

President McKinley, who succeeded Cleveland, was more willing to confront the Spanish diplomatically over their conduct in the war than Cleveland had been, but stopped short of advocating American intervention. Nevertheless, he was torn by conflicting domestic sentiments about the war. The business lobby, on the whole, disliked the idea of war while some politicians of both parties advocated more aggressive action. Much of the public saw intervention as a form of moral duty, while diplomats worried about the response of European powers to any sort of US involvement. McKinley attempted to strike a middle ground in his inaugural address by promising a foreign policy that was 'firm and dignified ... just, impartial and ever watchful of our national honor ...'. At the same time this foreign policy 'want[ed] no wars of conquest'. His inaugural address went on to warn against the 'temptation of territorial aggression'. The Yellow Press, nonetheless, continued to be filled with stories of Spanish cruelty in Cuba. McKinley, again trying to walk a middle line, put the Spanish government on notice that its conduct in Spain was unacceptable and that if it did not remedy the situation the USA would take further action. This threat seemed to have the desired result. The Spanish government recalled General Weyler and proposed some limited reforms. By the end of 1897, the Cuban insurrection had again appeared to recede from the public eye in the United States.

'Ever watchful of our national honor' took on a more immediate meaning in early 1898. The Yellow Press, in this case the *New York Journal*, printed a letter that had been leaked from the Spanish ambassador in Washington, Dupuy de Lôme, to the Spanish government in Madrid, in which he derides McKinley as a weak and pandering politician. Although the latter's political opponents in the USA made the same accusations, when they came from a foreign country they took on the robes of a national insult. Congress again took up the cause, dormant for some time, of recognition of the revolutionary government. A week later a more serious and deadly blow to 'national honor' occurred when the USS *Maine*, an American battleship, exploded in Havana harbour, killing 260 of her crew.

McKinley's response was, at first, measured. An inquiry was ordered into the causes of the explosion. The inquiry concluded that it had been an underwater mine that had ignited explosions in the ship's magazines. Congress allocated $50 million to the looming war and the press and the public increasingly called for aggressive action against Spain. Although still wary of war, McKinley went to Congress on 11 April for the authority to use force against the Spanish. The Teller Amendment, one of the resolutions that Congress passed authorizing the war, stated that the USA had no intention of annexing Cuba.

The USA invades the Philippines

On 19 April Congress authorized the use of force against the Spanish. Although Spain's colonial holdings included Guam, Puerto Rico, Cuba and the Philippines, the fighting was largely contained to Cuba and the Philippines. The US Navy was well prepared for the war. It was a modern fighting force that had developed a strategic plan should war with Spain come. Once the war broke, it put this plan into action. Commodore

Historiography
- Orthodox – follow traditional historical views
- Revisionist – see things from a newer different viewpoint

ATL Thinking skills

There has been considerable historic debate on the forces that led President McKinley to war with Spain in 1898. Some historians have argued that it was the Yellow Press that incited the public to pressure the government to take action. Others have argued that it was the business lobby that influenced the President. Analyse the arguments of historians such as:

- Walter Lefeber
- Julius Pratt
- Howard Zinn
- Robert C Hilderbrand
- John Dobson

Find one of these guys

- The Spanish Navy wasn't ready
- Still used wooden ships

▲ US troops crossing over a river, Philippines, 1899

Class discussion

What other regional crisis from 1880 to 1920 took on a global nature as a result of imperialism? How were these the same as the Spanish-American War? How did they differ?

Class discussion

How had industrialization changed the way that 19th-century armies prepared for war? How might this change the standard for measuring political "power?"

▲ Rough Riders charge up San Juan Hill

George Dewey assembled a squadron of seven ships of the American Asiatic Squadron in Hong Kong in February and with this force set out for Manila Bay in the Philippines in late April. The Spanish naval force defending the islands consisted of older ships that were outgunned and out-armoured by the American force, although the Spanish commander Admiral Montojo had hoped that shore batteries could support his ships in defending the islands against an American naval attack. The Spanish preparations were still underway when Dewey's squadron arrived in the Philippines on 30 April. Once they found Montojo's fleet, the Americans attacked at dawn on 1 May. After an hour and a half of action, the Spanish force was destroyed. But what to do now? Dewey had enough marines to hold the naval yards in Manila Bay, but not to wrest the city, much less the islands, from the Spanish troops stationed there. The US Navy held the waters around the islands and waited for a landing force to arrive, which it had by the end of the summer, and by 13 August the Philippines were in US hands. The first major success of the war, the Battle of Manila Bay, had been won half the globe away from the fight to free Cuba.

The US army was not the modern fighting force that the US Navy was in 1898. At the outbreak of the war, the regular army consisted of 28 000 soldiers and officers spread out across the continent. State militias were estimated to have less than 115 000 additional men, although the federal government's authority to press them into overseas service was debatable. Volunteers would be needed. In this instance the war fever that had gripped the country in the preceding months paid dividends. Citizens of the USA responded enthusiastically to the President's call for 125 000 volunteers. It was, however, one thing to call for 125 000 volunteers and quite another thing to clothe, arm, equip, train and transport that many men.

These problems were soon obvious. As regulars and volunteers assembled in Florida, Tennessee and Virginia for the anticipated invasion of Cuba, it became evident that the army was not prepared. The camps were rife with disease. Despite the fact that they were going to fight in a tropical climate, the majority of the men were issued with the traditional dark woollen uniforms. While the regular troops were issued with modern repeating rifles, much of the volunteer force had to make do with the Springfield single-shot 'Trapdoor' rifle.

Confusion also characterized the early command decisions made by the army. Lacking a coherent strategic plan prior to the Congressional resolutions, the army high command, led by General Nelson Miles, debated how to proceed and where to attack. Havana was considered and then rejected, as the bulk of the Spanish force was stationed there. Eventually it was decided to launch an attack from the Florida camp, in Tampa, on Santiago. The regular army units were in Tampa, as was the volunteer cavalry force led by its second in command Theodore Roosevelt, that became known as the Rough Riders. The Rough Riders, the regular army units and the state militia that embarked at Tampa on 6 June for the invasion numbered some 17 000 men and were led by General William Shafter. This force would face about 125 000 Spanish troops. Spain's land forces were augmented by a squadron of obsolete ships dispatched from Spain under the command of Admiral Cervera that had managed to elude the US fleet and slip into Santiago harbour, only to be subsequently trapped there.

After a chaotic landing in Cuba, the US forces moved towards Santiago. En route they fought the battles of El Caney and San Juan Hill, defeating the Spanish forces, and by early July found themselves in front of Santiago, exhausted and lacking supplies. Within days the Spanish fleet attempted to break through the US naval blockade and was destroyed, leading the Spanish commander to negotiate the surrender of his forces defending Santiago. Meanwhile, a force of 18 000 US soldiers embarked for Puerto Rico, another Spanish Caribbean possession defended by 9000 Spanish soldiers. After a series of battles in early August, the Puerto Rican campaign was cut short by an armistice signed by Spanish and US officials on 10 August. The war had lasted a matter of months and had cost the USA about 2500 dead, of which only about 16% were battle deaths, the remainder perishing from disease.

The aftermath: The imperial debate

From October to December 1898 American and Spanish representatives negotiated a treaty in Paris. The resulting Treaty of Paris ceded Puerto Rico and Guam to the USA. Cuba would gain its independence, as the Teller Amendment prohibited its annexation. It was the Philippines that proved to be a difficult point. The Spanish were less ready to relinquish it than they had been their Caribbean possessions, but had no realistic way of holding them against American demands backed up by a naval squadron in Manila Bay. The USA for its part recognized the strategic importance of the islands to the growing China trade. In the end, the USA agreed to pay $20 million for the Philippines. But the real debate was only getting started.

In the USA, the Treaty of Paris had to be ratified by the Senate with a two-thirds majority. Groups such as the **American Anti-Imperialist League** with prominent members like Mark Twain and Samuel Gompers formed to argue against the annexation of the Philippines. Many Democrats, sugar growers and isolationists joined them. The Republican Party, led by President McKinley, the Navy and those who would benefit from increased Asian trade lined up to press for annexation.

In early February 1899 the fate of the Philippines was discussed in the Senate. Annexation carried the day by the narrowest of margins.

While the Teller Amendment ensured Cuba's nominal political independence, the USA still maintained an occupation force on the island until 1902. During this period, American capital poured into Cuba. The infrastructure was modernized, while the occupiers renovated the financial system and government administration. American fruit and tobacco companies bought up huge tracts of land such that by 1901 much of Cuba's economy and trade was dominated by the USA. How could the USA protect these extensive interests while at the same time upholding the Teller Amendment in word if not in spirit? The answer came in the form of the Platt Amendment. Passed in 1901, the Platt Amendment 'guaranteed' Cuban independence by forbidding Cuba from entering into foreign treaties that would 'impair' its independence. The amendment further reserved for the USA the right to intervene in Cuba to protect this independence and to be sold or leased military installations on the island for this purpose. Amid popular Cuban protests, the Platt Amendment became a part of the Cuban constitution.

Class discussion

In other 19th- and 20th-century wars, what proportions of casualties were from non-military causes? Has this changed in the 21st century? How might governments and armies minimize these casualties?

American Anti-Imperialist League

An organization formed by a wide cross-section of US society to fight against the growing sentiment that favoured annexation of the Philippines after the US victory in the in the Spanish American War.

Class discussion

Samuel Gompers was a prominent organized labour leader in the USA. What arguments would organized labour have against annexing the Philippines?

ATL Research skills

Research the post Spanish–American War positions of Cuban nationalists or Filipino nationalists. Write a speech from your country's perspective. Then, with someone from the other perspective, compare and contrast post-war nationalism in Cuba and the Philippines.

The status of the Philippines was less complicated; it was part of the USA. In 1899 under the leadership of an erstwhile US ally Emilio Aquinaldo, Filipinos rose against their colonizers and conducted a brutal guerrilla war until 1901. By the time Aquinaldo was captured, the USA had come to understand the price of empire building. The war had occupied close to 100 000 soldiers and cost close to 5000 American lives. It is estimated that over 200 000 Filipinos died in the two and a half years of fighting. When William Taft took over the governorship of the Philippines in 1901, he embarked on a paternalistic programme of reform that involved the construction of schools and infrastructure to support the US-dominated industry and the creation of a political assembly to practise a limited form of self-rule. Despite this, it would take the severe dislocations accompanying the end of the second world war to secure Philippine independence.

Source skills

The imperial debate

Source A

The following is an excerpt from an essay written in August 1898 by Andrew Carnegie, a wealthy steel magnate and Vice-President of the Anti-Imperialist League.

To reduce it to the concrete, the question is: Shall we attempt to establish ourselves as a power in the far East and possess the Philippines for glory? The glory we already have, in Dewey's victory overcoming the power of Spain in a manner which adds one more to the many laurels of the American Navy, which, from its infancy till now, has divided the laurels with Britain upon the sea. The Philippines have about seven and a half millions of people, composed of races bitterly hostile to one another, alien races, ignorant of our language and institutions. Americans cannot be grown there. The islands have been exploited for the benefit of Spain, against whom they have twice rebelled, like the Cubans. But even Spain has received little pecuniary benefit from them. The estimated revenue of the Philippines in 1894–95 was £2 715 980, the expenditure being £2 656 026, leaving a net result of about $300 000. The United States could obtain even this trifling sum from the inhabitants only by oppressing them as Spain has done. But, if we take the Philippines, we shall be forced to govern them as generously as Britain governs her dependencies, which means that they will yield us nothing, and probably be a source of annual expense. Certainly, they will be a grievous drain upon revenue if we consider the enormous army and navy which we shall be forced to maintain upon their account.

Source: Carnegie, Andrew. 1901 'Distant Possessions: The Parting of the Ways.' *The Gospel of Wealth*. New York: The Century Co.

Source B

The following is an excerpt of a speech given by Albert Beveridge, a senator from Indiana.

The Opposition tells us that we ought not to govern a people without their consent. I answer, The rule of liberty that all just government derives its authority from the consent of the governed, applies only to those who are capable of self government. We govern the Indians without their consent, we govern our territories without their consent, we govern our children without their consent. How do they know what our government would be without their consent? Would not the people of the Philippines prefer the just, humane, civilizing government of this Republic to the savage, bloody rule of pillage and extortion from which we have rescued them?

Source: Beveridge, Albert J. 'The March of the Flag.' 1898. *History Tools.org: Resources for the Study of American History.* http://www.historytools.org/sources/beveridge.html.

Source C

President McKinley related the following to General James Rusling in 1899. Rusling recalled the conversation for an interview in 1901.

When next I realized that the Philippines had dropped into our laps I confess I did not know what to do with them … I walked the floor of the White House night after night until midnight; and I am not ashamed to tell you, gentlemen, that I went down on my knees and prayed to Almighty God for light and guidance. … And one night late it came to me this way. …

1 That we could not give them back to Spain—that would be cowardly and dishonorable;

2 That we could not turn them over to France or Germany—our commercial rivals in the Orient—that would be bad business and discreditable;

3 That we could not leave them to themselves—they were unfit for self-government—and they would soon have anarchy and misrule worse than Spain's war;

4 That there was nothing left for us to do but to take them all, and to educate the Filipinos, and uplift and civilize and Christianize them as our fellow men for whom Christ also died.

Source: Rusling, General James. 'Interview with President William McKinley.' *The Christian Advocate*. 22 January 1903. P. 17. Reprinted in Schirmer, Daniel and Rosskamm Shalom, Stephen. (eds.) 1987. *The Philippines Reader*. Boston: South End Press. Pp. 22–23.

Questions

1 What does Carnegie mean by 'glory'? (Source A)

2 What evidence is there of a practical approach to the issue of imperialism in each of the documents?

3 What evidence is there of ethnocentrism in the documents?

4 Compare and contrast how the people of the Philippines are regarded in Sources A and B.

5 What role did religion play in McKinley's decision to annex the Philippines, according to Rusling?

6 With reference to its origin and purpose, evaluate the value and limitations of Source C to historians studying McKinley's decision to annex the Philippines.

1.) He means pride in American power.

2.)

1.3 US foreign policy

Conceptual understanding

Key questions

→ To what extent was the foreign policy of the USA from 1900 to 1916 similar to its foreign policy in the years 1880–1900?

→ To what extent was US foreign policy driven by economic considerations in these years?

Key concepts

→ Continuity

→ Change

→ Consequence

→ Perspective

– Unequal treaties

While the USA seemed content to set up a colonial administration in the Philippines, it specifically disavowed such an approach to China. By the end of the 19th century, European powers were taking advantage of a weakening Chinese regime to expand their influence, direct and indirect, in the country. These expanding spheres of influence threatened to leave the USA behind, even though the significant focus of US Asian policies and territorial acquisition in the Pacific had been to protect or further China trade.

The Open Door Policy

John Hay, the US Secretary of State, had to devise a way to assert American trading interests in China without resorting to war. His answer was the Open Door Policy. The Open Door stated that there was to be no discrimination of foreign powers within a country's sphere of influence and that the existing tariff structure as set by the Chinese government was to remain in effect. Hay proclaimed the Open Door in diplomatic notes sent to the major European powers. With no military threat to back it up and no international authority to enforce it, the Open Door could be observed or ignored as the Europeans saw fit. It would take an international incident to give the USA the leverage to press the Open Door into reality.

Chinese nationalists had long bridled at the gradual erosion of their economic and political sovereignty at the hands of European powers. This growing rage erupted in 1900 when a secret nationalist society called the Righteous and Harmonious Fists or Boxers rose against Europeans in China, besieging the foreign diplomatic corps in the British embassy in Beijing. A multinational force, of which over 2000 were from the USA, eventually relieved the siege. This participation gave the USA a say in the resolution to the incident, with which they further pushed the Open

Class discussion

What were the relative positions of the Republican and Democratic parties on the question of the Open Door Policy? How have these parties changed their foreign policy stances in the 21st century? To what degree have they remained consistent with the late 19th and early 20th century?

Door Policy. Hay also insisted that the resolution must therefore include the territorial integrity of China – that China would stay nominally independent – but that this 'independence' must include free trade.

The Big Stick

When an assassin's bullet cut William McKinley's life and presidency short in 1901, it catapulted Theodore Roosevelt into the White House. Roosevelt, in many ways, typified a popular sentiment at the turn of the century. The Progressive movement, and the era that bears its name, was a diverse group of interests within US society that believed US ascendancy on the world stage depended on a modern, scientific and professional approach in everything from industry to the military and diplomacy. The return of economic prosperity helped fuel this optimism. Under Roosevelt, the US military would move from an *ad hoc* civilian army to a more centralized professional force. The diplomatic corps would be modernized with specialized training and examinations for those who would represent the USA to the world. Roosevelt also believed in the 'civilizing' obligation of the modern countries of the world – that it was their duty to bring the benefits of 'civilization,' as he saw them, to the 'backward' corners of the earth. Inherent in that notion was the principle that the USA would have to become more involved in international affairs.

Class discussion

How might the concepts of 'progress' and 'civilization' as espoused by Theodore Roosevelt be different for someone living in central Africa or China?

Warship tonnage of the powers, 1880–1914

	1880	1890	1900	1910	1914
United Kingdom	650 000	679 000	1 065 000	2 174 000	2 714 000
France	271 000	319 000	499 000	725 000	900 000
Russia	200 000	180 000	383 000	401 000	679 000
USA	169 000	240 000	333 000	824 000	985 000
Italy	100 000	242 000	245 000	327 000	498 000
Germany	88 000	190 000	285 000	964 000	1 305 00
Austria-Hungary	60 000	66 000	87 000	210 000	372 000
Japan	15 000	41 000	187 000	496 000	700 000

Source: Kennedy, Paul. *Rise and Fall of the Great Powers: Economic and Military Conflict from 1500 to 2000.* London: Fontana Press. P. 261.

▲ The Great White Fleet, USS *Connecticut* leading North Atlantic fleet off the coast of Virginia, 1909

When Roosevelt's progressive and internationalist inclinations were combined with his deep admiration for the military as an expression of a nation's strength, the result was Big Stick diplomacy – the notion that the USA could achieve its foreign policy goals if it backed its interests with a credible military threat. As an ardent follower of Alfred Mahan, Roosevelt understood this to mean primarily a large and modern navy. Between 1898 and 1913 the US Navy constructed 25 battleships and more than doubled its personnel. In 1907 Roosevelt paraded this portion of his Big Stick around the world. The Great White Fleet made stops at a number of ports, including Yokohama in Japan.

Class discussion

What was the purpose of the Great White Fleet's world tour? To what extent was it successful? How might the countries that it visited interpret the Great White Fleet and the purpose of its tour?

ATL

Research and communication skills

Research, create, and make a presentation to the class on why the Central American Canal should either be dug through Nicaragua or Panama from the point of view of the Panamanians and Nicaraguans. Be sure to include potential economic, military, social, and foreign policy benefits of the canal.

▲ Roosevelt on a steam shovel digging the Panama Canal

ATL

Research skills

Research the history of the Panama Canal in the 20th century. Evaluate the effect of the canal on the USA and Panama respectively. List the benefits and drawbacks for each country.

The full proverb from which the term Big Stick comes reads: 'Speak softly and carry a big stick'. On occasion, Roosevelt could speak softly. When Russia and Japan went to war in 1905, it was Roosevelt who helped broker the peace in an attempt to maintain some sort of a balance of power in Asia. Under his leadership, the USA grew closer to the United Kingdom than it had been in years. Roosevelt also helped to mediate a settlement on Morocco at Algeciras in 1906.

But there was also the Big Stick. Partially on the strength of the enlarged American fleet, the Americans and Japanese came to an agreement on the status quo in the Pacific. But it was in Latin America that the Big Stick would be the most evident.

The Panama Canal

The prospect of cutting through Central America to join the Pacific and Atlantic oceans had been discussed since the middle of the 19th century. The failure of a French attempt had brought scandal and political disaster to the French Third Republic. The two primary questions surrounding such a massive project were 'Who would build it?' and 'Where, exactly, would it be built?' The USA and United Kingdom had agreed to cooperate on the project, but by the time Roosevelt took office this had fallen out of favour in the USA and the McKinley administration had negotiated away this agreement. Where to locate this colossal project proved more complicated. The two leading contenders were Nicaragua and Panama.

In 1903, Congress and the President decided on the Panama option. The USA, however, had only purchased the rights to build the canal. It now had to acquire the land on which to build the canal, and this would require negotiations with the Colombian government, the country that owned Panama. The US Secretary of State Hay negotiated that the USA would lease the land for 100 years, pay $10 million to Colombia for the lease and pay $250 000 a year for the duration of the lease.

The Colombian Senate rejected the treaty, favouring as it did US interests. Roosevelt was enraged at the nerve of the Colombian government, standing in the way of his idea of progress and civilization. Since speaking softly had not seemed to work, Roosevelt prepared the 'Big Stick'. The fear that the USA might abandon the Panama option for the Nicaragua option drove the Panamanians to revolt against their Colombian overlords yet again. The fortuitous arrival of a US battleship and troops, a very real display of Roosevelt's Big Stick foreign policy, prevented the Colombian government from crushing the revolt. The USA was only too happy to recognize the newly independent Panama, the government of which agreed to the same payment as had been promised to the Colombian government for a strip of land 10 miles (16 kilometres) wide. When the canal opened in 1914, North Americans saw it as a testament to their ingenuity, hard work and industry – a crowning achievement of the Progressive Era. To others in the Americas, and indeed the world, it was another example of imperialism backed by Western technological advances. It also meant that the USA now controlled one of the most important waterways in the world. It needed to secure that ownership to achieve further control of the Caribbean.

Venezuela, Santo Domingo and the Roosevelt Corollary

While the Monroe Doctrine may have stopped European countries from physically intervening in the Americas, it did not stop European capital from flooding into the region through to the end of the 19th century. When, early in Roosevelt's presidency, Venezuela defaulted on loans to German, British and Italian creditors, these governments used force to secure payment by blockading Venezuelan ports and shelling the *[handwritten: ← Caused the Corollary ← some bombing occurred too]* port city of Puerto Cabello, something that Roosevelt, the USA and the Monroe Doctrine could not tolerate. To prevent any further incursions to collect debts on the part of foreign powers, Roosevelt articulated a policy that would come to be known as the Roosevelt Corollary to the Monroe Doctrine. While Monroe's original doctrine had been a warning to European powers to stay out of the USA's sphere of influence, the Corollary was an assurance that if the nations of Central and South America could not keep their financial houses in order and thereby threaten the 'civilized' world, the USA would step in and manage their finances for them, even to the point of collecting debts for the European powers. Roosevelt wanted to remove any pretext that European powers might have for military interventions in the Caribbean.

The Corollary was first used in Santo Domingo *[handwritten: (Dominican Republic)]*. To stop France and Italy from forcibly collecting money they were owed by Santo Domingo and thereby threatening American strategic interests in the region, the USA sent a financial administrator to manage Dominican finances, collecting duties on imports and using 55% of this revenue to pay foreign creditors. The remaining 45% was remitted to the Dominican government of Carlos Morales.

Class discussion

How might the other countries of Central and South America react to the Roosevelt Corollary? What options were open to them? How would the Corollary affect European countries? What advantages did the Corollary have over simply taking control of Santo Domingo?

Source skills

Backing down in Venezuela

Source A

Following is the view of historian Nancy Mitchell on the crisis in Venezuela.

President Theodore Roosevelt later claimed that it was only his big stick (wielded quietly) that stayed the Kaiser's hand [in Venezuela]. Analysis of German aims and ambitions in Venezuela, however, does not support this interpretation. It indicates that it was a withdrawal of British support, not Roosevelt's stick, that convinced Germans to end the blockade. It also reveals that, US fears and allegations to the contrary, Germany was exceedingly cautious before, during, and after the blockade. Its policy was far from recklessly aggressive. It was timid. ...

Theodore Roosevelt claimed, almost fourteen years after the fact, that he had delivered a secret ultimatum to the Germans that brought them to the bargaining table. The US naval exercises had been planned well in advance and were known to the Germans and the

English before the blockade began, yet not one document has been found to confirm the President's assertion, not in the United States, not in Germany, and not in England.

Source: Mitchell, Nancy. 1999. *The Danger of Dreams: German and American Imperialism in Latin America.* University of North Carolina Press. Pp. 65, 87.

Source B

Following is an alternative view put forward by the historian Edmund Morris.

The Venezuela incident of late 1902 is the locus classicus *[classic example] of [Roosevelt's] famously colloquial foreign policy, "Speak softly and carry a big stick."*

If Roosevelt expected an answer to his ultimatum of 8 December, he was soon disappointed. That Sunday von Holleben [the German ambassador] seemed interested in talking only about the weather, of all things, and tennis. Losing patience, TR [Theodore Roosevelt] asked if Germany was going to accept President Castro's arbitration proposal transmitted by Secretary of State Hay. The ambassador said no. Controlling his temper, the President replied that Kaiser Wilhelm must understand that he, Roosevelt, was "very definitely" threatening war.[11] Von Holleben declined to be a party to such peremptory language.

From there [New York], before midnight [16 December], certain words flashed to Berlin. ... The evidence suggests that von Holleben's cable [to Berlin] was burned after reading, in approved German security fashion.

... The reaction in Berlin was immediate [once it received the ultimatum]. On 17 December, the Reichstag decided to accept arbitration, acting secretly and in such haste that urgings from Secretary Hay in Washington and Metternich in London were redundant on receipt.

[11] TR (Theodore Roosevelt), quoted by William Loeb (witness) to Henry Pringle, 14 April 1930, Henry Pringle Papers, Harvard College Library, Cambridge, Mass. (Edmund Morris's citation)

Source: Morris, Edmund. "'A matter of extreme urgency': Theodore Roosevelt, Wilhelm II, and the Venezuela Crisis of 1902." *Naval War College Review*. Spring 2002.

Questions

1 Compare and contrast the views of why the Venezuelan crisis did not result in war in each document. Can you account for the differences?

2 Is it possible for both historians to be correct? Why or why not?

3 According to Source A, what was the role of Britain in the resolution to the crisis?

4 With reference to its origin and purpose, evaluate the value and limitations of Source B.

Responding to extraterritoriality

Extraterritoriality is a principle by which a country enforces its laws outside its own borders. During the late 19th and early 20th centuries this became an important tool of imperialism. Taken to its extreme, this principle held that British or US citizens living in a foreign country would still be governed by British or US laws regardless of the laws of the nation in which they were living. This could prove very handy for foreign businessmen trying to enforce contracts and a serious impediment to a country trying to exercise its sovereignty in the face of imperialism.

Two Latin Americans developed doctrines in response to the principle of extraterritoriality. In the late 19th century the Argentine jurist Carlos Calvo argued that extraterritoriality had no basis in international law. Initially, Calvo advocated that debt had to be enforced through the courts of the countries in which the money was lent. He later developed this idea into a doctrine stating that all sovereign countries should be entirely free to treat foreigners within their borders as they saw fit to the extent that there would be very little, if any, accepted international standards; in a sense, there was no such thing as international law. Argentine foreign minister Luis Drago later developed a more workable and specific doctrine by which countries could not use force to collect debts owed to its nationals. The Hague Conference of 1907 adopted a form of the Drago Doctrine in its conventions.

Source skills

Two views of Roosevelt

Source A

President Roosevelt standing atop Sagamore Hill (his home) wearing wings labelled 'Down With Peace' and 'Hurrah For War' while carrying a 'big stick.'

Source B

President Roosevelt 'speaking gently' to the Russian Tsar and Japanese Emperor in an effort to mediate an end to the Russo–Japanese War in 1905.

"GOOD OFFICES"

Questions

1 Compare and contrast the view of President Theodore Roosevelt in the two sources.

2 How might these two views be explained?

3 How might the domestic context in the USA, when each of these cartoons were published, have affected the cartoonists' opinions of Roosevelt?

Dollar Diplomacy

William Howard Taft succeeded Roosevelt as US President in 1908 and sought to hold the same foreign policy course as his predecessor. Taft, however, was less inclined to use the Big Stick. He looked to the apparent success of the Roosevelt Corollary and expanded on what he saw as the lesson gleaned from it. His approach would come to be known as Dollar Diplomacy. Dollar Diplomacy sought to replace US military might with the power of its strong economy and the financial know-how of Progressive Era financial wizards. Like the Corollary, Dollar Diplomacy wished to remove any pretext for European intervention in Latin America by managing the financial affairs of countries whose economies were 'backward' by US standards and thus ensure that European debts were paid. Loans from US bankers would be used to pay off European creditors. Financial managers would move in and remake the economy, if not on the US model, then to US advantage. Tax collection would become more efficient, budgets regularized, and a form of the gold standard adopted.

There developed a marked gap between the theory of Dollar Diplomacy and its practice. As rational and 'progressive' as the measures seemed to the USA, Latin Americans could not help but see them as thinly veiled imperialism. Costa Rica and Guatemala rejected it outright – refusing to sign treaties based on the principles of Dollar Diplomacy. Honduran nationalists persuaded their congress to do the same. This provoked a US-sponsored revolution, which installed a pro-American regime that was more amenable to the dictates of Dollar Diplomacy. The Dominican agreement also broke down in 1912, requiring the US military to restore the obligations of Dollar Diplomacy.

Nicaragua was another trouble spot for American diplomacy. In response to the nationalism of the Nicaraguan leader, José Santos Zelaya, American mining interests sponsored a revolution eventually backed by Taft's government and the US Marine Corps. When the US Senate would not ratify the Dollar Diplomacy treaty with Nicaragua, private US companies and banks acquired controlling interests in Nicaraguan banking and railroads. Such economic imperialism was bound to enrage already tense nationalist sentiments, and more marines were called upon to suppress another revolution in 1912. The marines would remain in Nicaragua for a further 13 years. Dollar Diplomacy was not restricted to Latin America. By 1908, Liberia in West Africa was deep in debt. Surrounded as it was by British and French colonies, the Taft administration feared that a bankruptcy would result in its annexation to one or more of the neighbouring colonial empires. To forestall this, Taft approved a loan and the menacing presence of a US warship. Nevertheless, Dollar Diplomacy did not stop Liberia's financial and political problems.

Taft also looked to Dollar Diplomacy as a means to curtail Japanese and Russian influence in China and Manchuria. As in so many other parts of the world, building an effective railroad system was the key to further economic expansion, and the US arranged to be an investor in the development of such a railroad system in Manchuria. Eventually Russia and Japan cooperated in dividing the Manchurian economic interests between them, and the Chinese government was not strong enough to oppose them. The USA, unable to secure the support of France (a Russian ally) or the United Kingdom (a Japanese ally), settled for more moderate financial intervention in China.

Moral Diplomacy

Despite the aggressive foreign policies of Roosevelt and Taft, there was still anti-imperialist sentiment in the USA and it was to this that Woodrow Wilson appealed as the Democratic presidential candidate in 1912. Publicly repudiating acquisitive foreign policies such as the Big Stick, Wilson promised a foreign policy that would encourage human rights and the development of 'constitutional liberty' in the world. Guided by a belief that the Christian precepts of the USA could offer a model to the rest of the world, and with little diplomatic experience and a very autocratic nature, Wilson set out to chart a new course for US foreign policy. In light of the actions of his Republican predecessors and the growing tension and later international chaos that would grip the world, this was going to be a difficult course to chart. Wilson, despite his idealistic intentions, would come to understand that, like Dollar Diplomacy, his new Moral Diplomacy would, in the end, depend on its ability to back up good intentions and moral precepts with military force.

There were, however, important elements of continuity between Wilson's foreign policy and those of his predecessors. He believed in the expansion of international trade and American financial interests and the role that the government can play in that expansion, with or without the consent of trading partners. When this belief was combined with his inability to understand the nature of nationalism and its role in revolutions in places such as China and Mexico, a gap emerged between Wilson's perception of the USA in international affairs and the perception that other countries had of the USA.

Wilson initially supported the Chinese Revolution that predated his presidency. As a reformer, he saw it as the birth of a modern state out of the ashes of a corrupt relic of a bygone era. He moved quickly, and unilaterally, to recognize the new government, even though it was by no means clear that this was the final form that the Chinese government would take. He also took the USA out of a banking agreement with China, in the hope of fostering Chinese independence, leaving the other signatories a free hand to benefit from Chinese instability. With the outbreak of the First World War, Japan further expanded its influence in China with little opposition from the US State Department. Again, although he sympathized with the revolution, Wilson's idealism was no match for the expansionist self-interest of the Japanese, and by 1916 he began to drift to a policy that bore some resemblance to Dollar Diplomacy in that it authorized private loans to China and promised action if the Chinese defaulted.

In the Dominican Republic, Wilson imposed free elections in 1913 but this brought the republic no closer to stability, with civil war and revolution constantly simmering just below the surface of Dominican affairs. Efforts by Wilson's Secretary of State William Jennings Bryan to appeal to the Dominicans to formally denounce revolution did no good. In 1915 a frustrated Wilson ordered the US military to intervene and establish order. They would occupy the country until 1924. In neighbouring Haiti, similar revolutionary upheavals, coupled with European financial interests, persuaded Wilson to occupy that half of Hispaniola as well. In the case of Haiti, the occupation lasted until 1934.

In Mexico too, Wilson favoured the reforming elements in the 1911 revolution that brought down the regime of Porfirio Díaz. Under Díaz, American oil and railroad concerns had prospered while the Mexican elite profited from this prosperity, alienating Mexican peasants and workers. Francisco Madero's reforming government was itself soon overthrown by General Victoriano Huerta. Wilson, however, was less enamoured of Huerta and his regime.

Wilson brought increasing pressure to bear on Huerta, soliciting international support from the likes of the United Kingdom and offering support to the opposition leader, Venustiano Carranza. Carranza, a Mexican nationalist, was hesitant to accept help from the USA. By 1914 the USA did not officially recognize the government of Mexico, but there

- Wilson doesn't like Huerta and wants to protect U.S. investments
- Backs Carranza up.

was no credible replacement that supported the USA. The quandary was that while recognizing that the Huerta government was repugnant to Wilson, if the USA intervened militarily it would anger, perhaps to the point of war, the Mexican nationalists who opposed Huerta. Moral Diplomacy had again run into the complicated realities of actual diplomacy.

After a minor diplomatic slight, Wilson ordered the US Navy to occupy Verecruz in April 1914, precipitating an attempt at mediation by Chile, Brazil and Argentina. Eventually Carranza's forces forced Huerta from office, but Carranza proved no more able to bring the country together than his predecessor, and the country again descended into civil war. During the course of this civil war, Pancho Villa mounted a raid into American territory. The punitive raid ordered by Wilson soon broadened. Wilson did not, however, let these events drag the USA into a longer, wider war. As relations with Germany deteriorated and it looked more and more likely that the USA would join the Allies in their war with Germany, Wilson ordered American troops out of Mexico in early 1917.

▲ US Navy occupies Veracruz

ATL Thinking skills

Evaluate the strengths and weaknesses of the three approaches to foreign policy used by the USA in the period 1900–1914. Use the following table to help you.

Policy	Proponents	Strengths	Weaknesses	Results
Big Stick Diplomacy				
Dollar Diplomacy				
Moral Diplomacy				

Q#3

Q#2

Q#1 ~~ubor to~~ write

- Source A ~~~~
  - British withdrew and the Germans followed afterwords
  - were slightly intimidated by the US Navy

- Source B
  - Germany's withdrawal didn't have anything to do with Britain
  - Submitted to arbitration w/o hesitation

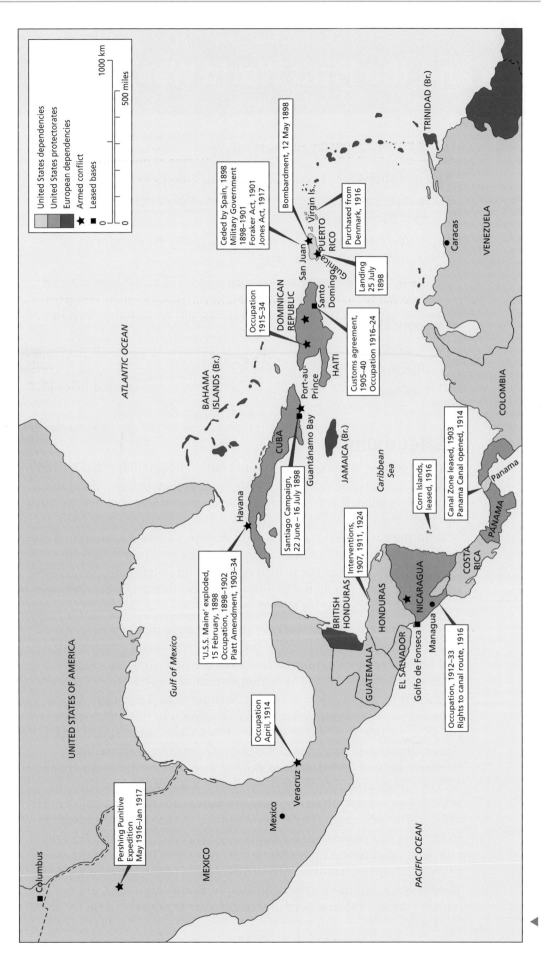

Map legend:
- United States dependencies
- United States protectorates
- European dependencies
- Armed conflict ★
- Leased bases ■

1000 km
500 miles

ATLANTIC OCEAN

Ceded by Spain, 1898
Military Government
1898–1901
Foraker Act, 1901
Jones Act, 1917

Bombardment, 12 May 1898

Purchased from Denmark, 1916

Virgin Is.

PUERTO RICO

San Juan

Guánica

Landing 25 July 1898

TRINIDAD (Br.)

VENEZUELA

Caracas

Occupation 1915–34

DOMINICAN REPUBLIC

Santo Domingo

Customs agreement, 1905–40
Occupation 1916–24

HAITI

Port-au-Prince

BAHAMA ISLANDS (Br.)

COLOMBIA

CUBA

Havana

Santiago Campaign, 22 June – 16 July 1898

Guantánamo Bay

JAMAICA (Br.)

Caribbean Sea

Corn Islands, leased, 1916

Canal Zone leased, 1903
Panama Canal opened, 1914

Panama

PANAMA

'U.S.S. Maine' exploded, 15 February, 1898
Occupation, 1898–1902
Platt Amendment, 1903–34

Interventions, 1907, 1911, 1924

BRITISH HONDURAS

HONDURAS

NICARAGUA

Managua

COSTA RICA

GUATEMALA

EL SALVADOR

Golfo de Fonseca

Occupation, 1912–33
Rights to canal route, 1916

UNITED STATES OF AMERICA

Gulf of Mexico

Occupation April, 1914

Veracruz

Mexico

MEXICO

Pershing Punitive Expedition May 1916–Jan 1917

Columbus

PACIFIC OCEAN

◀ The United State in the Caribbean, 1898–1934

1.4 The USA and the First World War

Conceptual understanding

Key questions

→ To what extent was it realistic for the USA to continue its neutrality as the First World War progressed?

→ How did participation in the First World War change the nature of the US government's role in US society?

→ To what extent was there domestic opposition to US participation in the First World War?

Key concepts

→ Causation

→ Change

→ Consequence

US Neutrality

While President Wilson was trying to craft a foreign policy that looked to morality as a guiding principle, Europe was embracing age-old notions of narrowly defined self-interest and balance-of-power politics. By 1914 this path saw Europe descend into the catastrophe of the First World War. In the early days of August 1914 European powers committed to war; in the case of the British Empire, this commitment stretched around the globe to all the British colonies and dominions. The USA did not feel the same gravitational pull of the war. In many ways, Wilson saw it as antithetical to his foreign policy.

The issues that drove Europe over the edge were not American issues and few Americans saw them as such. The rival alliance systems that had been developed in mutual fear over the preceding two decades did not include the USA. The nationalism that was hacking at the Austro-Hungarian Empire was of little concern to Americans. While imperialism was an important source of tension to European states, the Monroe Doctrine and Roosevelt's Big Stick, combined with Taft's Dollar Diplomacy, had kept European interests out of the western hemisphere, and US interests in the Far East did not significantly run foul of European interests. Besides, the USA did not see itself as an imperialist power in the same way the Europeans did, especially under Wilson. The militarism that gripped Europe in the decades leading up to the war was markedly absent from American culture. The US army, although modernized under Roosevelt, was still a fraction of the size of most European nations, with the exception of the United Kingdom. The US Navy, although gaining in size on European navies, did not pose a major threat to either Germany or Britain, its primary naval rivals in the world.

Any sort of official participation in the European convulsions seemed foolish to most people in the USA and the case for neutrality strong:

- In 1914, over a quarter of the population of the USA were immigrants. British and Russian Americans favoured the Allies, while German and Austrian immigrants held with the Central Powers. Irish Americans would not support any move to join the British. Choosing sides risked tearing the country apart.

- The monstrous appetite that modern war has for industrial goods promised to drag the country out of the depression of 1913, especially if US businesses could trade with both sides.

- The USA had traditionally remained out of European affairs in the same way it hoped that Europeans would stay out of the affairs of the Americas.

- Wilson despised the idea of war as a solution to international disputes and saw the war as an opportunity for the USA to illustrate the benefits of peace and emerge as a world leader.

But, as Belgium had so recently discovered, being neutral is far more than simply declaring neutrality. Neutrality without the ability to enforce it is only neutrality so long as other states allow it to be so. Belgium was unable to maintain its neutrality even with the guarantee of the United Kingdom and so was dragged into the war by virtue of its geographic position. The USA would find neutrality difficult for different reasons.

The USA had emerged into world prominence in the decades preceding the German invasion of Belgium, Luxembourg and France in 1914. Its economy was now tied more closely to a world economy than ever before and the disruptions caused by the war were sure to have ramifications on the domestic economy. US financial institutions caught a glimpse of these disastrous possibilities when the outbreak of the war caused a need for cash in belligerent nations. When these states began to sell off their US securities, Wilson suspended the sale of stocks to prevent a panic.

The Allied blockade

Early in the war both sides indicated that they were not willing to respect US neutrality. This situation laid bare the prejudices of Wilson and indeed most Americans in favour of the Allies at the same time that the commercial potential of staggering war demand began to dawn on American industry. Although international law prohibited the blockading of non-war material – non-contraband materials – such as food, this restriction would make the blockade useless as a tool of war, so both sides ignored it. The blockade was designed to prevent the importing of goods to enemy ports. Given the geography of the war, this was directed mainly at Atlantic shipping. The Allied blockade, enforced primarily by the surface fleet of the British Royal Navy, proved less deadly than the submarine warfare of the German Navy. Regardless, war orders from the Allies were more than enough to keep the US economy producing at capacity, especially when credit restrictions were eased and later lifted altogether.

▲ German U-boats in harbour

The deadly nature of a blockade enforced by German submarines, without the provision required by international law that adequate measures be taken to ensure the safety of passengers and crew, was brought into sharp focus in May 1915. A single torpedo fired by a U-20 struck the passenger liner RMS *Lusitania* as she steamed off the Irish coast. The *Lusitania* carried passengers as well as US-made munitions destined for Britain. She went down with 1195 of her passengers and crew, 123 of them US citizens. The Germans claimed that, as well as civilian passengers, the British ship was carrying munitions, which was true.

The sense of Allied outrage was partly due to the nature of the attack on a ship carrying civilian passengers: this, despite German notices printed in US newspapers that such attacks were possible and warning Americans that they travelled on British ships at their own risk. The outrage was also derived in part from the growing fear that Germany would ignore what the USA saw as its maritime rights as a neutral country, regardless of the position of the United Kingdom. Again, American neutrality meant nothing if the USA could not defend it. Having already acquiesced to the British blockade, Wilson felt he could not acquiesce to the German blockade. On the domestic front, Wilson began to feel pressure from Republicans, who might use any weakness shown in the face of German aggression to political advantage. After strongly worded warnings from Wilson and after other sinkings, the Germans called off unrestricted submarine warfare in May 1916.

As the war progressed the US economy, with its prodigious loans and exports to the Allies, was increasingly dependent on Allied success. The size of the US economic support alone made any blockade attempt that excluded it weak. While the Germans backed down in 1916, they could conceivably get to the point when it would take more than threats to stop them from attacking American ships.

The British were not above aggravating American neutrality. In 1916 Britain banned a number of American firms from doing business in the United Kingdom on the grounds that they also did business with the Germany. Although this enraged Wilson and many in his administration, the USA continued to supply the Allied war effort.

Getting ready

Wilson ran for re-election in 1916 partly on his record of keeping the USA out of the war. The reality, however, was that American neutrality was rather one-sided. Further, the first years of the war illustrated that if the USA wanted to maintain what neutrality it had, a credible military threat was going to be necessary. These arguments, anchored by Republicans and industrial interests, but also echoed by important members of Wilson's administration, fuelled a vigorous debate in the USA as to the extent to which a neutral country should militarize. On the other side of the question, pacifists, socialists and organized labour worried that expanding the military could provoke war and, should the USA be able to maintain its neutral position, would only serve to profit industrialists at the expense of the taxpayer. By the end of 1915, Wilson was coming around to the idea that the war, which was now revealing itself to be the long, bloody stalemate that it would remain until 1918, whether the US was neutral or belligerent, would require a larger and more modern military. Wilson took his argument to Congress and the people. By mid-1916, after difficult legislative wrangling, long debate and some compromise, Wilson guided his bills through Congress and into law.

National Defense Act, 1916

- Increased the army from 80 000 to 223 000
- Brought state militias under federal control
- Gave the President power to mobilize the National Guard
- Expanded the National Guard to over 400 000
- Established Junior Reserve Officer Training Corps

Naval Expansion Act, 1916

- Multi-year building plan
- 10 Dreadnoughts
- 16 Cruisers
- 50 Destroyers

Merchant Marine Act, 1916

- Federal government could own ships
- Increased federal power to regulate shipping

▲ British recruiting poster

Class discussion

Recruiters in all countries used emotional appeals to encourage men to enlist in the armed forces. Compare and contrast this poster with any US recruiting posters you can find on the Internet.

ATL Thinking, communication and social skills

Choose either to support or oppose the expansion of the US military in 1916. Research the arguments of those who supported each position and conduct a class debate on the question, 'To arm or not to arm?'

Against expansion:

- Farmers
- Socialists
- Organized labour
- Pacifists
- Others

In favour of expansion:

- Industrialists
- Military leaders

The drift to war

In 1916 the Democrats campaigned on Wilson's neutrality record. It is therefore understandable that the Republicans would attack this record, and in the process they began to be perceived as the party more likely to guide the country into the war. Wilson did his level best to encourage this perception. On a deeper level, this debate revealed the development of a foreign policy split that would continue for 40 years.

There was of course any number of variations on these two main themes. For example, some internationalists, represented generally by eastern industrial interests, advocated for a strong military to help 'police' the world, while other internationalists spoke more in terms of universal disarmament and the use of economic sanctions and collective security to enforce the peace. By 1916, Wilson was a committed internationalist. He attempted to bring the belligerents in the European war to the negotiation table, but to no avail. Early in 1917 he presented his vision for a post-war world, a world in which disputes between countries were negotiated, armaments were greatly reduced, ships plied the seas unmolested, and nations cooperated in an organization to ensure the stability of the international economic and political system.

The realities of the war were, however, conspiring against Wilson's lofty intentions. While he was putting the final touches to this plan, the German Chancellor, Bethmann Hollweg, was meeting with his military commanders. Generals Hindenburg and Ludendorff argued that if the German Navy could unleash its fleet of 100 submarines on all shipping bound for its enemies, they could strangle Britain within six months. This timeline was important, because all present at the meeting understood that should Germany resume unrestricted submarine warfare it would entail sinking American vessels and this would likely bring the USA into the war against Germany. The German High Command reasoned, however, that it could take up to a year for any American soldiers to materialize on the Western Front, and by this time Britain would have been brought to its knees. On 31 January 1917 the German ambassador in Washington announced that, starting the next day, all ships regardless of country of origin would become targets for their submarines.

While some of Wilson's administration urged an immediate declaration of war, the President could not bring himself to do it. He feared it would further divide his country and wreck prospects for a stable post-war settlement and his role in its construction. Apart from breaking diplomatic relations with Germany, Wilson did little. It would take a curious diplomatic episode to push him and the American public over the edge to war.

The Zimmermann telegram

On 25 February 1917 the British turned over to the USA a telegram that they had intercepted. In it, the German foreign minister Arthur Zimmermann promised that Mexico might regain territory lost to the USA in return for an alliance with Germany.

Regardless of how realistic such a prospect was or was not, it had a serious effect on public opinion. After the telegram was made public, Americans who had been ambiguous about the situation in Europe saw Germany as meddling and conniving. More serious than diplomatic intrigues, however, was the fact that German U-boats had been sending American merchant ships to the bottom of the sea throughout February and March. Wilson now believed that the USA would have to enter the war.

Source skills

The Zimmermann telegram

The following telegram was sent from the German foreign minister Arthur Zimmermann to the German minister in Mexico. It was intercepted by the British and turned over to the USA.

To the German Minister to Mexico

Berlin, January 19, 1917

On the first of February we intend to begin submarine warfare unrestricted. In spite of this, it is our intention to endeavour to keep neutral the United States of America.

If this attempt is not successful, we propose an alliance on the following basis with Mexico: That we shall make war together and together make peace. We shall give general financial support, and it is understood that Mexico is to reconquer the lost territory in New Mexico, Texas, and Arizona. The details are left to you for settlement...

You are instructed to inform the President of Mexico of the above in the greatest confidence as soon as it is certain that there will be an outbreak of war with the United States and suggest that the President of Mexico, on his own initiative, should communicate with Japan suggesting adherence at once to this plan; at the same time, offer to mediate between Germany and Japan.

Please call to the attention of the President of Mexico that the employment of ruthless submarine warfare now promises to compel England to make peace in a few months.

Zimmermann

Source: "Primary Documents: Zimmermann Telegram." 19 January 1917. http://www.firstworldwar.com.

Questions

1 How were the Germans 'endeavoring to keep neutral the United States of America?'

2 Given the situation of Germany in January 1917, how realistic was its pledge of support to Mexico?

3 Why might Germany be interested in an alliance with Japan as well?

4 What relationship does this telegram have to the Monroe Doctrine?

5 To what extent do you believe this telegram was an important catalyst for the US entry in the war? Explain your answer.

On 2 April 1917 Wilson gave a solemn address to Congress in which he outlined his case for war. He understood that it was a 'fearful thing to lead this great peaceful people into war ...'. The extent to which it was a fearful thing that still deeply divided his people was evidenced by the pro-war and anti-war speeches, marches and demonstrations that seemed to appear daily in cities across the country. Four days later, the formal declaration of war was signed.

▲ President Wilson addresses Congress recommending war with Germany in 1917

ATL Thinking skills

Read President Wilson's 2 April 1917 address to Congress in which he asks for a declaration of war. You can find a copy of the speech at http://www.firstworldwar.com/source/usawardeclaration.htm.

Use the following table to analyse Wilson's reasons for taking the USA into the war.

Immediate reasons for entering the war	Long-term reasons for entering the war

1 What evidence is there in the speech that Wilson was hesitant to go to war?

2 Why does Wilson say that 'Neutrality is no longer feasible...'?

3 What evidence is there that in asking for the declaration of war, Wilson is already looking to a post-war settlement?

4 What does Wilson mean when he says that 'The world must be made safe for democracy'? What implications does this have for the post-war settlement?

5 Write a reply to Wilson's speech from the perspective of the German government.

The Selective Service Act, 1917

In his address of 2 April, Wilson had clearly stated that in his view the massive mobilization required by the war must be managed by a strong central government centred in the **executive branch**. It would require a financial commitment that would mean higher taxes. Just as wealth would need to be conscripted, Wilson also argued for the draft to swell the ranks of the small US army.

Although the National Defense Act of the previous year had provided for an expanded army, the declaration of war required that this be drastically increased and expedited. Although Wilson's preference would certainly have been a massive volunteer army, he understood that time and sentiment would not permit one. He therefore urged the passing of the Selective Service Act, which would draft young men into the army. The debate that ensued proved that the divisions that had preceded Wilson's April address had not evaporated with the declaration of war. Despite the rancour, the act was passed in May and by June millions of Americans were registering for the draft.

Financing the war

Once the USA entered the war it became evident to Wilson and the US government how desperate the situation in Europe had become for the Allies who needed money, men and material. The U-boat campaign was biting deeply into Britain's food stores and all belligerents were close to bankruptcy. While Wilson wanted to finance the war with as little recourse to credit as possible, the dire need of his new allies could not wait for new taxes to make money available for loans to the Allies and at the same time mobilize and expand the armed forces. Congress authorized a loan of $7 billion to get mobilization moving and shore up France and Britain.

The issue of taxation was another element dividing the country that Wilson was trying to unite behind a war effort. Both the extent of a new tax regime and the distribution of the tax burden were hotly debated.

executive branch
The branch of government concerned with carrying out laws passed by the legislative branch. The executive branch of the United States government consists of the President, the cabinet and the civil service.

In the end, taxes provided for about 30% of the cost of the war. As in other belligerent countries, to income tax was added a wide variety of duties on a wide variety of goods and services. An extensive Liberty Bond campaign raised money from all quarters of the USA.

The scale of the First World War led all participants to expand government management of national economies to an unprecedented extent. In the USA this meant the creation of thousands of government agencies to shepherd the economy towards war production.

The Food Administration

Led by future President Herbert Hoover, this agency managed the production and distribution of food through largely voluntary measures. The administration bought crops at a fixed price that proved profitable to farmers. Hoover encouraged food conservation. Food production increased dramatically under the supervision of the Food Administration.

The War Industries Board (WIB)

The WIB led by Bernard Baruch coordinated the production and purchase of war materials. All industries involved in war production were subject to its direction in what would be produced and by whom. The board worked to fix prices and set wages and hours. Factories that had supplied consumer and other peacetime goods were converted to production of war materials.

Fuel Administration

Just as Hoover had guaranteed a profitable price for grain to encourage increased production, the Fuel Administration did the same thing for coal with a similar effect on production.

National War Labor Board

This organization, with representatives from government, owners and labour, sought to regulate labour relations without recourse to lockouts and strikes so as to keep wartime industries producing without interruptions.

Railroad Administration

This board coordinated the transportation of goods from mines, factories and fields by operating the various lines and spurs of American railways as one system. Again, money greased the wheels of coordination. The government provided funds for upgrading existing lines.

The Shipping Board

This body oversaw the expansion of shipbuilding to maintain the merchant fleet in the face of the U-boat campaign. Over the course of the war, American shipping tonnage increased by a factor of 10.

Committee on Public Information (CPI)

Just as war production was to be coordinated, the Wilson administration also attempted to coordinate public opinion. The CPI published

Class discussion

How does this level of government coordination compare to other 20th-century wars in which the USA participated?

pamphlets, posters and newspapers articles to gain support for the US war effort. Tens of thousands of its speakers trooped around the country presenting the government's case for patriotic support for the war. The propaganda effort extolled the virtues of the Allies and their cause, while demonizing the enemy.

Women and the war

As in other Allied countries such as the United Kingdom and Canada, women increasingly filled the jobs vacated by soldiers. While women had always played an important role in the industrial production of the USA, the war saw them enter occupations traditionally dominated by men and in numbers never seen before. These jobs were in the industrial sector such as munitions factories and in white-collar positions such as clerks. Women also flocked to more traditionally female occupations such as nursing, many thousands of them serving overseas.

Partially because of the independent income that accompanied these new economic roles, women found themselves with a greater degree of social freedom. While many of these jobs disappeared when the war ended, with the reduction in economic demand and soldiers returning to fill their old jobs, the contribution women had made to the war effort was significant and their social position altered permanently. Women's suffrage activists wished to capitalize on this importance and accelerated their demand for the vote. By 1920 they were successful with the passing and ratification of the **Nineteenth Amendment**.

▲ Women munitions workers in the United States

Nineteenth Amendment
This amendment to the United States constitution guarantees the right to vote regardless of gender.

Opposition and repression

Opposition to the war continued after Wilson's April address. This resistance could be issue specific while remaining pro-war. For example, there was widespread resistance to the imposition of the draft by many who were generally in favour of the USA entering the war. Critics could also be broad and deep in their resistance to the conflict as a whole. The Socialist Party maintained its opposition to any American participation in the war throughout the conflict.

ATL Research skills

Research the political platforms of each of the following US political parties active in the First World War period. Be sure to include each party's view on US participation in the war.

Party	Platform
The Democratic Party	
The Republican Party	
The Progressive Party	
The Socialist Party	

The Espionage Act, passed in June of 1917, provided a powerful club with which to keep dissent in check. The act allowed for prison sentences of up to 20 years for anyone who, in times of war, willfully caused or attempted to cause insubordination, disloyalty, mutiny or refusal to serve in the military. The act also stipulated that it could not be used to limit discussion, comment or criticism of the government's policies or actions.

In 1918 the Espionage Act was amended (called the Sedition Act) to include:

> ... whoever, when the United States is at war, shall willfully utter, print, write or publish any disloyal, profane, scurrilous, or abusive language about the form of government of the United States or the Constitution of the United States, or the military or naval forces of the United States, or the flag of the United States, or the uniform of the Army or Navy of the United States ... or by word or act [to] oppose the cause of the United States.

Such an ambiguous, and some would say contradictory, act was sure to be applied inconsistently and selectively, but the Supreme Court upheld its legality in the face of First Amendment challenges. Those who spoke out against the war generally, and the draft specifically, found themselves in court and often in jail on the force of the Espionage Act. Over 1500 people were arrested under these acts. Socialist leader Eugene Debs and hundreds of others were found guilty under the Espionage Act and Sedition Act and went to jail for speaking out against the war.

Other acts further expanded the government's reach and power over the spread of ideas during the war. The Trading with the Enemy Act of 1917 gave the government the power to censor any communications leaving the country. The Sabotage Act was used to suppress industrial action by organizations such as the Industrial Workers of the World (IWW).

By the end of the war there was also more mainstream opposition to Wilson's handling of the US effort. There was dissension within his Democratic Party. Eastern Democrats disagreed with measures proposed, and occasionally passed, by western Progressives in the party. Republicans who had put aside party animosity in the cause of a united war effort emerged from their truce as the end of the war neared. The end result of this inter- and intra-party wrangling was that the Republicans took control of both houses of Congress in the 1918 elections. This did not bode well for Wilson as he left for the Peace Conference at the end of the war.

American armed forces overseas

British and French hopes that the USA should be rushed as soon as possible to shore up the existing Allied positions became more acute when the Bolshevik Revolution and subsequent **Treaty of Brest-Litovsk** took Russia out of the war and made scores of additional German divisions available for action in France. The near collapse of the Italian army at the Battle of Caporetto and the French mutinies of 1917 made this situation even more desperate. The US government and army resisted this impulse. General Pershing, the US commander, wanted to enter the war with a US army distinct, intact and strong

Class discussion

To what extent has the US government used laws to curtail dissent in other 20th century wars?

Treaty of Brest-Litovsk
Signed between the new Bolshevik government of Russia and the Central Powers in 1918, the treaty stipulated that Russia would lose parts of Ukraine, the Baltic States and Finland to Germany in exchange for an end to hostilities between the Russia and the Central Powers. The treaty allowed the Germans to send troops that had been fighting on the eastern front to the western front.

enough to fight on its own terms alongside, not mixed in with, its new allies. In the face of Allied pleas, Pershing softened his position somewhat, but it would not be until early 1918 that US troops would move to the front in significant numbers – at about the same time that the German High Command would make one last attempt at breaking the stalemate.

ATL | Research skills

From early 1918, until the end of the war, the American Expeditionary Force contributed to Allied defensive and offensive operations. Research the following battles to complete the following table.

Battle	Dates	Commanders	Description	Significance
Battle of Cantigny				
Battle of Chateau-Thierry				
Battle of Belleau Wood				
Second Battle of the Marne				
Battle of St Mihiel				
Meuse-Argonne Offensive				

President Wilson and the peace of Paris

Wilson had advocated for a 'peace without victory' before the USA had entered the war. In many ways, Wilson's decision to enter the conflict was taken with a keen eye to the post-war world system as much as it was to the protection of US shipping. Wilson's notion of internationalism based on liberal democratic ideals, capitalism, freer trade and the dissolution of colonial empires, he believed, required US leadership, and to have a guiding hand in the peace required a contribution on the battlefield. Regardless, for these principles to prevail, Wilson believed that Germany had to be defeated.

While Wilson had floated a number of these ideas in public since 1917, they were crystallized as the 14 Points in a speech in January 1918. By October 1918 the Germans believed that the 14 Points were the best deal that they could hope for from what increasingly appeared to be an inevitable defeat. They appealed directly to Wilson with a proposition for an armistice based on his peace plan. Wilson found himself in the difficult position of potentially mediating between his enemy and his allies. Nevertheless, he spent the better part of October 1918 selling the British and French on his 14 Points with some limited success.

ATL Thinking skills

Read the synopsis of the 14 Points below:

1 Open treaties

2 Freedom of the seas

3 Free trade

4 Universal disarmament

5 Impartial adjustment of colonial claims with consideration of the wishes of the inhabitant and the governments in question

6 Evacuation of all Russian territory

7 Evacuation of Belgium

9 Italian border readjusted according to nationality

10 Autonomous development to be offered to the peoples of the Austro-Hungarian Empire

11 Evacuation of Serbia, Montenegro and Romania; Serbia to be given sea access

12 Autonomous development for the nationalities of the Turkish Empire; the Dardanelles Straits to remain permanently open

13 Establishment of an independent and free Poland with access to the sea

14 A general association of nations must be formed under specific covenants for the purpose of affording mutual guarantees of political independence and territorial integrity to great and small states alike

Answer the following questions:

1 On what points would the British have agreed? Which would they have opposed and why? What about the French?

2 What evidence is there of idealism and moral diplomacy in the 14 Points?

3 Analyse the 14 Points in terms of continuity and change in American foreign policy before and after the war.

4 To what degree do these points reflect the principle of collective security?

5 Draft a letter of response from the German government and the French government.

As the world limped towards the end of the war on 11 November 1918, it seemed that all parties had taken the 14 Points to be at least the basis for a peace settlement. But there was incredible resentment towards Germany on the part of the Allies and the grudging acceptance of the principles in the 14 Points could not overcome that. After the armistice, Germany evacuated its conquered territory in the west and surrendered its fleet, while the Allies maintained the naval blockade. Most significantly, the Allies denied to Germany any role in crafting the peace settlement. If Wilson had envisioned a 'peace without victory', the reality certainly appeared as though it would be a victor's peace.

As personally involved as he was in the decision to take the USA into the war and as closely linked as that decision was to the post-war settlement, Wilson felt the need to negotiate on behalf of the USA personally. He arrived in Europe in late 1918 and would stay for six months with only a brief return to the USA in that time. He left Congress in the control of the Republicans, a Congress whose approval he would need for any settlement he achieved at the Paris Peace Conference. Aggravating deteriorating domestic party politics, Wilson took no significant Republican politicians with him to Paris, leaving them to fume at the distant President and the treaty he was crafting without them.

The Peace Conference seemed to amplify Wilson's previous tendency towards autocratic decision-making. At various times he found himself at serious odds with the British prime minister, Lloyd George, and the 'Tiger of France', Georges Clemenceau, who at one point threatened to pull out of the negotiations. Wilson did not feel bound by secret treaties concluded by the other allies such as the Treaty of London with Italy nor to any promises made to Japan. Most of his objections to these agreements, apart from their largely secret nature, were that they amounted to a division of the spoils of war, violating his concept of national self-determination. The staggering number of national submissions by countries, territories and national groups complicated matters immeasurably and exposed Wilson's ignorance of European politics – the by-product of 150 years of American isolationist policies.

The First World War: Armies mobilized and casualties					
Countries	Total mobilized forces	Killed and died	Wounded casualties	Prisoners and missing	Total casualties	Casualties as % of mobilized forces
Allies and associated powers:						
Russia	12 000 000	1 700 000	4 950 000	2 500 000	9 150 000	76.3
France	8 410 000	1 357 800	4 266 000	537 000	6 160 800	73.3
British Empire	8 904 467	908 371	2 090 212	191 652	3 190 235	35.8
Italy	5 615 000	650 000	947 000	600 000	2 197 000	39.1
USA	4 355 000	126 000	234 300	4500	364 800	8.2
Japan	800 000	300	907	3	1210	0.2
Romania	750 000	335 706	120 000	80 000	535 706	71.4
Serbia	707 343	45 000	133 148	152 958	331 106	46.8
Belgium	267 000	13 716	44 686	34 659	93 061	34.9
Greece	230 000	5000	21 000	1000	27 000	11.7
Portugal	100 000	7222	13 751	12 318	33 291	33.3
Montenegro	50 000	3000	10 000	7000	20 000	40.0
Total	42 188 810	5 152 115	12 831 004	4 121 090	22 104 209	52.3
Central Powers:						
Germany	11 000 000	1 773 700	4 216 058	1 152 800	7 142 558	64.9
Austria-Hungary	7 800 000	1 200 000	3 620 000	2 200 000	7 020 000	90.0
Turkey	2 850 000	325 000	400 000	250 000	975 000	34.2
Bulgaria	1 200 000	87 500	152 390	27 029	266 919	22.2
Total	22 850 000	3 386 200	8 388 448	3 629 829	15 404 477	67.4
Overall total	65 038 810	8 538 315	21 219 452	7 750 919	37 508 686	57.6

Data supplied by the United States War Department, February 1924

Source: Trueman, John et al. 1979. *Modern Perspectives*. 2nd edn. Toronto: McGraw, Hill, Ryerson. P. 411.

As Wilson gradually gave way on some elements of the 14 Points, he seemed to place more and more confidence in his proposed League of Nations to mitigate what he saw as deficiencies in the broader treaty. Rather than creating the League under a separate treaty, Wilson sought to bind the participants more closely to it by insisting the Covenant of the League be included in the actual Treaty of Versailles.

Back in the USA, the Republican-controlled Senate saw aspects of the League to which they could not agree and political advantage in opposing it. While Wilson acquiesced on some Republican sentiments, such as allowing for the withdrawal of a member nation with two years' notice, and the maintenance of the domestic sovereignty of member nations, he stubbornly pressed on.

US reaction to the League of Nations

A tired and ill Wilson returned from Paris to lay the League, and by association the entire Treaty of Versailles, before the people of the USA. He returned to a country having difficulty adjusting to the new conditions of peace. The **Red Scare** and the impending 1920 presidential election compounded labour strife, unemployment and decreasing economic demand.

Opposition to the Treaty and the League came from a number of quarters. To the pettiness of partisan politics was added the voices of intellectuals, worried that the League would serve only to entrench the status quo of balance-of-power diplomacy in Europe. Some isolationists honestly believed that the interests of the USA were best served by disengaging from European matters. Other pragmatists thought the lofty goals of the League unrealistic and the best way to safeguard US interests was a strong military – not disarmament. Many were concerned that a strict reading of Article X of the Covenant of the League would violate US sovereignty and compel the USA to intervene when other nations' integrity was threatened. Italian Americans were upset at Wilson's stance on the Treaty of London. Irish Americans wondered angrily why 'self-determination' did not apply to their homeland. German Americans railed against Germany's humiliation.

A number of Republican senators – the Reservationists – saw the Covenant as more or less workable with revisions. Most of these agreed that Article X would need some alterations so as to protect what they saw as American freedom of action in the world and in its foreign policy traditions.

Those senators who opposed any form of the Treaty with the included League were known as the 'Irreconcilables', and a number of them sat on the Senate Foreign Relations Committee chaired by Senator Lodge. He held weeks of hearings, allowing all manner of dissenters to air their issues with the Treaty and the League – all duly reported in the press. For his part, Wilson rapidly became intransigent with regard to the League and especially Article X. His increasingly stubborn defence of the Treaty gave ammunition to his opponents who saw him as autocratic and arrogant. Perhaps it was this arrogance that led him to believe that if he could persuade the US public of the righteousness of his cause, the uncooperative senators would have to yield. To this end, and despite his frail health, Wilson embarked on an exhausting cross-country speaking tour to put his case for the League before the American people. The strain proved too much for his health and, after cutting the tour short, Wilson suffered a stroke in early October 1919. With Wilson incapacitated and unable to rally more support for the League, the Senate, in a series of votes from November 1919 to March 1920, voted against ratification of the Treaty. The end result of this Senate defeat was that the major treaty that concluded the First World War, and that was signed by America's European wartime allies, was not recognized by the USA.

Class discussion

Joseph Stalin is believed to have said "A single death is a tragedy; one million deaths is a statistic." What does this tell us about the relationship of numbers to reality? What light does it shed on the relationship of personal knowledge and shared knowledge?

Red Scare

A period of ideological repression in the United States. In the aftermath of the Bolshevik revolution in Russia a fear of radical left-wing politics gripped the United States. Socialists, communists, anarchists and labour organizers were harassed and arrested during this period.

Source skills

Lodge versus Wilson on the League

Source A

The following is an excerpt of a speech given by Henry Cabot Lodge in August 1919 addressing the issue of the League of Nations.

National I must remain, and in that way I like all other Americans can render the amplest service to the world. The United States is the world's best hope, but if you fetter her in the interests and quarrels of other nations, if you tangle her in the intrigues of Europe, you will destroy her power for good and endanger her very existence. Leave her to march freely through the centuries to come as in the years that have gone.

Strong, generous, and confident, she has nobly served mankind. Beware how you trifle with your marvellous inheritance, this great land of ordered liberty, for if we stumble and fall freedom and civilization everywhere will go down in ruin.

We are told that we shall 'break the heart of the world' if we do not take this league just as it stands. I fear that the hearts of the vast majority of mankind would beat on strongly and steadily and without any quickening if the League were to perish altogether. If it should be effectively and beneficently changed the people who would lie awake in sorrow for a single night could be easily gathered in one not very large room but those who would draw a long breath of relief would reach to millions.

We hear much of visions and I trust we shall continue to have visions and dream dreams of a fairer future for the race. But visions are one thing and visionaries are another, and the mechanical appliances of the rhetorician designed to give a picture of a present which does not exist and of a future which no man can predict are as unreal and short-lived as the steam or canvas clouds, the angels suspended on wires and the artificial lights of the stage.

They pass with the moment of effect and are shabby and tawdry in the daylight. Let us at least be real. Washington's entire honesty of mind and his fearless look into the face of all facts are qualities which can never go out of fashion and which we should all do well to imitate.

Ideals have been thrust upon us as an argument for the League until the healthy mind which rejects cant revolts from them. Are ideals confined to this deformed experiment upon a noble purpose, tainted, as it is, with
bargains and tied to a peace treaty which might have been disposed of long ago to the great benefit of the world if it had not been compelled to carry this rider on its back? 'Post equitem sedet atra cura,' Horace tells us, but no blacker care ever sat behind any rider than we shall find in this covenant of doubtful and disputed interpretation as it now perches upon the treaty of peace.

No doubt many excellent and patriotic people see a coming fulfilment of noble ideals in the words 'league for peace.' We all respect and share these aspirations and desires, but some of us see no hope, but rather defeat, for them in this murky covenant. For we, too, have our ideals, even if we differ from those who have tried to establish a monopoly of idealism.

Our first ideal is our country, and we see her in the future, as in the past, giving service to all her people and to the world. Our ideal of the future is that she should continue to render that service of her own free will. She has great problems of her own to solve, very grim and perilous problems, and a right solution, if we can attain to it, would largely benefit mankind.

We would have our country strong to resist a peril from the West, as she has flung back the German menace from the East. We would not have our politics distracted and embittered by the dissensions of other lands. We would not have our country's vigour exhausted or her moral force abated, by everlasting meddling and muddling in every quarrel, great and small, which afflicts the world.

Our ideal is to make her ever stronger and better and finer, because in that way alone, as we believe, can she be of the greatest service to the world's peace and to the welfare of mankind.

Source: Henry Cabot Lodge on the League of Nations. 12 August 1919. http://www.firstworldwar.com/source/lodge_leagueofnations.htm.

Source B

The following is an excerpt of the last speech given by President Wilson in his 1919 tour of the USA promoting the Treaty of Versailles and the League of Nations.

But the treaty is so much more than that. It is not merely a settlement with Germany; it is a readjustment of those great injustices which underlie the whole structure of European and Asiatic society. ...

It is a people's treaty, that accomplishes by a great sweep of practical justice the liberation of men who never could have liberated themselves, and the power of the most powerful nations has been devoted not to their aggrandizement but to the liberation of people whom they could have put under their control if they had chosen to do so. ...

At the front of this great treaty is put the Covenant of the League of Nations. ...

Unless you get the united, concerted purpose and power of the great Governments of the world behind this settlement, it will fall down like a house of cards. There is only one power to put behind the liberation of mankind, and that is the power of mankind. It is the power of the united moral forces of the world, and in the Covenant of the League of Nations the moral forces of the world are mobilized. For what purpose?

Reflect, my fellow citizens, that the membership of this great League is going to include all the great fighting nations of the world, as well as the weak ones. It is not for the present going to include Germany, but for the time being Germany is not a great fighting country. All the nations that have power that can be mobilized are going to be members of this League, including the United States.

And what do they unite for? They enter into a solemn promise to one another that they will never use their power against one anther for aggression; that they never will impair the territorial integrity of a neighbour; that they never will interfere with the political independence of a neighbour; that they will abide by the principle that great populations are entitled to determine their own destiny and that they will not interfere with that destiny; and that no matter what differences arise amongst them they will never resort to war without first having done one or other of two things—either submitted the matter of controversy to arbitration, in which case they agree to abide by the result without question, or submitted it to the consideration of the council of the League of Nations, laying before that council all the documents, all the facts, agreeing that the council can publish the documents and the facts to the whole world, agreeing that there shall be six months allowed for the mature consideration of those facts by the council, and agreeing that at the expiration of the six months, even if they are not then ready to accept the advice of the council with regard to the settlement of the dispute, they will still not go to war for another three months.

In other words, they consent, no matter what happens, to submit every matter of difference between them to the judgment of mankind, and just so certainly as they do that, my fellow citizens, war will be in the far background, war will be pushed out of that foreground of terror in which it has kept the world for generation after generation, and men will know that there will be a calm time of deliberate counsel.

The most dangerous thing for a bad cause is to expose it to the opinion of the world. The most certain way that you can prove that a man is mistaken is by letting all his neighbours know what he thinks, by letting all his neighbours discuss what he thinks, and if he is in the wrong you will notice that he will stay at home, he will not walk on the street.

He will be afraid of the eyes of his neighbours. He will be afraid of their judgment of his character. He will know that his cause is lost unless he can sustain it by the arguments of right and of justice. The same law that applies to individuals applies to nations. ...

Let us accept what America has always fought for, and accept it with pride that America showed the way and made the proposal. I do not mean that America made the proposal in this particular instance; I mean that the principle was an American principle, proposed by America. ...

Article ten is the heart of the whole matter. What is article ten? I never am certain that I can from memory give a literal repetition of its language, but I am sure that I can give an exact interpretation of its meaning. Article ten provides that every member of the League covenants to respect and preserve the territorial integrity and existing political independence of every other member of the League as against external aggression. . .

It may be that that will impair somewhat the vigour of the League, but, nevertheless, the fact is so, that we are not obliged to take any advice except our own, which to any man who wants to go his own course is a very satisfactory state of affairs. Every man regards his own advice as best, and I dare say every man mixes his own advice with some thought of his own interest.

Whether we use it wisely or unwisely, we can use the vote of the United States to make impossible drawing the United States into any enterprise that she does not care to be drawn into. ...

You will say, 'Is the League an absolute guaranty against war?' No; I do not know any absolute guaranty against the errors of human judgment or the violence of *human passions but I tell you this: With a cooling space of nine months for human passion, not much of it will keep hot. ...*

Source: President Woodrow Wilson's Address in Favour of the League of Nations. 25 September 1919. http://www.firstworldwar.com/source/wilsonspeech_league.htm

Questions

1   What evidence is there of Wilson's moral diplomacy in Source B? What evidence is there of a pragmatic approach to foreign policy?

2   What does Lodge mean when he says 'For we, too, have our ideals, even if we differ from those who have tried to establish a monopoly of idealism' in Source A?

3   Evaluate Wilson's use of the 'neighbour' analogy in making his argument.

4   On what points might have Lodge and Wilson agreed?

5   Evaluate the two arguments. Whose is more convincing? Why?

Class discussion

Is it possible that both Wilson and Lodge were correct? How does the perspective of each speaker influence his argument? How do subsequent events affect how a historian may evaluate the position of each man? What does this tell us about the role of the historian in evaluating the past?

Washington Treaty

Signed in 1922 by the United Kingdom, the United States, France, Italy and Japan, this treaty limited naval armaments including warship tonnage.

Dawes Plan

An economic recovery plan engineered by Charles Dawes, designed to address hyperinflation in Germany. US loans would be used to back the revaluation of the German currency. The plan also facilitated the flow of US capital into the German economy. The recovery was intended to allow Germany to resume reparation payments to the Allies.

Economic involvement: Impact of the war

Wilson would be the last Democratic President for over a decade. The Republicans who won the 1920 election, and those who followed, continued on the foreign policy course that had been charted by those who had defeated the Treaty of Versailles in 1920. They vigorously guarded American interests without becoming tangled in alliances and partnerships with other states. They relied on their apparent juggernaut of an economy and the private sector to speak for US interests on the world stage. A small group of Republicans – the Peace Progressives – modified a strictly isolationist stance adopted by others of their party; they opposed the role of business in both domestic and foreign policy while decrying imperialism and militarism. The war had made the USA the single biggest creditor nation on earth. This proved to be a mixed blessing. While, on the one hand, it gave the USA a great deal of influence in the world, it also meant that the USA had a huge stake in the economic stability of the world. This ran counter to the growing isolationist sentiments in the country.

Nevertheless, the legacy of the First World War was that the relative strength of the US economy meant that it dominated exports and capital markets around the world. Even with the growing sentiment towards higher tariffs in the USA through the 1920s, the USA was still an impressive importer. American capital, propping up the German economy and playing a substantial role in many others, meant that as went the US economy, so went the world economy. There were elements of continuity with the pre-war period. American companies continued to buy and lease huge amounts of foreign land in their voracious search for raw materials for the overheated American economy. The relative weakness of other economies meant that there was limited competition from overseas firms. But again, these 'incursions' into foreign countries and markets were piloted by private enterprise, albeit with a helping hand from the US government. The **Washington Treaty** helped short-term relations with Japan – an important trading partner – and the **Dawes Plan** helped rehabilitate the German economy such that it could resume payment of reparations to Britain and France, which would then find their way back to the Allies' American creditors.

1.5 Canada and the First World War

Conceptual understanding

Key questions

→ To what extent did participation in the First World War affect national unity in Canada?

→ What were the economic effects of the First World War on Canada?

→ How was Canada's place in the world different in 1919 than it had been in 1914?

Key concepts

→ Continuity

→ Change

Pulled into war

Having gained independence in domestic issues in 1867, Canada still laboured under a confusing foreign policy structure in 1914. As a dominion of the British Empire, with the British government essentially controlling Canada's foreign policy, Canada was bound by the course that the British would take in the July Crisis of 1914. When the United Kingdom declared war on August 4, 1914, Canada was automatically at war with Germany. Over the preceding 12 years, the Canadian military had been gradually drawn into a more centralized command structure in terms of imperial operations and by 1912 Canadian forces were integrated into imperial defence plans. Despite this integration, there were hints that the issue of British command of Canadian soldiers would prove contentious and in fact this would come to a head during the war. In 1904, Wilfred Laurier's government officially placed the country's militia under the command of a dominion-born officer. From 1907, however, integration continued, with advances in common training and standards among the imperial forces. On paper, Canada had a permanent force of about 4000 soldiers and about 50 000 militia with some training. The Navy consisted of two warships.

Mobilization

In the midst of a heated debate regarding the construction of the Canadian Navy, Wilfred Laurier had declared that when Britain was at war, Canada was at war. Although Canada had been debating its place in the British Empire almost since the signing of the British North America Act, with some advocating greater independence and others arguing caution and the benefits of 'dominion status', in 1914 the fact remained much as Laurier had characterized it. While it is true that Canada tumbled into the conflict with Britain's declaration of war in August 1914, the manner of Canada's participation was, as the South African War of 1899 had illustrated, a matter for the Canadian parliament to

ATL Research skills

Research the economic situation in Canada in the period 1912–1914. Use the following topic headings to guide your research:

- Manufacturing
- Unemployment
- Agricultural production
- Trade

1 How was the economic context related to Canada's ability to fight a war in 1914?

2 What effect might the unemployment situation have on recruiting efforts in the autumn of 1914?

3 What effect did this economic situation have on government revenues? How might this impact Canada's ability to equip an army and navy? What might be some possible solutions for the government?

decide. That said, there was little debate. Canada, with its population of 8 million, would commit to the total war effort. It would send men and material and mobilize the home front for the war effort. The initial commitment was a contingent of 25 000 men equipped and delivered to the European theatre at Canada's expense – initially estimated at some $50 million. To facilitate this mobilization, the government passed the War Measures Act at the outbreak of the war. The act reserved for the federal government the right to govern by executive decree in times of perceived 'war, invasion, or insurrection'.

The character of the Minister of Militia Sam Hughes, would dominate the mobilization effort. Hughes operated free from governmental interference, method and scruples. Within a month of the outbreak of the war, over 30 000 men had assembled at Valcartier, Quebec, for training. Assembling men was one thing, but a modern army had to be equipped and clothed and this proved a challenge. Khaki uniforms and the **Ross rifle** were ordered in huge quantities. Ships were contracted and preparations made, albeit at times in an unorthodox fashion and somewhat haphazardly. The embarkation of the first contingent of the Canadian Expeditionary Force bore a marked resemblance to the US army's chaotic departure for Cuba during the Spanish–American War. Nevertheless, the first contingent of 30 000 troops landed in England in mid-October 1914, and Robert Borden's Conservative government ordered a second contingent of the same strength be raised.

Ross rifle

The weapon that Sam Hughes decided would be issued to Canadian infantrymen at the outset of the First World War. The rifle proved to be a good target and sniping weapon, but was heavy and jammed regularly, especially in the trying conditions of trench warfare. Persistent criticism by frontline soldiers eventually led to its replacement by the British Lee-Enfield rifle.

▲ Canadian Ross rifle

ATL Thinking and communication skills

The initial volunteers for the Canadian Expeditionary Force came from all over Canada, although in markedly different numbers. For each of the following people, write a letter explaining your motives for volunteering or not.

- A farm boy from Southern Saskatchewan
- A lawyer from Toronto
- A French Canadian mill worker from Montreal
- A recent German immigrant living in Edmonton
- A Mennonite farmer from Steinbeck, Manitoba
- A logger from New Brunswick whose parents had emigrated from Scotland

The volunteer spirit was not limited to those seeking active service in Europe. Organizations such as the YMCA and other existing associations turned their efforts to raising money and material for the war effort. The Canadian Patriotic Fund was chartered to raise money that would bridge the gap between what soldiers would earn in uniform and what they had earned as civilians, thus taking some of the financial burden off those who remained behind. Schools, clubs and mutual benefit societies raised money to buy food, uniforms and even weapons.

Despite the enthusiasm with which most Canadians approached the war effort, there was, from the start, some quiet voices of dissent – voices that would grow in volume as the slaughter in France became more apparent and dragged on from year to year. Pacifist religious sects, such as the Mennonites and Doukhobors, remained opposed to the war although quietly so. But even among the religious groups that opposed the notion of war, such as the Methodists, some were won over to support the war effort on the grounds that it was becoming a moral crusade against those who would use war to further their national goals, namely Germany.

Recruiting remained relatively easy throughout 1914 and 1915, with close to 60 000 enlisting by the end of 1914. By June 1915, Canada had a force of over 100 000 soldiers overseas, with a goal of one man in reserve in England for every two at the front. This goal would be increasingly hard to maintain in the face of enormous casualty figures, the likes of which none of the belligerents had foreseen. By the autumn of 1915, Canada had two divisions with a total strength of over 40 000 fighting in France. Sam Hughes boasted an ever-expanding Canadian army, with all new recruits forming into new battalions, which in turn would coalesce into new divisions. The brutal arithmetic of the trenches, however, dictated that each division that was fighting would need replacements at a rate of some 15 000 men a year. The decentralized recruiting system continually lowered medical and height standards in order to meet the need for men. Volunteer recruiting peaked in early 1916 and fell off from that point. Nevertheless, when the Battle of Arras erupted in the spring of 1917 and the Canadians began their assault on Vimy Ridge, the Canadian Corps consisted of four divisions in France with a fifth waiting in Britain. But by this time, recruit numbers could not keep up with battle losses.

Quebec

Recruiting in Quebec had lagged behind English Canada from the beginning of the war. The reasons were numerous. There was one French-speaking regiment – the Royal 22 Battalion 'The Van Doos' – but it was primarily led by English officers. Demographically, men married earlier in Quebec, and this shrank the available pool of single men as compared to Western Canada and Ontario. Recruiting in the province was organized by a Protestant clergyman and thereby excluded the most influential social institution in the province – the Catholic Church – from the recruitment process. Anti-French education laws in Ontario and Manitoba epitomized an attitude that convinced many French Canadians that this was not their war. The growing employment opportunities afforded by increased war production, and the high wages that accompanied them, seemed to young Quebecers a more sensible decision than enlisting. Politically, Henri Bourassa, a leading Quebec politician, was expressing his opposition to the war openly by 1916, as were many of his *nationaliste* allies, and this curtailed Quebec recruitment even further.

▲ Canadian machine gunners in a shell hole during the advance at Vimy Ridge, near Arras, France, 1917

Class discussion

The Battle of Vimy Ridge is considered an important event in the development of Canada as in independent nation. How can the experience of war foster nationalist feelings?

Canada's willingness

Source A

The following is an excerpt by historians J Finlay and D Sprague.

At the beginning, mobilization had the effect of unifying the country around a sense of common danger that was far less artificial than anything Canada had experienced in the past. Earlier, in the case of John A. McDonald's attempt to create an atmosphere of national emergency around the building of the CPR, for example, the artificiality of the effort was only too apparent. Or later with the South African war, the episode was only English Canada's adventure.

Source: Finlay, JL and DN Sprague, 1984. *The Structure of Canadian History*. Scarborough: Prentice Hall. Pp. 298–99.

Source B

Wilfred Laurier, the leader of the official opposition, uttered the following to describe Canada's stance at the beginning of the war.

... when the call goes out our answer goes at once, and it goes in the classical language of British answer to the call of Duty: Ready, Aye Ready.

Source C

Stuart Ramsay Tompkins was a young Albertan working for the Department of Education when the war broke out in 1914. The following is an excerpt of a letter he wrote to his wife-to-be in September 1914.

The whole city [Edmonton] is now astir with a mild form of mobilization. Last night coming down town we passed a squad of citizens marching to the tune of "A Hundred Pipers ...". A whole regiment is being formed to train bellicose citizens. The civil service are forming a squad but in view of the announcement ... there is much less enthusiasm being displayed. Strong exception is being taken to the stand of the government in refusing to allow men any part of their salary while on active service.

Source: Stuart Ramsay Tompkins to Edna Christie, 10 September 1914. Cited in Ramsay Tompkins, Stuart. 1989. *A Canadian's Road to Russia: Letters from the Great War Decade.* Doris H Pieroth (ed.) Edmonton: University of Alberta Press. P. 36.

Questions

1 How does Source A contrast the First World War with earlier crises in Canada? Why was it different?

2 Why, according to Source C, are members of the civil service hesitant to enlist?

3 Compare and contrast the sentiments of Canadian citizens regarding enlisting as expressed in Sources B and C.

4 Using the documents and further research analyse military enlistment in Canada in 1914.

The home front

While the First World War was developing into a human tragedy of catastrophic proportions, it was fundamentally changing the short-term condition and long-term structure of the Canadian economy.
Like other countries, Canada entered the war while in the depths of a sharp depression. The increased production required by a European war and the prospect of a vastly expanded army meant that after a period of realignment – and in fact a brief deepening of the depression – unemployment would be a memory. When the massive increase in demand that accompanied a war of this magnitude was combined with the physical devastation and dislocation of established European national economies, it meant that Canada – its fields and factories safe on the other side of the Atlantic – could expand into this niche.

Initially in Canada this expansion would be in its traditional role as a supplier of primary resources. Acreage under cultivation increased dramatically early in the war and this pushed wheat production to new levels. Thereafter, production would stabilize at lower levels. The massive demand created by the disruption to European wheat supplies sent commodity prices higher. The net result was that the value of wheat exports doubled during the war, although they would never match the amount of grain produced per acre in 1915. Wartime necessity also buoyed the Canadian lumber industry, which had been hit hard by the building slump that accompanied the depression of 1913. Dairy products and meat also found new markets. Meat exports increased by some 1400% during the course of the war. Mineral extraction also increased during the period.

Munitions production was certainly not a traditional sector of strength in the Canadian economy. The expanded Canadian army, its British allies, the grinding nature of trench warfare, and the domineering personality of Sam Hughes all demanded that it become one. It was initiated in typical Sam Hughes fashion – ad hoc with a heavy dose of **patronage**. But such a 'system' was bound to collapse under the huge demands of a war of the scale which was developing in Europe. Initial war production suffered in both quantity and quality. Hughes' Shell Committee, set up in 1914 to manage munitions production, proved incapable of keeping up with purchase orders from both the Canadian and British armies, plagued as it was by Hughes' meddling, profiteering and old party patronage. The Imperial Munitions Board, over which Hughes had no control, was created to replace the Shell Committee in 1915. Quantity and quality of munitions improved almost immediately.

> **patronage**
> The practice of giving political positions and economic opportunities to political allies and supporters.

The issues with the Shell Committee and munitions production illustrated the fact that the Canadian government did not have an overall plan for wartime economic coordination. Rather, it responded to issues and situations as they arose. The War Measures Act gave the government a powerful tool with which to address these emergent situations. Nevertheless, as the war progressed, a patchwork of government intervention appeared in Canadian society:

1915 Imperial Munitions Board coordinated production of artillery shells and later other materials from ships to airplanes

1915 War Purchasing Commission coordinated military procurement

1915 Munitions Resources Commission supervised the conservation of natural resources for war production

1917 Fuel Controller coordinated fuel import, export, production and distribution

1917 Board of Grain Supervisors managed wheat marketing

1918 War Trade Board managed import and export licences

1918 Canadian Food Board supervised food distribution

Financing the war

With a massive war effort comes a massive financial burden. Canada, like all countries, had two means at its disposal to meet this burden – taxation and credit. Taxation was anathema to the finance minister Thomas White, but there really seemed no alternative. A multitude

> **British North America Act**
> A 1867 act of the British parliament that established and outlined self-government in Canada. It, in essence, formed part of the Canadian constitution until 1981 when the constitution became a solely Canadian document.

> **Class discussion**
>
> How does the level of taxation in 2015 compare to the level of taxation in 1918? What accounts for the differences?

of indirect taxes descended on the Canadian public. Steamship and railroad tickets were taxed, as were items such as coffee, sugar, tobacco, cheques and telegrams. Tariffs increased. It was clear from the beginning, however, that indirect taxation would not suffice and in 1916 the federal government passed its first direct taxation measure, a power that the **British North America Act** had reserved for the provincial level of government. It was a tax on profits made from war materials. It was not the last such tax and in 1917, with bills mounting, the federal government introduced Canada's first income tax, assuring the public that it was a temporary measure. The new taxation, however, came nowhere near meeting the government's wartime obligations. The rest would have to be raised by borrowing.

Canada was already in debt when the war broke out. Years of railroad construction and subsidies had pushed government expenditures well beyond its income. The problem with wartime debt was where was there money available to borrow? Britain, a traditional source of credit for Canadian enterprise, was strapped beyond its capacity to pay and indeed would become a debtor nation to Canada by the end of the war. The USA was an economy that, free from wartime expenditure and flush with war profits, became one source of credit. The other, more important source, however, was found within Canada. Starting in 1915 and continuing throughout the war, the federal government issued a series of bonds that would raise $2.3 billion. Provincial and municipal governments were also looking for credit during the war; when the resultant burden was added to the federal numbers, Canada emerged from the conflict with a debt of close to $5 billion.

While spending helps create employment; it also causes prices to rise. When this spending is undertaken by the government on a scale such as that required by the First World War, inflation is bound to be significant. The Borden government had taken Canada off the gold standard early in the war and began to print money. When this was added to the dramatically increased demand in the war years, prices almost doubled. The war also put strains on world supply that exerted an upward pressure on prices.

A question of leadership

The war brought into sharper focus an issue that Canada and its leaders had been grappling with increasingly over the preceding 20 years – namely the dominion's relationship with the United Kingdom. The simple fact that a declaration of war by the British parliament committed Canada to war highlighted the limited nature of Canada's independence, as did the fact that its constitution was in fact an act of the British parliament and would remain so into the 1980s. It is true that when the British parliament declared war in August 1914, there was no hesitation on the part of either Prime Minister Borden or Leader of the Opposition Laurier, the latter somewhat cool to imperial integration. Canada would commit completely to Britain's cause. But as Canada's commitment grew and the war dragged on in its vicious stalemate, questions of dominion sovereignty began to emerge. Nowhere was this clearer than in the matter of the leadership of Canadian troops.

At the outset of the war the British High Command gave brief consideration to the Canadian troops being distributed among existing British formations, but then determined to use the Canadians as a division led by a British general. Borden favoured the idea that Canadian officers would lead these units. While he was largely successful in these efforts, the Canadian Expeditionary Force (CEF) would become, for operational purposes, part of the British Army. Operationally, the Canadian troops would gradually come ever more under the Canadian commanders as the war progressed, with Sir Arthur Currie becoming the first Canadian-born commander of the Canadian corps in 1917. But the overall direction of military operations was another matter.

Throughout 1914 and the first half of 1915, Borden began to realize the fact the Canadian troops had essentially been turned over to the British government to do with as they pleased short of splitting them up. While this might have been inconsequential had the war been over by Christmas and Canada's contribution remained proportionally small, by the summer of 1915 it was becoming evident that the war was going to be a long, brutal and grinding affair and that the Canadian contribution was growing in significance. Borden found it increasingly difficult to accept that he and the Canadian parliament had no say in the policy and strategy that its troops would execute. Facing staggering casualty figures with no end in sight, Borden travelled to Britain in the summer of 1915 to assess the situation for himself and argue for a more significant decision-making role for his dominion.

Finding no answers and plenty of condescension from British government and military officials, Borden returned to Canada determined to raise enough soldiers for the cause that Canada's concerns could not be ignored. It was not until the horrific battles of 1916 decimated Allied ranks and David Lloyd George became the coalition leader of a new British government that this situation began to change. In January 1917 Lloyd George convened an Imperial War Conference and the dominion leaders formed into an Imperial War Cabinet. Two things became evident at the cabinet table. Britain expected even more from its imperial partners and, in turn, the dominions wanted a change in their status as a result.

A country divided: Quebec and the War Effort

The initial wartime consensus welded together by war fervour and patriotic outpouring soon began to show cracks; as might be expected, these were most evident in French–English relations. Wilfred Laurier, ever an eloquent advocate of Canadian unity, never wavered in his exhortations to cooperation. But as the war dragged on, recruiting numbers began to reveal a perceived gap between English volunteers and French volunteers. Lack of distinct French military units and a perceived prejudice against French officers combined with anti-French language legislation in both Ontario and Manitoba to further enflame a tense situation. The Quebec nationalists had furthered their alliance with the Conservatives early in the war by joining Borden's government. The *nationaliste* leader, Henri Bourassa, however, had turned publicly against the war by 1916.

Class discussion

To what extent is it important for troops to be commanded by people from their own country?

Much of this was brought to a head by the conscription crisis and subsequent 1917 federal election campaign. The Liberal Party under Laurier opposed conscription. Its power, which stretched across the Quebec–Ontario border, however, was severely split by the question of conscription. Many Ontario and western Liberals who either supported conscription or recognized the prevailing political winds crossed to join Borden's new Unionist government, leaving the ageing Laurier feeling betrayed and with but a few Quebec MPs.

In the streets, conscription proved deeply unpopular in Quebec. Riots and protests spread across the province and with them denunciations of treason by pro-conscription advocates. Order was restored with the help of the War Measures Act. When the dust of the 1917 election settled, Quebec found itself with its MPs in parliamentary opposition and with conscription a reality. While to the community of nation states the First World War had helped propel Canada towards nationhood, within its borders Canada was more divided in 1918 than it had been in 1914.

Political unity and division

When the British government entered the war in August 1914, dragging its empire over the edge, the news was greeted with pledges of cooperation and support from politicians on both sides of the House of Commons. Wilfred Laurier put aside his pre-war imperial misgivings and ranged his Liberal Party behind the Borden government. Henri Bourassa, although personally opposed to the war, would not speak against the war as a politician until 1916. His parliamentary followers backed the government, as many had in the years preceding the war. This united front, however, was built more on circumstances than it was on deeper political principles. There was agreement on the ends, but not the means. All could agree if not on the necessity of supporting the United Kingdom, then at least on opposing the dangers of 'Prussianism' and the evils of an unprovoked expansionary war. How that was to be accomplished was another matter.

The government's approach to meeting these ends was to place a great deal of power, money and trust in the controversial Sam Hughes, Minister of the Militia. Hughes was a bombastic, stubborn, energetic politician who had little use for the formalities of parliamentary government or his own prime minister. He did, however, have a great deal of use for people who supported him and the quirky ideas that took his fancy. His championing of the Ross rifle, a fine target weapon but unsuitable for the dirty rigours of trench warfare, left the riding (electoral district) in which it was produced flush with employment and the Ross Rifle Company flush with profits, but Canadian soldiers bereft of a workable rifle in France. His lack of a centralized recruiting system created chaos at the same time as tens of thousands of Canadians signed up. Mounting scandals and criticism finally pushed Borden to fire Hughes in 1916.

The corruption that accompanied Hughes' 'system', as well as non-Hughes related scandals, brought political opposition to the Borden government's handling of the war. A number of Liberals had been calling for a coalition government from early in the war and these calls increased in intensity as 1916, with its seemingly endless casualty lists, dragged on. Borden himself began to see that this was going to be necessary before the end of the war. It was the combination of dwindling enlistment numbers and growing casualty lists that would bring about the formation of a Union Government.

The conscription crisis

Unable to maintain voluntary enlistment numbers that could sustain the Canadian Corps in the face of battlefield losses, Prime Minister Borden decided that the only alternative was conscription and in May 1917 announced it to the House of Commons. After the announcement, he approached Laurier with the prospect of forming some kind of coalition government, not necessarily with Borden as prime minister. Laurier, struck by the fact that the prospect of conscription was raised before he was approached, essentially asking for his endorsement rather than his input, declined and set himself against conscription.

The Military Service Act was debated throughout the summer of 1917 and was passed by the end of August. It would call up single men first and provide for conscientious objectors. Borden hoped it would raise an additional 100 000 men for the Canadian Corps. He was unable to persuade opposition leader Laurier into a coalition government and his inability to get the opposition Liberals to consent to a further year's postponement of a general election meant that conscription would be decided largely at the polls. To bolster the chances of victory, the government drafted and passed the Military Voters Act. This act provided for soldiers serving overseas to cast a vote. As if to underscore the fact that it was essentially a one-issue election, they could cast either a 'yes' or a 'no' vote for the current government. Alternately, they could write in the name of a candidate if they knew of one. A helpful list of government candidates accompanied the ballots. The Wartime Elections Act significantly extended the franchise to female relatives of serving and deceased soldiers. The same act removed the franchise from those immigrants who had come to Canada from enemy countries after 1902.

As it became increasingly obvious that the pro-conscription forces would win the looming election, many English-speaking Liberals began to take Borden up on an offer to accept them into what he called a Union government in October 1917. Regardless of how these politicians read the prevailing winds, the general election of 1917 was a hard-fought affair that revealed the issue of conscription to be divisive across the country. In an effort to secure the western farm vote, Borden announced that farmers' sons would be exempt from military service. The outcome of the election returned a Unionist government with a 71-seat majority. Closer examination of the returns reflected the divided nature of the country that had emerged in the campaign. Quebec and the Maritimes had gone heavily against the Unionists, but Borden was able to carry the day on the strength of Ontario and Western Canada. In terms of the popular vote, Quebec had voted four to one against the Unionist government while the rest of Canada had voted in favour of it by a margin of almost three to one. Not surprisingly, serving soldiers voted overwhelmingly for the Unionists and by association for conscription.

In an effort to win the election of 1917, the Union government had promised a number of conscription exemptions – farmers' sons and Mennonites, for example – but the sheer number of those seeking exemption ran the appeals mechanism to a standstill. The conscription machinery in Quebec proved incapable of compelling a largely unwilling population to register for the draft. When Borden and his Cabinet, faced with the alarming casualties at the beginning of 1918, ended most exemptions, violence erupted in Ontario and Quebec. In the west the violence was often turned on those seeking exemptions. The divisions created by conscription would continue to the end of the war.

By the end of the war, some 24 000 conscripts had made it to the front and were assigned as reinforcements to existing formations within the Canadian Corps and many played an important role in the battles that took place in the last three months of the war. While it can be argued that conscription was necessary to maintain Canada's overseas fighting strength and that it did just that, it came at the cost of the national unity that appeared to be forming at the beginning of the war, and the division thus engendered would continue throughout the century.

ATL Research and communication skills

Choose to support or oppose conscription in Canada after some research. In class, conduct a debate on whether or not the Canadian government should pass conscription into law in 1917. In researching your position be sure to include a representative sample of perspectives including:

- The Maritimes
- The Western Prairies
- British Columbia
- English-speaking Quebecers
- French-speaking Quebecers
- Immigrants
- Families of soldiers
- Members of the Conservative Party
- Members of the Liberal Party
- Labour leaders

At the front

The first contingent of the Canadian Expeditionary Force arrived in England in October 1914 and soon began a haphazard training at their quarters on the infamous windswept, cold and wet Salisbury Plain. While the bulk of Canadian troops would serve as a distinct division and later corps in the British Army, some units served in other British formations. The Princess Patricia's Canadian Light Infantry, a unit raised in Canada at the outset of the war consisting of Canadians with British military experience, initially served within a British division. Some Canadian specialist units served in other theatres of war, but the vast majority was stationed at various points on the Western Front throughout the war.

ATL Research skills

From their initial involvement in 1915, the Canadians took part in numerous battles on the Western Front. Research the following battles to complete the following table.

Battle	Dates	Canadian commanders	Description	Significance
2nd Ypres				
St Eloi				
The Somme				
Courcelette				
Vimy Ridge				
Hill 70				
Passchendaele				
The 100 Days				

The Canadians arrived in France in February of 1915. After some minor engagements in March, in April the Canadian brigades were stationed in the Ypres Salient, a bulge in the British line near the ancient cloth-making town of Ypres. On 22 April the Germans positioned opposite the Canadians, who were flanked by French and Algerians, released chlorine gas for the first time on the Western Front. The ensuing Second Battle of Ypres was a chaotic and bloody affair that revealed the Canadians as inexperienced but courageous soldiers. The shortcomings of the Ross rifle were becoming dangerously evident and Canadian soldiers would abandon them for the more robust Lee-Enfield of the British Army whenever they could.

With the arrival of the second contingent in mid-1915, the Canadians were formed into a corps, commanded by a British general with the component divisions being commanded by Canadian generals. The Canadian Corps began to gain a reputation as skillful trench raiders and eventually as shock troops, leading larger assaults on German lines. By 1917, the Canadian Corps, by then consisting of four divisions, was given the task of capturing Vimy Ridge, a commanding position that the French army had been unable to wrestle from the German army. This operation, to commence on 9 April, was to be Canadian in conception, planning and execution. General Arthur Currie took note of previous failures and, determined not to repeat them, had his corps meticulously rehearse the plan behind the lines. Innovations such as platoon tactics, new methods for counter battery targeting, as well as ensuring that all men, especially non-commissioned officers, understood their objectives and how to find them both on a map and in reality, helped make the operation a huge success.

▲ Canadian soldiers move shells to the front during the Battle of Vimy Ridge, 1917

The peace

From Borden's first wartime visit to England it was evident that he believed the scale of Canada's commitment entitled Canada to a share in determining the direction of the conflict. While this was not immediately evident to the British authorities, by the time David Lloyd George formed the Imperial War Cabinet, it was fairly clear that the role of the dominions would have to be redefined.

The British assumed that the dominions would be consulted, but submit as subordinates to the British delegation at the peace conference. Borden would have none of this. Canada must have a seat at the conference on its own merits and the merits of its contribution to the Allied victory. Canadian delegates sat on committees that decided some aspects of the final treaty. Canada's position on the whole can be seen as a mixture of American and British sentiment. Borden refused the notion that Canada might benefit from German territorial concessions. While Borden may have seen Canada's new position in the world as ideal to act as the middle ground between Britain and the USA, Wilson saw it quite differently. Wilson and other US diplomats preferred to deal with Britain on matters involving Canada. Britain could be counted on to arrive at compromise more quickly than Canada, having little direct interests in much of Canada–USA relations. Article X of the League of Nations Covenant providing for international response to aggressive acts was also a major concern for Borden, much as it was for American opponents of the treaty. He was worried that this clause might drag Canada into another European war – its hands tied this time by the League as it had been by the British Empire in 1914. Canada also opposed any part of the League of Nations Covenant that might curtail its ability to limit immigration based on race or any other criterion. In the end, Canada became a signatory to the Treaty of Versailles separate from the British delegation. Likewise, Canada was admitted to the League of Nations as its own country.

Demobilization

Canada had mobilized close to 9% of its total 1914 population for the war effort. Almost 60 000 of these had not returned. Reintegrating those scores who did return into an economy that was no longer buoyed by wartime demand was going to be a difficult task. For the most part, the government made little provision for demobilized soldiers. They were given money for civilian clothing, access to medical care for a year and some help, depending on where they were, finding a job. Those so inclined and deemed good investments could apply for a low-interest loan to purchase farmland. What remaining free land could be found was made available to veterans, but this was far from prime agricultural land. Beyond this, the veterans were left largely to their own devices. Nevertheless, the veterans were reintegrated into the economy with fewer problems than might have been expected.

While the veterans integrated into society, organized labour struggled to adjust to the new ideological and economic landscape. When the Bolsheviks seized control in Russia in 1917, left-wing politics in Canada were invigorated. As it had with the US government this prompted a reaction by the Canadian government, which worked to shut down foreign-language newspapers and banned a number of 'radical' organizations in 1918. The economic disruption prompted by the end of the war helped spark a number of radical labour actions in the

Class discussion

How did Canada's handling of demobilization compare to that of its allies? How did it compare with Canada's own efforts after the Second World War?

immediate post-war period, the most significant being the Winnipeg General Strike of 1919, which shut this major western Canadian city down for six weeks and gave rise to sympathy strikes across the country.

Impact of the war

Economic changes

The Canadian economy had undergone a significant restructuring during the war. Manufacturing played a far greater role in 1919 than it had in 1914. Not only had existing sectors expanded, but new areas of activity also expanded. Textiles and chemical production had increased with the wartime demand and the decline of British imports. It would prove far less expensive to convert wartime industries to civilian production than to build these from scratch, and thus the war provided an important accelerant to Canadian manufacturing. Notwithstanding the advances in manufacturing, more land under cultivation, new forests and mineral deposits being exploited, the war had created another important structural shift in the Canadian economy. The relative weakness of the British economy and strength of the American economy meant that, increasingly, the USA replaced the United Kingdom as Canada's leading trading partner, creditor and foreign investor.

Diplomatic changes

On the world stage, Canada took its hard-fought independent membership in the League of Nations and the International Labour Organization very seriously. It did not take long after the war, however, for the reality of this independence to be tested. When, in 1922, Turkish forces tested the resolve of the British garrison at Chanak in the Straits, Britain summoned its dominions to its side once again. Canada's Liberal prime minister Mackenzie King discovered the British assumption of Canadian aid in the press before he heard from the British government. King responded by declaring publicly that it would be the Canadian parliament that would decide if Canada would participate, not the British government. While the Chanak crisis was resolved without recourse to arms, it prompted a further clarification of Canada's international position. The conference that assembled at Lausanne to negotiate with the Turks did not include Canada, to which King responded by stating that Canada would not be bound by any agreement to which it was not a signatory. In 1923 Canada signed the Halibut Treaty with the USA with no participation by the British – the first time that Canada had negotiated and signed a bilateral treaty on its own. By 1927 Canada had appointed a Canadian envoy to the USA who, for the first time, would officially act and work independently of the British embassy. The sovereignty that had begun on the battlefields of Flanders thus progressed throughout the 1920s.

> **ATL Research skills**
>
> Compare and contrast labour unrest in the following countries in the Americas in the immediate post-war period:
>
> - USA
> - Canada
> - Argentina
> - Brazil
> - Central America

1.6 The impact of the First World War on Latin America

Conceptual understanding

Key questions

→ To what extent did the First World War affect the economy of Latin American countries?

→ To what extent did the effects of the First World War vary by country in Latin America?

→ To what extent did the First World War change the relative national power structure of Latin America?

Key concepts

→ Continuity

→ Change

→ Consequence

Economic conditions prior to the First World War

The end of the 19th century saw an incredible integration of the world economy. Goods, people and capital moved around the globe with increasing ease and in ever-growing amounts. Technology allowed for a uniform system of commodity prices to exist and thus trade to be more globalized. While this integration allowed consumers and producers around the world to take advantage of foreign markets and prices, it also exposed them to the vagaries of these markets. Changes in livestock prices in Canada could affect the price of Argentine beef and thus the life of Argentine ranchers. A catastrophe the scale of the First World War was bound to have profound effects on this global economy and all its participants whether they were a belligerent or not.

Latin American countries were certainly a part of this global economy. Massive amounts of European capital flowed into the region. By 1914, the United Kingdom had poured close to 4 billion dollars' worth of capital into Latin America. Large sums were also invested by France ($1.1 billion) and Germany ($0.9 billion). Foreign capital was heavily invested in communication and transportation networks. The British enjoyed a telegraph monopoly in Argentina, Brazil and Uruguay, while the US-owned Central and South American Telegraph Company was also heavily investing in the region. British and US banks were scattered throughout the continent, facilitating the movement of this capital.

Latin America's major role in this global economy was as an exporter of commodities. Argentina exported wheat, corn, beef and wool. Foreign capital and technology fuelled the Chilean copper-mining industry at the turn of the century. Chile's production of nitrates for the world market was also expanding rapidly, as were its wheat and wool industries in

Class discussion

What are the comparative benefits and drawbacks of a large amount of foreign capital moving into an economy?

the years leading up to the First World War. Although Brazilian coffee production was volatile in the years leading up to the war, it was nonetheless an incredibly important part of the Brazilian economy, accounting for over half of the value of all Brazilian exports in the years 1870–1911. Significantly for the coming war, the primary consumers of Brazilian coffee were the USA, France and Germany. The Mexican export economy grew dramatically until 1911 and tended to be more diversified than other Latin American economies. Ranching, mining, as well as henequen and oil production were important elements in Mexico's export economy.

Latin America in the First World War	
Country	Status
Brazil	Declared war on Germany in 1917
Argentina	Neutral
Colombia	Neutral
Venezuela	Neutral
Peru	Broke diplomatic relations with Germany
Chile	Neutral
Uruguay	Broke diplomatic relations with Germany
Paraguay	Neutral
Ecuador	Broke diplomatic relations with Germany
Bolivia	Broke diplomatic relations with Germany
Nicaragua	Declared war on Germany in 1918
Guatemala	Declared war on Germany in 1918
Mexico	Neutral
Cuba	Declared war on Germany in 1917
Panama	Declared war on Germany in 1917
El Salvador	Neutral
Costa Rica	Declared war on Germany in 1918
Haiti	Declared war on Germany in 1918
Honduras	Declared war on Germany in 1918

Migration was also an important aspect of the pre-war global economy. Europeans moved to Latin America, and these people were increasingly from Germany. Germany was taking an ever-more aggressive approach to foreign policy with the Kaiser's imperial desire for 'a place in the sun' and this included Latin America. By 1900, well over 250 000 Germans had emigrated to Brazil and some 120 000 to Chile. German migrants could be found throughout the region. At the turn of the century, wherever German people, business and money went, the German army would not be far behind, most notably in Chile, where German officers instructed the Chilean army. The Germans also had a military presence in Argentina, Bolivia and Paraguay. The German

High Command mapped out contingency plans for a war with the USA during this period and these included operations in the Latin American region. German interest in South America raised the ire of the USA and was an important factor in its own ambitions to expand in the region throughout this period.

As war clouds gathered, there were signs that the world economy was beginning to change. Much of this had to do with the ascendance of the USA in international economic importance and the looming comparative decline of the British economy. While the British remained the most important foreign economic power in South America, the USA had made important inroads into the economies of South American countries, especially those on the Pacific coast. These were changes that were to be accelerated by the outbreak of the First World War. Seen in this light, although there were drastic changes in Latin America as a result of the war, there were also elements of continuity in terms of trends that had begun prior to 1914.

The economic impact of the outbreak of war

The outbreak of the war had been preceded by a short, sharp world economic recession. Although this represented a dramatic slowdown in economic activity, the war brought things to a near standstill. Part of the reason was that the war immediately affected the physical and financial apparatus by which world markets operated: credit was no longer available; insurance became scarce; there was an immediate impact on shipping as British ships, which carried the bulk of Latin American goods, waited for orders and naval escorts. Shipping rates skyrocketed with the reduction in availability. These effects were fairly immediate, but the increased demand that accompanies war had yet to be felt. The end result was that export economies dependent on foreign capital and foreign shipping, such as Latin American economies, were hit particularly hard very early in the war.

As they were reliant on foreign credit, predominantly from London, the outbreak of the war in which the United Kingdom had decided to participate placed immediate pressure on Latin American banks. Loans were called in. There were significant runs on banks and a number of governments responded by declaring 'bank holidays' and placing temporary moratoriums on debt. The short-term credit upon which day-to-day business in Latin America and indeed the world depended began to collapse, making even small domestic transactions difficult. The Argentine and Brazilian governments were also dependent on long-term loans, as were all the governments that ran deficit budgets as part of their national finances, and securing and refinancing these loans became extremely difficult.

It might be expected that export economies would fare well in wartime with its dramatically increased demand for everything from food to chemicals and minerals. But this took some time to filter through. For example, Chile was one of the world's leading producers of nitrates, which are key components in both fertilizer and explosives – two products in particular demand in wartime. But in the early months of the war, other factors conspired to hurt Chilean nitrate sales. The pre-war recession and slump in prices meant that many countries carried surplus supplies of nitrates into late 1914. Much of Chile's nitrate sales were to central European countries, with close to a third of these sales to Germany. The British naval blockade closed this market, creating a nitrate surplus in Chile as well. Only when the enormous destruction of the war continued into 1915 did the massive demand for nitrates, among other goods, erode the surpluses and increase exports.

By 1915, Latin American economies had begun to recover from the initial shock of the war. The massive demand for the raw materials of war fuelled this recovery. Although the volume of exports would not completely recover due to the interruption of shipping and capital, the demand drove prices dramatically higher and therefore the income from exports did recover by 1916. Wartime demand also sparked a rise in international inflation, pushing the price of imports higher. Eventually, as in most other national economies during the war, domestic inflation followed. The price of food in Argentina rose by 50% during the war and clothing in some cases tripled in price. Financial mechanisms such as currency exchange systems also began to improve in Latin America in the second year of the war, making it easier to conduct business than it had been when the war broke out. The international value of the US dollar and the pound sterling began to stabilize. Nevertheless, the amount of foreign capital that was directed at infrastructure and capital building projects did not recover. In general, the governments of Latin America responded to the unavailability of foreign loans by curtailing public works and other major projects. Some loans were secured by the USA and domestic bonds secured others, but on the whole austerity was the primary response.

The debt problem of many Latin American economies was compounded during the war by the fact that around 50% of states' revenues came in the form of duties. With the slump in imports, this revenue stream was cut dramatically. Some countries, such as Brazil, responded to this revenue shortfall by printing money, with the predictable inflationary effects, which were already extreme due to supply and demand issues created by the war.

The combination of fiscal austerity and domestic inflation created a volatile labour situation in a number of Latin American countries. By 1917, employment was rising in Argentina, as were consumer prices. Real wages were falling. Consequently, labour union activity increased significantly during this period. When the government seemed to side with the workers, it was quickly denounced as pro-German, especially by British business interests. In January 1919 Buenos Aires erupted in a violent general strike that started in the Vesena metal works and quickly spread to other sectors; a number of strikers and police officers were killed. In this case the government ordered the army to end the strike, and a week of violence, arrests and many deaths followed – a period known as the 'Tragic Week'. This week was followed by a period of popular reprisals against Russian and Jewish communities in the country, fuelled by the belief that the general strike was a prelude to a Bolshevik-like revolution. The war and related events seemed to spark unrest beyond the labour movement in Argentina. Student movements, influenced by the Mexican and Russian revolutions, staged strikes and

Class discussion

What other commodities are in higher demand during war? How did this change throughout the 20th century? What effect might this have on the balance of power in the world?

demonstrations calling for academic reform, and these demonstrations did find support from the Yrigoyen government despite its violent suppression of the general strike.

In the end, the effect of the war on the various economies of Latin America depended to a degree on the state of these economies at the outset of the war. Countries such as Brazil and Chile, which had begun to industrialize in the pre-war years, used the wartime demand to accelerate industrial output during this period. Peru, Colombia and countries with stronger trade ties with the USA built on these ties during the war and therefore had to substitute for lost imports to a lesser degree than those economies more dependent on European trade. The less industrially developed economies of Central America saw in the war a disruption to their regular economic activity to which they would return at the end of hostilities. Regardless, all these economies would return to export dependence after 1919.

Structure of pre-war and wartime exports 1910–12 and 1915–18		
Country	**1910–12**	**1915–18**
Argentina	Wheat 19.4%	Wheat 12.9%
	Corn 17.9%	Corn 9.6%
	Linseed 10.2%	Linseed 5.4%
	Hides 10.2%	Hides 9%
	Wool 12.9%	Wool 12.9%
	Frozen beef 7.6%	Frozen beef 15.3%
		Tinned meat 5.9%
Brazil	Coffee 54.2%	Coffee 47.4%
	Rubber 27.9%	Rubber 8.8%
		Hides and skins 7.7%
		Sugar 4.5%
Chile	Nitrates and iodine 86%	Nitrates and iodine 74.6%
	Copper 8%	Copper 17.3%
Peru	Sugar 17.5%	Sugar 27.6%
	Cotton 13.8%	Cotton 18.3%
	Copper 20.5%	Copper 26.3%
	Rubber 12.3%	Petroleum 7.5%
	Petroleum 6.3%	Wool 7%

Source: Albert, Bill and Henderson, Paul. 1988. *South America and the First World War: The Impact of the War on Brazil, Argentina, Peru and Chile*. Cambridge: Cambridge University Press. P. 59.

As with Canada to the north, one overarching result of the war in Latin America was the growth in importance of the USA at the expense of European economies, particularly the United Kingdom. US representatives, private and official, advocated this course from very early in the war. The US government used forums such as the Pan-American Financial Conference held in Washington in 1915 to make the point that the outbreak of the war highlighted the problem of relying on European countries economically and to suggest that a more hemispheric approach was desirable. Trade with the USA increased significantly during the war, especially in the west coast economies such as Peru and Chile. The flow of US capital also increased during these years. This increase was not uniform: Brazil and Argentina, for example, did not see much of an increase in US economic activity. In some ways the US economy was not predisposed to supplant the British economy either in the region or globally. As Bill Albert has pointed out, the USA would become increasingly protectionist in the post-war period. The USA also produced a great deal of primary products on its own and was interested in protecting and growing these industries, whereas the domestic British economy produced far less in the way of primary goods. These factors meant that although the USA would become more economically dominant in Latin America it would not replace the United Kingdom. Albert also contends that the immediate dislocation caused by the war spurred nationalist sentiments in a number of Latin American countries. In fact, once the USA joined the war, neutrality itself became a point of nationalism, as was the case in Colombia.

ATL Research and thinking skills

The experience of the war varied drastically across the Americas. Complete the table below to better understand the nature of these differences.

	Argentina	Brazil	Canada	USA
Reason for involvement/non-involvement				
Nature of involvement				
Military role				
Economic role				
Diplomatic role				
Impact on society				
Impact on economy				
Impact on hemispheric status				

Non-economic issues

Throughout the first years of the war, it was Latin America's strategic location that conditioned its role in the war. The terms of neutrality permitted the presence of ships for a 24-hour period in a neutral harbour, and both sides availed themselves of this provision in terms of Latin American ports. Naturally, it led to both abuse and accusations of abuse by both sides. German ships were seized on more than one occasion. Latin American goods and ships were subject to the German U-boat campaign and the British Royal Navy conducted operations in the territorial waters of some Latin American states such as Chile.

Brazil was the only Latin American country to participate in the war beyond a symbolic declaration of war. After the USA entered hostilities, and after a number of German attacks on Brazilian shipping, Brazil drifted to a more rigorous pro-Ally 'neutrality'. The sinking of the Brazilian ship *Parana* on 5 April 1917 resulted in anti-German rioting in Rio de Janeiro, the expulsion of the German ambassador and the severing of diplomatic ties between the two countries. By late October 1917, Brazil had formally declared war on Germany and the Central Powers. Brazil's main contribution would be to provide naval support in patrolling South American waters and minesweeping activities on the west coast of Africa. By mid-1918, Brazil sent a nominal number of troops to the Western Front as well as a medical detachment. Brazil's participation in the Paris Peace Conference provided the opportunity to argue for compensation for Brazilian goods confiscated by the Central Powers.

Source skills

Brazil's rationale for war

Letter from the Brazilian Foreign Minister Lauro Müller to the Imperial German Government, 6 February 1917.

The unexpected communication we have just received announcing a blockade of the wide extent of countries with which Brazil is continually in economic relations by foreign and Brazilian shipping has produced a justified and profound impression through the imminent menace which it contains of the unjust sacrifice of lives, the destruction of property, and the wholesale disturbance of commercial transactions.

In such circumstances, and while observing always and invariably the same principles, the Brazilian Government, after having examined the tenor of the German note, declares that it cannot accept as effective the blockade which has just been suddenly decreed by the Imperial Government.

Because of the means employed to realize this blockade, the extent of the interdicted zones, the absence of all restrictions, including the failure of warning for even neutral menaced ships, and the announced intention of using every military means of destruction of no matter what character, such a blockade would neither be regular nor effective and would be contrary to the principles of law and the conventional rules established for military operations of this nature.

For these reasons the Brazilian Government, in spite of its sincere and keen desire to avoid any disagreement with the nations at war, with whom it is on friendly terms, believes it to be its duty to protest against this blockade and consequently to leave entirely with the Imperial German Government the responsibility for all acts which will involve Brazilian citizens, merchandise, or ships and which are proven to have been committed in disregard of the recognized principles of international law and of the conventions signed by Brazil and Germany.

Questions

1 What is meant by 'the means employed to realize this blockade'?

2 How does this justification compare to the rationale for war in the USA and Canada?

3 Brazil would not declare war until October 1917. Why the delay?

4 With reference to its origin and purpose, assess the value and limitations of this document for historians studying the First World War.

5 Draft a response to this letter from the Imperial German Government.

Exam-style questions

1   Examine the effects of the Spanish American War on US foreign policy.

2   Evaluate the Canadian contribution to the Allied war effort in the First World War.

3   Compare and contrast the effectiveness of Dollar Diplomacy and "Big Stick" diplomacy in achieving the foreign policy goals of the United States.

4   Analyse the ideological reasons for US expansion at the end of the 19th century.

5   Discuss the effects of the First World War on any two Latin American countries.

6   Analyse the change in US foreign policy in the years 1880 and 1929.

Understanding the question

An effective essay response starts with a thorough understanding of what the question requires. Paper 3 consists of two questions set on each of the 18 topics. You are required to answer any three of these questions. Paper 3 questions are more specific than Paper 2 questions and will name content from the Guide.

What are the command terms in the question?

It is essential to understand the command terms used in the questions. The following table tells you what they mean you have to do.

Command term	Task
Analyse	Break down a topic in order to bring out the essential elements or structure.
Compare	Give an account of the similarities between two (or more) items or situations, referring to both (all) of them throughout. A thematic approach is the best way to tackle these questions: this means that you must first decide on which common components or themes you are going to conduct the comparison. These common components will be used to compare both elements of the question.
Contrast	Give an account of the differences between two (or more) items or situations, referring to both (all) of them throughout. A thematic approach is the best way to tackle these questions: this means that you must first decide on which common components or themes you are going to conduct the contrast. These common components will be used to contrast both elements of the question.
Discuss	Offer a considered and balanced review that includes a range of arguments, factors, or hypotheses. Opinions or conclusions should be presented clearly and supported by appropriate evidence.
Evaluate	Make an appraisal by weighing up the strengths and limitations. Like compare and contrast questions, this command term requires you to identify the criteria against which you are evaluating the subject of the question.
Examine	Consider an argument or concept in a way that uncovers the assumptions and interrelationships of the issue.
To what extent	Consider the merits or otherwise of an argument or concept. This requires you to examine multiple perspectives on the argument or concept. Opinions and conclusions should be presented clearly and supported with appropriate evidence and sound argument.

Developing a thesis statement

Broadly speaking, a thesis or thesis statement is your position on a given topic or answer to a question. While there are a number of ways to write one, strong thesis statements all have some things in common. A thesis statement should contain:

- **your position/answer to the question** – this indicates a focus on the task

- **any qualification to that position/answer** – because few historical issues/questions have a straightforward "yes" or "no" answer, some qualification is generally required. Using a qualifier also indicates that you are thinking deeply about the task and understand its complexity. A qualifier is particularly important in responding to a task involving the command term "to what extent".

- **an indication of how you will support your position/answer** – this provides structure to your response and an indication to the reader of the direction your response will take.

Here are some examples of thesis statements ranging from poor to sound, and the rationale for these levels.

Question: Discuss the extent of the United States' involvement in the First World War.		
Level	**Thesis statement**	**Rationale**
Poor	The United States was heavily involved in the First World War.	Vague. No indication that the candidate understands the complexity of the question. No indication of the evidence that the candidate will use to answer the question.
Adequate	The United States was involved economically, militarily, and politically in the First World War.	More detailed. Indicates how the question will be answered. Shows limited understanding of the complexity of the question.
Sound	The United States was involved economically and politically throughout the First World War, but only committed to total war after 1917.	A detailed thesis that indicates a position, how the question will be answered, and that it is a complex issue (that the involvement changed over time).

Addresses the task

An indication of how the position will be supported

A qualification to the position

2 THE MEXICAN REVOLUTION, 1876–1940

Global context

Early in the 20th century, fuelled by nationalism and industrialization, much of Europe was busy colonizing various overseas possessions in an attempt to expand their existing empires and find new economic markets to meet the needs of growing industries. However, this led to tensions among countries, and soon Europe collapsed into the First World War. The United States grew economically, fuelled by expanding railway and resource development, which caused it to push the nation's boundaries and discover outside markets through geographic expansion. This led to US involvement in regional events such as the Spanish–American War and the building of the Panama Canal. The Mexican Revolution would span a period during which the world was involved in the causes and effects of the First World War, the Great Depression and the Second World War.

Mexico's economic growth and political stability in the latter part of the 1800s and early 1900s drew the attention of many European and North American investors to the country. This economic growth and stability was spurred on by the investments of foreigners and created at the expense of Mexican labourers. President Díaz and the elite class who wanted a modern and industrialized Mexico heavily supported the foreign investment. However, Díaz ruled as a tyrant and allowed the exploitation of his people by foreign business in order to see his country progress. These social, economic and political problems gave way to Mexico's revolution in 1910.

Timeline

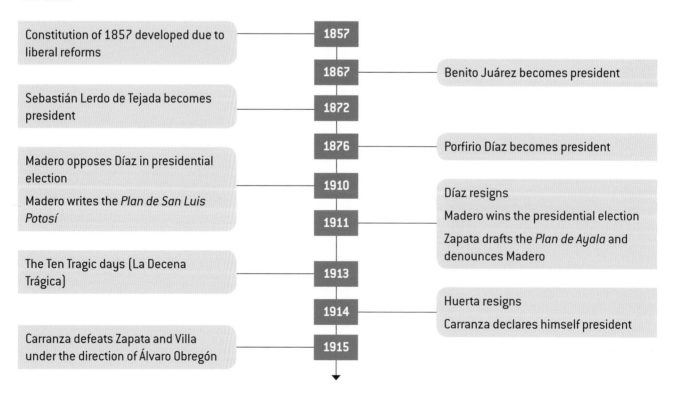

Constitution of 1857 developed due to liberal reforms	1857
	1867 — Benito Juárez becomes president
Sebastián Lerdo de Tejada becomes president	1872
	1876 — Porfirio Díaz becomes president
Madero opposes Díaz in presidential election / Madero writes the *Plan de San Luis Potosí*	1910
	1911 — Díaz resigns / Madero wins the presidential election / Zapata drafts the *Plan de Ayala* and denounces Madero
The Ten Tragic days (La Decena Trágica)	1913
	1914 — Huerta resigns / Carranza declares himself president
Carranza defeats Zapata and Villa under the direction of Álvaro Obregón	1915

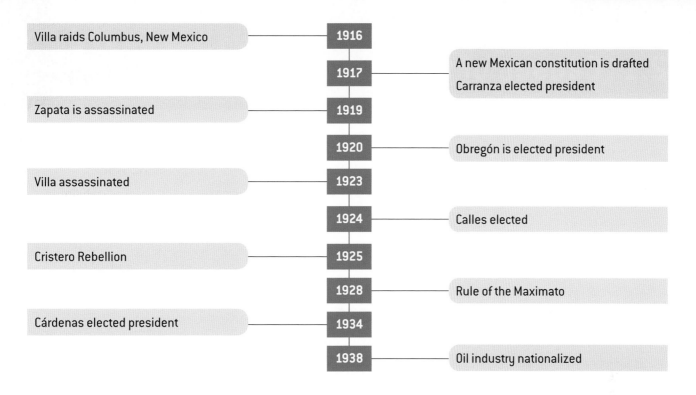

Villa raids Columbus, New Mexico	**1916**	
	1917	A new Mexican constitution is drafted Carranza elected president
Zapata is assassinated	**1919**	
	1920	Obregón is elected president
Villa assassinated	**1923**	
	1924	Calles elected
Cristero Rebellion	**1925**	
	1928	Rule of the Maximato
Cárdenas elected president	**1934**	
	1938	Oil industry nationalized

▲ Map of Mexico in 1910

2.1 Causes of the Mexican Revolution

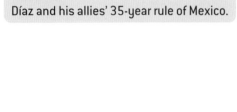

Conceptual understanding

Key question

→ What conditions in Mexico led to revolution?

Key concepts

→ Causation

→ Perspective

Porfiriato 1876–1911

Porfiriato
Díaz and his allies' 35-year rule of Mexico.

Mexico was rife with political and social chaos from the 1820s to the 1870s. Mexico lacked an identity and struggled as a nation, still embarrassed by the taking of its land by the United States in the Mexican–American War, the continual political fighting in the power vacuum left by Spain when it vacated Mexico, and the constant argument over the role of the Catholic Church in state affairs. War hero and President Benito Juárez served five terms and almost 14 years in the presidential office, from 1858 to 1872. He was loved by many for his sacrifice in military campaigns for Mexico and for advocating liberal policies, such as human rights and democracy. Many citizens struggled under his rule however, as he manipulated the electoral system to stay in office and centralized power to the federal government.

Fed up with the liberal policies of Juárez and the political and social banditry taking place in Mexico at the time, Porfirio Díaz opposed President Juárez in the 1871 election. Neither Díaz, nor Juárez, nor the third candidate received a majority of votes, forcing the election to be taken to the Mexican Congress. Being full of loyal Juaristas, President Juárez was named president and immediately General Díaz proclaimed himself in revolt. Díaz drafted the Revolution of La Noria, a demand for electoral freedom and no re-election for presidents. Very few people supported him and eventually he was stopped from campaigning. However, in 1872 President Juárez abruptly died of a heart attack and Supreme Chief Justice Sebastián Lerdo immediately stepped in as acting president, in accordance with the Mexican constitution of 1857. President Lerdo served for four years, closely following the ideas and policies set by his predecessor, Juárez. After Lerdo's term was up, Mexico held elections in 1876 for a new president. Lerdo decided to run for re-election and General Porfirio Díaz opposed him, standing again on the platform of "no re-election". Upon losing the election Díaz led a series of battles, accompanied by several other generals, eventually ousting Lerdo and proclaiming himself President of Mexico.

▲ Porfirio Díaz, President 1876–1911

22

Political rule

Finally in office, with military loyalty, President Díaz could now give the people of Mexico the peace and stability that they desired. During Díaz's 35-year tenure in office he furthered the country economically, socially and politically. Many citizens loved their country, and enjoyed the social stability and lack of political rebellion offered under Díaz. He helped raise the national economy by getting rid of the nation's debt, and commercializing and professionalizing industries like mining, textiles, ranching, banking and other economic sectors, thus pushing Mexico into the future. However, the progress of the nation that took place under Díaz's watch came at the expense of the people of Mexico.

Díaz ruled as a tyrant and as head of the military; he supported the elite in any way he could, in return for their loyalty and support politically and socially. In this way Díaz micromanaged Mexico, advised by a group of officials known as the "**científicos**", controlling every aspect of the country: politics, economics, the military and the justice system. Because of this, only a small portion of the population were able to take advantage of the economic progress while most Mexicans had to labour for low wages and long hours in bad conditions. Díaz also made political compromises in order to subdue the conflict between liberals and the Catholic Church. To make matters worse, much of the work done by the vast majority of Mexicans was for the benefit of the very small elite class or for foreign investors who Díaz had allowed to buy much of Mexico. This led to a widening class gap and created many problems between labour classes and industry across Mexico.

> **científicos**
> A group of administrators that advised Diaz during his regime.

Díaz and the Catholic Church

Church and state relations had been a centrepiece of politics for a number of years, even before Díaz took office. The reason for this was because of the large influence the Catholic Church held over Mexican economics, politics and culture. The constitution of 1824 did nothing to address the control the Church had on Mexico. The liberals of Mexico struggled with the Church holding property rights, controlling education and receiving so many business privileges. In 1854 there was a liberal political revolution, known as La Reforma, and Church control was at the centre of it. From this revolution two laws and a constitution emerged. This first law was the Ley Juárez law that eliminated the special exceptions for the Church, and limited their role in politics and economics. The second was the Ley Lerdo law, which forced the sale of any Church property used for profit. From this liberal revolution they created the 1857 constitution which would formally separate the Church and the state. Incorporating the Ley Lerdo and Ley Juárez laws into the constitution formally disallowed the Church from owning land, monopolizing education in Mexico and curbed the Church's influence. It focused on individual rights and giving the judicial branch power to support these rights; however, it also reduced some of the power held by the executive branch which allowed these laws to go unenforced for much of the next few decades.

When Díaz entered office his goal was to co-opt the Church. This was difficult as many priests still held influence in the community, especially in rural areas. Díaz did not appreciate the reach of the Church and tried to enforce the Ley Lerdo law when he entered office. He quickly realized that a more political approach was necessary to avoid direct and open conflict.

Díaz compromised heavily with both the Church and the liberals. He kept the land taken during La Reforma and kept the existing laws. However the enforcement of these laws was given to local authorities, allowing wide differences in enforcement across the nation. The Church in most areas was still allowed to do much of what it had always done, including implementing a variety of social welfare programmes. This helped improve people's opinion of the Church in Mexico. In this way, the Church slowly crept back into power under Díaz and eventually became a Díaz supporter.

Díaz allowed other non-Catholic denominations into Mexico, wanting to break the religious monopoly the Church held in Mexico. This encouraged foreign investment in Mexico helping the economy pick up. Ironically this population base would play a part in the future revolution as advocates for civil rights and the reduction of Church power.

Agriculture

When Díaz entered office he began commercializing and privatizing agricultural lands through the Terrenos Baldios law. The state surveyed the land all across Mexico, looking for deeds of ownership in order to identify who owned what sections of property and seizing any unowned land. Close to 50 million **hectares** of land were taken and auctioned off to bankers, land barons and foreign investors while Díaz was in office. Three US ranching companies became the owners of close to 13 million acres alone. These arable lands were taken from individuals and communities who could not find ownership paperwork, despite the fact that they may have been farming that very land for over a hundred years. These lands were then turned into **haciendas** and Mexican citizens were made to work the same land that had been taken from them. Haciendados ruled these vast plantations strictly and abusively, paying workers in scrip, a type of credit that could only be spent at the estate store, where items were expensive and unaffordable, forcing many workers into debt. Strikes were prohibited, the working day was long, there were no holidays and no compensation for injury or illness. The loss of land had a cultural effect as citizens had no money to celebrate certain holidays or celebrations. The haciendas also caused an economic problem. The foreign landowners gained access to vast resources on the land they had acquired, which in turn produced money. They used the revenue to buy more land, while poor Mexican farmers could not compete.

Mining and textiles

The mining sector of the Mexican economy during this period was similar to the agricultural sector, and was dominated by US and European corporations. Working conditions in the mines were poor, and miners from the US and Europe were better treated than those seen as Mexican by the management. So local Mexican laborers (even if they were of European ancestry) did all the low-level jobs, such as digging and hauling, while US and European workers were given superintendent jobs. These low level local workers were forced to train their foreign counter parts who then received better pay, better housing, food and medical care. These foreign workers were paid with gold dollars while local laborers were paid with silver pesos, adding to wage disparities. This became a bigger problem in 1905 when silver lost 50% of its value and import prices increased, causing serious unrest. By 1906, local miners walked out of work at the Cananea Consolidated Copper Company in Chihuahua. The workers demanded five pesos a day, as American workers were earning twice what they were. They no longer wanted to train American workers to become their supervisors, and demanded an eight-hour working day. President Díaz prohibited the company from negotiating with the strikers and sent federal troops, called **Rurales**, to restore order and get the employees back to work. A fight ensued and 23 people died. The Arizona Rangers, called for by the American company, came to help stop the strike, in complete violation of Mexico's sovereignty. The workers eventually returned to work with no change in policy. However, the strike planted the seeds of future revolution as citizens

hectares
A metric unit of square measure, equal to 2.471 acres.

hacienda
Large land estate, which could include plantations, factories or mines, where workers were usually indebted to the owner, facing a life of perpetual obligation.

Rurales
Rural police force in Mexico from the 1860s to 1914.

and workers alike were appalled at the support Díaz gave the US company over his own people, and the brazen disrespect the US had for Mexican autonomy.

The lack of decent wages made it hard for workers to feed their families. This eventually forced miners and textile mill workers to strike for increased pay and better conditions, however the generous climate Díaz had created for foreign investors showed just how much control foreign companies had gained. One strike in particular, the Rio Blanco textile strike (1907), showed this. The government told the foreign company to agree to the strikers' demands for improved wages and conditions. Instead, the company ignored the government and ended up firing shots at the protestors. The labourers returned to work with no change in pay or conditions. There was no punishment for the shots fired. This added revolutionary fuel against Díaz and foreign corporations.

▲ The Rio Blanco textile strike

Railway industry

All of the economic success experienced by the elite and foreign business in Mexico demanded the building of more railways across the country in order to ship more products to sea ports and north to the US. Díaz, of course, was more than willing to oblige as he could see the economic advantages. He gave subsidies and no-bid contracts to foreign companies to build the railways while allowing them major tax breaks and low cost deals on buying the land. Díaz and the elite reaped the economic benefits immediately as land values rose, more products could be sent to destinations quicker, more cheaply and more efficiently, and Díaz could now send his Rurales all over Mexico much faster. The railways meant that all Mexican industies, such as mining, ranching, farming and textiles, saw major increases in their income. However, the railway boom also added to the industries' strife as workers did not get a share of the profits. Citizens resented Díaz and the foreign companies for buying more Mexican land and receiving concessions in order to prosper at their expense.

Oil industry

The oil industry began to expand in the last years of Díaz's presidency. This was due to new oil discoveries, an increase in foreign investment and improvements in transportation. Notably, US investor Edward Doheny discovered a reserve in San Luis Potosi. He received some tax breaks and other assistance from the Díaz government in order to develop the reserve.

With US dominance of the existing oil industry in Mexico and Doheny making a large amount of money, Díaz feared the US was creating an oil monopoly in his country. To thwart this, Díaz courted British engineer Sir Weetman Pearson to develop oil fields and infrastructure. Weetman had already worked in Mexico and had a close relationship with Díaz. So, Díaz gave Weetman large concessions on oil development, including a 50-year contract for all of Veracruz, free exportation of oil, free importation of equipment, and limited federal and state taxes. With the business privileges granted to Weetman by the Díaz government, Weetman would create his oil company El Águila. Under this company Weetman built Mexico's first oil refinery, created the most productive oil well in Mexico and ended up controlling half of the foreign investors' oil developments in Mexico.

Oil production in Díaz's last years grew astronomically, and led to two problems that would have future implications. First, his intentional attempt to limit US control of the oil industry led to tensions between the US and Mexico. Second, the growth of the industry attracted workers from all over Mexico, initially paying wages higher than in other industries, but the treatment of workers and harsh conditions became a source of discontent.

Discontent leads to revolution

Díaz was committed to seeing Mexico enter the 20th century as a strong economic nation; he wanted industries to have new technologies and to be able to enter the global economy. As his country progressed economically, albeit on the backs of Mexican labourers, he kept a tight hold over Mexico socially and politically, and did not allow modern ideas of justice or democracy to take root. He consistently jailed or exiled political dissidents, put down any strikes or rebellions, and did not allow the Mexican citizens to speak out or allow them to be heard. For example, brothers Ricardo and Enrique Flores Magón felt Díaz's social and political injustices firsthand. Tired of the President and his policies, they became outspoken critics, forming the Mexican Liberal Party and wanting a return to the previous president Juárez's liberal policies of federalism and democracy. In 1906, the Flores Magón brothers called for revolution and was soon pursued by the Rurales, eventually caught and imprisoned, and later died in federal prison. Díaz would not allow citizens to vote and choose their local officials, which was something Mexicans had been doing for as long as they could remember. Local officials were now chosen by the governors and the governors were chosen by Díaz. This showed Díaz's lack of concern for locals and greater concern for the elite. Society was torn and disgruntled over Díaz's treatment; citizens – not just the labouring class, but the upper middle class as well – wanted a voice.

Although the labourers were taking the brunt of Díaz's dictatorial rule and foreign exploitation of Mexico, the upper middle class professionals and businessmen grew tired of competing in the unfair market that Díaz and his científicos had created. It was becoming increasingly difficult to compete with foreign companies that received preferential treatment from the Mexican government in the form of tax breaks, discounted licences, permits and no-bid contracts. As a result, the upper middle class would help fund and support the working classes' future rebellion.

The Mexican economy soon saw a downturn as demand for Mexican products fell on the global market. This forced harsher conditions as business owners worked people harder to produce more in the hope of making more money, and they laid off workers to save money, increasing unemployment. Meanwhile food prices started to rise as the price of silver decreased. This devaluation of silver hurt labourers significantly, as they were paid with a silver-based peso causing further resentment towards management and foreigners.

campesinos
Peasants, farmers, labourers in the rural areas of Mexico.

The following made Mexico ripe for revolution:

- harsh treatment and conditions for **campesinos**
- resources being exploited and shipped off to other countries

- foreign control of wealth made at workers' expense

- workers' desire for a voice in national politics

- workers' demand for an opportunity to gain wealth from their country's resources

- Native laborers receiving half the pay of US and European counterparts in most industries

- upper middle class lacked political opportunity

- Díaz's appeasement of the Catholic Church, violating the terms of the 1857 constitution

- increasing costs of food and other goods.

Long-standing political, social and economic problems would be the basis of discontent in Mexico and fuel the revolution in 1910.

Source skills

Source A

Excerpt from *Zapata and the Mexican Revolution* (1969) by John Womack, Jr. Womack is a retired Harvard professor of Latin American History and Economics.

Escandón's actions were in part only another episode in the oppression traditional in those districts of Mexico. Since the sixteenth century, sugar plantations had dominated life there; in 1910 it was an old story that they crowded villages and independent farms, that hacienda lawyers finagled lands, timber, and water from weaker but rightful users, that hacienda foremen beat and cheated field hands. Still prevailing as the excuse was the lordly racism of viceroyal times. For the young Joaquin García Pimentel, whose ancient and illustrious family owned the largest plantations in the state, it seemed that "the Indian…has many defects as a laborer, being as he is, lazy, sottish, and thieving." His pious and learned older brother, Luis, who managed the family's vast estates, felt the same way. The local villagers' "natural inclination toward banditry" impressed him deeply, and he often lamented that "Jacobin governments" had removed the villagers' "only restraint and guide: religion," leaving the planters to impose their own cruder controls.

Source B

Excerpt from Francisco Madero's *Plan de San Luis Potosi*, 5 October 1910. Díaz had Madero imprisoned, so as soon as Madero was released he fled to San Antonio, Texas, and issued the *Plan de San Luis Potosi*, nullifying the elections and calling on Mexicans to take up arms against the government.

Our beloved country has reached one of those moments. A force of tyranny which we Mexicans were not accustomed to suffer after we won our independence oppresses us in such a manner that it has become intolerable. In exchange for that tyranny we are offered peace, but peace full of shame for the Mexican nation, because its basis is not law, but force; because its object is not the aggrandizement and prosperity of the country, but to enrich a small group who, abusing their influence, have converted the public charges into fountains of exclusively personal benefit, unscrupulously exploiting the manner of lucrative concessions and contracts…the administration of justice, instead of imparting protection to the weak, merely serves to legalize the plundering's committed by the strong…

Questions

1 What is being proclaimed in Source B and how did it contribute to the Mexican Revolution?

(2 marks)

2 In Source A John Womack describes the treatment of hacienda workers. How did it contribute to the start of the Mexican Revolution? (3 marks)

3 Compare and contrast ideas in Sources A and B on what contributed to the start of the Mexican Revolution. (6 marks)

4 With reference to their origin and purpose, assess the values and limitations of Sources A and B. (6 marks)

ENTRADA DE MADERO A MEXICO

▲ Mexican politician Francisco Madero (1873–1913)

Maderistas
Followers of Madero.

Madero challenges Díaz's power

In 1908 President Díaz gave an interview with American journalist James Creelman in which Díaz told Creelman that he would be stepping down from the Mexican presidency at the end of his term in 1910 because he felt that Mexico was ready for a democracy and the formation of political parties. When the Mexican populace heard this they began to prepare for an election. Political parties attempted to form, candidates sought supporters, elites tried to link up with notable political figures, and political tracts and booklets were written (notably Francisco Madero's *La Sucesión Presidencial en 1910*, which set his political platform against the re-election of Porfirio Díaz for a sixth time). Díaz did not seem concerned with any of the parties or candidates because all were fairly small with little initial influence, and he believed he would be able to pick his successor or continue as president himself.

Díaz's decision to choose to continue as president forced Francisco Madero to act against him. Madero's campaigning was instantly successful; he stood on a moderate platform, was funded by his family's wealth, and promised democracy for the peasants yet limited social and economic changes, appealing to the elites and foreigners. It was under this rhetoric that Madero's followers increased. Concerned, President Díaz disrupted Madero's campaign in every way possible until they eventually threw Madero and the **Maderistas** that followed him into prison. As a result, Madero was ineligible to be voted in as president. Madero was soon released on bond with the understanding that he stay in San Luis Potosi where he could be watched. After the election, which Díaz won through corruption and fraud, Madero went to San Antonio, Texas where he wrote his *Plan de San Luis Potosi*, recalling the election as fraudulent, promising political reform, free elections, and a no re-election principle, and calling for Mexican citizens to rise up against the dictatorial rule of President Díaz.

Although it seemed ironic that Madero was calling for revolution from the safety of the United States, the rebels knew they needed organization and unification. Even though Madero and his call to arms did just that, there were two fundamental problems. Firstly, the plan never called into question the genuine problems citizens and labourers had with the Díaz regime – land rights and labour rights. Madero only called for political freedoms, which was not a top priority among labourers and campesinos. Secondly, many peasants were already rebelling and didn't need the plan to prompt them to do so: **Zapatistas** were already reclaiming lands in the south; Pascual Orozco was overthrowing local authorities in the north, increasingly becoming a military threat to Díaz; miners were protesting against abuses; and textile labourers were fighting for more pay and better conditions.

When Madero returned to Mexico from Texas he had no army or rebels to lead and was forced to recruit men. He joined local political boss Lucio Blanco and 500 men of various backgrounds and occupations. Northern rebel leaders Orozco and Pancho Villa joined Madero in early 1911 with their forces of 2500 men.

Orozco and Pancho Villa gained the revolution's first major victory against General Navarro at Ciudad Juárez despite Madero's passiveness. Navarro refused to hand over the federal garrison to Madero. Díaz sent representatives to establish peace terms and to buy some time. Annoyed with Madero's insistence on waiting for a deal that they believed was never going to come, Villa and Orozco attacked the garrison against Madero's wishes. After two days of fighting, General Navarro was forced to surrender. This allowed the rebels to gain control of a railway port of entry into the US for weapons, food and other supplies.

This rebel victory in the north, coupled with Zapata's men continuing to take back land in Morelos just south of Mexico City, forced Díaz to sign the treaty of Ciudad Juárez and go into exile. The treaty called for President Díaz and Vice-President Ramón Corral to resign, to pay damage reparations to foreigners, for all rebels to disarm and disband, for the retention of existing generals and for Francisco León de la Barra to be named provisional president, with open elections within six months.

> **TOK discussion**
>
> To what extent was emotion offered as a justification to rebel?
>
> In what ways was emotion a part of the rebels' style of persuasion towards their revolutionary goals?

> **Zapatistas**
> Followers of Emiliano Zapata under the banner of land reform.

▲ Orozco, Braniff, Villa and Garibaldi

▲ Morelos in 1910

> **TOK discussion**
>
> The peasants and labourers of Mexico rose up in opposition against the ruling class of Mexico for many reasons.
>
> Is it justifiable or moral for the oppressed to resort to violence rather than use civil means in order to free themselves from their oppressors?

Madero takes office

Upon Díaz's resignation the revolutionaries loyally followed Madero into office. This support soon faded as Madero kept many of Díaz's men in power, appeasing Porfiristas in the hope of getting their cooperation, and pushed away the men who got him into the presidency. Madero naively believed that if the political system was fixed and democracy adopted, then the social and economic problems would be fixed as a result.

Madero was glad the fighting was over and the Porfiristas were pleased that many of them had retained their government positions, but the revolutionaries were outraged at the compromise. The Treaty of Ciudad Juarez became the beginning of the end for Madero as revolutionary leaders wondered why the Federal Army that had persecuted the people was left in power, why revolutionaries had to lay down their weapons leaving them unable to protect themselves, and why nothing was done about land reform and other labour issues.

Madero had to address the problems of the nation. He put many conservatives in his cabinet who blocked all progressive reforms. This made him look as if he was maintaining the Porfirista agenda and ignoring the revolutionaries that put him in power, causing resentment among leaders who quickly turned against him. Asking all revolutionaries to lay down their arms and allowing all land in question to be handled by the court system forced Zapata to refuse to disarm or demobilize his men. Zapata had expected land reform immediately but did not get it from Madero. Instead, Madero put local Morelos elite Juan Carreón in charge and gave Zapata a list of haciendas to protect. Insulted, Zapata met Madero in Mexico City and demanded land reform. Refusing to compromise, Madero offered Zapata a ranch for his revolutionary efforts. Zapata would not be appeased; he returned to Morelos and launched a rebellion against Madero. Zapata then wrote his Plan de Ayala calling for a return of stolen land and the break-up of haciendas. He withdrew his support of Madero, declared the south was rebelling and named Orozco as the chief officer of the revolution. This gave legitimacy to Zapata's name and a new focus to the revolution as Orozco turned on Madero when he was not named Minister of War and claimed himself a rebel against Madero. In turn, Madero named General Victoriano Huerta as commander of the federal forces. Madero, tired of Zapata's resistance soon dispatched his federal troops south to Morelos under the leadership of General Victoriano Huerta, who had a hatred for all revolutionaries, to find and kill Zapata. Zapata escaped into the mountains and began his guerrilla warfare.

Rebel leader Pancho Villa remained loyal to Madero, unlike Zapata who argued against Madero's legitimacy to the revolution because of his lack of action towards land reform. Villa was made a colonel in the Federal Army with specific instructions to put down Orozco's rebellion. Villa, who lacked a real revolutionary agenda, was put under the direction of General Huerta in the hunt for Orozco. Huerta, however, immediately disliked Villa, seeing him as a bandit and not a real soldier. Huerta beat Orozco in a number of battles, which damaged Orozco's reputation as a general and also gave Madero a little more time as president.

▲ Revolutionary leader Emiliano Zapata

Class discussion

For what reasons do you think Madero abandoned the revolutionaries who put him in office?

While Villa was hunting Orozco in the northern desert of Mexico, Villa got into an argument with a federal officer over a horse. Villa asked Huerta if he could take the horse and an argument ensued. Villa departed from the army and the next day Huerta had him arrested and put in front of a firing squad. Madero stepped in to stop the execution, which Huerta viewed as Madero choosing the bandit over him – something he would always remember. So Huerta had Villa transferred to another prison where he eventually escaped. Villa then returned to Chihuahua to recruit men for the future rebellion against Madero and by year's end he had more than 7000 men under his command.

Madero focused on political reform, believing that changing the political system would eventually lead to economic and social reform. This, however, alienated key sectors of his initial support base. Zapata defected because of a lack of change in land reform, Orozco defected when he was snubbed for a ministry job and Villa defected when he was arrested and Madero chose not to release him. Madero's inaction concerned many other people besides these three and within 15 months of being voted into the presidency, Madero found himself facing a coup d'etat (known as La Decena Trágica, the Tragic Ten Days). Four generals, Victoriano Huerta, Félix Díaz (Porfirio's nephew), Manuel Mondragon and Bernardo Reyes (whom Madero defeated in the 1911 election), supported by US Ambassador Henry Lane Wilson, organized an assault on the Presidential Palace in Mexico City.

▲ General Victoriano Huerta

While Reyes and Díaz led their rebels in the fight for the palace, Huerta seemingly protected Madero. But this was a façade: Huerta met with Reyes and Díaz several times, and sometimes allowed fresh supplies in, in order to extend the battle and force Madero into negotiations. Huerta's apparent support for Madero, however, was certainly real for the many rebels, troops and innocent civilians who died. After 10 days, Huerta turned on Madero and overthrew him. Huerta immediately arrested Madero's brother, handing him over to General Díaz in order to force negotiations. Madero was forced to resign as president, after securing the promise of safe passage out of Mexico for himself and his family. Huerta proclaimed himself provisional President of Mexico.

▲ Bombed buildings during La Decena Trágica

Madero, initially under house arrest, was later moved to the federal prison. On the way to prison both Madero and Vice-President Pino Suárez were shot and killed. Huerta denied knowing anything about the murders, but quickly arranged for Congress to name him interim president. Assuming his militancy would bring back past economic successes, Porfirian elites, the Catholic Church, wealthy elites and federal officials were all supporters.

Huerta seizes power 1913–1914

As interim president, Huerta quickly made the changes he wanted. He used the Federal Army to control the central states by ousting local officials and replacing them with trusted military generals and demanded recognition from loyal governors, which all but three gave. One of those who refused was Abraham González, Pancho Villas' mentor, and Huerta had him thrown under a moving train. Huerta's main concern was a consolidation of power and increasing the size of the Federal Army, allowing him to control Mexico via intimidation and militarism. He also encouraged hacienda owners to put together their own private armies to protect their lands. Old Díaz supporters who were sidelined during the revolution came back to influence under Huerta. For example, the Catholic Church and foreign investors hoped for a return to prosperity, similar to the life they knew under the Porfiriato. Much of this desire was created by what would eventually become the First World War in Europe, increasing the demand for Mexican resources, from which foreign companies wanted to gain. Many western European countries and Latin American nations recognized Huerta, but only because their ambassadors pushed them to do so, influenced by foreign companies who could make money from Mexico with Huerta as President. Policies favouring foreign investors encouraged the same people and groups that opposed President Díaz to oppose Huerta. The main problem for Huerta was that US President Woodrow Wilson refused to recognize him, ultimately leading to Huerta's fall from power.

Wilson neither recognized nor opposed Huerta immediately. Wilson kept the existing arms embargo for all revolutionaries, but lifted it for Huerta. He also sent former Minnesota Governor John Lind to gather information on the situation, since former US Ambassador Henry Lane Wilson had other motives. Lind proposed early elections, without Huerta as a candidate. Huerta rejected this notion, became increasingly upset with Wilson's meddling in Mexico's affairs and established anti-US rhetoric. After this, Huerta's reign tightened on Mexico, arresting or assassinating political dissidents or anyone who opposed him. He soon abolished Congress and imprisoned any officials he thought opposed him. Huerta did hold elections, but through his intimidation the required amount of voters needed for an official election (51%) was not met so he remained in power. These actions lost Huerta further foreign and domestic support and only those holding on to a hope that Huerta would return Mexico to the Porfiriato still supported him. President Wilson could see Huerta losing power within his own country, so he turned to Venustiano Carranza as head of the **constitutionalists** to help topple Huerta.

Carranza, however, turned President Wilson down because he was opposed to US intervention and didn't believe he needed help in order to oust Huerta. Hoping Carranza would change his mind, Wilson lifted the arms embargo, and recognized Carranza as the Constitutionalist leader, which gave Carranza legitimacy and strengthened the various revolutionary armies. Carranza still refused to join Wilson, so the US President left Mexico, but still without recognizing Huerta's rule.

Carranza led the resistance against Huerta, organizing the northern revolutionary movement. He wanted to operate by the old constitution of 1857 and tried to pull the southern rebels into his cause, as well as leaders such as Álvaro Obregón of Sonora. Carranza entitled his call to arms the Plan de Guadalupe, rejecting Huerta as president and placing himself as the interim president until elections were held. In his plan he never addressed any social or political reforms, resulting in some revolutionaries choosing not to join him and making it difficult to raise an army. Huerta chased Carranza north with the Federal Army, forcing him into Sonora. It was here that Carranza allied with Álvaro Obregón who helped him recruit and lead the army. Carranza named Obregón Head of Military Operations and it was in this army that future president Plutarco Calles rose as a leader.

constitutionalists
Led by Venustiano Carranza, they were advocates for a strong president and central government, and a weaker form of federalism.

▲ Venustiano Carranza

A shared hatred for Huerta pulled together revolutionaries under Carranza's banner. Obregón, Zapata and Villa did not accept Huerta's claim to power as they saw him as a similar dictator to Díaz who would not fulfill the social, political or economic needs of the revolution. Villa fought alongside Carranza solely because of his hatred for Huerta. This proved critical for Carranza later as Villa won a series of battles in the north, forcing Federal troops into major capitals and out of rural areas. Zapata refused to deal with Huerta, never recognizing his control of Mexico as legitimate because of their differing views on agrarian reform.

Huerta faced much opposition at this point: non-recognition from the US; Carranza organizing the rebels and giving them a focus for which to fight; Obregón poised in the west with his army; Villa marching from the north capturing town after town, gaining legitimacy as well as key railway centres and towns like Torreón; and Emiliano Zapata still in open rebellion in the south near Mexico City. Seeing the futility of his situation, and the government on the verge of collapse, Huerta fled into exile on 12 August 1914, leaving a vacuum of power and bitter rivalry for the presidential seat. General Obregón was the first to arrive in Mexico City, courtesy of Villa's victory in the town of Zacatecas, and signed the armistice officially ending Huerta's reign. This armistice required soldiers along the southern perimeter to hold their positions, preventing Zapatistas, whom he did not trust, to enter Mexico City. This fight for power in Mexico City would lead the revolutionaries into another period of revolution.

▲ General Pancho Villa and his soldiers

Carranza and Civil War 1914–1920

Huerta made it to the United States where eventually he was imprisoned and died. The army he left behind came under the control of General Obregón of the Constitutionalists. With Huerta gone, the rift between Carranza and Villa opened up as Obregón protected Mexico's seat of power for Carranza to take. Zapata received representatives from both Carranza and Villa, eventually siding with Villa because of Carranza's opposition to land reform. Those in the inner circle knew the revolution would continue until Carranza and Villa came to terms.

After the battle of Zacatecas, Villa and Obregón met in Villas' camp, to see if they could agree on what the political state of the nation should be and to stop the fighting. However, Villa lost his temper, as he was prone to do, and tried to have Obregón executed twice. Once was because Carranza cut railway services, stranding Villas' army between Aguascalientes and Torreón. With nothing of significance achieved, Obregón left, distrusting Carranza and despising Villa.

On 1 October 1914, in an effort to settle differences, stop the continuing violence and try to establish a legitimate government, representatives from all facets of Mexico and representatives from all the major leaders (Carranza, Villa, and Zapata) met at Aguascalientes for a meeting on how to deal with the power vacancy and future government. The delegates represented the social and economic mix of Mexico and had the authority to establish a legitimate government. The meeting encompassed four main groups: Villistas who were surprisingly willing to compromise; Carrancistas who attended to impress the US, but were hard line in their desire to see Carranza as president; independents and

Zapatistas who focused on land reform. The meeting's moderates, led by General Ángeles and General Obregón, tried to push for what was right for Mexico and lessen the influence of Villa and Carranza at the meeting. The committee adopted Zapata's Plan de Ayala, agreeing to three major points: to seize foreign-owned land, take land from enemies of the revolution, and return land back to rightful owners. Many ideas, voices and proposals were heard, but in the end revolutionary party politics influenced the outcome.

The committee asked Carranza to step down as First Chief and Villa to give up command of the División del Norte, seeing this as a way to end revolution and get a legitimate government in office. Without delay Carranza rejected the committee's power to make any mandatory decisions. The committee immediately declared Carranza in rebellion, causing a split between delegates. Villa and Zapata formed an alliance and influenced the committee members to vote in Eulalio Gutiérrez, Governor of San Luis Potosi, as the interim president. His followers, including Villa, would become known as the **conventionalists**, the opposing party to Carranza's Constitutionalists. Carranza and his delegates dismissed the convention and Gutiérrez, and abandoned Mexico City for Veracruz where Carranza would be able to control a trade port. Obregón was left with a choice of who to join. He hated Villa for his earlier attempts to kill him and knew Villa didn't need him to win militarily. Obregón knew, however, that Carranza needed his military expertise, could get him political power in his home state of Sonora, and that Carranza distrusted, rather than hated, him. So a careful, thoughtful Obregón took his time, then strategically chose to side with Carranza, taking over the Federal Army and rounding out the Constitutionalists. These two parties engaged in a Civil War for the power of Mexico.

When Carranza left Mexico City, Villa and Zapata took the capital and neighbouring city Puebla, forcing Obregón to go to Veracruz to meet with Carranza and re-gather his army. Villa and Zapata then met to form a strategy to defeat Obregón's army. Oddly, a strategy was never developed, a formal alliance never signed; however, Villa promised to supply Zapata with weapons and Zapata agreed to attack the Constitutionalist army from the south and hold the city of Puebla. Neither of them desired national political prominence but rather control of their own spheres of influence. After the meeting, never tempted by national power, Zapata left for Morelos, leaving Villa in the capital. Zapata continued with his resistance in southern Mexico, raiding haciendas and redistributing lands back to peasants.

In January 1915, with no official government and various rebel factions throughout Mexico, both sides focused on the recruitment of men and military training in preparation for the impending battles between Carranza and Villa. After murdering Carrancistas and raiding and looting Mexico City, Villa left for northern Mexico where he had a strong following but failed to expand his political base outside of that region, mainly due to the lack of a true political platform. Carranza, however, did gather followers because he not only had a political

conventionalists
Loosely associated with Obregón, they were advocates for political freedoms, labour rights, a strong regional government, and wanted to implement parts if not all of the Plan de Ayala, Zapata's agrarian reform.

▲ Pancho Villa and Emiliano Zapata together in the capital

vision but also communicated it well. He hated the US and foreign imperialism within Mexico, a feeling that most Mexicans could support; he promised a political voice, land and better working conditions including wages. This increased Carranza's political followers and in turn increased Obregón's army.

Villa and Obregón face-off

Obregón was confident he could defeat Villa because President Wilson had not only just recognized the Constitutionalist government but had also just vacated Veracruz, leaving behind a cache of modern weaponry for Obregón's use. It was with this confidence that Obregón started preparations to engage Villa on the battlefield near Celaya in the spring of 1915, for a fight to establish the country's government and future.

First, Villa sent his army across northern Mexico to confront Constitutionalist armies, primarily in Sonora, led by General Calles. This spread Villa's army thin for the potential showdown with Obregón. Also, Villas' relationship with Zapata started to weaken because the promised armaments did not immediately arrive and when they did they were old and second-hand. Zapata heard rumors that previous Madero supporters had joined Villas' ranks and were saying Zapata would eventually have to be killed. From that point on Zapata protected Morelos but left Villa to fight Obregón virtually alone. Zapata and Villa's inability to work together was a significant detriment to the revolution, but their aims for the revolution seemed too different for a lasting alliance.

It came down to the battlefield. The warrior Villa, who everyone, including the United States, believed would win, faced the cunning politician Carranza and General Obregón. General Obregón moved first, taking his military north, away from his supplies and Mexico City. Villas' mentor and righthand man, the militarily brilliant Felipe Ángeles told Villa to move north and extend Obregón further, but Villa arrogantly did not listen and instead engaged him outside Celaya.

While confronting Obregón, despite Ángeles' advice, Villa asked Zapata to cut Obregón's railway supply lines. Zapata never did this, allowing Obregón access to continuous supplies. Villa fought Obregón on the outskirts of Celaya and, again ignoring the advice of Ángeles, sent infantry and cavalry in waves into an onslaught of trench warfare, machine guns and cannons. Villa faced two major defeats at Celaya, losing thousands of men, horses and artillery, and forcing him and his army to flee, many of them abandoning him permanently. Villa fought Obregón's army in a few battles as he retreated towards the north, mainly to Sonora and Chihuahua, and the once strong División del Norte was now only a remnant. Obregón's victory over Villa allowed Carranza to win the war, the Constitutionalists to govern Mexico, and increased Obregón's stature as a military general.

Villa made an attempt at one last fight, scraping together any men he could from the northern states and trying to establish control in Sonora. He believed that if he could control this town the US would reconsider recognition of Carranza, but he found stiff opposition in Sonora from General Calles. Incidentally, Calles was reinforced with troops and supplies from Obregón that went through US territory and had been allowed by President Wilson. When Villa was defeated he blamed Wilson and turned towards the US for revenge. Unsurprisingly, Villa didn't have many problems finding Mexican citizens who were angry at the US. They believed the US was responsible for many of their problems, especially economic. Once defeated by Calles he went back to Chihuahua City with only his most loyal generals. After much deliberation Villa came to realize that his army was all but finished. Obregón took advantage of the situation, offering amnesty to Villistas. Thousands of officers and soldiers took the offer, joining the ranks of Carranza and Obregón's army. Villa fled to the mountains.

Class discussion

At this point, what do you see as the most significant turning point of the revolution and why?

Villa and the United States

Subsequently two major incidences took place involving Villa and the US. The first incident involved Villista troops, but not Villa himself. On 17 January 1916 Villa's troops stopped a train and shot 16 US mining engineers and Commander Pablo López who were on board. Villa was not present but he was publicly held accountable. The second incident was more significant because it involved Villa personally and took place on US soil. Trying to spark an international incident to cause disorder for Carranza, Villa raided the New Mexico town of Columbus. Reasons included Wilson's recognition of Carranza, a series of losses to Obregón and because he was being cheated by his ammunition and gun suppliers. Balancing international opinion and US public pressure, Wilson responded to this brutal attack with an expedition led by General John J Pershing to pursue and capture Villa. Wilson asked for Carranza's permission, which Carranza never denied or gave, being careful to balance US relations with Mexican public opinion. Pershing and between 5000 to 10 000 men, pursued Villa for almost a year, but never caught him. The US attack revived Villa's legacy, allowing him to hold towns such as Torreón. This upswing in Villa's popularity alarmed Carranza and he asked the US to leave Mexico. Pershing and Wilson obliged, but the expedition has done the opposite to what was intended, hurting US–Mexico relations and making Villa as popular as ever.

Carranza as president

Carranza was elected president in 1916 and he immediately tried to structure a new constitution written by regionally elected delegates. The convention members reflected the diversity of interests and people in Mexico. Carranza presented them with a draft of a new constitution but it did not address land reform or labour rights. Carranza put a five-month deadline on the document, hoping the short timeline would increase the chances of his constitutional draft being adopted. The council ignored Carranza's requests and instructions and developed one of the most progressive constitutions of its time, addressing land issues, gender inequality, workers' rights and the role of the Church. Two parties emerged from this convention, one supporting Carranza's ideas and one side loosely identifying with Obregón.

During Carranza's presidency he continually struggled against the influence of Obregón and many of his policy decisions did not comply with the 1917 constitution, losing him support throughout his tenure in office. He continually opposed agrarian reform and never settled the issues that organized labour had experienced before the revolution. As a response, the trade unions in the north joined forces to form the Regional Confederation of Mexican Workers (CROM) to fight for better wages and conditions across multiple industries.

During the constitutional talks, Zapata put forward his "Manifesto to the Nation" which denounced Carranza and reasserted his Plan de Ayala. Carranza, tired of this continual nuisance in Morelos, sent Pablo González to Morelos to kill Zapata. He was unsuccessful, so he set a trap to assassinate him, which succeeded. This eliminated Zapata, but Carranza had other problems to deal with as well. The differences that emerged from the convention divided revolutionaries and politicians, Obregón's popularity and independence was a challenge, and caudillos looking for the leader who could give them the most were difficult to control.

The revolution had stirred up political and economic discontent among citizens and **caudillos**. The new constitution had given them a structure to address the issues. Along with political pressure from the people, Carranza faced competition within his own party. Obregón resigned as Secretary of War in 1917 and in 1920 ran for president.

In the 1920 election Carranza handpicked Ignacio Bonillas to follow him in office. Bonillas had been Mexico's ambassador to the United States and had been educated in the US as well. Despite this, it was Carranza that still had the influence to secure the votes. Realizing that Obregón's popularity was on the rise, accusing Carranza of political corruption and not serving the people of Mexico, Carranza attempted to undermine the whole election process. Obregón immediately delivered the Plan de Agua Prieta with fellow Sonoran's Plutarco Elias Calles and Adolfo de la Huerta, calling the nation to arms against Carranza. When the majority of political leaders joined Obregón and overtook the capital, Carranza fled to Veracruz, where he would try to set up a temporary government. On the way to Veracruz his train was held up and attacked a number of times, but he fled on horseback, making it to northern Puebla. That night, 21 May 1920, Carranza was killed while sleeping. Adolfo de la Huerta was appointed interim president from June to November of 1920. Carranza's death marked the end of the old regime; all the revolutionary leaders were now from a different generation and they wanted to see the 1917 constitution realized.

▲ Zapatistas in the south

caudillos
Military or political leaders.

TOK discussion

Many leaders gave speeches and put forward plans in order to communicate their beliefs or expectations about the revolution. Examples are the Plan de Ayala, Plan de San Luis Potosi, Plan de Guadalupe, Plan de Agua Prieta and Plan de Veracruz.

The way in which thought and experience is communicated can transform the way in which others shape their thought and action.

1   How does language used by the revolutionaries influence or change our understanding of the revolution?

2   What role did language play through these various speeches and plans by leaders in creating or reinforcing revolutionary ideals and goals?

Organize the information in this chapter using the table below. Once the table has been completed, use the information to analyse the leaders in terms of the revolution's goals and how well they met them.

	Madero	Villa	Zapata	Carranza
Leader background				Family politician, adorer of Benito Juárez and well educated
Aim(s)	Overthrow Díaz, install a new government that will eventually fix the economic and social needs of the country		To acquire and return land that was usurped by elite and foreigners back to its original owner	
Issues with aim(s)		His aims at times were contradictory and most of the time non-existent, like he was in permanent revolution mode. If Villa had a political agenda, it was not communicated well.		
Methods	Political ascendancy and when that didn't work, revolution		Political reform through his Plan de Ayala supported by revolution and war	
Outcome			Was assassinated near the end of the revolution by Carranza's men. His Plan de Ayala was adopted into the constitution of 1917.	
Student analysis of leader	Credit for starting the revolution, but made some pivotal mistakes once he ascended to the presidency. Many of these mistakes came from his personal aims, which did not align with the goals and desires of the people.			

2.3 The 1917 Constitution

Conceptual understanding

Key questions

→ Did the 1917 Constitution address the political, economic and social issues that the revolution was fought for? Why or why not?

→ What made the 1917 Constitution so "progressive" for its time?

→ For what reasons was the Mexican constitution of 1917 so significant?

Key concepts

→ Change

→ Significance

Constitution background

Three years after Mexico gained independence from Spain in 1821, the constitution of 1824 was signed and declared. This document set a structure for the government and established responsibilities but did not address the enforcement and application of the laws. The document was revised as a result of to these limitations as well as a liberal revolution demanding changes to Church influence. In response to the revolution, a convention of delegates met for a year in 1856 and produced the constitution of 1857 that included a bill of rights and anti-clerical laws. This constitution stood until Mexico called for a new one to answer the demands of the revolution in 1917.

With most of the fighting behind them and a desire to bring some legitimacy to the Mexican government, Carranza called for a Constitutional Convention in the town of Querétaro, just north of Mexico City. The delegates for the constitution of 1917 met from 10 November 1916 until 31 January 1917. The convention members were from various backgrounds, moderate and radical, with various philosophies and ideals stemming from their vast knowledge of Mexico's many problems and concerns.

Carranza gave the convention a draft drawn up by a group of his moderate politicians. His draft included modifications and reforms to various social issues but did not address any labour or agrarian reform, modelling it after the 1857 constitution. Even though he did not allow Villista or Zapatista delegates to participate, significant differences in political and social thought immediately divided the convention. There were those that backed Carranza and the constitution of 1857, as a party advocating the ideas of social welfare, limitations for the Church and its role, and individual rights. The other faction was more progressive and was associated, albeit loosely, with Obregón. They held strict views against the Church but wanted the government responsible to correct social and economic problems, pushing through legislation for reforms on labour, property, and relations between Church and state.

The convention members for the most part ignored Carranza's demands and instructions and developed the most progressive constitution of its time. Carranza did not want or expect the radical document that eventually came out of the convention, as he only envisioned a slight modification of his draft to reflect the demands of the revolution. The 1917 Constitution took on social injustices, economic issues, political participation problems, education concerns and role of the Church.

Article 27 – Land reform

One of the most pivotal issues that launched the Mexican Revolution in 1910 had been the issue of land reform. Initially championed by Emiliano Zapata, it was a concern because of the land that had been taken from peasants and farmers under Díaz and sold to the wealthy and foreigners.

The issue of land was dealt with in Article 27 as it established that land ownership ultimately rested with the nation and the nation had the authority to take control of and distribute property, but only in the public interest or due to national necessity. Article 27 placed conditions on foreign ownership of land and any issues involving foreign countries would be dealt with in Mexican courts. Given that Mexican land held vast mineral resources, the statutes for natural resource extraction under this article were changed, so Mexico had the power over mineral extraction rather than foreign entities.

This article reflected the concerns of Zapata and his followers. Most appreciated the section of Article 27 claiming Mexico's land was now under the power of the state including all subsoil rights. This gave any future president that chose to use it leverage against foreign ownership of land, and any conflict that arose from it would be settled by decisions made in the Mexican courts. This would come into play in the future under President Cárdenas.

Article 123 – Labour reform

Another major concern at the onset of the revolution was the harsh treatment of workers, not only in industry but also on haciendas. The treatment of labourers throughout Mexico had been brutal, oppressive and unjust. Article 123, probably the most progressive article in the 1917 Constitution would address these concerns.

Article 123 guaranteed workers and employers an opportunity to defend their interests through unionization. It gave labourers a limit on working hours, a guaranteed day off per week, fair pay, workman's compensation and improved work conditions. It also allowed labourers the right to receive payment in cash, not scrip, and payment for overtime; it outlawed child labour, guaranteed safety laws, certain holidays off and gave women maternity leave as well as equal pay for equal work.

This article would be used by labourers in every industry across Mexico in the following years as the number of strikes increased. Future unions would use it to represent workers to establish better conditions. These unions would play a major political role in the future of Mexico.

Articles 24 and 130 – Church reform

As mentioned before, the Catholic Church played a major role in the grievances of the populace at the start of the revolution. It had a significant influence in politics, economics and the social lives of most Mexican citizens. The Church did not stand much chance as even the moderates looked to lessen the power and role of the Catholic Church within Mexico. The political attachment of the Church to national politics was addressed in two articles of the constitution.

Article 24 had two main ideas. The first was freedom of religion, establishing that every person in Mexico could practise any religion they desired as long it did not involve a crime. It also established that the Church would be held to the laws of land ownership, allowing the Church to only own lands that were for worship purposes and not for monetary gain.

Article 130 addressed two additional concerns as well. The first was establishing the separation of Church and state, making clear the role of government and the role of Church. The second idea it established was limitations on the Church, limiting the number of priests in each state, taking political rights from Church officials, and making official ceremonies matters of the state not the Church. The Church no longer had judicial authority, nor could it criticize the government.

The enforcement of these laws took some time because of politicians' belief in Catholicism, their established role in society and the lack of organization it would take for the laws to take effect. Because the Church was tied to so much in Mexico it would take a large force to separate the two fully. This force later came with President Calles, and led to a revolt by the Church.

Article 3 – Education

Education issues were very much tied in with the position of the Catholic Church as education was not secular and was controlled by the Church. Many people in rural areas were illiterate and never received a proper education as the Church established most of their schools in urban areas and taught those that had money. This was vastly changed under Article 3.

Article 3 would make all education free of religion – it would be secular, nationalistic and based on the teaching of scientific progress and the institution of democracy. Under this article schooling would be mandatory but free, so even the poor could receive an education. The federal government would take control of what was taught in the schools.

Obregón was the first president to begin to change schools in Mexico. The enforcement of this article would very much coincide with the enforcement of the articles pertaining to the Church. The following presidents differed in their approach to education and the application of this article, but all desired to see the improvement of schools, especially in rural areas.

Other articles of note

Many other significant political, economic and social issues raised before and during the revolution were covered in the 1917 Constitution:

- **Article 4** gave women equality under the law
- **Articles 6 and 7** gave freedom of expression and freedom to the press

- **Article 8** gave the right to petition and assemble
- **Article 10** allowed citizens the right to own guns
- **Articles 13 and 14** addressed federal control of the courts, guaranteed due process and outlawed retroactive laws
- **Article 17** required all disputes to be resolved in a court of law
- **Article 22** outlawed cruel and unusual punishment
- **Articles 32 and 33** were concerned with social injustices as they declared that treatment of Mexican citizens trumped that of foreigners.

The document that came about from the convention was progressive and liberal in nature but stood to benefit the majority of citizens and gave the government power to make sure the social, political and economic benefits took effect. Although the application and enforcement of the constitution would vary greatly with the first few presidents after 1917, in many ways the people got what they wanted out of the constitution. The final document was signed on 31 January 1917 and released 5 February 1917. Immediately, Carranza called for elections to be held in March; he won and subsequently took office on 1 May 1917.

Opposition to the constitution

Naturally the constitution developed in 1917 was met with a range of opposition. A few large oppositional forces were the Catholic Church, foreign companies as well as land owners and large estate owners, because these were the forces the document intended to limit. Also most states throughout Mexico had developed laws and statutes of their own and were very apprehensive about changing their laws to align with the new constitution. Time had to be spent dealing with the political, economic and social ramifications of the revolution before it could be rightfully fulfilled.

2.4 Post-revolutionary state

General Álvaro Obregón 1920–1924

After Carranza's death, the three powerful Sonorans, Obregón, Calles and Adolfo de la Huerta, would all take their respective strengths and influence to the national government. De la Huerta, who had the most political experience of the three, was selected as the interim president for the six-month term that the constitution called for in order to set up national elections. Once in office de la Huerta immediately began to make some necessary changes, one of which was to get rid of Pancho Villa. Villa and de la Huerta ended up striking a retirement deal in which Villa was given a hacienda in Durango, 50 of his top generals were given payment by the government, and his other troops were given plots of land with one year's pay. While Villa took the deal and went into retirement, the deal incensed Obregón as he felt Villa could not be trusted to stay quiet and peaceful; Obregón would have preferred to see him dead.

De la Huerta set up the national elections, which Obregón and almost everybody else expected him to win. In fact Obregón did not face a serious opponent in the election and won by over a million votes, taking office in November 1920. Obregón had taken an unpredictable road to the presidential seat of Mexico, joining Madero in support of his call to arms, fighting his way to respectability on the battlefield, losing an arm during the revolution, fighting off Villa and his army to clear the way for Carranza and then eventually succeeding him as president. He faced a number of connected issues that required his immediate attention. The context in which he took office involved a troubled economy, partly due to the post-First World War global recession and partly due to the physical damage to agriculture from the revolution, the death of so many male citizens and population loss from emigration during the revolution. He found political success not in his ideologies or immediate reform but rather in his knack to establish relationships, gain compromises and form alliances, especially with the new-found force of organized labour, and ultimately compromise the ideals of the revolution for stability within his country.

▲ General Obregón

> ### CROM under Obregón
>
> In response to the 1917 Constitution a labour convention was held. Craft unions joined together to form the Regional Confederation of Mexico Workers (CROM). Although formed in 1918 under Carranza, President Obregón was the first to use the union as a wide base of support for his presidency. CROM was led by Luis Morones, who used his position to become the strongest labour leader in the country for the ensuing years. Obregón put CROM leaders into influential positions while relying on them to help address the labour turmoil resulting from the difficult economic conditions created by the revolution. Morones increased the membership from 400 000 in 1922 to 1.2 million members by 1924.

Military

Obregón very much relied on regional bosses, many of whom were revolutionary generals or influential businessmen. Since many of the generals in the federal military had been under the leadership of Obregón during the revolution, they remained loyal to Obregón. He knew, however, that many of them aspired to the presidency and for that reason he did not want them to gain too much influence in any one area. So he rotated his military generals every couple of months around the military zones that he had broken the country into, to diminish any major support or any build up of influence. He gave governors, businessmen and generals what they wanted in order to keep them loyal, whether it was tax breaks, government positions or money as he was once quoted as saying "no general can resist a cannon shot of fifty thousand pesos".

Labour

President Obregón increased his influence and control within the country when he made an alliance with organized labour. Carranza had suppressed the influence and operational ability of labour unions within Mexico, but Obregón intelligently made a deal with the Confederación Regional de Obreros Mexicanos (CROM) in order to gain political support. This worked to Obregón's advantage during his presidential tenure as layoffs and stagnating wages caused labour turmoil. He was able to call on CROM leader Luis Morones for assistance and strikes went to an all-time low under his leadership. Through CROM, labour now had a political voice locally and nationally in Mexico.

Agricultural reform

Obregón believed that the base of his policies had to be in agrarian reform, but he did not support of full agrarian reform and had no desire to cut up and distribute large estates if there were smaller plots to distribute. Obregón believed that large estates could produce more money if properly run, giving more tax money to the government and providing more jobs and better pay to workers. Land reform had political and social effects as well. Land distribution would appease the revolutionaries that saw land as their right after fighting in the revolution, and would also be a way of gaining the foreign recognition he needed to give legitimacy to his government. He started by implementing the Agrarian Regulatory Law of 1922. Giving power to local communities to establish lands to distribute.

These decisions were made locally but needed to be approved on all government levels; only then work its way up the government ranks until it eventually reached the President's signature. This made reform very slow, but protected the national government from appearing to just step in and take land. In the end most land received by **ejidos** was barely farmable and not located in geographically favourable locations. In total Obregón distributed just over one million hectares. Morelos, under heavy Zapatista influence, received much more attention than other places, firstly because of their demand for agricultural reform throughout the revolution and secondly because three Zapatistas were given influential government positions under the new president. It also kept Obregón's political influence in Morelos strong. The little land reform Obregón did implement ended up being enough to stabilize the discontent in rural areas, despite half of Mexico still being owned by just over 2500 families. Despite how little land Obregón parcelled out to villagers, much of which was done locally, it was much more than Carranza had ever done and was just enough to satisfy a population who saw his efforts as legitimate.

Economically, Obregón's presidency struggled, mainly because the country was slow to recover from the revolution. Much of the workforce was lost in the fighting, commodity prices were falling and much of the economic infrastructure was damaged. Obregón wanted and even invited much of the old Porfiristas back into Mexico because of their economic skills, business wisdom and large amounts of money. Petroleum reserves kept the country afloat economically during Obregón's tenure. Mexico had become the second leading oil producer during the First World War; global oil prices and demand continued to rise and much of the petroleum reserves were largely intact and functioning in spite of the fighting.

Foreign recognition

Foreign recognition was an immediate and very delicate issue for Obregón. He needed it to establish legitimacy for his government, but he could not allow his populace to feel that foreign governments or companies were taking advantage of Mexico. This became difficult as the US and Europe were the places he needed to win recognition because of their global influence, but they wanted Mexico to pay reparations for damages that took place during the revolution and also the repayment of loans. Because of the state of Britain after the First World War and its relationship with the US, it would not recognize Mexico's government unless the US did so. Obregón set about selling himself as someone foreign countries could trust. Foreign recognition eventually hinged on the outcome of talks between the US and Mexico, known as the Bucareli Accords. The US government and US companies had some major concerns with the legality of Article 27 of the constitution and wanted an agreement signed protecting US investments in Mexico before recognition was given. This was critical as petroleum production had jumped in the last 10 years in Mexico. The country produced 25% of the world's petroleum and three-quarters of it was sold to the US. Knowing that increased revenue through taxes on oil would help increase Mexico's economy, Obregón levied taxes that angered US oil companies and they demanded negotiations. De la Huerta was sent to establish terms and agree to a deal with the US, which he did. Obregón felt that de la Huerta had sold out on

ejidos
Community land for agriculture where individuals or individual families farm a specific portion of land.

ATL Research and social skills

Research an instance of foreign involvement in the Mexican Revolution and post-revolutionary state that you see as the most critical. For example, pre-revolution economics, President Wilson, Veracruz, President Coolidge, Pershing Expedition, oil nationalization, Bucareli Accords.

Next, prepare an attack or defence statement for foreign involvement, its necessity or justification. Take a side, you cannot be on both sides at once.

Mexico in order to make the deal, declaring the article was not retroactive; Mexico would pay back loans from oil taxes, putting that money back in the US and US land holdings would be secure. Recognition of Mexico was finally given within days by President Coolidge. Once recognition was established, loans, weapons and ammunition could be procured from the US and Mexico kept ownership of all its land and subsoil minerals. However, the disagreement between de al Huerta and Obregón was the beginning of the end for their relationship.

Education

While in office, Obregón established the Secretariat of Public Education (SEP), naming José Vasconcelos in July 1921 to lead the department. He immediately set to work, creating over 1000 schools across Mexico, especially in rural areas to which many recent college teacher graduates were sent. Many schools were constructed by the villagers and they had input into what was taught. New teachers had to adapt quickly to the culture of rural life. They taught Spanish, integrated national pride into teachings and used copies of the classics and primary readers, which Vasconcelos made cheaply available to help teach the illiterate. They also taught many of the students about nutrition and hygiene towards preventing disease. Vasconcelos established a vast network of libraries in the capital city. He was also responsible for the muralist movement of the 20s and 30s. He recruited artists to create representations of Mexican culture, history and the revolution on public properties for all citizens to enjoy.

Presidential succession

The end of Obregón's term caused some political turmoil for Mexico as the constitution forbid re-election. Knowing that he would face severe opposition, he decided to choose his successor in order to keep his influence vicariously through his appointee. His two choices were between de la Huerta, Treasure Minister and former interim president (although their relationship had begun to disintegrate), and Calles, the former General who was Obregón's Secretary of the Interior. Obregón chose Calles, believing that the military would not follow anyone except a military man. Initially even de la Huerta supported the choice, but revolutionary bandit Pancho Villa voiced his concern from retirement, stating that he would consider taking up arms if Calles was the next president. From that point on, Villa's life was in danger as both Obregón and Calles feared Villa joining de la Huerta in opposition to Calles. Interestingly, Pancho Villa was assassinated shortly afterwards by Salas Barraza who was a Durango legislator. Knowing that Villa would be travelling through Parral on his way to Chihuahua, Barraza ordered several men to open fire on Villa as he passed through the town. Barraza was found guilty and imprisoned for the crime but was released within the year by President Obregón.

De la Huerta resigned as Finance Minister and declared his candidacy for president, in opposition to Calles, throwing the entire election and successor process into turmoil. He quickly fled to Veracruz and offered the Plan de Veracruz, assuming the position of head chief of the revolution and listing a number of grievances against Obregón. Supported by just over a hundred generals and many Villistas, Huerta accused Obregón of controlling the courts and Congress, and guessed that Obregón would attempt to come back to the presidency after Calles. Obregón, with his history of military success, led the federal military against de la Huerta, while getting rid of a number of congressmen and soldiers that opposed him. Although the fighting was intense and bitter, Obregón defeated de la Huerta for several reasons: by this time he had obtained US recognition which allowed him to acquire weapons from the US; CROM gave him a strong base of allies; two-thirds of his army remained loyal and those that he had given land to did not fight against him. All of this allowed Obregón to defeat de la Huerta who eventually fled to Los Angeles. This brief civil war showed that in many ways the government could stay united and continue to operate as expected even under duress. It also put Obregón's influence above all else, and with his choosing of Calles it virtually put Calles in the presidency, and the impending elections would just be a formality. Calles won in a landslide victory, as did the congressmen that were loyal to Obregón and his ideals.

Obregón's presidency ended with violence and a struggle, but in many ways was a success for Mexico. His education programme, although largely the work of Vasconcelos, was very positive for the future of Mexico. His recognition from the US was monumental in establishing global legitimacy politically for the nation. Obregón's work to centralize authority helped provide practical solutions for problems hindering the nation and his work to begin agrarian reforms was a major improvement for Mexico.

Calles and the Maximato 1924–1934

Plutarco Elías Calles was inaugurated as president on 30 November 1924 in what would be the first legitimate election of a constitutional president. Calles immediately set up his new cabinet and federal positions, none more notable than the appointment of CROM leader Luis Morones as the Minister of Industry, Commerce and Labour. In his new political position, Morones increased CROM membership to two million, enforced an eight-hour workday and by 1927 minimized strikes across the nation to fewer than 10.

▲ Adolfo de la Huerta

Maximato

Six-year period in Mexico where Plutarco Elías Calles ruled Mexico behind the scenes through three "puppet" presidents.

CROM under Calles

The influence Morones had with CROM eventually ended as he and other CROM leaders gained wealth and influence while none of these benefits trickled down to the labourers of Mexico. As wages did not increase as expected and conditions did not improve due to the impending Great Depression, discontent among the working class increased. Because of these conditions and Calles' preference for business management over the workers, those labourers influenced by socialism joined other unions and left CROM. Most of them found the union led by the charismatic Marxist Vicente Lombardo. He formed the anti-CROM union known as the Confederación de Trabajadores or CTM. It would eventually unseat CROM as the leading union in Mexico.

Calles' time in office was dominated by his struggle with the Catholic Church. Since the development of the 1917 Constitution there was a liberal attack on the Church and it manifested itself as an issue of power, influence and control. For many deap-seated reasons, Calles opposed the Church and wanted to expand secular education and end Church

▲ Plutarco Elías Calles

influence in politics and education, encouraging a National Church that was independent of the Pope and Vatican City. He wanted to have control over the Church, rather than somebody else. In addition to national pressures, local pressures in some regions enforced the limit on priests, the registration of priests and the ban on clerical robes in public, which in turn forced the Church to denounce the anti-clerical articles of the 1917 Constitution. When mediation, led by a representative from Rome failed, rebellion was certain to take place.

The Cristero rebellion

In July 1926, the Catholic Church in Mexico went on strike, which meant that services were put on hold. Citizens rushed to hurry marriages, baptisms and other services. The strike would last for three years and dominate Calles' presidency. In response to the strike, Calles closed several Catholic schools and expelled a number of foreign priests.

Calles then gave the Church three choices, none of which it liked: it could follow the constitutional laws, appeal to the Congress or rebel. They refused the first, then a formal appeal was turned down by Congress, at Calles' urging. Subsequently, the Church rebelled against Calles and the government.

Cristeros
Rebels who fought the government as representatives of the Catholic Church.

The rebels, or **Cristeros**, numbered over 10 000 by 1927 and they supported the priests in their defiance of the government. Although the Catholic Church did not advocate violence, small pockets of violence emerged, especially in rural areas where they engaged government troops. At the time neither side would compromise or stop fighting, so the violence continued throughout the next few years, with many bishops leaving the country. The rebellion, however, was about to get worse.

In November 1927, as Obregón drove by Chapultepec Park in Mexico City, three bombs hit his car and were followed by gunshots. He was not killed but the assassination attempt worsened relations between the government and the Cristeros. An investigation found that the bomber had bought the car from Father Miguel Pro. He and his two brothers were convicted of the murders, even though evidence pointed to them playing a small part in the assassination attempt. Calles, however, wanted to make an example of the brothers and had them publicly executed. Although Calles made a last second phone call that saved the life of the youngest Pro, Humberto, the other two executions were photographed and widely circulated for all to see. The example had been made, but those in support of the Church hardened their resolve and internationally people reacted negatively to Calles' handling of the situation.

▲ Pro brothers' execution

US citizens were concerned about the events taking place south of the border, although they didn't fully understand the reasons behind them. The US government did not want to get involved and reiterated their support for the government because their main concern was the protection of land and investments, which was already on shaky ground. Dwight D Morrow, the recently appointed Ambassador to Mexico by President Coolidge, finally arbitrated an agreement between the two countries as far as subsoil rights were concerned. Morrow proclaimed that subsoil rights were a domestic, not foreign, concern and so Calles reassured him that the courts would rule in favour of the

US oil companies. This solidified Calles' and Morrow's relationship and the US was rid of a diplomatic problem that had the potential to lead the two countries to war. Following this, Morrow eventually got Calles and Church leaders to meet and try to reach an agreement. Although nothing official came from the meeting Morrow had at least attempted to bring the Cristero rebellion to an end.

Presidential succession

Calles was in office from 1924–1928 and near the end of his term had to think about presidential succession. At first Obregón, who had retired to garbanzo bean farming and various small business ventures, kept his political influence with occasional visits to the palace over the last two years of Calles' term. Gaining presidential office was not an option because of the no re-election clause in the constitution. But Obregón did not like it when Calles put forward the idea of CROM leader Morones as his successor. So Calles then put forward Veracruz military operations leader Arnulfo Gómez, and Obregón put forward his former Minister of War General Francisco Serrano. After some political events took their course to open a door for Obregón, he used his influence on Congress to amend the constitution in order to allow non-consecutive terms for presidents and to extend the presidential term to six years. When this happened he decided to run for another presidential term. Serrano and Gómez stayed in the election. Seeing it as political suicide not to back Obregón as president, Calles strongly supported him.

The three-way race for president soon became violent. Serrano decided to stage a revolt that went badly when over three-quarters of the army stayed loyal to Obregón. Calles then ordered Serrano to be found and executed, which he was along with his other conspirators in what became known as the Huitzilac Massacre. Shortly afterwards federal troops hunted down Gómez and shot him in Veracruz. The three-way race had quickly turned into a one-man show, featuring Obregón. He won re-election with no other incidents. To celebrate he had dinner with family members and supporters on 17 July 1928. Sketch artist José de León Toral made his way around the tables sketching caricatures of the guests. When given permission by Obregón to draw him, he pulled out a pistol and shot Obregón twice, killing him instantly.

Toral was captured, tortured and interrogated, and discovered to be a religious fanatic, supporter of the Cristeros and influenced by a charismatic nun called Madre Conchita. The trial of Toral and Madre Conchita ended with his execution and her imprisonment. Many people believed there was someone bigger behind the plot. Morones was instantly suspected as he was the only one left who had ambitions to run for the presidency. Others believed it was Calles and that he wanted to grab the presidency for himself. Morones left Mexico City so as not to be blamed, while Calles remained as President of Mexico, with the problem of what to do about a new president. He had to tread lightly as many were still upset about the assassination and the many Obregonistas were suspicious of Calles and his possible involvement in the murder.

In a stroke of political genius, Calles announced in his final outgoing state of the nation speech, that he would not seek another term as president. This not only gained respect from Obregonistas as they now believed he was not behind Obregón's death, but also allowed him to lead Congress in finding a candidate for provisional president as warranted by the constitution. After many names were put forward (and Calles received a guarantee from all the generals that none of them would put their names forward or lead a rebellion), Emilio Portes Gil, governor of Tamaulipas, was voted in by Congress as provisional president.

Emilio Portes Gil 1928–1930

Gil had many ideas for programmes and reforms that he wished to push through, none more so than those dealing with the Catholic Church. He invited Church leadership to a meeting and Rome-appointed Archbishop Ruiz y Flores was to remediate an end to the dispute, while US ambassador Morrow helped with the process as well. Gil did not blame the Church leadership for the rebellion nor did he intend to persecute any of them. In fact he wanted to see services running again. Even with these guarantees, talks went nowhere and both sides decided to trust the intentions of the other as good, allowing mass to be held again on 30 June 1929.

As Gil's 14 months as president came to an end, the next presidential election was on everybody's mind, especially Calles'. Using Morones' structure of CROM as an example, he formed a national party that could pull together various backgrounds, ideologies and economic classes into one party that would give him political power for the foreseeable future. Calles subsequently formed the Partido Nacional Revolucionario (PNR). As the power behind the PNR, General Calles would be known as Jefe Máximo.

The PNR, under the influence of Calles, subsequently chose their candidate for the presidential race: Pascual Ortíz Rubio. He was loyal to both Calles and Obregón and had plenty of foreign policy experience as he had just served as a diplomat in Europe. He was put forward because it was believed that he could be politically strong and had enough clout to keep the military in line.

However, in March 1929 a small section of the military split away, stating grievances against provisional president, Gil, and wanting him to be replaced with General José Gonzalo Escobar. In the Plan de Hermosillo Escobar was named Supreme Chief of the Army of Revolutionary Renewal and planned to make a quick strike against the capital and take Gil, Calles and the Minister of War, Amaro. However, Amaro had recently been injured and was absent, so Calles was named Minister of War in his absence and led over 70% of the military against the rebellion. Successful, mainly because of his use of aircraft against the rebels, Calles used this event as a tactic to strengthen his argument for the formation of the PNR, arguing that the political desires of the revolution still had to be fulfilled and a strong party could deliver them.

Near the end of Gil's term worldwide economic disaster struck, hitting Mexico as hard as any other country. Foreigners had no money to invest, bringing investment in manufacturing and mining to a decreased level not seen in recent history, prompting the government to look within the country to uplift the economic system.

President Ortíz Rubio 1930–1932

Rubio won the presidential seat against José Vasconcelos, but upon entering office was shot at while riding in his car with his family by a man named Daniel Flores. He had loose ties with the Vasconcelos re-election team but nothing solid was ever found. Yet Flores and about a hundred others associated with Vasconcelos' election campaign were gathered up, hanged and buried. The government then asked Vasconcelos to leave the country, which he did and he stayed away for the next six years. This episode displayed the strength of the PNR and how it was already becoming futile to challenge them politically.

As the US stock market collapsed and world trade came to a virtual halt, Mexico looked at self-sufficiency and revisited the idea of controlling its own resources under the banner of economic survival. Mexico quickly began to see the effects of the global depression as poor weather brought limited harvests, demand for Mexican commodities dropped, minerals brought much lower prices, with all of this negatively affecting employment and investment opportunities. The government took in far less taxes to help out and balanced the budget, but with less tax revenue and less money in circulation it only made the situation worse. All of this had a staggering effect on unemployment as more workers lost jobs or never got paid for the work they did. CROM stepped to the forefront and demanded action by the government to keep factories open and the railways running. Ambassador to France Alberto J Pani returned and accepted the office of Finance Minister, immediately producing silver coins to get more money into circulation.

Some peasants still held out hope that land distribution would come their way, as they saw it as a means of survival, but Calles had convinced the cabinet that it was not good for the economy and would curtail production, so they cut the distribution of land by almost 60%. Calles still held a lot of influence within the government, making it a real struggle for Rubio to lead his nation. In fact Calles never held more political influence than during Rubio's tenure as president. Because of the constant upheaval in Mexico, government seats were constantly being vacated and Calles influenced who filled them and who did not, and as Secretary of War he was constantly around to wield this influence. Many of the cabinet ran measures by Calles before acting on them, making Rubio seem inept, and he lacked the respect of his constituents as an effective leader. Rubio's tenure during the worst times of the Great Depression was doomed from the start and he never recovered. Calles felt Rubio had to be replaced, so he ensured that his loyalists did not accept any positions under Rubio. The President, nervous that he would not find anybody strong enough to help lead Mexico or anyone who was not connected with Calles, resigned. Rubio left for the US immediately so Calles now had to find a replacement. Calles put General Abelardo Rodriquez forward as a suitable replacement and the PNR found him acceptable.

General Abelardo Rodríguez 1932–1934

As the last political puppet of Jefe Máximo, it was during Rodríguez's tenure that Calles' influence began to decline. Although he was careful not to alienate Calles, he used him in cases when he needed him, but pushed hard to create a different culture in the presidency than his two predecessors had known; he did not want all of his cabinet and Congress passing everything through Calles instead of him. As soon as he took office he made it very clear that he wanted to be a fully independent functioning leader, telling cabinet members to only take issues to Calles if he allowed them to do so and to much surprise he immediately asked for Alberto Pani's resignation. This was unfortunate for Mexico as Pani was probably the most brilliant man in the cabinet, but Rodríguez saw him as being too loyal to Calles. Once Rodriquez had established his authority and influence he attempted to address issues that were taking place in Mexico.

He first set his focus on wages. Under his guidance Congress passed legislation for a three peso daily minimum wage across the nation. Rodríguez set up an Agriculture Department to address land redistribution. They put a stop to land injunctions so it would not slow down the process. Land redistribution spiked with about 1.2 million hectares being redistributed within half a year. Rodríguez also set up a new labour department that dealt with many of the labour issues the economic crisis had caused. They intervened in many strikes on the President's behalf, generally taking the side of the strikers. He also amended laws, increasing the amount of paid holidays for workers and getting the working week hours reduced.

At the end of his term, the PNR and Calles believed the next president needed to be more reform-minded in light of the global economic situation. Calles believed that Roosevelt's New Deal in the US was a good example for Mexico to follow. With this belief, Calles gathered concerns and current statistics from every department in the government and drew up a six-year plan for the next president to follow. With this, Calles put forward to the PNR delegates three names he felt would be legitimate for the presidential seat. Calles did not openly support any of them, allowing the convention to vote without his influence in the matter. During the convention, the issues of the Church, education and land reform were raised again, despite Calles' belief that land reform was bad for the economy. In the end the delegates voted and chose the man Calles had supported behind closed doors, General Lázaro Cárdenas.

General Lázaro Cárdenas

General Lázaro Cárdenas had a background in both the military and politics. He had followed and supported Calles through the military ranks, holding several significant posts. He also was the President of the PNR for a short time and governor of Michoacán. Cárdenas, however, was not considered one of the original revolutionary leaders, but was seen as the first of the new, young generation of revolutionary leaders, those that had grown up through the fighting. This young generation of leaders had seen the goals of the revolution stifled by the tight-fisted autocratic rule of Calles and the Maximato. Hope of bringing back to life any of these revolutionary aspirations had to come in the form of a man strong enough to rid Calles of his influence, bring together the peasants and labourers and have enough strength to defy the power of foreign companies.

Class discussion

What would drive Calles to keep control of the Mexican government during the Maximato, in light of all the sacrifices and goals of the revolution?

Ultimately the PNR saw Cárdenas as that man and nominated him for their president elect. With the backing of the PNR and support from his mentor, Calles set off on an electoral campaign that would take him over 15 000 miles through big cities and rural villages, using all modes of transportation from trains to donkeys. He used the PNR radio station to give reports of his travels as well as to give a speech on the eve of the election which he won by a landslide with over 2 million votes. He committed himself to the six-year plan given to him by the PNR and Calles, as the future plans for Mexico that he felt necessary to see through. It included improvements to transportation, land redistribution, agricultural infrastructure, education and nationalism. He envisioned a capitalism that did not exploit Mexico but rather worked for Mexico.

Cárdenas took the oath of office in 1934, and being empathetic to the situation of the peasants in the country did not move into the presidential palace, eventually turning it into a museum. Instead he moved into a common home built near the palace. He cut his salary in half and spent close to 500 days on the road visiting the people of Mexico. This allowed him to develop a personal relationship with them and build political support outside of Calles' control and influence. Creating this support base was a significant focus in his first two years and would pay off in the latter part of his tenure as president. It also allowed him to establish his own political agenda as he gathered those discontented with Calles and brought them into his inner circle, such as labour unions outside of CROM and peasants. He needed the support of these people behind him as political strife with Calles came to a head in 1935.

Cárdenas versus Calles

When Cárdenas came to the presidency two major problems developed. The first was a challenging split in Congress between Callistas and Cárdenistas, with older congressman loyal to Calles in the majority and the younger more progressive-thinking loyal to Cárdenas in the minority. Secondly, there was economic strife between labourers and management in several areas. The congressional problem was a struggle because Cárdenas wanted to shed the influence Calles had on his government. However, the second problem was welcomed by Cárdenas as he saw the fight between labourers and management as an opportunity to begin to address the labour issues of the revolution. But Calles disagreed as he saw the issues as a disturbance to economic prosperity and political solidarity, so Calles let his opinions be known in a public statement.

Tension between Calles and Cárdenas came to a head as Cárdenas interpreted these remarks as being in opposition to his presidency and Calles trying to push his influence through Cárdenas as he had done to the three previous presidents. Calles still had support from CROM leaders, some army generals, various cabinet ministers, his faction of Congress and some business leaders. Because of this, Cárdenas set out to consolidate his leadership and end Calles' influence for good.

Cárdenas purged the PNR of any Calles loyalists as he called the labour unions outside of CROM's influence to his side. He made military leaders, cabinet members and congressmen pledge their loyalty or step down. With the US ambassador Josephus Daniels in full support of the moves Cárdenas was making, he addressed the military, putting his trusted generals in political positions, gave junior officers raises and new positions, and rotated senior officers to new positions where they had no influence, or gave them the choice to retire. He put civilian experts in charge of agriculture and finance, and repealed a law that prevented him from removing federal judges.

He then crafted a public reply to Calles remarks, arguing that the strikes made the economy stronger and then subtly gave the country a choice between him and Calles. There was overwhelming support for Cárdenas, pressuring Calles to leave Mexico for a short time only to return a month later in December 1935. After a few months Calles made the decision that the ex-president could not be there without influencing decisions so he had Calles leave the country permanently. In April 1936 Calles, CROM labour leader Morones and a few other close associates were flown to Texas, eventually ending up in Los Angeles. Subsequently the Maximato and the power of Calles were over, and Cárdenas now had the country to lead by himself with the labourers and peasants as his support base.

Cárdenas's socio-economic programmes

By the time Cárdenas reached office the global depression had been in full swing for four years and Mexico had suffered, but not as badly as many other countries. In fact, Mexico had started to see some economic improvement in some areas and much of this was due to the fact that it was reliant on two major exports, oil and silver, both of which were fairly stable commodities. During his tenure he would see some positive economic results as GNP would grow more than 25% between 1935 and 1940. Manufacturing production rose over 50% in his six-year reign and government expenses would grow at an astronomical rate as his administration ditched the idea of a balanced budget and used government money to implement programmes to improve the social and economic infrastructure of Mexico, in the areas of education, land and labour. Although this stability and growth would change in 1937, for the first few years of his presidency these socio-economic plans helped.

Education

Cárdenas set out to change the education system in Mexico as he saw it as a way to include the future generations in the socialist revolutionary state. He expanded the number of schools by about 4000 so that more students had the opportunity of a basic free education. The government took over teacher training and changed the curriculum to include socialist, scientific, secular and nationalistic concepts. He also encouraged teachers to give lessons on hygiene, sex education and cleanliness to help address public health. The school led anti-alcohol campaigns for families as well as vaccination programmes and introduced new farming techniques. Cárdenas also had new textbooks printed that described Mexican history as a class struggle between peasant labourers and two forces: the wealthy capitalists and foreign businesses. They also brought attention to revolutionary heroes such as Emiliano Zapata. In many places where citizens were Catholic and held on to their traditions, the socialist ideas and sex education were not well-received and many teachers had to minimize the Cárdenas teaching agenda for fear of their lives.

Land Reform

President Cárdenas favoured ejidos over haciendas which he wanted broken up, so he could formed many ejidos out of land from large haciendas. He believed that the ejidos would free peasants from the oppressive life of **hacendados**, increase agricultural output and raise the standard of living, help feed the nation and build a base of political support. He redistributed more land than all of his predecessors combined at over 45 million acres, and much of it was irrigated land that was farmable. President Cárdenas also set up structures to assist them in the use of this land. He encouraged self-defence units in order for the campesinos to protect themselves and their newly acquired land from past owners and their cronies. He set up an agricultural bank, Banco de Crédito Ejidal, so that farmers and landowners could more easily get loans. The government also gave assistance for machinery and training. Although he gave out an unprecedented amount of land, much of it irrigated, problems arose, as the bank could not keep up with the demand and many of the farmers were now directly connected to the government instead of being independent farmers.

> **hacendado**
> Owner of a hacienda, a Spanish estate of significant size with plantations, factories or mines, and sometimes all three.

Labour

As mentioned earlier, Cárdenas had pulled together the various labour organizations that were disgusted with CROM and their leader Morones, in order for Cárdenas to gather political support. With CROM leader Morones and Calles exiled, President Cárdenas formed his own labour union to compete with the fledgling CROM and put it under the leadership of a well-known socialist, Vicente Lombardo. Under Lombardo, the Confederation of Mexican Workers (CTM) would boast more than 940 000 members at its peak, eventually becoming the leading labour organization, limiting CROM's influence. It would help consolidate the petroleum unions into one, the Sindicato de Trabajadores Petroleros de la República Mexicana (STPRM), which would prove vital in the future oil crisis.

Under the influence and encouragement of Cárdenas and CTM, strikes increased every year that Cárdenas was in office and they happened in all parts of the economy: oil, railways and streetcar workers, telephone workers and a general strike that included various professions. Two strikes of note were the 1936 railway workers strike and the 1937 oil workers strike. The railway workers strike is significant because after mediation and talks fell through, Cárdenas ultimately decided to nationalize the rail system. It had no real international backlash as the railways in Mexico had never been a lucrative enterprise. This ended unsuccessfully because the government could not run it properly, and Cárdenas ended up turning it over to a railway workers administration that did no better. However, this experience did give Cárdenas the knowledge and confidence he needed to navigate through the next major strike, which took place in the oil industry.

In 1937 Cárdenas faced a financial crisis. The cost of living in Mexico on average had jumped over 50% and to make matters worse wages fell behind inflation. All food supplies reached critically low levels, so much so that there was widespread fear of people not getting enough food to eat. Cárdenas responded by creating a wheat board to regulate the purchase, sale and storage of wheat. The board imported various crops to cover the shortfall of food and set minimum prices so that farmers would receive a fair income for their crops. Cárdenas' popularity began to drop with the 1937 recession and workers everywhere were stirring for better wages and opportunities, but none more so than in the oil industry.

Oil industry labour unrest

The oil industry workers in Mexico reached a fever pitch of unrest in 1937. The industry was seeing higher profits with global economic improvements and European war mobilization. However, the petroleum workers were not seeing any of these profits in their wages or treatment. So oil workers went on strike, demanding higher wages and better conditions. In 1935 they had pulled together to form one union and affiliated themselves with CTM, Lombardo's labour union that had the full support of Cárdenas.

The difficulty with this strike was that it would freeze Mexico's major export industry, causing more economic problems for the nation. Because the industry was dominated by foreigners, namely the US and Great Britain, it stirred up the revolutionary nationalism of the country, making it a headline issue in every corner of Mexico. For two reasons, nationalism and the nation's economics, the President felt he had to intervene and uphold the constitutional laws.

The workers were demanding a wage increase that would total 26.4 million pesos on average and a better workplace environment. So Cárdenas formed a commission to see if the companies could meet the pay increase demand. The commission found that in fact the companies could and so Cárdenas backed the workers and the commission, and demanded that the companies pay the increase. The companies refused, forcing the matter to go to the Mexican Supreme Court, which upheld the decision found by the commission and sided with the workers as well. The companies refused to pay the wage increase to the workers, forcing this labour conflict to turn into a political fight for national pride and sovereignty. The companies' inflexibility fired up Mexican nationalism across the country, giving Cárdenas the much needed political support to do what was necessary.

Roosevelt had already denounced US military intervention in Mexico because of the situation coming to a head in Europe and he desired solid hemispheric relations because of Europe's situation and did not want any country to be a future foothold for Hitler or Mussolini. With Cárdenas' knowledge of this and the companies' continued defiance over paying the wage increases, Cárdenas gave a radio address to the nation in March 1938 announcing that he was nationalizing the oil companies using the 1935 Expropriation Law that allowed him to do so as long as the companies were paid their fiscal value. The companies demanded 450 million dollars, but after many months of talks and dealings, and pressure from their respective governments, they ended up settling at 130 million dollars which Mexico would pay in annual installments over a four-year period. Companies took the money but made the transition as difficult as possible, withholding equipment and expertise, organizing a global boycott of Mexican oil, and the US stopping the import of silver.

Cárdenas formed the state-run oil company PEMEX to own and run the oil industry, and although it struggled at first, domestic demand for oil helped stabilize the company early on with oil sales to Germany, Italy, Japan and the Soviet Union helping too. Despite the difficulties and economic hardship oil nationalization caused, people were overwhelmingly supportive, donating money to the government in order to help pay the compensation owed to the oil companies. The US would eventually lift the boycott on oil and silver after Cárdenas put heavy taxes on the silver mines and hinted at nationalizing those as well, plus Roosevelt's desire to uphold his Good Neighbor Policy. With the impending Second World War Roosevelt had a strong desire for hemispheric solidarity.

▲ Mexicans celebrating oil nationalization

Mexican Revolutionary Party

Riding the wave of popularity after nationalizing the oil industry, just three weeks later Cárdenas disbanded the national political party, the PNR, and formed the Mexican Revolutionary Party (PRM) in 1938. There was a new relationship between the government and the workers, and Cárdenas wanted the political party to reflect this as he believed that the old PNR left out many of his supporting populace. The party encompassed four main sectors: the military, government employees, the labouring class and the peasants. This party empowered these groups, which were the most supportive of his progressive programmes, and it would become the party of the future for Mexico.

Cardenismo

Cárdenas' populist ideas and leadership would come to be known as Cardenismo, as he truly attempted to enforce the major concepts of the 1917 Constitution, including land reform, labour reform and ownership of subsoil rights. Oil nationalization was by far his greatest achievement, despite the economic damage that occurred, but that never could have taken place if not for his ability to gather the masses under his influence and his courage to stand up to foreign nations without warfare. Although his socialist education programmes were not received well by many, they did help reinvigorate nationalism and gave many the opportunity to improve their social situation. His land distribution and assistance to campesinos was unprecedented and would never be done again on that scale. President Cárdenas and his progressive and populist programmes showed how much he truly cared for the rebels of the revolution, and he wanted to pay them back for their sacrifice by enforcing the 1917 Constitution.

Class discussion

For what reasons did Cárdenas try to return to the original goals of the revolution when in office?

To what extent was he successful at achieving those goals?

TOK discussion

From the beginning of the revolution under Madero's Plan de San Luis Potosi and through the work of President Cárdenas, the meaning, expectations, reasons for revolution and results varied during this 30-year period.

Write a one-page response to either of the following questions.

1 To what degree did the two sides of this revolution find an equilibrium? What discourse helped them to achieve it or move away from it? In what ways did reason find a place in this revolution?

2 Discuss or think about the difference between reasoning about means and reasoning about ends. Is one more prevalent than the other in the Mexican Revolution?

In light of the Mexican Revolution and the opposing groups consider the following questions.

1 To what extent are the groups aware of each other's assumptions?

2 To what extent are the groups conscious of their own assumptions?

3 In what ways do the values in areas each group considers to be most important or most moral affect their knowledge of the revolution?

4 In what ways do the opposing groups differ in the set of facts they consider relevant or essential?

5 To what extent do they use different forms of justification to support their conclusions, and are these just?

In a one-page response answer the following question.

To what extent did the classification systems (peasants, labourers, business, military and government) affect the knowledge each class attained through the revolution?

2.5 Impact of the revolution on women, the arts, education, music and literature

Conceptual understanding

Key questions

→ In what ways did women and their role change due to the Mexican Revolution?

→ How did the arts change and incorporate the revolution?

→ In what ways did the revolution affect education?

→ How was music and literature changed due to the revolution?

Key concepts

→ Change

→ Perspectives

Women during the revolution

Soldaderas

When men left their homes to fight in the Mexican Revolution, they often left their families behind. In the rural areas of Mexico this left women susceptible to rape and kidnapping by bandits or marauding revolutionary armies. Because of this many women began following their men to the battlefield to be safer and also to continue their supportive roles as wife and mother.

These women became known as soldaderas, as they followed men around Mexico from battlefield to battlefield, doing a variety of tasks, including setting up camp, cleaning for the soldiers, cooking for when they returned from battle, hauling equipment, gathering water and firewood, building shelters to protect the men from the elements, caring for the horses and other animals they had brought along, and being in charge of medical care at times. Many would go so far as to say that without these women there may not have been a revolution as many of the men would have returned home. Many rebels were able to fight because these women literally carried their homes on their backs, brought their families and followed their men, doing all they could to make battlefield life easier.

▲ A soldadera

Some of the more ambitious soldaderas picked up weapons and swelled the ranks of the military, involving themselves in every capacity of the military except for the highest-ranking positions. They fought in many battles, fired weapons, distributed ammunition before battles, and became involved in espionage and propaganda for their armies. At times some of the soldaderas obtained battle reports, distributed gear and carried dispatches.

Some of these women became famous for their fighting, leading men into battle, fighting in over 100 different confrontations, some even forming their own brigade of women. None are as well known as Amelia Robles who fought her way up to the status of colonel, sleeping with her pistol, smoking a cigar and one of the few after the revolution to earn a veteran's pension for her efforts.

Not all women during the revolution lived the life of a soldadera. Many that stayed at home filled some of the jobs the men abandoned, worked to help their families and also to support the revolutionary efforts. Many found jobs on newspapers, founding girls' schools or working as telephone operators, forming the largest group of women in the economy under the telephone workers union, Sindicato de Telefonistas de la República Mexican. Many tried to keep their jobs after the revolution or moved to the city to find work. These working women and the soldaderas used their experiences to fight for women's rights from the 1930s.

Education policies

Before the revolution, schools throughout Mexico were run by the Catholic Church or regional governments, making them mainly accessible for the elite and wealthy. The various educational standards held by the different regional governments led to many inadequacies with devastating results such as an 80% illiteracy rate. For these reasons education became a major concern for presidents in the post-revolutionary era.

Obregón and education

President Obregón established the Secretariat of Public Education (SPE) and appointed José Vasconcelos to be its First Minister. He was in charge of all public education: primary, secondary, as well as state colleges and universities. He also ended up developing a network of vocational schools to help teach adults new skills like farming, reading and writing. Vasconcelos believed that the Indian population was a hindrance to social and economic progress and needed to be educated and assimilated, so he had thousands of new schools built, mostly in rural areas to help change the life and culture of the peasants and farmers. These schools taught the basics of education, hygiene and health care, the Spanish language and Mexican history and geography.

Vasconcelos also started a magazine called the *El Maestro* in order to assist rural teachers in their instruction and content. He reprinted "classics" like Homer and Cervantes and had thousands printed and taken to schools all over the nation, also supplying them with "readers" that helped people improve their reading. Vasconcelos also increased the number of libraries across the nation, giving people access to books to read. There were more than 1900 libraries by the time he left office. In opposition to the political beliefs of President Calles he resigned in 1924.

Calles and education

This left the office open for Calles to appoint José Puig Casauranc to the head of the SPE from 1924–1928. Casauranc was greatly persuaded by Under-secretary Moisés Sáenz who in turn was influenced by John Dewey, who believed in educating through practical experiences. He combined this theory of education with his ideas to stress nationalism and Mexican history, focusing on the positive goals of the revolution. Casauranc also wanted to expand rural schools and their access to education, which he did but he also gave them access to gardens, orchards and animals to take care of in order to make their education more practical. With the expansion of rural schools the number of teachers increased as well as regular student attendance. His focus was also on the assimilation of the Indian culture, teaching them Spanish and Mexican history. Schools under Casauranc became centres of their communities, offering classes in art, music and general health. He opened a small number of model primary schools in the capitals so that other schools would have a model of effective teaching methods. Arguably his greatest contribution was the building of a number of central agricultural schools that came with 2500 acres of agricultural land where new farming techniques were taught alongside general schooling.

While Vasconcelos allowed Catholic schools to continue to operate independently, President Calles shut down all Catholic schools. This coincided with the Cristero rebellion and caused major disruption to the student attendance that both Vasconcelos and Casauranc had built up.

Education in Mexico would struggle for a short time from 1928 to 1930, as the SEP saw four different ministers rotate through the office leading to a lack of cohesion in expectations and hampering any significant progress. This changed when Narciso Bassols came to the SPE for the last years of the Maximato, from 1931 to 1934.

Bassols was a socialist and had the responsibility of carrying out Calles' socialist education plan to include science and technology in schools. Like those before him, his goal also focused on the rural population, wanting to educate the campensino population in the hope that they would increase agricultural output, thus improving their local economies. He published *El Maestro Rural*, a teaching magazine assisting teachers in their classrooms, and a tool for communicating expectations to rural teachers and students. He also ensured the supply of better prepared graduates of the Escuelas Normales, the teacher training college to teach in schools.

Under Calles' socialist education plan, Bassols implemented a sex education curriculum that met stiff opposition in most places, especially in rural communities. With parents' consent and encouragement the students protested against the curriculum as they saw it as unnecessary and because it clashed with their religion and traditions. Teachers also began to protest and oppose Bassols when he wanted to begin to assess teachers. Facing such stiff opposition from students and teachers, Bassols resigned.

Cárdenas and education

Cárdenas came into office and appointed a new SPE leader, Gonzalo Vázquez Vela, who ran the office until 1940, throughout Cárdenas' tenure as president. Much of this is covered in the Cárdenas presidency section (page 102). Vázquez was given an increased budget of nearly 15% of the total national budget. With that he focused his attention, like those before him, on the rural population, especially after the disturbances of the Cristero rebellion. He would oversee the construction of more than 4000 rural schools and increase student enrolment by more than 50%.

Vázquez added to the common theme of the SPE of assimilating the indigenous population through education to make them more productive for the overall community and nation.

Arts

Muralist movement

The revolution sparked a burst of creative thought that manifested itself in images of Mexican history, experiences, traditions, culture, nationalism and the future. This creatively was best portrayed through the muralist movement, sometimes known as the Mexican Renaissance, led by Los Tres Grandes (The Three Great Ones): José Clemente Orozco, Diego Rivera and David Alfaro Siqueiros. These artists tried to define a new post-revolutionary Mexico through their art, in the hope of educating the illiterate population to instill pride in the past and yet focus on the realities of the present day. Their murals were large public displays so that more people could see them. They used Mexican culture, revolution and nationalism.

In 1922 SPE minister Vasconcelos recruited Orozco, Rivera and Siqueiros to paint large communal mural projects as a means to instill nationalism and give their analyses of the revolution and its influence on Mexico's current state. Vasconcelos gave them their first job – painting murals at the National Preparatory School in Mexico City – and it was here that the three established the Syndicate of Technical Workers, Painters and Sculptors. The group created a paper called *El Machete*, which became the official paper of the Mexican Communist Party as all three of these muralists were communists to varying degrees. Their works included communist symbols through the use of Mexican history and the people's daily struggles.

▲ "History of Mexico from the Conquest to 1930" by Diego Rivera

Rivera

Diego Rivera was touring Europe, gathering inspiration and ideas from frescoes, when Vasconcelos recruited him, getting him to return home and use his art in public spaces for the betterment of Mexico. After returning and touring the Yucatan he received his first job under Vasconcelos – a painting at the National Preparatory School. Here he painted his first large-scale mural called "Creation", showing the nature of arts and sciences. The students at the school, not used to such progressive ideas and art, were offended and tried to destroy the piece. He eventually finished within a year but was unhappy with the heavy European influence in it and wanted to include more Mexican ideals and influences in future pieces.

He completed other works at the SPE headquarters, the National School of Agriculture, the National Palace and the Cortés Palace in Cuernavaca under such titles as "Life of Zapata", "The Rural Teacher", "The Liberated Earth", "Natural Forces Controlled by Humanity", "Epic of the Mexican People", and the "Liberation of the Peon". They all portrayed the glories and injustices of the revolution and of Mexico through the peasants, indigenous population and revolutionary events. He worked hard to reflect Mexican social life as he interpreted it.

In the early thirties, while in exile in the US, he did a number of works, most notably for the Museum of Modern Art and the Rockefeller Center in New York. The pieces reflected the social abundances of the 1920s in the US, while showing the contradictions he saw in capitalism. His use of communist symbols got him fired and his piece at the Rockefeller Center was destroyed when he refused to change it. He would later return to Mexico to do more works of art after his short time in the US.

Orozco

Orozco began his career as a cartoonist in the press during the revolution. He lived through the revolution and saw the horrors of it, not only death, but also the dishonesty and deceitfulness of the generals and politicians getting more for themselves at the expense of the masses. His paintings reflected much of this through tragic images of human imperfection that evoke sadness and pity in their viewers.

▲ "Zapatistas Marching" by Jose Orozco

He was employed to do his first work at the National Preparatory Academy, and like Rivera's mural, his two murals were not widely accepted and nearly destroyed by the students. His two murals were "Reactionary Forces" and "Christ Destroys His Cross", the latter showing Christ destroying his cross because he was not happy with what people had become. He completed several other murals, "The Trench", "Cores and Malinche", "Omniscience", "The Destruction of the Old Order", "The Strike" and "The Rich Banquet While the Workers Fight" before leaving for the US.

Like the other two muralists, he spent the beginning of the 1930s in the US painting murals. He did several works in California, New York and Dartmouth College. In these works he proudly displayed the history of Mexico but also his critique of what he saw as the deception of capitalism. Later he returned to Mexico to do some of his most famous pieces: "Man on Fire", "Political and Ideological Exploitation" and "Hidalgo". These increasingly focused on Mexico's culture and proud history but also the unreliability of humans and how it led to greed and the exploitation of others.

Siqueiros

Siqueiros was a muralist but with a very different background and social agenda than the others. He was a revolutionary soldier who had fought and witnessed the tragedies of the revolution and was now a political activist. He found himself exiled from Mexico and in prison for his political activities on a number of different occasions. He spent time in Europe learning from the French and Italian influences and even spent time with Rivera in Italy.

▲ "Del Porfirismo a la Revolución" by David Siqueiros

He was contracted to paint his first mural for Mexico under Vasconcelos at the National Preparatory School just as the other two had. His mural "Burial of a Martyred Worker" showed the oppression of Mexican labour juxtaposed by the freedom of death. The students tried to destroy the work as they had Rivera's and Orozco's.

After this he was forced to leave Mexico because of his political activities, and went to the US where he was contracted to do work, mainly in California. He created two large murals, "America Tropical" and "Workers Meeting", both of which critiqued American imperialism and capitalist oppression, and displayed unions, interracial relations and racial unity, none of which were widely accepted in the US at that time. Subsequently both murals were covered and destroyed and his work visa was not renewed.

From here he left for South America where he started to develop the processes and techniques that would make him famous. He believed in continual experimentation with different techniques and new technologies. He developed a process of spraying a base for his murals out of pyroxylin paint and attempted to make his art stand out and not be so one dimensional by using polyangular perspectives. He returned to Mexico in 1939 at the end of Cárdenas' tenure in office and painted "Portrait of the Bourgeoisie", a visual struggle between the evils of fascism and democracy. Siqueiros created works that were full of political and social content, which later in his career included the struggle against emerging fascism.

The muralist movement was a large collection of historical reflections on Mexico that incorporated the impending concepts of industry and the future. All the muralists drew upon their connections with the revolution and the culture of Mexico, but they portrayed their interpretations differently. Although all of them showed Marxist influences, Rivera drew attention to the indigenous and labouring population in Mexico, while Siqueiros focused on political, social and future themes in his paintings, and Orozco drew attention to the flaws of humans and what those flaws could lead to. All of them drew ideas from the nation's past while also looking to the future realities of the industrial world.

ATL Thinking and social skills

Examine at least one photo of a revolution-inspired artwork. Discuss the points of revolution present and the underlying themes of the revolution in each work.

TOK discussion

Muralists and novelists shared their perceptions, realities and knowledge of the revolution through their art and writing.

1 In what ways were the artists' use of emotions necessary and/or problematic in their sharing of the revolution?

2 In what ways did the arts help others understand the history of the revolution?

3 In what ways did muralists use culture to understand the revolution and portray it in their murals?

Music

Music during and after the revolution very much reflected the ideals and sacrifices made by the soldiers and their loved ones during the fighting. They used the various ideas and themes of the revolution and coupled them after the revolution with the new emergence of mass media, namely radio and production.

During the revolution brass bands followed the armies, reflecting the regional traditions of music and instruments. Music and dancing were a significant component in the revolutionary armies as they would play music after wins, losses and even during battles to motivate the soldiers. Corridos, or Mexican ballads, were around before the revolution but their association with the fighting brought them to the forefront. These corridos incorporated simple language and became a communication tool to share stories and news of the revolution throughout the country. These narratives of social events were sung by soldiers around the fire at night, and usually had political undertones, themes of land reform, nationalism and women as a romantic theme. They used authentic and traditional musical instruments to accompany these songs. The revolution certainly popularized this style of music, but when the revolution ended and technology entered the world of music, it all started to change.

Styles started to change in the twenties and thirties. Girls started to cut their hair short, raised their skirt lengths and discovered the dance floor. This type of girl was known as "Chica Moderna", the modern girl. The radio was now delivering music to almost everyone across the nation and recording studios started to refine the sound quality. Radio stations not only helped the popularity of songs, artists and types of music but also helped foster a nightlife among young professionals, hence the Chica Moderna.

Mariachi was traditional rural music that used only stringed instruments and voice. In the 1930s they gained national popularity. The mariachi bands began to tour the country, and even the US. A mariachi band accompanied President Cárdenas across Mexico on his campaign tour. The mariachis soon adopted trumpets because of the influence of the big band in the US.

Music helped heal a torn nation during and after the revolution. It was an avenue in which polarizing populaces, whether it be government, Church, rural or urban, could meet on common ground. Much of the music development was pushed by technology, which improved the style, sound and delivery, but Mexico's most famous music stems from the influences of the revolution.

Literature

A new literary genre emerged from the revolution known as "Novels of the Revolution". This genre included hundreds of novels by as many authors inspired by the events of the revolution. One of the most famous authors of this genre is Mariano Azuela. He was a doctor during the revolution, and saw many of the tragedies that took place. He wrote *The Underdogs*, one of the first and most popular stories of its time. Most of these stories, like Azuela's, are based on the revolution and real events. They often dark, showing the loss and disorder that took place, but trying to show the heroic side of the revolution as well. Other stories in this genre are: *They Gave Us the Land* by Juan Rulfo, *The Edge of the Storm* by Agustin Yáñez, *The Shadow of the Caudillo* by Martin Luiz Guzman, and Nellie Campobello, a famous woman writer who wrote titles including *Cartucho* and *Notes on the Military Life of Francisco Villa*. A later generation wrote stories based on the events from the revolution as well, like Carlos Fuentes' *The Old Gringo*.

All of this literature was a reflection of and inspired by the events of the Mexican Revolution. While it was very much intended to bring people's attention to the dark but very real side of the revolution, it also revealed the authentic source of nationalistic pride the revolution inspired.

Conclusion

The 1910 revolution was brought about through the demands of lower classes who felt they were ignored by the oligarchy that dominated the Porfiriato. This attitude stemmed from unrealized desires set forth by the 1857 Constitution. They had forced their issues and problems to the forefront, although these would evolve as the revolution progressed. Revolutionary heroes would champion the revolutionary cause as many of them would rise and fall during this time in Mexican history. When the 1917 Constitution was created from the turbulence of the revolution, it addressed many of the initial issues raised when the revolution began. The post-revolutionary leaders in Mexico would use this document and their experience of fighting in the revolution to lead Mexico in the years ahead.

The post-revolutionary state in Mexico saw much of the political support come from the common labourer, rather than the wealthy elite and foreign investors. This gained Mexico respect from the masses but also foreign countries. During this time Mexican leaders like Obregón, Calles and Cárdenas would for the most part fulfill and enforce all that had been fought for, although this fulfillment of revolutionary goals would take time and to some degree be done through political control and economic development. This period, however, did see an increase in Mexican nationalism. Just as many of the issues that were raised in 1910 were being answered, the onset of technology and industry advanced Mexico into a technologically and economically developed country, which in turn caused new problems for the country. The revolution and all that came after, however, gave Mexico an infrastructure to handle these new emerging problems.

Exam-style questions

1. Who deserves the title of "Father of the Mexican Revolution" and why?

2. Evaluate the extent to which the leaders of the Mexican Revolution could be considered as either "revolutionaries" or "reformers."

3. Analyse the causes of the Mexican Revolution of 1910.

4. "By the end of the 1920s the original objectives of the Mexican Revolution had been abandoned." To what extent do you agree with this judgment?

5. Examine the major stages of the Mexican Revolution (1910–1920).

6. "The Mexican Revolution was a revolt of the impoverished many against the wealthy few." To what extent do you agree with this statement?

The introductory paragraph

Question

Discuss the aims and achievements of one of the following three leaders of the Mexican Revolution: Alvaro Obregon, Plutarco Calles or Lazaro Cardenas.

Analysis

Your answer to a Paper 3 essay question should start with an introductory paragraph. This introduction should be concise – no more than one paragraph long – and not take much time away from the body of the essay, but it needs to explicitly address the demands of the question. This means that you must establish the issue(s) of the question and form a thesis, but not waste time copying down the question. Your introductory paragraph should show that you clearly understand the question and the factors involved in answering it.

In your introductory paragraph you should do the following:

1   Clarify terms

You will need to define any major terms used in the question before you can answer it. (The terms in this example are "aims" and "achievements".) If the question uses a term that is ambiguous or could be used in multiple ways, it is important to clarify the way in which you will use and address that term. For example, if the question asks "To what extent was Pancho Villa a rebel or a revolutionary?" you should briefly lay out your understanding of the two terms, "rebel" and "revolutionary", before proceeding.

2   Establish the context

When you establish the context for the question, you prove to the examiner/reader that you understand that other events were happening before, during and after this question's time frame and that the topic of the question did not happen in a vacuum. If the question is "Evaluate the role and impact of the United States in the Mexican Revolution", it would be useful to mention the eras in which the Revolution occurred, according to the United States.

3   Outline the structure of your argument

To meet the demands of the question, you will also need to outline the structure of your argument. This will take up the bulk of the paragraph and is probably the most critical part, aside from the final thesis. Here you need to establish the main ideas, themes, factors, criteria or components you plan to address in the essay. For example, if you are going to break the question down and address it thematically (political, social, and/or economic), establish here the themes you will use to support the thesis. In this way, you can give the examiner the blueprint or structure in which you will address the question. Again, be brief: save the details for the body of the essay. Here you are simply showing how you intend to approach the question and support the thesis you will argue. Any counter-claims you will make to support or strengthen your answer can be mentioned briefly here as well.

4   State your position

The final piece of the introduction should simply be your overall thesis for answering the question. In one or two sentences, state clearly your explicit answer or position relating to the question. This will allow the examiner to clearly see not only your position on the question but also that you understand the question and are addressing it appropriately. The thesis should tie together all the components or main ideas in your argument addressing the question.

Here is a checklist of guidance for your introduction.

Do...	Don't...
• be as specific as possible as soon as possible	• use general phrases
• be concise and stay brief	• say more than is needed
• establish that you clearly understand the question	• say what you *won't* be addressing in the essay
• construct the main points in support of the thesis	• get bogged down in specifics
• set the thesis of the paper	• tell a story or "paint a picture" to lead into your paper
	• take significant and precious time from the body of your answer

Sample introductory paragraph

Obregón was a military leader of the Mexican Revolution following the fall of Madero; he successfully rose to power to become the President of Mexico in 1920. His role as both a military and political leader during the Mexican Revolution provides a basis for his aims and achievements as a revolutionary figure. Obregón aimed to gain support from the Mexican people as well as from political figures within and outside the country. He also aimed to advance Mexico as a progressive and developing nation and to increase his personal power. He achieved his goals of rising to power and maintaining citizen support. He also supported and followed through with his aim of creating progressive change within Mexico, although he did not achieve this to its full extent. Obregón's brilliance as a military general and politician allowed him to successfully gain a position of power and usher Mexico into the post-revolution as a progressive state.

Examiner comments

This sample paragraph shows an obvious understanding of the question in the choice of only one leader, Obregón, as the subject of the essay. However, other than giving the date of 1920, it lacks context. The candidate has given a structured outline of the main arguments to be addressed, and has included a thesis based on the main ideas. The candidate could have briefly explained what is meant by the terms "aims" and "achievements", or at least the difference between them.

3 THE GREAT DEPRESSION IN THE AMERICAS, 1920S TO 1940S

Global context

The Great Depression dominated the global economy from 1929 to the onset of war in the late 1930s. The economic recovery from the First World War proved to be illusory, dependent as it was on US credit. The Depression was met with different responses around the world. Germany embraced autocratic extremism and militarism. Italy's dictatorship sought self-sufficiency through violent expansionism. Japan would take a similar path, using its army to create what Japanese politicians called the Greater East Asia Co-Prosperity Sphere. Tariff walls sprang up around countries across the globe, shrinking markets even further, likely making things worse in the long run.

These years put an indelible mark on the psyche of a generation. While the Depression is often marked from October 1929, the reality is not so easily delineated. The underlying causes of the Depression date back to the end of the First World War and the economic and social chaos that followed it. To understand how the Depression set upon the Americas, its course and consequences, it is important to examine the context of the 1920s. For most countries, it was the onset of war in the late 1930s, if not direct involvement in war itself, that led to an end to economic depression, and the political consequences of the depression were even more far-reaching than the economic ones.

Timeline

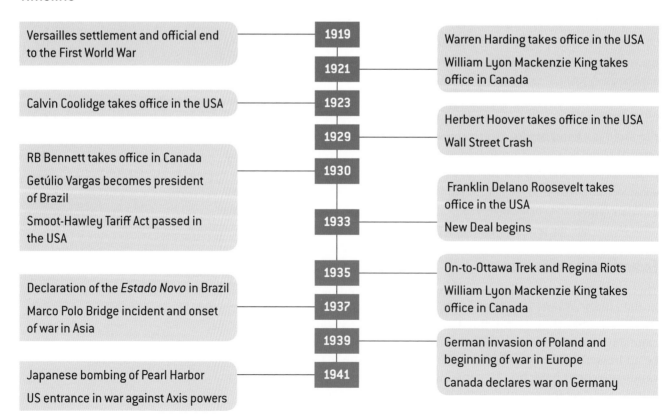

Versailles settlement and official end to the First World War	**1919**	
		Warren Harding takes office in the USA
	1921	William Lyon Mackenzie King takes office in Canada
Calvin Coolidge takes office in the USA	**1923**	
		Herbert Hoover takes office in the USA
	1929	Wall Street Crash
RB Bennett takes office in Canada	**1930**	
Getúlio Vargas becomes president of Brazil		Franklin Delano Roosevelt takes office in the USA
Smoot-Hawley Tariff Act passed in the USA	**1933**	New Deal begins
	1935	On-to-Ottawa Trek and Regina Riots
Declaration of the *Estado Novo* in Brazil		William Lyon Mackenzie King takes office in Canada
Marco Polo Bridge incident and onset of war in Asia	**1937**	
	1939	German invasion of Poland and beginning of war in Europe
Japanese bombing of Pearl Harbor	**1941**	Canada declares war on Germany
US entrance in war against Axis powers		

3.1 The Great Depression: Political and economic causes in the Americas from the 1920s and 1930s

Conceptual understanding

Key questions

→ How did the consumer culture in the USA contribute to the onset of the Great Depression?

→ To what extent was the Wall Street Crash a cause of depression in Latin America?

→ How did the prosperity of the 1920s help create the problems of the Great Depression in Canada?

Key concepts

→ Causes

→ Consequences

Latin America

The conditions that brought the Great Depression to Latin America had their roots in the economic policies of late 19th-century political leaders. The first 50 years after independence had seen the creation of largely self-sufficient agriculturally based units that mirrored the **latifundias** of Spain; here plantations produced the food needed for the immediate surroundings and handicrafts were produced by local artisans, mirroring the feudal systems that existed in Europe. However, with the onset of industrialization in the USA and Europe, Latin American commodities became more valuable. Industrialized countries focused on production, and the concentration of labour in factories meant that many of these countries became dependent upon exports to feed the growing urban population in their states.

> **latifundias**
> A large estate or ranch in ancient Rome, or more recently in Spain and Latin America, where peasants or slaves work.

This was especially true in the United Kingdom, which had established strong trade relations with Latin American states after the wars of independence. They capitalized on pre-existing relations to increase their importation of food; Argentina in particular profited from this change, exporting beef and wheat to the UK. There was also a growing market for the tropical fruits that were being produced on US-owned plantations in Central America. The onset of refrigeration on ships allowed this market to flourish and companies such as Standard and United Fruit Company profited tremendously as it could ship tropical fruits to its home base in the USA. Lastly, the demand for Latin American minerals and resources that had floundered in the post-revolutionary era once again became important; for example, Chilean copper and nitrates were exported to Europe as part of its industrialization.

While Latin American resources were thriving, there was very limited development in their own industries. Local entrepreneurs did create textile factories, construction facilities, food-processing and beverage industries but they were a very small part of the national economy. This meant that for most finished goods Latin Americans had to rely on imports. This set up the export–import dynamic: Latin American countries were dependent upon export of resources for income and were reliant upon foreign imports for industrial goods.

Also, in many countries, the elites in power felt that their own countries lacked the educational and technological skills needed to develop. Rather than nurture a local industrial sector, they encouraged foreign investment and ownership in such endeavours. This could be seen very clearly in Mexico, where the economic liberals called themselves the *científicos* and advocated for incentives for foreigners to invest in Mexico. US investors flocked to the country, buying land for mining and railway construction. While Mexico did benefit somewhat from these companies, the majority of the profits went back to the USA, and the government itself gained very little as the incentives came in the form of tax-free or reduced-tax status for foreign companies.

The USA was not the largest trading partner for most of Latin America, however. In 1913, two-thirds of investment in the region came from the United Kingdom, followed by the USA, France and Germany. During the First World War, Latin America as a whole benefited but the weakness of the system for them began to show after the war. As the European countries faced economic hardships and slow recovery from the war, the wealth that had previously been generated by the export–import model began to fade, and most Latin American imports had reached their peak values even before the Crash.

Supply of Latin American goods began to outstrip demand even before the onset of the Great Depression and provided some early warning signs for those who tracked global trade. Since their economies were dependent on the prosperity of those with whom they traded and the policy decisions made overseas, Latin American countries were very susceptible to the needs and wants of their partners. In May 1927 Argentina received its maximum price for wheat; for Cuban sugar it was March 1928 and Brazilian coffee hit the same apex in March 1929. This shows that most Latin American countries were already on a downward slope due to the policy decisions that were made by their leaders. The onset of the Great Depression served to exacerbate existing issues – it did not create them.

▲ Women working in the export sector in Honduras

Canada

Political fragmentation

The Conscription Crisis of 1917 had threatened to tear Canada apart. English-speaking Canada was once again pitted against French-speaking Canada. To this national division was added a rift in traditional party politics. Laurier's Liberals, a party that had largely transcended the linguistic–political divide that had plagued Canada since before Confederation, were torn into pro- and anti-conscriptionist factions. Based as it was on a single issue, Borden's Union government could not

be expected to outlast the war. With Laurier's death in 1919, and Borden's retirement a year later, it was clear that the political landscape was going to change. Few foresaw just how significant this change would be.

Before they could tackle any of the issues that accompanied the end of the war, the two mainstream national parties had to find new leaders. This was especially delicate for the Liberals. Not only would the new leader have to replace an icon of Canadian politics who had dominated his party since 1887, but the more pressing problem was that the new leader would have to stitch the party back together. He had to appeal to both the English-speaking and the French-speaking elements in the party and the country. The Liberals chose William Lyon MacKenzie King, a previous Minister of Labour, for this role, and he, like his predecessor, would dominate both his party and his country for 25 years. The Conservatives chose Arthur Meighen to pilot their party in the post-war years. As Borden's Solicitor General, Meighen had been instrumental in developing the War Measures Act, the Military Service Act and the Wartime Elections Act. Meighen had been at the forefront of the most difficult legislation of the war years.

The political situation may have settled down into established pre-war patterns had these two parties remained, with *Nationalistes* from Quebec, the only political choices for voters. The early 1920s, however, saw a remarkable surge in the popularity of non-traditional parties. Thomas Crerar, a former Minister of Agriculture from Manitoba, harnessed a growing sense of western prairie alienation and formed the National Progressive Party with other disaffected western members of parliament in 1919. They would form the official opposition after the federal election of 1921, although they declined the title. This same sense of rural discontent was the chief force that propelled the new United Farmers of Ontario into government in 1919. A similar story played out in Alberta in 1921, when the United Farmers of Alberta formed the government after the provincial election.

Throughout the 1920s, the progressives were divided. Moderate progressives advocated cooperation with the established parties while the more radical members of the party were not so inclined and favoured a radical change to the system of Canadian politics. In the mid-1920s a progressive member of parliament from Winnipeg named JS Woodsworth rose to the fore of the progressives, preaching tax reform that shifted the tax burden to business and the wealthy, the development of federal unemployment insurance and old-age pensions.

Regional discontent spread to the Atlantic coast as well. The Maritime Rights Movement developed in the early 1920s, arguing for greater subsidies to the Maritime provinces and tariffs to protect their coal and steel industries. When their Liberal members of parliament could not deliver on these demands, Maritime voters turned en masse to the Conservatives in the 1925 federal election. King and his Liberals nevertheless won the election on the strength of their support in the rest of the country. Although this fractured political landscape was short-lived, neutered in large part by the piecemeal compromises of King, it introduced a number of elements into the federal political discussion – the regulation of industry, financial support for farmers, social security, new political parties, federal versus provincial relations – ideas that would resurface during the difficult years of the 1930s.

Canadian Prime Ministers, 1920–48	
Prime Minister	**Years**
Arthur Meighen	1920–21
William Lyon Mackenzie King	1921–26
Arthur Meighen	1926
William Lyon Mackenzie King	1926–30
RB Bennett	1930–35
William Lyon Mackenzie King	1935–48

Class discussion

Were there any other political parties in Canada or other countries advocating for unemployment insurance and old-age pensions in the 1920s? Would any of the politcal parties in Canada today argue in favour of discontinuing such schemes? Why (or why not)?

Economic fragility

The roots of the Great Depression, in Canada and the rest of the world, can be traced to the economic changes that followed the armistice of 1918. The war had damaged most of the major industrial economies of the world. Only the USA would emerge from the First World War in a position of relative economic strength. As such, much of the world owed money to the USA. This position of strength spread American economic influence throughout the world to an even greater extent.

In many ways Canada was no different. The economic boom that was gathering pace in the USA throughout the early 1920s eventually dragged the Canadian economy out of its post-war slump. The surging demand for consumer goods such as automobiles and electronics, in turn, created a demand for minerals such as zinc and copper, a demand supplied by the Canadian mining industry. Exploration opened new areas of the **Canadian Shield** to mining interests, many controlled by US investors.

Pulp and paper also became vital new exports. US demand for newsprint was skyrocketing and it became economical for US paper companies to establish **branch plants** across Canada to feed the appetite of the US newspaper industry. Between 1920 and 1929 Canada tripled her production of newsprint.

The emblematic consumer product of the 1920s was the automobile, and its production was an important stimulus to the Canadian economy. By the middle of the decade, the major US carmakers had plants in Canada able to produce half a million automobiles a year. The growing car culture sparked the construction of some 57 000 kilometres of paved roads in the last five years of the 1920s – this despite the fact that only a quarter of the Canadian population was financially able to purchase a car at the time.

By the last years of the decade, agriculture was also recovering from a post-war slump. Prices had recovered and in 1928 Canadian farmers harvested a bumper crop of record proportions (close to 600 million bushels). While on the surface and at the time this seemed like good news, it concealed a troubling development. Canada's agricultural sector was not the only one that was recovering in the middle of the 1920s. Global competition in wheat production from places such as South America and Australia was accelerating, and world purchasers could now choose between a number of non-North American grain producers. Such a dramatically increased supply could not sustain high prices for long.

A similar story was beginning to play out in other economic sectors. Pulp, paper and mining production were beginning to outstrip demand by 1928. Tertiary industries such as railroads also began to feel the effect of declining trade volume. As economic activity slowed and world prices dropped, the short boom of the 1920s seemed to be coming to an end.

So, why did the boom end in Canada?

- Increased tariffs across the world meant a decline in trade.
- Supply of commodities and manufactured products exceeded demand, leading to a decline in world prices for commodities.

Canadian Shield
An exposed area of rock that covers much of central and northern Canada.

branch plants
Factories operating in Canada, but owned by non-Canadian companies.

Class discussion

What are the advantages and disadvantages of a branch plant system for the receiving country?

- Overdependence on staple products.

- Overdependence on the economy of the USA.

- Heavy debt burden carried by governments and individuals.

The USA

In the USA, the 1920s are often characterized as years of prosperity but, as is often the case, there was prosperity for some but not all. In fact, many historians now argue that the political and economic attitudes and actions of the 1920s ultimately led to the Great Depression.

After the Great War most of the world fell into a post-war slump without the driving force of war to stimulate domestic and colonial economies. Even countries that remained neutral experienced the boom, and then the habitual bust. The exception to this was the USA; the economic expansion that began with the war continued into the 1920s. Unlike other countries, the USA emerged as a creditor nation and was receiving loan payments from the belligerent countries. Added to that, the USA was experiencing a technological revolution that fuelled itself: assembly-line technology made goods cheaper and more widely available, stimulating demand, leading to increased employment and a larger consumer society. Finally, government policies freed businesses from taxation and regulation, allowing profits to increase dramatically.

The 1920 census demonstrated some significant demographic shifts, most notably that the majority of Americans were now urban dwellers even though most Americans still perceived of the USA as a country of small farmers. The war had been instrumental in the Great Migration, in which 500 000 African Americans moved from the agricultural south to the industrial north, settling in Midwestern cities such as Chicago, Detroit, Cleveland and Pittsburgh.

In 1921 the Republican Warren Harding took office as US President, advocating non-interventionist economic policies meant to keep the US economy growing. According to Harding and his successors, Calvin Coolidge (1923–29) and Herbert Hoover (1929–33), the goals of the government were prosperity, peace, efficiency and growth. At the centre of these policies was Andrew Mellon, who served as Secretary of the Treasury from 1921 to 1932. His fiscal policies were implemented during three Republican presidencies (with Republican-majority houses of Congress) and had far-reaching consequences. According to Mellon, as income tax rates were increased, money was driven underground or abroad, thus he concluded that lowering rates would increase tax revenues. This led to a series of new laws beginning in 1922 that decreased the tax rates on both individuals and corporations. The top marginal rate was reduced annually in four stages from 73% in 1921 to 25% in 1925, so that by 1927 only the richest 2% of wage earners paid any federal income tax. At the same time the corporate tax rate was reduced from 65% to 50%. Mellon's policies reduced the national debt from $24 billion to $16 billion, and seemed to work exactly as he envisioned them.

Additionally, businessmen were appointed to serve on the very commissions that had been created to regulate business. The Interstate Commerce Commission, Federal Trade Commission and Bureau of

Corporations were three such entities in which the regulatory agencies were headed by the very people they were supposed to limit. There was very little oversight of the banking industry. The Federal Reserve System was created in 1913 to help stabilize the economy by establishing a central banking system for the USA. However, not all banks were members of the system, and remained unregulated. This led to an expansion in the availability of both money and credit. Interest rates declined and the stock market escalated, as investors could borrow against future stock profits in a method known as borrowing on the margin.

The one area in which government policies were fiscally conservative was international trade. In 1922 the Fordney–McCumber Tariff Act raised tariffs above pre-war levels. It also authorized the President to adjust tariffs, largely to assist US farmers. Even in 1928, Hoover ran on a platform of higher tariffs designed to protect farmers from foreign competition.

As in other countries, the war brought important sociopolitical shifts in the USA: in 1920, the Nineteenth Amendment was passed. Although many states had already granted suffrage to women, this gave all adult women in the USA the right to vote, including the right to participate in presidential elections. In 1924 the Indian Citizenship Law finally gave Native Americans suffrage as well.

At the same time, the USA was in a renewed phase of xenophobia. In US legislation, this led to immigration quotas of 150 000 per year that excluded 'undesirable' nationalities, and in society more generally it led to a renewed expansion of the Ku Klux Klan (KKK), especially in the Midwest. While the KKK still targeted African Americans, it was also anti-immigrant and anti-Catholic, showing a wave of intolerance throughout much of the USA.

Most Americans saw an increase in their purchasing power in the 1920s. A technological revolution increased mechanization and it was faster and cheaper to mass-produce goods. In fuel consumption, many companies, especially the ones with large factories, saw the wisdom in increasing the wages of their employees so they could purchase many new goods. Formerly non-existent goods were seen as necessities almost overnight as the working and middle classes were convinced that they needed washing machines, blenders and, of course, automobiles. With the assistance of the emerging advertising sector, demand for these durable goods increased, and the industrial productivity of the USA increased by 70% between 1922 and 1928. In the 1920s unemployment averaged 3.7% and inflation 1%. This, plus the urbanization of the USA, led to a construction boom as new housing, schools, hospitals and roads needed to be built. Existing roads had been built for horses and carts and were not suitable for automobiles. This created new job opportunities for those willing to relocate to the appropriate areas.

However, the 1920s were a period of vast contradictions in the USA and the idea of the Roaring Twenties existed for some, but not all. In that decade there was a great disparity between rich and poor. More than 60% of the population lived below the poverty level while the richest 1% controlled 40% of the wealth. This same top 1% saw its disposable income increase 75% while the average increase for the remaining 99% was 9%. Even more telling, 80% of Americans had no savings.

▲ A poster for a silent movie during the Roaring Twenties

those who Dance must pay the PIPER!

Worst off were the farmers, and rural poverty was commonplace even before the onset of depression. Due to overproduction, farm incomes declined steadily in the 1920s and the price of farmland fell by over 50% between 1920 and 1930. In 1929 the average family income was $750 but for farm families it was only $273. Farmers and rural states began to petition the government for assistance, and, as the US identity was built on the idea of the family farm, the government eventually responded.

Small businesses were squeezed out by the pro-corporate policies. During the 1920s there were 1200 mergers, in which 600 companies ceased to exist. Most tellingly, chain stores replaced local businesses that could not compete with the economies of scale that large department stores were capable of.

One last looming problem was that of stock speculation. The lack of regulatory authority made it very easy to purchase stocks; an investor needed only 10% of the purchase price to complete the transaction. This led to falsely high stock prices that soared in 1929. As long as there was confidence in the market this fuelled a boom, but loss of confidence would prove disastrous.

Despite the uneven distribution of wealth, there was general confidence in the government, and in 1928 yet another Republican, Herbert Hoover, was elected president. He was more concerned with social welfare than his predecessors, and was willing to increase government intervention in the economy, but knew that any changes made would be seen as radical. Nonetheless, he ran on a platform of assisting farmers, and in 1929 the Agricultural Market Act was implemented, creating the Federal Farm Board. This agency had $500 million available for low-interest loans that would go to local cooperatives to build warehouses for surplus crops. He also worked to increase tariffs on agricultural products to protect American farmers, but the end result was disastrous.

The unprecedented extension of credit provided additional stimulus to the market, forcing prices up and bringing more people into the market. But the market was manipulated by large investors, who would combine money to make large purchases of stock, driving prices up further still. Small investors, seeing the price rise, bought the stock, hoping to ride the price up and make money quickly. When the price was high enough, the large investors sold and took profits, leaving only small investors holding stocks.

Expansion of credit also helped fuel consumer demand. Many new household appliances such as washing machines, refrigerators and air conditioners arrived in stores. The extension of consumer loans allowed manufacturers and retailers to move the new products into homes, but also increased personal debt. The banks' confidence in low-collateral loans followed the common thought of the time that the economy had changed permanently. The patterns of panic and recovery that had been the rhythm of the previous century no longer applied in the new economy. At the time, most economists of the era believed that the economic fundamentals had changed but there was also a minority that looked at the market fundamentals and felt that this growth could not be sustained.

There were signs of economic troubles. As a result of overproduction, farm prices dropped in the first half of 1929. In the spring of 1929, car sales, steel production and construction also declined. Still, over the summer months stock prices doubled, purchases funded by increased debt. High confidence in the market remained. On 3 September the stock market reached its all-time high.

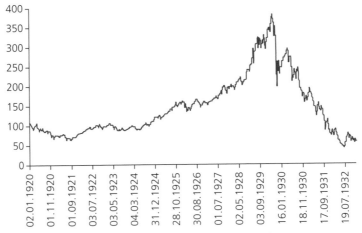

▲ United States stock market performance 1920–1932

The Wall Street Crash and the onset of the Great Depression in the USA

Stocks began to fall and the market took wild swings through the rest of the month. Still, bankers were convinced the market was a secure investment. The fluctuations continued though October. On 24 October, the market crashed and large banks responded by announcing that funds would be made available for purchasing stocks. The market appeared to stabilize. On 29 October, Black Tuesday, the market crashed and the banks' efforts could not stop the sell-off. Confidence in the market fell along with stock prices, increasing the sell-off and forcing prices down further. Small investors lost their life savings in a day. But, contrary to common thought, the Crash alone did not lead directly to the Great Depression.

Several trends occurred in the Twenties that, when combined, most likely caused the Great Depression. While gross domestic product (GDP) increased during the decade, so did income disparity. Uneven distribution of income resulted in wealth becoming concentrated in the upper class: by 1929 almost half of American families lived at subsistence level or below. The lack of wealth in the lower classes reduced purchasing power. Much of the economy depended upon the automobile and construction industries, and the growing aviation, motion picture and consumer-product companies were not large enough to take up the slack when construction fell by 20% in the three years preceding the Crash, along with the decline in automobile sales. Productive capacity continued to grow during those same years, eventually outstripping demand, resulting in lay-offs and lower wages and consequently accelerating the decline in purchasing power of the population. At the same time that American industries were suffering from domestic economic weaknesses, the market for American products

in Europe dropped. A combination of several European countries increasing production while other economies weakened because of turmoil, reparation payments, unpaid war debts and loan obligations caused a decline in demand for goods from across the Atlantic. All of these developments combined with the unstable underlying economic foundation in the USA to produce an economic free fall.

To sum up, the following factors contributed to the Great Depression, although their relative importance is debated:

- **Wall Street Crash**: Two months after the original crash in October, stockholders had lost more than $40 billion. Even though the stock market had begun to regain some of its losses by the end of 1930, it was not enough, and America truly entered what is called the Great Depression. On 3 September 1929 the Dow Jones was at a high of 381 points, and on 29 October 1929 it had fallen to 41 points after a week of panic selling.

- **Farm overproduction**: Due to surpluses and overproduction, farm incomes dropped throughout the 1920s. The price of farmland fell from $69 per acre in 1920 to $31 in 1930. Agriculture was in a depression which began in 1920, lasting until the outbreak of the Second World War in 1939. In 1929 the average annual income for an American family was $750, but for farm families it was only $273. The problems in the agricultural sector had a large impact since 30% of Americans still lived on farms.

- **Reduction in purchasing**: Individuals from all classes began to limit their purchasing. This was a natural process as many of the items that were purchased in the 1920s were durable goods that did not need to be replaced: automobiles, vacuum cleaners and irons, to name a few. This led to a reduction in the number of items sold, meaning that there was less production, which in turn reduced the workforce. As people became unemployed, they were unable to continue payment of their instalment plans and many of these items were repossessed. Ultimately this would result in massive unemployment, which further reduced purchasing.

- **Unequal distribution of wealth**: The wealthiest 1% owned between 33% and 40% of wealth in the USA – the same amount as the bottom 42%. Additionally, there was a disparity between relative urban prosperity and rural poverty.

- **Government policies that limited regulation in key industries**: Bank deposits were uninsured and thus, as banks failed, people lost their savings. Surviving banks, unsure of the economic situation and concerned for their own survival, were unwilling to create new loans. This exacerbated the situation, leading to less and less expenditure. Once the stock market crashed, fearful that banks would fail, millions of Americans began to withdraw their money. By 1933, more than 11 000 of the nation's 25 000 banks had collapsed. Between 1929 and 1933, 10 763 of the 24 970 commercial banks in the USA failed.

ATL Social skills

On this page there are five different causes of the Great Depression in the USA. Arrange these in hierarchical order from the most important to the least important cause in your opinion. Then, with others in your class, discuss your decisions and come to a consensus and present your findings.

Herbert Hoover's responses to the onset of the Depression, 1929–32

Herbert Hoover is often portrayed as the villain in the story of the Great Depression, but this analysis lacks depth of understanding of both his ideological view and the prevailing views of the time. Instead, popular culture focused on lack of government assistance to the vulnerable in society and much emphasis was placed on the creation of Hoovervilles – makeshift communities of people displaced by the economic crisis, and hoboes – itinerant workers who moved from place to place, often on the railroads, trying to find employment. However, Hoover was a far more complex leader than his reputation leads us to believe.

▲ Hooverville on the outskirts of Seattle, Washington, on the tidal flats adjacent to the Skinner and Eddy Shipyards, Port of Seattle, 10 June 1937 – one of many similar shanty settlements built by Americans who lost their homes during the Great Depression

Like many powerful men of his generation, he was a self-made man who believed that Americans were responsible for their own well-being and prosperity, an idea informed by the Protestant work ethic. He was well known as a humanitarian, responsible for the assistance the USA provided to Europe at the end of the Great War. Unlike other politicians of the time, he held only administrative posts, and the presidency was his first elected position. Hoover was profoundly optimistic regarding US economic growth; in a 1928 campaign speech he stated:

> 'We in America today are nearer to the final triumph over poverty than ever before in the history of any land. The poorhouse is vanishing from among us. We have not yet reached the goal but given the chance to go forward with the policies of the last eight years we shall very soon be in sight of the day … when poverty will be banished from this nation.'

A key component of Hoover's campaign promises in 1928 was the continuation of Coolidge's policies of minimal government involvement. When the Crash occurred Hoover, like many politicians and economists of the time, felt that it was the market self-correcting the economic bubble that emerged in the late 1920s. According to this line of thinking, the government's duty was to remain passive so that market forces could

take effect. Even after the Crash, the market was still higher than it had been a year previously, so this did not sound so outlandish.

It must also be kept in mind that Hoover's initial policies were consistent with the economic theories of the time. Governments felt that their mandate was to reduce government debt, tighten the money supply and protect domestic production. This meant that most countries raised taxes and lowered expenditures in the early 1930s. Federal Reserve monetary policy continued to take money out of the economy rather than increase the supply, mistaking deflation for inflation.

Despite his reluctance to involve the federal government in the economy, Hoover was sensitive to the plight of Americans. He summoned governors to the White House and encouraged them to accelerate infrastructure projects to employ workers. He urged corporations to keep employees on the job despite surplus inventories, and advocated that wages remain high to improve purchasing power. Despite how he is portrayed, Hoover was pro-union as he felt this stabilized the economic system.

Farms continued to lose money and rural banks continued to fail. Hoover believed that the American people would help each other, that members of communities would fix their own problems. He did not recognize that devastated communities did not have the resources to save themselves. While he did not feel that the federal government should assist individuals, he did see this as the role of individual states. Unfortunately, the states that were the worst off were unable to provide assistance to their struggling populations. The rural states had been losing income in the 1920s and this trend only worsened.

The situation was exacerbated by the onset of what came to be known as the Dust Bowl. A drought began in 1930 that would continue throughout the decade, affecting most of North America, but the central plains region in particular. Years of farming practices, including removal of native grasses and replacing them with seasonal crops, deep ploughing and failure to rotate crops to replace nutrients, made the area vulnerable to any rainless period. As the drought wore on, crops failed, and farm animals were brought to the slaughterhouse in a desperate attempt to make some money. Many farms in Oklahoma, Texas, Nebraska and neighbouring states were abandoned as the drought continued. The winds that often blow across the plains picked up the fine dust that a century before had been held down by tall grasses. The dust formed into massive clouds that darkened the sky, making breathing difficult and fouling farm machinery. The Dust Bowl was born. Over the next few years approximately 100 million acres (over 40 million hectares) of topsoil blew away. In May 1934 a dust storm darkened skies as far away as Washington, DC. The condition caused more than 2 million farmers, shopkeepers and white-collar workers to leave the plains for California and other destinations. The Dust Bowl was a terrible ecological disaster that added another dimension to the Great Depression.

Legislators reacted to economic distress by trying to protect the home market from foreign goods. In 1929 exports accounted for 7% of US GDP and, perhaps more importantly, trade accounted for nearly

▲ A deserted farm in the Great Plains region of the USA. As a result of land misuse, erosion and years of drought, the ecological disaster known as the Dust Bowl lasted through the 1930s, resulting in farmland becoming useless and hundreds of thousands of people becoming homeless.

one-third of US farm income. In an attempt to save domestic producers, the Congress passed the Smoot-Hawley tariff in June 1930. Smoot-Hawley, signed by Hoover, established a high protective tariff. Unfortunately, rather than saving farmers, it devastated the agricultural sector. As many as 887 existing tariffs were increased and the number of commodities subject to import duties rose to 3218. Although the average rate increase varied by sector, in most cases there was at least a 10% increase. The tariff caused other nations to retaliate with their own high tariffs, reducing exports by more than 50% and causing a deepening of the Depression.

As the farming industry collapsed, rural banks failed in record numbers and hundreds of thousands of customers lost their savings. The Federal Reserve System had little control over local banks, so there was no means of protecting customers or banks. People lost confidence in their banks and withdrew their money, fearing they would lose it. Most banks lacked liquidity and could not provide customers with the money they demanded, so even more banks failed. Between 1900 and 1933, over 9000 banks closed.

To combat this, Hoover provided monetary assistance to troubled banks, but the government lacked funds to prevent all bank failures. At the same time, the President established the Reconstruction Finance Corporation (RFC), an independent agency that granted loans to banks, railroads, states and local governments, and also spent more money on federal public works projects than any president before him. He hoped to create a solid infrastructure on which a stronger and more resilient economy could rise: during his presidency, the San Francisco Bay Bridge, the Los Angeles Aqueduct and the Hoover Dam all began construction. Programmes to provide credit to farmers and buy excess crops began, but these only motivated farmers to grow more crops – consequently prices did not rise and, once again, there was a problem of overproduction. Although Hoover is often seen as being fiscally conservative, federal spending increased by over 50% between 1929 and 1932, the largest increase in federal spending during peacetime. However, to fund these initiatives, the Revenue Act of 1932 increased taxes, doubling income so that the top tax bracket escalated to 63%. Further restricting the flow of money, the Federal Reserve contracted the US supply of money by one-third between August 1929 and March 1933.

Hoover did not give money to individuals as it was not the government's job to interfere with individual initiative. In fact, job loss and poverty was a sign of individual failure. To give money to the unemployed was to support failure: today that concept is called 'moral hazard'. It was resurgent American individualism that would get the country out of the economic downturn.

These policies were detrimental to the already dire situation and the US economy worsened from 1929 to 1933:

- From 1930 to 1931, the federal government's share of GNP soared from 16.4% to 21.5%.

- Production in US factories, mines and utilities fell by over 50%.

- Automobile production, which in 1929 reached an all-time high of over 5 million vehicles, fell to 3 million in 1930 and, by 1932, fell even further to 1 331 860.

- Consumer prices declined nearly 25% between 1929 and 1933.

- Wages on average decreased 15% and real disposable income dropped 28%.

- Stock prices collapsed to one-tenth of their pre-crash value.

- Unemployment in 1929 was 3.2% (1.6 million); by 1933 it hovered at 25% (12.8 million).

Most Americans agreed that Hoover needed to act to ameliorate the effects of the Depression. There was fear that if the government did not act the USA would be vulnerable to extremism like that being experienced in Europe at the time. As a result, Hoover implemented policies that were consistent with his moral and political views. The Agricultural Marketing Act created the Federal Farm Board to limit production and buy surplus, and the Hoover administration distributed $2 billion to states for them to spend as they saw fit, but these measures were not nearly extensive enough to affect the economic situation and the Depression worsened. As mentioned above, the Reconstruction Finance Corporation was created and allocated $500 million to assist the flailing economy, and the government was granted the right to borrow up to $5 billion more. This marked a shift to direct government action in the economy but it came too late and the general public turned against Hoover.

One public relations disaster pertained to veterans of the First World War. For their participation these men had been promised a bonus to be paid out in 1945, but given the economic situation they requested they receive it immediately. When their request was denied the so-called Bonus Army congregated in Washington DC to demonstrate. Two thousand veterans and their families camped in Anacostia Flats outside of the Capitol. When the situation became unruly, Hoover requested assistance from the US army and on 28 July General Douglas MacArthur dispatched troops. As the conflict intensified, MacArthur exceeded his authority and attacked the veterans and their families with tanks, tear gas and 1000 troops. Hoover defended the action by calling the marchers subversives, and his popularity plunged even further.

▲ Bonus Army veterans at their camp at Fort Hunt, Virginia

Unlike other presidents, Hoover was not a politician and did little to work on his image. A career bureaucrat and successful administrator and engineer, Hoover was seen as effective but not warm or empathetic. His view that the Depression could be reversed through traditional means did not work because the entire system had become unsound. His methods exacerbated the situation, rather than allaying the effects, and his unwillingness to provide relief made him seem uncaring.

Not surprisingly, Hoover was defeated by Franklin Delano Roosevelt in November 1932 by almost the same margin by which he had defeated Al Smith in 1928: Hoover received 15 million votes to Roosevelt's 22 million. The era of Republican dominance of politics ended and a new era began, in which one president was successfully elected four times, showing the country's confidence in, and support for, him.

The Hoover Dam

Large recovery projects employing many manual labourers are usually associated with Roosevelt's New Deal programmes, but in 1931 Herbert Hoover initiated a similar project that in some respects became a prototype for those completed by the Works Progress Administration and Civilian Conservation Corps.

The area of southern Nevada was in need of power and there was also a need to irrigate and control flooding of the Colorado River in the region, so the construction of a large dam was seen as an important step to help the expanding southwest. Plans for the dam began in 1928 while Calvin Coolidge was still president, but the project was activated in 1931, in the midst of the Depression. In addition to creating a dam, engineers had to divert the Colorado River to an area that was conducive to water catchment, and it took nearly six years after the dam was completed to fill Lake Mead.

Hoping to find work, tens of thousands of unemployed descended on Las Vegas, Nevada, then a town of 5000.

Dam construction employed over 5000 employees at any given time and 21 000 worked on it during its construction. Many of these remained in Nevada after the project was complete, increasing the size of Las Vegas. At the time, it was the tallest dam in the world at 221 metres and the largest producer of hydroelectric power. Lake Mead has 880 kilometres of shoreline, making it one of the largest man-made lakes in the world.

There was a tradition of naming dams after presidents, and the dam was named for President Hoover, who was responsible for beginning construction on it. This became very controversial as Hoover was increasingly blamed for the Depression, but attempts to rename it Boulder Dam were never successful and thus it remained the Hoover Dam.

Today, the dam's generators provide electricity for Arizona, California and Nevada.

▲ The Hoover Dam

Franklin D Roosevelt's responses to the Great Depression

Roosevelt's Depression-era presidency is usually divided into three periods: 1933–34 is that of the First New Deal; 1935–36 is the Second New Deal; and 1937–41 is the Third New Deal and Roosevelt Recession. In reality, Roosevelt's policies were not much different from those of Hoover's. When comparing the economic plans of the two we see a concurrency of ideas – both Roosevelt and Hoover recognized that there were both economic and psychological reasons for the government to intervene in an unprecedented manner. The difference was that of scope.

Roosevelt ran on a financially conservative platform, not the multitude of New Deal programmes that were to come over the next four years. When running for president, he called for a 25% reduction in federal spending, a balanced federal budget, the removal of government from areas that belonged more appropriately to private enterprise and an end to the 'extravagance' of Hoover's farm programmes.

Many political observers considered Franklin D Roosevelt (FDR) an intellectual lightweight, with little to offer a struggling nation, but Roosevelt took action. The new president, working with a largely cooperative legislature, tried many different programmes over the next two terms, some more successful than others. As important as his governmental programmes was Roosevelt's public persona: his warmth and use of the media, especially radio, contrasted greatly with his aloof predecessor. Roosevelt was sworn in on 4 March 1933.

First New Deal, 1933–34

Roosevelt acted quickly to reform a broken system, create a foundation for recovery, and provide much needed relief for the millions of suffering Americans. His inaugural address planted the seeds for immediate and bold presidential initiatives, claiming, 'This nation asks for action, and action now.' In the first few months he acted to reform the economic system, stimulate industry, and develop a sense of confidence in the American people. Two days after taking office, Roosevelt proclaimed a banking holiday, closing all American banks for four days. He subsequently submitted the first of many pieces of legislation: the Emergency Banking Act. Congress passed the bill in one day. The new law stabilized large banks, gave the Federal Reserve Bank additional powers, began the separation of the dollar from the gold standard, and mandated inspection of banks by the Department of the Treasury before they reopened. A second bill, the Economy Act, quickly followed. The new law attempted to balance the federal budget by cutting salaries and reducing pensions. The two bills reflected Roosevelt's fiscal conservatism and were in no way reflective of British economist John Maynard Keynes' theories on government and economy. In fact, cutting government spending acted as the opposite of a stimulus.

But there was another purpose to the first week's legislation: Roosevelt wanted to build confidence in the US economy after almost four years of decline. Building on a phrase from his inaugural address, 'Let me assert my firm belief that the only thing we have to fear is fear itself', he gave his first national radio address in the evening of 12 March. Over the radio Roosevelt explained to the American people how the new laws would work and what they could expect in the upcoming days. It was the first of 31 'fireside chats' over the 13 years of his presidency. The talks played an important part in building support for the President's initiatives and allowing time for the economy to turn around, and, due to this first talk, many Americans returned to the banks and deposited their savings upon their reopening.

Congress passed the Glass-Steagall Banking Reform Act, which was written to address a main cause of the Depression and to renew confidence in banks. A significant amount of the money that fuelled the stock market speculation of the late 1920s came from banks. The Glass-Steagall Act was to prohibit banks from underwriting securities. In other words, financial institutions had to choose between being a lender or a stock underwriter. The act also created the Federal Deposit Insurance Corporation (FDIC), an organization funded by banks that insured individual bank deposits up to $2500. The FDIC brought confidence to depositors, inviting trust in banks, thus helping to stabilize and rebuild the banking system.

To improve the competitiveness of American goods, the USA moved off the gold standard and forbade the export of gold except under licence from the Treasury. This brought down the value of the dollar, a desirable situation when the economy is struggling as it makes goods cheaper in relation to foreign goods.

To stabilize the farming sector, the Agricultural Adjustment Agency (AAA) was formed in May. The purpose was to raise farm prices so that farmers could survive and put a halt to the abandonment of farms. Even in the midst of the Depression, farmers produced more food than Americans could consume or purchase. The surplus put a downward pressure on prices and, combined with general deflation, resulted in prices well below the cost of producing food. The government identified corn, cotton, milk, pigs, rice, tobacco and wheat as essential to the economy and the plan stipulated that farmers would be paid not to grow. This would be subsidized by a tax on processed-food companies that was extended to consumers via price increases. However, there was still too much of a surplus in certain sectors. The USA produced over twice the world demand for cotton, so these crops were plowed under. In addition, the AAA ordered the slaughter of over six million pigs beginning in July 1933. Some of the pork was distributed to the needy, but the destruction of so much food at a time when millions of people were going hungry did not make sense to many Americans.

Generally the AAA was seen as preserving the viability of the farming sector and the government priority was the stabilization of the agricultural sector, rather than assistance to individual farms and farmers. The result was that the AAA made loans available to farmers but was predisposed to assist large scale farming operations. Some credit was granted to small farmers, but it was limited, and the tenant farmers in the rural south were completely left out of the assistance programmes. These farmers were the worst off of all farmers and often found themselves jobless when the farms they normally worked on were left fallow to conform to government programmes of non-growth.

On balance, the AAA achieved its objective of stabilization of the rural economy of the US. In 1935 farm income had risen to $6.9 billion from a low of $4.5 billion in 1932.

To assist industry, the National Industrial Recovery Act (NIRA) was passed by Congress in June 1933 to prompt economic recovery through promoting confidence among workers, industry and investors. The National Recovery Administration (NRA), directed by General Hugh Johnson, worked to end wage deflation through a minimum wage, establish a maximum limit to weekly hours to promote new hiring, end child labour, and restore competition to the marketplace through business codes that included the elimination of price fixing. Perhaps the most famous symbol of the New Deal was the NRA 'Blue Eagle', a sticker that cooperating businesses placed in their front window. Many companies agreed to abide by the NRA rules, but not all who professed compliance actually followed the codes. During the NIRA's tenure (before it was declared unconstitutional), industrial production rose by 22%. This act also saw the return of government oversight of industry. It established codes in all aspects of the economy to regulate and provide fair practices. Over 100 industries were involved in the creation of 557 different codes, affecting 22 million workers, and the NIRA even included a consumer advisory board so that those purchasing goods would have a voice and be protected. However, this was the beginning of conflict over the role of government in American public life. Some felt that the New Deal policies overstretched the boundaries of government, and lawsuits were filed against the new agency.

Another aspect the First New Deal concentrated on was relief. To a large extent, the Federal Emergency Relief Agency (FERA) that Roosevelt created was simply an expansion of the Emergency Relief Agency (ERA) formed by Hoover a year before. The purpose of ERA was to create new jobs through loans to states, but FERA did much more. Under the leadership of Harry Hopkins, who would become an important part of the Roosevelt administration's efforts to end the Great Depression and to fight the Second World War, FERA granted funds to state and local governments. In the two years of its existence, FERA created jobs for more than 20 million workers. Part of FERA was the creation of a sub-agency, the Civil Works Administration (CWA), which accelerated job creation in late 1933 and early 1934. Jobs included building roads, repairing schools and installing sewers. By mid-January 1934, more than 4 million people worked in CWA jobs. In addition to jobs through state and local governments, FERA provided funds for adult education, began projects that employed artists and writers, and placed women in jobs along with men. FERA ended when declared unconstitutional by the Supreme Court in 1935.

Other job creation programmes included the Public Works Administration (PWA) headed by Harold Ickes. A sum of $3.3 billion was made available for public works to employ people. The PWA employed 700 000 people and built 13 000 schools, 50 000 miles (over 80 000 kilometres) of roads, and numerous parks and public spaces throughout the USA. A very popular programme was the Civilian Conservation Corps (CCC) that enlisted men aged 17–24. They were paid $30 per month, $25 of which was sent home, and were provided with room and board. The CCC was involved in massive soil conservation, reforestation and forest management projects. Through the CCC, 1.3 billion trees were planted. It was initially funded to 1935 but proved so successful that it was extended until the outbreak of war.

▲ Civilian Conservation Corps logging camp, 1934

To provide relief and employment, the Tennessee Valley Authority (TVA) was created in 1934 to provide power and flood control. This project created a government-owned network of dams and hydroelectric plants to control flooding and produce electric power in part of the country where very few people had access to electricity. The idea of public ownership of utilities was debated and the creation of the TVA concerned a number of people who felt that the government was yet again overstepping its boundaries. These policies would result in a series of court cases to determine the extent of federal government involvement in the economy and lead to a showdown between FDR and the Supreme Court.

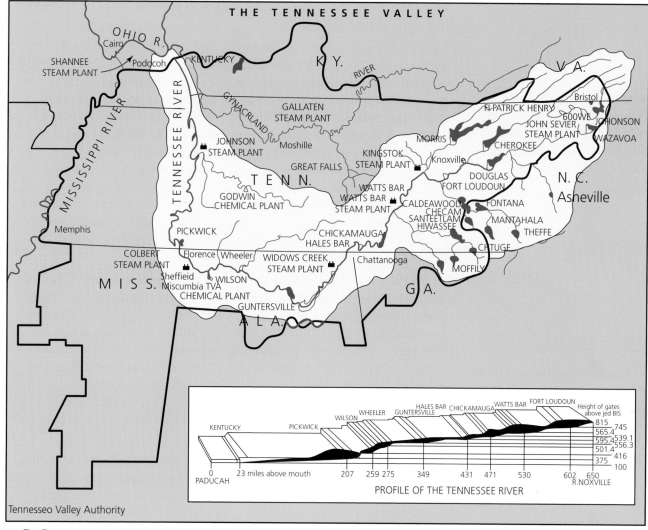

THE TENNESSEE VALLEY

PROFILE OF THE TENNESSEE RIVER

Tennesseo Valley Authority

▲ The Tennessee Valley

Roosevelt had several clear goals that were similar to those of Herbert Hoover. He wanted to stabilize the economic system, prevent extremism and rebellion, and reorganize the economy so that the USA could recover. However, his approach was very different and he was a savvy politician. For example, when members of the Bonus Army once again appeared at the White House they were given coffee, greeted by the President and met with one of his aides, who listened sympathetically but promised nothing. The Bonus Army response was to leave Washington DC peacefully; although they did not get their bonuses, they felt vindicated by Roosevelt's actions.

Second New Deal, 1935–36

In November 1934, US Congressional elections were held and returned an even more radical, Democrat-dominated House and Senate. As a result, a second wave of New Deal legislation passed that was even more ambitious, costly and interventionist than the programmes implemented in 1933 and 1934, as Roosevelt had to respond to demand for change. Programmes were proposed that would improve the use of natural resources; provide security against old age, unemployment and illness; and create a national welfare programme to replace state relief efforts.

Signalling this shift was the Emergency Relief Appropriation Act of 1935, which allocated $5 billion (equivalent to over $83 billion in 2013 dollars) for public works projects that would provide employment. A considerable amount of this money went to the **Works Progress Administration (WPA)**,which became one of the country's major employers. A total of 8 million people worked for WPA in various capacities between 1935 and 1943, at wages that averaged $52 per month. The idea was to pay workers less than the going rate in industry to give an incentive to move into the private sector, but employees would earn more than if they were simply on government assistance so there was also an incentive to work. The WPA tried to hire one family member per household to keep them out of poverty, and showed a preference for male heads of household.

The WPA was responsible for projects throughout the country; the agency built airport landing fields, schools, playgrounds, roads, bridges, courthouses, hospitals, post offices, parks, swimming pools, community centres and city halls, many of which are still in use today, which is a testament to the work ethic and construction methods used by the agency. WPA employees were also used in the **Rural Electrification Administration (REA)**. Private industry did not find rural electrification profitable, so the REA created 773 power grid systems and ran 348 000 miles (560 000 kilometres) of transmission lines in the Midwest and southwest of the USA.

A sub-component of the WPA was Federal Project Number One, which employed artists, musicians, playwrights and photographers. This sought to preserve historical records through oral history projects and film documentation but it also provided federal funding to the arts so they would be accessible to all Americans.

During its existence, the WPA cost the government $13.4 billion; it was dissolved in 1943 once US involvement in the war made it unnecessary. In many cases, the WPA projects emanated from public works projects that began under Hoover's RFC, demonstrating continuity with the Hoover administration.

Another agency created in the Second New Deal was the **National Youth Administration (NYA)**, which encouraged education through providing part-time work to young people aged 16–25 who stayed in school. It targeted African Americans, who were harder hit than the majority of the population, and – unlike the CCC – girls were employed. NYA employees lived at home and worked on local projects.

In an attempt to balance the power of big business over labour, Congress passed the Wagner–Connery National Labor Relations Act in July 1935. Wagner-Connery guaranteed workers the right to collective bargaining through unions of their own choice; it stipulated that workers could choose unions through secret ballot; and it established a three-man National Labor Relations Board to provide government oversight. This was the first law enacted in the USA that gave unions legal rights and committed the government to investigate the treatment of labour.

Works Progress Administration (WPA)
Formed in April 1935, the WPA was the largest of all New Deal agencies. It employed millions of previously unemployed people in public work projects across the US.

Rural Electrification Administration (REA)
A New Deal Agency created in May 1935. Its aim was to provide electricity to rural and remote areas.

National Youth Administration (NYA)
A WPA agency which focused on providing work and education opportunities for 16–25 year olds.

To provide relief to those who were not employable, Congress also passed the **Social Security Act (SSA)** in August 1935. This stated that direct government assistance was part of a worker's right. Old-age pensions were created, funded by both the employer and the employee, through payroll taxes, and unemployment compensation would be provided, financed through unemployment contributions of both worker and employer. This marked a break with the American tradition of self-financed retirement and reliance on family. The SSA was not a flat rate provided to all; it was based on the prior contributions of workers. However, it was not sufficient to meet the needs of the poor. For one thing, benefits would not be distributed until 1940 and the maximum unemployment benefits were $18 per week for 16 weeks. Additionally, farm workers and domestic servants were excluded from this legislation because southern lawmakers insisted on these exclusions to pass the law. Unfortunately, these groups were some of the hardest hit by the Depression and the exclusions affected a large number of African Americans.

By the 1936 elections, there had been dramatic changes as a result of Second New Deal legislation. Relief and recovery continued through the WPA and SSA; labour unions were given a voice through Wagner–Connery; and the Rural Electrification Act helped modernize rural areas. Not surprisingly, Roosevelt won by a landslide; he received 60.8% of the vote and won all states except Maine and Vermont. He felt this gave him a clear mandate to continue his policies, and a general sense that the government actually cared about the public was evident.

▲ This young girl carrying her brother highlights the poverty experienced by African Americans, especially in the south, during the Great Depression

Acronym	Agency name	Date
AAA	Agricultural Adjustment Administration	1933
CCC	Civilian Conservation Corps	1933
CWA	Civil Works Administration	1933
FDIC	Federal Deposit Insurance Corporation	1933
FERA	Federal Emergency Relief Agency	1933
FHA	Federal Housing Authority	1934
NRA	National Recovery Administration	1933
NYA	National Youth Administration	1935
PWA	Public Works Administration	1933
REA	Rural Electrification Administration	1935
SEC	Security and Exchange Commission	1934
SSA	Social Security Administration	1935
TVA	Tennessee Valley Authority	1933
WPA	Works Progress Administration	1935

Legal challenges to the New Deal

At the same time, the judicial sector challenged the constitutionality of New Deal programmes, targeting the NRA and AAA specifically. While the Supreme Court supported most New Deal legislation, it contended that some of it was unconstitutional. Prior to 1935, 60 laws were found unconstitutional by the US Supreme Court; in 1935 and 1936 alone, 11 laws were found unconstitutional.

The most damaging of these rulings was the unanimous decision that the NRA was unconstitutional in Schechter Poultry Corp. versus United States, known colloquially as the 'sick chicken' case. The Schechter brothers were kosher butchers, who were accused of selling bad poultry in violation of NIRA codes, and the company was forced to shut down. The case was a test of industry autonomy, and the plaintiffs argued that the issue was one of jurisdiction: since Schechter Poultry only operated in New York it should be subject to state, not federal, law and thus it was not subject to the Interstate Commerce Commission. The Court found in favour of the Schechters and ruled that the NIRA exceeded the limits of its authority. With this ruling, the NIRA was not reauthorized by Congress.

Roosevelt responded to these decisions aggressively. Since he had been re-elected with such a strong mandate, he felt that his decisions were more indicative of American public opinion than Supreme Court decisions. In his 9 March 1937 fireside chat, he argued that the US Constitution did not give the Court the right to determine constitutionality, but that it had taken this position as its right when initially conceived in 1803, and he accused the Court of overstepping its role: 'The Court has been acting not as a judicial body, but as a policymaking body.' He said that he needed 'to infuse new blood into all our courts' and provide assistance for overworked judges.

In this way he presented the Judiciary Procedures Reform Bill to the public. This bill proposed the mandatory retirement of justices at the age of 70 and an expansion of the Supreme Court by up to six additional justices. Despite Roosevelt's personal popularity, the US public opposed the measure and although both houses of Congress had strong Democrat majorities, the legislators were unwilling to grant such powers to the President. For many, this represented the road towards authoritarianism and while most congressmen were worried about the future of New Deal policies, the political ramifications of **court packing** were so potentially explosive that the Democrats chose the loss of economic momentum in favour of preservation of the power of the judiciary and sent the bill back to committee in July 1937 in a 70 to 20 vote.

On the other hand, Roosevelt was seen as representing the will of the people, so the Supreme Court became more amenable to New Deal legislation after the defeat of the Reform Bill. Fewer court cases challenging New Deal programmes came before the Supreme Court and the justices were more likely to uphold popular programmes. Political equilibrium in the USA was recovered.

Earlier in 1936, the AAA was also found unconstitutional. Once again, the Supreme Court ruled that compensation for farmers – and raising revenue for that compensation – belonged in the domain of the states, not the federal government. This halted a number of programmes but the success of the AAA was questionable. In many areas, powerful

court packing
A term used to refer to Roosevelt's 1937 plan to reorganize the US Supreme Court. According to this proposal, the president could appoint a new Supreme Court Justice every time one of the incumbents reached the age of 70. Critics of the plan argued that Roosevelt was using this to force through legislation ruled unconstitutional by the sitting justices and the proposal failed.

landowners made the decisions regarding production and these decisions benefited the wealthy. Farm income had yet to reach pre-First World War levels and so agriculture remained depressed.

Addressing the Dust Bowl

According to government statistics, 35 million acres (14 million hectares) of farmland was destroyed, 125 million acres (51 million hectares) exhausted, and an extraordinary 350 million tons of soil 'transplanted' by the drought and heavy winds. During the Depression, millions were left to starve; the plains states had no industry and so there were no alternatives to farming. Out of a population of 2.4 million, 440 000 people left Oklahoma, many of them heading to California in the hopes of finding employment as farmers there. Unemployment in the plains was over 30%, with a high of 39% in Arkansas.

As 200 000 migrant labourers arrived in California, the state was not certain how it could cope with the influx of workers. One reaction was to expel Mexican migrant workers who had been working in California for decades. This was the beginning of a wave of xenophobia that struck the American southwest, sometimes resulting in the expulsion of US citizens mistaken for Mexican nationals.

A radical attempt to allay the effects of the Depression on destitute farmers came with the Resettlement Administration (RA) of 1935. The Administration was headed by Rexford Tugwell, a university professor from Columbia University. The RA provided short-term assistance for 400 000 families in 1936 when a new drought hit, and established 95 relief camps with temporary housing and sanitary conditions for these families. But there were more ambitious programmes, as the RA planned to create new communities where 500 000 families could relocate on model farms. Casa Grande, Arizona; Greenbelt, Maryland; Greenville, Ohio and Greendale, Wisconsin were four such planned cooperatives called **greenbelt communities**. These projects proved to be too controversial – they were seen as too much like Stalin's collective farms – and even the cautiously supportive in Congress feared they were too socialist. The greenbelt communities also proved more expensive than envisioned as only 4441 families resettled. Thus, in 1937, the RA was integrated into the Farm Security Administration, which existed until 1946.

Congress established the Soil Conservation Service, which promoted farming practices intended to protect existing farmland and prevent the spread of drought. Further assistance was provided by the Shelterbelt Programme, which planted over 1 billion new trees in the Great Plains to keep soil stable. Farmers set up their own districts and provided communal regulation based on the needs of local areas that were subject to five-year reviews. Although conservation measures yielded a 65% decrease in the amount of soil displacement, the drought continued until 1939. Finally, in the autumn of that year, the rains came and it was only then that the Dust Bowl ended.

Third New Deal, 1937–41, and the Roosevelt Recession

There was one final wave of legislation between 1937 and 1939 but in reality Congress lost much of its momentum after the court battles of 1937. The Wagner-Steagall National Housing Act led to the building of public

> **greenbelt communities**
> These new towns were built by the RA. They were built with the aim of moving people away from exhausted farmland, to new model communities which combined the amenities of urban life with the open, green spaces of the countryside.

housing to eliminate urban slums. In an attempt at balance, only 10% of all funding could be used in any one state. Unfortunately, this meant that states with more urban blight had less money per capita and thus it was ineffective in many areas.

The Fair Labor Standards Act (1938) gave further rights to workers. It established a minimum wage set at 25 cents per hour and a maximum working week of 44 hours for all industries engaged in interstate commerce. While the wages of 300 000 workers increased and 1.2 million workers' hours declined, certain key groups were left out. There were exemptions for domestic servants and farm labourers, which prevented many African Americans and women from benefiting.

By 1937 the economy had recovered to levels not seen since 1930, and had risen considerably since bottoming out in 1933. GDP was up 80% and private investment went from a low of $1 billion in 1932 to $12 billion in 1937. Then, beginning in May, the growth of the economy reversed and a recession began. Unemployment rose back up to 19% from a low of 14%, as close to 3 million jobs were lost. Manufacturing fell to 1934 levels and private investment fell by 40%. GDP declined by slightly over 6% during the recession that lasted until June 1938. The reversal was a stunning setback to the American people and to the administration.

The causes of the recession are still debated. The monetarist school blames the Federal Reserve Bank for taking actions to tighten the money supply. The Federal Reserve always feared inflation and a growing economy seemed to threaten significant price rises. Anticipating a severe inflationary cycle, the Federal Reserve clamped down; this caused investment to drop and people to stop spending money, thus slowing the economy. The Keynesian school also blames the Central Bank, but blames the Roosevelt administration as well for abruptly attempting to balance the budget. FDR was concerned about increasing federal debt, just as he was when he first became president. Furthermore, the New Deal relief and recovery programmes were intended to be temporary measures to help the poor and to stimulate the economy. As the economy had grown steadily for four years, Roosevelt and Congress increased taxes and decreased spending, removing the stimulus. To those who believed in the principle of *laissez faire* markets and were sympathetic to business, the reform acts that put regulations on business were an annoyance. These people believed that the principle of *laissez faire* should be taken further, even though the Supreme Court had limited government intervention in business.

In response to the downturn, Roosevelt increased government spending to 1936 levels. The recession eased in July 1938 and the economy grew in the second half of the year. By the end of the year, GDP surpassed that of the year preceding the recession. The economy continued to grow in 1939 and 1940, when GDP reached pre-Great Depression levels. Unemployment did not dip below 14%. In 1941 federal spending, especially defence spending, increased greatly in response to the Lend Lease Act. That same year the US economy posted the largest GDP in its history, as output rose by more than 20%.

Then on 7 December 1941 the USA entered into the Second World War, and FDR switched from 'Mr New Deal' to 'Mr Win the War'.

ATL Thinking skills

▲ A political cartoon on Roosevelt's court packing, published 14 February 1937

What is the message intended by this cartoon?

To what extent do you agree with the perspective in this cartoon?

Historical perspectives on the New Deal policies

There are a number of ways to look at the Roosevelt response to the downturn. Looking at the numbers, the economy recovered over the decade and returned to pre-Depression levels; however, unemployment did not return to 1929 levels until war production absorbed millions of workers. The reform aspects, farm and industrial policy, as well as banking and stock market regulations, encountered significant opposition from interest groups, many members of Congress and the Supreme Court. The administration's policies were developed to prevent a reoccurrence of the events that led to the Great Depression. Programmes that lasted well beyond the Depression include Social Security and the **SEC**. While there was some success in reform, most efforts were watered down, leaving the agricultural, industrial and financial sectors with less freedom than in the 1920s, but more freedom than many members of the administration intended. The many relief programmes provided work in fields ranging from theatre to construction to conservation. Millions were employed, housed and fed. Parks, schools, hospitals and a variety of works of art were created, while environmental projects started many devastated areas on the path to renewal. But benefits to minorities were uneven at best, and some programmes caused more harm than good. Historians sometimes criticize Roosevelt for not providing economic stimulus and for removing it before recovery was complete, and for failing to enact major reforms. Other historians counter that his pragmatic, rather than ideological, approach was focused less on changing America and more on restoring America to prosperity. Some historians have even called that approach conservative. The effectiveness and legacy of the New Deal are still discussed and debated today.

During the 1920s, there were, on average, about 553 000 paid civilian employees of the federal government. By 1939 there were 953,891 paid civilian employees, and in 1940 there were 1,042,420.

In 1928 and 1929, federal receipts on the administrative budget averaged 3.8% of GNP, while expenditures averaged 3.04% of GNP. In 1939, federal receipts were 5.5% of GNP, while federal expenditures

SEC

The Securities and Exchange Commission is responsible for enforcing federal laws concerning any tradable financial asset. It was founded in 1934 largely to regulate the Stock Market.

had tripled to 9.77% of GNP. (The administrative budget excludes any amounts received for or spent from trust funds and any amounts borrowed or used to pay down the debt.)

Although the expansion of the government was not nearly as large as it would be during the Second World War, this expansion was unprecedented, and both federalists and conservatives were alarmed by the growth, fearing that it would lead to centralization of government authority at the expense of states' rights, one of the most divisive themes in US history.

Another effect of New Deal policies was that the Keynesian view that government could and should stabilize demand to prevent future depressions became the dominant view in the economics profession for at least the next 40 years. Traditional liberal economic policies that saw the economy as self-correcting were cast aside for this new view, and this new approach was viewed with fear and suspicion. The American economist Milton Friedman felt that this put the USA on the wrong economic course and that the government became too involved in the economy.

On the other side, the idea emerged that the people were the responsibility of the government. William Leuchtenburg argues that the New Deal was a compassionate response to economic crisis. Roosevelt might have advocated fiscally conservative policies but the situation at the time demanded more radical policies than he anticipated. The unintended consequence was an expansion of government.

The New Left political movement of intellectuals in the 1960s and 1970s saw the Great Depression as a missed opportunity for radical change. From its perspective, the New Deal was not a significant change from previous policies and the capitalist system continued to prevail, only with government assistance.

Howard Zinn argued that only radical socialists ever noted that there was a genuine threat to the political and economic systems that existed. The poor, receiving little assistance from Hoover, began to organize themselves and protect each other against the middle and upper classes that exploited them. In urban neighbourhoods, people banded together to prevent evictions. Throughout the country, groups created barter systems that circumvented capitalism. In Seattle, fisherman, farmers and lumberjacks created exchanges to provide food and fuel without monetary exchange. In Western Pennsylvania and West Virginia, coalminers illegally mined coal and sold it at below-market prices. When caught, no juries would convict them. There were 330 self-help organizations with approximately 300 000 members in 37 states by the end of 1932; these with the onset of Roosevelt's programes most of these collapsed in 1933. Conventional historians argue that there was too much economic distress for small organizations to handle but Zinn asks us to consider whether they might have been undermined by New Deal policies that favoured big businesses.

In 1934, amid the first New Deal, 1 500 000 workers went on strike in the USA. In California, these strikes paralysed the state (and San Francisco especially) because the **Teamsters** participated. At the same

Teamsters
A Labour union in the US and Canada formed in 1903 that encompassed all kinds of industries. In the old days a teamster was a person who drove a team of horses. In the 20th century this evolved to include truck drivers.

147

time 325 000 textile workers in the south went on strike, and industrial action soon spread to New England – by September 421 000 textile workers were on strike in the USA. According to leftist historians, the American Federation of Labor set up the Committee for Industrial Organization to address the needs of strikers and then absorbed them and neutralized them so that they would not challenge the traditional economic dominance of the upper classes.

Contemporary critics of the New Deal

Critics of the New Deal came from all parts of the political spectrum. The political left was represented by men as diverse as Upton Sinclair, Huey Long and Floyd Olsen. Sinclair sought to end poverty in California and supported state-run cooperatives along the lines of the Seattle exchange. He won the Democratic nomination for governor but was defeated by Republicans who had the support and financial resources of big business, especially Hollywood, and its accompanying propaganda machine. Long's programme was called 'Share Our Wealth' and included the redistribution of wealth – for example, he felt that there should be a cap of $50 million in personal income, with the rest to be distributed among the poor. He was very popular in his native Louisiana where he was responsible for creating massive public works projects that included the development of 3000 miles (4000 kilometres) of highway and the erection of public buildings for schools and colleges. He also advocated old-age pensions and the development of adult literacy programes. The Thunder on the Left was Minnesota Governor Olsen's programme. He felt that the state should take control of idle factories and employ people, and he advocated the nationalization of utilities and the postponement of farm foreclosures. These men were **populists**, who represented their regions well and were very popular, but found little support beyond their states.

populist
Someone who appeals to the interests and world view of the general public.

Another New Deal critic was Father Charles Coughlin, a Roman Catholic priest in Michigan with a radio programme. He initially supported Roosevelt but in 1934 became a strong critic of what he saw as Roosevelt's pro-banker policies and created the National Union for Social Justice to advance his ideas. His weekly radio show had nearly 30 million listeners each week, so there was broad potential support for his ideas. As time went on, his views became increasingly anti-Semitic and pro-Fascist, so with the onset of war in Europe in 1939 Roosevelt cancelled his broadcasts.

Additionally, there were large groups that opposed Roosevelt's policies for a number of reasons. Industrialists felt that his policies were too pro-labour and limited their ability to recover fully from the Depression. Farm labourers and sharecroppers in the south opposed him because his policies excluded them, and free marketeers opposed such extensive government intervention. Communists and socialists felt that he did little to help the working poor and reserved his assistance for the wealthy and privileged in society.

Source skills

The Great Depression

In the modern era, historians usually have access to the same historical records, but their use of them – and the evidence that they find most important – affects their interpretation of the reasons for events such as the Great Depression.

Below are four excerpts regarding the Great Depression in the USA.

The first two look at the reasons for the Great Depression: *[handwritten: & Blames poor government action]*

What then caused the Depression? … the deepest problem was the intervention, the lack of faith in the marketplace. Government management in the late 1920s and 1930s hurt the economy. Both Hoover and Roosevelt misstepped in a number of ways. Hoover ordered wages up when they wanted to go down. He allowed a disastrous tariff, Smoot-Hawley, to become law when he should have had the sense to block it. He raised taxes when neither citizens individually nor the economy as a whole could afford the change. …

Roosevelt's errors had a different quality but were equally devastating. He created regulatory aid, and relief agencies based on the premise that recovery could be achieved only through a large, military-style effort.

Shlaes, Amity. 2008. *The Forgotten Man: A New Approach to the Great Depression*. Harper Perennial. New York, USA. Pp. 7–8

Monetarist doctrine held that the New Deal, which *[handwritten: → Could've been done better]* *created a large number of government jobs and social welfare programmes was costly and a useless sham. … [However, t]here is no reason why a properly functioning Federal Reserve cannot function a* *[handwritten: → Had more faith in the Federal reserve]* *complement to a properly functioning social state and a well-designed progressive tax policy. … the fact that the Fed followed an unduly restrictive monetary policy in the early 1930s says nothing about the virtues and limitations of other institutions.*

Piketty, Thomas. 2013. *Capital in the 21st Century*. Belknap/Harvard University Press. Boston, USA. P. 549

[handwritten top: saving the democracy; balance of power]

It was to the immediate interests of the Democratic Congress and Senate to pack the court and ensure that all New Deal legislation survived. But … congressmen and senators understood that if the President could undermine the independence of the judiciary, then this would undermine the balance of power in the system that protected them from the President and ensured the continuity of pluralistic political institutions.

Acemoglu, Daron and Robinson, James A. 2012. *Why Nations Fail*. Crown Business Publishing. New York, USA. Pp. 328–29

When the New Deal was over, capitalism remained intact. The rich still controlled the nation's wealth, as *[handwritten: → not enough change]* *well as its laws, courts, police, newspapers, churches, colleges. Enough help had been given to enough people to make Roosevelt a hero to millions, but the same system that had brought depression and crisis – the system of waste, of inequality, of concern for profit over human need – remained.*

Zinn, Howard. 2003 (first published 1980). *A People's History of the United States*. Perennial Classics. New York, USA. Pp. 403–04

Questions

1. Compare and contrast the views of Amity Shlaes and Thomas Piketty on the reasons for the development of the Great Depression in the USA.

2. Compare and contrast the views of Acemoglu and Zinn on the effect of elected politicians on the outcome of the Great Depression.

Conceptual understanding

Key questions

→ To what extent did Prime Minister King maintain the policies of Prime Minister Bennett when he took office in 1935?

→ To what extent did the Great Depression encourage the development of new political ideas in Canada?

→ How did Canadian citizens attempt to cope with the hardships of the Great Depression?

Key concepts

→ Continuity

→ Change

The Crash of 1929

The economic developments that brought about the Great Depression were well underway before 1929. There were structural problems in the economic boom that made it inherently unstable, both in Canada and in the USA. The problem was compounded by the world's reliance on the health of the US economy. US capital permeated nearly all aspects of the Canadian economy, making Canada vulnerable to instability in the USA. This growing instability was dramatically accelerated by the stock market crash of October 1929. Although the Toronto Stock Exchange did not suffer a calamity of the scale that befell its New York counterpart, the vast amount of US capital invested in the Canadian economy meant that the effects of the New York crash were soon felt north of the 49th Parallel, just as they were around the world.

The economic impact of the Great Depression

The Great Depression of the 1930s was not the first economic slump to hit Canada. In 1873 Canada had been hurt by the global economic stagnation. Just prior to and immediately after the First World War, Canada experienced short, sharp economic downturns. The factors that would set the Great Depression apart from the other slumps were its severity, scope and length. The fact that it was coupled with one of the most severe droughts in Canadian history only served to spread the misery and make recovery more difficult. In the years between 1929 and 1933:

- imports fell by 25%

- exports fell by 55%

- wheat prices fell by 75%

- unemployment reached 27%
- 20% of Canadians were on some form of relief.

The Depression manifested itself in different ways across the country. In rural Canada, collapsing prices were not matched by falling production costs. Agricultural and fishing products flowing out of the Maritimes faced slashed commodity prices. Agricultural and manufacturing products from central Canada were met by restricted trade policies. The economic disaster was exacerbated by misguided economic policies around the world. Many countries, such as the USA and Canada, had already started building ever-higher tariff walls before 1929. This movement spread around the globe after the stock market crash. Italy, Germany and France all increased tariffs in an effort to protect their own industries, blocking potential markets for Canadian agricultural and manufacturing products.

> **Class discussion**
>
> How did Canadian tariff policy compare to other countries. What accounts for any differences?

The Prairie Provinces were hit doubly hard in the 1930s as the economic disaster of the Depression was compounded by ecological disaster, as in the USA. The devastating drought that gripped the prairies from 1930 to 1937 turned the fertile land into a dust bowl. Scores of farms were simply abandoned, the families that owned them leaving to become part of the growing legions of unemployed in the cities. Those who did remain faced the same depressed commodity prices as all farmers. In Saskatchewan, the total provincial income fell by close to 90% and two-thirds of the population was on social welfare.

The picture painted by the Depression in urban Canada was more complex. Factory workers were laid off in droves and those who kept their jobs saw their wages slashed in the absence of any minimum wage legislation to protect them. Wage rates varied across the country, but the growing labour pool meant that they were all headed in one direction – down. The middle class and those in the professions who managed to maintain a stable source of income during the Depression saw their living standards improve on the back of a falling cost of living. This was, however, not the case for the majority of Canadians.

> **Class discussion**
>
> What forms of relief were available to Canadians during the Great Depression? What does the form of this relief tell us about Canadian's attitude toward poverty and its causes?

Social impacts of the Great Depression

While on the surface the Depression was an economic crisis, the reality is that it struck deep into every aspect of life in 1930s Canada. That it was coupled with the worst drought in memory meant that the family farm, often a source of relief during industrial downturns, suffered along with the rest of the economy. In a nation that was built largely on the promise of land ownership, losing family farms to foreclosure called into question the identity and character of western Canada. Newfoundland, although not a part of the Canadian Dominion until 1949 and an independent British Dominion at the outset of the Depression, suffered so acutely from the decline of fishery, an unemployment rate that reached 50%, and political scandals that it dissolved its legislature and reverted to colonial status later in the decade.

Accustomed to self-reliance, workers took long-term unemployment badly as it struck at their sense of self-worth. Marriages were postponed and birth rates declined. Once-prosperous prairie towns ceased to exist. Migration significantly changed the demographics of the country, as

Class discussion

How did Canada's immigration policy compare to that of other countries in the region?

What are some arguments in favour of decreasing immigration during hard economic times? What are some arguments in favour of increasing immigration during hard economic times?

▲ RB Bennett won the 1930 election by promising vast public works programes and employment

people moved in search of employment or precipitation. Immigration was sharply curtailed and people lashed out at new Canadians in eruptions of xenophobia. Such divisions bit into the labour movement, pitting English-speaking workers against recent arrivals from eastern and northern Europe in the Maritimes and other parts of the country.

Government responses to the Great Depression

The Depression set upon Canada during Mackenzie King's second term in office. King, not unlike his counterpart in the White House, was initially at a loss as to what to do about the stagnating economy. Other economic slumps had occurred in King's lifetime, but they had proven temporary. King therefore approached the early stages of the Depression as he approached politics in general – cautiously. When he was pressed for government action to alleviate the growing misery, he hid behind the British North America Act. King claimed that the type of action required was constitutionally the responsibility of the provinces. But he then refused to increase subsidies to provincial governments – all but two of which were Conservative. He believed that this fiscally vigilant approach was what prudent Canadians expected of him, and he took this faith to the polls in 1930. King miscalculated. The Conservatives, under the leadership of RB Bennett, won a majority government on promises of action and relief.

Bennett's responses

Once in office, Bennett succumbed to conventional wisdom and his campaign promises. He increased tariffs by 50% and allocated $20 million for relief programmes. All at once he pushed prices higher with the tariffs and gave people money to cope with the higher prices – in broad terms a zero net gain.

The relief 'system' that developed in the early 1930s consisted of a patchwork of municipal, provincial, federal and private efforts. Single unemployed men, for instance, were directed to work camps operated by the Department of National Defense and located in the wilderness, far from urban centres. While they toiled in these camps, the men earned 20 cents a day and the nickname the Royal Twenty Centers.

The system of relief, such as it was, consisted of federal and provincial funds making their way into municipal coffers from where they would be redistributed to those in the most need. Initially, most were 'work for relief' schemes of public works, but this eventually gave way to direct relief. Nevertheless, federal and provincial funds were rarely enough to sustain the growing numbers of people in need. The economic downturn shrank the tax base in cities across the country at the same time that the cities' costs were ballooning. Cities such as Montreal tried to meet the need by raising taxes, but to no avail. Montreal slid into bankruptcy in 1940. As the Depression deepened, it became evident that its economic costs were to be borne disproportionately by local governments.

At the federal level, Prime Minister Bennett established a number of other measures to fight if not the causes then the symptoms of the Depression:

- **The Canadian Wheat Board**: a marketing board designed to rationalize the marketing of grain on the world market and provide a measure of shelter for prairie farmers.

- **The Farmer's Creditors Arrangement Act**: a law to help debt-ridden farmers restructure their loans.

- **The Prairie Farm Rehabilitation Act**: an act that set up an organization to seek solutions to the devastating ecological conditions of the Dust Bowl.

- **The Bank of Canada**: Canada's first central bank; it was designed to coordinate the government's monetary policy.

- **The Canadian Radio Broadcasting Commission**: a body designed to foster the growth of the Canadian broadcasting industry.

In all, despite his personal responses to the letters he received regularly asking for aid and his halting intervention in the economy, Bennett's approach to the economic crisis was largely consistent with his belief in the free-enterprise system and his belief that people, not the government, are ultimately responsible for their own well-being. As the Canadian economy limped into the fifth year of the Depression, Bennett shocked many in the country and his own party by advocating a more comprehensive and aggressive approach to the crisis. Taking a cue from Roosevelt's plan, this package became known as Bennett's New Deal.

ATL Research and thinking skills

Bennett's New Deal came at the end of his tenure as Prime Minister. His New Deal included laws to govern the following areas:

- wages
- hours of work
- farm credit
- natural resource marketing
- unemployment insurance.

1 Research each of these measures. To what extent do you think Bennett saw them as a repudiation of the free-market system or rather temporary measures to correct a defect in the system?

2 To what extent do you think Bennett genuinely supported these measures or was he just trying to appease the voting public in the face of the 1935 election?

Sources you can use for your research:

Waite, Peter B. 1992. *Loner: Personal Life & Ideas R.B Bennett*. University of Toronto Press.

Gray, H. James, 1991. *R.B. Bennett: The Calgary Years*. University of Toronto Press.

Boyko, John. 2010. *Bennett: The Rebel Who Challenged and Changed a Nation*. Toronto: Key Porter Books.

King's responses

The federal election campaign of 1935 pitted King's Liberals, out of office during the worst years of the Depression, against Bennett and his New Deal, as well as the Cooperative Commonwealth Federation, the Social Credit Party, the remnants of the progressives and a number of smaller parties. King's Liberals won a huge majority on the slogan 'King or chaos'. But now the problem of the Depression was his.

The reality is that King had no more of a plan to fight the Depression in 1935 than he had had in 1930. He was not, however, willing to see if Bennett's New Deal would work. He had attacked the New Deal in the election as being extravagantly expensive at a time that called for prudence. Not wanting to be the politician to cut this direct aid and risk incurring the wrath of the unemployed, he referred the measures to the Supreme Court, which duly found that most of the New Deal tread on provincial jurisdiction and thus contradicted the British North America Act. To compound the delay caused by the court challenge, King then created his own commission to study the extent to which the act could be altered to accommodate the type of measures pioneered by Bennett.

It was during this period of study that another of King's commissions reported that what the Canadian economy needed was an infusion of government spending and tax cuts. Just as Bennett's relatively radical reforms had split the Conservative Party in 1935, the unity of the Liberal Party was threatened by this revolutionary departure from accepted economic theory during the budget discussion of 1938. A scheme of public works helped address some unemployment issues, while a National Employment Commission was established in 1938. A compromise allowed the Liberal Party to remain intact as the Canadian economy stumbled towards the recovery that the Second World War would bring.

Political responses to the Great Depression

Just as the profound economic dislocation brought on by the Depression led to a radical rejection of liberal democracy in parts of Europe, so too did it bring out ideas for a radical reordering of the political economy in North America. In Canada this was expressed in the creation of some new and innovative political parties. In many ways these new parties were a continuation of the populist politics that appeared in Canada during the 1920s.

The Cooperative Commonwealth Federation

The Cooperative Commonwealth Federation (CCF) was born out of a meeting between workers and farm activists in Calgary in 1932. Within a year there was another meeting in Regina, during which the CCF adopted its platform as expressed in the Regina Manifesto. In many ways what separated the CCF and its manifesto from other ideas about how to fight the Depression was its underlying assumption that the system could not or should not be fixed, but rather replaced. It represented a rejection of the basic tenets of the free-market system and as such was branded as dangerous socialism or even communism.

ATL Research and thinking skills

John Maynard Keynes was a British economist who studied the problems of the Great Depression. He formed the opinion that the ultimate issue in the Depression was a lack of overall demand. Although this business cycle of booms and recessions was common, his worry was that the Depression had lasted so long that there was not enough purchasing power left in traditional sources of demand to bring the economy back to close to full employment. He feared that the business cycle might find equilibrium at a lower level of employment. Keynes believed that the only institution with enough purchasing power to boost demand out of the Depression were national governments.

He therefore advocated that governments should spend money on public works and anything that put money in the pockets of potential consumers during periods of economic decline. During times of economic expansion, governments should take in money in the form of increased taxation. Booms would not be as high but nor would recessions be as deep.

Research the economic history of five countries in North, Central, and South America in the decades after the Great Depression, 1936–2000. What evidence is there of Keynesian economics? What are the results of these policies? Are there any patterns to the adoption and or rejection of these policies in the region?

Country	Years	Keynesian policies	Results

The CCF would run as a democratic socialist party in the established Canadian political system – it sought reform not revolution. It chose JS Woodsworth, progressive Member of Parliament, as its leader and managed to elect five candidates in the 1935 federal election. The CCF ran candidates successfully in provincial and municipal elections as well. This provincial and local success makes sense in that, as King's court challenge to the New Deal would prove, matters of direct relief, unemployment insurance and similar measures were the purview of provincial governments and it was in these areas that the CCF and its policies were most appealing to the voting public. By 1944 the CCF would form the provincial government in Saskatchewan under the leadership of Tommy Douglas, a former Baptist minister. This was the first socialist government elected in North America. The CCF, which merged with organized labour to form the New Democratic Party (NDP) in 1961, governed Saskatchewan for 40 years during the 20th century.

Social Credit

While supporters of the CCF looked to collectivism as the solution to the misery of the Depression, others looked to improving the spending power of the individual as the magic bullet. William Aberhart was another Baptist minister who was moved to enter politics by the suffering heaped on the people of the west by the Depression. Aberhart, or 'Bible Bill' as he was known, found a solution in the complicated doctrine of Social Credit and brought it to Alberta in 1932, publicizing

▲ *All the World Loves a Lover*, May 1938, Cameron Stewart, Calgary Herald, commentary on the Social Credit Party and William 'Bible Bill' Aberhart

it on his popular radio programme. In short, Social Credit sought to increase consumer spending by issuing credits worth $25 a month to citizens. Not intended to encourage idleness, these dividends could be suspended if people refused available employment. While Aberhart did denounce the greed of the banking system, Social Credit was designed to operate within the market economy.

It is not hard to understand why Social Credit struck a chord with the impoverished farmers of Alberta. Aberhart seemed to be promising $25 a month to all Albertans, and this promise carried the movement to decisive electoral victory in the 1935 Alberta election. The financial mechanics of such a payment, however, delayed its implementation. The 'Socreds' did bring some debt relief to farmers and a reformed farm insurance scheme. When Aberhart tried to regulate the banking industry and bring in the $25 social dividends, however, the laws were struck down as unconstitutional in that monetary policy and banking were federal powers. Nevertheless, with a modified, practical and largely conservative platform, the Social Credit Party would govern Alberta for 36 years until 1971.

Source skills

The Regina Manifesto vs the Social Credit League of Alberta 10 Plank Platform (1935)

Source A

The Social Credit League of Alberta 10 Plank Platform (1935)

The following excerpt is from a document that was issued by the Social Credit League of Alberta in 1935 as a summary of its platform.

1 Finance and the Distribution of Goods

   c The establishment of a Just Price for all goods and services, and the regulation of the price spread [price mark up] on all goods sold or transferred within the bounds of the Province [Alberta].

This Just Price is to be just and fair:

1 To the producers and to the distributors. They should not be required to sell goods for less than the cost of production or of import.

2 To the consumers. They should not be exploited of unduly deprived of fair returns for their purchasing power.

3 The Present Problem of Debt

   a Private, or Mortgage and Tax Indebtedness

      1 The Distribution of Basic Dividends [Social Dividends] and the Establishment of a Just Price will at once begin to give our citizens the ability to cope with Mortgage Indebtedness at present against their farms and their Homes.

Source B

The following is an excerpt from the Regina Manifesto, a founding document of the Cooperative Commonwealth Federation (CCF).

2 Socialization Of Finance

Socialization of all financial machinery—banking currency, credit, and insurance, to make possible the effective control of currency, credit and prices, and the supplying of new productive equipment for socially desirable purposes.

Planning by itself will be of little use if the public authority has not the power to carry its plans into effect. Such power will require the control of finance and of all those vital industries and services, which, if

they remain in private hands, can be used to thwart or corrupt the will of the public authority. Control of finance is the first step in the control of the whole economy. The chartered banks must be socialized and removed from the control of private profit-seeking interests; and the national banking system thus established must have at its head a Central Bank to control the flow of credit and the general price level, and to regulate foreign exchange operations. A National Investment Board must also be set up, working in co-operation with the socialized banking system to mobilize and direct the unused surpluses of production for socially desired purposes as determined by the Planning Commission.

Insurance Companies, which provide one of the main channels for the investment of individual savings and which, under their present competitive organization, charge needlessly high premiums for the social services that they render, must also be socialized.

Source: Zakuta, Leo. 1964. *A Protest Movement Becalmed: A Study of Change in the CCF.* Toronto: University of Toronto Press. http://economics. uwaterloo.ca/needhdata/Regina_Manifesto.html.

Questions

1 Explain the following references:

   a 'Basic Dividends' [Source A]

   b 'Socialization of all financial machinery' [Source B]

   c 'Socially desirable purposes' [Source B]

2 How do 'Insurance Companies . . . provide one of the main channels for the investment of individual savings'? [Source B]

3 How do the two documents differ in their approach to debt?

4 a What evidence is there of collectivism in each of the sources?

   b What evidence is there of individualism in each of the sources?

5 With reference to their origin and purpose, what are the values and limitations of each source for historians studying political responses to the Depression in Canada?

6 What are the strengths and weaknesses of the arguments presented in these two sources?

7 Research the subsequent political history of Saskatchewan and Alberta. How do these sources help explain that history?

Union Nationale

While on the prairies the impulse was to look to either new collectivist models (the CCF) or to modifications on traditional individualist themes (Social Credit), in Quebec the desperation created by the Depression found expression in renewed nationalism. Profiting from an ideological split in Quebec's Liberal Party and the growing popularity of French Catholic social action groups such as *École Sociale Populaire*, Quebec's Conservative Party leader Maurice Duplesis brought these groups together in a new party called the Union Nationale, which formed the Quebec government after the 1936 election. Strictly provincial and populist, the Union Nationale established a conservative regime that championed Quebec francophone interests against the federal government in Ottawa and a nebulous traditional Quebec Catholic rural ethic. Duplesis ruled Quebec and the Union Nationale as a demagogue, taking aim at political opponents and anyone suspected of socialist or communist sympathies. This hardline approach to left-wing opponents was best illustrated in the controversial Act Respecting Communist Propaganda, known as the 'Padlock Law', passed by Duplesis' government in 1937. This law empowered the government to shut down any organization deemed by the government to be promoting 'communism'. The wording was vague enough for Duplesis to use it against any number of moderately left-wing groups.

157

Comintern

Short for Communist International. This was an organization developed by the Soviet Union to co-ordinate the activities of national communist parties around the world. From 1928, Stalin chaired the organization and used it as a tool of Soviet foreign policy.

Class discussion

What directions did the Comintern give to national communist parties in Canada and other countries during the Great Depression?

How might this affect the attitude of Canadians toward communism?

The Communist Party of Canada

As in other parts of the world, economic crisis bred extremist politics and Canada in the 1930s was no exception. The Communist Party of Canada, founded in 1921, approached the Depression from two angles. It ran, and in some cases elected, members to public office at the provincial and municipal levels, and in the 1940s elected Fred Rose to the federal parliament. The party was also an important force in organized labour and was instrumental in the Workers Unity League and the On-to-Ottawa Trek. The centralized control of all communist parties imposed by Stalin through the **Comintern**, however, meant that the Communist Party of Canada could not fashion a platform that responded to the Canadian context, and its popularity suffered as a consequence. Government repression also bit deep into its popularity. Duplesis used the Padlock Law liberally against the party in Quebec. In 1931, the National Party's headquarters was raided and its leader Tim Buck was arrested and sentenced to five years in prison.

Ontario Liberals

The crisis of the Depression put strains on the relationship between traditional provincial parties and the federal government. In Ontario, Mitchell Hepburn, the Liberal premier, clashed regularly with Prime Minister King, a fellow Liberal. Although elected on a moderate reform platform, championing higher wages and business regulation to combat what he described as the privilege of the elite, Hepburn had little time for unionism and governed the province from a fairly traditional centre-right perspective. This perspective was well illustrated in 1937 when he created an army of strike-breakers, 'Hepburn's Hussars', to smash a large strike at the Oshawa General Motors plant when Prime Minister King refused to use the Royal Canadian Mounted Police (RCMP) to break the strike.

ATL Research skills

Compare and contrast the policies of Canadian political parties during the Great Depression. To what extent do these policies represent continuity with past policies? To what extent did they represent a break with traditional policy? Use the following table to help you.

	Liberals	Conservatives	CCF	Socreds	Communists
Government ownership					
Relief/welfare					
Monetary policy					
Fiscal policy					
Tariffs					

Unionism

The principles of supply and demand in the labour market generally dictate that unionism is at its weakest during periods of recession and depression, and the 1930s more or less bore this out in Canada. There were, however, some important innovations developed by working people to cope with the hardships of the Depression.

Canada's traditional labour organizations, groups such as the Trades and Labour Congress (TLC), responded to the Depression by retrenching and turning their attention to what remained of their employed membership. In fact, union membership in Canada only declined by 15% during the 1930s. Much of the militant industrial action that erupted during this period was guided by a new broad-based labour organization led by committed communists.

The Workers Unity League (WUL) was instituted in Canada in 1929 at the behest of the Comintern. Its goal was to organize disparate unions into a larger association and to use this as a weapon for large-scale industrial action. The WUL and its energetic and active organizers led a number of strikes across the country between 1930 and 1940 in both primary industries, such as mining, and secondary industries, such as manufacturing. But the WUL was a tool of international communism and, despite its successes in championing the rights of working Canadians, it was denounced and broken up by those in government and rival labour organizations who saw it as a threat to the essential principles of society.

ATL Research skills

Research the outcome of the strikes listed below.

Industrial action in the 1930s in Canada		
Location	Union	Year
Bienfait, Saskatchewan	Mine Workers Union of Canada	1931
Stratford, Ontario	Chesterfield and Furniture Workers' Industrial Union	1933
Rouyn, Quebec	Mine Workers Union of Canada	1934
Montreal, Quebec	Industrial Union of Needle Trades Workers	1934
Oshawa, Ontario	Committee for Industrial Organization	1935
Vancouver, BC	Vancouver and District Waterfront Workers' Association	1935
Quebec (Province-wide textile industry strike)	Catholic Confederation of Labour	1937

The On-to-Ottawa Trek

From 1930 to 1935 Bennett's government clung stubbornly to its contention that relief was the business of provinces, municipalities and private charities. For their part, provinces and municipalities preferred to spend their limited resources on the welfare of family breadwinners. The end result of this haphazard and paltry relief system was that as the Depression deepened the legions of single unemployed men swelled to huge proportions. In an effort to find work, these masses of resentful and desperate men took to the rails, hopping on freight cars and travelling across the country in search of what limited employment opportunities might exist elsewhere. Shanty towns grew up outside Canadian cities just as they did outside US cities. While in the USA they were called Hoovervilles, they were the Bennett Boroughs in Canada. These growing encampments and the prospect of throngs of rootless men inundating communities led the federal government to establish a system of 'relief' camps deep in the wilds of Canada, far from urban centres and 'respectable' citizens. The work camps were administered by the Department of National Defense with military discipline. The discipline, work conditions, low wages and sense of hopelessness that permeated the camps made them a natural environment for the growth of radicalism.

The communist WUL recognized this potential to organize and radicalize the unemployed in the relief camps. WUL members soon infiltrated the camps and began to organize and direct the seething discontent there, forming the Relief Camp Workers Union. By the beginning of 1935 men began to leave the camps in British Columbia to descend upon Vancouver. They lived in the streets and supported themselves with handouts, clashing with police regularly. Following their leader Arthur 'Slim' Evans, 1000 of these Royal Twenty Centers climbed aboard trains to take their complaints to the seat of the federal government in Ottawa. As the On-to-Ottawa Trek passed through the towns and cities of British Columbia and Alberta, the number of Trekkers more than doubled.

The spectre of thousands, perhaps tens of thousands by the time the Trek reached Ottawa, of unemployed men invading the capital scared Bennett into negotiating with Evans and other leaders of the Trek. In reality, Bennett was simply buying time while the Trek moved out of his home riding of Calgary. He had already decided that the Trek would be stopped before it reached Winnipeg, the scene of the Winnipeg General Strike of 1919 and hotbed of union activity. Conveniently, the RCMP training depot was located between Calgary and Winnipeg in Regina, the next stop on the Trek. On 1 July 1935 police and Trekkers clashed in what became known as the Regina Riot. After a day of bitter fighting, over 100 Trekkers were arrested and the rest dispersed.

▲ On-to-Ottawa Trekkers in Regina

▲ Regina Riot, July 1935

The role of religion in the Great Depression

In times of crisis people often turn to traditional sources of comfort. Victims of the Depression looked to religious movements, established as well as new, for succour. The crisis also politicized religious movements during the Depression. While some saw in the ecological and economic catastrophe divine retribution for the material sins of humans and preached repentance, men such as 'Bible Bill' Aberhart used their religious pulpits to preach not patience, but rather reform. The Depression gave new life to the Social Gospel movement that had flourished at the end of the previous century. The Social Gospel of the 1930s was the belief that Christian principles such as charity and compassion should be the centre of government action, rather than a fortunate by-product of a non-interventionist government. This conviction was essential to many of those who helped found the CCF, such as JS Woodsworth and TC Douglas. Tommy Douglas, a Baptist minister, however, did not advocate reckless spending. Instead, he believed that the economy could be actively managed for the equal benefit of all while observing the equally Christian principles of prudence and restraint. The Fellowship of a Christian Social Order brought together Christianity and socialism for members of the United Church. The Catholic Church, especially in Quebec, sought to give its congregation support in the form of charity while at the same time railing against the evils of communism. It saw the Depression as a call to moral rebirth and championed a back-to-the-land movement as a remedy for the wanton consumerism bred by unbridled capitalism.

The Canadian government passed the Indian Act in 1876. It was designed to identify those First Nations people who were subject to the terms of the various treaties signed by the government and First Nation bands across the country – 'status Indians' – and to regulate the relationship between the government and these people. In practice the Indian Act became the chief tool by which the government of Canada sought to assimilate the First Nations people. The Indian Act was amended numerous times between 1884 and 1938. The Indian Act still exists although not in the form it did throughout the 19th and 20th centuries.

The act and subsequent amendments in 1938 established the following:

- 'Indian Agents' had the power of magistrates and administered Indian affairs in their respective districts.
- 'Status Indians' could only sell agricultural produce including livestock with the permission of the Indian Agent.
- Ceremonial dances and celebrations such as the potlatch were banned.
- First Nations people could be removed, without recourse, from reserve land that was close to centres with a population over 8000 people.

- First Nations bands would be compensated up to only 50% for the sale of reserve lands.
- Western First Nations people could not appear in ceremonial dress without permission from the Indian Agent.
- 'Status Indians' were banned from pool halls.
- 'Status Indians' were not permitted to vote. (They would not be allowed to vote until 1961).

Questions

1 How did the Indian Act try to assimilate First Nations people?

2 In establishing its relationship with the First Nations of what would become Canada, the Canadian government signed a series of treaties with groups of First Nations peoples at the end of the 19th and beginning of the 20th centuries. Use the Aboriginal Affairs and Northern Development website (www.aadnc-aandc.gc.ca) to analyse these treaties and the extent to which the Indian Act reflects or contradicts the provisions of the treaties.

3 Compare and contrast the treatment of Canada's First Nations people in the 1920s and 1930s with the treatment of African Americans and Native Americans in the USA during this same period.

Depression-era culture in Canada

The same forces that have structured Canada's economy – colonial heritage, geography and proximity to the USA – have dominated its cultural landscape. In this sense there was a great deal of cultural continuity with earlier periods. There was also continuity with the First World War period, in which Canadian nationalism germinated. The growing importance of the radio as a cultural disseminator meant that Canadians were exposed to those elements of US culture that could be broadcast, most notably music. Jazz and country music made their way into Canada during the 1920s and this continued throughout the Depression years. Musicians crossed the border in both directions, including popular Canadian big bands such as Guy Lombardo and his Royal Canadians. US musicians such as Woody Guthrie were using their art to respond to the Depression, and these responses found an audience in Canada, expressing as they did the same struggles facing Canadians during this period.

In the years prior to the First World War, a group of visual artists shared a vision of what would become a particularly Canadian approach to aesthetic representation. The artists Fredrick Varley, Franklin Carmichael and JEH MacDonald came together with Arthur Lismer, Lawren Harris, AY Jackson and Franz Johnson in the early 1920s to demonstrate their distinctly Canadian sensibility, drawing on an expression of national identity that grew out of Canada's participation in the First World War. Known as the Group of Seven, these artists, with some changing

membership, exhibited together into the early 1930s. Although the Group of Seven itself did not exist beyond 1931, its influence and nationalist sentiments had an important and lasting impact on those artists grappling with the bitter reality of the 1930s.

The economics of the Depression had a stifling impact on Canadian art during this period. Money for all luxuries dried up and art was no exception. Nevertheless, the Depression was an important context for painters such as Illingworth Kerr and Carl Schaefer. While on the one hand the nationalism of the Group of Seven had an important impact on this generation of painters, the regional character of the Depression helped foster distinctly local approaches to painting style and subject matter. Much of Kerr's work is rooted in the Saskatchewan prairies and the paintings of Emily Carr have become iconic of the Pacific coast.

In terms of literature, there were significant Canadian works developed during the Depression. Morley Callaghan and Emily Carr (who worked across both art forms) produced period pieces. One of the lasting impacts that the Depression had on Canadian literature is its enduring influence on writers who grew up during this period – writers such as WO Mitchell and Max Braithwaite. Mitchell's *Who Has Seen the Wind* (1947) offers, in a distinctly western Canadian voice, a deep insight into a boy's coming of age during the Depression on the Canadian prairies and the lives of ordinary Canadians as they responded to the reality of the drought and the hardships of rural life.

Canadian popular culture in the Great Depression: The emergence of hockey as a national pastime

The national passion that hockey would become in Canada during the course of the 20th century was becoming evident early in the century. Like so many other aspects of Canadian society, sports in general and hockey in particular were fundamentally altered by the upheaval of the First World War. Professional hockey, however, as it emerged in the post-war era boomed in much the same way as the broader economy did, both in Canada and in the USA. Hockey franchises appreciated dramatically in value during the 1920s, in some cases by a factor of three. Easy credit, high employment and stable income levels left Canadians with money to spend on entertainment and, in many centres, this meant the local hockey team. As part of the growing consumer culture, hockey also benefited from the growth of mass media and advertising, which in turn was becoming increasingly national in nature. As such hockey, which until the 1920s had largely been dominated by local and regional teams and leagues, became a national phenomenon. By the end of the 1920s, the NHL was the dominant professional hockey league and consisted of 10 teams.

The National Hockey League (NHL) was and is a business and as such was not immune to the economic disaster of the Depression. The NHL expanded, as did many businesses in the 1920s, on easy credit, and as this dried up the league would contract into a body of six smaller but very successful teams. Cities such as New York and Montreal found that they could financially support only one team, each losing their second franchise during the 1930s. Other teams found ways to continue and even expand. When Con Smythe tried to build Maple Leaf Gardens in 1930, he garnered some of the building costs by offering shares to the construction trades as partial payment. Tickets sales were but one way a professional hockey franchise made money; when national radio broadcasts began, this opened a number of other revenue streams such as endorsements and advertising that allowed the teams to remain profitable in the Depression.

When Canada slid into economic depression in 1929 and unemployment lines lengthened and family farms, and in some cases whole communities, were swept away, Canadians across the country took refuge in what was fast becoming the national pastime – hockey.

While comparatively few could go to see a top-level hockey game due to cost or living too far away from one of the major professional hockey teams, the beginning of national radio broadcasts in 1933 brought the game into the homes of people across Canada, and within a year these broadcasts had an audience of over a million. As Richard Gruneau and David Whitson have pointed out, this mass marketing of the game and its incredible popularity in Canada kept hockey a distinctive part of Canadian culture despite the fact that many of the teams were from the USA, albeit with mostly Canadian players.

Imbedded within the NHL were two dominant sides of the national culture. The Montreal Canadiens became emblematic of French Canada and later the Toronto Maple Leafs would, to a lesser degree, represent English Canada; they met in ritualized competition on Saturday nights for the whole country to hear. The escapism of *Hockey Night in Canada*, as the national broadcasts were known, allowed Canadians to forget the economic gloom of the 1930s, if only for a couple of hours a week, in the same way that Hollywood musicals did. It did so in a manner that was culturally unifying – the Toronto Maple Leafs, New York Rangers and Detroit Red Wings had fans in Saskatoon, Edmonton, Prince Albert and countless small prairie towns as well as in Toronto, New York and Detroit. Thus hockey established itself in the 1930s as an enduring national cultural factor.

Class discussion

How did sports become unifying elements in other countries in the region during the Great Depression?

To what extent can sport fuel nationalism?

▲ The Canadian ice-hockey team from the 1936 Winter Olympic Games, who came second in the tournament having been undefeated since 1924

3.5 Impact of the Great Depression on Latin America

Conceptual understanding

Key question
→ How did the Great Depression change the political structure of Brazil?

Key concepts
→ Consequence

→ Significance

The initial effects of the Great Depression in Latin America were similar to what was seen elsewhere. As the demand for goods declined, there was an outflow of capital. This in turn meant internal deflation, the fall in value of Latin American currencies and a rise in unemployment. There was a fall in foreign investment and most countries found themselves in financial trouble as they were significantly indebted to foreign banks. As the banks themselves faced collapse, they demanded an immediate return of the money they had invested but in most cases this was impossible. Protectionist measures in other countries also left Latin American goods unaffordable; local products could not provide the revenue to repay debts or keep the governments afloat. There were exceptions: Venezuela's oil and Honduras' bananas kept them solvent, but these were the anomalies. Most countries were facing economic collapse.

The immediate effect of the Depression in many countries was political change. Placing blame on the existing governments, there were a number of *coups d'état*. In the year after the Wall Street Crash, the military took power in Argentina, Brazil, Chile, Guatemala, Honduras and Peru. While their treatment of the population and respect for the rights of individuals were dubious at best, they had at their disposal the mechanisms to change economic policies to address the crisis. From the Depression onwards, state intervention in the economy became the norm.

Brazil

Prior to 1929 the Brazilian economy was dependent on agriculture, particularly coffee. While rubber, cotton and cocoa were also key cash crops, coffee dominated Brazilian exports. In the 1920s coffee exports were the source of over 70% of the country's revenue. Brazilian producers had to strike a delicate balance to prevent overproduction yet have enough to maximize profits; this was not always easy as the trade was reliant on the vagaries of the international market, over which Brazilians had no control.

To take more control, in 1925 Brazil created the São Paulo Institute for Permanent Defense of Coffee. To keep coffee prices high, the institute would purchase and withhold its goods from the world market. To pay for the coffee, the institute received the revenue from a transportation

valorization
Increasing the value of a product through government policy.

tax and took out loans from foreign banks. This policy – known as **valorization** – held potential dangers, however; coffee producers wanted to expand to increase their revenues and at the same time other Latin American countries were increasing their production of coffee, thereby limiting Brazil's dominance of the international market. Manipulation of supply might have short-term success, but in the long run it would fail as Brazil would not keep its goods competitive.

However, the policy seemed successful in the 1920s. In 1927, Brazil produced an all-time high of 27 million bags of coffee and, as world prices began to fall, the institute bought coffee and prevented a substantial decrease in the price. Then, in 1928, when the coffee crop was small, the stocks they had purchased were placed on the market and not only did prices hold, but there were substantial reserves of coffee to be sold.

There was a small, emerging industrial base in several cities, but it was limited; most manufactured goods came from overseas, meaning that most profits from export were spent overseas, and there was a substantial outflow of capital. While some Brazilians advocated protectionist tariffs and tax credits to stimulate domestic industrialization, they were largely ignored by policymakers.

On the eve of the Depression, Brazil's foreign debt was $900 million and it paid out approximately $175 million per year in repayment of loans, relying on its international trade to make its annual payments. As long as coffee values remained high, the system worked to Brazil's advantage. But in May 1929 the price of coffee began a very fast decline. In Brazil there had been two years of bumper crops, leading to a huge surplus at home; at the same time other countries also saw a leap in their output, flooding the market. This weakened Brazil's economic standing and foreign lenders began to limit credit to them. Brazilian banks, in turn, began to cut back on their liberal lending to coffee planters. Nonetheless, the institute declared that its policies were sound and no changes would be made, giving Brazilians a sense of security that turned out to be ill-founded.

After the Wall Street Crash

Although the problems existed before the Wall Street Crash, the Crash highlighted the shortcomings of the economic system that Brazil had in place and was devastating to the export economy. In September 1929 coffee was being sold at 22 cents per pound; by 1 December it had fallen to 15 cents. This dramatic fall meant that national income declined and government revenue was limited. The government tried to curtail the effects by exporting its gold reserves to London and New York, which had the short-term result of preventing a downward spiral.

The state of São Paulo was in especially dire straits and faced bankruptcy. It appealed to the federal government for assistance but was denied by President Washington Luis. He had been an opponent of coffee valorization earlier in his political career (as governor of São Paulo) but when elected had said that the economy was dependent upon valorization. With the Wall Street Crash, he reverted to his previous outlook and stated that an unhealthy economic situation had been created that would be difficult to recover from. Instead, he favoured development of the small commercial and industrial sectors.

This national economic decline had profound effects on local businesses. In an informal report to the São Paulo opposition paper *Diario Nacional*, shop owners reported a 40% decline in sales in December 1929. Imports ceased coming to the country, trade stagnated and the small industrial sector sat idle. Planters, who often lived in the city, returned to their plantations. They were resentful of Washington Luis' policies, seeing the decline in prices as temporary, and his unwillingness to help them changed their political orientation.

At the same time, a new presidential race was looming between Getúlio Vargas and Julio Prestes – the handpicked successor of Washington Luis. In an astute political move, Vargas stated support for both coffee valorization and the financial propositions of the Washington Luis administration. This increased his popularity among most Brazilians but even so, in the March 1930 elections, Prestes won a narrow victory, giving assurance to foreign lenders of Brazil's political solvency. Almost immediately credit was extended to the ailing state of São Paulo, which was supposed to use the money that was not borrowed to service debts (almost 50%) to buy coffee surpluses and stabilize the price. Instead, a record-breaking 29 million bags of coffee were produced and prices – which had stabilized at 14 cents per pound – dropped again.

With coffee prices down to 10 cents per pound, the economy was dangerously close to collapsing. At the same time, Brazil's debt had increased to $1181 million, three-quarters of which was owed by the government. Brazil had seriously depleted its gold reserves, which stood at $70 million. Additionally, the overthrow of governments in neighbouring states made European and American lenders reluctant to engage in trade with Brazil.

The situation affected not only those in power; approximately 1 million Brazilians suffered as a direct result of the economic crisis. Most Brazilian rural workers were landless labourers who planters could no longer afford to pay. They began to subsist on food that they planted between coffee trees and faced hunger. Those who could often migrated to the cities in search of work, but just as many remained behind, unemployed and disgruntled. Unemployment was also rife among urban workers, including civil servants. Those who retained their positions were often unpaid for months at a time. While there were few civil disturbances, the country seemed poised for a change.

Political repercussions

Vargas took advantage of the situation and, in October 1930, revolts took place under his leadership. The government could not halt the rebel forces and on 24 October a revolutionary junta was formed. On 4 November Vargas was installed as provisional president. While there were deep-seated political problems that led to this *coup d'état*, the economic crisis created the conditions that made it viable. Those who had previously advocated democracy saw in Vargas a strong, charismatic leader who could make decisions to improve Brazil's economy. From 1930 to 1945 (and again until 1954) Vargas ruled Brazil. His political dominance was clear, and many argue that it was his charismatic personality that created political stability and allowed for a change in economic policies.

coup d'etat
Sudden and illegal overthrow of the government, usually by military means.

The rule of Vargas during the Depression included several attempts to overthrow his regime, one of which led to the creation of the Estado Novo, or New State, in 1937. Although his policies were largely consistent up to this point, the Constitution implemented at that time gave him authoritarian powers. For the economy, that would mean varying degrees of government intervention.

The political and economic effects of the Great Depression in Argentina

The initial economic effect of the Great Depression was a near-immediate fall in the demand for Argentine exports. As Europe and America suffered from crises of their own, they implemented protectionist policies to keep their farmers solvent. For Argentina, this led to an imbalance of trade and a 43% fall in the value of its cash crops, accompanied by a 40% devaluation of the Argentine peso. At the same time, businesses were forced to lay off workers, creating high unemployment in the cities. Civil servants did not lose their positions but often the government did not have enough money to pay them – customs duties were a main source of revenue for the government and the slowing of export and import made income non-existent.

Generally, then, most people blamed the Radicals for the dire economic straits. On 6 September 1930 the Radical Party President, Hipólito Yrigoyen, was overthrown and a military junta under General José Felix Uriburu was established. No one really opposed the military as they marched to Buenos Aires, and no one supported Yrigoyen, who was placed under temporary house arrest. Uriburu took control of the country and attempted to impose hardline military rule, but a potential rival, General Agustín Justo, was waiting to challenge him. Without consensus among the military, Uriburu was forced to hold elections in 1932 and Justo became president, relying on a mix of anti-Yrigoyen Radicals, National Autonomous Party (PAN) conservatives and socialists. This coalition, called the Concordancia, maintained its power only through electoral fraud and corruption. Despite reigning over what was later called the Infamous Decade, the Concordancia ruled Argentina from 1931 to 1943.

▲ Soldiers in Buenos Aires, Argentina, on 17 September 1930, holding pictures of the new president, General José Félix Uriburu

Conceptual understanding

Key question

→ Why did Brazil recover from the Great Depression more quickly than the USA or Canada?

Key concept

→ Consequence

There were several approaches to addressing the crisis. The first was government regulation to stabilize the local economy; governments set prices and established maximum levels of production (sometimes this included destruction of surplus goods). This was done to bolster the existing economies and help them regain their strength. The second was Import Substitution Industrialization (ISI). The goal was to encourage the creation of homegrown industries to replace Latin American dependence on foreign manufactured goods. Finally, governments tried to keep their international markets open by engaging in bilateral trade agreements with industrialized countries.

In many cases the policies led to a rapid recovery; mining and agriculture were not as hard hit as the industrial sectors, so these products could be used to bring about recovery. Additionally, the economic model that had been adopted prior to the Depression included a close relationship between banks and the government. Financial reforms of the 1920s included the creation of central banks and regulatory institutions with clearly defined rules. This made government intervention in the financial sector easier to implement than in other countries. Many countries left the gold standard and pegged their currencies to the US dollar, aiding their recovery. Despite difficult financial times, Latin American countries did not default on their loans, and used non-payment as a temporary measure to bring about recovery and keep faith in their currencies.

Ultimately, these policies brought Latin America out of the Depression but the issues of class and race that had plagued the region since independence remained and were in fact heightened by the economic distress. The leaders who came to power as a result of the Depression did not simply have to bring about economic recovery; they also had to address social and labour issues that had languished for over a century. To be successful, many leaders adopted a populist stance to co-opt the working and middle classes; the degree of success of these men varied and the results of their rule were contentious.

To make a more decisive determination on the success and failure of political leadership and economic policies during the Depression it is best to examine some countries in detail to see if there is consistency in the policies, their application and their effects. To this end, Brazil will be examined further.

Brazil

Economic policies of Getúlio Vargas

To address the economic crisis, Vargas implemented a series of policies that supported the coffee industry but at the same time sought to wean Brazil off its dependence on this crop. Honouring his promises during his presidential campaign, he created the National Department of Coffee, which was under his control but had considerable flexibility to act as it saw fit. Effective immediately, a reduction in coffee-tree planting was ordered. In 1920 there had been 1.7 billion trees; that figure had then risen to 3 billion, causing in part the glut in production. By 1939, the slow reduction brought the number of trees down to 2.5 billion, thus curtailing production. In 1931 the government also introduced a programme of coffee burning, and it is estimated that 60 million bags were burned by 1939. While these were nominally successful, the industry only recovered with the onset of the Second World War.

More importantly, the government tried to diversify the economy. Agricultural incentives were provided, which led to significant increases in livestock and cotton production. In the 1920s cotton consisted of only 2% of exports; in the 1930s it rose to 18%. While coffee would remain an important part of the economy, history and culture of Brazil, its dominance was fading fast. Even in São Paulo, planters diversified their crops and limited coffee production so that they could farm other crops. Sugar production was also reduced; it could no longer compete on the international market so the government decided to free up the land for more profitable cash crops.

▲ Mixing coffee into tar to be used in building new roads and highways

Import Substitution Industrialization

The Brazilian government reduced its imports by 75% between 1929 and 1932 – from $416.6 million to $108.6 million – and while exports also fell, they did not fall as fast, leaving Brazil with a favourable trade balance despite the economic crisis. Additionally, Brazil's agricultural policies kept a large sector of society employed. Thus, domestic demand for manufactured goods remained relatively stable while foreign supply was no longer available. With nowhere else to invest surplus capital, Brazilians (especially the coffee barons) began to invest in the industries which produced goods that had previously been imported. The government assisted, providing tax exemptions and long-term loans with low interest rates. Although most imports were subject to tariffs of up to 40%, exceptions were made for machinery or raw materials that were used to help build new industries.

Vargas strongly supported the growth of industry but it was growing international belligerence and the coming of war that led to the greatest growth spurt of the era. In 1940, the National Steel Commission was established, followed by the National Steel Company, which built Brazil's first large steel plant. Similar corporations were founded for

the production of iron, aircraft and truck engine production, and river valley development. These corporations were mixed, in that they were funded by both direct public investment and private investment. The government reserved the right to intervene directly in the affairs of these corporations if it was considered to be in the national interest.

Another area of economic development came in the realm of transportation. Recognizing the increasing importance of air transport – considering Brazil's topography, this was logical – Vargas encouraged commercial aviation. By 1939 there were 9 Brazilian companies flying routes that covered over 43 000 miles (nearly 70 000 kilometres), carrying 71 000 passengers, 223 tons of mail and 490 tons of freight, accounting for three-quarters of all commercial traffic in South America. This nascent industry was encouraged by the military and in 1941 Vargas created the Air Ministry. Railroad expansion also took place at this time, but there were half as many miles of train track as air routes. Instead, Vargas focused on road construction, leading to the construction of 258 390 miles (nearly 416 000 kilometres) of roads by 1939.

Trade and war

In the late 1930s, Germany became the biggest consumer of Brazilian cotton, provided the second largest market for coffee and the third largest for cacao. Vargas wanted a positive relationship with Germany but wanted to hold Nazism at bay; he was, at heart, a Brazilian nationalist, uninterested in European domination in any form, but had to strike a delicate balance to encourage German trade.

At the same time, the USA was courting Brazil. Despite his economic nationalism, Vargas encouraged foreign investment in Brazilian firms. Immediately after Pearl Harbor, Brazil remained neutral in the war, but as the Battle of the Atlantic accelerated, this position became less sustainable. Initially unwilling to provide weapons to Brazil, the USA increasingly made concessions in the hopes of gaining an ally in the southern Atlantic. Vargas was able to use this to gain a $20 million loan from the Export-Import Bank to help develop the Volta Redonda plant for the newly created National Steel Company. In August 1942, Brazil declared war on Germany after the Germans torpedoed Brazilian ships. To show support for the Allied effort, Vargas committed Brazilian troops to the war in Europe and sent 25 000 to fight in the liberation of Italy in 1944.

Labour policies

In one of his first actions as head of state, Vargas created the Ministry of Labour and integrated the unions into the Ministry. Union leaders had the right to bargain with management, with the government as an intermediary that would choose the resolution that best fitted the needs of the state. As part of legislation, the government provided a fixed minimum wage, a maximum working week of 48 hours and an 8-hour day in some industries. In addition, Vargas established a social security system, which provided a pension plan, retirement, paid annual vacation and health care. For women, maternity benefits were provided to help women remain in the workplace. In factories, safety and health standards were established, and educational opportunities – focused largely on literacy – were provided after work. The rights and privileges of Brazilian labour now eclipsed those of the industrialized states and by 1944 there were 800 unions with over 500 000 workers.

These were all positive steps but there were a number of limitations associated with the rights of labour. First, unions were allowed to organize by plant and industry but not on a statewide or national basis lest their power become too great; this seriously diminished the autonomy that trade unions enjoyed prior to the creation of the Ministry of Labour and the Labour Code (1943), and they lost the right to strike unless it was authorized by the government. As the system continued, union leaders tended to put the needs of the state ahead of those of the worker in an attempt to take the long view but this did little to help the workers. Perhaps more damaging was that the laws were applied unevenly. Since the government was given the jurisdiction to determine how the labour code was enforced, Vargas and the Ministry of Labour often used labour law to take action against individual owners or particular states that were not cooperating with the Vargas regime. Lastly, labour legislation only applied to industrial workers; the rural, agrarian workers were not protected, so their working conditions and salary remained poor. As over 80% of workers were in rural areas, labour policies applied only to the lucky few.

The reasons that Vargas decided to implement such sweeping legislation are complex. On the one hand, it seems that he had a genuine desire to improve the lives of the urban poor that predated the Depression. He saw that, in improving their lives, they were less likely to become a revolutionary force and that there were far more workers who could potentially purchase Brazilian-produced goods if their salaries were sufficient. E Bradford Burns notes that one key reason was that Vargas recognized that he could use urban workers as a tool against the traditional elites. While they were not yet powerful, urban workers were a growing force that Vargas sought to co-opt; by establishing a relationship with the working classes, he limited his reliance on the Brazilian upper classes and military to remain in power.

Education

Another linked area of social policy that Vargas considered important was education; once again, the importance to Vargas can be seen by the creation of the Ministry of Education under Francisco Campos. Illiteracy hovered around 60% of the population – a problem when trying to create a skilled workforce. In 1930 only 3% of children completed primary school, largely because there were few schools beyond the cities, and the urban poor often had to send their children to work before completion. There was no federal structure to education (although the right to free education was guaranteed in all Brazilian constitutions) and little incentive to create state schools. As late as 1940, there were only 12 free secondary schools in Brazil. There were some privately funded schools – interestingly, the Ford Motor Company had such a system in place in Belterra to attract workers to such a remote area – but many of these were founded by immigrant communities, and once it was illegal

to educate Brazilians in foreign languages (1938), they were forced to close their doors. Those who were wealthy enough sent their children to private, Catholic schools.

Under Campos, new schools were created, teacher training was required, teachers' salaries were increased and primary education was made compulsory. There was a wave of infrastructure development in rural areas that often included health centres and schools, in an attempt to increase literacy and improve public health. Even so, only 25% of school-age children were attending schools because the children were needed to contribute to the family income.

More successful was the expansion of the university system. New universities were established in São Paulo and Rio de Janeiro, increasing student enrollment. In 1920 there had been 13 200 university students in Brazil; in 1940 that number had climbed to 21 200.

Popular mobilization and repression

More due to domestic politics than the Depression, the 1930s introduced a wave of repression in Brazil. Vargas had seized power with the support of many Brazilians upset with the inadequate policies of Washington Luis, but some did not feel that he was meeting the needs of the country. Not surprisingly for the era, strong movements on the Left and Right arose in the 1930s and then were repressed by the regime.

On the Left, the *Aliança Nacional Libertadora* (ANL) formed as a coalition of leftist parties that opposed what they saw as the fascist, repressive policies of the Vargas regime. The Brazilian Communist Party spearheaded this coalition, and was taking its orders from Moscow via the Comintern. This ultimately caused the breakdown of the coalition as the communists took a revolutionary position against the government and the emerging Fascist Party.

Integralismo was the Brazilian response to fascism; its doctrines borrowed from the different European versions of the time. Much like the Iberian forms, there was strong nationalism centred in Roman Catholicism and traditionalism, but the Integralists were firmly anti-colonial and sought to distinguish themselves as distinct from, even superior to, their European colonizers. Like Nazism, there was a strong anti-Semitic strain to Integralism, although not all leaders adopted this. Like Italian fasciscm, at the core of Integralism was the idea that the human self was at its best when serving the common, national good. The Integralists adopted the paramilitary approach of European fascism and as Mussolini had his Black Shirts and Hitler had his Brown Shirts, the Integralists had their 'Green Shirts', who increasingly engaged in street fights against their communist counterparts. Both extremes were tolerated only as long as they were beneficial to the Vargas regime.

Initially, the Brazilian Communists seemed capable of mobilizing the working classes, but their potential strength was neutralized by the government's labour policies. With strong support from labour for government initiatives, the communists lost their momentum, and attempted an armed insurrection against the government in November 1935. The government's reaction was swift and brutal. Communist and

ANL leaders were arrested and sometimes tortured, and leftist parties were banned. Suppression of socialist and communist leaders continued into the late 1930s, convincing the Integralists that they had a special position in the state.

This, however, was contradicted by the 1938 ban on paramilitary agitators. As a result, a group of Integralists attacked the presidential palace in an attempt to take power, but found they had very little support and the attempted coup failed. From this point forward, the Integralists were banned, as were all political parties. Vargas would be the unquestioned leader of Brazil until the end of the Second World War.

During this time, security forces affiliated with the police were used against subversives repeatedly and the jails were overcrowded, full of political dissidents; suspect foreigners were deported without cause. The government engaged in press censorship to the point where there was one official version available for newspapers and journals to use when reporting the news.

Results of the Vargas regime

Vargas' economic policies proved to be very successful; between 1924 and 1939 industrial output grew at an average rate of 6% and the 1930s were marked by very strong increases. In 1941 there were 44 100 plants employing 944 000 workers, meaning that most work was still done in small-scale factories and plants, and that production was often reliant on hand labour rather than machinery. Although they primarily produced consumer goods, these industries successfully provided substitutes for goods previously imported, and they helped to diversify the economy. Due to the Second World War, Brazilian goods were being exported, and a push towards heavy industry was in place.

This growth was not even throughout the country, however. Most of Brazil's population (40 million) was still rural and still dependent upon cash crops for their livelihoods. Unlike their urban brethren, the rural working class was still subjected to harsh living conditions that included low wages and debt peonage, a condition in which rural labourers were indebted to the plantation owners to the extent that they often worked to pay off an ever-increasing debt rather than for wages.

Brazil continued to rely on coffee as a major source of revenue, and foreign reserves. Five states employed 75% of factory workers, and had most of the industrial wealth concentrated in their environs, and São Paulo alone had 41% of all workers. The interior was largely untouched and untapped; Vargas tried to encourage migration to these areas by offering 50-acre (20.25-hectare) tracts to those willing to populate the west and the Amazon Valley.

As the war against the Axis progressed, Brazilians did not miss the irony of fighting a war against a tyrannical regime while having a similar one in place in their own country; the military put pressure on Vargas and he understood that his regime would end with the war. In 1943 Vargas began to move towards the renewal of democracy and even helped develop the Brazilian Labour Party that emerged in 1945. Vargas was deposed in October 1945 in a bloodless coup and free elections took

place on 2 December 1945, with General Eurico Gaspar Dutra elected president in free and fair elections by secret ballot that included women. A tenuous democracy was in place in Brazil; Vargas would be re-elected president in 1950 and take office in 1951, continuing the Vargas regime for a bit longer.

▲ Men and women polishing Chevrolets on the assembly line at the General Motors plant, São Paulo, Brazil, in 1939

Research skills

All of Latin America was affected by the Great Depression. Most countries were affected as much as Brazil but the responses and recovery were different. Choose one country in Latin America and examine the following:

Before the Depression

1. Was there one dominant crop?
2. Was the population primarily rural?
3. What percentage of the population was indigenous, mestizo or criollo in each group?
4. How large was the middle class?
5. What was the form of government?

Responses to the Depression

1. Which sectors of society were affected the most severely?
2. What happened to the economy?
3. Did the political system change?
4. What policies did the government introduce to alleviate the effects of the Depression?
5. How successful were government policies? At what point can we say that your country of choice had come out of the Depression?

Panama in the Great Depression

Historically, Panama's economy was based on farming and fishing for local consumption, and much of Panama remained so in the early 20th century. However, the completion of the Panama Canal led to a shift for the areas surrounding it. To maintain control over the canal, the USA annexed the Panama Canal Zone – an unprecedented US territory within the country of Panama – and had troops stationed there. The Panamanians in the surrounding areas relied on commerce with Americans in the zone for their livelihoods.

With the onset of the Depression, the US government reduced the number of Americans living in the zone. Panamanian professionals found their jobs taken by 'Zonians' – Americans living in the Panama Canal Zone. There was also unemployment in the surrounding Panamanian cities and a migration of urban dwellers back to the countryside to engage in subsistence farming. However, there was also a large number of West Indians residing in the area who were laid off too, and the Panamanian government insisted that the USA pay for their repatriation to their home countries.

The Panamanians had adopted the US dollar as their currency and this tied their prosperity to the US economy. When the dollar was devalued on the international market, the $250 000 annual annuity that Panama received for the canal lost 40% of its value, vastly reducing government income.

This gave rise to a secret political organization called Acción Communal that deposed the government. The goal of Acción Communal was to decrease US influence, and its rallying cry was 'Panama for the Panamanians'. It put pressure on the USA to share its profits from the canal. Leading this nationalist cause were Harmodio and Arnulfo Arias Madrid, brothers who came from the rural, mestizo middle class and represented a new political faction in the country.

They appealed to Roosevelt and his Good Neighbor Policy, and in 1936 the Hull-Alfaro Treaty removed US protection over Panama, enabling it to pursue independent foreign policies. While they found the Roosevelt administration sympathetic to their requests for a greater share in canal profits and equitable treatment for Panamanians in the zone, they ran into opposition from the 40 000 American Zonians who did not want to pay more for services. This was a critical interest group as their expenditures constituted one-third of Panama's GNP at the time.

In negotiations Panama managed to increase its annuity to $430 000 annually, end the US right to acquire Panamanian land and receive approval to have its own radio stations. However, with war looming in both Asia and Europe, ratification of these agreements stalled in the US Congress and were not approved until 1939 when it was determined that granting concessions to Panama would keep it in the Pan-American sphere.

▲ Aerial view of the Panama Canal

Focus on the impact on women and minorities in the USA

An overview of the effects of the Great Depression on Americans must examine the consequences for African Americans, Hispanics and women. Overall, the 1930s set all groups back; the vast majority of the economic gains of previous decades were lost.

African Americans

In some areas of the USA, African Americans had seen improvements during the 1920s, mostly in the northeast, as the Harlem Renaissance flourished. But in many ways the twenties represented stagnation, as most blacks gained little from the economic growth of the decade. Violence against blacks continued into the decade, although attacks were less frequent than the number of killings at the turn of the century.

When the economy collapsed, African Americans lost the little economic status they had obtained. One-half of all blacks lived in the south. Rural southern blacks lost farms as cotton prices and other agricultural products dropped in price. In the cities, blacks lost jobs as white men took the low-pay, low-status jobs such as street cleaners and janitors. The farmers' first move was often into southern cities, where they joined other unemployed African Americans. Some whites formed groups to keep blacks out of work. The sign 'No Jobs for Niggers Until Every White Man has a Job!' is representative of the mood and obstacles that blacks faced. By 1932, 75% of blacks were unemployed compared to 25% of all workers in the USA. Relief programmes run by local governments went to whites first, leaving many black families malnourished and homeless. All was not negative; African Americans did benefit from several federal programmes, including the Public Works Administration, the Works Progress Administration and the Farm Services Administration. Blacks comprised a quarter of residents in federal housing projects.

Hiring within the agencies often, but not always, followed non-discrimination regulations. Other federal divisions harmed African Americans. The Agricultural Adjustment Administration, whose policy enforcement favoured landowners over tenant farmers, penalized blacks, who were mostly sharecroppers. The National Regulatory Authority's industrial non-discrimination wage policy encouraged businesses, especially in the south, to fire African American workers who had been paid significantly less. Federal programmes, administered by local whites, often denied relief to African Americans. Intimidation, including lynching, increased as the Depression deepened. Efforts by the National Association for the Advancement of Colored People (NAACP) to have a federal anti-lynching law foundered as southern Democrats prevented its passage in the Senate. Black women were also affected; those with jobs as domestic servants were fired and their positions went to white women. As a result of the worsening economic and social conditions, close to half a million blacks moved to northern cities to find work (in addition to the millions who moved north during the **Great Migration** of 1915–30). When they arrived, they found few jobs, as the cities were already devastated by factory closings and failed businesses.

African Americans in northern urban cities lost jobs as well. Men and women suffered high unemployment as factories and businesses closed, and as service and domestic work dried up. As elsewhere, job-loss rates for blacks significantly exceeded those for whites. Black women's jobless rates were often greater than for men. An interesting development took place, however, one that has been termed 'survivalist entrepreneurship' among women. The new female entrepreneurs were an extension of a common practice of running boarding houses in residential homes. During the 1930s, a third of black women workers were laundresses, a quarter worked in beauty occupations, just over a fifth operated or worked in boarding houses, and a tenth were dressmakers and seamstresses. Very few black women found work in retail or restaurants, where many job-seeking white women found work.

One bright spot for African Americans was the labour movement. Some factory owners attempted to use blacks as strike-breakers. The NAACP supported the all-white labour unions' job actions. As a result, 500 000 blacks joined labour organizations during the 1930s; in some unions blacks comprised a fifth of the membership.

Hispanic Americans

The Great Depression devastated Hispanic Americans as well. At the start of the Great Depression there were between 1.5 and 2 million Latinos in the USA. The majority were of Mexican heritage and most lived in the southwest. Other Hispanics traced their heritage to Cuba, Puerto Rico and the Dominican Republic, among other origins. Latinos lived in many northern cities as well. Although some Mexican Americans were long-established within communities, most Hispanics worked the

Great Migration
Movement of 1.6 million African–Americans out of the rural South to the urban Northeast, Midwest, and West between 1915 and 1930.

lowest paying jobs, whether in agriculture or industry. The agricultural jobs were often geographically transient, as workers followed crops, planting and harvesting. Low wages, long hours and poor working conditions were commonplace. In southwest USA Hispanics occupied similar socio-economic status to African Americans in the south. When the Depression hit, Latinos suffered substantial job losses, as they were 'last hired, first fired'. White programme administrators prevented Latinos from taking advantage of relief programmes on the grounds that they were foreigners – regardless of their American citizenship. The ill-treatment went further as their children were not allowed to enroll in school and hospitals often refused to admit them when ill or injured. There were a few exceptions, for example, the head of the Texas division of the National Youth Administration, Lyndon Baines Johnson, the future president, made sure that Hispanics benefited from the programme. But, because they were often treated as unwelcome aliens, regardless of their citizenship status, as well as the difficulty they had in creating stable institutions due to labour movement, Latinos frequently had little or no support from either outside or within their own communities.

In the face of poverty and ill-treatment by employers, and local and state governments, Hispanics relocated. The mass movement within the USA resulted in a rise in the Latino urban population. The move into cities simply relocated their poverty into urban ghettos. As the city populations swelled, local governments tried to force Mexican Americans out. In states including California, *barrios* were raided: Americans were rounded up as well as non-citizens, and they were deported to Mexico without checking legal status. A climate of fear motivated many to move; intimidation and deportation led nearly half a million Latinos to move to Mexico during the Great Depression.

Even more telling as to the desperate situation of Latinos, was the estimate that half of all Hispanic–Americans relocated to other parts of the US during the Great Depression.

Women

The Great Depression affected women by sending many into poverty, often forcing them to fend for themselves and their families when their husbands went on the road to find work. In the Dust Bowl region entire families packed up their belongings and moved west, women fulfilling the traditional role of taking care of the family, even in migrant camps and on the side of the road. As stated above, some women became entrepreneurs, but most remained in traditional roles of wife and mother; a prevailing view that jobs should go to men as the primary wage earner was solidified by the falling economy.

▲ Women working at a breadline during the Depression

Research skills

It can be difficult to separate women in the Great Depression from other subsets of society. With women, as with men, it is often important to differentiate the class and race to which a woman belongs rather than making generalizations.

Choose a region of the United States and investigate how the Depression affected a particular subset of women from the following list: African-American, Latina, Native American, government employees, married, single or head of household. To what extent did the Great Depression affect these women?

Write a 1500-word research paper using proper research methods and formats. The resources below can help you with your research. (You may wish to find these resources using the Internet.)

Baker, Carolyn. *On Robert S. McElvaine's "The Great Depression"*, Speaking Truth to Power, 2007.

Hapke, Laura. *Daughters of the Great Depression: Women, Work and Fiction in the American 1930s*. Athens: University of Georgia Press, 1995.

History, Art and Archives, U.S. House of Representatives, Office of the Historian, *Women Representatives and Senators by Congress: 1917-Present*, U.S. Government Printing Office.

McElvaine, Robert S. *The Great Depression: America, 1929–1941*. United States: Three Rivers Press, n.d.

Swaine Thomas, Dorothy, and Dudley Kirk. *Demographic and Economic Change in Developed Countries*. N.p.: Universities-National Bureau, 1960.

Walker, Melissa. *Women in the 1930s: Workers or Homemakers?* H-Net Reviews, 1996.

Ware, Susan. *Women and the Great Depression*. The Gilder Lehrman Institute of American History.

United States Department of Labor. *Handbook or Labor Statistics: 1936 Edition*. Washington D.C. Government Printing Office, 1936.

Woolner, David. *Feminomics: Breaking New Ground – Women and the New Deal*, Roosevelt Institute, 2011.

Focus on the arts in the USA

During the Great Depression, the arts did not disappear. For the first time the Federal Government took a significant interest in the fine arts, as exemplified by Federal Project Number One (FPNO). Eleanor Roosevelt, the first lady, well known for her promotion of civil rights, was also a strong proponent of the arts. The government launched several programmes, ranging from theatre to music to photography.

The private sector, including novelists and movie studios, created many works, some addressing the Depression while others provided escapism. Other diversions included music and cartoons. Folk music and blues became more visible. The radio also played an important part of popular culture as radio stations penetrated rural America, as well as the cities. The plethora of arts expanded America's cultural landscape.

The federal government and the arts

There were several federal arts programmes. Urged by his wife Eleanor, who felt that the arts should not be just for the elites, President Roosevelt supported the arts for another reason: it would employ a great many people. Initial involvement began with the Public Works of Art Project (PWAP) division of the CWA. A major focus was murals on public buildings such as schools, libraries and other public buildings. Artists were offered commissions first if they were on relief, and second for their skill. Artists included Thomas Hart Benton, Jackson Pollock and Grant Wood. The programme was short-lived, and ended when the CWA was abolished in 1934. The PWAP was followed by a painting and sculpture programme housed within the Treasury Department. Artists competed for funds. In the short life of the programme, upwards of 1000 works of arts were commissioned. In 1935 the Treasury Relief Art Programme (TRAP) was created. In response to complaints from the established arts community, TRAP focused less on relief and more on the skill of the artist, not adhering to the Works Progress Administration (WPA)'s standards. But TRAP continued the placement of art in public buildings, including a mural in at least one post office in every congressional district.

The most significant arts programme, Federal Project Number One, began under the auspices of the WPA, also in 1935. This programme was much larger than the previous arts programmes and encompassed many different fine arts including theatre, music and writing; it would also be involved with documenting local culture, along with gathering and organizing historical records. A year after Number One began, more than 40 000 people were employed in various projects across the country.

FPNO had a significant dramatic arts section that operated until 1939. Not only did it remove over 12 000 people from the relief rolls, but it established community theatre in communities, large and small, across the country. Ethnic production companies produced African American, French, German, Italian and Yiddish dramas. The projects even crossed into CCC camps. Joseph Cotton, Orson Welles and Burt Lancaster were among the participants. The visual arts section contributed more than 20 000 works of art, ranging from stained glass to sculpture, from artists such as Jacob Lawrence and Mark Rothko. Arts education was an important component of the Federal Arts Project with 100 arts centres that served millions. Writers such as Studs Terkel, Ralph Ellison and Margaret Walker were among the thousands of writers who wrote fiction, guidebooks to every state, and collected folklore. One of the most historically significant projects was the recording of narratives from former slaves. Additionally, artists created more than 2000 different posters to publicize theatrical and musical performances and on subjects such as health and safety, and education.

▲ 'Migrant Mother', Dorothea Lange's iconic photo of migrant farm workers

An unlikely agency, the Farm Services Administration (FSA), was the source of many of the iconic images of the Great Depression. The FSA hired scores of photographers, including some of the finest of the era: Esther Bubley, Walker Evans, Dorothea Lange and Gordon Parks are among the notables. They were sent out to document conditions for workers on the road, in camps and on farms. Dorothea Lange's 'Migrant Mother' portrait, for many the image of the displaced Dust Bowl farmer, is but one of thousands of photographs that the FSA used to tell the story of rural America.

Commercial arts

Popular art forms in the 1930s included movies, radio, music and literature. Two themes emerge: art that addressed the times, and art that allowed audiences to escape for a little while. Authors such as John Steinbeck, who portrayed the plight of migrant farmers in *The Grapes of Wrath* (1939), depicted the conditions in fiction. Richard Wright contributed essays, poetry and novels, and edited *The Left Front*, a Communist Party publication. Movies ranged from Frank Capra's *Mr Deeds Goes to Town* (1936), *Lost Horizon* (1937) and *Mr Smith Goes to Washington* (1939), to adventure films such as *Tarzan the Ape Man* (1932) and *Captains Courageous* (1937) to spectacularly choreographed Busby-Berkeley musicals. The end of the decade brought *Gone With the Wind* (1939) and *The Wizard of Oz* (1939). For the first time, radio penetrated rural areas and shows such as *The Lone Ranger*, *Superman* and *Dick Tracy*, and comedians Jack Benny and Burns and Allen filled the airways. Forms of music that continued into the 1930s, either as live acts or over the radio, included folk, blues and jazz. Folklorist John Lomax (also director of the ex-slave narrative project) made field recordings of thousands of songs, preserving examples of the various musical forms. Lomax wrote books, is often credited with discovering Lead Belly, and elevated folk music as an art form.

Despite the dire living conditions of millions of Americans, entertainment did not disappear. Commercial entertainment survived, and the federal government stepped in to create a role for the government that brought fine arts to millions of ordinary people and preserved vast amounts of Americana for future generations.

ATL Research skills

Choose a place in the USA – it can be a city, county or rural area – and investigate what was created in that location through the New Deal programmes.

New Mexico in the Great Depression and the New Deal projects

In 1930 the population of the entire state of New Mexico was just 423 000, yet the state was home to a number of New Deal projects. Of those, 203 remain and are under the stewardship of local organizations which aim to help preserve this legacy.

In 1930 there were 167 known artists in New Mexico, and the WPA Art Project allowed them to survive and continue their crafts. One such artist was Pablita Velarde from the Santa Clara Pueblo, whose works centred on pueblo life. One goal of WPA art was to preserve traditional forms, and in New Mexico that included the work of santeros – those who recreate traditional religious art.

The most high-profile projects were in Albuquerque on the campus of the University of New Mexico. Here, John Gaw Meem, the architect who would come to be associated with Pueblo Revival style, designed a number of buildings, including the Zimmerman Library. In it, a local artist in residence, Kenneth Adams, painted three murals to represent the different cultures in New Mexico: Native American, Spanish and Anglo, and the union of the three that made the state unique. These works are continuing reminders of the quality of workmanship of New Deal projects and are available to the general public.

▲ The Zimmerman Library at the University of New Mexico was a New Deal project designed by architect John Gaw Meem

▲ Kenneth Adams' 'Three Peoples' murals were painted in 1939 and decorate the interior of the Zimmerman Library

Conclusions

The desperation that North American politicians felt was unmatched. In the rest of the hemisphere, governments sought more radical, less democratic solutions to the Great Depression. Without a strong history of pluralism, countries other than the USA or Canada were willing to experiment with autocratic forms of government and economic models that borrowed freely from socialist and fascist systems.

In the southern hemisphere, the Great Depression had profound economic effects, but those are often overshadowed by the political changes that were brought about. While a number of countries recovered relatively quickly from the economic distress, it was under newly established military dictatorships and/or populist regimes that directed the economy and funneled money where they thought it would best serve the country.

Traditional, agricultural products continued to dominate the economies but the economic power of the landowners was waning, as a new urban elite emerged with the onset of ISI. The corporatist policy adopted in the 1930s by Brazil would become a popular model for developing countries to escape from economic dependence on the Western, industrialized nations. While ISI prevailed until the 1960s, its success would be challenged and argued by economists and historians alike.

Latin American political systems also shifted and the period was marked by authoritarianism. There were some exceptions to the rule, but from this point forward, military leadership was predominant in the region.

Ultimately, the aggressive policies of dictators in Europe and Asia led to war, which brought the Americas out of the Depression. Canada and the USA felt this most directly; their employment skyrocketed along with the demand for arms and other war-related goods. Latin America also profited as its resources were once again desired commodities. After over a decade of economic distress, the region recovered quickly, just as its countries prepared to enter the war.

Exam-style questions

1 Examine the claim that the Great Depression was caused by political rather than economic factors.

2 Compare and contrast the responses to the Great Depression of Herbert Hoover and Franklin D Roosevelt in the USA.

3 Evaluate the political impact of the Great Depression on the USA.

4 To what extent were RB Bennett's policies successful in ameliorating the effects of the Great Depression in Canada?

5 To what extent did the onset of the Great Depression lead to the collapse of democracy in any country in the region (excluding the USA and Canada)?

6 Analyse the impact of the Great Depression on the arts in one country in the Americas.

"To what extent…"

Question

To what extent did one country in the Americas (other than the US or Canada) respond successfully to the Great Depression between 1929 and 1941?

Analysis

As explained at the end of Chapter 1, "to what extent" implies that there are multiple sides to this question, which you should weigh up before formulating an answer. There is nothing wrong with a direct answer using the command phrase itself.

There is no magic response that will score better than any other one. You can argue completely on one side or another, or take the middle ground. It is important to acknowledge that there are different views, but your answer will depend on the evidence you use to advance your arguments. Different historians may use exactly the same evidence to advance different arguments, depending on what they choose to emphasize, and why.

To illustrate how you might answer this question, we will choose Brazil as the example of "one country". When brainstorming, you need to consider the following questions:

- How hard was Brazil hit by the Great Depression?
- What economic measures did the government take to deal with the Depression?
- How successful were these measures?
- What were the political consequences?
- What were the consequences for society and culture?

Once you have identified the different aspects of Brazil's response, you will see that there are multiple answers, all of which are accurate assessments:

1   Getulio Vargas was very successful in his response to the Depression, as evidenced by Brazil's economic recovery (diversification of crops, ISI, new trading partners).

2   To deal with the Great Depression, Vargas implemented a dictatorship limiting the rights of individuals that lasted until the end of the Second World War.

3   While there were general economic improvements, the rural majority of the population remained impoverished and did not benefit much from the policies.

4   The urban working classes saw improvements in their standards of living.

5   A number of social policies were implemented to benefit the urban poor.

6   The elite, landowning class became the elite, industrial class, with very little shift in class structure in Brazil.

Sample introductory paragraph

The Wall Street Crash in October 1929 led the way to an international depression that further depressed Brazil's already weakened economy. In an effort to protect their domestic economies, countries were forced to enact tariffs that led to an overall decline in international trade that affected Brazil's export-based economy. In addition, Brazil faced political unrest that led to the establishment of the populist dictatorship of Getulio Vargas. In an effort to battle the Depression, Vargas implemented numerous policies that were intended to move Brazil away from its dependence on coffee, such as crop diversification and Import Substitution Industrialization (ISI). These policies, along with the stabilization of coffee production, ameliorated the economic effects of the Depression and some income redistribution but at the cost of political freedom and unequal development of an economy that still relied on an underpaid, underrepresented majority of peasants.

1   Based on that introduction, how did the author prioritize the bullet points above?

2   Do you think there is sufficient support for this line of thinking?

3   What evidence would you use to support the thesis?

Now write a brief introduction, using the dos and don'ts in the previous Skills section to make a different argument.

4 THE SECOND WORLD WAR AND THE AMERICAS, 1933–45

Global context

It is with the engagement of the Americas that a world war truly came into being. Before this, there were two continental wars – one in Europe and one in Asia – and while there was some localized fighting in Africa and the participation of troops from all inhabited continents, this was due largely to colonial considerations. Thus, war raged in Europe and Asia, however the Americas were insulated from the effects of the war and most claimed neutrality.

Prior to 1939 in the Americas, countries were much more concerned with domestic issues and solving the grave economic problems brought on by the Great Depression, rather than examining the rise of authoritarianism in Europe and East Asia in the 1930s. While some mistake the rise of authoritarianism in Latin America as mimicking the Europeans, many countries in the region had a long tradition of *caudillismo* and were adapting economic and social policies that they thought could address the needs of their countries but they were suspicious of the motives of fascist groups in their countries.

In Brazil, Getúlio Vargas admired German and Italian economic policies yet he suppressed the fascist-like Integralist party in his consolidation of his own power. He was a populist dictator in his own right, and not reliant upon right-wing European rhetoric. Latin American responses to escalating conflict in Europe were based firmly on realpolitik – they took advantage of the circumstances to maximize their position as trading partners with European dictatorships and used Hitler (and to a lesser extent Mussolini) against traditional British and US trade to improve their international economic position.

For the most part, foreign relations were focused on the hemisphere in the 1930s as countries sought to improve relations as a response to the Great Depression. Even Canada, arguably the most European-oriented country in the region, was focused more on intercontinental relations and its main trading partner was the USA. Canada maintained close relations with the UK but it no longer dominated its foreign policies. In 1939, when the UK declared war, the Canadian parliament voted to do so as well, but Canadians did not participate as enthusiastically as they had in 1914. As we shall see, Canadian participation was very important to the British war effort, and the Canadians were very involved in the war.

The rest of the continent remained neutral, waiting to see what would happen. Even the onset of Operation Barbarossa did not change the non-interventionist orientation of the Americas. It was only the bombing of Pearl Harbor that jarred the region out of this perspective, and effectively changed the course of the war.

Timeline

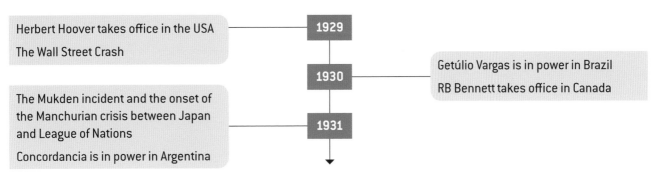

Herbert Hoover takes office in the USA
The Wall Street Crash

1929

1930

Getúlio Vargas is in power in Brazil
RB Bennett takes office in Canada

The Mukden incident and the onset of the Manchurian crisis between Japan and League of Nations

1931

Concordancia is in power in Argentina

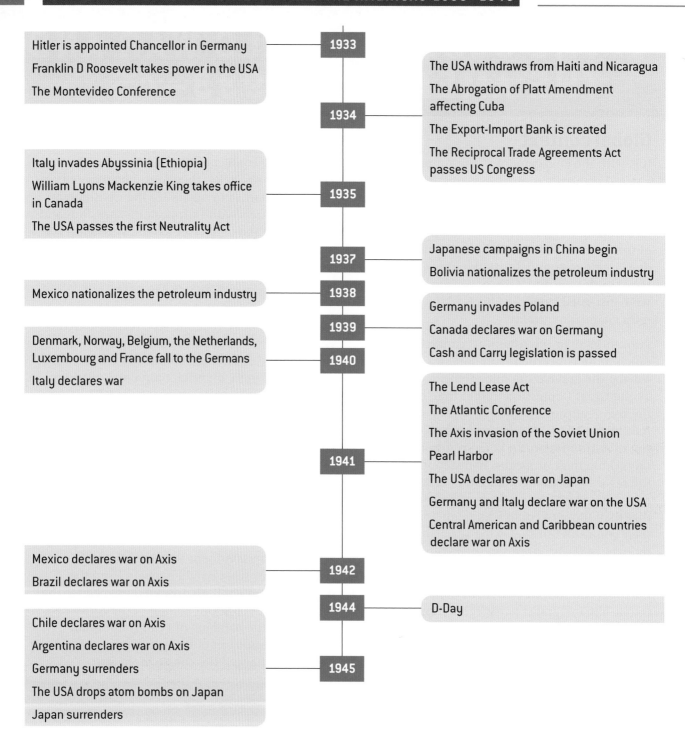

Hitler is appointed Chancellor in Germany Franklin D Roosevelt takes power in the USA The Montevideo Conference	**1933**
	1934	The USA withdraws from Haiti and Nicaragua The Abrogation of Platt Amendment affecting Cuba The Export-Import Bank is created The Reciprocal Trade Agreements Act passes US Congress
Italy invades Abyssinia (Ethiopia) William Lyons Mackenzie King takes office in Canada The USA passes the first Neutrality Act	**1935**
	1937	Japanese campaigns in China begin Bolivia nationalizes the petroleum industry
Mexico nationalizes the petroleum industry	**1938**
	1939	Germany invades Poland Canada declares war on Germany Cash and Carry legislation is passed
Denmark, Norway, Belgium, the Netherlands, Luxembourg and France fall to the Germans Italy declares war	**1940**
	1941	The Lend Lease Act The Atlantic Conference The Axis invasion of the Soviet Union Pearl Harbor The USA declares war on Japan Germany and Italy declare war on the USA Central American and Caribbean countries declare war on Axis
Mexico declares war on Axis Brazil declares war on Axis	**1942**
	1944	D-Day
Chile declares war on Axis Argentina declares war on Axis Germany surrenders The USA drops atom bombs on Japan Japan surrenders	**1945**

Key questions

→ Why did Franklin D Roosevelt implement the Good Neighbor policy after coming to power in 1933 and what were its effects for the Americas up to 1941?

→ How and why did Canada's role both in the Americas and as part of the Commonwealth change in the 1930s?

→ To what extent were the countries in the Americas (other than Canada) truly neutral up to 1941?

Key concepts

→ Causation

→ Consequences

Franklin D Roosevelt's Good Neighbor policy, its application and effects

US diplomacy in the Americas was centred around the Monroe Doctrine of 1823. The doctrine was first developed to prevent European powers from reasserting themselves in the region once countries achieved independence. The idea was further extended to mean that the USA would use military force, if necessary, to prevent European powers from reasserting themselves in the region but this corollary was used to justify US intervention in the region, especially in Central America and the Caribbean, during the early 20th century.

When Herbert Hoover took office in 1929 one of his goals was to improve the relationship between the USA and Latin America; he even embarked on a goodwill tour of Latin American countries immediately after the 1928 election. However, the Wall Street Crash and subsequent Great Depression altered his course. Instead of improving hemispheric relations, they were damaged by the implementation of the **Smoot-Hawley Tariff Act** of 1930.

> **Smoot-Hawley Tariff Act**
> US law enacted in June 1930 that raised import duties on over 20 000 goods to protect US agriculture and industry from the effects of the Great Depression.

Franklin D Roosevelt concurred with Hoover's opinion on Latin America and was determined to improve relations with the countries south of the border – a position he made clear in a 1932 article he published in the journal *Foreign Affairs*. In his inaugural address on 4 March 1933 Roosevelt articulated his desire that the USA would become a 'good neighbor', thereby launching the eponymous policy. Concretely, it meant that the USA would not intervene unilaterally in the affairs of other states in the Americas. Initially, the political leadership in Latin America was doubtful, but the actions of the US Secretary of State Cordell Hull bore out Roosevelt's stated intentions.

In December 1933 at the Seventh International Conference of American States, the USA declared the Good Neighbor policy operational. By its terms, no sovereign state in the region had the right to intervene in the affairs of other sovereign states. Although it was stated in general terms, it was really a sign from the USA to the rest of the region that the USA would not intervene militarily in other countries. The Montevideo Convention on the Rights and Duties of States was signed by 19 countries in the Americas, and asserted their sovereignty. It went into effect in 1934, advocating a position of non-interference, with Hull stating 'no government need fear any intervention on the part of the US'. Demonstrating that the USA would uphold the terms of the convention, it withdrew the US marines from Haiti and Nicaragua and **abrogated** the Platt Amendment, giving Cuba a free hand in its own domestic affairs. Even when a military junta under the government of Ramón Grau San Martín came to power after a coup, the USA pursued a policy of non-recognition, rather than its traditional action of sending in the marines to facilitate a change in government. It appeared that the USA had changed its course.

abrogate
To repeal or do away with, usually in reference to laws.

The intentions of the Good Neighbor policy were further strengthened in the 1936 Buenos Aires Conference where it was explicitly stated that force would not be used for the protection of property or citizens abroad. To the consternation of US business interests, its citizens and investments had to adhere to laws of the host countries. Argentina and Mexico in particular were insistent that the Americas not be driven by US interests or agendas, openly challenging US dominance. In response, the USA agreed that it could not act unilaterally in affairs in the Americas or dictate inter-American policy.

This Buenos Aires Convention was very controversial in the USA where business interests felt threatened. The USA held $5 billion in investments in Latin America ($1.5 billion in portfolio, $3.5 billion in direct investment) including $1.5 billion in Cuba alone. Thus, the question of the defence of US economic interests was raised. The government response was that US intervention to defend these '[w]ould not constitute intervention in internal affairs of another state. It would be simply a matter of protection'. This was seen as a potential threat to US agreements of non-interference, but the USA chose to use diplomatic pressure – including the tactic of diplomatic non-recognition – rather than use of force, as in the case of Cuba.

US non-intervention was welcomed but the other countries had a more complicated agenda: they desired easy access to US markets and were hoping that the Montevideo Convention would lead to an improvement in this area. To this end, the US government established the Export-Import Bank to facilitate commercial loans to companies that imported goods from the USA. It also passed the Reciprocal Trade Agreements Act which allowed the government to negotiate bilateral agreements that would reduce tariffs and therefore negate the damaging effects of Smoot-Hawley. It recognized that the USA largely imported raw materials in the form of minerals for manufacturing and non-competitive foods (bananas, cacao and coffee); since the USA did not produce the desired commodities, the tariffs were mutually disadvantageous. Brazil was one of the countries that benefited the most from these tariff revisions. In 1935 a reciprocal trade agreement placed 90% of Brazilian exports on the duty-free list; it became the fifth largest supplier to the USA.

As a result of this series of agreements, by 1938 the USA was the main trading partner for all independent countries in the region except Argentina, which had agreements with the UK and saw its future aligned more to Europe than to the region. This was particularly surprising as Germany wanted to improve its trade relations with the region and its trade with Brazil doubled between 1933 and 1938. However, the Germans paid in 'compensation marks' which could only be used to purchase German goods, so the income was less desirable than income that yielded fully convertible US dollars.

There were definite benefits to the economic agreements, but they had the unintended consequence of binding these countries' economies to the USA. Regional economies were increasingly reliant on the US market, which led to serious complications after the Second World War.

One area of conflict between the USA and Latin America arose in the 1930s – oil. Bolivia and Mexico were oil-rich countries but the concessions were owned by foreign nationals. This was a potential source of extraordinary income for these countries, and Bolivia and Mexico in turn challenged foreign ownership. First, in March 1937, Bolivia confiscated the properties of Standard Oil Company. According to the Bolivian government, Standard Oil committed illegal actions by selling its oil to Argentina, thereby cancelling its agreement with the Bolivian government. Since this was a cancellation, and not an **expropriation**, Bolivia argued that it did not have to compensate Standard Oil for its losses. To put pressure on Bolivia, it was denied loans from the Export-Import Bank and negotiations lasted over three years. In 1940, with Europe and Asia at war, the USA was much more willing to concede, and an agreement was reached in which Standard Oil received $1.5 million for the sale of the company to Bolivia.

In March 1938 the Mexican government announced the expropriation of US, Dutch and British oil companies after months of labour disputes and court cases regarding the treatment of Mexican nationals by foreign oil companies. Bowing to domestic pressure, US Secretary of State Cordell Hull accused Mexico of violating international law, demanded immediate compensation for US companies and implicitly threatened US intervention. However, Roosevelt had made it clear that US intervention would not occur, so Mexico chose not to respond to the veiled ultimatum and instead proceeded with negotiations as if it had not happened. At that time, Mexico was refused loans from the Export-Import Bank and the USA terminated a long-standing agreement to purchase 5 million ounces of silver per month; it later recanted and purchased the silver on a day-to-day basis (due to the needs of the US Treasury). US business interests boycotted Mexican oil, but rather than force the Mexican government to settle, this led to an agreement with the Axis powers. Urgency to come to an agreement intensified with the onset of war in Europe; the final straw for the USA was the fall of France in June 1940. It then agreed to a $24 million payment from Mexico plus 3% interest, for a total of $29 million.

The willingness of the USA to negotiate with Bolivia and Mexico was indicative of a shift in the Good Neighbor policy due to the onset of war in Asia and Europe. Between 1939 and 1941 the USA would return to the idea of hemispheric solidarity, more in terms of military assistance than economic.

expropriation
An action in which the state takes possession of private property.

191

There was also a strong cultural component of the Good Neighbor policy. Throughout the 1930s government agencies were devoted to promoting a positive portrayal of the USA throughout the Americas. Passenger lines to South America were developed that sailed from New York to Argentina, Brazil and Uruguay to establish cultural understanding. Motion pictures, radio and the press in the USA were all encouraged to showcase Latin American culture to further the Good Neighbor agenda. Even the 1939 World's Fair in New York was an instrument to highlight unity, and many of the countries in the Pan-American Union sent delegations. This only intensified when war broke out in Europe and the USA sought to negate the growth of what was seen as a pro-Axis position in Latin America.

The results of the Good Neighbor policy until 1939 are viewed as mixed by historians and politicians. Peter Smith refers to this as a 'golden era of US relations with Latin America', while others see it as a way for the USA to maintain regional dominance through diplomatic and economic pressure. In the midst of the Great Depression, the USA could reduce its military costs through withdrawal of troops.

Those who see it as positive feel that the economic cooperation of the 1930s promoted stability and put countries on the road to stable democracies. However, this ignores the number of dictatorships that developed during the Good Neighbor era; by August 1939 Cuba, the Dominican Republic, El Salvador, Guatemala and Nicaragua all fell to dictators and the authoritarian regimes in Argentina and Brazil persevered, leading the Peruvian reformist Victor Raúl Haya de la Torre to call the USA 'the good neighbor of tyrants'.

▲ A meeting of the Pan-American Union

Canada's inter-Americas diplomacy

Most of the focus of inter-Americas diplomacy is on the Good Neighbor policy and its effect in the region, but that focus ignores Canada and its relations with the other states in the hemisphere. Historically, Canada's foreign relations were subordinate to the UK and it only had five diplomatic **legations** prior to the 1930s. However, Canada's position within the empire began to change during the First World War and autonomy regarding diplomatic affairs evolved in the inter-war period.

The defining moment for this change was in April 1917 at the Battle of Vimy Ridge. Canadian divisions representing all of Canada and commanded by Lieutenant-General Sir Arthur Currie, a Canadian, overran the Germans and took this strategically important site. While there were more definitive battles involving the Canadian corps, Vimy Ridge is representative of the birth of Canadian national unity and separation from the empire. As a result of its performance in the war, Canada was awarded its own seat in the Paris Peace Conference and, later, in the League of Nations. In the 1920s Canada began to take responsibility for its own foreign and military affairs. In 1931 this increase in autonomy was formally recognized by the British with the Statute of Westminster in which Canada along with Australia, New Zealand, the Irish Free State, South Africa and Newfoundland were 'fully independent dominions equal in status to but closely associated with the mother country as part of the British Commonwealth of Nations'. From this point forward, laws passed by the British parliament did not apply to Canada and it could pursue its own independent foreign policy.

At the same time, there was an economic shift in Canada where the USA began to replace the UK as its primary trading partner. This shift was logical; it was much less expensive to engage in trade with a contiguous country, and Canada had necessary resources while the USA provided relatively inexpensive manufactured goods. Canadians traditionally feared US encroachment and even cross-border conflict but this sentiment waned in the 1920s and in 1927 Canada sent its first ambassador to the USA, William Phillips.

These positive relations were negated by the onset of the Great Depression and the Smoot-Hawley Tariff. Canada retaliated with its own tariffs and US–Canadian trade fell by 75%. Prime Minister William Lyons Mackenzie King understood the need to improve trade relations and Canada signed the Reciprocal Trade Agreement with the USA in 1935 to regain US trade and ameliorate the harsh effect of the Smoot-Hawley Tariff in USA–Canada trade. Once again, the relations between the two countries began to improve.

Canada also had an interest in hemispheric relations that went beyond the USA, and it tried to improve its ties with Latin America and the Caribbean. In the 19th century there had been economic relations with other imperial possessions in the Caribbean, and Mexico and Brazil but Canada had little latitude to act due to British imperial policies. When the Pan-American Union was formed only the USA opposed Canadian membership, fearing that it would represent British colonial interests, in violation of the Monroe Doctrine and against the goals of the Union.

legation
A diplomatic representation lower than an embassy.

The USA's argument was that Canada was neither independent nor a republic, and was therefore ineligible for membership.

In the 1930s, during the Good Neighbor tenure, Canada made a series of trade agreements with South American countries and even became Argentina's third-largest trading partner, despite competing for grain markets. There were Canadian investments in the fields of insurance and infrastructure development but this was not significant; roughly 2–3% of Canadian world trade was with Latin America and Canada remained loyal – and deferential – to British interests in the region.

In the late 1930s, given the improved economic relations in the hemisphere, and attempts to establish political and social solidarity, proposals were advanced to create an inter-American economic cartel, but these had to be quashed due to the implications for East Asia. Solidarity was at its high point when events in Asia and Europe intervened, changing the course of hemispheric relations.

Hemispheric reactions to the events in Europe and Asia

In the midst of the Great Depression most states were focused on their internal affairs and concerned themselves with foreign policies mostly when it might help alleviate the suffering of their people. European countries initially diminished their trade with the region as they imposed taxes to benefit their national businesses. With the Great Depression, however, extremism intensified and in both Europe and Asia the establishment of authoritarian regimes was accompanied by increased militarism and aggression. Despite attempts to remain aloof from such events the USA and Canada were drawn into the crises of the 1930s. As members of the League of Nations, 15 countries in the Americas voted on these issues. Despite its non-membership in the League of Nations, the USA had a profound effect on League decision-making; as it was not bound by League decisions, all agreements within the organization had to weigh the League's position against the impact that the USA could have.

In September 1931 a section of the Japanese-controlled Southern Manchurian Railway track was damaged in an explosion that the Japanese military then used as a pretext to invade Manchuria and occupy the resource-rich area. Despite its reputation as isolationist, one of the first countries to complain was the USA, which refused to recognize Manchuria as a Japanese territory. US policy remained focused on registering diplomatic disapproval and non-recognition in the hopes of reversing what it saw as an illegitimate action but the Japanese did not respond, and went about consolidating their control over Manchuria.

As members of the League of Nations, member states in the region found themselves drawn into the dispute between two League countries. In December 1931 the League established the Lytton Commission to investigate the causes and determine whether Japan was indeed guilty of aggression. Surprisingly, the USA appointed General Frank McCoy to serve on the commission even though it was not a member of the League. Not surprisingly, the Lytton Commission found Japan guilty of aggression and the next step was to determine what actions to take.

In the USA, President Herbert Hoover believed that economic sanctions would lead to war, and counselled moral condemnation and international pressure rather than overt actions. His position, however, became irrelevant as the League's decision-making was delayed until 1933. It would fall to Roosevelt and Secretary of State Hull to influence a decision. The League made its decision and upheld the commission's condemnation of the action but would not go as far as imposing economic sanctions against Japan; in this decision, the USA and Canada were both important.

Most of the League countries were unwilling to impose economic sanctions on Japan, largely due to the USA's non-membership. In their estimation they would be risking the already tenuous economic health of their countries and potentially give the USA a free hand in East Asia. Additionally, the UK had numerous territories in East Asia and was afraid that economic sanctions might lead to retaliation on the part of the Japanese, and in the worst case, war in East Asia against Japan. However, the British were not certain how publicly they could state their case, and enlisted the assistance of the Canadian delegate and Secretary of State Charles Cahan, who gave a speech that accepted the recommendations of the Lytton Commission but sounded pro-Japanese and in line with conciliation with Japan.

Cahan's speech seemed out of step with the stated Canadian position, but in reality it illustrated it well: Canada was torn between the USA and the UK. While the foreign policy of RB Bennett was focused on the Commonwealth (he thought that Canada should not have a foreign policy separate from the British one), he was also aware of the importance of the USA to Canadian affairs. Cahan tried to straddle both positions and failed, but in the end, his speech led to direct dealings between London and Bennett. The British position of conciliation contrasted with the US position of moral condemnation and non-recognition. The British soon felt that conciliation was impossible and supported the findings of the Lytton Commission; with other members of the League, they condemned Japanese aggression in accordance with the USA's findings. This response did nothing to reverse Japanese actions and in March 1933 Japan withdrew from the League. This was the beginning of the end for the League and it marked a shift in US foreign policy.

When Hitler was appointed Chancellor in Germany, the response in the Americas was mixed. There was no clear consensus in any one country; some saw him as Germany's saviour and sought to imitate his brand of nationalism through their own populist movements. This was much more prominent in countries with large German immigrant populations, but his ideas found some support throughout the Americas. On the other side were those who feared his racial policies and authoritarian control – President Roosevelt fell into this category – and still others saw policies they could borrow and use to their advantage – such as Getúlio Vargas. Most people waited to see how he implemented his policies and ideas, and there was growing discomfort with his methods even as there was admiration at Germany's apparent recovery.

In 1935 the US Congress bowed to public pressure and passed the first of a series of Neutrality Acts consistent with the traditional US fear of foreign entanglements. The 1935 act specified that the USA would not sell arms or war materials with any country involved in war. This was the first of a series of acts that had expiration dates; it was renewed in 1936, 1937 and 1939 with further provisions attached.

Roosevelt first invoked the act with the Italian invasion of Ethiopia, the action that would deal a death blow to the League. When Italy declared war and invaded Ethiopia, the USA prevented arms and ammunitions sales to both countries.

Canada was divided on the issue: Ottowa instructed its representative to abstain in a decision of condemnation but the delegates were appalled by this – it would put them in the same camp as Austria and Hungary, making it appear pro-fascist. Instead, the delegation worked within the framework of the Commonwealth and volunteered to work on a committee to determine sanctions, expressly against Ottowa's instructions. Shortly thereafter, Bennett's government was defeated. After the election on 15 October 1935 newly re-elected Prime Minister Mackenzie King made arrangements to meet with President Roosevelt to determine the US position on the war. Walter Riddell, Canada's representative to the League, urged sanctions, and although King agreed he felt that condemnation had to be accompanied by some action demonstrating the strength of the opinion – but once again Canada was caught between the US and British positions. Riddell's perspective was more aligned with the British while the US view counselled restraint.

Shortly thereafter, civil war erupted in Spain. Most official government policies were clear: this was an internal matter to be determined by the Spaniards themselves and the USA invoked the Neutrality Act. However, US businesses worked overtly with the nationalists, most notably the Texas Oil Company (Texaco) which supplied gas on credit to Franco.

Mexico was the only country in the region to participate actively in the Spanish Civil War: the Cárdenas government supported the Republicans against Franco's forces, but this was more important in terms of morale, rather than strategic or economic assistance – its $2 million and negligible resources comforted the Republicans but did not help with victory. Most Latin American countries and the US territory of Puerto Rico were sympathetic with the nationalists but maintained an officially neutral position.

When conflict erupted again in Asia, Roosevelt decided he would not implement the Neutrality Act. It had been further expanded in 1937 but Roosevelt was sympathetic to the nationalist (Guomindang) government of China and did not want to limit its ability to purchase US arms. Since there was no formal declaration of war in the Japanese campaigns in China, this was possible. US neutrality was increasingly questioned by US isolationists as it was clear that Roosevelt had preferences and was seeking to pass legislation that would benefit the countries he supported.

One of the reasons that Ottowa was ambivalent in determining whether its primary loyalty was to the USA or the UK was that the USA took a much stronger stance against German aggression than the UK. When Roosevelt was visiting Kingston, Ontario in 1938 he gave a speech in which he stated that the USA would be willing to defend Canada to defend itself, and that it did not see Canada as a threat to US security in any way. This willingness to defend Canada concerned nationalists who worried that the USA might set its sights on the country to its north, but many Canadians were reassured that the USA could be relied upon as a potential ally.

Roosevelt was increasingly on the side of intervention but appeasement became the prevailing policy throughout the world. The Munich conference of September 1938 was hailed as a success for appeasement and war was avoided over the central European country of Czechoslovakia. British Prime Minister Neville Chamberlain appeared to be a hero for those interested in peace and his determination to solve disputes without war looked successful until the March 1939 occupation of the remainder of Czechoslovakia. The world was horrified as Germany established a protectorate in the Czech regions of Bohemia and Moravia, and Slovakia became a satellite state. In response Roosevelt sent a telegram to Hitler in April 1939 demanding that he not invade a series of countries which Hitler used to his advantage by reading it aloud to his government, making Roosevelt's demand sound silly rather than serious. Roosevelt appealed to the US Congress once again, once again unsuccessfully.

On 1 September 1939 Germany invaded Poland. France and the UK had guaranteed Poland so they declared war on Germany and began to mobilize, but they were unprepared for combat and Germany rolled through Poland, only stopping when the Soviets also launched their attack and took the eastern section of Poland. Hemispheric responses were somewhat divided, but it was clear that most of the region was anti-Axis even if neutrality was maintained. Canada was the exception and shortly entered the war against Germany.

Canada at war, 1939–41

In 1939 there was still a sense of loyalty to the British and with the invasion of Poland, Canada's participation seemed a foregone conclusion, but with the Westminster Statute the decision was Canada's to make. The decision to enter the war occurred only after debate and vote in the Canadian parliament and, on 10 September 1939, Canada declared war on Germany – its first independent declaration of war.

The Canadian army was poorly equipped and small; in the face of economic depression military spending was very unpopular. The Munich crisis precipitated an increase in spending and in the year before the declaration of war, military spending nearly doubled, and then nearly doubled again in the following year: by 1940 the defence budget was $64.3 million. Half of that went to the Royal Canadian Air Force (RCAF); in December 1939 the British Commonwealth Air Training Force was established, because the British Isles were vulnerable to enemy attack. In addition to establishing a training site in Canada, it called for the training of 13 000 Canadian airmen per year. All Commonwealth airmen received elementary training in their home countries before transferring to Canada for advanced training. Throughout the course of the war Australians, New Zealanders, South Africans, Southern Rhodesians and Americans received training in Canada.

These forces were important in the Battle of Britain when Germany launched its aerial offensive on the UK in July 1940. Canada was among the 13 countries that also sent pilots that flew missions to protect the

▲ Canadian bomber squadron, 1941

island. The 7th British Army Corps consisted of Canadian, New Zealand and British troops. It planned a counter-offensive against the Luftwaffe and helped in the victory over the Germans. In October 1940 the Germans abandoned their aerial battle and instead began the Blitz – night raids on civilian areas designed to undermine British morale.

Canada's Navy also rose to prominence during the war. When German offensives in spring 1940 caused the defeat of most of western Europe, the Battle of the Atlantic became critical. From this point the British were reliant on supplies from overseas and Canada's small Navy was made responsible for patrolling the north Atlantic for German ships and submarines and was instrumental in protecting convoys as they crossed the ocean. Canadian naval construction was expanded to meet the need of the battle.

Hemispheric neutrality 1939–41

Although the USA hoped to remain aloof from the aggressive actions unfolding throughout the war, Roosevelt recognized the need for self-defence and in the 1930s requested from Congress $1 billion for defence and the development of a two-ocean navy. As New Deal policies were being cut back as too costly, even the most isolationist politicians saw the importance of a strong military.

The invasion of Poland further demonstrated the dangers of authoritarian expansion so once again Roosevelt approached Congress with the intention of altering the Neutrality Act that lapsed in May 1939. He presented neutrality as a dilemma that could indirectly assist the aggressive powers, just as neutrality in the Spanish Civil War assisted Franco against the legitimate Republican government. After much discussion the policy of 'cash and carry' was implemented. It allowed the sale of arms to belligerent countries as long as the recipients arranged the transportation themselves and paid cash for the armaments. This prevented Germany, which was cash poor, from purchasing arms from US businesses while assisting the French and British in obtaining weapons. Additionally, US ships and citizens were prohibited from entering war zones.

After rolling rapidly through Eastern Europe, in the winter of 1939–40 activity was so limited that US journalists often referred to the war as the 'phoney war'. This changed in April 1940 when once again the Germans launched their offensives, taking Denmark, Norway, Belgium, the Netherlands and Luxembourg, and attacking France. As a result of the Norwegian defeat, the British government fell and Chamberlain was replaced by Winston Churchill and a war cabinet. In June 1940, French forces surrendered; France was divided – the northern and coastal region was occupied territory while the south and east became the collaborationist government with its capital in Vichy. Spain, Switzerland and Sweden were officially neutral and had economic agreements with the Axis to protect their neutrality. The UK was now alone against Germany in Europe, reliant on its colonies and the Commonwealth countries for assistance.

The British maintained trade relations with the Americas and ships were constantly crossing the Atlantic to facilitate this trade, not just in war materials but in all commodities. German submarines patrolled the Atlantic, hoping to prevent this from continuing, torpedoing any ship they thought was engaged in trade with its enemy; as a result a number of US, Mexican and Brazilian vessels were damaged or sunk, but neutrality remained the prevailing policy. Latin America was ambivalent – Germany had helped a number of countries out of the Great Depression through trade, and still others (such as Peru) had engaged German officers to help train their own troops. There was discomfort with the brutality of the regime, but the Nazis were also admired. Like the USA, at this time the Latin American countries found it was most favourable to maintain a neutral position regarding the war in Europe.

In 1940 Roosevelt broke with tradition by running for an unprecedented third term in office. He soundly defeated his opponent, Wendell Wilkie, even though the Revenue Act of 1940 raised the debt ceiling to $4 billion and the Select Service Act began the first peacetime draft (conscription) in US history. Americans were clearly afraid of being unprotected in the event of war.

Shortly after the election, Churchill wrote to Roosevelt and informed him that the British could no longer afford to pay for war materials and requested assistance. To address British needs, Roosevelt developed what came to be known as Lend Lease Aid, a programme by which the USA would lend or lease equipment to the British in their fight against the Germans. It was approved by Congress in March 1941 and $7 billion was allocated to begin the programme. This act stipulated that the US could sell, lease, loan, or transfer war materials to any country that the president determined was critical to US interests.

There was some concern that Canada would lose out economically due to Lend Lease, so the Americans and Canadians worked together to create a programme that benefited both countries while helping out the British. The Hyde Park Declaration, signed by Mackenzie King and Roosevelt, allowed US war materials that were made in Canada to be included in Lend Lease Aid. Although Canada only received $20.3 million from this agreement, it created a triangular agreement with Canada emerging as a junior partner in the Grand Alliance that had significant political ramifications after the war.

Lend Lease Aid to the Allies eventually totaled $50 billion, and while the majority went to the UK, the Soviet Union, China and France, Latin America also benefited. The belligerence in Asia and Europe solidified the concept of hemispheric solidarity, and the USA saw Latin America and the Caribbean as critical to its defence. With the fall of France and the Netherlands, a decision of the **Pan-American Union** stated that, in adherence to the Monroe Doctrine, Dutch and French colonial possessions in the region would not be recognized as Axis possessions. Only Argentina dissented, afraid that the US would use this as an excuse to annex these territories. Furthermore, the outbreak of war was the critical reason that the USA became amenable to solving the petroleum disputes with Bolivia and Mexico in 1940.

In 1940 Roosevelt created the Office of the Coordinator of Inter-American Affairs (CIAA) to further promote hemispheric solidarity and prevent or end Axis espionage in the region by emphasizing inter-American relations. The CIAA had departments dedicated to motion pictures, radio, journalism and museum displays. On the political side, the CIAA

Pan-American Union
An organization of American republics dedicated to peace and understanding founded in 1890.

199

emphasized an inter-American heritage of independence and democracy (ignoring the proliferation of dictatorships of the time). Culturally, the CIAA sought to find common ground and create the idea of a common Americas way of life, distinct from the European, fascist one. Citizens in the USA were presented with sympathetic, identifiable neighbours to the south, and the USA was presented as open and egalitarian. The CIAA targeted Brazil, with large Japanese and German populations, and Argentina and Chile – also with large German populations but also pro-fascist proclivities.

The cultural component of the Good Neighbor policy was more effective at home than the US government realized – while most Americans remained isolationist regarding the war in Europe, a majority believed that Latin America must be defended in the event of an Atlantic attack. In a series of public opinion polls in 1940, 72% of Americans thought that Cuba should be defended and 53% were willing to send troops to defend 'Brazil, Chile or any South American country'; however, a mere 17% were willing to do so to defend the UK.

One other aspect of solidarity was economic; war in Europe also meant an end to Latin American trade with Europe. Argentina and Brazil also established Import Substitution Industrialization (ISI) and could absorb some of these losses but the majority of countries had to turn to the USA for both import and export trade. Manufactured goods now came almost exclusively from the USA although Canada also benefited somewhat. The USA also needed raw materials from Latin America due to the war. Copper from Chile, cotton from Peru, oil from Mexico, Bolivia and Venezuela, and platinum from Colombia were all necessary for the war effort and the USA often made agreements to buy at above-market values, but this was temporary. Once the USA became involved in war, shipping became more difficult, and US goods were more difficult to obtain, driving prices up. The net result for most of Latin America was inflation, but there was also growth and economies stayed afloat.

Military assistance was also forthcoming, especially for those countries seen as important to regional defence. Brazil, Panama, Cuba and Mexico, at least initially, were courted. Brazil in particular benefited: US air bases were built in Natal to provide a southern defence force; its ports were used to patrol the Atlantic between US and African shores; and Brazil eventually received one of the largest portions of lend lease arms assistance. Colombia, the Dominican Republic and Ecuador, gatekeepers to the Panama Canal, received funds to modernize and enlarge their militaries, with most of them emphasizing their air forces.

The anti-Axis position of the USA was further established in the summer of 1941 by the extension of Lend Lease assistance to the Soviet Union and the Atlantic Charter, an Anglo-American statement of eight global principles agreed upon by Churchill and Roosevelt. Although most of the principles were general statements opposing military aggression to make political or territorial changes, the sixth objective explicitly sought 'the final destruction of … Nazi tyranny'.

Still, the USA maintained neutrality and did not enter the war. It was aggression against its military (as opposed to its civilian) vessels that propelled the USA, and then the rest of the hemisphere, into war.

Pearl Harbor and its aftermath

Japanese aggression continued largely unchecked in East Asia. In 1940 Japan signed an agreement with Vichy France that allowed it to establish military bases in Indochina. The Dutch East Indies were occupied; independent Thailand was officially neutral; and British and US possessions were vulnerable. Japan was surprised, however, when the USA renounced the 1911 Japanese–American Commercial Treaty in July 1941 and stopped the shipment of steel and scrap iron to countries outside of the western hemisphere except for the UK. This was considered an aggressive act by the Japanese who received half of all oil, iron and steel from the USA.

The Japanese responded by offering diplomatic concessions: they promised neutrality if the USA went to war with Germany and Italy, and promised not to attack the Soviet Union. However, the USA demanded withdrawal from China, which was unthinkable to the Japanese, who in turn demanded that the USA cease aiding the nationalist government of Chiang Kai-shek. After months of negotiations, the Japanese determined that it was a fruitless course and planned a pre-emptive strike against the USA.

On 20 November 1941 the Japanese Navy dispatched aircraft carriers to Hawaii, maintaining radio silence until they reached their destination. On 7 December (8 December in Japan) Japanese bombers took the US naval base at Pearl Harbor by surprise and attacked. The results were devastating. It was Sunday morning so there was little activity and most of the ships were docked: 19 ships were sunk or damaged, including all 8 battleships; 188 airplanes were destroyed and 2471 people were killed. This was followed in quick succession by attacks on Guam, Midway Island and the Philippines. On 8 December 1941, after approval from Congress, the USA declared war on Japan. On 11 December Germany and Italy declared war on the USA in compliance with the terms of the Tripartite Pact.

After the USA declared war, all nine independent Central American and Caribbean countries followed suit while Colombia, Venezuela and Mexico immediately severed ties with the Axis powers. In January 1942 the Pan-American Union held a conference of foreign ministers in Rio de Janeiro. Here they reaffirmed the concept of hemispheric solidarity and passed a resolution to sever ties with the Axis powers. All but Argentina and Chile complied. The German response was to target not just US but Mexican and Brazilian vessels. Mexico declared war in May 1942 and by August 1942 the Germans had sunk 18 Brazilian ships, including five between August 15 and August 17. This led directly to a Brazilian declaration of war on 22 August, Brazilian participation in the Battle of the Atlantic and the development of the Brazilian expeditionary force, which sent ground troops to Italy and dispatched over 25 000 Brazilians to Europe.

Chile was in the middle of presidential elections and did not want to alienate its substantial German population. Additionally, it feared attacks on its lengthy coastline by Japanese or German vessels if it complied with this agreement, and argued that the USA lacked the strength to defend the entire Pacific after Pearl Harbor. The Germans and Japanese used Santiago as an important espionage site in the Americas, a fact that infuriated the USA. Although they knew that Nazi cells existed, US counter-intelligence was undeveloped and uncoordinated at the very least. By late 1942 the USA began to intercept messages from Berlin and Tokyo, and put pressure on the Chilean government to oust the spies, leading to the deportation of three German nationals.

Allied successes in the Pacific and North Africa were more effective in ending Chilean neutrality however, and hostile German actions in the southern Atlantic pushed Chile increasingly towards the Allies. After Brazil declared war Chile relaxed its interpretation of neutrality and allowed its ships in port to take on cargo – an action already granted to the USA and Mexico. In 1943 Chile finally adhered to the terms of the Rio Declaration, and while it severed ties with the Axis, it did not declare war and in fact Axis espionage continued flagrantly despite attempts to halt it. Chile only declared war in February 1945, when Allied victory was assured and the USA threatened to block Chilean membership in the newly created United Nations.

The final holdout was Argentina, a country with a response to war far more complicated than is often portrayed. While it was true that Argentina was firmly pro-Axis and its government bore similarities to the fascist regimes of Franco and Mussolini, the choice was not simply ideological. Throughout the 1930s Argentina was the country that expressed the greatest fear of US domination of the region and did not want to bow to US pressure. Even a US boycott of Argentine goods was unsuccessful in swaying the government's view. In 1943 Ramón Castillo, the leader of the government, died. This was followed by a military coup. Allied countries severed diplomatic ties, putting pressure on Argentina to end its neutrality. Juan Perón, the politically astute, pragmatic general, consolidated power in 1944 and maintained neutrality to maintain support of both pro-Nazi and pro-Allied forces within Argentina. However, economic necessities prevailed and Perón saw the wisdom in re-establishing ties with the USA. In March 1945 Argentina was the last country in the Americas to declare war on the Axis.

Class discussion

US foreign policies prior to Pearl Harbor are discussed in very different terms by different constituencies. Do you think that the USA was isolationist between 1933 and 1941? Why or why not? Write a one-page defence of your position. You must choose one side or the other – you cannot take the middle ground.

4.2 Involvement and participation of Canada and Mexico in the Second World War

Conceptual understanding

Key question

→ Why and with what results did Mexico and Canada participate in the Second World War?

Key concept

→ Significance

All independent countries in the Americas declared war on the Axis powers but only four sent military forces into battle. Canada was involved from the beginning, but the USA, Mexico and Brazil only declared war when they themselves were attacked by Axis forces. By the end of 1942 these four countries had committed troops and undergone training to fight enemy forces, but their effect on the course and outcome of the war were dramatically different. While Canadian and US forces were critical to Allied success, the results for Brazil and Mexico were more profound domestically.

Canada

Canada had one of the largest participation rates of any country in the Second World War. With a population of only 12 million, 1 million Canadian citizens served in the military, and by the end of the war Canada possessed the fourth-largest surface fleet and third-largest air force in the world. The RCAF's role in training Commonwealth airmen was important not just in the Battle of Britain but in most of the bombing campaigns in Europe, and it provided support in Asia. Canadian forces participated in many major offensives of the war, initially in Europe, but as the war widened, they were also present in the Asian battles.

Due to the successes of Canadian participation it is easy to forget that the Canadians were unprepared for war in 1939. Most of Canada's equipment was outdated, and the regular army consisted of only 45 000 men. There were over 50 000 reservists to call up for service, but this was still a very small force. This war was not nearly as popular as the First World War, so Canadian soldiers were initially given the option to remain in Canada as part of the National Defence Force or go to Europe.

Canada's participation in the war furthered the idea of *Canadianization*: the Canadian military would fight with the British, but in its own army, navy and air force units, with its own leadership. In the early stages of war, the army remained a volunteer army: the conscription crisis of 1916 still resonated throughout the country so King held off with conscription as long as possible. Even with a volunteer army, 250 000 men and 2000 women enlisted by 1941, most coming from 'English Canada'. Once again, the Quebecois were reluctant to be embroiled in a war in Europe.

Battle of the Atlantic

The Battle of the Atlantic was launched by the Germans to prevent the UK from receiving imports. After the rest of Europe was knocked out of the war, the Germans focused their submarine forces on this battle in an attempt to create shortages and discomfort in the UK so that public opinion would turn against the war and force British politicians to negotiate a peace settlement with the Axis. The British were determined to withstand this pressure even though the population was stretched thin, and Canada became critical to British survival. The Canadian Navy began a process of rapid modernization and development of its fleet so that it could assist the British. The Canadian Navy began the war with a mere six destroyers. By the end of the war it had 471 warships and over 100 000 sailors.

As German submarines trolled the north Atlantic to prevent the transport of goods to Britain, the Canadians served as escorts and protected the coastline, sinking 33 Axis submarines in the process.

The Battle of the Gulf of the Atlantic (1942–44) was part of the larger Battle of the Atlantic and it centred on the St Lawrence Seaway where the Germans kept submarines on constant alert in an attempt to interrupt trade. The St Lawrence River was the gateway to Montreal. During the war that city exported more tons of shipping than all of the other ports on the eastern seaboard combined and transporting materials from Montreal to Liverpool shaved valuable time off the duration of the journey. German submarines were so successful that they prevented roughly one-quarter of all materials from reaching the UK; receiving war materials was a key component of the Allied ability to launch a counter-offensive against the Axis, making this battle important for North Africa, Italy and eventually D-Day. By the end of the war in Europe Canadians escorted 25 343 merchant ships to the British Isles to help the UK continue its war effort and keep morale high during the Blitz. This came at a cost, however, as over 100 Canadian ships were destroyed by German submarines and approximately 3600 Canadians died in the protection of convoy routes.

To make the protection of convoys more effective, Canada, the USA and the UK convened the Atlantic Convoy Conference in March 1943. At this point the Canadian Northwest Atlantic Command based in Halifax, Nova Scotia was established. It gave the Canadian Navy the responsibility for patrolling north of New York City and had the distinction of being the only area of operation commanded by a Canadian, Rear-Admiral Leonard Murray. This was one of a series of meetings that established Canada as a junior member in the **Grand Alliance**.

Grand Alliance
The Second World War alliance of USSR, UK and USA.

Battles with significant Canadian participation

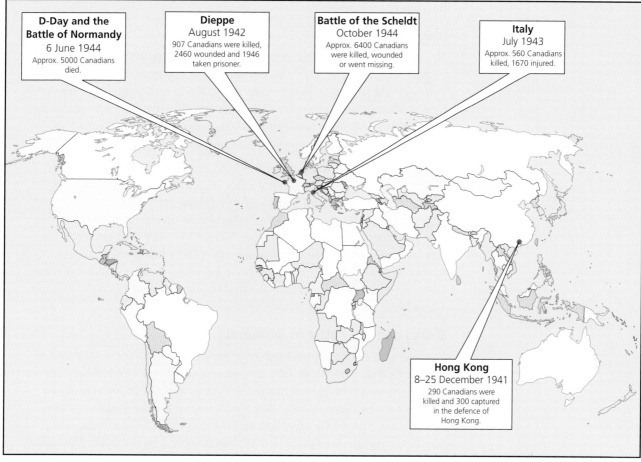

D-Day and the Battle of Normandy
6 June 1944
Approx. 5000 Canadians died.

Dieppe
August 1942
907 Canadians were killed, 2460 wounded and 1946 taken prisoner.

Battle of the Scheldt
October 1944
Approx. 6400 Canadians were killed, wounded or went missing.

Italy
July 1943
Approx. 560 Canadians killed, 1670 injured.

Hong Kong
8–25 December 1941
290 Canadians were killed and 300 captured in the defence of Hong Kong.

▲ Canadian involvement in the Second World War

Hong Kong

In November 1941, Canadian forces arrived in Hong Kong as reinforcements to assist in the defence of the British protectorate. On 8 December the Japanese attacked and quickly overran an overwhelmed garrison by 25 December. Of the 1975 Canadians sent, 290 were killed and 300 captured in the defence of Hong Kong. The Canadian force was made up of a bilingual regiment from Quebec – the Royal Rifles – and the Winnipeg Grenadiers, representing a cross-section of society and sparking outrage across Canada as it was learned that the UK government had determined that Hong Kong was expendable and had decided against providing its own reinforcements for the 20 000 troops already stationed there.

Dieppe

The Soviet Union was still on the defensive in Eastern Europe and was demanding that the other allies open a second front in Western Europe to take pressure off its stretched forces. This led to the Canadian army's first major engagement in Europe. In August 1942 the Second Canadian Infantry attempted to take the French port of Dieppe and establish a foothold on the continent. The raid proved to be a disaster for the Canadians – of 5000 troops, 907 were killed, 2460 wounded and 1946 taken prisoner. The Allies used the disaster to evaluate Axis strength on the mainland and plan a larger offensive to re-take France that eventually resulted in the D-Day invasion and Battle of Normandy.

Italy

Nearly one year after the debacle at Dieppe, Canadian forces were dispatched to North Africa to participate in the attack on Sicily that commenced in July 1943. Unlike Hong Kong or Dieppe, this was to be a sustained battle; as victories occurred, the armies were instructed to advance, and once Sicily was taken, the next move was to the Italian mainland.

Italy surrendered on 3 September but the Germans took over the defence of the peninsula. With other Allied forces, the Canadians did battle from south to north, slowly taking Italy from the German forces and establishing Allied bases on the Tyrrhenian and Adriatic seas. Canadian forces fought for over 20 months, city by city through the mountains and plains but they were not involved in the final surrender; on 1 February 1945 Canadians were transferred to north-western Europe to join the rest of the Canadians serving in Europe.

D-Day and the Battle of Normandy

Canada's best-known performance in the Second World War came on the first day of the D-Day invasion. On 6 June 1944, Allied forces landed on a series of beaches on the French coast at Normandy in a massive offensive to establish a beachhead on the continent and launch a counter-offensive against the Germans in the west. The Royal Canadian Air Force (RCAF) participated in the inland bombing campaigns meant to help prepare the beaches for invasion; Canadian paratroopers landed ashore to assist the amphibious landing; and the Canadian divisions landed on Juno beach, getting further on the first day than any other Allied landing force. Canadian forces then moved along the coastline, providing assistance in the occupation of Caen and then, appropriately, taking Dieppe in September. After the coastline was secured, the Allies then began to move inward with the goals of liberating Belgium, the Netherlands and Luxembourg and launching an attack across the Rhine River to take German territory.

Battle of the Scheldt

In late October 1944 the Canadian army reached the coastal frontier and crossed into Belgium. Separating it from important Belgian and Dutch port cities was the German army stationed on the Scheldt River. It launched the battle on 16 October but the area was well defended and the Germans flooded the Scheldt estuary, making any Canadian advance difficult. After five weeks of bitter fighting with a high number of casualties, the Germans were defeated on 8 November, and Antwerp was now open to Allied shipping, meaning that supplies could get through that led to the final Allied push into Germany early the following year.

▲ Canadian posters from the Second World War supporting the British Empire effort

A second conscription crisis

The Battle of Scheldt was complicated by a new conscription crisis in Canada. Conservatives in the government had been urging it as early as 1942 but King managed to avoid the issue of conscription until 1944. In 1942 the government held a plebiscite to ask the Canadian people to release it from its 'no conscription' promise that the government would not introduce conscription if further troops were needed to fight overseas. Although 70% of Canadians agreed to the proposition, in Quebec only 20% of voters agreed. Mackenzie King did not wish to incite the Quebecois, however, and enough Canadians volunteered to make sending conscripts overseas unnecessary until 1944. The high number of casualties in Italy, France and the Lowlands or Low Countries changed the situation and the government saw the need to implement overseas conscription. In November the government authorized the dispatch of 16 000 conscripts to go abroad, and 13 000 were sent to the UK to prepare to fight on mainland Europe. Until the surrender of Germany only 2500 conscripts saw battle and the Quebecois, due to domestic politics, did not challenge the decision. In reality, Canadian participation in the overseas war effort was borne overwhelmingly by volunteers, and conscripts only saw battle when it became absolutely necessary – and only for a short period of time in early 1945.

The end of the war

From February until April 1945 the Canadian army was responsible for the liberation of the Netherlands and crossed into German territory. In May, Canadians entered Germany, participating in the defeat of the Germans on German soil. The Canadian participation in the Asian theatre after Hong Kong largely consisted of assisting US troops in clearing Alaska of Japanese forces that occupied the Aleutian islands of Attu and Kiska in 1942 and 1943. After a long hiatus, the Canadians returned to the Pacific where one Canadian cruiser and two RCAF squadrons provided support to the Allies. With the bombings of Hiroshima and Nagasaki, the Canadians returned home.

Results for Canada

The war was costly for Canada both economically and socially. Government spending skyrocketed from $118 million in 1939 to $4.6 *billion* in 1945. A total of 42 042 Canadians died in the war, most in north-western Europe, and 54 000 returned home as casualties of war. The conscription crisis once again highlighted the tension between French- and English-speaking Canada that would erupt in the 1960s.

On balance, however, Canada emerged as a transformed country. Its industry finally recovered from the Great Depression and it possessed one of the most modern, efficient economies in the world. Canada itself was untouched by the war, except for several German submarine attacks, its productive capacity had increased and full employment was reached as early as 1942.

It was also considered an important power with its large navy and air forces, and the military contributions of its soldiers. The concept of the middle power emerged due to Canada's performance in the Second World War. These were countries that would never achieve superpower status (nor did they desire it) but that had sufficient strength to influence diplomacy and even policies adopted by the United Nations.

Lastly, in spite of the conscription crisis, the war consolidated the idea of a Canadian national identity as Canadians – regardless of language or ethnic background – fought together in numerous battles under Canadian leadership.

Mexico

Mexico remained studiously neutral when Europe went to war, but as the Germans became increasingly aggressive in the Atlantic Mexico saw it would be in its best interest to side with the USA, if not through a declaration of war then through the policy of hemispheric solidarity that had been introduced in 1933 and developed further throughout the 1930s. The populist President Lázaro Cárdenas supported US efforts to assist the British and went so far as to expel known German agents in June 1940. When Manuel Avila Camacho succeeded Cárdenas in December of that year, his attitude was one of increasing sympathy to the countries fighting the Axis: the UK, its Commonwealth and a China that was bordering on collapse. The issue of Mexican nationalization of foreign oil companies had yet to be resolved but steps were being taken towards that end.

There was some support for the Axis powers in Mexico, partly born of anti-Americanism, and partly from Italian and German immigrants, but Avila Camacho used Nazi ideology to galvanize the population against the Axis. He argued that the indigenous and Mestizo populations would certainly be oppressed with the implementation of Hitler's racial policies, and that all Mexicans might be seen as low on the racial scale designed by the Nazis.

At the same time that the USA was firming up its agreements with the UK via Lend Lease, it also used the war as a means to improve its relations with Mexico. In April 1941 there was a reciprocal agreement concluded regarding mutual defence and the use of each other's air bases. In practical terms, this allowed the USA to use Mexican air bases and in return it helped train Mexican pilots.

In an action intended to show hemispheric solidarity, in August 1941 Mexico closed all of its German consulates, expelled the German diplomatic staff and recalled Mexican diplomats from Nazi-occupied Europe.

Finally, in November 1941 the USA ignored oil company demands and settled the issue of Mexican oil. This was a signal of the importance of Mexican support for the coming war. Furthermore, the two countries agreed that Mexico would sell all of its strategic minerals to the USA, arranged a loan of $40 million to the Mexican government and issued a long-term guarantee to purchase Mexican silver – an economic boon to a country that was still reeling from nearly 25 years of revolution and civil war.

The Pearl Harbor attack shook the Mexican government. Its policy was one of neutrality unless Mexico was attacked directly, but the Mexicans feared a Japanese attack on its west coast. Approximately 9000 Japanese resided in Baja California and they were forced to relocate to Mexico City or Guadalajara. Former president Cárdenas was made commander of the Pacific Defense Zone in a move to increase support for the Allied cause. The largely ambivalent or apathetic population now saw the Axis as aggressive for no reason and Mexico was one of the largest supporters of breaking relations with the Axis at the Pan-American Union conference in January 1942.

Avila Camacho saw the war as a way to unify the population in a common cause against a common enemy. He also thought that the war could be a catalyst for economic nationalism and exhorted Mexicans to show their patriotism through increasing their productive capacities. While Mexicans were willing to increase productivity to assist the Allied cause, they were still reluctant to become involved in yet another armed conflict. This changed, however, in May 1942.

On 13 May 1942, the Mexican oil tanker *Potrero del Llano* was sunk by a German submarine in the Gulf of Mexico, killing and wounding those aboard. Still hoping to maintain neutrality, the government demanded an official apology and compensation for the destruction. Instead, the Germans responded on 21 May, torpedoing another ship and killing seven sailors. With this act the Germans showed that they were unwilling to negotiate with what they perceived as a pro-Allied Mexico, and Mexican public opinion changed dramatically. Avila Camacho addressed the Mexican Congress, calling for a declaration of war against the Axis but stipulating that the country would not commit its military to fight in the European theatre.

He declared Mexico to be in a state of emergency, suspended civil rights such as freedom of speech and freedom of the press, and urged the people to begin the process of mobilization. In his opinion, all sectors of society needed to respond to this call, and he argued that the German enemy was stronger because its concept of national unity was stronger than that of the Mexicans, hoping to prompt nationalism.

The Mexican Navy patrolled the Gulf of Mexico to keep German submarines at bay but the threat of a Japanese invasion seemed less and less likely, especially after US success in the Battle of Midway (in June 1942). Intensive training of the Mexican military began, yet only one branch of the service would serve overseas: the Escuadrón 201, or Aztec Eagles. This squadron consisted of 300 men who were trained in the USA and were sent to the Philippines in March 1945. The Aztec Eagles flew 59 missions, logging 1200 hours of flight time in less than six months of combat. They participated in the battles of Luzon (Philippines) and Formosa.

The military impact of the Aztec Eagles was negligible, but their active engagement increased domestic support for the war. Once the Aztec Eagles were sent to the Pacific, Mexicans felt a more personal stake in the outcome of the war, and they were hoping that this would provide them with a voice in the post-war settlement. They did not desire territorial concessions or reparations; Mexicans wanted continued improvement of regional relations, especially with the USA. Escuadrón 201 also contributed positively to the idea of a Mexican national identity.

▲ Escuadrón 201 (the Aztec Eagles)

Results for Mexico

From the perspective of Avila Camacho the Second World War achieved his goals of industrialization and developing the idea of national unity and identity. Although its sojourn to the Pacific was short, the Escuadrón 201 squadron distinguished itself and provided a tangible reason for national pride. The war put Mexico on the road to industrialization as it saw infrastructure improvements, especially with highways and ports, and both agriculture and the military prospered.

Not all results were positive, however. Inflation and corruption soared as a result of the rapid pace of modernization and large government contracts, and the war made Mexico dependent upon US markets once again.

Occupied colonial possessions in the Americas during the Second World War

Colonies remained in the Caribbean and Latin America during the Second World War. None were German or Italian, but after the defeat of the Netherlands and France, the issue of sovereignty became key for some of these territories. The independent American states debated the status of Dutch and French possessions, with the majority refusing to recognize them as conquered territories, citing the Monroe Doctrine as the rationale for non-recognition.

All islands in the Caribbean were strategically significant and could be used as a gateway to the Panama Canal so most countries preferred that they be possessed by the Allies. The Netherlands Antilles, Aruba and Suriname were occupied by British and US forces with the consent of the Dutch government in exile. Suriname was especially desirable to the Allied cause due to its bauxite mines, and Curaçao's oil reserves made it a target of German submarine attacks, especially in the early stages of the war. In 1942, Queen Wilhelmina gave a speech in which she presented the idea of autonomy for all Dutch overseas territories. Dutch colonial rule was re-established temporarily after the war, but there was a strong push for autonomy and while these territories remained part of the Kingdom of the Netherlands they were considered constituent countries that had equal status to the Netherlands proper.

The situation regarding French possessions was more complicated. Initially, Guadeloupe and Martinique declared their loyalty to the Vichy government due to its official policy of neutrality, but when General Charles de Gaulle established Free France, support grew for this government in exile against the Vichy regime which cooperated with the Nazis and did little to reject their racial policies, and in 1943 both islands recognized the Free French.

In sum, the Dutch and French Caribbean territories were much more sympathetic to the Allied cause and aligned with the hemispheric rather than their imperial political perspectives.

ATL Research skills

Since only four countries in the Americas sent forces to participate in the Second World War, the question that arises is how did the other countries participate in the war effort if they declared war on the Axis but did not send their armies?

Choose one non-combatant country in the region and research how it participated in the war, and if that participation had a significant effect on the course or outcome of the war.

The Second World War brought profound changes to all the countries in the Americas. In various ways, the Second World War governments had to mobilize their populations so that they could serve in the military, increase industrial productivity and/or increase agricultural production. As noted in the previous unit, it was the war that solved the unemployment created by the Great Depression. In most of Latin America, the governments granted concessions to industrial workers or appealed to their patriotism to increase productivity. In the USA and Canada, with so many men in the military, industry needed to enlist sectors of the population that were not usually recruited: women, minorities and immigrants. These conditions prompted changes in social hierarchy, at least temporarily, and these historically oppressed groups experienced newfound prosperity and responsibility.

The USA

In 1940 the population of the USA was just under 133 million, and during the course of the war 16 million men and women served in the military. From a demographic perspective, the Second World War marked a turning point in the USA: absent husbands made women the *de facto* head of households, the need for skilled labour in the factories led to training for minorities and with most factories located in the Midwest and West, nearly one-tenth of all Americans moved permanently to a new state.

President Roosevelt appealed to US patriotism: there was a sense that everyone was making one concerted effort to defeat the Axis powers in a war that was characterized as good versus evil. People reduced their use of goods needed for the war effort, and reused and recycled wherever possible. This included periodically collecting scrap iron and creating victory gardens – small vegetable, fruit and herb gardens that families and individuals planted in urban areas so that they could grow their own food. Nearly 20 million of these were planted in front yards, on rooftops and in local parks, harvesting 9–10 million tons of produce, much of which was then canned and preserved.

The Fruits of Victory

Write for Free Book to
National War Garden Commission
Washington, D.C.
Charles Lathrop Pack, President   P.S. Ridsdale, Secretary

▲ Propaganda poster encouraging citizens of patriotism to get involved in growing victory gardens

The home front was fully mobilized and the USA was in a state of total war. Although attacks on the mainland were extremely limited (involving German submarines in the Gulf of Mexico and the Japanese occupation of some of the Aleutian Islands) the war affected the daily lives of nearly all Americans; one could not forget there was a war – it permeated the news, entertainment and the way in which people lived their lives.

Minorities

African Americans

Arguably, the Second World War was the most transformative event for African Americans at home and at the front. Although African Americans were hypothetically equal to all other citizens, the reality was much different. Segregation prevailed throughout the USA, not just in the south, and the Great Depression had worsened the condition of minorities in the USA. The Red Cross separated blood by colour of the donor in addition to the blood type, and most establishments were designated 'White' or 'Coloured'.

African American political leaders saw military service as a way to bring about equal rights and agitated for the right to be drafted proportionate to their percentage of the population – 10% in 1942 – and over 2.5 million answered the call and registered for the draft. At the height of the war there were 700 000 African Americans in the army as well as 187 000 in the navy, marines and coast guard, all the while facing discrimination on all levels. During the Second World War African Americans served in segregated units but they fought on front lines for the first time and were no longer relegated to menial tasks and service and support positions.

Race riots ensued on military bases even though the military advocated a position of segregation and separate-but-equal quarters. Both black and white military personnel were housed in similar conditions, but the commanders where white. In the south, white civilians assaulted black soldiers and there were no repercussions. In one of the most notorious cases, a black soldier named Booker T Spicely was murdered by a white bus driver in North Carolina for not moving to the back of the bus quickly enough. The driver claimed self-defence and was acquitted. Such actions were a common occurrence; law enforcement did little to protect African American soldiers and some of the worst violent offences were against blacks. In many cases it appeared that Italian and German prisoners of war were receiving better treatment than African American soldiers. Between 1942 and 1945 an estimated 200 racial military confrontations occurred; in 1943 alone there were 68 acts of racial violence on military bases.

An example of contribution in the face of discrimination was the Tuskegee Airmen. In 1939, the War Department appropriated funds to begin the training of African American pilots. It was deliberately designed for failure: there were only 124 qualified African American pilots in the USA. However, a large number of civilian pilots had been trained at Tuskegee University and they applied for entrance in the

▲ A poster featuring a member of the 99th Pursuit Squadron designed to convince African Americans to purchase war bonds

programme, leading to the creation of the first all-black squadron – the 99th Pursuit Squadron. Most Americans did not think that African Americans were sufficiently capable to serve as pilots, so psychologists set up testing areas at the training facilities that included intelligence testing, only accepting those who performed at an acceptable level. These tests proved to be so successful in predicting success that they were then given to all potential pilots, regardless of race. In 1943 the 99th Pursuit Squadron was considered ready for combat and was deployed to North Africa, where it would fly missions to clear the sea lanes in anticipation of the invasion of Sicily in July 1943. Tuskegee airmen subsequently flew missions over Italy, Austria, Hungary, Czechoslovakia, France and Germany.

While the Tuskegee Airmen had an admirable record – according to government records they did not lose a single bomber they escorted – they were treated in a humiliating manner. After being relocated to Freeman Field in Indiana in 1945, the airmen were categorized as 'trainees' (and not the officers they were) as a means of treating the black airmen differently even though some had logged nearly 1000 hours of flying and served in Europe. They responded using civil disobedience that led to the arrest of 162 officers. While their attempts at desegregation were not successful in the short term, the actions (known as the Freedom Field Mutiny) led to the airmen being placed under African American Commander Benjamin O Davis, and the military re-evaluating its racial policies.

▲ Second Lieutenant Jack R Robinson faced court martial in 1944

Some of the African American officers involved in acts of passive resistance throughout the US military later became important in the civil rights struggle on a number of levels. Coleman Young was a labour leader who became the first black mayor of Detroit, and the most visible of these men was a young officer at Fort Hood, Texas who was court martialled in 1944, Second Lieutenant Jack R. Robinson, who would later become the first baseball player to break the color barrier in the USA.

For its part, the National Association for the Advancement of Colored People (NAACP) saw the war as an opportunity 'to persuade, embarrass, compel and shame our government and our nation into a more enlightened attitude toward a tenth of its people'. For the NAACP the war was about a double victory – over the foreign enemies and against inequalities at home. People were more insistent about their rights as individuals and more willing to protest, and support grew – in 1940 there were 50 000 members of the NAACP; this number grew to 450 000 in 1946.

Civilians saw a shift in the attitude towards African American workers. During the war 1.5 million blacks migrated to the north and west to work in factories that had expanded and were in need of labour to replace those serving in the military. Roosevelt was a proponent of civil rights and issued Executive Order 8802. It stated that employers in defence industries that were accepting contracts from the government had to make jobs available without discrimination. Around 500 000 African Americans became active in unions, and many became Democrats in support of Roosevelt's policies.

This was important as the African American population constituted a vital swing vote in northern states; in southern states, Jim Crow laws were in effect and this limited the political impact of African Americans there. While their labour was seen as necessary for the war effort, violence in civilian life was just as prolific as in the military. In 1943 there were 250 racial conflicts in 47 cities. The worst of these took place in Detroit on 20–21 June. This was due in large part to the living conditions in Detroit at the time. To meet production demands, the factories needed to hire more people than ever before, and they lived in very crowded, ethnically segregated neighbourhoods that offended the long-time residents, regardless of the race of the newcomers. All workers, including blacks, were demanding better conditions and wages as they had the upper hand against the managers. In addition, the weather was hot, leading to short tempers. Beginning on 20 June, racial tension erupted into a riot that lasted 36 hours, and by the end of it 34 were killed (25 blacks and 9 others), 433 people were injured, damage to property amounted to $2 million, 1000 people were arrested and over 1 million manpower hours were lost.

Despite claims to protect workers, the federal government did nothing to prevent further racial violence. While African Americans were critical to the war effort, little was done to protect their rights as citizens. However, civil rights leaders in the African American communities learned a number of lessons regarding passive resistance, strength in numbers and the power of the working class when labour is scarce. These leaders would later harness the energy and anger created in the Second World War to mobilize the African American community in the 1950s and 1960s.

Native Americans

In 1940, the US Congress passed the Nationality Act, finally granting citizenship to Native Americans. According to the US census, there were 333,969 'American Indian, Eskimo and Aleutian' people living in the USA. Most of the Native American population lived in the west, many on reservations.

Through circumstance, a number of the reservations had resources that became increasingly important during the war effort, particularly after the decision was made to construct an atom bomb. Many Native American lands were deemed 'essential natural resources' and the federal government began to appropriate minerals and land to help with the building of war materials and military technology. The resources found on Indian lands included asbestos, coal, copper, gypsum, helium, lead, natural gas, oil and zinc. Still other lands were used as internment camps for Japanese Americans, or were taken as military bases expanded. In Alaska, the Unangax people met an even worse fate when, fearing Japanese aggression, the US military burned eight villages to the ground to prevent their occupation. At the same time Aleutians were recruited to help patrol the outlying islands after the Japanese took two of them. Their skills as kayakers and trackers made them incredibly useful to the US military and they participated in the liberation of Attu and Kiska.

Just as African Americans were needed to work in the factories in the cities, Native Americans were seen as necessary to the war effort due to their proximity to the resources and their ability to work in the local mines. Another 40 000 men and women left the reservations to work in the defence industry. During the war, even the most traditional patrilineal societies saw tremendous change as women took over traditionally male leadership roles. As in the rest of the USA, Native American women became firefighters, mechanics, welders and farmers.

What may be surprising is the number of Native American men who participated in the war. In 1942, 99% of all healthy, qualified Native Americans aged between 21 and 44 were registered for the draft and over 44 000 served. This was over 10% of the Native American population at the time and one-third of all men aged between 18 and 50. The reason for such extensive Native American participation is subject to speculation and little has been written on it. Some have argued that, despite feelings against the US government, the warrior culture prevailed and Native American men felt that participation was not an option; it was predetermined due to their own traditions and a dedication to the protection of the land.

The Navajo Nation was of particular use to the US army. During the First World War the US army had developed a code using the Native American Choctaw language that the Germans could not break. Prior to the Second World War, a large number of German anthropologists came to the USA, ostensibly to learn about the different cultures, but they expressed a very keen interest in the languages, so the USA suspected that these were agents trying to prevent something similar from happening again.

Alphabets (English)	Code language (English)	Code language (Navajo)	Modern spelling
A	Ant	Wol-la-chee	Wóláchííʼ
B	Bear	Shush	Shash
C	Cat	Moashi	Mósí
D	Deer	Be	Bįįh
E	Elk	Dzeh	Dzeeh
F	Fox	Ma-e	Mąʼii
G	Goat	Klizzie	Tłʼízí
H	Horse	Lin	Łííʼ
I	Ice	Tkin	Tin
J	Jackass	Tkele-cho-gi	Téliichoʼí
K	Kid	Klizzie-yazzi	Tłʼízí yázhí
L	Lamb	Dibeh-yazzi	Dibé yázhí
M	Mouse	Na-as-tso-si	Naʼatsʼǫǫsí
N	Nut	Nesh-chee	Neeshchʼííʼ
O	Owl	Ne-ash-jsn	Néʼéshjaaʼ
P	Pig	Bi-sodih	Bisóodi
Q	Quiver	Ca-yeilth	Kʼaaʼ yeiłtįįh
R	Rabbit	Gah	Gah
S	Sheep	Dibeh	Dibé
T	Turkey	Than-zie	Tązhii
U	Ute	No-da-ih	Nóódaʼí
V	Victor	a-keh-di-glini	Akʼehdidlíní
W	Weasel	Gloe-ih	Dlǫʼii
X	Cross	Al-an-as-dzoh	Ałnáʼázdzoh
Y	Yucca	Tsah-as-zih	Tsáʼásziʼ
Z	Zinc	Besh-do-gliz	Béésh dootłʼizh

▲ Terms in English and the Navajo language

▲ Navajo code talkers

However, the idea of using a language known by few outsiders as the basis for a code was reconsidered. When evaluating the different languages, it appeared that there were only 30 non-native speakers worldwide who spoke the Diné – or Navajo – language so a group of 29 Navajo recruits were charged with coming up with a dictionary and memorizing the terms they devised. They encoded 413 commonly used military terms and the Navajo were trained as radio operators so they could communicate with one another. There were 410 code talkers in the Pacific, working as part of the Marines; two were assigned to each battalion – one went ashore and the other remained on board. In this way the ships could talk to the landing expeditions, and they took part in every battle in the Pacific from 1942 to 1945, and the Normandy invasion in 1944. Their code was never broken during the war and was used in the Korean War as well. After the war, the work of the code talkers was classified so even their relatives were unaware of the valuable work done by the code talkers in the Second World War until 1968 when the code was declassified.

It is estimated that nearly half of all Native Americans participated in some aspect of the war effort. After the war, many Native Americans did not return to the reservation but instead assimilated into mainstream society, finding that life preferable to the subsistence lifestyle they had left.

Those who returned after the war sometimes felt a calling to return to the reservation to integrate the education, business and industrial techniques they learned into traditional society to both preserve and expand their native communities. The returning populations saw opportunities for an improved standard of living, modern healthcare and infrastructure development. Those on the reservation felt that these ideas threatened their traditional way of life and put that above material gain. This led to tensions between those who rejected what they saw as a foreign incursion into their culture, and an attempt to destroy it. In 1940, only 8% of Native Americans lived in urban areas, compared with 56% for the USA in general, so most lived far from non-Native Americans and it was the mobility brought on by war that made them realize they were discriminated against in the workplace and as citizens. Even though it took them nearly 25 years to organize themselves, the war made Native Americans aware of their lack of civil rights and they began to take steps towards improving the conditions of Native Americans throughout the USA.

Hispanic Americans and Mexicans

Like all other ethnic groups in the USA, Hispanic Americans participated in all aspects of the war. An estimated 500 000 served in the US military, including 53 000 Puerto Ricans, and Hispanic labour was greatly valued during the labour shortages. Since most Hispanics resided in the west, they were employed in the shipyards and nearby factories in California. Women often took the positions of absent males, giving them a new, higher status. However, the effects for Hispanics were similar to those of other minorities.

Bilingualism was highly valued during the war, so Latino Americans were desired, and as Latino men served in the military at relatively high rates, that meant that Hispanic women and youths were recruited. Women worked in communications and cryptology, largely as linguists and nurses, serving in the Red Cross and various branches of the military.

During the Great Depression, a number of Mexicans had been repatriated to Mexico during a wave of xenophobia, including those who were US citizens. With the labour shortages, once again there was a demand for migrant workers, and the USA established the Bracero programme in August 1942 that allowed for the temporary importation of labour on short-term contracts. Initially, agricultural workers were hired, but the programme was later expanded to include all types of unskilled labourers, including railroad workers. To participate in the programme, businesses had to agree to pay certain wages and provide decent housing and

▲ Mexican–American women working on the Southern Pacific Railroad during the Second World War

medical care for the workers so that their standard of living would be higher than it had been in Mexico. At the height of the programme, 75 000 Mexicans were working throughout the USA. The programme continued until 1964.

Of the Mexican Americans working around Los Angeles, 17 000 worked in the shipyards and there was ethnic tension between them and the **Anglo** sailors serving on the naval bases there. The tension hit its peak and during 31 May to 8 June 1943 the 'Zoot Suit Riots' broke out, named after the type of clothing worn by the Mexican American men called Pachucos. The Pachucos were underage, and so too young to be drafted, and fighting broke out between them and the servicemen. The servicemen beat the youths, stripped them of their flamboyant clothes and cut their hair while the local police looked on. Like the riots that took place elsewhere that summer, these riots interrupted worker productivity and destabilized the area. On 8 June, recognizing how damaging the riots were to the war effort, the federal government quietly insisted on an end to them. The Navy responded by cancelling shore leave for all sailors in port and declared downtown Los Angeles off limits to all military personnel.

Latinos were among the first to see battle after Pearl Harbor. Fearing an attack in the Pacific – but not expecting it as far east as Hawaii – the US government deployed two units from the New Mexico National Guard to the Philippines as many of them spoke Spanish and could work with the local populations, many of whom still spoke Spanish. This group was poorly supplied and outmatched by the Japanese when they launched their attack on the Philippines in December 1941. A substantial number of Latinos were present for the Bataan Death March of US prisoners of war, where the Japanese forced Filipino and US soldiers to march in harsh conditions without food and water, killing those who could not continue.

While there was a general feeling of equality in terms of service for the USA, most Hispanic Americans were dissatisfied with their lower social status after the war. Although there had been economic opportunities, discrimination, violence and political oppression continued. After the war, Hispanic Americans took advantage of the **GI Bill** to gain an education and push for greater civil rights.

> **Anglo**
> Americans for whom English is the primary language.

▲ A Pachuco youth

> **GI Bill**
> Originally named the Servicemen's Readjustment Act of 1944, this law clearly enumerated the benefits that returning World War II veterans would receive. The most popular benefits included university tuition and living stipends while attending university, but there was also assistance available to start small businesses or claim a year's worth of unemployment compensation.

Women

Women participated in the war effort at an unprecedented level. This trend began during the First World War but as such a large sector of the US male population was serving in the military, women were even more necessary than previously. Not only did they work in industry at home and as nurses for the military but they also formed their own branches of the military. These included the Women's Army Corps (WACs), the US Naval Women's Reserve (WAVES), the Women's Air Force Service Pilots (WASPs) and Women's Coast Guard Reserve. These women served as air traffic controllers, clerical support, teletype operators, communications experts, flight instructors and test pilots. During the course of the war, nearly 200 000 women served in these roles and another 75 000 served as nurses.

▲ A group of Women Airforce Service Pilots

At the same time 6 million women entered the labour force, an increase of 57%. Whereas the employment of women was a point of contention during the Great Depression, it was now seen as a woman's patriotic duty to work. Women filled 2 million clerical jobs but more surprising were the 2.5 million women who went into manufacturing. The percentage of working women over the age of 45 increased the most and married women were the primary means of bolstering the labour force.

This change in attitude was critical as women were necessary for industrial jobs and it was thought that labour shortages threatened the war effort. During the war, women were trained to become crane operators, riveters, shell loaders, welders and tool makers. In rural areas lumberjacks were replaced by lumberjills and cowgirls replaced cowboys on the range. As many as 7 million women voluntarily moved to war-production areas and African American women quit their jobs as domestic helpers and moved into industrial jobs with better pay and benefits. Even then, women received lower pay than men in the same position, but accepted this as part of the effort to win the war. There was a social contradiction in place: people frowned upon women working while at the same time expecting them to do so.

This was especially true for women with children. Childcare centres were in short supply in war-boom areas and many women had to work swing shifts, late at night, to keep production moving at a sufficient pace. To cope with this, the Lanham Act provided federal aid to communities that absorbed large war-related populations. It provided childcare centres in addition to other infrastructure developments. In 1943, 60 000 children were in Lanham Care; in 1944 this number had increased to 130 000, but even so this was grossly insufficient. In reality, most children were with extended family members, usually grandmothers who took on the role of caregiver as part of their service to the country.

Extended school services also offered care for children before and after school; 320 000 children were enrolled at its peak in 1943. Older youth were also coopted in the war effort – in 1940 only 900 000 people aged between 14 and 19 were in the workforce but by 1944 that number had increased to 3 million – roughly one-third of that age group. Unfortunately, high school enrollment dropped at that time so in 1944, when the war reached its turning point, the government launched a back-to-school drive to encourage the youth to return to school.

Demography changed; after the low marriage and birth rates of the Great Depression, there was an upswing in both of these during the war. In 1939, there were 73 marriages per 1000 people; this rose to 93 per 1000 in 1943. In the same years the birth rate climbed from 2.1 million to 3.1 million. Men and women married at record paces, often after very brief courtships. Married couples often wanted 'goodbye' babies who were born after their fathers had been deployed. The suddenness of these decisions, however, also led to an increased divorce rate. In 1939, there were 25 000 divorces; that number rose to 359 000 in 1943 and 485 000 in 1945.

Although all of this led to a brief period of progress for women, there was little social support for these initiatives. Newspapers and magazines were full of articles about what they termed 'eight-hour orphans', and they mourned the loss of family values.

There were social problems after the return of servicemen. Women had been independent and taken charge of their home economies, proving they could function without their husbands and accustomed to being heads of household. The returning husbands felt irrelevant because their families had thrived without them. With the war's end women were pushed out of the roles they had held during the war by industry, government and society. When the war began, women saw these changes as temporary and intended to return to their previous positions as homemakers and caregivers. However, when the war ended most women were unhappy with resuming their previous positions. In one poll, 75% of women in Detroit and 85% of women in New York wanted to keep their jobs. They were dissatisfied with the inequality they felt.

Conscription

Registration for the Selective Service began in 1940 and allowed for peacetime conscription. This decision was made by President Roosevelt after the fall of France, Scandinavia and the Low Countries. All men between the ages of 21 and 40 were required to register for the draft, and 50 million did so. A lottery was held and those selected served in the military for one year. A cap was set so that no more than 900 000 men would be in training at any one time.

Further legislation changed the time of service from 18 to 12 months and eventually to six months beyond the end of the war. At the same time, the age requirements were changed and all men aged between 18 and 65 were required to register, although initially only men aged between 18 and 45 would be called up.

In a final change, in December 1942, voluntary enlistment was terminated and the age range for conscription was moved to between 18 and 38. The goals were to have one man in five in the military service and to have a military that totalled 9 million personnel, with 200 000 being inducted each month. By the end of the war, 36 million men were classified and 10 million inducted into the armed forces.

There were pacifists in the USA but the number was small. Certain religious groups – Quakers, Mennonites and Brethren – were historically conscientious objectors and there was limited conflict with the US government over this. However, the militant African American Nation of Islam opposed conscription on political grounds and received very little support; its leader, Elijah Mohammad, was convicted on charges of inciting draft dodging. The 37 000 who received the status of conscientious objector served, as medics in battle, acted as fire jumpers and worked Civilian Public Service (CPS) camps beyond the duration of the war, paying $35 per month for room and board. In the camps there was little meaningful work; the main objective was to keep conscientious objectors out of the public view, and they were kept in the camps until final release in 1947.

ATL Communication skills

Choose a country in the region other than the USA and present to the class the effect that the Second World War had on conscientious objectors, women **or** a particular minority. If it is a multimedia presentation there should be no more than seven slides and there should be no more than 25 words on each slide. The presentation should not last longer than 10 minutes, including some time for questions.

4.4 Treatment of Japanese Americans, Japanese Latin Americans and Japanese Canadians

Conceptual understanding

Key question

→ Why were citizens of Japanese descent ostracized, moved and/or interned after Pearl Harbor?

Key concept

→ Comparison

The bombing of Pearl Harbor set off a wave of hysteria in the Americas. The hemisphere saw itself as immune to attacks from outside and the damage done to the US Navy in Hawaii made the Americas feel vulnerable. While other foreign nationals were targeted, Japanese were especially singled out. In the Americas Japanese were categorized as either Isei: immigrants born in Japan or Nisei: children of Japanese immigrants. Laws were passed in most countries that made these Japanese Americans subject to arrest, internment, confiscation of property and humiliation.

Japanese and Japanese Americans in the USA

From the late 19th century until the Japanese attack on Pearl Harbor in 1941 over 275 000 Japanese immigrated to Hawaii and the continental USA. On the west coast there were 113 000 Japanese, two-thirds of whom were US citizens. On the mainland, the white population had long-held prejudice regarding Japanese Americans.

US intelligence was aware of pro-Japanese propagandists and sympathizers in Hawaii and along the west coast. For example, the San Francisco Japanese Military Servicemen's League supported the Japanese army and was seen as intensely nationalistic. A December 1941 memo from the Office of Naval Intelligence expressed fear that such societies were vehicles for espionage and sabotage, and that Japanese Americans who received their secondary or university education in Japan had been indoctrinated.

After the bombing of Pearl Harbor, on 7 and 8 December, Roosevelt issued presidential proclamations addressing the issue of enemy aliens. Almost immediately approximately 3000 enemy aliens were identified and detained by the US Department of Justice, roughly half of whom were Japanese. This initial move was provoked by fear of enemy agents within the USA, but the situation regarding the Japanese was far more complex than initially thought. The historic prejudice against the Japanese erupted and both beatings of Japanese and property damage occurred, largely against innocent civilians with little or no connection to the Japanese government. However, Roosevelt was unsure how to proceed.

Pressure came from General John DeWitt, Commander of the Western Defense Command, and Henry Stimson, Secretary of War, both of whom advocated the evacuation of people of Japanese descent from the Pacific Coast area. Thus, on 19 February 1942, Roosevelt issued Executive Order 9066 which empowered the Secretary of War (or any military commander authorized by him) to designate military areas of strategic significance and remove 'any and all persons' from these areas. Most of the west coast was designated one of two military zones and first-generation Japanese immigrants, along with second- and third-generation Japanese Americans were excluded from these zones. However, the issue then became where they should go.

On 18 March 1942, President Roosevelt issued Executive Order 9102, establishing the War Relocation Authority (WRA) as part of the Department for Emergency Management. The WRA would remove Japanese Americans from designated military zones and relocate them, mostly to internment camps.

Although only 2% of the west coast population was Japanese, the transfer was disruptive for thriving businesses. The registration of Japanese Americans began on 27 March; once they were registered, they were given between 48 hours and six days to pack necessities such as toiletries and clothing, and dispose of the rest of their possessions. Many of the evacuees were successful business people and homeowners. Some asked friends to look after their possessions but most had to sell all but what they could carry quickly, thus they lost their affluence in this brief window as houses and businesses were sold at a fraction of their value. By 2 June 1942 most Japanese and Japanese Americans from the first zone were in army custody.

Most Japanese Americans were first sent to assembly centres while it was determined where they would go from there. These centres tended to be small and underprepared, so the conditions were chaotic. These makeshift centres were in Civilian Conservation Corps (CCC) camps abandoned by the war, stables or even on racetracks. Families were kept together as much as possible, and the majority were eventually placed in internment camps located in seven states. There were 117 000 interned in these camps, two-thirds of whom were US citizens.

The internment camps were located on unused government lands in regions with harsh climactic conditions, such as high temperatures in the summer and freezing conditions in the winter. The camps were encircled by fences that had barbed wire, and there were guard towers and patrols to prevent people from leaving. The camps had schools and hospitals, and were intended to be self-sufficient. Initially, the occupants were housed in very sparse single-family barracks but had communal areas for washing, laundry and eating, which went against their traditional values. Since these were not work camps, families used their time by improving their housing to make it more personal, often transforming the oil stoves given to them for heat to cooking stoves so they could prepare family meals.

However, this was not the only fate for the Japanese and Japanese Americans. Those considered a threat to US national security, especially those who met with Japanese nationals on a regular basis, were detained in the Department of Justice (DOJ) detention centres. Throughout the course of the war, 17 477 such people were imprisoned. They were mostly men and community leaders. A number of them were ministers who were seen as having undue influence over their local communities. These detentions were based on intelligence gathered prior to the war on individuals, many of whom lived in Hawaii, and many of whom were arrested on 7 December, the day before the US Congress declared war.

Initially, draft-age men were prohibited from serving in the military but in 1943 the government reversed its position and allowed the enlistment of Nisei – second-generation Japanese American citizens. Like African Americans, they were segregated and served in their own unit – the 442nd infantry. The government was hoping for 1500 recruits; instead 33 000 served during the war, 2100 of whom came from the internment camps. These recruits were forced to complete and sign a loyalty questionnaire that many found humiliating.

The 442nd infantry participated in the battles to liberate Italy and France. They also served in the military intelligence division, acting as interpreters and translators once encrypted documents were deciphered and, in the late stages of the war, they calmed civilians on the Japanese islands taken who had been told to expect atrocities at the hands of US soldiers. While valued in the field, they faced the same discriminations as other minorities once they returned to the USA.

In Hawaii, roughly one-third of the population was Japanese, yet of these 157 000 people less than 2000 were interned. The decision was based on the economic situation of the time: Hawaii could not function if its Japanese population was interned, even though the Japanese there had much closer ties to Japan than the mainland Japanese. As Hawaii was a territory and not part of the USA, strictly speaking, this dilemma was solved by declaring martial law in Hawaii and turning its administration over to the US army until war ended in 1945.

While the internment continued, cases were making their way through the courts on the legality and constitutionality of the internment camps. On 7 December 1944 the US Supreme Court determined that the west coast exclusion order should be rescinded and the internment camps closed within the year. On 2 January 1946 the order was completely rescinded and Japanese Americans could return home. However, they received no support and many had little to return to; their homes and businesses were gone and they had to rebuild their lives.

One of the main reasons for internment came from DeWitt who argued that the evacuation was a 'military necessity'. Another reason given was the protection of Japanese Americans due to the virulent and often violent anti-Japanese sentiment felt on the west coast. While there was some truth in this, a detainee noted that the guards were keeping them in, not keeping others out.

In its findings, the Commission on Wartime Relocation and Internment stated in 1982 that Executive Order 9066 was not justified by military necessity, Supreme Court and 'historical causes [...] were race prejudice, war hysteria, and a failure of political leadership'. In 1988, the US government, under President Ronald Reagan, officially offered an apology to the internees and offered $20 000 in restitution to all survivors.

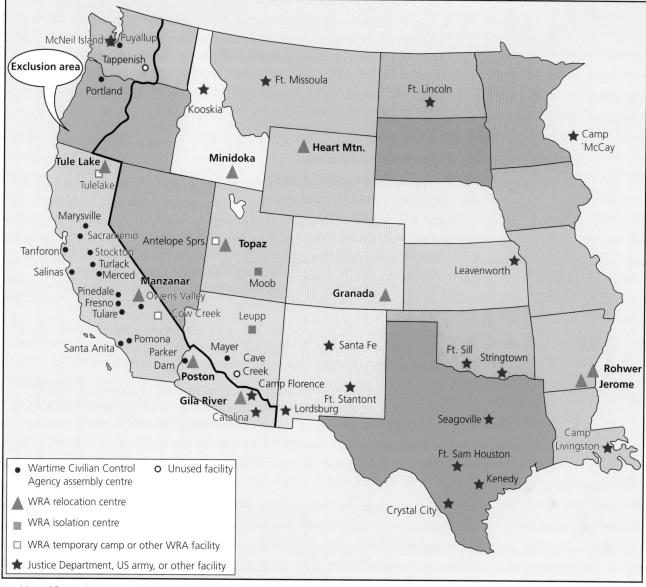

▲ Map of Second World War Japanese American internment camps

Japanese Canadians

As in the USA, most Japanese Canadians lived on the west coast of the country; 22 096 lived in British Colombia and three-quarters of them were naturalized citizens or native-born Canadians. Many worked in the lucrative fishing industry and anti-Japanese racism was prevalent in the west. The reasons for Canadian internment were similar to those in the USA: the government was fearful that they were working for the Japanese as enemy agents. Their loyalty to Canada was questioned. Although not eligible to vote (suffrage would be implemented in 1947) Japanese Canadians participated fully in Canadian life and there were even those of Japanese descent who had fought in the First World War for Canada.

In 1942, in reaction to Pearl Harbor, prominent members of British Columbia society called for action against the Japanese residing in the province. They argued that the large number of Japanese fishermen could be consorting with the enemy and providing intelligence that could facilitate an invasion of Canadian territory. Although there was no proof of espionage, the Canadian government passed the order that authorized the removal of 'enemy aliens' within a 100-mile of the coast of British Columbia. On 4 March 1942, Japanese Canadians were given 24 hours to pack and then were moved inland. Their property was confiscated, including valuable fishing boats. The government auctioned off the property, often authorizing sales well below market value, and the proceeds raised were used to pay for the Japanese Canadians' internment.

As in the USA, they were initially placed in an assembly centre before being moved to a camp. The Canadians interned women, children and the elderly in the interior of British Columbia. Men were sent to road construction camps or they had the option of working on sugar beet farms and their families would be relocated with them. While not legally interned, it was illegal for them to work anywhere other than in designated areas, and it was illegal for the children to receive a provincially subsidized education.

Japanese Canadians were housed in 10 internment camps. Three were road camps, two were prisoner of war camps, and five were called self-supporting camps that were considered low security.

The living quarters were small and families had to share stoves and other basic necessities. Most of the camps were not established for such high numbers so Japanese were placed in tents until housing became available but those houses were poorly made and badly insulated; they were not sufficient to cope with the Canadian winter, especially when located next to a lake.

▲ An internment camp for Japanese Canadians in British Columbia, 1945

The internees petitioned for better conditions, and, in particular, more stoves. After several petitions families were allowed to have vegetable gardens and create additions to their houses for extra rooms. The government of British Columbia refused to fund education in the camps so the federal government intervened, along with the Roman Catholic Church, Anglican Church and United Church. This joint church–state enterprise allowed for a complete primary and secondary education system within the camps.

Before the Second World War Japanese Canadians could enlist in the Canadian army but after Pearl Harbor, British Columbia would not allow it. To counter this measure, some Japanese Canadians enlisted in the British army but that caused some problems in the Canadian parliament where it was argued that Japanese Canadians could not leave the country in foreign uniforms. This led to Japanese Canadians being conscripted into the Canadian army as privates and serving in Europe that way.

Another indignity suffered by the Japanese Canadians was the threat of repatriation. Any Japanese Canadian could be deported to Japan if found in British Columbia, even though in 1944 King said 'it is a fact no person of Japanese race born in Canada has been charged with any act of sabotage or disloyalty during the years at war'. During the war, 4000 Japanese Canadians were stripped of citizenship and deported, and after the war another 6000 were sent to Japan. Those Japanese who moved east to avoid deportation were not allowed to buy land, and if they were farmers and chose to lease land, they needed a special license to farm.

When the war ended it remained illegal for Japanese Canadians to return to Vancouver; this remained in place until 1949. It took until 1988 for Canada to admit fault and apologize for the detention. Prime Minister Brian Mulroney offered $21 000 for each internee or internee's survivor.

Japanese Latin Americans

Just as the USA was fearful of Japanese Americans prior to Pearl Harbor it bore similar reservations regarding those of Japanese descent living in Latin America and even made plans to build an internment camp near the Panama Canal so that the USA had a place to detain potential enemy agents. Beginning in 1942 the US government pressured Latin American countries to turn over any potential spies or saboteurs and 13 countries did so, arresting 2300 – nearly 80% of whom came from Peru. The two countries with the largest Japanese populations were – and continue to be – Brazil and Peru. Peru was the first South American country to recognize Japan and accept Japanese immigrants. Brazilians welcomed the Japanese in the early 20th century as they were seen as having a strong work ethic that could be beneficial in the coffee fields.

Initially, Brazilian reactions to Axis aggression were diplomatic and it severed relations with Japan in line with US requests. However, the Vargas government had its own agenda of national unity and felt it needed to deal with its large Japanese population, most of whom read and wrote in Japanese and had not, in the opinion of the regime, assimilated sufficiently. Japanese was banned as the language of instruction (along with all other languages other than Portuguese) and Japanese newspapers were forced to cease publication.

After Brazil declared war on the Axis powers in August 1942 Japanese Brazilians could only travel throughout the country if they were permitted to do so by the police and it was illegal to drive motor vehicles unless they too had police permission. Japanese schools were closed and Japanese-owned businesses had their goods confiscated. On 10 July 1943, Japanese immigrants who lived in the port city of Santos were given 24 hours to vacate the coast. Japanese immigrants were arrested or deported from Brazil on suspicion of espionage yet no breach of national security due to the presence of Japanese Brazilians was ever proved.

Peru's Japanese were targeted by both the government and the USA during the war. In Peru the Japanese population was 26 000, and 1800 Japanese Peruvians were arrested and deported to the USA where they were put in Department of Justice camps with other Issei and Nisei, mostly in the camp in Crystal City, Texas, but also in Santa Fe, New Mexico and Kennedy, Texas.

Japanese Latin Americans were singled out for an express purpose distinct from Japanese Americans and Japanese Canadians: they were used in prisoner exchange programmes with the Japanese government. To do this with Japanese Americans would have violated their civil rights, but as foreign nationals the Japanese Latin Americans had no US constitutional rights. Two prisoner exchanges took place involving over 800 Japanese Latin Americans in 1942 and 1943, many of whom had never been to Japan.

The remaining 1400 were in US internment camps until the end of the war; at this point they were considered illegal aliens and subject to deportation. Their home countries refused to repatriate their citizens so 900 were deported to Japan. Those remaining stayed in the USA, challenging deportation and eventually obtaining US residency. The USA only acknowledged these actions as the result of a lawsuit filed on behalf of Latin American internees, citing the 1988 payment of restitution for Japanese Americans. Living Latin American internees and their heirs were offered compensation but had a limited opportunity to apply.

Detention of Europeans in the Americas

Much emphasis has been put on the detention of those of Japanese descent in the Americas but Italians and Germans were also interned during the Second World War. In Canada 26 internment camps were established to detain those considered to be 'enemy aliens' according to a 1940 Order in Council. Anyone who became a naturalized British citizen (there was no Canadian citizenship yet) after September 1922 who was of German or Italian descent was suspect, as were Communist Party members. Approximately 30 000 people had to register with the Royal Canadian Mountain Police and check in monthly. Approximately 850 Germans, 500 Italians and 100 communists were interned during the Second World War in Canada.

A less well-known component of Executive Order 9066 was that Germans and Italians were also asked to relocate away from sensitive zones. However, the order remained voluntary for them, and few adhered to this. Initially, all Italian- and German-born residents of the USA were considered enemy aliens but there were over 1 million residing in the USA – 695 000 Italians and 315 000 Germans – who were required to register according to the Smith Act of 1940 and, like the Japanese, could be sent to War Relocation Centers and internment camps. The numbers were vast and it was difficult for the government to keep track of them, especially the Italians. 1521 Italians were arrested and 250 were detained in military camps, many targeted for their involvement in the Fascist League of North America, but after the defeat of Mussolini in September 1943 they were released. More extensive was the detention of Germans; over 11 000 were interned in camps throughout the USA.

The USA was more fearful of espionage outside of its borders; the FBI compiled a list of Italian and German Latin Americans that they suspected of having links to the Axis regimes and requested that the governments detain them and send them to the USA. Close to 4300 were sent to the USA and 15% were identified as having links to the Nazi Party – including 12 who were reportedly recruiters. Some recent refugees were erroneously sent to the internment camps, including Jews who had recently escaped Hitler's racial policies only to find themselves interned in the USA.

Another goal that the USA had was to ensure proper treatment of US prisoners of war in Axis camps. In the hopes of reciprocity it treated these enemy aliens as enemy combatants according to the terms of the Geneva Convention. Lastly, there was an economic rationale: to prevent Axis trade with Latin American countries by eliminating any direct connections with Italy and Germany.

As with the Japanese internees, few German or Italian internees were found to have links with the fascist regimes and there was no compensation for detention. In recent years there have been campaigns for reparations similar to those for the Japanese and their descendants but this is a lesser-known component of the treatment of people who had lived in immigrant communities, sometimes for decades.

ATL Thinking skills

How does the treatment of particular minorities affect you and your country today and how would you react if one of your classmates was treated in this way? Who in your culture would be ostracized and why?

▲ Japanese–Canadian men in a road camp

Conceptual understanding

Key questions

→ Why did the USA decide to develop the atom bomb?

→ Why did the USA decide to drop the atom bomb on Japan in 1945?

Key concepts

→ Significance

→ Perspective

In May 1945 war came to an end in Europe but was continuing at a very slow pace in the Pacific. The Japanese were on the defensive, but each Allied victory was brutal for both sides, and the spectre of a land invasion of Japan seemed imminent and potentially bloodier. At Yalta, Roosevelt was so determined to gain Soviet support in the war that he granted a number of concessions to Stalin to secure the promise that the Soviet Union would declare war on Japan 90 days after victory in Europe but after the death of Roosevelt and defeat of Nazi Germany there were fissures in the Grand Alliance.

The Manhattan Project

The story of the atom bomb is compelling, riveting and immensely scientific. There was drama and pathos and, at the same time, there were scientists working 12-hour days, jotting notes on cocktail napkins and arguing abstract possibilities. The US military, President Roosevelt and a group of scientists had a clear objective – to develop a nuclear weapon before the Axis could do so.

In 1939 Albert Einstein, then a professor at Princeton University, signed a letter sent to President Roosevelt explaining recent German technological developments that included splitting the atom in 1938 and explaining how this information could be used. He outlined the potential for a new form of weaponry and urged Roosevelt to be proactive and produce new technology prior to German success in the endeavour.

A Hungarian physicist, Leo Szilárd, recognized that splitting a uranium atom, and the resultant process of fission, could be used to create a chain reaction that might result in a large amount of energy that could then be used to generate energy and perhaps form an atom bomb. Roosevelt used this information to convene the aptly named Advisory Committee on Uranium, later renamed the National Defense Research Committee (1940) that included physicists, scientists and members of the military who were tasked with exploring the potential uses of nuclear fission, but only in 1942 was it decided to try and develop a nuclear weapon.

The project was initially managed by the US army corps of engineers in the Manhattan Engineer District with Columbia University but that was eventually seen as too small and the project expanded to the University of Chicago and University of California at Berkley. It was at Chicago, under the (American) football field where Enrico Fermi successfully created a nuclear reaction in December 1942.

Work on the project took place throughout the USA; approximately 120 000 Americans were involved in the production of the atom bomb, and the British and Canadian governments also provided assistance in developing the weapon. However, only a handful of scientists actually understood the scope and mandate of the project, and they were centred in Los Alamos, New Mexico.

When Dr Robert Oppenheimer of Berkley was asked to head the project, which had become known as Project Y, he chose the site of the Los Alamos Ranch School. It was very isolated but accessible with a nearby water supply which was necessary for the experimentation that took place there. The Ranch School had sufficient infrastructure to house the 30 scientists, their families and the support staff needed to work on weapons assembly in secret. The residents' official address was Box 1663 Santa Fe, New Mexico and the one road to Los Alamos was protected by military personnel. The scientists were a multinational team, many of whom had escaped Nazi Europe. Einstein, however, was not part of the team – he was denied security clearance due to pacifist leanings, even though his letter initially prompted the development of the project.

The scientists determined that about 40 kilograms of uranium would be needed for a bomb, and thus facilities in Oak Ridge, Tennessee and Hanford, Washington worked non-stop to produce enough enriched uranium, and heavy water facilities were developed in Morgantown, West Virginia, Newport, Indiana and Childersburg and Sylacauga, Alabama. After two years of trial and error, Dr Oppenheimer felt that the team had succeeded and a test of the new weapon was planned. The southern New Mexico desert site of Trinity was the chosen location for the detonation of the bomb.

At Trinity Site a number of explosions were detonated to test the effectiveness and power of the bomb. On 7 May 1945, to measure against the new weapon's potency, 108 tons of TNT were exploded. Then, on 16 July 1945, the first successful detonation of the atom bomb occurred, visible for nearly 300 kilometres. The heat of the explosion melted the soil around the explosion, creating a new element called trinitrite, and rather than the expected 100 tons, the explosion equalled 18,000 tons of TNT, vastly exceeding the expectations of the scientists involved in the weapon's development. 'The Gadget', as it had been called by the scientists, was now a weapon, not an abstraction or a concept, and the USA was its sole possessor.

▲ Trinity test, first successful detonation of the atom bomb, July 1945

Decision-making: Reasons for dropping the atom bomb

The scientists continued to work tirelessly as they feared that a similar type of weapon could have been used against the USA. The war in Europe had been won in May, however. On 8 May 1945, the Allies formally accepted the unconditional surrender of the German army and German people. With the death of Roosevelt in April 1945, President Truman was only recently informed of Project Y, and was meeting with Stalin at Potsdam when news of the Trinity detonation reached him.

Despite consistent victories against the Japanese in the island-hopping campaign, the Battle of Okinawa – the last of these – was also the bloodiest battle of the war for the Americans, with over 12 000 Americans killed, 36 000 casualties and the destruction of 34 ships, largely through kamikaze raids by the Japanese.

Until 16 July 1945 the military plan that the USA was pursuing involved starting with the southern-most island of Kyūshū in October 1945. General Douglas MacArthur advised Truman to expect 30 000 US casualties in the first 30 days of fighting. Some members of the joint chiefs of staff put the numbers at over seven times this amount and later analysts have argued that a land invasion would have resulted in millions of casualties on both sides.

There were four notable alternatives to the use of the atom bomb against the Japanese. These were to:

- rescind the demand for unconditional surrender and retain Emperor Hirohito

- wait for the Soviet declaration of war and an invasion of Manchuria by the Soviet army

- intensify the bombing campaign and naval blockade on Japan, in the hope this would destabilize the country and force internal collapse

- detonate an atom bomb on an uninhabited island in the Pacific with Japanese leaders as spectators so that they could see the potential for destruction.

The decision on whether or not to use the atom bomb was ultimately Truman's decision and his top priority was ending the war quickly. The decision was made in late July, and plans were developed to drop the bomb in early August once the weapons were ready.

Results

On 6 August 1945, the Enola Gay bomber dropped the atom bomb called 'Little Boy' on Hiroshima. This city was chosen as it was considered an important army depot and port, but was located in the middle of an urban industrial area. A government report stated that it was 'a good radar target and it is such a size that a large part of the city could be extensively damaged. There are adjacent hills which are likely to produce a focusing effect which would considerably increase the blast damage'. The Hiroshima blast killed between 70 000 and 80 000 people instantly and another 70 000 were injured. The USA estimated that 12 square kilometres of the city were destroyed and Japanese officials reported that 69% of the buildings were destroyed. Over 90% of doctors and nurses were killed; they worked in the city centre, which received the greatest damage.

The Japanese government did not react, but the Soviet government did by declaring war on Japan and beginning its invasion of Manchuria in accordance with the agreements it made with the USA.

TOK discussion

Although he did not receive it until 7 August 1945, Truman was sent a letter that is now known as the Szilárd petition. In it, 68 atomic scientists counselled Truman against using the bomb in the war with Japan. Rather than use the bomb, they suggested that he explain or demonstrate to the Japanese the potential damage they would suffer if the bomb were used against Japan. It was a plea to look at the moral considerations of using the weapon against the Japanese public.

These scientists had participated in the development of the weapons, most of them in Oak Ridge, Tennessee and at the University of Chicago. Given that they participated in the development of the bomb, was this the right thing to do? Why or why not?

Present an argument, a valid counter-claim and supporting evidence. Using these, present a conclusion consistent with the material you have presented.

On 9 August 1945, another bomb named 'Fat Man' hit Nagasaki, one of the largest ports in the south and, like Hiroshima, an industrial area. Unlike Hiroshima, almost all of Nagasaki's buildings were traditional wood structures. The city of Kokura was the original target but the city was obscured by clouds, so the site was shifted. In Nagasaki, immediate deaths were approximately 40 000, and one-third of the city was immediately destroyed.

On 15 August 1945, Emperor Hirohito addressed the Japanese population by radio – the first time they had ever heard his voice – and announced that Japan had surrendered unconditionally to the Allies.

▲ Replica of the Fat Man bomb

ATL Social and research skills

There are three prevailing views regarding the USA's decision to use the atom bomb against Japan:

- There are those who argue that the bombs caused the Japanese surrender, preventing massive casualties on both sides in the planned invasion of Japan.

- There are those who argue that the bombs were an extension of the conventional bombing campaign that included the firebombing of Tokyo. With the sea blockade and the collapse of the Axis countries' power in Europe, they argue that the atomic bombings were militarily unnecessary.

- There are those who argue that the atom bombs were not simply directed against the Japanese. They were a US show of force to deter further Soviet aggression.

There are numerous resources available online and in libraries on these perspectives so some research on each of these positions should be done before class. The class should be divided into three positions, and the merits of each argument should be presented to the entire class. Although only three people will present the positions, others in the class – representing all groups – should contribute by asking clarifying questions and should present counter-arguments.

Each panellist should present the initial argument in approximately five minutes, starting with a thesis that supports that person's position, and should be supported with relevant factual detail.

Useful resources include the following:

- 'The decision to use the bomb: a historiographical update'. *Diplomatic History*. January 1990. Vol 14, issue 1. Pp 97–114.
  http://onlinelibrary.wiley.com/doi/10.1111/j.1467-7709.1990.tb00078.x.

- Tsuyoshi Hasegawa. 2006. *Racing the Enemy: Stalin, Truman, and the surrender of Japan*. Belknap Press of Harvard University Press. Cambridge, MA.

- Nathan Donohue 'Understanding the decision to drop the bomb on Hiroshima and Nagasaki'. Center for Strategic and International Studies.
  http://csis.org/blog/understanding-decision-drop-bomb-hiroshima-and-nagasaki.

- Truman Library: 'The Decision to Drop the Atom Bomb'.
  http://www.trumanlibrary.org/whistlestop/study_collections/bomb/large/.

▲ Enola Gay, the B-29 bomber that dropped the atom bomb

Conceptual understanding

Key questions

→ How and why did the Second World War affect the economies of Canada and Mexico?

→ To what extent did the Second World War change the international diplomatic role of Canada?

→ Why did Mexico emerge from the Second World War with improved relations with the USA and Canada?

Key concepts

→ Consequences

→ Change

Canada

Even before the Second World War began, Canadian Prime Minister Mackenzie King established a close relationship with US President Roosevelt. Initially, it was the Great Depression that led to the promotion of intercontinental cooperation, followed by mutual defence agreements such as Ogdensburg that were intended to deter Axis aggression against Canada. While Canada's position as a Commonwealth country made US politicians wary of integrating it into the Pan-American Union, it also made Canada the ideal intermediary between the USA and the UK. An example of this was the Quadrant Conference held in Quebec in August 1943 in which Roosevelt and Churchill discussed plans to launch a cross-channel invasion to liberate France and discussed developing an atom bomb with Canadian assistance, including a secret agreement to share nuclear technology. King organized the conference but was mostly on the sidelines as Roosevelt and Churchill engaged in secret meetings; Canadian politicians and military leaders had little influence in the prosecution of the war. However, King's facilitation of the conference and willingness to assist those men served Canada well and gave it a position of strength that would be important after the war ended.

The home front and a war economy

At the beginning of the war the government passed the War Measures Act that gave the central government the authorization to implement whatever policies were necessary for Canada to succeed in the war. Through this act wages and prices were frozen and in 1942 rationing of sugar, meat, gasoline, rubber, coffee and textiles began. Salvage campaigns were launched and Canadians contributed scrap metal and newsprint to the war effort.

As British demands for Canadian goods escalated, Ottowa recognized the need to organize the economy effectively. The Department of Munitions and Supply was created with CD Howe as its minister, with wide-sweeping powers to expand industry, fund and build new factories and adapt older ones to the production of war materials. It coordinated all purchases of war materials by the USA and UK. Another result of this department was the expansion of Crown corporations. These were federally or provincially owned corporations that were structured like private firms so that they were free from direct political control. Most production was of different types of military transport: ships, planes and vehicles were produced – a remarkable 815 729 – but also parachutes, uniforms, mine-sweeping equipment and hospital supplies.

This level of production required workers, but the people needed incentives to move to where the work needed to be done. In all, over 1 million were employed in essential war industries and another 2 million in 'essential civilian employment': agriculture, communications and food processing.

To encourage relocation, the government also established the Wartime Housing Ltd Crown Corporation in 1941. From then to 1947 it constructed 32 000 rental homes for industrial workers, servicemen and their families and returning veterans. The majority of children were cared for by family members but the federal government also assisted the provinces in establishing free childcare facilities so that mothers were able to work in the war industries. With so many men overseas, women were necessary to fill all the positions that were newly created or vacated by men serving in the military. Since most materials were going to the UK, which was unable to pay, the Canadian government subsidized British purchases. During the course of the war Canada provided over $3 billion in assistance to the UK. This not only benefited the war effort but helped Canada overcome the Great Depression once and for all.

Through the Crown corporations, the Canadian economy emerged as mixed: the government controlled 28 major firms and had dabbled in social policies through the family allowance, subsidized housing and childcare it provided.

Diplomacy

Roosevelt and King met and created the Ogdensburg Agreement in August 1940. They advanced a plan, developed by Roosevelt, to establish mutual defence in the event of an attack on either country. This led to the creation of the Permanent Joint Board on Defense, an advisory body composed of US and Canadian civilians and military officials who would consult to come to mutually agreed-upon strategies.

Until 1941 its contribution was valued among the Commonwealth countries but within the Americas Canada felt isolated. Not only were all the other countries neutral but with the onset of war the Pan-American Union established a 300-mile neutrality zone around the Americas.

While this was meant to deter German incursions, it left Canada unsure of how the other countries would react to its actions. In reality there was little to fear. The USA was firmly pro-British and the other independent countries either followed suit or confirmed neutrality.

One possibility was to join the Pan-American Union, but this was discouraged by the USA which saw this as a European encroachment in the region that potentially violated the Monroe Doctrine. Realizing the position of the Soviet Union on this issue, Mackenzie King decided he would not pursue this course, and Canada never joined the Union.

However, the rest of the Americas were eager to have good relations with Canada and, as the historian Ogelsby wrote, it became 'the belle of ball'. Due to its affiliation with the British Commonwealth, Canada often worked through the British embassies and legations, rather than establishing its own, and had no Latin American missions until after the outbreak of war in Europe in 1939.

Canada's lack of representation was based on pragmatism rather than philosophy: the Canadian government suffered from a lack of sufficient funding and qualified diplomats. It had diplomatic representatives in the UK, the USA, Japan and France prior to the Second World War. Throughout the course of the war, Canada established formal, independent relations with Brazil, Argentina and later Chile. With these missions, the Canadians exhausted their list of qualified diplomats and had to pursue interested parties from the business sector, rather than the public sector. Interestingly, most of the representatives were French Canadian and there was limited interest from English Canada.

The country's diplomatic advantage came as a successful middle-man between the USA and UK, which was reflected in the positions of future Prime Minister Lester B Pearson. During the course of the war, Pearson was stationed in London, and was then posted to Washington in 1942, eventually becoming ambassador to the USA. His movement demonstrated the changing orientation of Canada away from the empire and towards the hemisphere. Its ability to work equally well with the USA, the UK and even Latin America poised it as a middle power that would possess strength through the ability to serve as a go-between.

Mexico

Mexico's primary role in the war was to produce strategic goods, and this translated into the acceleration of industry and mining, with an emphasis on zinc, copper, lead, graphite, cadmium and mercury which was sent to US factories and ammunitions plants. In a show of hemispheric solidarity, the Mexican government instituted price controls that prevented the value of these desired resources from becoming inflated. As a result, there was an influx of US capital for the first time since the revolutionary period.

During the war, Avila Camacho and his administration equated good citizenship with worker productivity. Both agricultural and industrial workers were targeted in the propaganda, but it was clear that industrialization was seen as the key to victory. Defence of democracy and personal freedoms were equated to financial security for private investors. Despite the predominance of industrialization in Avila Camacho's propaganda, he presented agriculture and industry as inextricably linked sectors; both needed to prosper for Mexico to succeed.

Mexicans were once again encouraged to cross the border and work in the USA through the Bracero programme. Initially implemented as a guest worker programme to help US farms cope with the absence of agrarian workers, the programme provided workers with free transportation to and from their homes and a guaranteed minimum wage of 46 cents per hour. Mexican labour officials were encouraged to make periodic inspections to ensure that the terms of the agreement were upheld. It was so successful – and labour was in such short supply – that in 1943 it was expanded to include non-agricultural workers and the minimum wage was raised to 56 cents. The Bracero programme was controversial in Mexico as industrialists feared that labour shortages would occur at home and lead to demands for higher salaries on the part of factory workers. The Catholic Church, already feeling the effects of an anti-clerical government, was also opposed to the programme; it feared the programme would break familial ties and weaken workers' loyalty to the church. Nonetheless, Mexican workers enthusiastically joined the programme, sending money home, and receiving higher wages than they would have received, especially the agrarian workers. In all, 300 000 Mexicans worked in 25 states during the war, wherever needed, and when the programme expired in 1947 it was renewed by both the US and Mexican governments.

The Bracero programme did not hinder industry substantially. The war resulted in shortages of manufactured goods previously imported from the USA and Europe, so there was a market for consumer goods and demands for import substitution. To facilitate industrialization, the government expanded the Nacional Financiera, Sociedad Nacional de Crédito, Institución de Banca de Desarrollo (NAFINSA), which was established in 1934. This was a government-owned bank that, during the war, provided loans to nascent and expanding industries and also provided government oversight of the development of these industries. The government provided tax exemptions and tariff protection, just as the Brazilians and Argentinians had done in the 1930s. Special emphasis was placed on industries that used Mexican raw materials and natural resources, and the long-term goal was to establish a new export sector of manufactured goods. The textile, food processing, chemical and cement industries saw rapid growth during the war, and the production of pig iron and steel increased, as did electrical output. Initially, the government was hesitant to accept foreign funds but there was a shortage of Mexican capital available for investment, so in 1944 foreign participation was permitted and US investment in Mexico once again increased.

Part of the reason for the success of these economic programmes was the participation and support of the labour movement. The Confederación de Trabajadores de México (CTM) – or Confederation of Mexican Workers – under Fidel Velásquez, was in a much more moderate phase, and supported job creation through voluntary (if temporary) emigration and industrial expansion. The CTM's position at this time was that the masses would remain impoverished unless there was a greater focus on industrialization, leading to a demand for labour and improved conditions. Cárdenas emphasized agrarian reform and Avila Camacho shifted the focus to industrial development.

During the war the Mexican national income nearly tripled from 6.4 billion pesos in 1940 to 18.6 billion in 1945. Per capita income at the time also increased from 325 pesos to 838 pesos, although the distribution of this income was far from equal and the countryside remained impoverished. After over a decade of socialist programming, the economy was focused on industrial capitalism that promoted economic growth but did not necessarily provide social benefits to the less affluent in society.

Diplomacy

In 1941 Mexico suspended its commercial relations with Germany and withdrew its consuls assigned to Germany, France and the Netherlands. It continued to recognize the diplomatic representatives of the countries invaded and occupied by the Germans and refused to recognize German conquests as legitimate.

After Pearl Harbor, Mexico broke off all diplomatic ties with Axis powers and allowed all boats and naval ships from all American countries to anchor in Mexican ports and waters with simple prior notification. The Mexican Congress also gave the president the power to authorize other American countries' forces to cross through Mexican territory if there was a military need to do so.

In January 1942, Mexico participated in the Inter-American Conference of the foreign ministers of all the independent republics of the Americas in Rio de Janeiro and supported US initiatives for all countries to sever diplomatic ties with the Axis. Strained relations with the USA were improved during the war and Avila Camacho resumed relations with both the UK (severed due to Mexican nationalization of British petroleum firms) and the Soviet Union (Calles severed relations and accepted Trotsky's request for asylum). The marked improvement in US–Mexican relations was evident in Roosevelt's visit to Monterrey to meet with Avila Camacho in November 1943 – the first face-to-face meeting of heads of states of the USA and Mexico since *Porfiriato*.

Porfiriato
The era of Porfirio Diaz's government in Mexico 1876–1910.

Mexico was a key supporter of the Pan-American Union and in March 1945 hosted the conference in Chapultepec which led to the Inter-American Treaty of Reciprocal Assistance and Solidarity. This treaty reiterated the ideas of national sovereignty and non-intervention and reinforced the Good Neighbor agreements of the 1930s; as the war drew to a close the Americas were closer than ever and Mexico approached this agreement with optimism.

▲ Franklin D Roosevelt and Avila Camacho

Conclusion

While only Brazil, Canada, Mexico and the USA sent troops to countries in the Americas to participate in the Second World War, the war transformed the entire region. The Good Neighbor policy that began with Roosevelt as, to a certain extent, an economic initiative to cooperate and allay the effects of the Great Depression allowed a high degree of collaboration on the continents during the war, and contributed to Allied success in both Europe and Asia.

Canada was not part of the Pan-American Union or the Good Neighbor policy but it, too, saw the benefits of regional cooperation and emerged more connected than it had been prior to the war. This was seen economically, politically and socially. In addition, through the Office of the Coordination of Inter-American Affairs, there were cultural exchanges promoting unity and understanding that emphasized hemispheric similarities.

The war also led to economic dependence on the USA for the rest of the region. With Europe blockaded and at war with most of Asia, European countries had little opportunity to engage in trade. The USA was far more important to the other countries than they were to the USA, due largely to its economic strength. This was not seen as worrisome to the other countries, and they saw themselves as emerging from the war as equal states with similar goals. However, the end of the Second World War became the beginning of the Cold War and US priorities shifted. The Americas were eclipsed by fear of communism and, less amorphously, the Soviet Union.

ATL Self-management skills

'Even citizens and countries in regions where no fighting took place or that were not central to the actual war had their society and their history significantly altered.'

Bratzel, JF. 2007. *Latin America During the Second World War*. Page 1. Rowman and Littlefield. Plymouth, UK.

Based on this chapter, and the research you conducted in the activity in Section 4.2, how far do you agree with this assessment?

Present an outline of an essay that shows evidence of planning. Include a thesis, supporting evidence in the form of a table, Venn diagram or spider diagram and a concluding statement.

Exam-style questions

1 To what extent were inter-American relations transformed between 1933 and 1945?

2 Examine the involvement and participation of any two countries in the Americas.

3 Evaluate the social impact of the Second World War on women and minorities in one country in the Americas.

4 Analyse the treatment of Japanese Americans, Japanese Canadians and Japanese Latin Americans during the Second World War.

5 To what extent do you agree with the assertion that the dropping of atom bombs at Hiroshima and Nagasaki were necessary to end the Second World War?

6 Compare and contrast the economic or diplomatic effects of the Second World War on two countries in the Americas.

"Compare and contrast..."

Question

Compare and contrast the involvement and participation of any two countries of the Americas in the Second World War.

Analysis

As you saw in the Chapter 1 Skills section, "compare" is to explain the similarities between given items and "contrast" is to explain the differences between those same items.

Many students approach answering the question by giving information first on one item and then on the other, linking the two together in a culminating paragraph that is part conclusion, part analysis. Rather than a comparative format, this sequential, descriptive format does not lend itself to scoring above the 7–9 mark band.

To write an effective compare and contrast essay, you should tackle the items both thematically and in an integrated fashion.

Using a diagram

A useful way to outline or plan an essay is to draw a diagram, and for compare and contrast questions a Venn diagram is very useful. Use the one below to make a plan for this question.

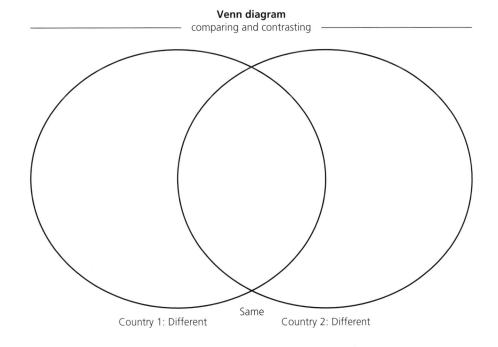

Venn diagram
comparing and contrasting

Country 1: Different   Same   Country 2: Different

A comparative approach

To show how to achieve a comparative rather than a descriptive approach, we will use the United States and Canada as our two countries and we will use the same evidence in both examples.

A sample plan for the *descriptive approach* looks like this:

Canada: Entered war in 1939 by an act of Parliament, fought in multiple fronts, trained pilots, helped feed the UK, accepted British children, advanced the most of all the D-day forces at Juno Beach, fought in the Battle of the Atlantic, Italy, North Africa, helped liberate the concentration camps, 10% of population participated in armed forces.

USA: Entered war in 1941 after bombed by Japanese, fought on multiple fronts, supplied Allies through Lend-Lease Act, helped in victories in Italy, North Africa, France, Battle of the Bulge; part of the Grand Alliance, very active in the Pacific, island hopping, atom bomb.

Conclusion: Similarities of the two are where the battles were fought, and assistance to their allies; differences are reasons for entering the war, scope of involvement (Canada – a lot of its population; USA – more men and available resources), US focus on the Pacific, island hopping and the atom bomb.

This descriptive approach also leads to a lot of repetition in the conclusion, which is a waste of words – and a waste of time.

A sample plan for the *comparative approach* is topic-based, like this:

1   Reasons for involvement – different (Canada supporting its ally UK; USA bombed)

2   Mobilization of population – different (Canada mobilized a tenth of its population)

3   Assistance to Allies – similar (both provided food and materials to the Allies but USA provided billions in Lend-Lease Aid)

4   Theatres of operation – both similar (Europe) and different (Asia; there were Canadian forces but much smaller in scale than European participation)

5   Technology – different (USA atom bomb; Canada training RAF pilots)

6   Diplomacy – different (USA in Grand Alliance; Canada a junior partner)

7   Conclusion – although they joined at different times, the level of involvement was similar yet the scope was different because the USA had a lot more resources and a larger global role than Canada.

5 POLITICAL DEVELOPMENTS IN LATIN AMERICA AND THE CARIBBEAN, 1945–1980

Global context

Like the rest of the world, the 30 countries and dependencies in Latin America and the Caribbean experienced social, economic and political changes and challenges between 1945 and 1980. The geopolitical forces of the Cold War certainly affected Latin America and the Caribbean. Political responses to these forces varied from country to country, from the continuation of democracy to 'populist' movements to outright conflict, revolution and the establishment of authoritarian regimes in the 1960s and 1970s. Areas of study include: conditions for the rise to power of new leaders; economic and social policies; and the treatment of women and minorities.

Timeline

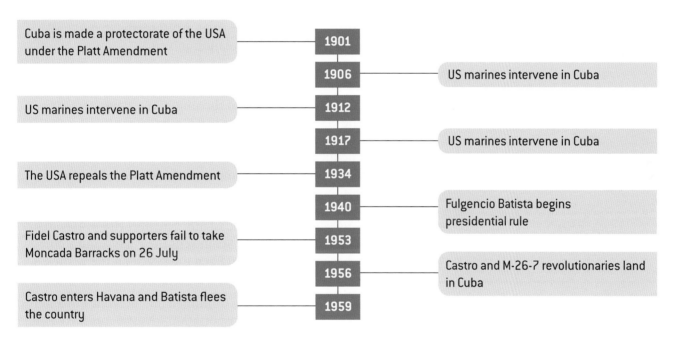

Cuba is made a protectorate of the USA under the Platt Amendment	**1901**	
	1906	US marines intervene in Cuba
US marines intervene in Cuba	**1912**	
	1917	US marines intervene in Cuba
The USA repeals the Platt Amendment	**1934**	
	1940	Fulgencio Batista begins presidential rule
Fidel Castro and supporters fail to take Moncada Barracks on 26 July	**1953**	
	1956	Castro and M-26-7 revolutionaries land in Cuba
Castro enters Havana and Batista flees the country	**1959**	

Background

Cuba is the largest island in the Caribbean Sea, with a current population of over 11 million people. Since colonial times, beginning in the late 15th century, it was the entry port of Spain to the Americas. As the indigenous Taíno population was destroyed, African slaves were transported for labour. Over time, as was the case all over the Americas, the population mixed.

▲ Cuba

In the 19th century, Cuba's proximity to the USA made it attractive to that young country, which was interested in buying Cuba and adding it to the union as a slave state, before the US Civil War. Cuba is 97 miles from the US coast of Florida. As other Spanish colonies in the Americas fought for independence in the 19th century, Cuba's independence movements failed. Despite impassioned intellectuals who fought for it, many Spanish royalists fleeing other newly independent countries came to Cuba, adding a strong pro-Spanish sentiment to the island. The port city of Havana was the first place to which Spain sent their navy and troops to claim back the empire and keep the peace on the islands, so independence movements were effectively quelled in Cuba.

Sugar plantations and African slavery continued and grew in Cuba in the 19th century. Large US sugar and transportation investments increased, even though slavery was abolished in Cuba in 1886. In 1898, when the US cruiser *Maine* was blown up in Havana harbour, allegedly by the Spanish according to the US press, the USA invaded Cuba and ended Spanish rule. This was the emergence of the USA on the world stage. Cuban intellectuals who had fought for independence from Spain had also sought economic independence from the USA, but Cuba was made a protectorate of the USA under the Platt Amendment in 1901. This was repealed in 1934, but by then US hegemony was firmly established.

The Platt Amendment and the subsequent deep US involvement in the island's affairs created simmering resentment in Cuba in the first half of the 20th century. The Cuban government was prohibited from entering into any international treaty that would compromise

Cuban independence or allow foreign powers to use the island for military purposes. However, the USA reserved the right to intervene in Cuban affairs to defend Cuban independence and maintain 'a government adequate for the protection of life, property, and individual liberty'. The Cuban government also had to improve sanitary conditions on the island and relinquish claims on the Isle of Pines (now known as the Isla de la Juventud). It had to sell or lease territory for coaling and naval stations to the USA. This clause ultimately led to the perpetual lease by the USA of Guantánamo Bay. The Cuban government had to make a treaty with the USA that would make the Platt Amendment legally binding by incorporating its terms in the Cuban constitution.

Political causes

Given the legacy of the Platt Amendment and the enormity of US investments in Cuba, in the sugar industry, banking, telecommunications, tourism and more, the USA intervened with marines in 1906, 1912 and 1917 to defend these interests from unstable governments. By the 1940s US intervention changed to supporting authoritarian politicians who perpetuated the status quo, while keeping up the pretence of democracy and elections. One especially corrupt politician was a former sergeant named Fulgencio Batista, who was alternately in power as president or ruled through puppet presidents in 1940–44 and 1952–59.

The Batista government corruption created mounting resentment against the USA, as university students and workers demonstrated for 'Cuba for the Cubans'. Batista's crackdown was brutal, and many dissidents were imprisoned and tortured. James DeFronzo, a US academic historian, has characterized the 1940s and 1950s in Cuba as enacting minor reforms in agriculture, labour and education, but nothing that challenged US businesses. In addition, he notes that the Cuban governments under Batista's aegis, when he himself was not president, were 'corrupt and notorious for theft of public funds'.

Once the USA repealed the Platt Amendment in 1934, Cubans were disappointed to see that US interests and influence continued, as the Cuban business leaders and political leaders supported it. Some disgruntled Cubans, following the intellectual **José Martí's** ideas, formed the **Auténtico Party**, calling for true, authentic reforms, and an end to corruption and dependence on the USA. By 1947, when Auténtico politicians proved ineffectual, many members left to form the **Ortodoxo Party**. They vowed to disclose corruption and restore honour to a Cuba truly independent of entrenched US influence. One member, running for Congress, was a charismatic young lawyer called Fidel Castro.

Another political party that was slowly making headway among industrial and manufacturing workers, especially Afro-Cubans, was the Communist Party of Cuba (PCC). Its members were particularly active and successful in producing union leaders and pressuring businesses and the government to accept some labour demands.

By 1952 Batista felt sure enough of USA support to end the 'presidency' of Carlos Prío Socarrás with a military coup, pre-empting elections and taking over the government. This became the political trigger to the revolution.

▲ Cuban dictator Fulgencio Batista circa 1935

José Martí
Cuban national hero during the 1890s and leader of the independence movement from Spain.

Auténtico Party
Cuba's largest opposition party to Fulgencio Batista, in power from 1944–1952.

Ortodoxo Party
Splinter party from the Auténtico Party in 1947. They had nationalist ideals and were fed up with government corruption.

Communication skills

On YouTube, find the film *El Mégano* (1955), by Cuban film director Julio García Espinosa, about wood coal burners. Starting 12 minutes into the clip, watch about five minutes of the film.

What does this excerpt tell you about the harsh life of the charcoal makers? How are the 'rich folks' portrayed?

boom and bust
Refers to economies that are dependent on exporting one product, and who are therefore vulnerable to prices rising or falling, usually with devastating national results.

Communication skills

On YouTube, find the hotel scene from the film *Our Man in Havana* (1959), set in pre-revolutionary Cuba.

What does this clip tell you about the hotel scene in Havana?

Social causes

Social inequality grew in Cuba as a result of the seasonal nature of the sugar industry. Both Cuban and foreign-owned sugar plantations and mills let their workers go for part of the year, creating a wandering class of workers who then crowded the cities, desperate for any kind of work, but generally as domestic servants in the tourist industry. Unemployment figures were between 20% and 30% between 1943 and 1957, adding to social inequity.

Land ownership also compounded the social situation, as sugar plantations and cattle ranches owned one-third of agricultural land. This created a large group of landless peasants, who were habitually underemployed and earned less than one-fifth of Cuba's per capita income in 1956. Statistics show a skewed panorama: overall the literacy rate in Havana was 88%, but it was only 50% in the countryside. Amid the opulence displayed in Havana at hotels and gambling casinos, the disparity was obvious to all and fuelled resentment and social malaise.

Middle-class Cubans were also feeling underpaid and exploited working for US businesses when compared to US standards at the time. The US per capita income in 1956 was US$2000 a year, but the Cuban per capita income was only US$374. Cuba's national statistics relating to the availability of medical services, communications (telephones) and transportation (automobiles) as well as to food intake were among the top in Latin America, but this was a reflection of the Havana tourist industry and not spread out in Cuban society. Indeed, all classes felt the pinch in lack of food supplies and fuel, as the government could no longer purchase them.

Cuban and US business owners felt increasingly annoyed with Batista as social protest in the form of guerrilla warfare from the 26 July Movement (M-26-7) burned mills, industries and public works to force Batista out. Batista and the army were unable to prevent this.

Economic causes

In the early 20th century sugar constituted 80% of Cuban exports, which often suffered '**boom and bust**' cycles. The island was especially hard hit during the Great Depression in the 1930s. There was more stability, albeit at lower prices than the world market value, after the Second World War when Cuba had a guaranteed 28% access to the US market. Cuba provided a safe environment for US investment so that by the first third of the 20th century the USA controlled 75% of Cuba's sugar production, as well as banking. By the 1950s, the USA owned 85% of all foreign investments. This also included a growing concern: tourism. Cuba became known as the playground of the Caribbean.

Vast land tracts were used for sugar cane, which forced Cuba to import food, as internal agricultural production was insufficient to feed the population. Sugar plantations and mills hired dependant farmers and farm workers. These workers were only employed for parts of the year and became part of the urban proletariat at other times.

By the middle of the 20th century an uneven distribution of wealth was apparent in Cuba. Statistics showed high income among professionals, especially in medicine. There was great advancement in communications development (telephones) per capita.

Rule of Fidel Castro (1945–80)

Cuban nationalism

Elections in 1952 did not take place, because Batista, with the support of the army, took over the government. Dissident groups planned a revolt. This was the ill-planned attack on the Moncada Barracks, led by Fidel Castro on 26 July 1953. These were young people, some from the Ortodoxo Party, who were sick of the Batista government corruption and were steeped in the independence movement of 1898 and the ideas of the poet José Martí.

The revolt failed; some rebels were killed and others imprisoned. Castro and his group used the ensuing trial to expound on the corruption of the government. Castro used his oratory skills in an impassioned speech titled 'History will absolve me'. Nonetheless, he was found guilty and jailed until 1955, when he was exiled to Mexico. The exiles now called themselves 'The 26th of July Movement, (M-26-7)' in remembrance of the failed Moncada attack.

▲ Fidel Castro (on the left) and his companions being convoyed to Vivac prison in Santiago de Cuba, 1953

The Cuban Revolution

From Mexico, with his brother Raúl Castro and the Argentine revolutionary Ernesto (Che) Guevara, Castro planned a landing in Cuba in 1956, but it failed. The M-26-7 survivors, including the Castro brothers and Che Guevara, fled to the Sierra Maestra Mountains in south-eastern Cuba.

ATL Communication skills

On YouTube, find the video clip of *Cuba before Fidel Castro's Communist Revolution*, Part 1/12.

Watch this clip with one or two classmates and discuss the following.

1 What impression does this 1950, US-made film give of Cuba?

2 How does this fit with the following quote?

'Cuba is a rich country with too many poor people' (Fidel Castro).

ATL Research and communication skills

On the Internet, find and read Castro's *History will absolve me* speech.

What were Castro's main grievances against the Batista government?

ATL Research and communication skills

▲ Fidel Castro and Che Guevara

What does this photograph convey about Castro and Guevara?

The group of rebels resorted to guerrilla warfare until they were able to gather enough support among the peasants and the urban proletariat. As the Cuban military realized that Batista had few supporters, his troops abandoned him; even the USA no longer backed him. Castro and his M-26-7 supporters were able to take over and enter Havana in January 1959.

Political issues

A major priority became institutionalizing the revolution in order to create a more equitable Cuba. As the dominant classes lost power and emigrated, mass mobilization of volunteers stepped up to help. This led to the creation of the Junta Central de Planificación (JUCEPLAN) – the central planning committee – in 1960. Castro knew that Cuba needed reform to create a more equitable society, and thought a centrally planned government and economy would be more efficient in instituting broad changes and facing opposition, especially from the USA. A major political consequence of the revolutionary government led to the **expropriation** of US property valued at US$1 billion. In addition to US antagonism, Castro also alienated many middle-class Cubans who found his measures too radical and left the country (10% of the population).

expropriation
When property is taken by the state for public use, with or without approval of the owner and with or without compensation.

Close to Castro was his brother Raúl and the Argentine Che Guevara, who were Marxists. Through them, Castro used the organizing power of the Communist Party of Cuba (PCC). This proved to be a useful alliance once the revolution succeeded, although members of the party had not supported him before. Castro used their discipline and labour organization to help restructure the government, thus uniting M-26-7 guerrillas and leaders with communist ones. This relationship was strengthened once the Soviet Union conveniently stepped in to support Castro when the USA pulled out and **boycotted** Cuba.

boycott
The ban on all commercial relations with a country as a form of punishment.

Economic issues

Another major structural change in the government dealt with the farm hands in the sugar industry. This led to the formation of the National Institute for Agrarian Reform (INRA) in 1959. Its target was to nationalize the mostly US-owned sugar mills and land. The INRA began by limiting the size of landholdings, breaking up the huge sugar plantations, many of them foreign-owned. The land was distributed to rural workers.

Although rural worker conditions improved, the overall production goals were not achieved. By 1970 Castro wanted to produce a record harvest, or **zafra**, of 10 million tons. This was a symbolic figure and meant to be a moral victory, but the target was not reached, and greatly disappointed idealists and volunteers from all over the world who came to help.

A poster by Eufemia Álvarez, produced in 1970, had a caption: 'tras el fracaso de la zafra de los diez millones, este afiche llama a convertir ese revés en una victoria', which translates as 'After the failure of the 10 million tons *zafra*, this poster calls for turning that setback into victory'.

Castro did succeed in raising wages for workers, gaining approval among both rural and urban workers. He also established highly successful literacy campaigns. Students took one year off and taught people to read and write. For a year, 300 000 volunteers collaborated in this campaign, which generated results as well as a sense of unity and purpose to the first years of the revolution.

Consolidation of the Cuban Revolution

In 1960 small businesses were nationalized, about 58 000 in total, including businesses producing most goods and services. However, labour absenteeism was high – between 20% and 50% – as there was little incentive to work and little to buy. In addition, when middle- and upper-class Cubans left Cuba for the USA, they left a gap in both capital for new business and professional expertise.

Oil for fuel and electric power became scarce as the Cold War world sided with the USA in boycotting all economic transactions with Cuba. This was a setback for industrial and agricultural production. As some countries (Canada, Mexico, Spain and others) slowly broke away from the boycott, joint ventures carefully planned by the Cuban government set up new enterprises and industries to spur the economy.

Although the moral imperative of social equity worked for a while to motivate Cubans to work selflessly for the benefit of all, by the 1970s wage incentives began to be used, as they tend to produce better long-term results. By 1976 small-market economy measures were introduced, such as establishing farmers' markets, in an effort to make the Cuban economy grow. These measures worked well – perhaps too well – and by the 1980s were rescinded to prevent corruption of revolutionary and socialist ideals.

In any case, the military and economic assistance of the Soviet Union from the 1960s to 1990, as the major buyer of Cuban sugar, certainly helped stem the greatest effect of the US boycott of Cuba. At first the USA used its clout to convince many countries to join the embargo, but by the late 1990s most countries had decided to ignore it. In 2009, 187 countries in the UN General Assembly formally voted against the US embargo of Cuba.

> **zafra**
> Spanish word meaning 'sugar-cane harvest'.

▲ Volunteers trying to reach their 10 million ton harvest target

> **Class discussion**
>
> Under what conditions will people rally behind causes for ethical reasons? Why are material rewards needed for people to continue to support them?

As Fidel Castro aged and became ill, he delegated power to his younger brother Raúl Castro. Since being elected President by the Cuban National Assembly in 2008, Raúl Castro has opened up the acquisition of consumer goods, such as computers and mobile phones. He has improved the quality of public transportation with Chinese buses and continued to allow small private enterprises, such as restaurants, taxis and the lease of state land by farmers.

Social and cultural policies

Castro's social programmes were definitely in favour of the working classes. A countrywide literacy campaign, where students and literate volunteers travelled to rural locations in 1961 to teach other Cubans how to read and write, became emblematic of the first social policies of the revolutionary government. New schools were built and teacher-training institutes founded. The campaign was a resounding success and increased the government's popularity. Other popular measures included building rural hospitals and clinics and opening private beach resorts to the public. Even so, despite an initial rise in wages, living standards became uniformly low.

▲ Young women working for a literacy campaign, parading with big pencils in the streets of La Havana during the Cuban Revolution, 1 May 1961

As the guerrilla fighters began to take over the Cuban army, many pro-Batista officers were tried and executed in public trials. Although the world watched this gruesome display in disgust, the retribution sat well with many Cubans, who were tired of torturers and assassins in their military and police forces.

An important social development in revolutionary Cuba had to do with gender. As the 'playground of the Caribbean' and the site of mafia-owned gambling and prostitution rackets, Havana in the 1950s had been known for its 100 000 prostitutes, reputedly the highest amount of prostitutes per capita in the world. By 1961 the rehabilitation of prostitutes had begun. They were sent to boarding schools, often with childcare centres for their children, to be trained as seamstresses, textile workers in factories, workers in workshops and banks, and as drivers. They were given healthcare and psychological support. Some went on to further their studies.

The Federation of Cuban Women (FMC) was founded in August 1961 by Vilma Espín, guerrilla fighter in the Sierra Maestra. She was a chemical engineer who had studied at the Massachussets Institute of Technology when she joined the M-26-7. Later, she married Raúl Castro and became deeply involved in the Cuban government, especially in advancing women's education and equality. Under her leadership until her death in 2007, the FMC began by rehabilitating prostitutes, but soon Espín convinced Fidel Castro of the necessity of gender equality and opportunities if Cuba was to progress and socialism succeed. Women had to be incorporated into the workforce.

The FMC grew to 3 million members. Schools were organized all over Cuba, with a strong impetus to convince women to study. They were trained as office workers, mechanics, tractor operators and chicken producers, and received instruction on the tenets of socialism in Cuba. The FMC also organized centres for sex education, childcare facilities so that women could work outside the home and organized public health brigades where women were trained in vaccinating children.

▲ Vilma Espín (centre, in plaid skirt), President of the Federation of Cuban Women, welcomes Soviet cosmonaut Valentina Tereschkova, 1 November 1973

The FMC was also responsible for creating cultural campaigns among Cubans to end racial discrimination and prejudice against Afro-Cubans, as well as gender bias in the Cuban population. By 1974 the FMC began working on the Family Code, a truly revolutionary change in culture

ATL
Communication and thinking skills

Read Vilma Espín's obituary, *Vilma Espin de Castro; Politician Empowered Women in Cuba*, in the US newspaper *The Washington Post*, 19 June 2007.

Compare this to the obituary issued by the Cuban Communist Party (PCC), *Vilma Espin, 1930-2007: A Heroine of the Cuban Revolution, A Builder of a New Society*, as well as Fidel Castro's words at the time of her death in 2007.

TOK discussion

How far can we say that the different political perspectives of these obituaries agree or disagree with Vilma Espín's life and accomplishments?

Research skills

Trace the course of persecution of other minorities, for example, Jehovah's Witnesses, in Cuba after the revolution.

that called for both spouses to share fully in household and child-rearing tasks. Discussion groups were formed all over the country to explain and convince Cubans of the importance of gender equality in daily life, not just the workplace. Women faced fathers and husbands who traditionally had not allowed them to work outside the home. In 1953 only 13.5% of Cuban workers were female. The needs of the revolution turned out to be a strong argument. Some jobs could be done near home in the country, such as beekeeping, raising rabbits and chickens, and growing vegetables. Others required more study, for example, the professions. By 2012, females made up 46% of the Cuban workforce.

In addition, the Family Code attempted to change the culture of the double standard where men and women worked all day at a factory and came home for the woman to cook, care for the children and do laundry while the man rested. Although the double standard has diminished, if not entirely, women have an ear in the FMC should they require support at home.

Although the Family Code was revolutionary in changing traditional gender roles, this was done within the framework of traditional values of heterosexual marriage and family. Homosexual behaviour was punished in the penal code and during the 1960s the gay community was persecuted. Military Police raided beaches and gay bars and detained gays in re-education concentration camps. Gays and lesbians revoked their membership of the Communist Party. By the early 1970s the brutal raids and homophobia began to ease and public policy was liberalized by decriminalizing homosexuality in 1979. Vilma Espín's daughter, Mariela Castro, now heads the National Center for Sex Education where lesbian, gay, bisexual and transgender issues, such as homophobia, are openly discussed starting in 5th grade classrooms.

The Cuban poet and novelist Reinaldo Arenas was persecuted for his homosexuality under Fidel Castro's regime. His writings were banned in Cuba, he fled the country and published numerous works in France and the USA. Suffering from AIDS, Arenas committed suicide in New York in 1990.

Treatment of opposition

At first, in 1959, support for Castro was overwhelming for his toppling of the hated Batista. As months went by, however, some moderates began to wonder about democratic elections. Castro avoided the issue of elections by giving in to popular demands relating to issues such as wages, universal education, agrarian reform and calling this more important. Fidel Castro said 'Politiquería (politicking) is as odious as tyranny'.

By April 1961, when Castro publicly announced that Cuba would be governed by the Communist Party of Cuba (PCC) under his leadership, many M-26-7 and more moderate leaders in the government protested. When they resigned, they were joined by anti-communist Cubans, landowners and former Batista soldiers, forming a counter-revolutionary guerrilla army in central Cuba. The CIA assisted them with air-dropped supplies. Still, support for Castro was enormous, and men and women joined in the defence of the revolution. The counter-revolutionary forces were defeated and thanks to **Committees for the Defense of the Revolution (CDR)** in the cities, dissent was starkly reduced. Even so, in Castro's Cuba, political dissidents left the country or were jailed.

Successes and failures

Free and accessible education for all through to university and complete health coverage have been the much-touted successes of the revolution. Certainly, compared to conditions in 1959, this is so. Cuba has the lowest infant mortality in all of the Americas, for example. As for social and cultural changes, gender equality has improved markedly – 63% of university graduates are women, over 40% in scientific and technical fields. In the government, women comprise 40% of Cuban leaders.

By 1976, a new constitution entrenched the PCC rule with a state administration and popular organizations. These consisted of assemblies with elected officials and secret ballots who chose delegates to the National Assembly, 90% of whom were PCC members. The purpose was to practise daily socialism. Cuba has also continued to maintain strong armed forces.

After the 1980s and the end of Soviet support, there has been more economic liberalization, as manifested in farmers markets, fairs and private real estate. However, corruption has spread too, leading to many trials and jailings, including apparatchiks (members of the Communist Party) and dissidents.

In the 1991 Fourth PCC Congress, Fidel Castro unequivocally expressed: 'We are the only ones and there is no alternative'.

In 2000 the government began liberalizing agricultural cooperatives, legalizing self-employment and home-based tourist restaurants, trying to diversify the economy. However, the country is still dependent on the income from sugar.

As for failures, despite educational access for all, professionals find that this does not make for material improvement or good salaries. Until 1990, consumer goods were poor quality Soviet or Soviet bloc manufactured goods. Hard times for Cuba occurred after the end of Soviet subsidies in 1990 with the break-up of the Soviet Union. This also affected repairs of Soviet machinery and spare parts.

Another failure of the revolution is providing free, popular elections of leaders and representatives. More political participation in local cadres and block committees has occurred in the 21st century, but no national elections have been allowed and dependence on Fidel Castro's charismatic leadership has now switched to dependence on his brother Raúl. It has been hard to keep up revolutionary fervour for half a century, despite the Castros' ability to sense the needs of people and to inspire them with a common purpose; this fervour wears thin after 50 years.

Committees for the Defense of the Revolution (CDR)
Militias formed in Cuba by Castro in 1960, when foreign invasion appeared about to happen.

In addition, despite the negative associations with the past when Havana was the playground of the Caribbean under Batista, Cuba has had to allow tourism and hotels to be built by Spain and other European, Korean and Chinese hotel chains. Through this, the island's tropical beauty and lovely climate can attract tourists and much-needed revenue.

The Cuban Revolution has proven more far-reaching than any in the Americas, including the Mexican Revolution in 1910. Cuba's economy was drastically changed to a classic communist model: central planning with very few private enterprises. It has a one-party communist system. An objective of communism is a classless society, and this was also a goal of the PCC. This has been changing in the last few decades with political connections or revolutionary pedigree creating some privilege.

On the positive side, the levels of literacy and professionalism as a result of education for all, free medical care and extended life expectancy all compare favourably with western European countries. Rural Cuba has profited from this especially and has avoided rural to urban migration, thereby supporting sugar and agriculture.

In the final analysis, it can be ascertained that the revolution succeeded in spreading the wealth in the country and providing equity among Cubans, as demonstrated by excellent medical coverage and educational opportunities for all. This also includes other areas of achievement, such as sports. Cuban athletes have excelled in boxing, as well as in other Olympic sports. Literacy levels are one of the highest in the world: 99.8%, according to the 2010 census.

Impact of the Cuban Revolution

US reaction

In 1960, Fidel Castro made a trip to the USA. As retaliation for Cuban expropriations of US investments in Cuba, the Cuban Airlines airplane that brought him to New York was taken over by the US government.

At first the USA waited and observed, but by 1961 decided to act by supporting, financing and training a group of Cuban exiles covertly by the CIA. President Eisenhower broke diplomatic ties with Cuba in January 1961. After intelligence reports affirmed that once an invasion took place Cubans would all join the exile army against the Castro regime, he authorized an invasion of Cuba with US support in April 1961 at the Bay of Pigs. The results were a fiasco, as the Cuban people were organized and able to repel the attack.

The Cuban reaction reaffirmed and strengthened Castro, who then came out as a socialist '**Marxist-Leninist**', but also as a nationalist defending Cuba from foreign invasion. This led to the creation of the Committees for the Defense of the Revolution (CDR), a popular militia that surged from 300 000 to 800 000 members. Cuba got closer to the Soviet Union and, especially in the 1970s, adapted Soviet institutions and models to Cuban reality.

Castro was always afraid of another US invasion. By 1962 the Soviet Union was actively arming the Cuban defence system. The USA sent U-2 spy planes to take photographs in Cuba and these showed that the Soviet Union was installing a nuclear missile base in Cuba, to defend it from

Communication skills

Watch the video clip called *Fidel Castro speaks English to American reporters* on YouTube.

Listen carefully to Castro protesting the US takeover of the Cuban Airlines airplane.

Despite his English language difficulties, how successfully does Castro convey his feelings and opinions?

Marxist-Leninist
Term used to refer to someone who adheres to the communist principles espoused by Karl Marx and Vladimir Lenin.

another US invasion (see page 405 for information on the Cuban Missile Crisis). The world watched aghast, as US President John F Kennedy and Soviet Premier Nikita Khrushchev were 'eyeball to eyeball' on the brink of nuclear war. After intense negotiation, the Soviet Union removed missiles and the USA promised not to invade Cuba.

The Cuban revolution prompted Kennedy's **Alliance for Progress**, as a way of promoting peaceful instead of violent revolution. Later it was deemed more practical to support anti-communist governments and dictatorships that were willing to receive US aid to suppress communist guerrillas in their countries (see, for example, El Salvador).

After 1975 the USA was unable to keep countries such as Italy, Mexico, Canada and Spain from trading with Cuba. Between 1970–75 eight Latin American countries established diplomatic relations with Cuba. In 1996 the USA passed the Helms–Burton Act in order to put more pressure on countries that wanted to trade with Cuba. This included suing international companies that used former US-owned businesses in Cuba. Due to firm opposition abroad, as well as a strong anti-Castro Cuban lobby in the US state of Florida, US Presidents Clinton, Bush and Obama have not implemented these measures fully. So far, no US Congress has allowed for the lifting of the embargo on the grounds of Cuba's lack of democracy and human rights abuses. However, these serious issues have not stopped the USA from supporting the military dictatorships in Guatemala and Chile, or authoritarian oil-producing governments in the Middle East and Africa.

In 2009 President Barack Obama lifted travel bans and money remittances to Cuba by Cuban Americans, but at the time of writing, his administration has not been able to lift the embargo. However, diplomatic relations between the two countries are now on the road to normalization, after Presidents Obama and Raúl Castro met at the Summit of the Americas in Panama in April, 2015. Party politics and losing precious Cuban American votes appear to be the causes.

Alliance for Progress
US aid program offered to Latin American countries by US President John F. Kennedy in 1961 to help improve the social and economic conditions that would encourage socialist revolutions.

ATL Communication and thinking skills

Look at this contemporary cartoon about the Missile Crisis.

1   Where is Cuba in this cartoon?

2   What message does this convey about Cuba's role in the crisis?

Effect on Latin America and the Caribbean

An important immediate effect of the Cuban Revolution in Latin America and the Caribbean has been the sheer vitality of the revolutionaries in engaging popular support to topple an abusive regime. Soon after, as Cuba became a communist country defying US geopolitical hegemony in the Americas, the Cuban example caused admiration and, in some cases, desire for imitation. This caused members of the new Cuban revolutionary government to consider exporting the revolution as inspiration for young revolutionists all over the continent in the 1960s and 1970s. The Argentine Che Guevara was one of the strongest proponents of this, although Fidel Castro, ever mindful of US retaliation, was more cautious. For Che Guevara, it ended in death in Bolivia in 1968 while he was exporting the revolution there.

▲ Erich Blossl was a German aid worker in 1967 when Bolivian military officers asked him to photograph Guevara's corpse. His photograph circled the globe and remains a haunting image to this day.

Cuba continued to inspire leftist revolutionaries after the creation of OLAS (the Organization of Latin American Solidarity) to support communist parties and revolutionists such as the Tupamaros in Uruguay and Salvador Allende's socialist government in Chile in 1970 and in Angola in Africa in the mid 1970s.

Impact on the world

In the 1960s and 1970s at least 50 000 Cubans in the military were sent to assist African rebels in Angola and South Africa. It can be said that they helped to overturn the apartheid government in South Africa.

Cuban doctors and health workers have been sent abroad starting in 1963, when the first medical workers were sent to Algeria. Cuban doctors were the first responders in the Haiti earthquake in 2010. The Cuban government has also sent teachers, nurses and engineers as advisers to developing countries, particularly in Africa.

ATL Social and communication skills

Find out if there are Cuban immigrants in your community and interview them as to their opinions on the Cuban Revolution's successes and failures.

5.2 Populist leaders in two countries (1945–80)

> ## Conceptual understanding
>
> ### Key questions
> → What conditions in Argentina and Brazil led to the rise of populist leaders?
>
> → How successful were they in solving national problems?
>
> ### Key concepts
> → Change
>
> → Significance

Case study 1: Argentina

Argentina is located in the southernmost section of South America, on the Atlantic Ocean. It is the fourth-largest country in the Americas. Its grassy plains, or pampas, have long fostered enormous cattle and sheep ranches. The capital city of Buenos Aires developed in the late 19th century as an increasingly urban and cosmopolitan industrial and port city, harbouring a third of the country's population. Argentina's industrialization in the early 20th century occurred at the same time as 2.5 million European immigrants arrived, between 1870 and 1930. Political leaders tried to mobilize and control this group of workers and use them as a broad popular base to challenge the landed oligarchies that had ruled Argentina since independence in 1818.

Background

Since the late 1930s, Argentina, like most Latin American countries, had been promoting national industry through the ISI model in order to add to traditional grain and meat exports started in the 19th century. After the Second World War, the country had a large manufacturing sector, textile mills and metalworks. Falling grain and meat exports and laid-off agricultural workers due to the Great Depression had already propelled a shift of agricultural labour to rural–urban migration, creating new Argentine workers. This group had grown from 500 000 in 1935 to 1.4 million workers moving to Buenos Aires by 1947. By then the labour force also included the children of European immigrants, who were steeped in **unionism**.

Rising expectations of social equity generated a strong momentum toward change in Latin America. The politics of the 1940s saw alternating **oligarchic parties** supported by the army, frustrating many who had hopes for a more fair Argentina. When the military split between the old school elitists and the younger officers from more modest backgrounds, who disdained democratic procedure toward change as a farce, the situation in Argentina became ripe for **populism**.

▲ Argentina

unionism
Movement to encourage workers to join unions and become powerful political players.

oligarchic parties
Conservative political parties in Latin America, stemming from the late 19th century, generally tied to land, agrarian or mining interests.

populism
Power strategy used by leaders who represented the common people using emotional speeches and feelings of nationalism.

Juan Domingo Perón

Rise to power

Following the military split, the young officers formed a group called the Grupo de Oficiales Unidos, United Officers Group (GOU) who, apart from disdaining democratic procedure to promote urgent social change, professed admiration for Franco's Spain. By 1943 the GOU had enough power to establish a military regime in Argentina. One of the members of the GOU was Colonel Juan Domingo Perón, who held the posts of army secretary, minister of labour and, in 1944, also war minister.

It was Perón's position as minister of labour that enabled him to unite the weak and disparate workers unions in order to achieve better wages for them. At the same time, he promised entrepreneurs that he would control the workers. This was how Perón became a populist: he was all things to all people.

Legitimacy

By 1945 Perón was Vice-President in the military government headed by General Edelmiro Juan Farrell. Perón continued to stand up for the workers by controlling the union leaders. During strikes, he sided with workers forcing the owners of factories, for example, the US-owned Swift and Armour Meat Packing Plants, to give concessions to the workers, such as better job security and safety. Perón established labour courts and social security benefits for factory and railroad workers. In this way, he bound workers and union leaders to him with debts of gratitude and personal loyalty. Soon the word 'peronistas' in Spanish, meaning Perón supporters, became popular.

The military government of Argentina, for all its labour advances, however, was criticized regarding its legitimacy. US ambassador Spruille Braden called the government fascist. The Argentine oligarchy attacked the government for its 'social agitation'. The middle classes demonstrated for democracy and freedom of speech.

By October 1945 the Farrrell-Perón government had come to an end. Perón was allowed one last impassioned radio speech and he was imprisoned. The popular reaction to his detention was overwhelming.

Although Perón won power by acclamation, he was keenly aware that democratic legitimacy was paramount. He resigned from the army, formed the Labour Party and ran for president on the platform of social justice. He campaigned with his wife Eva Perón, who with her charisma and enthusiasm became an invaluable political asset to him. Perón was elected by 52% of Argentines in February 1946. His party and allies won 66% of the congress, so his government could now easily pass reform laws in favour of Argentine workers. He won an election that even US contemporary observer, John Moors Cabot, admitted was the 'fairest in Argentine history'. There was no question about the legitimacy of his government. He then was re-elected in 1952, but this presidency lasted only until 1955, when he left the country. After his return from 17 years of exile in Spain, Perón ran for president again in 1972 and was re-elected.

Self-management and thinking skills

On YouTube, find a video clip entitled *17 de octubre de 1945* which shows newsreel footage from October 1945 and the massive crowds shouting "We want Perón!"

Even if you do not understand Spanish, the documentary footage showing the crowds of workers taking over the streets of Buenos Aires will give you a visual idea of the support for Perón.

▲ Juan Domingo Perón with his wife Evita (Eva)

Ideology

As a populist leader, Perón exercised authoritarian means to contain popular mobilization and to increase profitability for the country. Since his GOU days, Perón had observed that the agrarian oligarchy remained intact as a class, and that the landed interests found themselves still able to veto progressive development projects and workers' rights. In many Latin American countries, post-war political instability derived from the continuing tensions over agrarian reform and the mobilization of peasants and workers.

As a populist leader, Perón made it his ideology to represent the common people, the workers, and their imperative need for a change toward social justice. As such, he was not above being a demagogue and a shrewd manipulator. He gave impassioned radio and balcony speeches, using Argentine slang and popular phrases, and consciously united agricultural and urban workers to widen his power base.

Perón's views included ultra-nationalistic statements, articulated in his speeches, touching a sensitive note in Argentines, who increasingly reesented foreign investment, particularly from the USA and Britain. Anti-foreign sentiment, as well as rhetoric exalting the poor and disenfranchised workers, was evident in his wife Eva's writings and radio speeches. Perón also appealed to part of the middle class, who approved of Argentine nationalism. He also courted the Catholic Church and campaigned for religion classes in public schools, another source of appeal for part of the middle class in Argentina. Corporatism embodied Perón's ideology. Corporatism can be defined as the organization of a society into industrial and professional corporations serving as organs of political representation and exercising control over persons and activities within their jurisdiction. This was how Perón ran his government.

After his exile in Spain, Perón ran for president again in 1972. His old platform of social justice and economic independence now included a 'third position' between communism and capitalism, reflecting the intensity of the Cold War at the time.

Social policies

Perón's social policies were meant to continue to support industry, while at the same time make life less harsh for workers. In this, he followed the Catholic Church's doctrine: the Church had issued a stern indictment of brutal capitalism in 1891, and demanded just wages and labour conditions for workers, the right to unionize and strike and the duties of the state in brokering social justice. This ideology certainly fitted well with Perón's and gave it moral legitimacy.

Regarding Perón's social policies, it is important to emphasize the supportive role of his wife Eva. True to her roots in rural poverty, she sided with the *descamisados* or 'shirtless ones' of Argentina. She set up a foundation to help the poor, built hospitals and housing projects and received voluntary percentages from workers wages, lottery proceeds, private donations and taxes to fund the social projects of the Perón government. She was the first to admit her deep resentment of the moneyed classes, who repeatedly snubbed her. She actively intervened in labour, bargaining on the side of the workers.

descamisados

Spanish word for *shirtless ones*, who could not afford new clothes. This term was used in Argentina by Eva Perón to refer to the poor.

By 1952 Argentine workers had achieved an enviable standard of living in Latin America. They had decent homes thanks to government housing projects and access to schools, hospitals and sports facilities. They wore clothing and used appliances manufactured in Argentina. They enjoyed paid vacations, cheap access to beachside resorts, as well as social security and disability benefits. Workers' conditions improved in other cities, as well as Buenos Aires, notably Córdoba and Rosario, where new factories sprang up. The worker was king, gaining in dignity and self-esteem. US historian Peter Winn calls this self-confident working class Perón's most enduring legacy.

Eva Perón also made a major contribution to women's suffrage in Argentina. She convinced Perón to give women the vote in 1947. This also turned out to be a shrewd political move, as 60% of Argentine women voted for Perón in the 1952 election.

The elite always despised Perón because under his government they had lost power and social standing. The oligarchic landed classes and agriculture had lost sway to industry. They especially loathed Eva Perón, and when she was ill with cancer, coined the nasty phrase '¡*Viva el cancer*!'. Eva Perón died in 1952, and although her social work was by then institutionalized in the Perón government, her charisma and energy were sorely missed.

Economic policies

Argentina had undergone a change from an agricultural to industrial economy between the 1930s and the 1960s.

Source skills

The economy in Argentina

Study the following table.

	1960 prices		1937 prices	
	1927–29	1963–65	1927–29	1963–65
Agriculture	27.4	17.1	30.5	18.4
Oil and mining	0.3	1.5	0.6	3.5
Manufacturing	23.6	33.7	13.4	18.6
Construction	4.2	3.6	3.1	2.6

▲ Argentina: Percentage distribution of gross domestic product according to principal sectors Díaz-Alejandro (1970)

Questions

1   What areas of the economy show the most growth?

2   What areas show the least growth?

Even if the statistics above are impressive, they pale next to the incredible growth shown after Perón's election in 1946 and the end of his first term in 1952. The good state of the post-war economy allowed Perón to fulfill his campaign promises. Congress passed his reforms and legislation. Perón's five-year plan for economic independence from foreigners and

social justice for lower-class Argentines was widely acclaimed. Perón now sought to win influence with industrialists, with high tariffs to protect their products and awarding them lucrative government contracts to Argentine industries.

Between 1945 and 1948, manufacturing in Argentina increased by 50%. Industrial employment rose by 30%.

TOK discussion

Modern societies seek an ideal state of happiness and social justice for their citizens.

Did Argentines under Perón achieve equity at last?

Some economic indicators are given below to help you consider this question:

- By 1950, foreign goods had been practically replaced by national ones. The few items for industry that were imported constituted only 10% of foreign expenditures. Manufacturing made up 25% of the national product, growing much faster than agricultural production.

Industrial workers were 25% of the labour force by 1951, accounting for 1.5 million workers.

- The country's foreign debt was paid off. Foreign enterprises, such as the US-owned Telephone Company and the British-owned railways, were bought by the government, creating huge popular approval. Between 1945 and 1949 workers' wages rose by 50%. As for equity in sharing Argentine wealth, workers now had 25%. Economic growth was experienced by entrepreneurs and the middle class, as well.

Political issues

The popular outpouring of affection and approval for both Juan and Eva Perón was manifested in election results. In the 1946 election, Perón ran against a candidate from the Radical Party, who had the support of the oligarchy allied with a part of the middle class. The landed oligarchy saw the burgeoning power of the workers as a threat. Other segments of the middle class, especially those in the countryside, supported Perón. The USA also backed the Radical Party candidate, as more amenable to its business investments.

As Perón's government continued to improve the standard of living of Argentine workers, the government was not above using political propaganda to promote itself. Perón used the celebration of the 131st anniversary of Argentina's independence from Spain to publicly sign a unilateral declaration of economic independence for Argentina in 1947. Particularly symbolic cases of foreign investment were the British- and French-owned railway systems. The British received US$600 million and the French US$45 million for their companies. Perón made sure these purchases by the Argentine state were amply publicized.

There were cracks in the system even while the government achieved results. Perón alienated socialists and communists who had lost workers' support as union leaders.

As President between 1946 and 1952, Perón's focus on improving workers' status while at the same time promoting Argentine industry had great success. In his second term, world economic trends, as well as internal affairs, would take their toll, culminating in Perón's exile to Spain in 1955.

He was re-elected in 1972 upon his return to Argentina from Spain, but he was too elderly to succeed in exercising power. He died in 1974.

PERON CUMPLE

YA SON NUESTROS!

1º DE MARZO DE 1948

Question
Study this poster. What is the poster's message?

◀ Ministry of Education of Argentina poster, 1 March 1948. This image of a man holding a train says 'Perón keeps his word: now they are Argentine!'

The treatment of opposition

Perón's government became increasingly authoritarian, even though he had the popular mandate through elections. He did not tolerate opposition to his government, and censored the press, controlled universities, stopped student demonstrations, weakened politicians in congress and controlled the judiciary by appointing *peronistas*. He co-opted the support of reluctant or even opposing industrialists by handing out or withholding government contracts, credit, industrial machinery imports and labour unions.

During the years 1952–55, Perón's government had increasing opposition. The treasury was running out of the money accumulated during the Second World War, selling beef and grain to the belligerents. With Perón's unabashed privileging of industry, agricultural products had decreased. In fact, large farmers and cattle ranchers became an increasingly disgruntled opposition to Perón's government.

Industry required foreign industrial machinery, and this was expensive. With workers' wages raised and a decreasing treasury, inflation was growing. In an unpopular and highly criticized move, Perón began to court foreign investors, in order to generate funds. To attract them, wages were frozen. These measures, which went against his campaign promises in years past, created widening opposition.

Perón, whose **personality cult** had became increasingly apparent over the years, now felt secure enough to repress opponents. This was done through the use of a secret police, who produced detainees and used torture to weaken perceived enemies of Perón. Workers began to demonstrate and strike, especially when wages were frozen.

After Perón's wife Eva died in 1952, his personal life became less than exemplary. This quickly brought the opposition of the Catholic Church. Perón then took up an anti-Church stance, causing his person to be excommunicated by the Pope.

Only when the navy revolted in opposition in 1955, did Perón recognize that he had gone too far; he resigned and left for exile in Spain. Upon his re-election in 1972, Perón had new opposition groups to deal with, which had formed during his 17-year exile while military and civilian governments of little success had ruled the country.

> **personality cult**
> National propaganda used to praise and uplift a political leader's position and create a group of supporters who admire the leader.

Case study 2: Brazil

The Great Depression had a worldwide effect, but in Latin America there was an enormous impact, as countries depended on exports. These were reduced by 50% to 75% between 1930 and 1934, leaving a sequel of enterprises, farms and mines that had to close and fire their workers. In Brazil this was the backdrop to the social unrest and political control used to keep the peace. The country's economy was particularly vulnerable to boom and bust cycles because of its dependency on coffee exports. The traditional oligarchies that had led the export economy and controlled politics were now in question for being unable to solve the nation's economic and social problems. This situation gave rise to populism in Brazil, and the **caudillo** leader Getúlio Vargas.

The political system of Brazil, which was a loose federation of states in the 1930s, allowed the states the independence and power to impose taxes and grow crops according to their resources. This growth, however, became very unbalanced as two states, São Paulo (the leading coffee producer) and Minas Gerais (the leader in dairy products), became powerful enough to alternate their candidates for the presidency of the country. São Paulo became a particulary powerful powermonger, supported by the fact that its coffee exports accounted for nearly 40% of Brazil's national product.

▲ Brazil

> **caudillo**
> Term used for a political leader or strongman, usually with military origins, who rules in an authoritarian manner with little regard for democratic processes.

Getúlio Vargas

Vargas was from the southern state of Rio Grande do Sul. He was a member of a landowning family and was in the army as a young man, but left to study law. He became part of the *Gaúcho* traditional, landed Brazilian *caudillos* from the south, who were tired of the corrupt power system of the two leading states. The party that wielded power in Vargas' state was the Partido Republicano Rio-Grandense (PRR) and strong-arm politics was its hallmark. In particular, the party was antagonistic to the São Paulo (*paulista*) political elite, made up mostly of large coffee growers and exporters, who controlled the Brazilian government.

> **Gaúcho**
> South American cowboy, traditionally from the pampas.

▲ Getúlio Vargas, pictured wearing 'gaúcho' dress, circa 1950

Rise to power

Getúlio Vargas became involved early on in politics and the fraudulent use of votes. He represented his state in Rio and was made finance minister in 1926 by President Washington Luís. Vargas won the Rio Grande do Sul gubernatorial race in 1928 with no one running against him. As the Great Depression began to affect Brazil after 1929, President Luís insisted on maintaining the gold standard to accommodate foreign lenders, thereby depleting Brazilian treasury reserves. The country's balance of payments was in the red and public disapproval mounted, especially among the coffee-growing elite, who had a product to sell to the world and no buyers. To this group of disgruntled citizens was added an opposition group consisting of politicians from other states who resented the alternating presidential leadership of São Paulo and Minas Gerais. Military officers joined in the plot to bring down the President. Vargas was part of the conspiracy, calling for a constituent assembly and the writing of a new constitution.

The military removed President Luís from office and installed Vargas in his place in November 1930. It is a tribute to Vargas' charisma and strong leadership that he was able to push aside military officers who wished to rule and consolidate power in the presidency, ruling exclusively by decree. In classic *caudillo* fashion, he began to centralize power by appointing new state governors who answered directly to him. This was a distinct change for Brazilian state politics, which before had autonomy to run the states with little interference from Rio.

Not all states fell into line and Vargas had to deal with dissent in the powerful state of São Paulo. Vargas' appointed governor had been unable to co-opt the power elites in that state, which by 1932 staged what was called the Constitutionalist Revolution, demanding that Vargas call a constituent assembly for a new constitution. The armed confrontation between federal and *paulista* troops lasted four months and ended when the federal troops succeeded by surrounding the city of São Paulo.

Vargas also concentrated on neutralizing military groups that posed a possible threat to his power. One such group of officers known as the October 3rd Club who advocated for strong social reforms was disbanded by police raids to the club. Vargas continued to concentrate power using clientelist moves, skillfully choosing loyal politicians to form the constituent assembly that hammered out a new constitution between 1933 and 1934. Power was vested in the central government, not the states, and this included controlling interstate taxation which had previously greatly enriched each state. A legislature with two chambers and elected presidents would rule. The first president, Vargas, was elected by the Constituent Assembly.

After opposition groups to Vargas emerged, he suspended the new constitution and legislature and cracked down on challengers to his power. By 1943 he suspended elections, citing the world war as a reason, and postponed elections until 1945. Every aspect of Vargas' rise to power put the legitimacy of his government into question. A different situation arose in 1950, when he ran for and was elected president by legitimate means.

Ideology

Getúlio Vargas was among those who resented the power politics of 1930s Brazil, overwhelmingly controlled by coffee exporters in politics. He believed that Brazil's future lay not in an economy dependent on world prices of coffee especially, but also sugar and tropical fruits.

By the time Vargas had consolidated his power in 1934 with the new constitution, he also began to show his populist ideology by making sure the constitution included strong nationalism. Foreigners were restricted from owning land and entering certain professions.

Brazil was very much inserted in the world context of the 1930s, with the winds of war brewing in Europe and Asia, and the competing ideologies of fascism and communism. Vargas dealt with opposition groups piecemeal. He first attacked the left by jailing leaders. He dealt with armed insurrection in 1935 in several cities by suspending constitutional rights. This allowed him to use high-handed tactics such as torture, swift trials and jail to eliminate opposition entirely.

Fascist groups felt that Vargas supported them since he had destroyed communist opposition, but this was not exactly correct. By 1937 Vargas had hammered out an ideology by suspending the constitution yet again and creating the **Estado Novo** (or New State), the embodiment of a new ideology. Certainly, this ideology borrowed from elements of fascist leaders in Italy, notably Mussolini and Salazar in Portugal, but it also included a strong brand of Vargas as an authoritarian leader. In fact, by 1938 Vargas had also eliminated the fascists in Brazil. He could now rule as a dictator.

The context of the times certainly shaped Vargas' ideology during his dictatorship between 1937 and 1945. He surrounded himself with technical experts to take in hand Brazil's comparative advantage in selling resources and services essential during the Second World War, to gain from the war for the benefit of the country. In doing so, Vargas wanted to make sure that Brazil gained support from the belligerents in building its military-industrial complex, as well as who paid the most for what Brazil had to sell. Certainly, capitalism was an important part of Vargas' ideology and Brazil traded heftily and bought armaments from the Allies and the Axis until well into the war. In 1942 Brazil ended its neutral stance and joined the Allied side.

As an ideology, the Estado Novo concentrated on making Brazil a modern state. It promoted industrial and economic development though a centralized administration.

Social policies

Vargas' Estado Novo was meant to garner popular support for his government among the middle class and the workers. This was achieved by labour legislation that guaranteed a minimum wage, weekly rest, an eight-hour workday and work security after 10 years on the job. A social security system was established for all workers. Soon, the controlled press was touting Vargas as 'the father of the poor'. Centralization included school reform and centrally produced school textbooks.

Nationalism is always a good way to gain the public's favour, and Vargas certainly cultivated this art. In particular, like his much-admired Mussolini, and other fascist European dictators of the 1930s, he wanted

> **Estado Novo**
> Authoritarian state in Brazil 1937–1945, instituted by Getúlio Vargas, who ruled with dictatorial powers.

ATL Social and communication skills

It is often assumed that political parties have an ideology that they wish to promote. Brazilian political parties after 1945 positioned themselves among three groups: the left-leaning União Democrática Nacional (UDN); the Partido Social Democrático (PSD), which included bureaucrats and industrialists; and Vargas' Labour Party, the Partido Trabalhista Brasileiro (PTB).

In a group of three, research their ideologies and discuss this evaluation by US historians:

'These three remained Brazil's principal parties until 1964. They were often described as nonidelogical, personalistic, and opportunistic – in short, not to be regarded as modern political parties' (Skidmore *et al*, 2005: 163).

large construction projects that showed Brazilian greatness. The influence and visits to Brazil of one of the most famous architects of the 20th century Le Corbusier helped to found architectural movements and modern buildings in São Paulo, Rio de Janeiro and Belo Horizonte.

Even as the Estado Novo sought to make Brazil a modern industrial nation by building steel plants and other heavy industry factories, Brazil remained mostly underdeveloped and rural. In these factories, unionism was carefully monitored, preferring the use of corporatism to mobilize people to support the Vargas regime.

After he was elected president in 1950, in an effort to garner support through populism, Vargas raised low salaries by 100%, generating opposition among the industrialists and the landed elite. Despite the wage increase, prices rose and inflation with them, from 11% in 1951 to 20% a year later. The balance of payments was negative and, at the same time, an expected US loan was not forthcoming.

Vargas tried to solve the impasse by appointing a new minister of finance to stabilize the economy. Minimum wage increase became the bone of contention and produced a confrontation between the minister of finance's austerity measures and the minister of labour, who called for a wage increase. When Vargas interceded between the two, he sided with the finance minister and fired the labour minister.

Economic policies

Vargas made a huge effort to industrialize in the 1930s. The Estado Novo was a blueprint for improving the life of Brazilians, and he began to implement it by stopping all payments on the national debt. To generate more state funds, he decreed a tariff on coffee exports, as well as a new income tax. To stimulate industry, he privileged industries in petroleum, hydroelectric power and engines. These and other Brazilian industries received a protective tariff for national manufactured products.

With a rise in industry and workers, more Brazilians improved their purchasing power, thereby generating consumption of consumer goods. Vargas increased income for the nation by centralizing the tax system by the federal government. This move weakened the states by eliminating state taxes.

When Brazil declared war on the Axis powers in 1943, the Vargas government became closer to the USA. This was an economic boon to Brazil, as the USA helped to finance a huge steel plant in Volta Redonda, which greatly stimulated all heavy industry in Brazil. In addition, Vargas' Estado Novo organized international lobbies, or **cartels**, for Brazilian resources such as coffee, sugar, tea, natural rubber and so on, as well as promoting state-owned enterprises to build aircraft, engines and trucks. As Brazil joined the Allies in 1942, trade with Europe was replaced by trade with the USA.

Although Vargas had used **clientelism** as a way to converge power, his Estado Novo fostered a merit-based system in its administration. The Labor Code of 1943, however, held that workers in factories and their labour unions were controlled directly by the government in the person of the minister of labour.

▲ Worker opens the nozzle of a ladle to pour molten steel into ingot moulds in Volta Redonda, Brazil, 1995

cartels
Groups of competing producers (of oil, copper, manufactured goods etc.) who get together to fix prices at the highest level to insure profit.

clientelism
A political system that creates a dependence between supporters who provide financial and political backing to politicians, who in turn promise to support supporters' interest when elected.

Once elected president in 1950, Vargas created Petrobrás, a state-owned oil works and Electrobras, a state-owned power generation and distribution company.

Political policies

Due to Vargas' shaky national and political support, he used authoritarian and populist practices to rule. He suspended the constitution and ruled by edict. He quickly alienated the *paulista* (from São Paulo) oligarchy who accused him of being a dictator and tried to stage a coup in 1932. However, Vargas organized a constitutional committee who made a more modern constitution than the 1889 one, including giving women the vote in 1933 (to vote for the constitution of 1934).

Vargas was elected president. Using the violent 1937 clashes between communists and fascists to call for order, he suspended the constitution again and dealt harshly with both groups, but especially the communists.

The new constitution made by Vargas this time would be voted in by referendum for an Estado Novo. However, in the end it was a hand-picked assembly that voted in the new constitution, giving Vargas the absolute power he wanted. He eliminated political parties and labour unions.

When Vargas decided to postpone the 1943 elections, he began to build a populist labour party, presumably to run for president. He promoted strong nationalist sentiments, culminating in a decree restricting foreign firms in Brazil. After the war ended in 1945, however, this sentiment was not popular with Brazilians who felt that foreign investment would help to continue Brazil's development. In another populist move, Vargas freed jailed leftists and allowed the Communist Party to organize without police interference. If many had thought that Vargas was sympathetic to fascism, now people began to think he was sympathetic to the left.

The end of the 15-year dictatorship of Vargas' government came when he was deposed by a military coup in 1945, to initiate a democratization process for Brazil. Although Vargas left Rio for his ranch in Rio Grande do Sul, he did not stay out of power entirely and was senator for the state, waiting in the wings.

Elections were held and General Enrico Dutra, an Estado Novo participant, was elected. He called together another Constituent Assembly to produce another constitution in 1946, which returned to the decentralized tenets of the 1934 constitution and upheld citizens' rights. In addition, the Dutra government undid the Estado Novo push toward industrialization and diversification of the Brazilian economy, and once again coffee returned as the top product. The Cold War world also manifested itself in the growth of the Communist Party's growing participation in election results and labour unions.

New constitutional rights notwithstanding, Congress voted to outlaw the Communist Party in 1947, thereby persecuting its members and sympathizers. Vargas began to rally supporters to the PTD, including many from the PSD.

Social and thinking skills

Vargas and Perón were by no means the only populist leaders in Latin America and the Caribbean. Make a grid of the social, economic and political ideas of the following populist leaders:

- José Luis Bustamante in Perú
- Carlos Ibáñez del Campo in Chile
- José María Velasco Ibarra in Ecuador
- Lázaro Cárdenas in Mexico
- Jorge Eliécer Gaitán in Colombia
- Carlos Andrés Pérez in Venezuela
- Rafael Ángel Calderón Guardia in Costa Rica
- Errol Barrow in Barbados
- Maurice Bishop in Grenada

In 1950 he ran for and was elected president with 48.7% of the popular vote, for the first time through legitimate means. Brazil again returned to a push for industrialization and technology, even asking the USA to join in an economic study of Brazil for future development. The results pointed at weaknesses in the energy and transportation sectors. The USA was willing to invest in these areas, but as a populist and nationalist Vargas wanted more control of foreign firms in Brazil. His populist measures and authoritarian ways alienated the military, which began to plot for a coup to oust him in 1954. By then, the serious financial crisis of the country and the impasse within the Vargas government regarding minimum wage became inextricably mixed with the Lacerda scandal (see below). In an ultimate gesture, Vargas committed suicide and left a note saying:

'Nothing remains except my blood. I gave you my life, now I give you my death. I choose this way to defend you, for my soul will be with you, my name shall be a flag for your struggle.' It ended: 'I take the first step to eternity. I leave life to enter history.'

The treatment of opposition

Vargas considered communists a menace to Brazil and persecuted them severely, particularly their leader Luis Carlos Prestes, who was jailed in 1936. Vargas also used the spectre of communism as a means to scare the public into destroying them and augmenting his power. Starting with Vargas' dictatorship in 1937, the press was censored. Security forces were able to act with impunity, as all constitutional rights were suspended. As the Second World War forced Brazil to take sides, Brazilian security forces apprehended 'enemy aliens', in the form of German entrepreneurs and Japanese Brazilians.

By the early 1950s dissatisfaction with the Vargas government had risen. There was protest because he censored the press and suppressed all opposition. A particularly nasty example of this was the bungled assassination attempt of an opposition newspaper journalist Carlos Lacerda by a member of Vargas' bodyguards, although Vargas himself was not implicated. A military officer was accidentally killed instead, which caused uproar among the military, who called for Vargas' resignation.

5.3 Democracy in crisis (1945–80)

Conceptual understanding

Key question

→ What were the multiple causes for democracy to break down in Latin America between 1945 and 1980?

Key concepts

→ Causation

→ Perspectives

Reasons for the failure of elected leaders

Economic reasons

In the post-war period **Import Substitution Industrialization (ISI)** proved successful and brought an expansion of industry improvements in employment and real wages, as well as the transfer of technology into the region. In Chile new industry created a powerful entrepreneurial class that in part came from and initially allied with the landed oligarchy. In Mexico and Argentina the industrialists were not related to landed oligarchies, so had different political aspirations. In any case, the new class of industrialists brought new power brokers to the political scene by the 1950s and 1960s, who demanded control of labour and governments that supported capitalism. This system worked for a while, as long as there was no economic crisis.

Between the 1960s and the 1980s the ISI system began to break down and create economic distress in Latin America. Despite industrial output in Latin America, manufacturing, machinery, spare parts, patents and technology continued to be bought from developed countries, thus creating a dependency. The system could easily fail if these vital items became too expensive or were withheld for political reasons. This situation could easily arise in the Cold War world, as the case study below shows.

Consumer goods produced by national industries had limited markets, since income inequality precluded mass consumption. At the same time, technology and automatization both in industry and agriculture began to affect unemployment figures, further lowering purchasing power and limiting the market. Unemployment would create a restive social component after the 1960s. Ailing democratic presidents sought palliatives by taking out loans from the **International Monetary Fund (IMF)**, but this obliged governments to follow strict and unpopular economic austerity measures that often ended up creating more social discontent.

Political reasons

Many countries experienced intense struggles over distribution, led by populists such as Perón in Argentina and Vargas in Brazil. The expansion

Import Substitution Industrialization (ISI)
Economic program implemented by many Latin American countries 1930–1970 to develop national manufacturing and industry to avoid dependency on developed countries for their products.

International Monetary Fund (IMF)
An international organization created by the UN to maintain financial stability by loaning money to countries. This obliges the governments to follow strict economic austerity measures.

of urbanization and industrialization created large and increasingly powerful classes of workers, industrialists, the middle classes and the urban poor. In Mexico and Brazil these classes were a political resource utilized by populist leaders as well as politicians in general. Controlling labour organizations and their votes were certainly vital to Brazilian, Argentine and Mexican politics in the 1950s and 1960s.

The larger backdrop of the Cold War was also a strong factor in the breakdown of democracies, as political parties became polarized along leftist or rightist ideologies. With the example of Cuba becoming a communist country and a role model for socialist and communist parties in many Latin American countries, the USA overtly and covertly began to support and train military officers in counter-revolutionary measures. In addition to covert actions by the CIA in Cuba, Bolivia, Ecuador, Brazil, Peru, the Dominican Republic, Uruguay, Chile, Nicaragua, Grenada, El Salvador and Haiti, the USA made overt efforts to help attenuate social malaise, such as President John F Kennedy's Alliance for Progress and **United States Agency for International Development (USAID)**. The results of these efforts are mixed and can be viewed in different ways. As politics became polarized in the Cold War period between 1960 and 1980, political parties in Latin America tried to develop a middle ground between the left and right. The Christian Democrats tried unsuccessfully to become the party of the middle, taking a moderate course with some social reforms, but maintaining the values of capitalism and free enterprise. They had mixed success in different countries.

> **United States Agency for International Development (USAID)**
> Foreign aid program created in the Kennedy administration in 1961, to ensure that basic human needs in developing countries are met, thereby avoiding a socialist revolution.

Social reasons

Unemployment rose and social malaise ensued in the 1960s as political parties divided along left and right ideologies, and began to co-opt voters and organize demonstrations. The perception of social chaos mounted in many countries, as Cold War polarization of leftist and rightist parties strove to represent their constituencies. It is a testament to the rigid tenets of the bipolar Cold War world that many countries in the world replaced democratically elected governments for military or authoritarian dictatorships. In Latin America the list is long:

- Cuba: Fidel Castro 1959–2006
- Bolivia: René Barrientos 1964–69, Hugo Banzer 1971–78
- Chile: Augusto Pinochet 1973–89
- Paraguay: Alfredo Stroessner 1954–89
- Peru: Juan Velasco Alvarado 1968–75
- Haiti: François Duvalier 1957–71
- Nicaragua: Anastasio Somoza Debayle 1967–79
- Panama: Omar Torrijos 1968–81
- Brazil: Humberto Castelo Branco 1964–67; Arturo da Costa e Silva 1967–69; Emílio Garrastazu Médici 1969–74; Ernesto Geisel 1974–79
- Argentina: Jorge Rafael Videla 1976–81
- Uruguay: Juan María Bordaberry 1972–76

5.4 Rise of a military dictatorship in one country (1960–80)

Conceptual understanding

Key question

→ What conditions inside and outside of Chile caused democracy in the country to break down?

Key concepts

→ Causation

→ Perspectives

Case study: Chile

The Cold War period after 1960 affected the entire world, but this section focuses on the country of Chile, located in the southern cone of the Americas. This is a nation that prided itself on its democratic traditions. By the late 1950s, popular and rural worker sectors expressed their demands in labour conflicts and strikes. A rise in the cost of living and an annual inflation rate of 51% were made worse by straitened circumstances forced by loans from the IMF.

As the 1960s approached, the moderate Christian Democratic Party (PDC) offered the middle ground. The left offered socialism and communism, while the right proposed capitalist values as a solution to economic ills. Cold War alignments were expressed in the news media as Chile reflected global polarization tensions. The left focused on conflicts as part of a historic struggle against systematic exploitation that had to be replaced by a new and more equitable system. The right focused on conflicts as an attack on democracy that had to be defended by upholding principles such as private property and what it considered anti-communist western values.

▲ Chile

Allende's rise to power

Social, economic and political reasons

The moderate PDC won the presidential election in 1964. President Eduardo Frei's government, however, was plagued by miners' strikes and student demonstrations for educational reforms, especially by 1965. Yet part of Frei's domestic policy included the encouragement of workers' unions, the membership of which increased markedly even as the extreme right and left divide continued to grow, with the PDC in the middle. The left accused the PDC of slowing progress towards a more just Chile and of serving the interests of the upper classes. The right, on the contrary, saw the PDC as encouraging revolutionary changes that seemed in keeping with the left. Extreme parties were born on both sides: the Revolutionary Leftist Movement or Movimiento de Izquierda

271

Revolucionario (MIR) and the rightist National Party or Partido Nacional. Civilian–military relations became tense in 1969 due to low salaries and poor military equipment and supplies. Frei's government attempted to improve this situation.

An important constitutional reform was presented by the Frei government as a concession to the young people that helped to elect Frei. After much debate, Congress agreed to lower the voting age from 21 to 18, which by the presidential elections in 1970 meant nearly 1.5 million new voters. Frei's other new support, women voters, were strongly encouraged to join 9000 '**Mothers Centers**'. Nearly 500 000 women did so and received work training and 70 000 sewing machines bought with easy credit to start businesses.

Frei's foreign policy followed a narrow road continuing domestic reforms, yet avoiding direct confrontation with US hemispheric hegemony. There was internal political pressure to nationalize US-owned copper companies. Frei opted for a middle way, the '**Chileanization**' of the mines, and with the backing of Congress opted to buy part ownership of these companies and invest profits in improving processing plants. The results of this process were not as profitable as planned, as the US companies retained lucrative contracts. Still, Chile benefited from pro-USA leanings following the Cold War and was able to receive loans from the **World Bank** and the **Inter-American Development Bank (IADB)**.

By the time of the presidential elections of 1970, Frei had been unable to comply fully with his campaign promises. The PDC had tried, in a Cold War world, to create an alternative proposal to solve deep social, political and social issues; a middle position between capitalism and communism. It did not work. With the country deeply divided in three camps, Salvador Allende, the leader of the leftist coalition Popular Unity or Unidad Popular (UP) received the largest percentage: 36% of the popular vote in the 1970 elections. The traditional congressional approval of the candidate with the largest plurality was bitterly debated this time. The centrist PDC was crucial in supporting Allende, if he would guarantee respect for constitutional democratic process. US covert pressure to not confirm Allende was unsuccessful.

With Allende as President, the sociopolitical climate in Chile became highly charged. The upper and middle classes demonstrated their fears of a leftist government with massive removal of capital, creating financial chaos. Some even opted for leaving the country immediately, closing factories and firing employees and workers.

Mother Centers
Women's organizations created by the Chilean government in 1954 to support rural and urban women by teaching them household skills, for example, sewing, and later used by succeeding governments to co-opt women as political supporters.

Chileanization
Process initiated by President Eduardo Frei between Chile and the US for the gradual purchase by Chile of 51% of the shares of US-owned copper companies.

World Bank
UN financial institution created to lend money to developing nations, but can also put financial and political pressure on them.

Inter-American Development Bank (IADB)
Established in 1959, this organization was created to alleviate poverty in Latin America and the Caribbean, providing grants and technical assistance for development projects.

Research and thinking skills

Find the Chilean left-leaning musical group 'Quilapayún' on YouTube.

Listen to their song 'La batea' (the basin) in which they sing about the effect of the Allende election on the rich, leaving the country on the road to neighbouring Argentina. They refer to them as 'momios' or 'momiaje', 'mummies' that cling to ancient, dried-out traditions.

Listen also to leftist singer Victor Jara's songs 'Plegaria a un Labrador', 'Prayer for a peasant', and 'El Arado', 'The Plough', where he dignifies the downtrodden farm worker.

What emotions do these musicians try to evoke? Analyse their song lyrics to see their messages to the young people who listened to their music and attended their concerts during the Allende government.

Allende and his UP party wanted to institute deep changes in the social, political and economic system of the country and build socialism in Chile. This included a people's assembly and a replacement of capitalism for more state-owned enterprises, including mines, banks, insurance and foreign commerce. However, the next three years, between 1970 and 1973, were characterized by deep divisions in the six leftist parties that made up the UP on how and when to implement these radical changes: through legal and constitutional means versus immediate revolution. Although Allende preferred the former, his UP party was anything but united behind him. The centrist PDC became split in factions and the rightist National Party warned of a socialist takeover. Even the Catholic Church was unable to call for more conciliatory language and debate to avoid civil war.

Allende began to implement a domestic policy that enlarged government social services and the nationalization of key industries to the state, thereby alienating entrepreneurs. He continued the agrarian reform started by his PDC predecessor Frei. Despite congressional opposition and the US financial blockade of the Chilean economy, Allende followed through in nationalizing the copper mines and processing plants, as well as many banks and financial institutions. By 1971, however, the lack of coordination within the disparate factions of the UP started to become evident in the agrarian reform, which seriously threatened the private sector in agriculture, as expropriation of large landholdings created violent confrontations. Allende's foreign policy included reaching out to countries in the Soviet bloc, as well as inviting Fidel Castro to Chile. This was during the tense period in the Cold War when the Cuban-supported guerrilla Che Guevara had been killed in Bolivia in 1968, while exporting the communist revolution. The beginning of the 1970s brought an increase in third world countries that challenged the predominance of the two superpowers. Allende also visited the Soviet Union, where he was warmly received. Certainly Allende's socialist government in Chile became a focus for the bipolar conflict.

▲ Santiago, Chile, 1 October: Chilean President Salvador Allende (centre) waves to his supporters in Santiago a few days after his election, 24 October 1970. The car with Allende is escorted by General Augusto Pinochet (on the left).

▲ Moscow, 11 December 1972: Chilean President Salvador Allende (1908–73) (with glasses) meets Soviet Premier Alexei Kosygin (on the left), General Secretary of the Communist Party Leonid Brezhnev (second right) and Chief of State Nikolai Podgorny (right) during his visit to the Soviet Union

Social and communication skills

In a small group or in class, watch the film *Machuca* about schoolchildren at a Catholic boys' school during the Allende years.

How did the political situation affect the two friends and their families?

shock groups
Armed band of extreme political parties, who supported political demonstrations and engaged in violence with opposing groups.

Research and communication skills

In a small group, search the US National Security Archives for transcriptions of calls titled *Nixon Vetoed Proposed Coexistence with an Allende Government*, between Secretary of State Henry Kissinger and President Richard Nixon on the situation in Chile.

What was the extent of US covert operations between 1970 and 1973 according to these documents?

Escuela Nacional Unificada (ENU)
The National Unified School system promoted by President Salvador Allende in Chile in 1972, which was perceived by the Catholic Church as anti-religion, and by the right as being against family values.

External pressures quickly became felt by the end of 1971, and as currency reserves diminished and inflation soared, the US blockade was felt as Chile was unable to receive loans. Agrarian reform and industry expropriations diminished consumer goods as well as foodstuffs and a black market began to grow despite the government's attempt to fix prices. The opposition staged an increasing number of protest demonstrations against the UP government. The extreme left and the extreme right organized violent **shock groups**, who invariably met and fought in street demonstrations. Political polarization and extremism penetrated the entire Chilean society, in the cities and in the countryside. It affected schoolchildren and university students, all work spaces and the media, touching every aspect of daily life.

Allende's domestic policies regarding salary hikes and price fixing helped poorer Chileans especially and brought short-term political benefits. The UP obtained 50% of the posts in the March 1971 municipal elections. With a view to obtain a congressional majority, in 1972 Allende resorted to populist tactics, creating Neighborhood Supply and Price-control Committees, or Juntas de Abastecimiento y Control de Precios (JAP) to distribute basic foodstuffs. In October 1972, the dearth of supplies in the cities was further complicated by a truckers' strike, which was covertly financed by the USA.

Allende's control of his own coalition grew weaker, so that he began to distance himself from its members. Even the PDC now became allied with the rightist National Party in an opposition block, presenting opposition candidates to the congressional election in order to stop Allende's reforms. Like some of his predecessors, Allende resorted to decrees in order to pass laws. One particularly controversial reform, aimed at creating Unified National Schooling or the **Escuela Nacional Unificada (ENU)** in January 1973, upset the country and its traditional divided education of private and public schools. This prompted demonstrations all over Chile so powerful and violent that the President had to declare a state of emergency in 20 provinces to keep the peace. The ENU did not go through. Even so, by the time the congressional elections were held in March 1973, 54% of the Congress was pro-UP and 44% in opposition. The opposition parties wanted to impeach Allende for violating the constitution. The copper miners began a long strike for two months, thereby slowing production considerably. Extreme leftist groups continued to call to arms and revolution. In an effort to alleviate the strained civilian–military relations, Allende appointed several armed forces officers to his cabinet. The political conflicts however, did not lessen. The PDC and the National Party argued that Allende had exceeded his attributions and had gone beyond the constitutional and legal framework of the country. The UP, especially its most radical sectors such as the MIR, insisted that the process of transferring private enterprises and large landholdings to the state could not be halted.

By August 1973 Allende's government had gone through 10 cabinet changes in three years. The media, especially from the right, spoke increasingly of civil war. The Commander-in-Chief of the Chilean Armed Forces General Prats came under increasing pressure for his conciliatory stance in broaching civilian–military relations. Finally, he resigned and General Augusto Pinochet became Commander-in-Chief.

On a daily basis, Chileans were finding it increasingly more difficult to buy groceries, appliances and household supplies. Chilean women, in particular, two-thirds of whom were housewives at the time, were incensed at not being able to provide for their families and staged an enormous street demonstration in downtown Santiago. This protest was strongly supported by the PDC–National Party coalition and 'defended' by extreme-right shock groups, which led to violence and arrests. The most important newspaper in Chile, the conservative *El Mercurio*, gave particular coverage to this event, as women were not expected to have political agency at the time.

Source skills

Allende and the UP

This is a photograph from the front page of *El Mercurio* on 6 September 1973.

▲ Political demonstration by women in downtown Santiago on 6 September 1973

Thousands of women congregated beating pots and pans with wooden spoons or lids to signify that they had no food to feed their families due to the ineptitude of Allende and the UP. The headline says 'Feminine Repudiation (disavowal; rejection) of the Government'. The two subtitles say 'Marxists attack the (female) demonstrators' and '50 injured in incidents'.

Questions

1 Why would this female demonstration have been so shocking at the time?

2 How is the Right using gender roles to generate support?

▲ President Salvador Allende waves to his supporters – the last civilians to interact with him – from a balcony at La Moneda, at 9.20 a.m. on 11 September 1973, some 40 minutes before the Chilean military, led by General Augusto Pinochet, started bombarding the presidential palace in downtown Santiago, Chile. President Allende was overthrown and committed suicide.

▲ Admiral Toribio Merino, General Augusto Pinochet (in the middle) and Air Force General Leigh salute while walking to join the Te Deum on 18 September 1973, Independence Day, a week after military coup d'etat in Santiago on 11 September 1973

On 11 September 1973, much to the shock of Chileans, a military coup led by General Pinochet took over the country. It was a bloody, violent end to the conflicted government of Allende, who shot himself as the presidential palace was being bombed and burned by the Chilean Air Force.

Some Chileans celebrated, some mourned, but the internal political divisions remained, now suppressed as the presidency was replaced by the military junta of the army, navy, air force and national police. Congress was dismissed and closed. The judiciary appeared to have survived, but were unable to defend Chileans due to the 'state of siege' declared by the military which suspended the rights of citizens, like freedom of the press, the right to assembly and so on. All political parties were prohibited; elections were suspended indefinitely.

Economic and social policies

The supply of foodstuffs improved, but Chileans now had to get used to curfews every night for many years, as well as censorship of the press, radio and television. Public offices and universities were purged of leftist functionaries and replaced by the military. The judiciary was also purged and many judges opted for silence or open support of the military government. Worse, government became a series of edicts and decrees for the control of the population.

To turn back Allende's economic reforms toward a mixed socialist–capitalist economy, the Pinochet government attempted to stop galloping inflation and lack of consumer goods. By 1975, they turned to the 'Chicago boys'. These were male Chilean economists who had received higher degrees at the University of Chicago and followed the tenets of economics professor Milton Friedman, who promoted a neoliberal free-market economy. These economists, working with the

military government, privatized state-owned concerns (except copper), inserted Chile into global markets by lowering or eliminating tariffs, enacted economic, banking and fiscal reforms and promoted Chile's entrepreneurial sector. They helped to diversify from the traditional Chilean export, copper, to exporting fruit and promoting tourism.

These measures produced the desired effect after some years of application; per capita income in Chile rose two and a half times and inflation decreased from 500% per year to around 8%. The strict monetary and fiscal policies applied, however, had a great social cost in unemployment, as government bureaucracies were dissolved and factories, mines and farms became leaner and more competitive. The military government had to install a minimal employment programme, where heads of households were given preference in jobs such as street cleaning and gardening in public parks. When prices of consumer goods and food rose, the urban poor organized soup kitchens where resources were shared to cook for several families or city blocks.

In 1975 two-thirds of women in Chile were in the home, caring for their families and houses or apartments. Many had vociferously demonstrated against the Allende government, as they had been unable to feed their families due to lack of food available for purchase. These women were co-opted into the military government through 200 nationwide volunteer organizations, for example, the Mothers' Centers, lead by Lucía H de Pinochet, General Pinochet's wife.

Source skills

Pinochet visits local school

Look at this photo of Lucía de Pinochet greeting a teacher, while bringing a truckload of materials to a school.

▲ Materials delivered to a school, accompanied by Lucía de Pinochet

Question

How far can good work obscure human rights abuses?

These aid organizations were made up of volunteers who supported the Pinochet dictatorship. The government used them to march in their support. Pinochet insisted women had wanted a military coup and that women were his staunchest supporters. These organizations did an enormous amount of volunteer work, helping the aged,

ATL Research and thinking skills

Research the formation and objectives of the School of the Americas in the Cold War context in general and Chile in particular. If possible, watch *School of the Americas: an insider speaks out*, by Joseph A Blair and Linda Panetta.

children's hospitals, the blind, the disabled and many other people in need of assistance in Chile. They also held courses for members, in sewing, arts and crafts, food preparation and hygiene. The members were from all social classes, although the leadership tended to be made up of middle-class women and military officers' wives. There was also political indoctrination in meetings, bringing up the spectre of communism and how the military had saved the country from it.

Repression and treatment of opposition

Leftists, sympathizers of the Allende government, real or not, were detained, often tortured and sometimes 'disappeared'. The military organized systematic persecution of the 'subversives' it considered responsible for the political chaos of Allende's three years in the government. The infamous National Intelligence Directorate, or **Dirección de Inteligencia Nacional (DINA)**, working in the country and in covert operations with Argentine and Brazilian military governments, searched, found and detained political personages, sometimes murdering people as far away as Argentina, Italy or the USA. The director and many officers involved in the DINA were graduates of the US counter-insurgency training school, knows as the School of the Americas.

By 1978, human rights abuses in Chile became public with the discovery of bodies in the rural area of Lonquén. The murder of union leader Tucapel Jiménez in 1982 stunned the labour world and the murder of two teachers from the teachers' union in 1985 greatly disturbed educators. These, and the burning alive of two university students in 1986, were the most notorious cases of the more than 100 000 Chileans who were tortured or exiled, as well as the approximately 4000 who 'disappeared' when they were killed in military detention camps.

Pinochet acted harshly, yet sought legitimacy to his dictatorship by using *consultas* or plebiscites to document support and so respond to UN human rights abuse accusations. In 1978 he claimed 70% support. Under pressure also from the Catholic Church, Pinochet eventually lifted the 'state of siege' and the curfew and declared an amnesty, in an effort to improve his government's foreign image. However, the detentions, tortures and disappearances continued. The Church responded by excommunicating perpetrators in these crimes.

By 1980 the military dictatorship had elaborated a new constitution, presented to Chileans in a plebiscite for their approval. This included a slow process for the end of the military government and was approved by the population. The new government would be an authoritarian democracy to guarantee protection from what the military considered subversive influences. However, it would not be long until public opinion, dismayed at human rights abuses and the changing circumstances of the waning Cold War, would have Chileans voting no in 1988 on a plebiscite to end the Pinochet government.

Pinochet would finally leave office in 1989, when Patricio Aylwin was elected President in the first democratic election since 1969.

Dirección de Inteligencia Nacional (DINA)
Chilean secret police during the Pinochet dictatorship in Chile, responsible for many human rights abuses.

Class discussion

Why does the suspension of civil liberties in military dictatorships lead to human rights abuses?

▲ A guard of Villa Grimaldi, a known torture centre run by the military junta during Augusto Pinochet's dictatorship (1973–90), shows drawings done by detainees of the regime on display at the centre, 9 December 2005. Chile's current (2014) President, Michelle Bachelet, was held here with her mother for nearly a month in 1975.

ATL Social and communication skills

In class, watch the film *No!* (2013) on YouTube. This film is about the marketing campaign to canvass the 'no' vote during the referendum held by Pinochet to ask Chileans if he should continue in power.

Why did Pinochet accept the results and step down a year later?

5.5 Guerrilla movements in one country (1960–80)

Conceptual understanding

Key questions

→ What conditions caused El Salvador to become embroiled in civil war?

→ Can a guerrilla group, such as the FMLN in El Salvador, create change through violence?

Key concepts

→ Change

→ Consequence

→ Perspectives

→ Significance

Case study: El Salvador

A tragic case study is the Central American country of El Salvador. It is located on the Pacific Ocean and has a population of about 6 million people. Its only resource is the rich farmland it has to grow crops. The Cold War context and deep social injustices created conditions for insurrection, repression and civil war.

Background

By the middle of the 20th century El Salvador was plagued by severe land tenure problems that impeded most Salvadorans from owning land and producing food. In fact, 2% of the population owned 60% of the land. This small oligarchic group was known as the 'fourteen families'. The main cash crop was coffee, which was vulnerable to international prices and created havoc in the hiring and firings of agricultural workers. Some agricultural workers were *ladinos*, with a blend of Spanish and Indian cultural characteristics, but mostly the workers were Indians, who dressed in traditional attire and spoke Maya or Nahuatl.

By the 1930s Indian communal lands had been taken over by coffee plantations. When the Great Depression struck, coffee prices sank and when workers were fired, they had nowhere to go. At the same time, leaders such as the intellectual Farabundo Martí, from a landowning family, became imbued in Marxist ideas and began organizing the restive Salvadoran peasants. When the starving popular and indigenous movement rebelled against poverty and injustice in 1932 under Farabundo Martí, however, it was crushed by the army. Thousands of peasants were killed and Martí was caught and executed. This would provide the inspiration for the future guerrilla group, the FMLN (Farabundo Martí National Liberation Front).

▲ El Salvador

ladinos
Term used in Central America to denominate a person of Spanish and indigenous ancestry and culture.

Central American Common Market (CACM)
Created in the 1960s to establish regional protective tariffs to protect ISI manufacturing, but did not flourish.

In the context of the Cold War, the results of this massacre led to continual support from the USA of anti-communist military dictators in El Salvador. Reformers would be jailed, tortured and exiled. By the 1970s the economic situation in El Salvador worsened. Neighbouring Honduras expelled Salvadoran workers, who returned to find no work available. The incipient **Central American Common Market (CACM)** failed and Salvadoran trade with it. Per capita income in El Salvador fell 2.5% every year from 1970 to 1974. Landless peasants increased threefold. In the cities the situation was not much better. Industry had grown under the Central American Common Market, but wages were low. In 1972, when a Christian Democrat moderate ran for president promising some reforms, the military faked election results and took over. They received assistance from Nicaragua's Anastasio Somoza, from Guatemala and from the USA. When protests and demonstrations ensued, they were met with military fire. Popular outrage led to the formation of five different revolutionary movements, of leftist orientations, to organize peasants and Indians against the military.

▲ Mural showing Farabundo Martí painted in East Los Angeles, CA, USA

Rise of the revolutionaries

The largest and leading group of revolutionaries was the guerrilla group called the Farabundo Martí Liberation Forces (FPL). Cayetano Carpio, a labour organizer, had led the Communist Party of El Salvador, but left to form a guerrilla group. He felt that violence was the only way to eliminate the military and revolutionize El Salvador. To buy arms, the revolutionaries kidnapped members of the landowning families, exacting huge ransoms. It has been estimated that these totalled US $50 million. In addition, the guerrillas held up banks. Other groups included the People's Revolutionary Army (ERP) and the Armed Forces of National Resistance (FARN). They all believed that violence and guerrilla warfare was the only way for El Salvador, although they differed in approach, such as urban versus rural warfare and also on short- or long-term warfare.

Some guerrilla groups were supported by students and more moderate protestors. All were pursued hard by the military governments for threatening the established order. Even teachers who joined unions were suspect, and as many as 150 of them 'disappeared', some turned up dead. The military also viewed priests and religious workers with suspicion (see unit 5.6) and many were targeted, assassinated or exiled, although not always by the military. Right-wing death squads were formed, as well as private security forces, killing demonstrators and leftist sympathizers and committing political assassinations with the approval and non-intervention of the ruling military.

Consequences

The most dramatic consequence for El Salvador was the devastating escalation of violence. As a reaction to military oppression, leftist guerrilla groups resorted to escalating violence. The military repressed them with greater force and allowed paramilitary rightist groups to proliferate. One particularly virulent group was **ORDEN**, its name based on the Spanish word for 'order'. It would prove fanatical in terrorizing rural areas with gruesome exemplary killings and in its single-minded attack of priests and religious workers.

In addition to the polarized Salvadorans, however, the involvement of the USA added military equipment, counter-insurgency expertise and money to the mix. Military missions and experts were sent to El Salvador and, as with many other future military dictators in Latin America, Salvadoran officers were trained in counter-insurgency at the School of the Americas. US aid in the form of helicopters and airplanes for transporting troops between 1974 and 1976 made the Salvadorans more efficient in attacking guerrillas and peasants in rural areas. After 1976 and a corruption scandal involving Salvadoran military selling US weapons, US President Gerald Ford stopped military aid. This did not stop the violence, however, as the military was able to procure arms from Western European and Middle Eastern arms dealers.

After the success of the Sandinistas in Nicaragua in 1979, US President Jimmy Carter resumed aid to the Salvadoran military and President Ronald Reagan continued it. This policy was known as **KISSSS** ('Keep it simple, sustainable, small and Salvadoran'). The guerrilla forces increased kidnappings for money for arms, even of US businessmen. With the assassination of Archbishop Óscar Romero in 1980, who had been pleading with the military, the guerrillas and the death squads to stop the violence, the violence escalated to become a civil war that lasted from 1979 to 1992. He was beatified by the Pope in May, 2015 as a first step to sainthood.

By the end of 1980 five guerrilla groups had fused into the Farabundo Martí Liberation Front, FMLN. Their purpose was to depose the military/oligarchy alliance and institute urgent land reform for a more equitable El Salvador. Newly elected US President Ronald Reagan saw the civil war in El Salvador in stark Cold War terms: the guerrillas were Marxist and likely aided by Cuba and the Soviet Union and only strong military aid to the Salvadoran army would eliminate the guerrillas from converting El Salvador into another communist state in Latin America. Military dictatorship, rigged elections and human

Organización Democrática Nacionalista (ORDEN)
An anti-guerrilla paramilitary organization that coordinated and trained death squads and intimidations, led by Colonel José Alberto Medrano.

KISSSS
US principle on dealing with leftist guerrillas in El Salvador in the 1980s, amounting to sending Special Force Soldiers, arms, money and advisors, as well as setting up a counter-insurgency training camp in Honduras.

rights abuses did not enter into this view. Although the US press and pundits completely dismantled this perception and proved that there was no Cuban or Soviet arms provision to the FMLN, the Reagan administration persevered and by 1984 was sending US$196 million to the Salvadoran military. Countries such as France and Mexico disagreed with this bipolar view and recognized the FMLN as a political force to be reckoned with, not obliterated.

President Reagan also tried to stimulate what he called 'the magic of the market' by stimulating trade with El Salvador. This approach did not work in the polarized civil war climate, but resulted in one-third of Salvadorans receiving US food and agricultural products by 1988. This was the last straw to the few surviving Salvadoran farmers who could not compete with subsidized US food products. They migrated to urban areas. Meanwhile, the FMLN continued to grow and hold parts of the countryside. The USA also assisted the Salvadoran military with covert CIA operations against the guerrillas, often smuggled in through El Salvador's neighbouring countries, Honduras and Guatemala. The FBI also went to El Salvador to investigate various solidarity organizations and seeking answers about people who had disappeared, although this action was condemned in 1988.

Efforts by other nations, for example, Mexico, Panama, Venezuela and Colombia, to establish a peace plan for El Salvador and Nicaragua were rejected by President Reagan, who felt total destruction of Marxist guerrillas was the only option. Sandinistas from Nicaragua were also aiding the FMLN with arms, so the Salvadoran civil war became inextricably mixed with Reagan's policy in Nicaragua, and its ensuing Contra scandal. By the late 1980s El Salvador was the third largest beneficiary of US aid, behind Egypt and Israel. The USA sent US$5 billion to El Salvador to destroy the FMLN.

Cuba's Fidel Castro approved of the FMLN, although he sent little aid. The Soviet Union did not want to get involved either, and did not send aid to El Salvador or Nicaragua. Although the Reagan administration and the Salvadoran military government continually announced the FMLN's demise, by the late 1980s they commanded a force of 9000 guerrillas and controlled territory in every province of El Salvador, despite the Salvadoran army's 50 000 troops and massive US aid. The corruption of the Salvadoran military impeded its efficiency, while the FMLN continued its armed attacks, expanded in 1990 to include the Ministry of Defense in San Salvador. It was evident that their power was increasing, but also evident that they could not prevail against the Salvadoran military. The only solution was to negotiate.

Only as late as 1990 did the FMLN agree to begin talks with the UN to end the civil war, setting conditions such as the dismantling of rightist death squads and bringing torturers and assassins in the military to trial for human rights abuses. With the intercession of the UN, the two sides agreed to form a police force with equal parts guerrillas and right-wing para-military groups and planned a reduction of the army by 50% and a removal of the most corrupt and ruthless army officers. Respect for human rights and land reform were promised.

The UN sent peacekeepers to supervise the process of laying down arms and engaging in free elections, so the FMLN ended its insurgency and promised respect for the Salvadoran constitution. With the return to democracy in El Salvador after the UN-brokered accord in 1992, former guerrilla groups turned into political parties and won presidential elections in 2010.

The most tragic consequence of the civil war was the death of about 75 000 Salvadorans as well as foreigners, mostly priests and churchwomen. Nearly a million Salvadorans fled the violence to other countries. After 30 years of repressive military rule in the name of anti-communism, massacres and other human rights violations, and the retaliation of armed guerrilla groups like the FMLN, it has been hard to rebuild El Salvador.

A particularly unfortunate sequel to the Salvadoran civil war is that sweeping changes are still not accepted by ultra rightist landowners and that 80% of the country is under the poverty line. Acute social exclusion persists and violent crime has soared. Gangs or *maras* were formed by young gang members from Salvadoran refugee communities in southern California, thousands of whom were deported by US authorities. In cities such as Los Angeles, the *maras* met to support each other and their identity as refugee Salvadorans, some becoming involved with drugs and crime, while their parents worked to make ends meet. When the gang members were deported to El Salvador starting in 1996, they stuck together and grew in members, as the fragile country was trying to regain civil society after 12 years of civil war. By 2003 the Salvadoran police was able to crack down on the *maras,* which were outlawed, and to jail many members. Unfortunately, jails became hubs for propagating the gangs and for leaders to meet and organize criminal activities, for example related to drugs. By 2011 there was estimated to be over 28 000 *mara* members, more than one-third of them jailed. However, fear and extortion push the number of Salvadorans involved with *maras* to 10% of the population of 6.3 million. The *maras* have made current conditions increasingly violent, again producing a Salvadoran exodus, often of youngsters whose parents want to protect them from having to join the gangs. El Salvador, 12 years after the war ended, is trying to rebuild its government and control this violent consequence of the civil war.

> **ATL Social and thinking skills**
>
> Watch the film *Innocent Voices* (2004), directed by Luis Mandoki, about the life of a Salvadoran boy and the practice of recruiting children to fight in the civil war.
>
> What does the film show about the disruption of normal daily life during a civil war?

OP

Abbreviation meaning 'Order of Preachers' in Latin, and used to denominate Catholic priests belonging to the Dominican Order.

Background

In the 1960s, Gustavo Gutiérrez, **OP**, a Peruvian Dominican priest studying in Europe, became involved in a group of priests who wanted to apply the wisdom of the Second Vatican Council to conditions in Latin America. These religious reformers looked at the problem of poverty from a wide perspective, including Marxism and economic dependency theories in vogue at the time. In 1968 the Conference of Latin American Bishops met in the city of Medellín, Colombia. Gutiérrez was instrumental in producing the proclamations emanating from this conference. These called for more engagement in liberating the poor from their condition by condemning the gross inequity in economic and social conditions in Latin America. Although Pope Paul VI spoke to the bishops in Medellín to prevent a split between the Church hierarchy and the clergy, the proclamations were controversial. The Vatican censured the documents, as did more conservative elements of the Church, who especially condemned violence.

After Medellín, there was a change in how Catholic priests and nuns ministered to the popular masses, within their moral authority as religious workers among the poor. The Church now focused on the poor, instead of the rich. Factory workers, poor farmers and other low-income Latin Americans began to realize that the socio-economic situation they were in was not morally acceptable within their Catholic faith. Religious workers supported this view, as younger members of the clergy and religious orders of nuns and priests added messages of social justice and equity to their spiritual work. This perceptible and widespread change is called 'liberation theology', after Gutiérrez published his seminal book *Liberation Theology* in 1971. Gutiérrez, now a professor of theology at Notre Dame University in the USA, called for a definite commitment of Christian theology to building a more equitable society. This was to be achieved by raising consciousness in the congregations, who then would themselves take action to improve their lives.

Growth of liberation theology

Priests and nuns working with the poor were much inspired by liberation theology, especially in Brazil, Chile, El Salvador, Guatemala and Nicaragua. Parishioners became conscious of their plight and began to organize and actively seek solutions to endemic poverty. This was achieved by parishioners forming *comunidades de base* (faith-based communities) and meeting with clergy or nuns to discuss religious, social and political issues. As these groups met in churches and were sanctioned and funded by the Church, they initially remained under the protection of the Vatican and international Catholic foundations.

When the Conference of Latin American Bishops met in Puebla, Mexico, in 1979, the more conservative hierarchy insisted on community work without political involvement for the clergy. They officially condemned all violence, be it from Marxists, capitalists or rightists. Yet the clergy assisting reaffirmed that poverty continued to worsen among the poor in Latin America: peasants, Indians, women and the urban poor. They did not hesitate to point fingers at multinationals, which sought cheap resources from countries at great profit, while charging great sums for manufactured goods. According to research by US Catholic journalist Penny Lernoux, between Medellín (1968) and Puebla (1979) an unprecedented 850 priests and nuns in Latin America were tortured, murdered, expelled, or arrested. Commitment to liberation theology was proving dangerous, as the following case study will show.

The first area in Central America where liberation theology was tried was in El Salvador. It split the Salvadoran bishops and clergy into conservative and liberal camps, but they were united in asking the government to promote agrarian reform as a way of improving standards of living. The ruling oligarchy promptly labelled the Catholic clergy 'communist'. In the late 1970s and especially after the Salvadoran Civil War began in 1979, priests and nuns suspected of advocating liberation theology in their parishes routinely were attacked, imprisoned, exiled or deported, tortured and even killed. Right-wing paramilitary groups advertised the slogan 'Be a patriot; kill a priest!' When the Archbishop of El Salvador, Óscar Romero, denounced these excesses and demanded a stop to human rights abuses in El Salvador by asking the international community to intervene, he was assassinated while officiating mass on 24 March 1980.

Unfortunately, the violence against Catholic clergy continued. Ten months after Romero's death, US Catholics Dorothy Kazel, an Ursuline nun; Ita Ford and Maura Clarke, Maryknoll mission sisters; and Jean Donovan, a young laywoman missionary, were abducted, raped and killed by Salvadoran National Guard. This was part of the Salvadoran government's crackdown on liberation theology and the religious missionaries' community work among the poor. Other Latin American countries would also begin to curb liberation theology.

In Guatemala there was the additional religious controversy fuelled by the influence of US-based fundamentalist Protestant sects. They canvassed supporters and conversions while aiding victims of the 1976 earthquake there. One convert later became military dictator of Guatemala, Efraín Ríos Montt, who was quick to label Catholic priests and nuns as the enemy, to be treated accordingly.

ATL **Social and communication skills**

Find the video clip of *Canción para un mártir* (Song for a martyr) by Monseñor Romero on YouTube and listen to the song. It relates Archbishop Romero's works and commitment to the Salvadoran poor. If you do not understand Spanish, try to find an English translation of the lyrics.

1 What aspects of liberation theology are evident in the lyrics?
    Now find and watch the English trailer for the US biopic *Romero* (1989) on YouTube.

2 How does the film portray the growth of liberation theology in El Salvador?

In Brazil, Franciscan priest Leonardo Boff's work among slum-dwellers in Petropolis, Brazil radicalized his views in the 1970s. Boff, through his writings, appealed to many Brazilian clergy. He identified with liberation theology and became an important theologian in this regard, focusing on the poor and the Church's commitment to the community. During the Brazilian military dictatorships after 1964, Boff denounced the government's persecution and jailing of clergy who worked among the poor, especially when priests were shot while supporting demands for land grants. He also criticized the accumulation of wealth among the few, while many Brazilians lived in poverty struggling for social justice.

▲ Leonardo Boff preaches in 1986 from a raised platform outside a church to a crowd of followers of liberation theology in Brazil. The promotion of direct social action for the poor and oppressed lies at the heart of liberation theology.

Boff's written work was censured by the Vatican, especially when Boff openly criticized authoritarian governments and the Catholic Church hierarchy. Boff was tried at the Vatican for his criticism of Church doctrine and silenced for a year. After that, he published another critical book in 1992 and when silenced by the Vatican chose to resign from the Franciscan order. His popularity among liberation theologians has grown and he is a professor of philosophy, ethics and religion at the Universidade do Estado do Rio de Janeiro, Brazil.

Impact

The impact of liberation theology was important because it created such enormous frustration among peasants and workers in Latin America. They became convinced that it was not right, it was not moral and it was just not Christian that they were so poor while some people were so rich. Further, it created a desire for change – in fact, immediate change – so that the traditional oligarchies and power elites needed to relinquish economic and political power and share it with the entire population. This was quickly perceived by these elites as a threat to their leadership and a threat to capitalism. In other words, in the Cold War context, it quickly came to be seen by power elites, the military institutions in nations and the USA as an ideology infused in communism and therefore dangerous to the status quo.

Case study: Nicaragua

A particular case in point is Nicaragua where young priests and nuns, both from Nicaragua and missionaries from other countries, took upon themselves to spread liberation theology in the 1970s. With the message of the Roman Catholic faith, they instilled a sense of moral righteousness in the peasants, workers and the poor in general. They reinforced the message that the poor deserved a right to fair pay for their labour, education for their children, medical care for their families and governments that would support these rights. This awareness became massive enough that Nicaraguans expected to receive these rights from their government. When this did not happen under the Somoza dictatorship, Nicaraguans became more willing to support revolutionary leaders and groups who would fight for these rights, for example, the **Sandinistas**. Liberation theology certainly had a strong impact as one more influence in the Nicaraguan Revolution of 1979. A strong proponent of liberation theology was the Nicaraguan priest Ernesto Cardenal, who actively resisted the Somoza dictatorship and joined the Sandinistas.

Not all Nicaraguans supported liberation theology or the Sandinistas. In fact, the Nicaraguan Catholic Church became deeply divided into liberation theology and conservative elements. The Sandinistas would succeed, with popular support, in toppling the Somoza dictatorship in 1979 and instituting the changes demanded by the population. The Nicaraguan Catholic Church remained divided after the Sandinistas came to power, some supporting the revolutionary government by working within it in leadership or diplomatic positions or spearheading literacy campaigns. The Church hierarchy was not in agreement with such a radical departure from the role of the Church as separate from the state and dedicated exclusively to spiritual matters. Archbishop Miguel Obando y Bravo also objected strongly to the mixing of Marxist ideology and Christian values. In the Cold War world of the 1980s this carried overtones of Cuban and Soviet atheism and imperialism. The situation was exacerbated when Pope John Paul II visited Nicaragua in 1983. The Pope personally reprimanded Ernesto Cardenal for not following the Vatican's injunction for priests to refrain from getting involved in politics.

The impact of liberation theology continues to this day, and it has deeply affected the Roman Catholic Church and its mission the world over. During the Cold War it was inextricably mixed with Marxist ideas of social equality and anti-capitalism, so its proponents were often persecuted because of this. After 1989, this theology is less political and has remained a strong part of the Church's mission to eradicate poverty in the world.

> ### Sandinistas
> Name given to members of the Nicaraguan guerrilla group, Sandinista National Liberation Front (FSLN), who defeated the dictator Anastasio Somoza in 1979 and took over the government.

> ### Communication and thinking skills
> ATL
>
> Find and read the article *Nicaragua: Catholics Caught in the Middle of a Power Struggle* by Stephen T DeMott, MM on the Internet.
>
> 1   What are the issues that divided the Nicaraguan Catholic Church in 1983?
>
> 2   To what extent did liberation theology affect the rift?

Exam-style questions

1 Assess the importance of Cuban nationalism, Castro's leadership as a revolutionary and social malaise in creating the right conditions for revolution in Cuba in 1959.

2 To what extent was the context of the Cold War influential to the success and institutionalization of the Cuban Revolution?

3 How far can we say that the revolution liberated Cuban women and minorities?

4 How did Juan Perón use populism to change social justice in Argentina?

5 Some historians have called Vargas and Perón 'fascists', others have called them 'communists' and others say they are 'populists'. Compare and contrast the authoritarian methods of Perón and Vargas.

6 Why was Vargas concerned with legitimacy in 1950?

7 How far can we say that the military coup in Chile in 1973 was rooted in the Cold War polarization and US influence?

8 Analyse the conditions in El Salvador that caused the FMLN guerrillas to take up arms against the military government.

9 Why did the Roman Catholic Church change its approach to poverty in Latin America?

"Evaluate..."

Question

Evaluate the importance of Cuban nationalism, Castro's leadership as a revolutionary and social malaise in creating the right conditions for revolution in Cuba in 1959.

Analysis

To analyse the question, you must think about what the question is asking. Begin by looking for the command term. This will give you the framework for planning your answer, beyond the details of the topic at hand. For this question, the key command term is "evaluate" – making an appraisal by weighing the importance of the different elements included in the question. In this case the three specific elements in creating the right conditions for revolution in Cuba in 1959 are:

- Cuban nationalism

- Fidel Castro's leadership as a revolutionary

- social malaise.

The question also wants us to limit the time frame to events before 1959.

After formulating a general introduction (see page 118), your answer should begin to focus in turn on the three elements in the question: Cuban nationalism, Castro's leadership as a revolutionary, and social malaise. Given that the question asks you to evaluate three specific elements, you should write one paragraph about each of them. The answer should then end with a conclusion (see page 498).

Sample paragraph

Below is a possible paragraph dealing with the first element, Cuban nationalism:

Cuban nationalism had been growing as events unfolded in the first half of the 20th century, with increasing resentment against the United States. When the US intervened by defeating Spain in the war in 1898, Cuba became free of Spanish colonial rule, but had to accept the Platt Amendment (1901–34), allowing a preponderant US role in Cuban affairs. This was the first blow to Cuban nationalism, as the Platt Amendment was made legally binding by incorporating its terms in the Cuban Constitution. Among other things, it prohibited the Cuban Government from entering into international treaties, except with the US, and led to the perpetual lease by the US of Guantánamo Bay for its naval station. It also gave the US the right to intervene in Cuba and they did so, with US Marines, in 1906, 1912 and 1917, to defend growing US interests in the sugar industry, banking, telecommunications and tourism. By the 1930s US intervention changed to supporting authoritarian politicians who perpetuated the status quo, while keeping up the pretence of democracy and elections. Once the US repealed the Platt Amendment in 1934, Cubans were disappointed to see that US interests and influence continued, as many Cuban business leaders and political leaders supported it. By the 1940s the US controlled 75% of Cuba's sugar production, as well as banking. By the 1950s the US owned 85% of all foreign investments. Under the rule of Fulgencio Batista, whose government corruption in favour of US investments created mounting resentment against the US, university students and workers began to express Cuban nationalism in the streets demanding "Cuba for the Cubans". By the late 1950s, Cuban nationalism and anti-US feeling were becoming increasingly important. More elements would be needed, however, for creating the right conditions for revolution.

This paragraph begins with a general introduction to Cuban nationalism in the first half of the 20th century. The first sentence deals directly with the command term "evaluate"; it makes an appraisal of Cuban nationalism as "growing" during that time. The rest of the paragraph is packed with detailed evidence to support this appraisal. The last sentence on the paragraph corroborates the appraisal in the first sentence. Further, it ties it to the larger question of Cuban nationalism and the other two elements in *creating the right conditions for revolution in Cuba in 1959*. (This last will be evaluated in the concluding paragraph of the essay.)

6 POLITICAL DEVELOPMENTS IN THE UNITED STATES AND CANADA, 1945–1980

Global context

The Second World War left over 60 million dead and displaced millions more. Of the Great Powers that went to war between 1937 and 1945, only the United States and the USSR remained as such in the Cold War era. In North America this time period could be characterized as one of progress and reaction, particularly between and within the dominant political parties.

There was an economic boom in both US and Canada that led to greater global interconnections, however, not all of the nations or citizens of the societies involved benefitted equally. During the Cold War era there were ramifications (both peaceful and violent) for the social, economic, political and military actions that various governments took, both internationally and domestically. By 1980 both countries became more conservative after significant periods of liberal change, although many of the most impactful reforms that had been made after 1945 remained.

Timeline

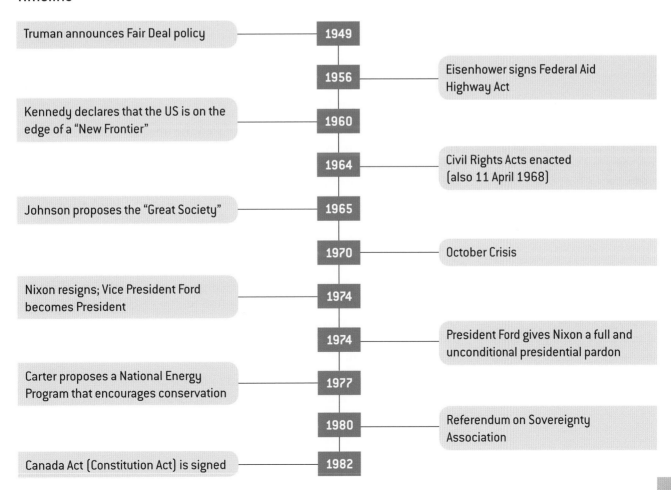

Truman announces Fair Deal policy	**1949**
	1956 — Eisenhower signs Federal Aid Highway Act
Kennedy declares that the US is on the edge of a "New Frontier"	**1960**
	1964 — Civil Rights Acts enacted (also 11 April 1968)
Johnson proposes the "Great Society"	**1965**
	1970 — October Crisis
Nixon resigns; Vice President Ford becomes President	**1974**
	1974 — President Ford gives Nixon a full and unconditional presidential pardon
Carter proposes a National Energy Program that encourages conservation	**1977**
	1980 — Referendum on Sovereignty Association
Canada Act (Constitution Act) is signed	**1982**

6.1 The Truman administration

Conceptual understanding

Key questions:

→ In what ways did Truman effectively transition the US government from a wartime footing to a domestically focused one?

→ To what extent did Truman successfully implement his agenda?

→ Why was Truman so unpopular at the end of his presidency?

Key concepts:

→ Change

→ Continuity

Presidency during the Second World War

On 12 April 1945, after only 82 days as Vice-President, Truman was summoned to the White House and was sworn in as President. Could he successfully win the Second World War? His approach was quite different from Roosevelt's. After the German surrender in Europe on 8 May 1945, he focused on Japan and the conflict finally ended on 2 September 1945 with an Allied victory; he became, according to McCullough, "the most powerful man on earth". Truman said at the time, "Never in my wildest dreams did I ever dream or wish for such a position".

Post-war domestic policies

reconversion
The process by which the US economy shifted from being focused mostly on military production for the Second World War to being redirected to meet domestic consumer needs.

After the Second World War, Truman faced the immense challenges of **reconversion** as he tried to shift the country from being geared toward total war. During the Second World War many groups had established their power in Washington, and a new system of connections had been established between the government bureaucracy and varied special interests in order to have an economy that could meet wartime production targets. Under immense pressure to "bring the boys home" and successfully re-integrate them into society, as well as slow down economic production in line with the 1944 **GI Bill**, Truman rapidly demobilized the military and tried to maintain some wartime economic regulations; he succeeded with the former, but in a conflict with Congress he failed with the latter and, as a result, some corporations profited disproportionately as privatization occurred, which had a negative impact on labour.

GI Bill
This gave substantial federal support to veterans to enable them to re-enter domestic society, including job re-training, education, housing subsidies and healthcare.

As a part of reconversion, Truman had to decide to what extent his government would follow the New Deal ideals, as the federal government had taken control of many aspects of the economy to try to make sure that as many Americans as possible could be taken care of.

In September 1945, Truman presented to Congress a proposal that followed the ideals of the New Deal: legislation trying to prevent unemployment and expand the Fair Employment Practices Committee (which included new public works programmes), raise the minimum wage, extend Social Security and create national health insurance. While he was able to get the **Employment Act of 1946** passed, the measure did not have a clear enforcement mechanism. Republicans and conservative southern Democrats in Congress were opposed to most of Truman's other proposed reforms, and the public was divided regarding the maintenance of a **welfare state**. Reconversion ended up being incredibly difficult to implement.

Organized labour, one of the backbones of the Democratic Party, also made it difficult for Truman to implement his vision of reconversion. Unions wanted to make sure that their workers were adequately compensated, but this was proving to be difficult owing to some of the reconversion programmes. Consequently, from late 1945 through to 1946, there were strikes in the railroad, steel, coal, and automotive industries. For example, in January 1946, 3% of the labour force was on strike. Truman refused to compromise, forcing compulsory mediation and arbitration, threatening to draft striking railroad workers (which was an unprecedented move and, ironically, occurred after the strike issues had been resolved), and taking the United Mine Workers to court. These conflicts were eventually settled, but a rift was created within the Democratic Party.

Americans were also anxious to be able to begin to buy the goods they had been deprived of during the war. It proved to be difficult to retool the American economy to producing consumer goods, which led to frustration. When price controls started to end in June 1946, prices skyrocketed. This caused the highest **inflation** rate in the country's history: farm prices rose 14% in a month and had reached 30% by the end of the year. The combination of high prices and scarcity angered consumers and voters, who often blamed the President.

In the 1946 congressional mid-term election campaign, Republicans highlighted the problems of the Truman programme with phrases such as, "To Err is Truman", and ended up successfully taking over Congress for the first time in 15 years: their relationship was mostly confrontational. With the assistance of conservative Democrats they had the unique power to overturn a presidential veto. This situation enabled Truman to blame Republicans for their own policies as they did not resolve the numerous difficulties associated with reconversion. A key example of this was how to deal with organized labour. In his January 1947 State of the Union address, Truman suggested the need for legislation to end the conflicts, but did not offer a specific remedy other than the fact that he would not sign a bill that hurt labour. In response, the Congress passed the **Taft-Hartley Act,** and in June Truman vetoed it. Congress overrode his veto (a rarity led by Ohio Republican Senator Robert Taft), and Truman implemented some of its laws, but by initially vetoing it, he got the support of some labour unions back.

Truman was also able to make inflation a Republican problem. When Congress passed economic controls and rationing, particularly regarding

Employment Act of 1946
The Act created the Council of Economic Advisors (CEC) which became a key bipartisan advisory group to the President.

welfare state
A system whereby the state undertakes to protect the health and well-being of its citizens, especially those in financial or social need, by means of grants, pensions, and other benefits.

Class discussion

Watch the clip *Action against striking workers* from the PBS American Experience website (http://www.pbs.org/wgbh/americanexperience).
Discuss whether you think what Truman did was best for the US at the time.

inflation
A general increase in prices and fall in the purchasing value of money.

Taft-Hartley Act
This act limits the power of unions by strictly monitoring their actions. It was created by overriding Truman's presidential veto; unions condemned it, as did Truman, though the latter did use it several times in his presidency.

meat prices, the public began to reject measures that would lead to privatization of basic needs. On the other hand, Truman was seen to support housing for the poor, a higher minimum wage, federal assistance for education, new labour legislation (the first union contract with a sliding wage scale was agreed upon between General Motors and the United Auto Workers (UAW) on 25 May 1948) and civil rights, with various initiatives building on his creation of the Civil Rights Commission in 1946.

The 1948 election

Owing to the continued problems with reconversion, his conflict with Congress and his own party, it seemed unlikely Truman would win the 1948 election. His weakness as a candidate led some Democrats to consider offering the party nomination to General Dwight D Eisenhower (who had been the Supreme Allied Commander in Europe in the Second World War), however, Eisenhower refused the endorsement. In response, during his campaign for the Democratic nomination, Truman evolved into a passionate, charismatic political presence. In July Truman won the Democratic nomination and chose liberal Kentucky senator Alben Barkley for Vice-President (after Supreme Court Justice William O Douglas turned him down).

Division within the Democratic Party

As a result of Truman's nomination, the Democratic Party split, with some right-wing southerners being in favour of segregation. Strom Thurmond, Governor of South Carolina, and a group of southern delegates walked out of the Democratic Convention when the civil rights laws were passed. Together they formed the States' Rights Party in July 1948, and its members came to be known as Dixiecrats. Left-wing members supporting Henry Wallace's Progressive Citizens of America Party also deepened the split in the Democratic Party. After the convention, Truman ordered the army to be integrated, partly bowing down to pressure from civil rights leader A Philip Randolph. Truman's stance on civil rights won him many votes from black voters in 1948, and some would say, the presidential election.

In addition to having problems within his own party, the Democrats had formidable opponents: New York Governor Thomas Dewey and his running mate California Governor Earl Warren. Dewey had lost a close race to Roosevelt in 1944 and was still popular. He was strongly anti-communist and anti-New Deal. However, he did not share Truman's folksy yet direct nature, with many finding Dewey aloof and elitist. Regardless, he had the support of a strong Republican Party.

Most debated only how large the Dewey victory would be and failed to pay attention to the fact that Truman was actually proving to be an effective campaigner. After the party's summer conventions, Truman called Congress into a special session and challenged them to enact their proposed programmes – they didn't, undermining the effectiveness of the Republican Party. In contrast, Truman issued executive orders desegregating the military and ending discrimination in the civil service. He then launched a whistle-stop national campaign that included many liberal promises delivered with fiery rhetoric.

As a result voters began to see Dewey as bland and arrogant, while they saw Truman as feisty and down to earth. Still, the final pre-election poll from October, which became public the day before the election itself, gave Dewey a solid lead of 49.5% to Truman's 44.5%. On the eve of the election, even the press were hailing a Dewey victory and *The Chicago Tribune* ran the headline "Dewey Defeats Truman" It would become one of the greatest, unpredicted American presidential upsets.

Truman won with the backing of key components of Roosevelt's New Deal support base: rural and urban labour unions, Midwestern farmers, African Americans who had the right to vote and southern Democrats (despite the Dixiecrat split). By finally being elected, he felt that he now had a mandate to govern due to his own merits, despite the fact that more Americans had voted for Truman's opponents than for him – a portent of a difficult second term to come.

▲ 1948 election "Dewey Beats Truman!"

Analysis of votes in the 1948 presidential election

Despite the fact that the split in the Democratic Party had lost Truman some votes, he won the popular vote with 24 million to Dewey's 21 million, with 303 seats to 189 respectively. Thurmond and Wallace each received 2.4% of the vote, although Thurmond also took four southern states and their 39 electoral votes.

The Electoral College consists of 538 electors, with a majority of 270 electoral votes required to elect the president. A state's entitled allotment of electors is the same as the number of members in its Congressional delegation: one for each member in the House of Representatives plus two for Senators. Electors are not required to vote according to the results of the popular vote in their states, although it is rare for electors to disregard the popular vote by casting their electoral vote for someone other than their party's candidate. Electors generally hold a leadership position in their party or were chosen to recognize years of loyal service to the party.

McCarthyism
A campaign against alleged communists in the US government and other institutions carried out under McCarthy in the period 1950–1954. Many of the accused were blacklisted or lost their jobs, though most did not in fact belong to the Communist Party.

Korean War
UN troops, dominated by US forces, countered the invasion of South Korea by North Korean forces by invading North Korea, while China intervened on the side of the North. Peace negotiations begun in 1951, and the war ended two years later with the restoration of previous boundaries, currently at the 38th parallel.

debt
A government is said to be in debt if the amount of revenue that it takes in is less than what it expends over several years.

fiscal policy
Policy where members of government in charge of creating economic policies try to regulate the economy; this is often done by the setting of tax rates and the creation of budgets for government spending.

Truman's second term (1948–1952) and the Fair Deal

Truman's second term faced continued difficulties, as he was unable to work with a conservative Congress. There was also dissatisfaction with the turmoil that **McCarthyism** was causing in American society, as well domestic fallout from the **Korean War**.

The focus of Truman's second term was a Fair Deal at home and containment of communism abroad. With the Fair Deal, Truman was able to enact some key legislation that had a significant positive impact on the lives of many Americans. On 5 January 1949 he stated, "Every segment of our population and every individual has a right to expect from our Government a fair deal". This was the most progressive social legislation since the New Deal. It reaffirmed that with growing prosperity the country had an obligation to help those less fortunate through government-sponsored social programmes.

Truman's Fair Deal

Truman's Fair Deal had several key components, some of which were:

- Truman centralised the Federal Security Agency (FSA) and within it the newly renamed Social Security Administration.
- After complex negotiations with Congress, he reformed the Minimum Wage to increase it in 1949 to 75 cents an hour.
- The Housing Act of 1949 helped to deal with the housing crisis that occurred after the Second World War, particularly regarding urban renewal with new and renovated infrastructure.
- The Fair Deal continued to support already established civil rights legislation, and went further supporting the NAACP's chief counsel, Thurgood Marshall, to enact Fair Employment Practices Commission (FEPC) laws in several north-eastern US states: the Supreme Court later broadened the coverage of these laws to include non-segregated professional schools.

Truman continued to support already established civil rights legislation, and went further, supporting the NAACP's chief counsel Thurgood Marshall to enact Fair Employment Practices Commission (FEPC) laws in several north-eastern US states. However, Truman was unsuccessful in getting most of his proposals passed, such as unemployment benefits, federal education aid, low income tax cuts and national health insurance. Post-war United States was entering a more conservative period as many Americans were affected by the beginning of the Baby Boom in 1946 and preferred to spend their time and effort on their own family and community than seeing the bigger picture of American society. This resulted in limited public support for government public assistance schemes than there had been in the past. Truman had to deal with a massive **debt**, and he had a contradictory **fiscal policy** as he wanted to create new programmes, but did not want to fund them as it would create more debt.

In addition, the Taft-Hartley Act led to continued anger from labour forces with a soft-coal strike in September 1949 and the United Steel Workers strike on 1 October 1949. On 27 August 1950 the army seized the railroads to prevent a strike, leading Truman to declare a state of national emergency in December of that year. In one of his most legally controversial moves, Truman ordered the seizure of steel mills to prevent a strike in April 1952, as America was at war with Korea and Truman believed a steel strike would severely threaten the US military. The seizures immediately prompted the steel owners and lawmakers to question Truman's exertion of presidential power. Truman's presidency ended with a reputation of being ineffective at finding diplomatic solutions to conflicts with labour.

Truman also changed the power of the presidential office. In 1950 Congress added to the executive branch's authority by giving the president the right to appoint the chairman of several new regulatory commissions such as the Civil Aeronautics Board (CAB), Federal Communications Commission (FCC), Federal Power Commission (FPC), Federal Trade Commission (FTC), Interstate Commerce Commission (ICC) and Securities and Exchange Commission (SEC). However, Truman also restricted the presidency with the 22nd Amendment of the 27 February 1951 that limited the presidency to two terms.

End of presidency and Truman's legacy

Truman's presidency was tainted by a foreign conflict that had failed to find a resolution, that being the Korean War and the accompanying fallout (including McCarthy's Red Scare) – one of the reasons why Truman left office with such a low public approval rating. However, his *New York Times* obituary from 26 December 1972 summarized his domestic impact by stating, "Truman led the nation's conversion from war to peace, while maintaining a stable and prosperous economy". He himself, reviewing his actions in December 1952, said: "The Presidents who have done things, who were not afraid to act, have been the most abused... and I have topped them all in the amount of abuse I have received".

Conceptual understanding

Key questions:

→ To what extent were the Truman and Eisenhower administrations different?

→ Why did Eisenhower have so much popular support throughout his presidency?

→ To what extent did the Eisenhower administration bring prosperity to all Americans?

Key concepts:

→ Causation   → Continuity

→ Change   → Significance

→ Consequence

Eisenhower's presidency (1953–1961)

Eisenhower liked to describe his philosophy as "Modern Republicanism". His government generally continued enforcing the New Deal and Fair Deal programmes, while also trying to maintain a balanced budget. The Miller Center at the University of Virginia aptly summarized the cultural legacy of the Eisenhower era: "Although there were dangerous moments in the Cold War during the 1950s, people often remember the Eisenhower years as 'happy days', a time when Americans did not have to worry about depression or war… Americans spent their time enjoying the benefits of a booming economy. Millions of families got their first television and their second car and enjoyed new pastimes like hula-hoops or transistor radios. Young people went to drive-in movies or malt shops". There were challenges regarding how to continue to develop the economy, bring equal rights to everyone in American society, and wage the Cold War, both at home and abroad, and Eisenhower tried to deal with those challenges with proposals consistent with his philosophy.

The 1952 and 1956 elections

Eisenhower swept to power in 1952 with the slogan, "I like Ike!" He defeated Senator Robert Taft for the Republican nomination on a more conservative platform. Despite the fact that Taft led an alliance of conservative Republicans and southern Democrats, and had orchestrated the defeat of Truman when the Taft-Hartley Act overrode his veto in June 1947, Taft was still a part of the Congress, and the country was in the midst of economic instability and the continued war in Korea. Eisenhower, in contrast, had "won" the Second World War with an impressive military record, effectively using both strategy and diplomacy. His bilateral approach to foreign affairs and the fact that he was a war hero seemed the answer to resolving the Korean War and dealing with future Cold War issues. This strength made him appear an ideal candidate to lead the country domestically as well globally.

In the presidential election, Eisenhower defeated Democrat Adlai E Stevenson who voters perceived as being too intellectual and ineffectual against communism. Eisenhower won 33.8 million votes (55% of the popular vote) to Stevenson's 27.3 million votes, and the Republicans maintained their control of the House and split the Senate. The Republicans held the presidency for the first time since 1933, but it was more due to Eisenhower's personal popularity than the appeal of the conservative Republican platform.

Despite suffering a heart attack in 1955 and general concern regarding his health, Eisenhower ran for a second term in 1956. Doubts began to appear about his ability to survive a second term, which generated a short-lived movement to remove Richard Nixon (see page 303) from the 1956 ticket as Vice-President. Eisenhower remained silent on this issue, so the movement lost steam and Nixon remained. Running on a platform of "Peace, progress and prosperity", Eisenhower beatDemocrat Stevenson again in the 1956 election. Eisenhowerremained immensely popular throughout his presidency.

Eisenhower's domestic policy

Even though part of his election platform criticized **Big government,** he was a moderate Republican, so Eisenhower continued and expanded upon some of the programmes of his predecessors. He strengthened the Social Security programme and on 1 September 1954 Social Security coverage was extended to 10 million more people including farmers and independent professionals. He also the minimum wage. He continued construction of low-income housing, and under the Truman administration the executive was given the power to appoint the chairmen of the "Big 6" intergovernmental agencies: Civil Aeronautics Board (CAB), Federal Communications Commission (FCC), Federal Power Commission (FPC), Federal Trade Commission (FTC), Interstate Commerce Commission (ICC), Securities and Exchange Commission (SEC).

On 11 April 1953 he created the Department of Health, Education and Welfare (HEW) managed by one director appointed by the president. Clearly, the executive branch was now at the centre of bureaucratic control of essential components of the government. For all of the legislation that was passed, Eisenhower was also able to produce balanced budgets: three of his eight budgets were "in the black". This was due to several factors, but significantly the reconversion process started by Truman had been completed.

Eisenhower often got his way with Congress, especially during his first term. However, in his last years as president, and with Democrats in control of both the House and the Senate from the mid-term elections of 1956, Congress was spending far more on domestic programmes than Eisenhower liked and he used his veto to block those that were expensive. In spite of this, the Miller Center reported that "domestic spending still rose from 31% of the budget in 1953 to 49% in 1961. During the Eisenhower years, federal spending as a percentage of Gross Domestic Product (GDP) declined from 20.4% to 18.4%. No presidency since has seen a decrease of any size in federal spending as a percentage of GDP".

▲ "I like Ike" campaign poster for Eisenhower. Ike is short for Eisenhower.

Big government
Government perceived as excessively interventionist and intruding into all aspects of the lives of its citizens.

McCarthy's domestic inquisition was another legacy of the Truman administration, and Eisenhower was initially conflicted regarding how to act. After years of not criticizing McCarthy (in reference to his attacks on George C Marshall, former Secretary of State and Eisenhower's mentor), and even supporting some of his decisions (such as not giving clemency to the Rosenbergs (see page 483), he finally made decisions that helped to end the McCarthy era after McCarthy turned on the military. Eisenhower forbade members of his administration to testify at the McCarthy hearings. On 2 December 1954 the Senate voted to condemn McCarthy for his conduct.

Throughout his second term in office Eisenhower created new infrastructure and territorial acquisition legislation. On 29 June 1956 Eisenhower signed the Federal Aid Highway Act (National Interstate and Defense Highways Act) that authorized $25 billion for the construction of 41 000 miles of highways. The Interstate Highway Act strengthened the country by linking urban areas, enabling economic development and benefitting American culture. However, it also hurt inner cities as it facilitated the growth of suburbanization. (By 1960 one third of Americans lived in a suburb.)

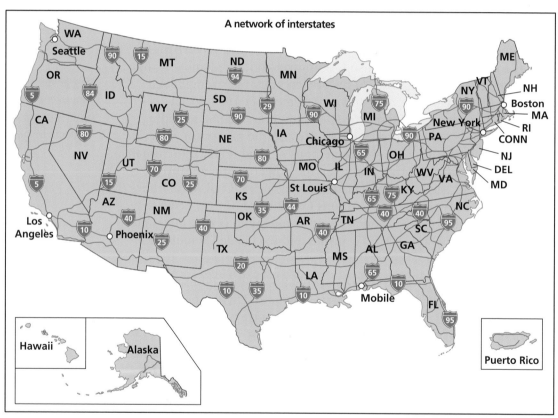

▲ The roads created from the 1956 Interstate Highway Act connected Americans: they were able to travel more domestically, and begin to appreciate the unique demographics of each region of the country, in many ways uniting the country.

Domestic airlines also began to connect different parts of the country, expedited by the Federal Aviation Administration (FAA). Between 1947 and 1957 passenger air travel grew significantly, and airlines became a normal means of transport. A new term – the jet set – entered common usage, referring to the wealthy elite whose international lifestyle depended upon air travel.

In 1959 – in partnership with Canada – Eisenhower opened the St Lawrence Seaway (from Montreal to Lake Ontario), which helped to facilitate trade from the Great Lakes region, improving the economies of cities like Detroit, Cleveland and Chicago. Gross ship registered tons for the 1959 season amounted to $25.1 million.

In addition to leisure and industrial transport developments, and in response to the Soviets launch of Sputnik in 1957, Eisenhower authorized funding for the Advance Research Projects Agency (ARPA) in 1958. ARPA had a clear mission to prevent further technological surprises and develop revolutionary technologies. During the 1960s it was responsible for the creation of ARPANET, the precursor to the Internet. Eisenhower also created the National Aeronautics and Space Administration (NASA) in 1958.

On 3 January 1959, Alaska became the 49th US state, and on 18 March Hawaii was proclaimed the 50th. This territorial acquisition was followed by the elections of the first Asian Americans in the federal government. Hiram Leong Fong, a Chinese American, was elected to the Senate, and Daniel K Inouye, a Japanese American, was elected to the House of Representatives.

According to historian Bernard Bailyn, during the 1950s a combination of "government spending, private investment, consumer borrowing, and a nearly 30% expansion of the population (Baby Boom) allowed the US, which represented only 6% of the world's people, to produce and consume about 33% of the world's economic output". Part of this was due to new agricultural techniques that boosted output. The1956 introduction of the Soil Bank (Title I of the Agricultural Act of 1956), strove to reduce production of basic crops, maintain farm income and conserve soil. Additionally, billions of dollars were invested in **heavy** and **light industry**, and the development of new materials, such as plastics and aluminium.

A mass market for cheap consumer goods developed as personal income increased by 45%, and American consumers wanted to use their new purchasing power. According to Bailyn, "in the 1950s America's largest corporations averaged $500 million/year in sales, ten times that of the 1920s". Cheap consumer credit helped to facilitate the nation's spending spree, including the introduction of the first credit cards to purchase new luxury consumer items such as televisions. On 4 September 1951 the first nationwide television broadcast occurred, and by 1960 90% of American households had televisions.

In contrast there was also a substantial segment of the population who came to be known as the invisible poor. John Kenneth Galbraith stated that during the 1950s the US had become "the affluent society". However, Michael Harrington's *The Other America* (1962), described the 20–25% of Americans who did not participate in the new "American Dream". Although the poverty rate declined during Eisenhower's tenure, 40 million Americans would be defined as poor by its end.

A substantial percentage of the invisible poor were African American, and Eisenhower, despite the fact that he had been raised in a segregated society and fought in a segregated military, ordered the desegregation of all public facilities in Washington, DC, and enforced the desegregation of

heavy industry
The manufacture of large, heavy objects and materials in bulk.

light industry
The manufacture of small or light objects and materials.

Social and thinking skills

Find and read Maurice Isserman's essay *Michael Harrington: Warrior on poverty* on the New York Times website (http://www.nytimes.com).

To what extent do you agree with Harrington's remedy regarding poverty, and has the United States been successful in its "assault on poverty"?

the armed forces (Truman's Executive Order 9981). His highly influential appointment of Earl Warren, a liberal Republican, as Chief Justice of the Supreme Court on 1 October 1953 would change civil rights history.

The "Warren Court" came to be synonymous with helping to bring more legal rights to non-whites throughout the country. Even though Eisenhower didn't comment publically on many of the pro-civil rights rulings, he was an advocate of slow desegregation. He only met with African American leaders once in his presidency, often empathizing with white southerner complaints about their changing lifestyles. However, he made it clear that he was going to uphold the Constitution, so signed the Civil Rights Acts of 1957 and 1960, and sent the National Guard in to help to enforce the law in various situations (see page 451).

Famously known for his foreign policies, such as ending the war in Korea in 1953, and the New Look policy implemented by Secretary of State John Foster Dulles, Eisenhower's refocusing of the economy towards fighting the Cold War led to the "military-industrial complex" domestically. He warned against this situation as he left office in his famous farewell address on 17 January 1961, however, he and his government's policies were instrumental in creating it by his authorization of defence spending, particularly to support programmes led by the CIA to undertake covert operations against communism around the world – military expenditures rose to 60% of the national budget. As American corporations such as General Electric, General Motors and Douglas Aircraft expanded and made substantial profits, they subcontracted part of their military contracts to others, leading to the problem that if the government cancelled a big defense contract, it would have huge ramifications for substantial sections of the economy. This meant that politicians who had such businesses in their districts would be adverse celling these contracts. Instead, politicians welcomed this new industry to develop in their communities.

Eisenhower also encouraged the American population to believe that the US could win a nuclear war, so civil defense drills began to be implemented, with the first on 12 June 1954, followed by others, such as the "duck and cover" drills implemented in schools nationwide.

Overall assessment of Eisenhower's presidency

Eisenhower was at that time the only Republican, other than Ulysses S Grant, to have served two full terms as president. According to one of his biographers Robert J Donovan, "Eisenhower was the only President in the 20th century to have presided over eight years of peace and prosperity, as well as a balanced budget and an economy with negligible inflation. He was dignified, fair, appealing. When he left office, his popularity had, if anything increased".

Eisenhower's Farewell Address also recommended restraint in the consumer habits that proliferated during his presidency, particularly with regard to the environment. "As we peer into society's future, we – you and I, and our government – must avoid the impulse to live only for today, plundering, for our own ease and convenience, the precious resources of tomorrow. We cannot mortgage the material assets of our grandchildren without asking the loss also of their political and spiritual heritage". Interestingly, it would mostly be Democrats who would implement legislation to try to address his concerns.

Class discussion

In *Bracing for Armageddon: Why Civil Defense Never Worked*, Lora D Garrison wrote about the significance of the small number of protests against these drills: the fact that their purpose was to scare the population into submission, making them believe they could survive a nuclear war when it was not possible.

Why do you think people didn't protest against these drills? Would you have protested against them?

6.3 Kennedy and the New Frontier

Conceptual understanding

Key questions:

→ To what extent were the Kennedy administration policies consistent with those of Eisenhower's?

→ Why did Kennedy have such a difficult time passing his legislative agenda?

Key concepts:

→ Causation   → Continuity

→ Change   → Significance

→ Consequence

Overview of the Kennedy presidency (1961–1963)

John F Kennedy's presidency lasted "A Thousand Days", and had a number of firsts. He was both the youngest elected president (at 43) and was Catholic. His presidency has been expansively documented: according to Jill Abramson (2013), executive editor of the *New York Times*, more than 40,000 books have been written about him. However, many have felt that it has been difficult to write effectively on Kennedy. As Kennedy biographer Robert Dallek (2003) stated, "Historians see him more as a celebrity who didn't accomplish very much" and that "there is editorial pressure to find sensationalist material instead of having the ability to seriously focus on his achievement record, particularly domestically, as many of Kennedy's most impactful acts regarded foreign policy such as the Cold War in Europe, events in Cuba and Vietnam. Most of his domestic legislative proposals were not enacted until after his death; however, that does not negate the fact that he should be given partial credit for their achievements".

The 1960 election

In 1960 the Democratic National Convention nominated Kennedy on the first ballot, with Lyndon Baines Johnson as his Vice-President. The Republican National Convention nominated Eisenhower's Vice-President Richard Milhous Nixon as their presidential candidate and Henry Cabot Lodge as Vice-President. The election campaign was close, but the televised Kennedy–Nixon Debates, particularly the event on 26 September 1960, seemed to have been decisive. As Professor Alan Schroeder stated, "It's one of those unusual points on the timeline of history where you can say things changed very dramatically – in this case, in a single night". Kennedy had been professionally prepared by media consultants, and projected calm confidence, whereas Nixon had been ill and had not recovered. By the end of the first debate, momentum had clearly shifted Kennedy's

Find and watch the first ten minutes of the Kennedy–Nixon debate (First Kennedy–Nixon Debate, 26 September 1960, from www.jfklibrary.org). Try to do this in pairs with one person watching and the other listening. Who do you think won and why? Can you relate your argument to the senses that you are using?

How can we know if our senses are reliable? What is the role of expectation in sense perception? What is the role of language in sense perception?

way. A CBS News poll stated that 57% of people voting in November felt that the debates were decisive for them regarding how they would cast their ballot. Nixon later became president, having learned from these mistakes.

▲ The last of the four Kennedy–Nixon Debates, 1960

During the campaign, the fact that Kennedy was a Catholic caused some concern in the media and some feared that he could be somehow influenced by or beholden to the Pope. There was also significant debate regarding his support for civil rights, leading to some southern conservative Democrats to vote for "unpledged Democrats" who became aligned with Senator Harry Flood Byrd from Virginia. However, Kennedy effectively defused this issue throughout the campaign, and instead focused on other issues such as the economy, campaigning with the slogan "Get America moving again".

Results of the 1960 election

Kennedy won 56% of the electoral votes against Nixon's 41% with Kennedy receiving 34.2 million votes to Nixon's 34.1 million. Byrd's "unpledged Democrats" won 3% of electoral votes (116,000 votes). In 1960 a significant popular vote in Alabama and Mississippi went to unpledged Democratic electors. The South in 1960 was still largely Democratic, the heritage of the Civil War. Most voters in the 11 states of the old Confederacy blamed Abraham Lincoln's Republican Party for the war. When conservative Democratic voters in the Deep South wanted to go against the national party's presidential candidate, they preferred to follow a local hero rather than the Republican alternative (such as going with Thurmond in 1948). In 1960 Kennedy was seen as being too pro-Civil Rights, so in Mississippi and Alabama, 'unpledged Democratic electors' ran."It is still debated whether Nixon actually won the popular vote if you examine what happened in Mississippi and Alabama. Kennedy's victory by such a small margin meant he did not have a mandate to push some of his more controversial measures through Congress.

▲ Kennedy is overwhelmed by supporters during his presidential campaign trail in Los Angeles

The New Frontier

Following Eisenhower's moderate presidency of the 1950s, Kennedy took office as more of a domestic liberal (particularly regarding civil rights), but he also felt there was a need to take a decisive stand against communism abroad. Once in office, he set about trying to implement his liberal platform.

In his speech at the Democratic National Convention accepting his nomination for president on 15 July 1960, he said that the nation was at the edge of a New Frontier, "The New Frontier of which I speak is not a set of promises – it is a set of challenges. It sums up not what I intend to offer the American people, but what I intend to ask of them". Once his presidency began, many Americans responded to his call for a more liberal America.

Kennedy took office during a major recession. Business bankruptcies had reached levels not seen since the Great Depression and 5.5 million people were unemployed. Kennedy decided to invest money in domestic and military spending, lower taxes and give investment tax credits. He also increased the minimum wage in May 1961 from $1.00 to $1.25 over a two-year period. Kennedy provided more support for the unemployed, business and housing industries. To overcome the 7% unemployment rate inherited from the Eisenhower administration, he signed a number of congressional bills that promoted economic expansion. By 1962 the recession had ended but Kennedy continued to reform The Trade Expansion Act of 1962 reduced tariffs on goods exchanged between the US and its major European trading partners, leading to increased commerce and prosperity for both sides.

TOK discussion

Ted Sorenson was Kennedy's famous speechwriter during Kennedy's presidency. Historian Douglas Brinkley wrote, "Ted Sorenson was the administration's indispensable man".

Find Kennedy's Inaugural Address (1961) written by Ted Sorenson, on the Internet, before reading Sorenson's obituary from the *Washington Post* which describes his impact and the influence of presidential speechwriters.

In what ways and for what reasons did Kennedy's Inaugural Address impact American culture?

Class discussion

Read Kennedy's political credo on the American Experience section of the PBS website, where he defines his attitude of liberalism.

Discuss the techniques Kennedy employs in order to make his argument more persuasive and his vision more appealing to the general public.

Although he dealt with the challenges by working in cooperation with some in the business community, he sometimes faced resistance. In the spring of 1962, the US Steel Company raised the price of steel by $6 a ton (an increase of 3.5%), as did others in the industry. Kennedy called the price increase an "utter contempt for the public interest" as it could contribute to increased inflation, however, US Steel President Roger Blough responded that steel prices had not increased since 1958 and that profits were at a record low. Kennedy ordered a federal investigation into the possibility of price-fixing, as well as anti-trust lawsuits and the end of some government contracts. Under pressure, US Steel and other companies backed down, but this conflict in the business community contributed to the stock market falling the steepest drop since 1929. In response, Kennedy did not take action when steel prices were later increased twice in one year.

To deal with continued economic challenges, he proposed a general tax cut in 1963: a $13.5 billion cut in taxes over three years. This would reduce government income and create a budget **deficit**, but Kennedy believed that the extra money consumers would have to spend would stimulate the economy and bring added tax revenues. In addition, increased business investment would lead to noninflationary economic expansion, more jobs, and greater prosperity for all. Both conservatives and liberals opposed this, and economist John Kenneth Galbraith claimed that the deficit would not address serious national problems. The tax cut proposal became stuck in congressional committee and had not passed Congress by the time of his death in November 1963.

After its enactment in 1964, the tax cut led to greater consumer spending and business investment: deficit spending worked. Regardless, Kennedy's economic policies produced an average annual GNP growth rate of 5.6%, inflation at 1.3%, and reduced unemployment from 7% to 5%. "In terms of economic management", wrote Arthur Schlesinger Jr, historian and chief aide, "Kennedy was a most effective president". The economy boomed for the rest of the 1960s, helping to provide the money that would be used to finance the social reforms in the Johnson administration.

The president also proposed new social programmes. These included advocating for the new idea of **Medicare**, providing research into mental illness, federal aid to education, assistance to needy rural areas, more funds for expanded urban mass transit, and a new Department of Urban Affairs. One of his more notable achievements was signing the Housing Act of 30 June 1961. The President's Advisory Council on the Arts was established by Executive Order on 12 June 1963.

deficit
An excess of expenditure or liabilities over income or assets in a given period, usually one year.

Medicare
Medicare provides government health care for those over the age of 65 as it was difficult for people in that demographic to get coverage privately. It was advocated for by Kennedy and finally enacted by Johnson. It is now one of the biggest elements of the US budget.

Housing Act, June 1961

For the first time, as Kennedy himself stated, this housing act provided Federal aid to preserve "rapidly disappearing open land and to improve inadequate public transportation in our growing urban and metropolitan areas. It recognizes, through a new program of low interest loans, the forgotten families – those who are ineligible for public housing on the one hand and those whose incomes will not allow them to pay for decent housing on the other. It provides, at the same time, expanded opportunities for private industry to meet the housing needs of families of moderate income. It authorizes new tools long needed to cope with blighted housing and neighborhoods. Finally, it extends the principle of experiment and research to the problems of mass transportation and both public and private housing".

▲ Kennedy signing the Housing Act, 1961

Lacking congressional support, Kennedy's success was mixed. He was successful in increasing the minimum wage, providing funds for regional development in Appalachia, and cutting taxes to an extent, but Medicare was rejected, as was the creation of an urban affairs department as southern Democrats feared that an African American would be in charge of it. His education bill was also rejected as it was surrounded in controversy regarding **parochial schools** getting equal support (although Kennedy, a Catholic, would come out against this).

Although many of Kennedy's proposals were blocked by Congress, he had the ability to use executive action, but he was cautious. Kennedy had said in his campaign that he would end discrimination in public housing "with a stroke of the pen", but he did not do so until a flood of pens arrived in the White House mail throughout 1961 and 1962. His Executive Order on 20 November 1962 against racial discrimination in federally aided housing was a positive reform, but it only covered future public housing.

Kennedy wanted to take action against poverty. In his first two years in office he hoped he could help the poor by stimulating the economy, but some felt that he was out of touch with the brutal realities of poverty. In 1962 author Michael Harrington publicized this problem in *The Other America:* white, middle class Americans were enjoying 1950s prosperity, but 15% lived below the poverty line. After reading the book, Kennedy decided to aid the poor directly. However, he acted too late in his term and was never able to push legislation through Congress. Johnson followed up his concerns in his War on Poverty.

On 1 March 1961, Kennedy signed Executive Order 10924 which established the **Peace Corps.** Thousands of Americans joined this organization and brought the experiences they learned abroad back home, which helped to contribute towards the civil rights movement as more people saw the need to create a more just and egalitarian society.

parochial schools
Schools related to or financially supported by church parishes.

Peace Corps
An organisation that sends young people to work as volunteers in developing countries.

Many were inspired by the Peace Corps, but chose to volunteer in America to work toward social justice, such as joining such organizations as the Freedom Riders (see page 450).

No frontier seemed too distant, and this was reflected by Kennedy's focus on the space programme. On 25 May 1961, in reaction to Soviet cosmonaut Yuri Gagarin becoming the first man to orbit the Earth, Kennedy asked Congress to deliver a special message on "urgent national needs": he requested $7–$9 billion through 1966 for the space programme, proclaiming that "this nation should commit itself to achieving the goal, before the decade is out, of landing a man on the moon and returning him safely to the earth". Congress responded enthusiastically. During Kennedy's administration Alan Shepherd became the first American to enter space (5 May 1961), John Glenn became the first American to orbit the earth (7 February 1962), and the Telstar II communications satellite was launched. Even though Kennedy had already died, many recalled his goal when Neil Armstrong and Buzz Aldrin became the first humans to walk on the moon on 20 July 1969.

By far the most volatile and divisive domestic issue Kennedy had to deal with was civil rights (see page 450). Kennedy had a mixed record regarding civil rights: his administration enforced existing civil rights laws more than it passed new ones. He ended up appointing southern conservative Democratic judges and federal officials due to pressure from his party (more than Eisenhower had before him as he had not faced such pressure from the Republican Party). However, Kennedy did use federal authority to send in troops to try to enforce the end of segregation, and by allowing for conservative Democrats to have their way with some appointments, he was able to get Thurgood Marshall, black general counsel for the NAACP, appointed to the Federal Circuit Court. The Justice Department under his brother, Attorney General Robert F Kennedy, did make more efforts to enforce black rights than previous administrations, but they gave only "limited assistance" to southern blacks and civil rights activists attacked by white racists. As Martin Luther King Jr said, while southern blacks had "marshalled extraordinary courage to employ non-violent direct action, they had been left – by the most powerful federal government in the world – almost solely to their own resources".

There are some who speculated that Kennedy was delaying pushing harder for his civil rights proposals until he had won a second term in office. In 1963 when civil rights demonstrators were attacked in Birmingham, Alabama, Kennedy sent in the National Guard to help forcefully integrate the University of Alabama, which was greatly opposed by Alabama Governor George C Wallace (leading to his political campaign). Addressing the nation on television on 11 June 1963, Kennedy stated, "We preach freedom around the world, and we mean it, and we cherish our freedom, here at home, but are we to say to the world, and much more importantly, to each other that this a land of the free except for the Negroes? The time has come for this nation to fulfill its promise", and that the grandchildren of the slaves freed by Lincoln "are not yet freed from the bonds of injustice".

He proposed modest voting rights reforms and school desegregation, and stronger legislation prohibiting segregation in public places by banning discrimination wherever federal funding was involved. It was the most comprehensive civil rights measure ever endorsed by a US president and

public approval was initially 61%, but Congress, dominated by influential white southerners, was resistant and prevented the bill from being voted on. This lack of consistent support for African Americans led to the March on Washington on 27 August 1963 and King's rallying cry, "I Have a Dream", as well as increasing the rift in the civil rights movement with the rise of Black Nationalism. Kennedy's bill did not pass in his lifetime but much of it formed Johnson's 1964 Civil Rights Act.

Kennedy's foreign policy decisions in the Cold War had a significant domestic impact. In the 1960s there was a campaign against the Soviets to 'win' the missile gap, although it was never proven that there was a gap. This led to the largest peacetime military build-up in American history. To demonstrate that Americans were willing to actually fight a nuclear war, the administration continued the civil defence programme started by Eisenhower, and made additions such as a fallout shelter programme that was supposed to save 97% of the population.

On 22 October 1962 the American population was notified of events in the Cuban Missile Crisis (see page 405), and that a blockade had been prepared. This caused immense concern throughout the United States, particularly in cities or military locations that were within firing range of Soviet missiles, which led to some even evacuating the cities. On 23 October the Soviet ships turned back, but the impact of a possible Third World War left an immense sociocultural impact on the US, as well as countries throughout the world. These actions also led to the beginning of a détente towards the USSR such as the 1963 ban on atmospheric and underwater (but not underground) nuclear explosions, supported by 80% of the country according to polls at the time. At the start of 1950 the total US budget was $40 billion, with a military allocation of $12 million; the 1960 military budget alone was $45.8 billion and by the end of the Kennedy administration it was nearly $55 billion.

On 22 November, while Kennedy was on an election campaign for his second term in office, he was assassinated in Dallas. The event was broadcast on television for the next four days, setting a record as the most watched television event in US history to date. For a time the assassination created a "Kennedy myth", as the "six seconds in Dallas" were engrained in society's collective memory. Vice-President Johnson made use of the spirit of hope and desire for liberal change, and saw enacted much of the legislation that Kennedy had failed to push through Congress.

Overall assessment of Kennedy's presidency

According to historian Bernard Bailyn, "Kennedy's advocacy of the New Frontier and of the need to get the country moving again turned out to be more rhetoric than substance". His rhetoric was passionate, but for various reasons he did not live to see most of his proposals enacted. He was considered too liberal for conservative southern Democrats, and too moderate for those who wanted more action, who felt betrayed that he had not worked hard enough to achieve his purported goals. It's difficult to speculate what would have happened had he lived, but it is important to note that many of his domestic goals were eventually achieved in the Johnson administration.

ATL **Thinking and social skills**

Watch the first 15 minutes of the video clip "1963 Interview with Malcolm X", on C-Span.org. Malcolm X was one of the leaders of the Nation of Islam, while Professor John C Leggett was one of the leaders of the Free Speech Movement at UC Berkeley. Malcolm X rejected the efforts of Leggett and other white liberals to help effect change.

Why does Malcolm X feel the way he does? To what extent is he justified? After doing some further research, compare and contrast how much has changed or stayed the same in American society since this interview?

6.4 Johnson and the Great Society

Conceptual understanding

Key questions:

→ Assess how successful Johnson was in having his legislative agenda implemented.

→ To what extent were the policies that Johnson enacted ones that Kennedy had created?

→ Why are many of Johnson's domestic achievements not remembered as much as his foreign policy decisions?

Key concepts:

→ Causation → Continuity

→ Change → Significance

→ Consequence

Overview of Johnson's presidency (1963–1969)

Johnson's presidency was among the most influential in the modern era. Johnson sought to not only complete Kennedy's unfinished legacy, but to create his own "Great Society" whereby "men are more concerned with the quality of their goals than with the quantity of their goods": he was able to pass more social legislation than any other president since Roosevelt. However, much of this domestic success was overshadowed at the end of his presidency by his administration's decisions regarding the Vietnam War, and he left office with some of the lowest approval ratings for any president.

Johnson's presidency: domestic issues

On the day of Kennedy's assassination (Nov 22) Vice-President Lyndon Baines Johnson had been in the presidential motorcade. He was whisked to Air Force One, where he was given the Oath of Office. Following the theme of "Let us continue", on 27 November in an address to Congress he pledged to continue Kennedy's policies, particularly regarding civil rights and tax cuts. He was well prepared to take over running the country due to his political experience, both in the White House and Congress. Some, such as former Secretary of State Dean Acheson, thought him "not a very likeable man". This was due to the nature of how he tried to achieve his goals: politicians were annoyed by, and some even feared, the Johnson treatment, but it was effective for him in accomplishing his agenda.

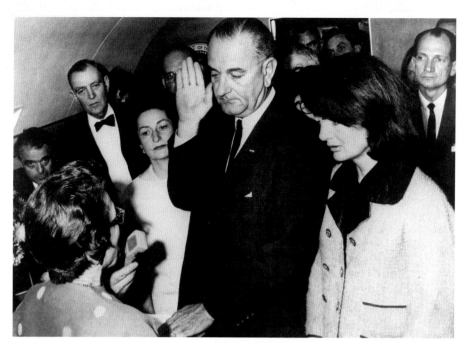

▲ Johnson taking the presidential oath on board Air Force One

In addition to finally getting Congress to pass much of Kennedy's civil rights and tax cuts bills, Johnson set about creating his own Great Society. Much of Congress, aware that the American people needed some action that would heal the wound, realized that it would have to respond to Johnson's appeal to fulfil Kennedy's legacy as well as some of Johnson's own goals. Among his first presidential decisions were federal spending cuts and new investments.

On 12 December 1963 Secretary of Defense Robert McNamara curtailed the construction of 33 military installations to save money (although this saving was soon countermanded in May 1964 when he asked Congress for $125 million in additional aid for South Vietnam, the first of many requests), and on 16 December Johnson signed a bill creating a $1.2 billion construction programme for colleges (for building classrooms, laboratories and libraries). In his 1964 State of the Union address, he announced a reduction in the federal budget, and urged that the nation take action against poverty and racism. During a commencement address at the University of Michigan on 22 May 1964, Johnson coined the phrase "Great Society". As a part of this initiative, he tried to have his Civil Rights Act passed. However, some House members tried to tie up the Act in the House Rules Committee, and a 57-day southern **filibuster** in the Senate ensued. However, this was finally defeated and on 22 July 1964 the Civil Rights Act was enacted. The Civil Rights Act sought to end discrimination in all public facilities and public housing, and forbade federal funding for some public facilities if there was discrimination. It also protected the African American right to vote and expanded federal aid to education, urban mass transit, and the food stamp programme.

▲ Johnson shakes hands with Martin Luther King Jr after signing the Civil Rights Act

filibuster
An action such as prolonged speaking which obstructs progress in a legislative assembly in a way that does not technically contravene the required procedures.

311

Find and examine the Civil Rights Act. Examine one section (title), give an example of racial discrimination and describe how this act tried to end it. In addition, carry out further research to find an example from contemporary times, and analyse to what extent the Civil Rights Act has been effective.

Johnson's attack on poverty, which affected one fifth of the nation's population at the time, can be broken down into three major weapons, as listed below. Research one aspect of one of these weapons, and discuss to what extent Johnson achieved his goals.

Weapon 1: Education

Weapon 2: Income maintenance

Weapon 3: Job creation

In his 1964 State of the Union address, Johnson declared, "This administration today, here and now, declares an unconditional war on poverty in America". Johnson said that he was inspired by Michael Harrington's book *The Other America* and invited him to Washington as a consultant. Johnson felt passionately that something needed to be done to assist the estimated 25% of the population living below the poverty line. On 20 August Johnson signed the $974.5 million Poverty Bill and created a new department: the Office of Economic Opportunity. The Economic Opportunity Act created Volunteers in Service to America (VISTA) which sent volunteers to help people in poor communities with community action programmes (CAP) to give the poor a voice in helping to define housing, health and education policies in their neighbourhoods.

On 9 October 1965, Johnson signed another $1.785 billion anti-poverty bill that doubled the previous appropriation, and on 23 September 1966 increased some welfare benefits and raised the minimum wage to $1.60. The number of Americans living below the poverty line fell by 50% to 11% during the Johnson administration. However, the war on poverty was not wholly successful. The annual budget for the war on poverty averaged $2 billion, less than one quarter of 1% of GNP. "For a mere $11 billion", economist Robert Lekachman stated, "we could raise every poor American above the poverty line". But Johnson was against a programme based on handouts. One view is that it was not fully funded because the Vietnam War drained potential resources, whereas others say it did not focus enough on creating jobs. Regardless, Johnson did make the first federal attempt to end poverty.

There were also advances in women's rights (see page 465) during the first Johnson administration. Johnson recognized the need to start to codify rights for women. In 1964 Congress passed Public Law 88-352 that "forbade discrimination on the basis of sex as well as race in hiring, promoting, and firing". Title VII of the Act created the Equal Employment Opportunity Commission (EEOC) to implement the law. The National Organization for Women (NOW) was formed in 1966 and continued to advocate for fair pay and equal job opportunities (see page 471).

Johnson was also able to take action on the environment. Kennedy had tried to protect millions of acres of wilderness lands from development, but Congress had blocked his proposals. In 1962 Rachel Carson had published *Silent Spring* exposing the deadly nature of chemical pesticides, especially DDT. A Special Presidential Advisory Committee under Kennedy had determined that there was a legitimate concern. DDT was banned and other chemicals had to follow stricter guidelines. There was, however, continued concern about air pollution, oil spills and toxic waste. Starting in 1964, Johnson passed 18 environmental acts, including the Endangered Species Conservation Act, a $3.9 billion water pollution control bill, and several air and land pollution control acts.

The 1964 election

Even though he had less than a year to prove himself to be a worthy president, his early successes led to a landslide victory over Republican Barry Goldwater in 1964. Goldwater was seen as too reactionary for many; for example, he opposed civil rights and believed that military commanders should be allowed to use nuclear weapons in combat. Goldwater had told the Republican National Convention, "Extremism in the defence of liberty is no vice". When Goldwater bumper stickers came out stating "In your heart you know he's right" regarding his advocacy of using nuclear weapons, the Democrats produced their own in response that said "In your heart, you know he might".

On 3 November 1964 Johnson won 42 million (compared to Goldwater's 27 million) votes and 61% of the popular vote, which is the highest percentage any president has received (up to 2012). Johnson and the Democrats also won 90% of votes in the Electoral College and large majorities in both Houses of Congress. "Landslide Lyndon" now had a mandate to continue to implement his Great Society.

Johnson's second term and the Great Society

Johnson would need to find a way to continue to pay for the Great Society and he agreed with Kennedy's controlled deficit spending programme. To gain conservative support for Kennedy's tax cut bill, Johnson agreed to cut spending. The GNP rose 7.1% in 1964 to 9.5% in 1966 and 10 million new jobs were created. The deficit, which many people thought would grow, in fact shrank, and inflation was manageable.

Following on from Truman's initial proposal of Medicare Johnson focused on decreasing the cost of medical care. In justifying his policy he said, "No longer will older Americans be denied the healing miracle of modern medicine. No longer will illness crush and destroy the savings that they have so carefully put away". Medicare became law on 30 July 1965. Additionally he introduced a policy called Medicaid that assisted poor Americans of any age who could not afford private health insurance.

Johnson helped provide further federal funding for elementary and secondary education. Trying to find success where Kennedy had failed, on 11 April 1965 Johnson signed a $1.3 billion elementary and secondary school aid bill that included the Head Start Program for disadvantaged preschool children. It started as a summer programme for children from low-income communities going into public school in the autumn, and helped 560,000 children with preschool classes and medical care. On 8 November 1965 he signed the Higher Education Act that authorized further federal aid and created a national Teacher Corps. He also formed the Neighbourhood Youth Corps for unemployed teens, Job Corps for school dropouts, and Upward Bound to help the underprivileged go to college.

The federal department of Housing and Urban Development (HUD) was finally created under Johnson in 1965. On 11 August Johnson signed a $7.5 billion housing bill that provided for rent subsidies, and on 31 August HUD became a cabinet position, with Robert Weaver becoming its first secretary. In 1966, the Demonstration Cities and Metropolitan Development Act — the Model Cities Program — began to fund pilot projects as a part of the War on Poverty. Johnson asserted that the goal of the programme was "to build not just housing units, but neighborhoods; not just to construct schools, but to educate children; not just to raise income, but to create beauty and end the poisoning of our

Research and communication skills

Have a look at the current Head Start Program in your community using the NHSA website. To what extent was Johnson successful in achieving his goals? What are some strengths/weaknesses of the Head Start Program? Discuss.

Problems with the Model Cities Program

Dick Lee was voted in as New Haven mayor in 1954 to create the first slumless city in the country. Federal money was pumped into New Haven for urban renewal, where projects ranged from slum clearance to historic preservation. Results, however, were mixed. While President Johnson's Secretary of Labour called New Haven's efforts "the greatest success story in the history of the world", by the end of his tenure, Lee was quoted as saying, "If New Haven is a model city, God help America's cities".

environment". The Model Cities Program helped provide cleaner, safer and cheaper living conditions for many low-income families, although there were problems. On 11 April 1968 Johnson signed another Civil Rights Act that prohibited discrimination in the sale or rental of housing.

During the Johnson administration the Consumer Protection Movement began. In 1964, Secretary of Labour Daniel Patrick Moynihan hired attorney Ralph Nader as a consultant on auto safety standards. His report became an exposé in 1965 called *Unsafe at Any Speed: The Designed-in Dangers of the American Automobile* that stated, for example, "A 1959 Department of Commerce report projected that 51,000 persons would be killed by automobiles in 1975. That figure will probably be reached in 1965, a decade ahead of schedule". Nader called cars "coffins on wheels" and decreed that the auto industry had knowingly done nothing. On 9 September 1966 Congress passed the National Traffic and Motor Vehicle Safety Act, and Johnson created the Department of Transportation on 25 October to better regulate safety. This included the Federal Aviation Administration, Coast Guard, Civil Aeronautics Board, Bureau of Public Roads, and the Interstate Commerce Commission. Finally, on 21 March 1966 and 15 February 1967 Johnson submitted broader consumer protection programmes to Congress.

The Great Society also reformed immigration. The Immigration Act signed on 3 October 1965 eliminated "national origins quotas" that had discriminated against all immigrants save those from north-western Europe. In the 1960s immigration into the US expanded, with people coming from diverse backgrounds, approximately 350,000 a year throughout the 1960s. These changes began to alter the demographics of American society, creating more tolerance, but also more xenophobia.

The Warren Court (see page 12) generally supported Johnson's vision. From the beginning of 1964, the Supreme Court took action to try to promote more equality. It ruled regarding equality in elections: on 23 January the 24th Amendment was ratified that banned poll taxes for federal elections; on 17 February it ruled that congressional districts had to be equal in population; and on 15 June it stated that state legislatures had to have districts that were equal in population for both houses. It upheld many measures aimed at guaranteeing citizen rights and demonstrated that discrimination would no longer be tolerated. The Supreme Court also enforced many laws supporting African American rights. However, the Warren Court alarmed conservative Americans who were against the outlawing of prayer and Bible reading in public schools and feared street crime in many urban cities. "Impeach Earl Warren" became a slogan for those conservative elements. For all of that had been accomplished, by 1965 little had changed in practice: few African American children were in integrated classes in the US South, Christianity was still being taught in most schools, and police mostly continued to act as they had previously. A new movement began that fought for traditional rights, for example, for white Catholic schools in New Orleans and Boston, and the Crime Control Act of 1968 was seen as a victory for continued strong police action against civil rights rioters.

Johnson continued to expand the space programme, which had a significant domestic impact. Texan politicians lobbied for the establishment of a spaceflight laboratory in Houston and Johnson, an enthusiastic supporter of the space programme, helped to make this happen in 1962 when NASA moved to Houston and the space programme was expanded. Some argued against sending humans to the moon and argued that robots could fulfil the mission goals more effectively. Costs for sending an American to the moon were estimated at $30–40 billion, money that could have been used for domestic programmes. However, there were those who saw that this could help the economy as there would be thousands of jobs created for the aerospace industry, as well as profits in other science, industry and education fields. On 20 July 1969 Neil Armstrong and Buzz Aldrin were the first Americans on the moon, fulfilling Kennedy's 1961 goal of getting an American on the moon within 10 years.

Johnson's attempt to bring more equality to African Americans had mixed results. On 21 June 1964, during the "Freedom Summer" (see page 456), three civil rights workers were murdered. There was massive upheaval as a result of this and other civil rights-related violence. Recently enfranchised African Americans began to assert their power. Some newly registered Mississippi voters, along with members of Student Nonviolent Coordinating Committee (SNCC), organized the Mississippi Freedom Democratic Party (MFDP) and sent delegates to the August 1964 Democratic National Convention to challenge the pro-segregationists who were there. Johnson tried to offer them concessions, but they wouldn't accept. Following Johnson's landslide victory in the 1964 election he followed up on the MFDP's concerns.

After overcoming a filibuster, Congress passed the Voting Rights Act of 1965 in August which authorized the Attorney General to appoint federal examiners to register voters where local officials prevented African Americans from exercising their constitutional right. The goal was to have 50% of the voting age population registered in 1964, and up to this point several states had failed to meet this quota. Due to the Voting Rights Act, by 1966 over 400,000 African Americans had registered to vote, and by 1968 1 million had done so. This Act created a new voter base in the US South, and eventually led to African American representation at all governmental levels.

However, violence continued. There continued to be a split in the civil rights movement as many felt that federal actions were not going far or fast enough. The movement further radicalized after Malcolm X was assassinated in February 1965. Despite the landmark event of Thurgood Marshall being appointed to the Supreme Court on 1 September 1967, there was still great dissatisfaction regarding the state of race relations in America. The Kerner Commission noted in February 1968, "Our nation is moving toward two societies, one black, one white: separate and unequal".

When Martin Luther King Jr was assassinated on 3 April 1968, Johnson declared a day of national mourning for Sunday 7 April and said that he condemned the "brutal slaying" and implored Americans to "reject the blind violence that has struck Dr King, who lived by nonviolence". Violence exploded in 125 cities, with the most destruction occurring in Washington, DC, Baltimore, Chicago and Kansas City, with 50 people killed, more than 2,600 injured, 21,000 arrested, and property damage exceeding $65 million. On 11 April 1968 Johnson signed the 1968 Civil Rights Act that "provided for equal housing opportunities regardless of race, color, religion, sex, disability, familial status, or national origin", and it also included an "Indian Bill of Rights" to extend protections to Native Americans.

The Johnson presidency faced student protests (see page 457) throughout its tenure, particularly regarding the Vietnam War. US combat troops had been in Vietnam since 8 March 1965, but as more soldiers were called up due to increasing casualties, resistance against the war grew. These protests were led by various groups such as Students for a Democratic Society (SDS), the Teach In Movement, the Free Speech Movement, conscientious objectors, and **draft** dodgers. In May 1964 young people started burning their draft cards and used the slogan "We Won't Go". By May 1966 there were overt controversies regarding the draft and US policy in Vietnam, leading to Johnson appealing for national unity on 17 May. In October 1967 there were organized draft-card "turn ins" all over the country and in San Francisco alone, 300 were returned to the federal government.

In the first six months of 1968 more than 200 major demonstrations occurred on college campuses, most dramatically at Columbia University where student groups took over the President's office. Johnson privately called dissenters "crazies" and publicly denounced them as "nervous Nellies" ready to "turn on their own leaders, and on their own country, and on our own fighting men". On 13 June 1967 the House approved a $70 billion defence bill, the largest single appropriations bill ever passed by either house. The negative reaction against this massively increased military funding, in addition to increasing American casualties in the war, caused Johnson to lose popular support. Although in a 1965 Gallup poll, 62% felt that Johnson was handling the war as well as could be expected, by 1968 50% disapproved of Johnson's actions and 49% felt the US had made a mistake in sending troops to Vietnam. After the Tet Offensive on January 30 1968, where the North Vietnamese showed they could continue to attack South Vietnam (see page 486), Johnson realized he could not win a second term as a majority of public opinion was against his handling of the War. After Eugene McCarthy achieved success in the Democratic primaries as an anti-war candidate (where he won 42% of votes to Johnson's 49%), and only 15 days after Robert F Kennedy entered the presidential race, Johnson made a surprising announcement on 31 March 1968 on national television that he would not seek re-election.

Johnson's legacy

Johnson's domestic achievements were, unfortunately, overshadowed by his actions regarding the Vietnam War. The Johnson administration passed an unprecedented amount of legislation that protected Americans, but many of his proposals angered conservatives, and his inability to stop the chaos that resulted from the Vietnam War in many ways contributed to Nixon's election.

Since the end of his administration, his reputation has been re-evaluated by biographers and political commentators. A 2014 Tony Award-winning Broadway play, *All the Way*, covering the period from 22 November 1963 when Johnson replaced Kennedy to his election in November 1964, has, to an extent, re-popularized Johnson in American culture; as stated by Peter Osnos (2014) of *The Atlantic*, "If only Johnson had been persuaded not to engage the Vietnam War with the same energy that he deployed in his domestic initiatives, he would rank among the great presidents".

draft
This was used to fill vacancies in the military that could not be filled voluntarily 1948–1973. Draft dodgers refused to register for the draft and refused to be inducted if they were called. Due to the vast unpopularity of the draft of the general public, there has not been one since.

Conceptual understanding

Key questions:

→ In what ways was the Nixon administration ideologically consistent with the previous Democratic presidencies?

→ Evaluate the reasons that Nixon had to resign.

Key concepts:

→ Causation   → Continuity

→ Change   → Significance

→ Consequence

Overview of Nixon's presidency (1969–1974)

Many Americans respected Richard Nixon for his abilities and his skilful handling of the vice-presidency under Eisenhower, but throughout his career many people did not trust or like him. Nixon biographer Arthur Schlesinger Jr called his administration an "imperial presidency" as his executive branch dominated the other branches of government to an extreme degree, and had a reputation as being secretive and inflexible to outsiders.

The characteristics of his presidential firsts embody the contradictions during his tenure: Nixon had the largest presidential victory margin in US history (1972) indicating overwhelming popular support, but in his downward spiral, he was the first president to utilize the 25th Amendment to nominate a vice-presidential successor, the first president to resign, and the first to be pardoned by his successor for possible offences against the country.

1968 Election

Nixon was not sure that he wanted to run for government office again after his 1960 loss to Kennedy and the subsequent run for the governorship of California in 1962. However, he formally announced his candidacy on 1 February 1968 and created a conservative coalition, particularly in the south and western US. Johnson's announcement that he would not run in 1968, Robert F Kennedy's assassination after winning the California primary and Eugene McCarthy's pacifistic platform versus Vice-President Hubert Humphrey's more moderate proposals combined to split the Democratic Party, significantly contributing to Nixon's election.

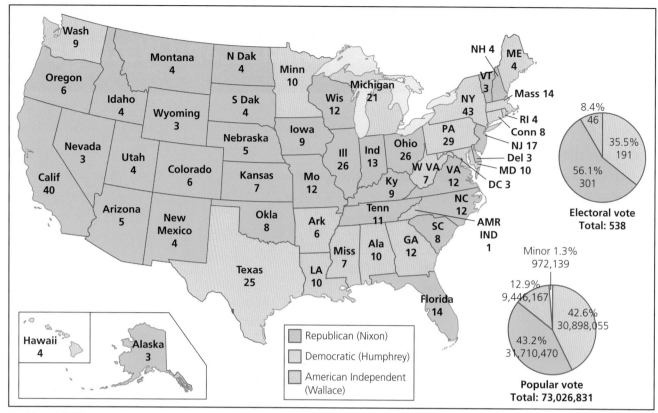

▲ Map of 1968 election comparing the Electoral College vote and popular vote

Further splits within the Democratic Party

Although Humphrey won the Democratic nomination easily against McCarthy (as McCarthy was seen as being too anti-war), the split inside the party regarding the Vietnam War was mirrored by the violence outside the 1968 Democratic National Convention as antiwar demonstrators clashed with police.

Nixon won the Republican endorsement over Nelson Rockefeller and Ronald Reagan on the first ballot at the Republican National Convention in August, however, he faced another conservative, George Wallace, with his segregationist platform. Southern white racists voted for Wallace's cause, but Nixon also constructed a "Southern Strategy" to win over the Democratic conservative white south. Nixon won the support of Senator Strom Thurmond's southern conservative Democrats and the selection of Spiro Agnew as Vice-President was made in response to Wallace's candidacy as Agnew had not been a supporter of civil rights. The Nixon and Wallace conservative campaigns increased Vice-President Humphrey's attractiveness to moderates. When Humphrey said he would stop bombing Vietnam, actioned by Johnson just before the election, Humphrey nearly won, but his involvement with Johnson's Vietnam policy proved to be too much for citizens voting for all parties or not voting at all (many disillusioned Democrats did not vote) and Nixon won.

Nixon's presidency: domestic issues

As President, liberals continually criticized Nixon, bringing up his "red baiting" as Senator and Vice-President, but Nixon ended up being quite moderate. In his Inaugural Speech in January 1969 he positioned himself as a centrist domestically. By being a centrist, however, he was more right wing than Kennedy and Johnson, and went about changing the New Frontier and Great Society.

Nixon called for a "New Federalism" regarding the structure of American government. This system reduced the federal bureaucracy by prioritizing state and municipal governments. In 1971 he urged for a "New American Revolution", and introduced the concept of "revenue sharing" which directed federal tax money to state and local governments for them to spend, creating federal fiscal efficiency. The 30 October 1972 State and Local Assistance Act gave $4 billion per year in matching funds to states and municipalities, and gained Nixon national popular support. He modified Johnson's Model Cities Program with his proposed **planned variation urban renewal plan** of 29 July 1971.

▲ Nixon surrounded by supporters 5 August 1968

Nixon's economic policies were surprisingly flexible for an economic conservative. Inflation had gone up at the end of the Johnson administration, so Nixon initially tried a traditional conservative approach of reducing federal spending and slowing the growth of the money supply. However, this led to a sharp economic downturn from 1969 to 1971 with unemployment doubling to 6%, inflation rising to 5% and no accompanying price decrease. Larry O'Brien, head of the Democratic National Committee, called it "Nixonomics: All the things that should go up – the stock market, corporate profits, real spendable income, productivity – go down, and all the things that should go down – unemployment, prices, interest rates – go up". Faced with such difficulties, he adopted the deficit spending techniques of his predecessors. He introduced wage and price controls and devalued the US dollar to boost American exports in efforts to stop the **trade deficit** (the first since 1893). His new policies contributed to an economic rebound in 1972. However, he did continue to try to stop spending. On 19 October 1972 he impounded funds appropriated by Congress to limit federal spending to $250 billion for the fiscal year 1973. However, on 12 April 1973 the US Court of Appeals ruled that Nixon should not have been allowed to impound funds for Missouri highways, and eventually, on 18 February 1975, after his presidency had ended, the Supreme Court ruled that Nixon had not had the right to impound funds voted by Congress. Although **stagflation** persisted throughout his first term, his policies did make some improvement to the US economy.

Nixon also created new laws regarding political campaign financing. On 7 February 1972 Nixon signed the Federal Election Campaign Act requiring all campaign contributions to be reported. Ironically, the Federal Election Campaign Act was one of the Acts that the members of the Nixon White House, including the Committee to Re-Elect the President, ended up violating and contributed to the end of his presidency. A series of government bills were passed in the wake of the Watergate revelations

planned variation urban renewal plan
This plan's aim was to give more autonomy to local governments by limiting federal government statutes and requirements.

trade deficit
The amount by which the cost of a country's imports exceeds the value of its exports.

stagflation
Persistent high inflation combined with high unemployment and stagnant demand in a country's economy.

and Nixon's resignation to try to continue to reform campaign financing and to improve public confidence in the American political process.

The welfare state was reorganized by Nixon. He increased Social Security funding by 50% and authorized more federal aid for medical education through grants. In August 1969 Nixon proposed the Family Assistance Plan (FAP). This plan got rid of many federally administered programmes such as Aid to Families with Dependent Children (AFDC), food stamps and housing subsidies, and replaced them with direct cash payments to single-parent families and the working poor. It guaranteed all welfare recipients a minimum income. However, all recipients, except for the mothers of preschool age children, would be required to work or undertake job training.

The War on Poverty had led to 20 million people being on some sort of government assistance and although the economy was doing well and there was low unemployment, there was the potential for the collapse of the welfare system in some areas. Pro-welfare radical groups like the National Welfare Rights Organization (NWRO) actively encouraged people to apply for public assistance. In 1960 only a third of Americans who were eligible for welfare actually received it whereas by the early 1970s this figure had risen to 90%. FAP received criticism from almost all segments of the population and Nixon continued to push for it until the 1972 election campaign season when he let it expire as there was so much controversy. Conservatives did not like that those who did not work would be guaranteed an annual income while liberals felt that that income, $1,600 per year for a family of four, was insufficient. Nixon also cut and restricted other Great Society policies; notably, on 9 December 1971 he vetoed the Economic Opportunity Act Amendments.

Nixon pledged to restore law and order. He delivered his Silent Majority Speech to the nation on 3 November 1969 in which he laid out a plan for the end of the Vietnam War through the process of diplomatic negotiation and Vietnamization. At the close of the speech, he requested the support of the **silent majority** for his plans. Nixon represented a strong conservative backlash against student radicals, anti-war protestors and youth counterculture as many Americans held them responsible for what seemed to be a cultural crisis exemplified by a rising crime rate, increased drug use and more permissive attitudes towards sex.

Women's rights moderately improved during the Nixon administration. He campaigned in favour of the Equal Rights Amendment that the Senate approved in March 1972 (although it had still not been ratified by the states), however, he did not actively promote it during his presidency. Nixon undertook several reforms to fight gender bias: he had a number of women in his administration; he launched a Presidential Task Force on Women's Rights; and sex discrimination lawsuits were filed enforcing the Civil Rights Act. Warren Burger's appointment as Chief Justice on the Supreme Court after Earl Warren died led to a woman's right to abortion in the Roe versus Wade case in 1973, although states still had the right to restrict abortions.

Nixon changed national civil rights policies. He had the voting age lowered to 18 with the 26th Amendment in 1971, increasing the electorate substantially. In 1969 he launched the federal Office of Minority Business Enterprise (OMBE) to redress the balance towards black capitalism and to promote minority economic development.

silent majority
The majority of people, regarded as holding moderate opinions but rarely expressing them.

As a part of his "New Federalism", he advocated for desegregation at a local level run by biracial state committees. Between 1968 and 1972 **affirmative action** programmes were implemented with some effect. For example, schools with all black children in southern states declined from 68% to 8%. However, when the Supreme Court desegregated busing in Swann versus Charlotte-Mecklenburg Board of Education in 1971 he went on television to say he would ask Congress to halt it and allowed the Department of Health and Education and Welfare (HEW) to restore federal funding to school districts with segregation. He supported southern segregationists when he opposed the extension of the Voting Rights Act of 1965, asking instead for a law that would remove a federal commitment to enforce it in the South, however, Congress passed the extension. He also tried to appoint to the Supreme Court jurists who were white supremacists, but the Senate rejected both. The NAACP stated, "For the first time since Wilson we have a national administration that can be rightly characterized as anti-Negro".

Nixon had a mixed record on the environment. Some of his policies were quite progressive, such as the 1970 signing of a bill that created the Council on Environmental Quality. On 21 April 1970 Americans observed the first Earth Day demonstrating against environmental pollution, and the Environmental Protection Agency (EPA) was established on 2 December 1970 to enforce environmental protection measures. Adding on to proposals passed by Eisenhower, Kennedy and Johnson, on 31 December Nixon passed the **Clean Air Act** of 1970, one of the most important pieces of environment legislation that has been created. However, Nixon insisted that all environmental proposals meet the cost-benefit standards of the Office of Management and Budget, and in 1972, he vetoed the Clean Water Act, not because he was philosophically against it, but because it cost $18 billion. When Congress overrode his veto, he used his presidential powers to prevent half of the money from being allocated.

The 1972 election campaign focused on Nixon's solid record of achievement domestically and internationally. However, the campaign was initially difficult, as Democratic Senator Edmund Muskie was even with him in the polls and George Wallace had a strong showing in the primaries with those who felt that Nixon had not been conservative enough. In May 1972, following an attempted assassination, Wallace pulled out of the race. Then the Democrats erred when they selected the left-wing liberal George McGovern for the Democratic ticket, who many saw as too liberal. Nixon was leading the country during an economic boom period, and had started drawing down the war in Vietnam, reducing protests against him. Instead of being able to focus on Nixon's failings, McGovern had to spend a large amount of time in his campaign appeasing conservative Democrats and defending his ability to be able to lead. Nixon won by a landslide 46.7 million votes to McGovern's 28.9 million, but the Democrats kept Congress, making Nixon the only president up to that time to win two terms with the opposition dominating both houses of Congress. McGovern only won 37.5% of the popular vote and 17 electoral votes, which was worse than Goldwater had done against Johnson in 1964.

affirmative action

A policy that attempts to end race and sex discrimination by setting goals for admitting women and minorities into higher education institutions and having a priority to obtain a job with a federal contract. Affirmative action helped many minorities and women attain positions that had been difficult to attain in the past, but there was a strong reaction against it, particularly in a time of economic competition for jobs.

Clean Air Act

A comprehensive law that imposed federal regulations regarding various environmental issues, including setting up emissions standards and limits.

ATL Thinking and research skills

How did McGovern change the Democratic Party? Read the article "Remember and thank George McGovern" from The Nation's website (www.thenation.com). Analyse the impact that McGovern's reforms had on the Democratic Party.

Nixon had a clear second-term mandate to continue to implement his policies, however, they were not fully successful:

- In 1973 he signed the International Convention for the Prevention of Pollution from Ships (MARPOL), but it was not fully implemented during his presidency.

- Unrest in the Middle East led to the 1973 Organization of Petroleum Exporting Countries (OPEC) oil embargo. As a result the price of oil soared (and continued to rise even after the embargo ended in 1974). Consequently, inflation rose, and there was 9% unemployment, the highest rate since the Great Depression, so Nixon introduced various conservation measures. On 25 November 1973 Nixon introduced a programme to save energy by reducing speed limits, banning Sunday gas sales, and reducing non-essential lighting.

- The Indian Self-Determination and Education Assistance Acts were created (but implemented under Ford). These acts upheld Native American autonomy and let local leaders administer federally supported social programmes for housing and education.

- On 8 April 1974 Nixon raised the minimum wage to $2 per hour.

- In January 1973 a ceasefire was finally signed for the Vietnam War, ending America's longest war to that time. Frustrated with the increased executive powers of the "Imperial Presidency", particularly regarding the commitment of troops to Vietnam by presidents over 10 years, including Cambodia in April 1970, Congress passed the **War Powers Resolution** on 7 November 1973 over Nixon's veto. (The war in Afghanistan which started in 2002 is, as of 2015, the United States' longest conflict.)

Watergate and possible impeachment

Many of the policies of his second term were implemented while his administration was embroiled in the Watergate scandal: the investigation of a break-in on 17 June 1972 at the offices of the Democratic National Committee (DNC) in the Watergate building during the 1972 presidential campaign that led to the end of Nixon's presidency.

The Watergate break-in was traced to officials of the Committee to Re-elect the President (CRP or CREEP) from the 1972 campaign. Members of what became known as CREEP had created an "Enemies List", collated by special counsel Charles Colson, of prominent people deemed to be unsympathetic to Nixon including politicians, entertainers and members of the press. To win the election campaign they had resorted to **"dirty tricks"**.

War Powers Resolution
A resolution allowing Congress to either approve or disapprove a president's proposal to send troops overseas or bring forces home.

dirty tricks
CREEP's dirty tricks included leaking a fabricated letter that caused Democratic contender Edmund Muskie to break down on national television, irreparably damaging his reputation; planting Republicans to pretend to be campaigning for the Democrats; and sending hecklers to disrupt Democratic campaign events.

Watergate timeline

DNC headquarters in the Watergate building is broken into by "plumbers".

17 June 1972

23 June 1972 — "Smoking gun" Oval Office tape discussion between Nixon and Haldeman where they propose asking the CIA and the FBI to halt the Watergate investigation, claiming the break-in was a national security operation. (This was not revealed until 1974.)

Nixon landslide re-election victory over George McGovern.

7 November 1972

10 October 1973 — Vice President Agnew resigns and pleads guilty to tax evasion to avoid imprisonment.

"Saturday Night Massacre" of White House resignations and firings.

20 October 1973

4 January 1974 — Nixon refuses to comply with Senate Select Committee subpoena of Watergate tapes and documents.

House Judiciary Committee opens hearings on **impeachment**; receives transcripts of Watergate tapes.

9 May 1974

24 July 1974 — Supreme Court upholds order that presidential tapes and documents be surrendered to the Watergate special prosecutor.

After months of nationally televised hearings, the House Judiciary Committee recommends to the full House three articles of impeachment: obstruction of justice in the Watergate cover-up, abuse of presidential powers and contempt of Congress in refusing to supply subpoenaed papers.

27–30 July 1974

30 July 1974 — Nixon surrenders 11 subpoenaed tapes that the Supreme Court had ordered to be turned over.

Transcripts of 23 June 1972 "Smoking gun" conversation reveal the President had ordered the CIA to stop the FBI investigation of the Watergate break-in.

5 August 1974

CREEP also proposed wiretapping key Democratic politicians before the Democratic National Convention (DNC); Attorney General Mitchell initially refused, but he finally approved the tapping of the DNC's phones in mid-1972. The second attempt to break in to the DNC headquarters to install a wiretap on 17 June 1972 led to the arrest of five men; the FBI traced money from these men back to CREEP. Top officials including Nixon had to decide how to act. Nixon directed the CIA to stop the FBI investigations on the grounds of "national security". Although Nixon had not been involved in planning the DNC break-in, he was now part of an illegal cover-up. Nixon authorized money to keep those involved quiet and some top officials, including Mitchell, committed perjury to protect Nixon.

Seven people were indicted by a Federal Grand Jury on 15 September 1972 regarding the break-in and attempted bugging of the DNC offices (the five burglars who were part of the White House "plumbers" and the two who organized it: G Gordon Liddy and Howard Hunt). One conspirator from the Watergate Seven told the US District Court Judge John Sirica that high-ranking officials were involved in the cover-up. In early 1973 the Watergate burglars either pleaded or were found guilty, but Judge Sirica did not believe that the incident stopped with these men, and said during sentencing, "I hope that the Senate committee is granted the power by Congress… to try to get to the bottom of what happened in this case".

The origin of the White House plumbers

Richard Nixon moved to end the Vietnam War, and his actions had a tremendous impact on his presidency domestically. Nixon stated in 1969 that he would secure "peace with honor" when he ended the War, and on January 27, 1973 he signed a peace agreement. However, before the War had ended, on June 13, 1971 portions of the *Pentagon Papers* that Daniel Ellsberg had given to the *New York Times* were released. In reaction, White House staff created the "plumbers" to find information on Ellsberg to discredit him, and then went on to harass other political opponents, eventually breaking into the Democratic National Convention offices in the Watergate building.

Nixon's staff were characterized by their loyalty, and helped to make the Executive branch the most powerful in the government (hence, the imperial presidency moniker). Nixon relied on key appointees within his cabinet for advice:

- Henry A Kissinger, a Harvard government professor, who joined the Nixon administration and became the head of the National Security Council (NSC) and Secretary of State in 1973

- John Mitchell, a lawyer who managed Nixon's campaigns and became Attorney General (he was nicknamed "El Supremo" as the top aide), then head of Nixon's re-election committee March 1972–July 1972 (he resigned right after the Watergate break-in)

- John Dean, White House Counsel

- Charles Colson, Special Counsel

- Ronald Ziegler, Nixon's Press Secretary

- HR Haldeman, Nixon's Chief of Staff, and John Ehrlichman, his legal counsellor then Chief Domestic Advisor. These two became known as the Berlin Wall, protecting Nixon's interests.

However, several members of Nixon's staff became implicated in the Watergate scandal.

On 7 February 1973, a Senate Select Committee on Presidential Campaign Activities, what became known as the Watergate Committee, began its investigation. James McCord, a burglar, testified. Rumours grew that the White House was involved, and in an effort to protect himself, on 20 April 1973 Nixon announced three Watergate-connected resignations (Attorney General Richard Kleindienst, chief White House aides John Ehrlichman and HR Haldeman) and one dismissal. He then went on national television and said that he would take responsibility for the mistakes of others. However, Nixon continued to profess his innocence.

In May 1973 the Watergate Senate Committee began televised public hearings and millions of Americans watched the story unfold on a daily basis. John Dean revealed that Nixon knew about the cover-up and other staff described other illegal activities at the White House. The most dramatic moment came when an aide revealed the existence of a secret taping system in the President's office. During the Watergate investigation, more than 25 individuals and important corporations were found to have conducted illegal actions, such as illegal corporate campaign contributions, illegal wiretaps of many individuals including journalists, and the illegal break-in of the office of psychiatrist Daniel Ellsberg in September 1971. Ellsberg had released the Pentagon Papers.

On 18 May 1973, Nixon appointed special Watergate prosecutor Archibald Cox. Cox asked for the President's tapes, but Nixon refused, citing executive privilege. Nixon refused a Court of Appeals order on 14 October to release the tapes. When Cox insisted, Nixon ordered Attorney General Eliot Richardson and then Deputy Attorney General William Ruckelshaus to fire Cox. The two men refused and resigned, so Nixon demanded that Robert Bork fire Cox, which he did on 20 October. This series of resignations and firings became known as the "Saturday Night Massacre". After Cox was fired, Nixon appointed Leon Jaworski to replace him, yet he also asked for the tapes. Nixon released edited transcripts of some conversations, but on 4 January 1974 he refused to comply with a subpoena of Watergate tapes and documents requested by the Senate Select Committee. Nixon continued to deny any personal involvement.

On 1 March 1974 seven former presidential aides and officials were indicted in the Watergate cover-up conspiracy: Mitchell, Haldeman, Ehrlichmann, Colson (charges dropped 3 June 1974), Mardian, Parkinson (acquitted 1 January 1975) and Strachan (charges dismissed 10 March 1975). In a separate sealed report that was delivered to the White House Judiciary Committee, Nixon was named as **unindicted co-conspirator** although this charge was not publically disclosed until June 1974.

On 30 April 1974, edited transcripts of the Oval Office tapes were released to the public, and **impeachment** proceedings followed. At the end of July 1974 the House Judiciary Committee, after months of nationally televised hearings, found grounds for presidential impeachment. Nixon's public approval ratings plummeted. Republicans were divided regarding Nixon's actions. The Committee voted to impeach Nixon: to remove him, a full House of Representatives would have to vote for impeachment, and then the Senate would hold a trial.

Nixon's presidency ended in early August 1974. On 30 July Nixon obeyed a Supreme Court order and released the tapes, and on 5 August transcripts of conversations that occurred on 23 June 1972, the "smoking gun" tape, revealed that the President had directed his staff to have the CIA order the FBI to end its investigation of the Watergate break-in: the tapes showed Nixon had led a cover-up, which was a clear obstruction of justice criminal charge. Nixon resigned on 9 August and left for California; he did not stay to see Vice-President Gerald Ford

TOK discussion

Find and read the newspaper report "President refuses to turn over tapes" from the *Washington Post*, 24 July 1973. Using the historical perspective of the time, and what you, as a public citizen, would have known at that time, what do you think your opinion would have been of Nixon's actions? Note in particular the various legal interpretations of presidential power at the time.

unindicted co-conspirator

Someone who is legally named to have been associated with other conspirators charged with a crime, but has not been charged for that crime themselves.

impeachment

Nixon was impeached based on three factors: obstruction of justice in the Watergate cover-up, abuse of presidential power and contempt of Congress in refusing to supply subpoenaed papers.

being sworn in as President. On 8 September Ford granted Nixon an unconditional presidential pardon regarding all federal offences that he "committed or may have committed or taken part in" while in office.

What brought about Nixon's downfall were not merely the tapes of the conversations after Watergate, but the complex misconduct at the highest levels:

- CREEP's actions

- attempting to cover up CREEP and White House staff actions

- paying of "hush money" to obstruct justice

- misusing the FBI and CIA to stop the investigation with false claims regarding issues of national security

- knowing of and even encouraging his staff to commit perjury

- using domestic surveillance and intelligence operations against political opposition

- fraud in relation to the donation of his Vice Presidential papers

- misusing the Internal Revenue Service (IRS) for both personal and political benefit, particularly to persecute those on his "Enemies List" by ordering their audits amongst other abuses

- huge undisclosed campaign contributions by large corporations

- a secret bombing campaign in Cambodia

- failure of Nixon's allies to cooperate with numerous investigations.

▲ Photo of a newspaper headline confirming Nixon's resignation

Source skills

Source 1

Jonathan Bernstein, the *Washington Post*, on the 40th anniversary of the "smoking gun" tape.

> *(Watergate) tells us volumes about the limits of presidential power. The president may be presented in the civics books as sitting at the top of a pyramid, with executive-branch departments and agencies below him, but in reality the people at the next level down, such as Cabinet secretaries, are also responsive to Congress and to the permanent bureaucracy below them. In short, that means that presidents cannot give them orders and assume they'll be carried out. Indeed, looked at through the lens of presidential authority, the roots of Watergate are all about the limits of presidential ability to get the bureaucracy to respond to presidents' policy preferences. Nixon hired the 'plumbers' to operate out of the White House as part of his policy of harassing anti-war protesters and other political enemies precisely because the FBI refused to implement a White House plan to do that sort of thing... That doesn't mean that presidents should simply accept their limited influence; to the contrary, effective presidents work hard to increase their influence over Congress, over the courts — and, yes, over the bureaucracy. But that takes hard work. And it only works, Watergate tells us, if the president accepts that the inherent constraints of the office — and the other players in the policy-making system — are just as legitimate as the occupant of the Oval Office.*

Source 2

Henry S Ruth, special prosecutor during the Watergate probe (second in command under Cox, and in charge of the investigation until Jaworski was appointed).

> *The sad residue of Watergate was so many people saw that their president had lied for 15 months and saw it so vividly and directly that a basic cynicism started in this country that has deepened, and deepened in a way where ... many don't believe anything that comes out of Washington.*

Analyse the legacy of Watergate regarding presidential authority.

Nixon's presidential legacy

Historian Stephen Ambrose, who campaigned for George McGovern, believed that Nixon had many lasting, liberal domestic achievements, "Nixon was proposing things in 1973–1974 that he couldn't make the front pages with—national health insurance for all, greatly expanded student loan operations, and energy/environmental programs". But clearly he had a mixed record in trying to implement his agenda. In the years following his resignation, Nixon sought to restore and enhance his legacy, which was not achieved during his lifetime. Nixon died on 22 April 1994, but there is still debate regarding the overall long-term success of the domestic agenda he implemented.

ATL Research and communication skills

Joan Hoff Wilson argues that Nixon, despite defining himself as a political conservative, could be considered a great liberal president. To what extent do you agree with her assertion? Research and discuss this statement.

Overview of Ford's presidency (1974–1977)

When Gerald R Ford was made President on 9 August 1974, he declared, "I assume the Presidency under extraordinary circumstances.... This is an hour of history that troubles our minds and hurts our hearts". Ford was the first and only president to hold America's top two political posts without being elected to either of them. He was the first vice-president chosen under the 25th Amendment, the first vice-president to succeed to the presidency due to a presidential resignation, and the first president to issue a presidential pardon to a former president. Betty Ford described her husband as "an accidental Vice President, and an accidental President, and in both jobs he replaced disgraced leaders". Ford's reputation for integrity and openness had made him popular during his 25 years in Congress, so he had the potential to repair some of the damage that had been done. His presidency has been termed "the Custodial Presidency"; he had to help the country with this scandal in a time of economic difficulties and the Vietnam War ending in defeat: it was an incredibly difficult challenge.

Ford administration

One of Ford's first jobs was to try to re-instil American confidence in the political system. Particularly during the 18 months of the Watergate investigations, public cynicism about politicians in general increased dramatically, with four out of five Americans saying that, while Nixon may have been lying, Nixon was no more corrupt than his predecessors, and in 1976 only 17% of the polled public indicated that they respected members of Congress.

There were also questions about Ford's ability to lead. Richard Rovere wrote in *The New Yorker*, "That he is thoroughly equipped to serve as Vice President seems unarguable; the office requires only a warm body and occasionally a nimble tongue. However... neither Richard Nixon nor anyone else has come forward to explain Gerald Ford's qualifications to serve as Chief Executive. He altogether lacks administrative experience. If his knowledge of foreign affairs exceeds that of the average literate citizen, that fact has yet to be demonstrated".

Ford's pardon of Nixon

One of Ford's first acts of office, one month after Nixon resigned, was to pardon Nixon on 8 September 1974. Nixon was given a "full, free and absolute" presidential pardon. There has been much debate regarding what happened in the first month of Ford's presidency, and how that affected Ford's decision to pardon Nixon.

Richard Nixon was still facing possible prosecution when he resigned Aug 9 1974. In March 1974 Nixon was charged as an unindicted co-conspirator so they could introduce all of his conversations as evidence against the others who had been charged. Jill Wine-Banks, former Watergate Assistant Special Prosecutor from 1974–1975, stated that all of the younger lawyers on the prosecution team wanted to indict Nixon, but Special Watergate Prosecutor Leon Jaworski, the head of her team, did not.

Ford faced difficulties in the presidential transition almost immediately that affected his decision regarding the pardon. Within 24 hours of Nixon leaving office, Nixon called his former Chief of Staff Alexander Haig (now Ford's Chief of Staff), and requested that 900 reels of tapes and all of his papers should be sent to him in California. Ford heard the plan and said that the Attorney General should be consulted, as the tapes could be used as evidence in a trial and it was unclear if Nixon would still be tried. Attorney General William Saxbe said to Ford that the tapes and papers belonged to Nixon, but special adviser to Ford, attorney Benton Becker, said to Ford that if he sent the records, "the only thing people will say is that Ford did the last act of the Watergate cover up". Consequently, Ford said that the papers had to stay until legal issues were resolved, which caused a break between the Nixon and Ford teams.

Ford had to figure out how a pardon could be justified. John Logie, former legal counsel to Ford, stated that there was fear that Ford himself could be impeached "if the pardon was not on solid ground". But as Nixon had not been indicted for a criminal offence, it was clear that the President could possibly justify a pardon. Ford asked Becker to try to find justification in order to secure public acceptance. Although Becker was against the pardon, he fulfilled Ford's request and found Burdick versus United States (1915), a case that set the precedent that the acceptance of a pardon is an admission of guilt.

The next question was would Nixon accept Ford's pardon? Becker went to California and presented the pardon. Ford wanted Nixon to publically apologize, but he refused and Nixon wanted his presidential papers and tapes as a part of the pardon deal, but Ford also refused this. Becker negotiated a deal whereby Nixon had access to his papers and tapes although they would remain in the National Archives. There was extensive disagreement regarding the wording of the acceptance of the pardon, with Nixon insisting on blaming the White House staff. According to Ken Gormley, Becker let Nixon know of the Burdick precedent, "He informed Nixon of the Ford White House position on the Burdick precedent and he made it clear that it would be said in public, that Nixon had the right to refuse that pardon, and he understood that an acceptance of the pardon constituted an acknowledgment of guilt". Nixon did not initially agree, but when Becker, after consulting with Ford, threatened to leave with the pardon deal, Nixon agreed.

▲ Ford signs Nixon's presidential pardon

ATL Thinking and communication skills

Find and read Nixon's speech accepting Ford's pardon. Did Nixon admit his guilt or take responsibility fully for what had happened?

Class discussion

Was the Ford pardon justified?

There was immediate outrage at the pardon. Most Americans felt that the pardon was wrong, and that the president was "above the law". Ford's approval rating fell dramatically from 71% to 49%.

The pardon of Nixon

There was little media coverage of the Burdick guilty precedent. Instead, there was more focus on the fact that Nixon did not admit his guilt and that he would not be prosecuted for his crimes. There was even more controversy over Ford making a deal regarding a pardon with Nixon before Nixon resigned. However, in an interview on the 25th anniversary of the pardon in 1999, Ford once again said that he had no need to make a deal with Nixon as he knew that he would become president regardless. He had pardoned Nixon simply because it was the "right thing to do for the country".

Ford's domestic policies

After the pardon of Nixon, Ford began to name his own cabinet. His nominee for vice-president, former Governor Nelson Rockefeller of New York, was confirmed on 19 December 1974. Rockefeller became the second vice-president to be appointed under the 25th Amendment. Gradually, Ford created a cabinet that was a mix of both Nixon and Ford appointments; Kissinger stayed on as Secretary of Defence, but Attorney General William Saxbe was replaced by Edward Levi.

In spite of his well-regarded 25-year service in Congress, Ford would have a confrontational relationship with it. Just months after taking office, on 5 November 1974 during the mid-term elections, the Democrats won by a landslide, which placed the White House and Congress further apart. During his two and a half years in office, Ford vetoed 66 bills regarding the economy, education, housing and health care, but Congress was able to override his veto 12 times.

Ford was more conservative than Nixon regarding economic measures. Three days after taking the oath of office, he addressed Congress and said that inflation was "public enemy number one". Inflation was at 11% per year and unemployment was at 5.3%. Home building had stalled, and on 8 October 1974 the Franklin National Bank failed: one of the largest bank failures in US history.

As the recession worsened, Ford tried different measures to stimulate the economy, and vetoed non-military spending bills so as to continue to fight the Cold War, but to not additionally increase the large budget deficit. He vetoed 39 spending proposals, but some of them were overridden. Unfortunately for Ford, stagflation worsened. On 8 October 1974, in an attempt to restore public confidence, Ford started a campaign called "Whip Inflation Now" (WIN) where people were encouraged to wear red and white WIN buttons, start savings accounts and even grow their own food in their backyards. However, without incentives the campaign failed. A policy to curb inflation by controlling the money supply led to the worst recession since the 1930s with unemployment skyrocketing to 9% throughout 1975, the stock market falling and a drop in GNP. Congress backed anti-recession spending, Ford increased unemployment benefits and offered a $22.8 billion dollar tax cut and rebates, but economic problems continued. Controversially, Ford refused to bail New York City out when it declared bankruptcy, and purportedly told the city to "drop dead".

Ford offered inconsistent support of civil rights. On 22 August 1974 he signed a $25.2 billion dollar education bill. However, it put limits on **busing**, stating that a student could not be bused to the next closest school district unless a court ruled that the child was being denied their constitutional rights; it also banned the use of federal education aid for busing. Ford said that he would "oppose excessive funding" of the legislation due to inflation. On 12 September 1974, Boston students began to get on buses for court-ordered busing, and this led to chaos. State police were called in, but, unlike presidents before him who used federal powers to stop civil strife, Ford refused to mobilize US marshals, saying it was up to federal court judges to enforce the desegregation order. Violence and protests continued until 1976.

In contrast, on 16 September 1974, Ford implemented a plan granting conditional amnesty for Vietnam War draft evaders and military deserters, even those who had already been convicted. In an earned re-entry programme, those who agreed to work for up to two years in public service jobs would be given amnesty. The programme lasted until 31 March 1975 after 22,500 men participated out of 120,000 who were eligible.

There was a crisis within the CIA and FBI. During the Watergate investigations the CIA and FBI were implicated in the White House cover-up, and there was a belief that more illegal actions may have occurred or were occurring. The Rockefeller Commission was set up by Ford on 4 January 1975 to investigate possible illegal, covert actions. Its findings were considered along with the larger Senate Church Committee investigations. Regarding the CIA, in addition to revelations that it had tried to assassinate Castro, it was announced that it had conducted domestic spying after the **family jewels** were exposed. This led to CIA Director William Colby's dismissal on 2 November 1975. The CIA would be reorganized under (future president) George HW Bush. On 18 February 1976 Ford gave an executive order that limited the surveillance of American citizens. The FBI was censured for violating the civil rights of various groups. Secretary of State Kissinger was removed as head of the NSA Nov 3, 1975, but kept him as Secretary of State. The FBI was also reorganized but Clarence Kelley remained director.

Foreign policy was not Ford's strength, and this had a domestic impact. Ford proved to be quite weak in his knowledge of foreign affairs, which played a key role in his loss to Jimmy Carter in one of their presidential debates as well as in the 1976 presidential election.

Overall assessment of Ford's presidency

The American bicentennial celebrations on 4 July 1976 brought a short, bright respite to an otherwise difficult presidency. During the 1976 presidential campaign, Nixon's pardon became the focus again. A Carter campaign badge said, "Pardon Me Mr Ford, if I Vote for Carter". Ford's advisors had been correct that the pardon proved too hard to overcome and this ended Ford's political career.

Ford might have won had it not been for the fact that the US was in a period of significant economic difficulties that Ford had failed to remedy. However, Ford did take steps to try to deal with some of the problems regarding the American political system that were exposed in the wake of the Watergate scandal. On Inauguration Day, President Carter began his speech: "For myself and for our Nation, I want to thank my predecessor for all he has done to heal our land".

busing
The transport of a child of one ethnic group to a school where another group is predominant, in an attempt to promote racial integration.

family jewels
Findings that were published about the series of investigations uncovering illegal activities that took place within the CIA from the 1950s to 1970s.

TOK discussion

Find and read the document "The family jewels" from the CIA website (www.foia.cia.gov). With reference to its origin, purpose and content, analyse the value and limitations of one of the family jewels for historians studying the domestic policies of the Nixon administration. In addition, to what extent did the revelation of this information hurt the Ford administration?

Overview of Carter's presidency (1977–1981)

James Earl Carter's presidency was the first full single term presidency since Herbert Hoover. Carter was determined to eradicate the corruption that continued to emerge after Watergate and he believed that his Baptist faith would keep him from taking on "the same frame of mind that Nixon or Johnson did: lying, cheating and distorting the truth". He worked hard in favour of human rights, both at home and abroad. While he had tremendous success with some of his foreign policies, his administration was limited to one term primarily due to dire economic times, and his inability to resolve the Iranian hostage crisis.

Carter administration

During the 1976 election Carter's campaign focused on the fact that he was a Washington outsider who could bring a fresh perspective to federal governance. As Governor of Georgia from 1971 to 1975, Carter had worked against racial discrimination. Nationally unknown, he won over many voters with his youthful, engaging demeanour. Carter played on the Watergate backlash, campaigning that he was not a lawyer (like Nixon and Ford had been) but a peanut farmer (he omitted the fact that he was also a nuclear physicist and naval officer, among many other occupations). Carter easily defeated Walter Mondale, a progressive senator from Minnesota, who became his vice-presidential candidate at the Democratic National Convention in June 1976.

Ford's campaign had liabilities: while people liked him, he did not seem fully presidential and he had not solved many of the problems that plagued his presidency. At the Republican National Convention in August 1976, Ford narrowly won the nomination over Ronald Reagan, the popular, charismatic Governor of California who represented the more conservative wing of the party who were against détente and

Ford's economic policies. Nixon had replaced his relatively liberal vice-president, Nelson Rockefeller, in November 1975 with Robert Dole, but Dole was also a choice that divided the Republican Party. In addition, Dole was a wooden speaker who did not always seem well informed on important issues.

Carter started with a huge lead of 30% but it eroded. While campaigning he was hard to pin down regarding his opinions on specific issues, which led to frustration. Until the decisive television debate in October it seemed like Ford could catch up; however, when Ford said in error, "There is no Soviet domination of Eastern Europe" it seemed clear that he was unqualified to continue to govern. With the smallest percentage of eligible voters (53%) going to the polls since 1948, Carter won 51% of the popular vote (40.8 million) to Ford's 48% (39.1 million) with the Electoral College division being 297 to 241, the narrowest margin since 1916. While Carter won the election with the support of most of the old New Deal coalition (organized labour, minorities, urban liberals), taking most of the South and industrial north-east, interestingly the liberal Eugene McCarthy (page 28), who ran for the Independence Party, won 760,000 votes, showing there was still a divide in the left-leaning electorate.

Carter's domestic policies

Carter faced difficult challenges regarding an economy that was being negatively affected by high energy prices. When he became president in 1977 the unemployment rate was at 8% and inflation was at 5.5% (half of what it was in 1974), so Carter concentrated on trying to expand the economy.

Carter created a new National Energy Policy, announced on 20 April 1977, which aimed to:

- reduce the growth rate in energy consumption to 2% per year

- reduce gasoline consumption by 10%

- cut imports of foreign oil to less than 6 million barrels a day, about half the amount that would otherwise be imported

- establish a strategic petroleum reserve supply of at least 1 billion barrels, which could meet all domestic needs for 10 months

- increase coal production by more than two-thirds, to over 1 billion tons a year

- insulate 90% of American homes and all new buildings

- use solar energy in more than 2.5 million homes.

Although he had support in the House, he faced resistance in the Senate from Republicans and southern Democrats who supported the oil and natural gas industries. In addition, Carter's proposals did not have enough support from the general public to overcome opposition. In fact, many opposed the National Energy Program because they did not want to change their lifestyles and did not believe that there was an urgent crisis. Even though many of his proposals were not

ATL Self management and thinking skills

Carter was not able to achieve many of the goals in his energy policy, including getting more Americans to conserve energy during his administration. Choose one of the principles and research to what extent his goal has been achieved today.

You may use Carter's "Proposed energy policy" speech on the PBS American Experience website (www.pbs.org/wgbh/americanexperience) to help you.

▲ The Arab oil boycott caused serious shortages of fuel in the United States

enacted, by the end of his presidency Americans had reduced their consumption of oil, leading to a lowered dependence on foreign oil, and there was an energy consumption shift towards coal, which the US had large reserves of.

Related to the National Energy Program, which encouraged nuclear energy, an anti-nuclear energy movement developed. "No more nukes" protests began in the late 1970s with Christian activists who had first protested against the Vietnam War. After the Three Mile Island nuclear reactor accident on 28 March 1979, Physicians for Social Responsibility and anti-nuclear activists like Dr Helen Caldicott taught the public about the harm of nuclear energy. Carter proposed the Nuclear Regulatory Commission on 30 June 1980 to be in charge of nuclear power and demanded that utility companies improve energy-efficiency standards. There were some improvements, but criticism of the nuclear industry (energy and weapons) was strong throughout the 1980s.

Carter prioritized preserving the environment. On 1 October 1977 the Department of Energy was created to bring together dozens of departments and agencies in an effort to better coordinate various programmes. In addition to the conservation measures in the National Energy Program, on 24 March 1977 the Energy Research and Development Administration established the Solar Energy Research Institute: Carter even had solar panels installed on the White House (which Reagan then removed). On 15 March 1978 fluorocarbons in aerosol sprays were banned. Taxes were imposed on gas-guzzling cars. On 15 July 1979 Carter proposed an $88 billion decade-long programme to produce synthetic fuels from coal and shale oil reserves. He also notably expanded the national parks system and protected 103 million acres in Alaska.

Carter worked with Congress to try to stimulate the economy. In 1977 he proposed $34 billion in tax cuts and an investment of $14 billion in public works and services, including a new national youth employment programme. He also raised the minimum wage by 50% and increased support for farmers and unprofitable industries. Some of Carter's policies found success and unemployment fell to 5.8% in1979.

However, his energy proposals largely failed as his responses to the energy crisis were not effectively implemented by Congress to promote conservation. As Americans remained dependent on imported oil, the Arab oil boycott caused serious shortages of fuel in the United States, and many citizens protested. There were long lines at gas stations and people could only buy on certain days of the week. By the late 1970s more than 40% of American oil was imported and as OPEC continued to raise prices, inflation in the US rose to 9.6% in 1978. It was announced on 28 January 1978 that the trade deficit for 1977 was the biggest ever, principally because of higher prices for imported oil.

The Carter administration's Department of Energy negotiated a lawsuit with Gulf Oil that cost the country millions of dollars. Carter reduced some of his proposed tax cuts and tried to cut government spending by vetoing congressional appropriations for defence spending and public works, which angered Republicans and Democrats and did not stop the economy from worsening.

By the end of 1980 unemployment had risen to 7.4%, the prime interest rate was at 20% and the federal debt was at a record high. Presidential historians Frank Freidel and Hugh Sidey summarized Carter's economic programme, "By the end of his administration, he could claim an increase of nearly eight million jobs and a decrease in the budget deficit, measured in percentage of the gross national product. He dealt with the energy shortage by establishing a national energy policy and by decontrolling domestic petroleum prices to stimulate production. He prompted government efficiency through civil service reform and proceeded with deregulation of the trucking and airline industries. Unfortunately, inflation and interest rates were at near record highs, and efforts to reduce them caused a short recession". Economist Robert J Samuelson said, "What was most consistent about the Carter administration was its inability to make a proposal in January that could survive until June… the Carter administration never projected a clear economic program or philosophy because it never had one". This situation would play a key role in his loss in the 1980 presidential election campaign.

None of Carter's policies significantly affected the continued inequitable distribution of wealth in America. Carter was also not able to make progress against poverty. Marian Edelman, Director of the Children's Defense Fund, said that in 1979 one in seven American children (10 million) had no regular source of health care, and one in three under the age of 17 (18 million) had never seen a dentist. She stated in *The New York Times*, "The Senate Budget Committee recently… knocked off $88 million from a modest $288 million administration request to improve the program that screens and treats children's health problems. At same time the Senate found $725 million to bail out Litton Industries and to hand to the Navy at least two destroyers ordered by the Shah of Iran".

However, Carter did fight for human rights issues, both abroad and at home. In his first day in office on 21 January 1977, Carter granted unconditional pardons to hundreds of thousands of men who had evaded the draft during the Vietnam War by fleeing the country or by failing to register. Ford had offered conditional amnesty to some draft dodgers but Carter set no conditions (although military deserters and violent political protestors were ineligible). Carter personally enforced affirmative action. He appointed record numbers of women, African Americans and Hispanics to work in federal institutions. However, this was in the face of some "white backlash" against affirmative action. Allan Bakke sued UC Davis for reverse discrimination that reserved enrolment spaces for minorities: in Regents of the University of California versus Bakke (1978), the Supreme Court ordered that Bakke must be admitted, but also upheld the essential essence of affirmative action while not allowing for actual quotas.

Carter also attempted to improve federal social services:

- 9 May 1977: he moved to reform Social Security to "eliminate the Social Security deficit"

- 6 August 1977: he proposed reforms to the national welfare system that involved a combination of increased benefits and tax cuts, but also included a work requirement

- 2 February 1978: As New York City was still experiencing a dire financial crisis, he gave more federal aid to the city

- 27 September 1979: The Department of Education was created when the Department of Health, Education and Welfare (HEW) was separated into autonomous sub-organizations.

However, Congress would not work with Carter, which affected his re-election chances. His advisors had mostly come with him from the South and the team did not try to build bridges with those entrenched inside the institution that was Washington, DC. This made it difficult for him to pass key elements of his programme, including his National Energy Policy. On 6 June 1980 the Democrat-controlled Congress overrode a presidential veto, the first time since 1952 that a Congress controlled by a president's own party had done so.

1980 election

The 1980 election was as much a defeat of Carter's liberalism as it was a signal of the rise of the New Right. The roots of the New Right came from the anti-communism of the 1950s, and Reagan seized on this fear again in the last decade of the Cold War. In addition, Reagan, a neo-conservative, stated regarding government-assisted social programmes (but not regarding defence spending), "Government is not the solution to our problem. Government is the problem". The Moral Majority, founded by Baptist Minister Jerry Falwell in 1979, supported Reagan with his religious conservative tele-evangelism. (Millions of Americans were converted to the "Reagan Revolution" and financially supported Reagan's campaign.)

The media was used effectively by the Republicans, particularly with the rise of new "spin doctor" political pundits who seemed like they could be objective journalists, but turned out to be political operatives promoting their candidates on national television. Reagan attacked Carter saying there was a "litany of broken promises", and criticized Carter's economic record by stating, "A recession is when your neighbour loses a job. A depression is when you lose yours. A recovery is when Jimmy Carter loses his".

Changes in the Democratic Party

The evolution of the Democratic Party began when it lost traditional southern conservatives with the civil rights movement, starting with the Dixiecrats' departure in 1948 and continued throughout the 1960s. In the 1970s the alliance among labour, urban and ethnic minority groups and different regional constituencies was thrown into question when left-leaning George McGovern was nominated in 1972. His pacifistic, social welfare views were rejected by most labour unions and other groups. This situation led to a split in the Democratic Party and independent voter interest waned. Interestingly, a key reason McGovern had been nominated was that he had reformed the Democratic Party after the 1968 Democratic National Convention with the McGovern–Fraser Commission of 1969–1970. The new nomination procedure, while being more democratic, led to, according to Scott Piroth, "McGovern being able to win the nomination on the strength of his success in caucus states, despite winning only about one-quarter of the vote in Democratic primaries… Ideological candidates with a committed base of activists, like McGovern, Jesse Jackson and Republican Pat Robertson, have been particularly successful in caucuses".

Although the Democrats retained their solid majorities in Congress (except for the Senate in 1980, 1982 and 1984), the national conservative coalition built by Nixon was sustained by Reagan from 1980 to 1988 and George HW Bush until 1993. It seemed that Carter won in 1976 more because of the problems with the Ford administration and the wake of Watergate, than a national ideological liberal shift.

On 24 April 1980 John Anderson split with the Republican Party and ran for president as an independent. He ended up taking Democratic votes in northern states as well as some Republican ones. Carter's campaign was not successful. Carter suffered during the Democratic primaries as Senator Edward Kennedy ran a tough campaign against him and although Carter won, the experience further divided the party. As with Nixon and Ford in previous presidential campaigns, Carter badly lost his televised debate to the former actor Reagan. Carter was also embarrassed by his brother Billy's behaviour, when on 14 July 1980 Billy registered as an agent of Libya after it was known that he received $220,000 from Libya. Right before the election on 2 October a Senate inquiry found that the President had "shown poor judgment in regard to his brother's activities". Carter was also embroiled with the Iranian hostage situation, and his inability to resolve it played an essential part in him losing re-election. Even Eugene McCarthy endorsed Reagan over Carter.

On 4 November 1980, Reagan won a landslide victory. Reagan won with 51% of the popular vote (43.9 million votes) to Carter's 41% (35.5 million votes), outpolling Carter in the Electoral College 489 to 49 (John Anderson received 5.7 million votes). Republicans took control of the Senate for the first time in 26 years. A new policy of "Reaganomics" or supply side economics reversed the **Keynesian theory** that had mostly dominated economic policy since Kennedy. Carter had been ousted, and the neo-conservative era of the 1980s began.

Carter's legacy

Freidel and Sidey summarized Carter's legacy: "Carter aspired to make Government 'competent and compassionate, responsive to the American people and their expectations. His achievements were notable, but in an era of rising energy costs, mounting inflation, and continuing tensions, it was impossible for his administration to meet these high expectations". Carter has gone on to become an impressive international statesman, winning the Nobel Peace Prize in 2002. He was honoured with it for "his decades of untiring effort to find peaceful solutions to international conflicts, to advance democracy and human rights, and to promote economic and social development". Many agreed that the award was in recognition for what he did and tried to do during his presidency, as well as for redefining how much an ex-president can achieve.

> **ATL Thinking and research skills**
>
> Assess the changes that the Democratic and Republican parties went through from the 1960s up to the 1980 election. In what ways did those parties remain similar and become different?

> **Keynesian theory**
>
> Based on the work of English economist John Maynard Keynes, Keynesian economics rests on the theory that full employment is determined by effective demand and requires government spending on public works to stimulate this.

▲ Carter receives the 2002 Nobel Peace Prize

6.8 Domestic policies of Canadian prime ministers

Conceptual understanding

Key questions:

→ To what extent did St Laurent strengthen the Canadian economy?

→ To what extent was Diefenbaker an effective leader?

→ How did Pearson attempt to modernize federal/provincial relations?

→ To what extent did Trudeau's autocratic nature impact Canadian society?

→ To what extent did Trudeau's policies change Canadian society?

→ What issues of federal/provincial relations remained or were created by Trudeau's policies?

Key concepts:

→ Change

→ Continuity

Louis St Laurent

When Canada went to war in 1939, Mackenzie King's government dusted off the **War Measures Act** first passed in 1914 and invoked its power. From that point King's Liberals worked to concentrate and coordinate social, economic and political power in the federal government, reducing provincial governments to subordinate partners in the Confederation. The massive coordination demanded by the war effort ballooned the size of the federal civil service. Even within the federal parliament, debate was curtailed and decision-making streamlined in the cause of wartime efficiency. King's government made unprecedented use of **Orders in Council** to push through legislation. The result of this was to alienate the provinces and transform the federal government into a bureaucratic machine as much as a governing machine. Louis St Laurent, King's successor as Liberal Leader and Prime Minister, was a product of this system.

St Laurent had joined the government in 1941 at the behest of King. He came from a successful legal career and saw eye-to-eye with King on matters of federal-provincial relations and the technocratic nature of the federal government. He continued with many of King's wartime ministers such as CD Howe and Brooke Claxton and brought Lester Pearson into cabinet after a successful career in the civil service. St Laurent saw himself as the steward of the bureaucratic, civil service-centred machine that King had established.

Economic development under St Laurent

Wartime demand had more than doubled Canada's GNP between 1939 and 1945 and this expansion would continue in the years after the war. The war had also boosted manufacturing's share of this expansion

War Measures Act
An act of the Canadian parliament that gives the federal government power to regulate the economy and suspend civil liberties in times of war or perceived insurrection.

Orders in Council
A order of the government of Canada that passes through the executive and the Governor General and becomes law without passing through parliament.

and this too continued under St Laurent. The value of manufactured goods produced in Canada rose from $8 billion in 1946 to $20 billion in 1955. A massive new smelter in Kitimat, British Columbia helped make Canada one of the world's top aluminium producers. While primary industry was still dominated by agriculture, lumber and mining were also becoming important sectors.

The geography of economic development transformed the structure of the Canadian federation. Uranium was discovered in northern Saskatchewan, exposing that part of the country to previously unseen economic development. In 1947, a massive oil field was located south of Edmonton, Alberta at Leduc. By the time St Laurent left office, oil was the single most valuable natural resource exploited by the Canadian economy. From this point forward, Alberta's character would steadily change to encompass this new wealth and the power that it believed should accompany it. This was a belief that ran counter to the centralizing instincts of the St Laurent administration.

It was the sheer size of Canada that posed the biggest challenge to exploiting these new discoveries. Oil, uranium and other commodities were found far away from the traditional processing areas of the country. Transportation was the challenge and it was to this that the St Laurent administration turned its attention. Pipelines were built both west and east out of Alberta, each passing through the US making Alberta oil available there. This solution was not necessarily ideal for Alberta. Successive Alberta governments sought greater refining capacity within the province for its oil. Alberta was likewise hesitant to export her natural gas. Eventually the massive Trans-Canada Pipeline would be built, but not before it would help bring down St Laurent's government in 1956. Construction of the Trans-Canada Highway was also initiated under St Laurent's government with similar hopes of opening new transportation options for Canadian industry.

While the pipelines would address the transportation issues regarding oil and gas, they did nothing for prairie grain or northern minerals. The long discussed seaway through the St Lawrence–Great Lakes system would be the answer. While the St Laurent government was in favour of the project, the US Congress had serious reservations and continually delayed approval. Frustrated, St Laurent and his cabinet decided to proceed with an all-Canadian route and this seemed to rouse the US to action. By 1954 US and Canadian diplomats had hashed out an agreement by which a portion of the route would move through the United States. The US section of the seaway would be paid for by the US while keeping the possibility of an all-Canadian route open. Canada agreed to pay $336.5 million of the $470.3 million with the US picking up the rest of the cost. Between 1954 and 1959, 19 lock systems were built to allow deep draft navigation along 3,700 kilometres from the Atlantic to Deluth, Minnesota.

This expansion required money, capital that increasingly came from the United States, which had replaced Great Britain as the main source of foreign investment in Canada. This investment raised questions about Canada's economic independence that would plague successive governments through to 1980. US interests controlled 50% of Canada's mining industry, 75% of her oil industry and virtually all of the car industry through the branch plant system that had developed in the

Class discussion

How did the construction of the seaway impact on the communities through which it passed?

1920s. St Laurent set up a commission, headed by Walter Gordon, to examine the extent to which Canada's economic landscape was controlled by foreign interests. His findings were predictable, namely that a good deal of the Canadian economy was dominated by US businesses. While this situation was vaguely unsettling to some Canadians, even a cursory examination of the Canadian economy in 1956 revealed that US capital was essential to maintain the pace of Canadian economic growth. St Laurent's government certainly recognized this and continued with the **continentalist** approach of previous Canadian governments.

First Nations – The Indian Act

The Indian Act is a series of laws that govern the relationship between the federal government and the people of Canada's **First Nations** registered under the *Indian Act* as "status Indians". It controls all aspects of First Nations existence including who is and who is not an "Indian". It was an act of the federal parliament which had been created and amended through the years with no input from the First Nations themselves.

After the Second World War attitudes to human rights began to change. The atrocities that accompanied this conflict led to the concept of Crimes Against Humanity and would lead to the proclamation by the United Nations of the Universal Declaration of Human Rights in 1948. Instrumental in the drafting of the Declaration was the United Nations Human Rights Division headed by Canadian John Humphrey. The stark contrast between the plight of Canada's First Nations people and the spirit of the Declaration became more and more apparent in the years after 1948. Native leaders again agitated for a revision of the *Indian Act*.

By 1951 St Laurent was ready to amend the Act. Some important revisions were made such as lifting restrictions on First Nation's culture like the **potlatch**. These 1951 amendments were the first in which native leaders were consulted. The overall tone of the document and its goal of assimilation nevertheless remained. **Indian agents** working for the federal government still controlled the lives of status natives. Perhaps most importantly they were still not permitted to vote – they were still far from full Canadian citizens.

continentalist
Continentalism is an approach that emphasizes and builds the ties – economic, military and cultural – between the United States and Canada.

First Nations
A term that refers to the native peoples of Canada, both status (registered under the Indian Act) and non-status (not registered under the Indian Act).

potlatch
A communal feast important among the First Nations of North America's pacific northwest.

Indian agents
Federal officials empowered by the *Indian Act* to administer its provisions and restrictions

Research and communication skills

The fact that St Laurent was a keen continentalist did not mean that he was blind to the dangers of the massive influence the United States was having on Canada's culture. In April 1949 he established the Royal Commission on National Development in the Arts, Letters and Sciences to investigate the extent to which Canadian culture was threatened and what could be done to further develop it. Headed by Vincent Massey and thereafter known as the Massey Commission, the inquiry took two years. It made several significant recommendations.

Research Massey's recommendations and their effect on Canadian society in the years 1951–2005. Use the following table as a guide.

Area	Recommendation?	Results to 2005?
Education		
Arts		
Sciences		
Telecommunications		

Should public funds be used to support culture?

- Choose one area from the table above and advocate a pro- or anti-government position.
- Discuss the question and debate with others of opposing viewpoints as it applies to all the cultural areas.

National devence

The global context in which St Laurent developed his national defence policy was unlike any that had preceded it. Canada had emerged from the Second World War as an important military power with the third largest navy in the world. By 1949 the Soviet Union had exploded its first atomic weapon, inaugurating the arms race. The Cold War would structure all major national defence decisions in Canada until 1990.

In 1949 Canada became one of the founders of the North Atlantic Treaty Organization (NATO). NATO would become Canada's first peacetime military alliance. Although there were 11 other signatories, the dominance of the United States was evident from the beginning and this was especially apparent for Canada, her closest neighbour. Nevertheless the Cold War reality and Canada's location meant that there was a degree of mutual dependence between the United States and Canada, one that St Laurent, unlike his successor, did not shy away from. Under St Laurent, Canada sought to continue this mutuality by negotiating the North American Air Defense Command (NORAD) agreement pledging to share joint command in terms of the defence of the air space of North America. As a result of this agreement a series of radar bases were built in Canada to detect Soviet attacks.

St Laurent's defeat

By 1957 the Liberal party had governed Canada for 22 years. In the last years of King's governments, and increasingly under St Laurent, they managed the country as it saw fit with limited interference from parliament and with the help of a civil service that it had largely created. This increasingly autocratic style came to a head during the debates surrounding the construction of the Trans-Canada Pipeline. Sections of the pipeline through Northern Ontario were to be jointly funded by the Ontario government and the federal government, with the federal government providing most of the money. The rest of the pipeline would be built and run by a company 85% of which was US owned. The Conservative opposition railed against Canadian public funds being used to enrich a US business. In the face of this opposition, St Laurent's government used its parliamentary majority to end debate and pass the required legislation in 1956.

Canadian voters did not forget this arrogance when the next federal election came around in 1957. A fiery lawyer named John Diefenbaker from Prince Albert, Saskatchewan led the Progressive Conservative Party to a minority government, capturing 112 seats to the 105 of the Liberals. While the pipeline debate was certainly an important factor in the Liberal's defeat, other factors played a role. Low wheat prices and high taxes led to a general feeling of western alienation, a feeling on which Diefenbaker, himself from a prairie province, capitalized during an energetic nationwide campaign. Diefenbaker's first government lasted less than a year. After the resulting general election in 1958, Diefenbaker's Progressive Conservatives emerged with the largest majority in Canadian history.

> **Class discussion**
>
> What is the command structure of NORAD? What does the United States contribute to the agreement? How does Canada contribute? To what extent is this an equal partnership?

Research one of the following Canadian populist political parties. Make a presentation exploring the extent to which Diefenbaker represented a continuation of older approaches to western alimentation and to what extent he represented a change in dealing with this issue.

- Cooperative Commonwealth Federation (CCF)
- United Farmers of Alberta
- The Alberta Social Credit Party
- The British Columbia Social Credit Party

John G Diefenbaker

Diefenbaker was a western populist. In opposition and as Prime Minister of a minority government he had decried Liberal arrogance and increasing complacency as leading to incompetence. In the campaign of 1957 he countered the Liberal message of sound management with a vision of a united, new Canada, a nation with a purpose, a nation with prosperity for all. While Diefenbaker's vision was long on enthusiasm it was certainly short on detail. He campaigned on a platform of northern development, better relations between federal and provincial governments, greater independence in North American affairs, and renewed ties with the British Commonwealth. The lack of a plan was compounded by the fact that when he swept to victory he did so with 207 other Members of Parliament who had no experience in running a country.

Economics

Trying to make good on his promises of northern development, Diefenbaker initiated programmes to find and exploit mineral resources in the Yukon and Northwest Territories. Highway and railway construction stretched into the north with minimal effect. His other economic policies did little to alter the cyclical nature of the economy. Diefenbaker came to power as a recession was beginning to take hold, a recession that would see unemployment reach a post-war high of over 11% in 1961 and put massive strains on Canada's unemployment insurance scheme. But it was the business cycle more than anything the Diefenbaker government did that brought the recession to an end.

Allowing his emotional affinity to the British Commonwealth to override practical economics, Diefenbaker proposed diverting 15% of Canadian exports to Great Britain, something that delighted Britain, which immediately proposed a free trade agreement between the two countries, and horrified the US, which noted that this was protectionist folly and violated the recent General Agreement on Tariffs and Trade. In the end, nothing came of Diefenbaker's scheme and in fact he took some steps to expand trade with the US during his time in office. Natural gas began to flow south under Diefenbaker's government and defence production was rationalized between the two countries. In this sense, Diefenbaker represented a certain continuity with previous Liberal governments despite his public disdain for them.

True to his prairie roots, Diefenbaker gave considerable focus to agriculture. *The Farm Credit Act* made money available for farmers to modernize and expand their operations while the Agricultural Stabilization Board sought to mitigate the effects of fluctuating prices in farm commodities. Cold War hostilities and the fact that Canada still did not officially recognize the Chinese Communist government did not stop Diefenbaker's government from benefiting from Chinese crop failures. The Canadian Wheat Board sold $450 million worth of Canadian grain to China in 1961–1962, trebling Canadian farm income in the process.

One Canada

Diefenbaker saw himself as the political ancestor of Sir John A MacDonald, even collecting MacDonald memorabilia and furniture. He called his broad policy vision and his memoirs "**One Canada**" evoking MacDonald's ambitious National Policy.

An example of the conflict between this core belief and the nature of Canadian federalism was the Canadian Bill of Rights passed by the Diefenbaker government. On the surface this was a landmark piece of legislation, guaranteeing civil rights for all Canadians regardless of ancestry, religion or beliefs. It granted the vote to First Nations people who previously had not been allowed to vote for the first time. Unfortunately it was only an act of parliament and as such could be superseded by any other act of parliament. In other words the rights that the Bill guaranteed were not seen to be inalienable. Further, the Bill only applied to areas of federal responsibility. It was not binding in areas such as education and health care that the *British North America Act* designated as provincial responsibilities.

As in other countries, the post-war period in Canada saw a steady increase in government-provided social programmes and this continued during Diefenbaker's tenure. The nature of the division of powers in Canadian federalism placed many of these responsibilities under the purview of provincial governments. Nevertheless, Diefenbaker's government supported increased pension payments and, through transfer payments, the beginnings of socialized health care.

Nationalism: the United States and the Avro Arrow

Closer economic, defence and cultural ties between Canada and the United States was an underlying trend in the Liberal policies of King and St Laurent. Broadly known as continentalism, this trend was reality by the 1960s. Canada and the US shared the longest undefended border in the world across which goods, gas, oil, water, radio and by the 1950s television signals flowed regularly. Canada and the US were bound together in both NATO and NORAD. Against this practical reality, Diefenbaker's attempts to assert his vague notions of nationalism were superficial and ultimately resulted in little change in continentalism.

Yet there were times when practicality overrode the Prime Minister's distrust of continentalism. In an effort to assert a degree of national defence autonomy and to foster Canada's fledgling aerospace industry, the Canadian government under St Laurent contracted AV Roe, a Canadian aircraft research company, to build an all-Canadian fighter interceptor jet, capable of protecting North America from Soviet nuclear bombers attacking over the North Pole – the CF-105 Avro Arrow. The idea was that by building a jet with all Canadian components, Canada would become an important exporter of air defence technology. As costs soared, the project became bogged down. The Canadian-made Orenda Iroquois engine that was to power the Arrow was scrapped in favour of a US engine, fueling unfounded speculation of US influence in the project. When the final price tag for each aircraft approached $8 million, Diefenbaker balked. In the interest of fiscal responsibility Diefenbaker and his cabinet decided to cancel the contract, essentially shutting down AV Roe and putting its 14,000 employees out of work.

One Canada

A belief that all Canadians were equal regardless of ancestry, language or province. The nature of Canadian federalism, however, made such a vision difficult to realize.

Research skills

Research Sir John A MacDonald's National Policy. To what extent was Diefenbaker's vision consistent with MacDonald's?

TOK discussion

Compare and contrast the provisions of the Canadian Bill of Rights (1960) with the Canadian Charter of Rights and Freedoms (1982). Using these documents, write a question relating to the use of language in these documents, then answer it.

▲ The Royal Canadian Air Force Snowbirds acrobatic team flies over a replica of the Avro Arrow. To what extent were the arguments against cancelling the Arrow based on emotion?

Thinking and communication skills

Assume the role of a government representative or an AV Roe representative. Research your position regarding the cancellation of the Avro Arrow project.

Then, as a journalist, develop a set of questions to ask your chosen representative that will help you write a story about the cancellation.

Class discussion

What made the CF-105 Avro Arrow an advanced aircraft in 1958?

Research and thinking skills

What military alliances has Canada been a member of during the 20th century? How was membership in these alliances related to domestic issues and policies at the time? What can this tell us about the relationship of domestic policy to foreign policy?

While unpopular with the public, many scholars believe this to be the right decision, but poorly handled. Regardless, it did leave the issue of Canadian defence unresolved – if not the Arrow then what? The solution would highlight inherent problems in trying to maintain independence while being geographically and ideologically tied to the US. Anti-communism in the context of the Cold War meant that Canada required close cooperation in matters of continental defence. The market economy's demand for free trade linked the two countries economically. Such realities lent a degree of superficiality to Diefenbaker's nationalist efforts. In answer to the question of what would replace the aborted Arrow, the Diefenbaker government purchased the CF-101 Voodoo jet from the US, further fueling unsubstantiated rumours of US interference in the Arrow decision. The Diefenbaker government also built missile sites for the US BOMARC nuclear missile. This too proved problematic. Diefenbaker had declared Canada a nuclear-free zone and US law prohibited nuclear weapons from being transferred to other countries. The end result was the installation of US nuclear missiles in Canadian-built sites without their nuclear payload – satisfying neither Canada's defence needs nor its nationalist desires.

From June 1962 Diefenbaker had led a minority government. The indecision with which he approached the issue of continental defence especially in light of the Cuban Missile Crisis, united opposition parties by February 1963 and they brought down his government. In the ensuing federal election, Lester Pearson and his Liberals defeated Diefenbaker's Conservatives. In Pearson, Diefenbaker faced a Nobel Peace Prize-winner who had built much of his career on the idea of international cooperation and fulfilling the commitments that such cooperation demanded – a stark contrast to "Dief the chief".

Lester Pearson

More of a career diplomat than a politician, Lester Pearson had a gift for negotiation and compromise. After winning the Nobel Peace Prize for his handling of the Suez Crisis and the creation of the United Nations peacekeeping forces, he inherited the Liberal Party on the retirement of St Laurent, but in his five years in office was unable to secure a parliamentary majority. Nevertheless he presided over a period of national confidence, albeit a confidence that thinly covered age-old issues of national unity.

Practical continentalism

Pearson wasted little time in traveling to the United States to reassure President Kennedy that Canada would honour and strengthen its international commitments. He quickly reversed Diefenbaker's position on the BOMARC missile, arming them with nuclear warheads and recommitting Canada to its NATO responsibilities. Attempts at limiting foreign investment through taxation aimed primarily at US capital went nowhere. In this sense, Pearson was continuing the policies of previous Liberal governments after the rhetorical nationalism of Diefenbaker.

Although leading a minority government, Pearson managed to move some important pieces of legislation through parliament. In 1965 the government implemented the Canada–US Automotive Parts Agreement

(**Auto Pact**). This allowed branch plants in Canada to specialize in certain models thus making production more efficient and theoretically maintaining Canadian jobs.

Where Diefenbaker had railed against "hyphenated Canadians" in his vision of "One Canada", Pearson saw the country differently, at least at the beginning of his term. In an effort to appease a Quebec growing in sophistication, industry and assertiveness, Pearson established the Royal Commission on Bilingualism and Biculturalism to examine all aspects of French–English relations in the country. The commission met for six years and its report, when delivered in 1969, would spark widespread and often controversial changes to Canadian society.

Pearson continued the Medicare work that Diefenbaker had begun with his signature diplomacy and notions of "cooperative federalism". Understanding that a single "all or nothing" system for the whole country would not work, but nonetheless committed to socialized Medicare for the whole country, Pearson's government crafted a set of broad standards of comprehensive government-supplied health insurance, which, if adhered to by provincial health ministries, would make them eligible for federal funding. By 1972 all provinces and territories had signed on to the scheme.

Further broadening Canada's growing commitment to social security based on the principle of universality and cooperative federalism, Pearson's government created the Canada Pension Plan in consultation with the provincial governments. This was a scheme that collected contributions from employers and employees toward old age security. Quebec established its own separate, provincially administered pension scheme.

Pierre Elliot Trudeau

Trudeau was one of three so-called "wise men" brought into federal politics by Pearson to shore up the Liberal Party's Quebec representation. When Pearson retired, the globe-hopping, highly educated lawyer from Montreal won the Liberal leadership in a hard-fought leadership convention. As the new Prime Minister, Trudeau immediately called a federal election and was swept into office on the power of his charismatic and youthful campaigning style.

Economic policy under Trudeau

Trudeau's tenure was marked by difficult economic circumstances. The difficult economic circumstances of the 1970s were built on years of growing spending, international events such as wars in the Middle East, and decades of expanding union membership and power. When these circumstances were combined with Trudeau's vague notions of nationalism and autocratic style of governing, the result was bound to be confused and contradictory.

Trudeau cut spending in national defence, highlighted by a 50% cut to Canada's NATO commitment. At the same time, he dramatically expanded the size of the civil service, continuing a long Liberal tradition of technocratic governing. These technocrats had to face several disruptions to the international economic system that had profound

Auto Pact
The Auto Pact essentially created free trade in automobiles and automobile parts between the US and Canada. While this agreement did little for consumers, it allowed automotive manufacturers to rationalize production. They agreed to maintain Canadian production relative to sales. In other words, for every car produced in Canada, one had to be sold in Canada, but it did not have to be the same car and there was no maximum placed on Canadian automotive production.

ATL Thinking and research skills

In the early 1960s when Medicare was proposed, first in Saskatchewan, it was bitterly opposed. One prominent Catholic priest predicted that if the Medical Insurance Act passed the legislature there would be "blood in the streets". How is it that over the course of the following 40 years socialized medical insurance has become an important component of Canadian identity?

Are there examples from other countries in the Americas where social legislation has become a defining value for that country? What can we learn about national identity from studying a country's legislation, policies and budgets? What are the dangers when this happens?

▲ Pierre Trudeau announces the resignation of his government in 1974. What factors led to this resignation?

effects on the Canadian economy. A weakening US dollar, crop failures in various parts of the world and expanding social programmes within Canada combined to push prices higher in the early 1970s. Inflation was further inflamed by the 1972 Middle East conflict. OPEC placed an embargo on oil that raised the price of oil radically. This had a ripple effect throughout the economy, increasing prices on everything dependent on oil for production or transportation. As prices increased, demand for goods decreased creating the strange coincidence of inflation and unemployment, so-called stagflation.

Trudeau's response to the energy crisis and the subsequent stagflation was a mixture of economic nationalism and autocratic government control of the economy. He announced subsidies to provinces that imported oil – namely Ontario and Quebec, the manufacturing heartland of Canada. These subsidies were paid for through a tax on oil exported from oil-producing provinces – namely Alberta. He founded Petro-Can, a new crown corporation to counter the fact that US companies dominated Canada's oil industry.

Much of the federal election of 1974 was fought over how best to deal with the growing economic recession. Robert Stanfield's Conservatives advocated a system of wage and price controls as the only effective solution to the combination of inflation and unemployment. Trudeau won a majority partially by deriding Stanfield's plan. Nevertheless, the next year Trudeau announced wage and price controls.

While Diefenbaker had talked a good deal about economic nationalism but actually done very little about it, Trudeau took more concrete action. During his time as leader of a minority government, he established the Foreign Investment Review Agency to scrutinize foreign takeovers of Canadian-owned businesses, reserving the right of the federal government to approve or deny them.

After a brief period in opposition, Trudeau returned to office and by 1980 announced another measure to combat the lingering energy crisis. The National Energy Policy (NEP) was designed to ensure that half of the Canadian energy sector was Canadian owned and that Canada was energy self-sufficient within ten years. An important part of the plan was increased federal taxes on oil. As the price of oil is set by international supply and demand, this tax increase would have to be borne by the provinces and the producers. Alberta was outraged and threatened to curtail oil production. As the world settled into another recession and the price of oil dropped in the early 1980s dropping tax revenue, Trudeau was forced to negotiate with Peter Lougheed, the premier of Alberta. The resulting compromise lowered taxation rates and limited this taxation to oil discovered before 1980. The NEP died when Brian Mulroney's Conservative Party won a majority in the 1984 federal election. Mulroney had campaigned on removing the NEP and this helped win support in western Canada, enough to carry the 1984 election.

Trudeau's social policy

Trudeau took office just as Pearson's Royal Commission on Bilingualism and Biculturalism delivered its report. As a result of its recommendations Trudeau's government passed the Official Languages Act in 1969, which ensured that all services offered by the federal government

were available in both English and French. While Canadians broadly supported the policy, this support was regionally based. Eastern Canada was largely in favour while western Canada was vehemently opposed, foreshadowing a sense of western alienation that would grow throughout Trudeau's tenure.

As a young man, Trudeau had travelled extensively and had developed a distrust of ethnic nationalism. As a result of this distrust, he worked to create a mosaic approach to multiculturalism in Canada. He saw in the melting pot approach of some countries, in which ethnicities were assimilated into one monoculture, a recipe for the ethnic nationalism that he abhorred. To that end, his government passed the **Multiculturalism Act** in 1971. Immigration reform encouraged immigration based on the economic needs of the country rather than the ethnicity of the applicants.

Trudeau's government also examined the place of First Nations as a dominant ethnicity in Canadian society. The results of this examination were published in 1969 and by 1971 Trudeau responded. True to his distrust of ethnic nationalism, his policy advocated the abolition of the reserve and treaty system, essentially placing First Nations on a par with all other ethnicities in the country. First Nations groups across the country greeted the report and Trudeau's response with outrage. The Prime Minister quickly retreated and from that point much of his government's initiatives in terms of First Nations concentrated on developing a framework through which First Nations land claims could be discussed and settled, but this was complicated by Trudeau's fundamental belief that there could be no special place for First Nations Canadians in the same way there could be no special place for Ukrainian Canadians or Quebecers. Predictably this contradiction led to limited progress being made in federal First Nations relations during Trudeau's time in office.

Constitutional patriation

From 1867 the Canadian "**constitution**" was actually an act of the British Parliament and any amendments had to pass that body. By the end of the 1970s Trudeau had grown increasingly interested in making this fundamental document a Canadian document. This became both more important and more complicated as Quebec asserted what it saw as its authority in relation to the federation. In 1976 a separatist provincial government came to power in Quebec and in 1980 held a referendum on independence. Although the question of independence was defeated in the referendum vote, establishing federal/provincial relations and how changes to this relationship would be handled in the future was becoming more urgent.

When the provincial premiers and the Prime Minister prepared to meet in Ottawa in 1980 to negotiate the conditions under which they would agree to a Canadian constitution, it became evident that there were a number of obstacles that would have to be overcome, including the personalities of some of those participating. Trudeau had a long history of autocratic rule. René Lévesque, the separatist premier of Quebec, was doubtful any agreement was possible. While Trudeau was determined that the federal government retain overarching power over

TOK discussion

What other countries are officially multilingual? What is the connection between language, culture and identity?

Multiculturalism Act 1971
This act funded activities that celebrated and encouraged the ethnic identities of all Canadians and established government agencies to monitor the development of multiculturalism in Canada.

constitution
The fundamental laws that govern a political unit. Constitutions usually form the basis around which other laws are passed and to which they must adhere. Constitutions can be written, unwritten or some combination of the two as in Canada.

economic and social policy, Lévesque was just as determined that social policy should be the sole prerogative of the provincial governments. Newfoundland's Brian Peckford, Alberta's Peter Lougheed and Saskatchewan's Alan Blakeney were all just as determined to retain or increase provincial control over natural resources. The western provinces were opposed to any amending formula that gave Quebec and Ontario a veto, while these two provinces, in which the majority of the population lived, were concerned that in any amending formula based on provincial vote they would be disadvantaged. In the autumn of 1980 the prospects for agreement were not promising.

Indeed the first meeting did end in failure. As a result, Trudeau announced that the federal government was willing to patriate the constitution without the consent of the provinces and that the new constitution would include a Charter of Rights and Freedoms in the document. The Supreme Court ruled that while unilateral federal action was indeed "legal", it violated established convention. The provinces saw a Charter of Rights as unwarranted federal incursion on provincial powers. The Premiers and Prime Minister agreed to meet in November of 1981. In a series of dramatic negotiations the Premiers, with the noted exception of Lévesque, and the Prime Minister agreed to a compromise. The constitution would include a Charter of Rights and Freedoms, but these rights and freedoms were subject to a provincial opt-out on a case by case basis – the so-called "notwithstanding clause". In other words, provincial legislation could violate the Charter if the province invoked the "notwithstanding" clause. The constitution could be amended on the agreement of seven of the ten provinces as long as these seven provinces contained 50% of the national population. Queen Elizabeth II and Prime Minister Trudeau signed the *Constitution Act of 1982* on a rainy day in Ottawa over the objections of Quebec and Lévesque who had been excluded from the final negotiations that brought about an agreement.

TOK discussion

Since 1982, how many times has the "notwithstanding" clause been invoked? What were the circumstances? What does this clause tell us about the nature of human rights? To what extent are human rights "universal"?

ATL Research and thinking skills

Complete the following table to compare constitutional rights of countries in the Americas.

	Rights protected	Limits on rights
Canada Constitution Act, 1982		
Brazil Constitution of the Federative Republic of Brazil, 1988		
Cuba The Constitution of the Republic of Cuba, 1976		
United States Bill of Rights, 1791		

6.9 The Quiet Revolution and the October Crisis

Conceptual understanding

Key questions:

→ How did the Quiet Revolution change Quebec society and Quebec's place in the Canadian federation?

→ How did the 1960s and 1970s reflect a growing sense of Quebec nationalism?

Key concept:

→ Change

Causes

By the time Maurice Duplessis died in 1959 he had dominated Quebec politics for 20 years. Under Duplessis, Quebec remained a province of smallhold farmers and outdated industry. The Catholic Church exercised broad control in areas of social policy and education. Duplessis' Union Nationale maintained control through patronage, heavy spend during election campaigns, low taxation and draconian laws. Labour action was strictly curtailed by the Padlock Law, which was also used to silence any organized dissent. The labour minister had sweeping power to ban labour unions that had communist members or were deemed "too socialist". While Duplessis resisted any federal incursion into what he considered provincial jurisdiction, he did so more out of an isolationist tendency than a nationalist tendency. Although the 1950s may have been a dynamic period in English Canada, Quebec in 1959 looked very much as it had in 1949 or 1939.

Jean Lesage's Liberal Party wrested control from the Union Nationale in the Quebec provincial election of 1960. Duplessis had died in 1959 and the Union Nationale was in disarray. The disorganization was in sharp contrast to Lesage's energetic campaigning and bold vision. His slogan *"Il faut que ça change"* (Things must change) resonated with many Quebecers. He campaigned on a platform of modernization – economic, social and cultural. This change would come to be known as the Quiet Revolution.

Economic change

Lesage's government inherited a sizable budget surplus from the Union Nationale, a byproduct of parsimonious spending – except during election campaigns – and non-existent economic development schemes. Lesage's government embarked on an ambitious scheme of public ownership. Nowhere was this more evident than in the energy sector. Quebec nationalized about 30% of the electricity companies operating in the province and brought them under the publically owned Hydro-Quebec. Lesage sought to use public control to modernize electricity distribution in the more remote parts of Quebec. While similar efforts in steel production were less successful, it marked a sharp departure from Duplessis' idea that the government had no part to play in the private enterprise system.

separatist
A term denoting Quebecers who favour independence from Canada.

TOK discussion

How was the pension issue finally resolved? What does this tell you about the nature of the Canadian federation?

Lesage's Liberals created the General Investment Corporation. This was a government organization designed to provide money for Quebec firms looking to rationalize, consolidate or modernize with an underlying goal of increasing francophone participation in the economy at all levels. In this sense, it is easy to see in the Quiet Revolution important nationalist seeds, even though Lesage was by no means a **separatist**. Perhaps this can be seen more clearly in Quebec's approach to Pearson's national pension scheme. The Quebec scheme as presented in 1964 reaffirmed pensions as a provincial jurisdiction. However, rather than completely shelving the federal scheme, Lesage negotiated an opt-out clause. In that way he carved out a distinct place for Quebec while allowing the rest of the provinces and the federal government to do as they wished.

The interventionist policies of Lesage's government required a larger and modernized civil service. New public enterprises, agencies and even government ministries – six in total – were created to put the changes into motion. These new approaches also required more money. Lesage had demanded that Quebec, indeed he argued the same for all the provinces, have a greater share of direct taxation and hinted that if this concession was not forthcoming from the Pearson government, Quebec was prepared to act unilaterally. Even increased taxation, however, could not stop Lesage's government from running a huge deficit by 1966.

Social changes

One of the most salient elements of Duplessis' tenure was the degree of control the government ceded to the Catholic Church in the area of education. Religious leaders dominated even Protestant schools. Students who did not fit into the broad categories of francophone Catholics or anglophone Protestants had to fit in as they could. Education reform thus became a central element of the Quiet Revolution. For Lesage, education was about socializing students to a modern society and preparing them for Quebec's new economy and for this to happen, education in Quebec had to be secularized. He appointed a Royal Commission to investigate the state of education in Quebec and make recommendations for reform. The sweeping changes recommended by the Parent Commission in 1963, not the least of which was the establishing the Quebec government's first department of education, would prove to be one of the most important aspects of the Quiet Revolution.

From 1963, Quebec's education system:

- limited the involvement of Catholic and Protestant churches

- offered a wider range of options for students

- provided for the creation of non-religious schools

- emphasized technical as well as general education

- standardized education requirements across the province

- established local school boards to take over control of schools from church officials

- created a system of schools, *Collèges d'enseignement général et professionnel* (CEGEP), designed to transition students from high school to business school, technical institute or university.

Effects of the Quiet Revolution

Like most periods of rapid change, the Quiet Revolution brought with it social and economic dislocation, especially for those who had enjoyed positions of influence during the Duplessis years. The secularization of local governments displaced traditional elites just as it had in education. New education requirements were expensive and difficult for some rural areas to afford. The expansion of the civil service as a whole was expensive, requiring tax increases unheard of in the previous regime. Less surprising was the discontent of those contractors, businesses, and local officials accustomed to the system of patronage and graft that had flourished under Duplessis.

Lesage's confidence and posturing made an impression among young Quebecers beyond pensions, education and taxation. When the election of 1966 threw Lesage and his Liberals out of office in favour of Daniel Johnson and the Union Nationale, in some ways it was a response to the fast and dramatic change of the Quiet Revolution. But Johnson, unlike Lesage, while stopping short of demanding separation, was less committed to a partnership with the federal government and thus struck a chord with Quebec nationalists. In creating a more modern and confident Quebec, the Quiet Revolution set the stage for the radicalization of Quebec nationalism that would be seen in the years after 1966.

Quebec Nationalism

There was some indication of this radical turn when the Quebec electorate turned out the Liberal Party in 1966 and returned the Union Nationale to power. The new premier, Daniel Johnson, may have been a conservative when it came to economic policies, but he took a stronger stand when it came to Quebec's relationship with the federal government. Johnson demanded that Quebec be given sole control over cultural affairs, employment, direct taxation, banking, and the right to negotiate directly with foreign states. Such demands suited many of the radical nationalists in Quebec. There were, however, those who believed that these demands did not go far enough, or at the very least kept the current situation a federation in name only. These people argued that if Quebec was functionally independent, it should be actually independent.

It was into this constitutional quagmire that Charles de Gaulle stepped mischievously in 1967. It was a given that de Gaulle would be among the world leaders who would visit Canada as part of the World Fair in Montreal (Expo '67) and Canada's centennial celebrations. But, even the circumstances of his invitation were controversial. Ironically, it was Johnson who directly invited de Gaulle to visit Quebec as part of Canada's centennial celebrations and de Gaulle's acceptance was sent directly to Johnson as premier of Quebec. Protocol, and indeed the *British North America Act*, said that this should have all been channeled through the federal Department of Foreign Affairs. Always a champion of all things francophone, de Gaulle supported the idea of a more sovereign Quebec and his visit to Canada in 1967 was designed to show it. Huge crowds of Quebecers greeted him enthusiastically wherever he went, in response to which he quipped that it reminded him of Paris on its liberation from the Nazis in 1944. The implication,

351

first past the post
A single-member electoral system in which a general election consists of a collection of single-riding elections. In such a system it is possible for a party to win an election with less than a plurality of total votes.

sovereignty association
The idea that Quebec would be independent politically with its own monetary policy, Supreme Court and foreign policy, as well the power to protect the French culture and language, while at the same time remaining economically tied to Canada and its resources.

of course, was that Quebec was an occupied territory. He was speaking to such a crowd in Montreal on 23 June 1967 when he concluded his speech with the separatist rallying cry *"Vive le Quebéc libre"*. The crowd thundered its approval. This was all too much for Prime Minister Pearson and the federal government. De Gaulle's visit was cut short. The incident polarized Quebec society. English politicians and newspapers decried de Gaulle and his remarks. Separatists such as René Lévesque, a former Liberal cabinet minister turned ardent separatist and later founder of the new Parti Québecois took heart from de Gaulle's support.

Lévesque's movement grew stronger between 1968 and the next provincial election in 1970, an election that Lévesque hoped to win by virtue of the Liberal and Union Nationale vote splitting. Instead his party was to be a victim of the vagaries of the **first past the post** electoral system. The Parti Québecois managed to secure about 20% of the popular vote, but received only 5% of the seats in the legislature. The Parti Québecois increased their popular vote by about 10% in the 1973 election, but actually lost seats. The message that Lévesque took from these defeats was that separatism had to be downplayed in favour of the party's social policy platform.

Sometimes it is better to be in opposition than in government. The 1970s proved to be such a time in Quebec. The ruling Liberals limped from one problem to another, all within the context of tough economic times, and Lévesque's emphasis on social and political issues rather than separatism seemed to make the Parti Québecois the logical choice for a disgruntled electorate. On 15 November 1976 Lévesque's Parti Québecois formed the government.

Between 1976 and 1980 Parti Québecois prepared for the referendum that Lévesque had threatened. They passed the controversial Bill 101, which established the French language as the legally dominant language in the province. The new law went so far as to stipulate that French lettering be physically larger on business signs than that of any other language. As Trudeau's Liberals' popularity fell, culminating in them being turned out of office, the time seemed ripe to proceed with the referendum. But what exactly would the referendum be on?

Parti Québecois hit upon the concept of **sovereignty association**. The referendum would ask Quebecers, in a convoluted way, if they wanted sovereignty association. Lévesque campaigned vigorously and felt confident of a strong "YES" vote. Trudeau and the federal Conservative leader Joe Clark pointed out that Quebec already had the power to protect its culture and language – Bill 101 – and that the federal government was committed to reforming Quebec's place in confederation. In the end, the uncertainty of what exactly sovereignty association meant for Quebec and its economy spelled defeat for the *"Oui"* forces. When the votes were counted on 20 May 1980, 60% of Quebecers had voted *"Non"*.

Source skills

A cartoon from the *Calgary Herald*, April 1980, entitled "The possible two roads the citizens of Quebec could travel".

Questions

1 What is the political message of the cartoon?

2 With reference to its origin, purpose and content, analyse the value and limitations of the cartoon for a historian studying the referendum campaign.

Radical nationalists

It is hard to say that the Quiet Revolution caused the rise of radical Quebec nationalism as it developed in parallel with the modernization of the province. The most active of the radical groups was the Front de liberation du Québec (FLQ). Founded in the early 1960s, the FLQ was a loose association of radical sovereigntist groups advocating the use of violence to achieve Quebec independence based on a vague Marxist platform. From 1963 the FLQ began a campaign of terror. Bombings and robberies accompanied public statements and pamphlets. The police responded with raids, surveillance and arrests. As the 1960s wore on, the FLQ's terror campaign accelerated along with general public instability. Demonstrations, sit-ins and even riots were not uncommon in Montreal in these years. When Prime Minister Trudeau attended the annual St Jean Baptiste parade in Montreal in 1968, he was pelted with bricks, rocks and garbage, but defiantly refused to leave his seat. This was an early indication of Trudeau's approach to Quebec separatists whether they were violent or peaceful.

The October Crisis

FLQ activities reached a peak in October 1970. A section of the group broke into the home of the British Trade Commissioner James Cross and kidnapped him. They demanded $500,000 in gold and the release of FLQ members that had been imprisoned since 1963 as well as safe transport to Cuba or Algeria. Two days later the FLQ kidnapped Quebec's minister of Labour, Pierre Laporte. This represented, especially in terms of the demands, a serious escalation in the FLQ's activities.

This is where Trudeau's uncompromising approach, hinted at in the face of rocks and garbage in Montreal, revealed itself. To restore public confidence and allay the fears of public officials fearing more kidnappings, Trudeau deployed the Canadian Armed Forces to protect public officials and buildings in Ottawa and throughout Quebec. Shortly after soldiers began patrolling the streets; Quebec Premier Robert Bourassa asked the federal government for help in finding the kidnapped officials and rounding up those responsible. Six days after a second kidnapping, that of James Cross, a British diplomat, the House of Commons convened to debate the first peacetime invocation of the War Measures Act. The measure passed with the dissent of only the 16 New Democratic Party MPs – 190 MPs voted in favour. This support reflected a wider public support for Trudeau's tough approach – 87% of Canadians, both in Quebec and in the rest of Canada, were in favour of using the War Measures Act, despite the contention of Tommy Douglas, the leader of the NDP, that it was "using a sledgehammer to crack a peanut".

The War Measures Act:

- was invoked only three times – First World War, Second World War and during the October Crisis

- applied across Canada, not just in Quebec

- allowed police unlimited powers of search and seizure

- allowed police to arrest people under suspicion

- permitted suspects to be held incommunicado and without access to legal counsel for 21 days

- resulted in the detention of 468 people, of which 408 were released without charge

- outlawed the FLQ, making membership a criminal act.

The sledgehammer worked, but not before Laporte was murdered, found strangled in the trunk of a car. Cross was released in exchange for safe passage to Cuba for the kidnappers. By December, the FLQ members responsible for the Laporte murder were apprehended. Although there were isolated FLQ activities into 1971, the movement had been broken.

Source skills

The FLQ and the October Crisis

Source A

Impromptu interview between Prime Minister Trudeau and a CBC reporter on the steps of Parliament Hill, 13 October 1970.

Trudeau: "… this isn't my choice, obviously. You know, I think it is more important to get rid of those who are committing violence against the total society and those who are trying to run the government through a parallel power by establishing their authority by kidnapping and blackmail. And I think it is our duty as a government to protect government officials and important people in our society against being used as tools in this blackmail. Now, you don't agree to this but I am sure that once again with hindsight, you would probably have found it preferable if Mr Cross and Mr Laporte had been protected from kidnapping, which they weren't because these steps we are taking now weren't taken. But even with your hindsight I don't see how you can deny that".

Reporter: "No, I still go back to the choice that you have to make in the kind of society that you live in".

Trudeau: "Yes, well there are a lot of bleeding hearts around who just don't like to see people with helmets and guns. All I can say is, go on and bleed, but it is more important to keep law and order in the society than to be worried about weak-kneed people who don't like the looks of ..".

Reporter: "At any cost? How far would you go with that? How far would you extend that?"

Trudeau: "Well just watch me".

Source: Saywell, John. 1971. *Quebec 70. A Documentary Narrative*, University of Toronto Press, Toronto, Canada.

Source B

▲ Trudeau running towards the post of unemployment. Uluschak, Edd, *Edmonton Journal*, 24 November 1970.

Source C

Reaction of the FLQ to the Invocation of the War Measures Act (17 October 1970).

Communiqué from the Liberation cell; released on 8 December 1970.

> The present authorities have declared war on the Quebec patriots. After having pretended to negotiate for several days they have finally revealed their true face as hypocrites and terrorists.
>
> The colonial army has come to give assistance to the 'bouncers' of Drapeau (the Mayor of Montreal) the 'dog'. Their objective: to terrorize the population by massive and illegal arrests and searches, by large and noisy deployments, and by making shattering statements on the urgent situation in Quebec, etc.

Source: Bélanger, Claude. 1999. *Documents on the October Crisis*. Marianopolis College, Quebec, Canada. http://faculty.marianopolis.edu/c.Belanger/quebechistory/docs/october/flqreact.htm

Source D

Excerpt from the Manifesto of the Front de liberation du Québec. (Original translation as made available in English by the Canadian Press in 1970.)

> The Front de liberation du Québec is not a messiah, nor a modern-day Robin Hood. It is a group of Québec workers who have decided to use every means to make sure that the people of Québec take control of their destiny.

> The Front de liberation du Québec wants the total independence of all Québécois, united in a free society, purged forever of the clique of voracious sharks, the patronizing "big bosses" and their henchmen who have made Québec their hunting preserve for "cheap labour" and unscrupulous exploitation.

> The Front de liberation du Québec is not a movement of aggression, but is a response to the aggression organized by high finance and the puppet governments in Ottawa and Québec . . .

http://faculty.marianopolis.edu/c.Belanger/quebechistory/docs/october/manifest.htm

Questions

1 **a.** According to Source D, what does the Front de liberation du Québec claim is the key problem facing Quebec?

   b. What is the message conveyed by Source B?

2 With reference to its origin, purpose and content, analyse the value and limitations of Source C for a historian studying the October Crisis.

3 Compare and contrast what Sources A and C reveal about invoking the War Measures Act in October 1970.

4 Using the sources and your own knowledge evaluate the extent to which the federal government was justified in invoking the War Measures Act in October 1970.

Exam-style questions

1   Evaluate the successes and failures of Truman's domestic policies.

2   Robert J Donovan stated that Eisenhower had "everything most Americans wanted in a President". Evaluate this statement.

3   "The New Frontier of which I speak is not a set of promises – it is a set of challenges. It sums up not what I intend to offer the American people, but what I intend to ask of them". To what extent did Americans meet Kennedy's challenges?

4   To what extent were the goals of Johnson's Great Society fulfilled?

5   Discuss the success of Nixon's domestic policies.

6   Evaluate whether Gerald Ford should have pardoned Richard Nixon.

7   Compare and contrast Jimmy Carter's domestic policies with another post-war president to 1980.

8   Examine how the Democratic or Republican Party changed from the late 1940s to 1980.

9   Compare and contrast the domestic policies of Diefenbaker and Trudeau.

10 To what extent was Diefenbaker's vision of "One Canada" achieved in the years 1957–1980?

11 Examine the relationship of the Prairie Provinces to the rest of Canada in the years 1957–1980.

12 Discuss the causes and consequences of Quebec's Quiet Revolution.

13 To what extent was Canada's economy based on primary industries in the years 1957–1980.

Source analysis

Question

With reference to its origin, purpose and content, analyse the value and limitations of Nixon's resignation speech for historians studying the Nixon Administration.

Analysis

To answer this question, you will need to read *President Nixon's resignation speech*, which can be found on the PBS website.

Document analysis is a fundamental skill every historian undertakes. For DP History, it is a skill that students will be specifically examined on in Paper 1, the Internal Assessment and Extended Essays in History, but should also be integrated into every assessment's answer.

A primary source may be:

- information about an event by an eyewitness or participant

- information about a person by someone who knew that person

- a statement of information or ideas given by someone who lived at the time of the event

- a government or legal proclamation or publication

It is essential that you evaluate a primary source to determine its reliability and the bias of the information provided. While primary sources are valuable because they bring the reader as close as possible to the event or time period under discussion, you can never be sure whether even an honest eyewitness is presenting an accurate picture. Four people all watching the same event – such as a road traffic accident – may interpret the event in four different ways as a result of their subjective experience, which may include limitations such as memory loss, an obstructed view or a heightened emotional response.

A secondary source may be:

- information taken from many sources and constructed by an historian

- information not directly from a witness to an event, such as, for example, the diary of the great-great-granddaughter of Mussolini talking about his March on Rome.

A secondary source must be evaluated as critically as a primary source: the author who constructs or presents the information will undoubtedly have a perspective they are attempting to present.

Start by thinking about what the question is asking. As you begin your analysis, you may find that the accuracy of the investigation varies when using primary or secondary sources, depending on the documents' nature. There is a huge range of sources and these can be used as major forms of evidence when developing an argument.

Topic	Must answer	To consider in your answer
Origin	Where did the source come from? What is it? Is it a primary or secondary source, and what are the ramifications?	Who produced it? When was it produced? How was it produced (e.g. textbook, monograph, memo, email, diary, memoir, newspaper, textbook, cartoon, speech, meeting minutes, government research or census data, eulogy, campaign, state of the union or state propaganda poster)?
Purpose	Why was the source created in the first place? What was the intended audience?	What was the author trying to do by creating it (e.g. to educate students or the public, inform government or bureaucracy, keep a record, collect memories, sell newspapers or report, laugh, critique, inform, satirize or serve as an immediate account)?
Content	What material does this cover?	How can the content of the source be integrated into my explanation of its origin, purpose, value and limitations?
Value	What did you specifically learn from the source?	How is it specifically related to your research question (e.g. overview or background, in-depth view or research, eyewitness, satire and humour in the society)?
Limitations	What are the specific issues regarding bias and reliability, as related to your research question? For example, specific nouns or verbs that were biased. What perspective is the source created from? Can bias be introduced in this way?	How reliable is the source? Determine this by asking: • How/why did the document come into existence? Through free will or under duress? • Was the source made genuinely or deceitfully? • What role did the person who created the document play in the event? Important or obscure? Was he or she in a position to know? • Is translation involved that could change the source's meaning? • What could be an alternative perspective? • Is the source internally consistent? • Is the source consistent with other sources from the period? (e.g. translation, excerpt, access to country's secret files from previous period, memory, speechwriter, world politics at the time)

7 THE COLD WAR AND THE AMERICAS, 1945–1981

Global context

The Cold War is often studied as a contest of ideology, diplomatic movements, military activities and political actions involving two protagonists, the USA and the Soviet Union, locked in a contest for dominance across the Eurasian land mass, focused on central Europe and far eastern Asia. From their beginnings, the Cold War policies of the two superpowers, especially the USA, had significant and continuing effects on the countries of the Americas, from Argentina and Chile in the south, to the islands of the Caribbean, and to Canada in the north but the effect was far from uniform.

While the USA pursued policies designed to solidify the region as a bulwark against the Soviet Union and communism, some nations of the region chose to oppose the USA, others to closely ally themselves with their large northern neighbour, and several charted a neutral path. Regardless, Cold War pressures affected all countries in the Americas regardless of their ideological orientation, significantly contributing to domestic agendas and the response to international events, from economic policies through to intervention in civil wars.

Timeline

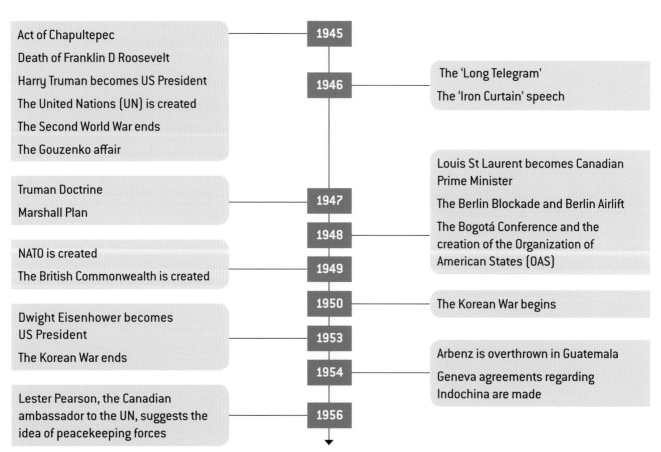

Act of Chapultepec	**1945**	
Death of Franklin D Roosevelt		
Harry Truman becomes US President	**1946**	The 'Long Telegram'
The United Nations (UN) is created		The 'Iron Curtain' speech
The Second World War ends		
The Gouzenko affair		
		Louis St Laurent becomes Canadian Prime Minister
Truman Doctrine	**1947**	The Berlin Blockade and Berlin Airlift
Marshall Plan	**1948**	The Bogotá Conference and the creation of the Organization of American States (OAS)
NATO is created	**1949**	
The British Commonwealth is created		
	1950	The Korean War begins
Dwight Eisenhower becomes US President	**1953**	
The Korean War ends		Arbenz is overthrown in Guatemala
	1954	Geneva agreements regarding Indochina are made
Lester Pearson, the Canadian ambassador to the UN, suggests the idea of peacekeeping forces	**1956**	

1957
John Diefenbaker becomes Canadian Prime Minister

The North American Aerospace Defense Command (NORAD) is created

1959 — Castro takes power in Cuba

1961
John Kennedy becomes US President

The Bay of Pigs invasion

The Alliance for Progress is created

1962 — The Cuban Missile Crisis

1963
Lester Pearson becomes Canadian Prime Minister

Kennedy's assassination

Lyndon Johnson becomes US President

1964 — The Gulf of Tonkin Resolution (US)

1965
Pearson's speech at Temple University criticizing US involvement in Vietnam

1968 — The Tet Offensive

1969
Pierre Trudeau becomes Canadian Prime Minister

Richard Nixon becomes US President

1970 — Salvador Allende becomes Chilean President

1973
US military withdrawal from Vietnam

Allende is overthrown in Chile

Augusto Pinochet becomes Chilean President

1974 — Richard Nixon resigns

Gerald Ford becomes US President

1975
Fall of Saigon

1978 — The Sandinista Revolution in Nicaragua begins

1977
Jimmy Carter becomes US President

The Panama Canal Treaties are signed

1979 — Joseph Clark becomes Canadian Prime Minister

1980
Pierre Trudeau becomes Canadian Prime Minister

Archbishop Romero is murdered in El Salvador

The Salvadoran Civil War begins

> ## Conceptual understanding
>
> ### Key questions
>
> → Why did the US Good Neighbor policy towards Latin America change after the end of the Second World War?
>
> → Why were Americans so afraid of communism in the 1940s and early 1950s?
>
> → How did the 'Red Scare' affect the arts and society in the USA?
>
> ### Key concept
>
> → Change

Truman's foreign policies after the Second World War

Looking back 20 years after the dismantling of the Soviet Union, the effectiveness of President Harry S Truman's foreign policies as a means of combating the influence of Soviet-style communism appears to be confirmed. The policy that became known as **containment** influenced relations between the USA and its hemispheric neighbours, dominating attitudes towards Latin America. The battle against communism was located not only in the official defence and foreign policy of the USA, but also in a multifaceted effort to rid the homeland of any influences of communism, an effort that began long before the Second World War with the 'Red Scares' of the 1920s, and peaked with McCarthy's actions in the 1950s. The fight against communism influenced popular culture, making its way into films, plays, and even television cartoons. The Truman years set the stage for the Cold War abroad and at home.

When the Second World War came to a close, the leaders and peoples of the nations of Latin America believed their contributions to the war effort, including subordinating and linking their economies to the needs of the USA, had earned them the right to greater recognition and influence in the hemisphere. This was confirmed by the Inter-American Reciprocal Assistance and Solidarity agreement of March 1945. They looked forward to a return to, and enhancement of, Franklin Roosevelt's Good Neighbor policy. The Act of Chapultepec, as it was called, guaranteed each nation's national sovereignty and diplomatic equality. On the other hand, especially after George Kennan's Long Telegram (1946), the leaders of the USA focused much more on Europe and Asia, where they worried about the threat of Soviet expansion. Rather than the expected hemispheric solidarity, all countries except Canada saw their influence diminish throughout the 1940s. As the Cold War developed, the Truman administration and the nations of Latin America and the Caribbean met diplomatically several times, including two international conferences in Rio de Janeiro (1947) and Bogotá (1948). At the conferences and in

containment
US foreign policy developed in the 1940s to prevent the further spread of Soviet expansionism and communism.

other forums the differences in the views of the USA and its southern neighbours, most significantly in terms of the relationship between economic aid and development and hemispheric defence concerns, became increasingly apparent.

While the countries of Latin America looked at post-war relations with the USA in a hemispheric and global context, for the most part the Truman administration saw them through the lens of the Cold War. Stability, not democracy, became the most important goal in the fight against communism. The USA assisted Latin America, but only when it felt threatened in the region. From 1946 to 1950 Latin America received only 2% of US overseas aid, and almost all was military in nature; this, despite the emphasis of the US State Department on greater economic support for hemispheric neighbours. Just a year after signing the Act of Chapultepec, the USA violated several provisions by interfering in the internal affairs of Argentina, Bolivia and Chile. In the following year, 1947, the Inter-American Treaty of Reciprocal Assistance (commonly known as the Rio Treaty) was signed at the conference in Rio de Janeiro. The Rio Treaty moved more towards hemispheric military cooperation with a shared vision that was anti-communist, at least from the point of view of the USA; unofficial fears of possible communist advances were communicated to US diplomats by Argentina and Brazil. That year Brazil, Chile and Cuba banned communist organizations and cut off diplomatic relations with the Soviet Union. Over the next year, several South American and Caribbean governments turned away from democratic systems to more autocratic and right-leaning regimes. The US government interpreted the Rio Treaty as allowing a larger role for itself, essentially rolling back some of the provisions of the Act of Chapultepec. The Truman administration felt it was imperative that Latin America remain non-communist and friendly towards the USA, so its importance began to increase somewhat. To many people in Latin American the Rio Treaty was a potential disaster. As Narciso Bassols García a Mexican jurist and political commentator wrote, the worst thing about the treaty signed in Rio de Janeiro is that Latin American countries became 'compulsory automatic allies of the United States'. In the eyes of many Latin Americans, the nations of the region were conforming to Truman's containment policy without any choice, and without receiving any reciprocal benefits.

While Latin American nations were clamouring for economic assistance, the USA continued to press for a united approach to hemispheric defence and paid scant attention to social and economic issues. The policy planning staff of the State Department understood the Latin American perspective, enunciated in a February 1948 anonymous memo that expressed the need for grants in aid, technical assistance and an easing of the policies of the **Export-Import** Bank. But despite awareness of these issues, the Truman administration approached the spring 1948 Pan-American Conference in Bogotá, Colombia, with a sole focus on defence issues, leading to the formal formation of the Organization of American States (OAS) as a regional defence pact similar to NATO that superseded the Pan-American Union. In fact, US diplomats attending the conference were advised to avoid any financial commitments. The difference in perspectives was clear in responses to the riots that occurred

Export-Import
The official export credit agency of the US government, established in 1934 to facilitate foreign trade without private companies assuming too much risk.

in Colombia during the conference. Sparked by the assassination of the Liberal Party leader Jorge Eliécer Gaitán on 9 April, violent demonstrations took place across the country. Most Latin American leaders understood that the demonstrations were a clear confirmation of the desperate state of the Colombian economy, but the US representatives believed that communist instigators were behind the riots.

The overwhelming emphasis on hemispheric defence at the expense of socio-economic advancement and support for democracy within the region might have improved after Truman's inaugural address on 20 January 1949. In what became known as 'Point Four programmes' (as these were outlined in the fourth main point of the speech) Truman announced scientific technical assistance and monetary aid to developing nations. Unlike Africa and Asia, Latin America received little benefit from Point Four as the administration promoted private enterprise reminiscent of long-discarded and discredited pre-FDR **Dollar Diplomacy**. Truman's attention was focused on Europe and the victory of the Mao-led communists in China. The monolithic approach to Latin America prompted a response from Louis Joseph Halle of the State Department's policy planning division, who wrote an anonymous article in the July 1950 issue of *Foreign Affairs*, the same periodical that published George Kennan's Mr X piece. Halle, writing as Mr Y, took the administration to task for its lack of economic support for Latin America but the article was to have little effect as events in Asia commanded Truman's attention and once again marginalized hemispheric relations.

On 25 June 1950, North Korea invaded South Korea. The Korean War brought the threat of communist advancement to another country in Asia and the administration worried that it was a Soviet-planned diversion designed to draw US attention away from Europe. Truman focused on containing communism in Asia, but the administration feared increased Soviet attempts to penetrate Latin America, and used an emergency meeting of the OAS in early 1951 to proclaim communism as a threat to the people of the Americas.

A new law, the Mutual Security Act of 1951 (a follow-up to the Mutual Defense Assistance Act of 1949), provided $38 million of military assistance specifically designated for Latin America. Surplus Second World War weaponry was made available, either as aid or for purchase, as well. More emphasis was placed on government stability and internal security, even as public declarations of support for democracy and non-intervention were being issued by the State Department. In the eyes of Latin America, developments in 1951 showed that the USA was continuing to ignore calls for economic assistance and assumed hemispheric support for US Cold War policies.

The last year of the Truman administration saw little change in policy. Following a legitimate election in 1951 in Bolivia that was annulled by the ruling rightist government, and a subsequent revolution in April 1952 to remove the dictatorship the Truman administration withheld formal recognition of the left-leaning Bolivian government of Victor Paz Estenssoro, a government that brought universal suffrage as well as land reform. The threat of instability and a left-leaning government caused concern in the White House. Later the same year, the National

Dollar Diplomacy
The method by which the US achieved its foreign policy aims in the Americas, East Asia, and the Pacific through loans and economic assistance to foreign countries.

Security Council issued the secret document, NSC-141. In line with the earlier NSC-68, defence against communism was the focus, but this time in Latin America. The policy of the USA should 'seek first and foremost orderly political and economic development which will make the Latin American nations resistant to the internal growth of communism and Soviet political warfare'. The call for stability confirmed Narciso Bassols Garcia's caution following Rio, as NSC-141 continued advising the administration to 'seek hemispheric solidarity in support of our world policy'. By the end of Truman's term the attitude of the USA toward Latin America, framed within its policy of containment, resulted in weak and growingly contentious hemispheric relations. In the view of Latin American nations the colossus to the north continued to ignore economic and social needs to the detriment of the region's peoples, while expecting those very same countries to solidly support the USA's mission of combating communism around the world.

▲ El Bogotazo, 9 April 1948

The rise of anti-communism and its effects on US domestic and foreign policies

Joseph McCarthy's public crusade against communists is often portrayed as the greatest violation of civil liberties and civil public discourse in the history of the USA. However, the 'Red Scare' of the late 1940s and early 1950s was not an anomaly and should be viewed in the wider context of a pattern of anti-immigrant sentiments and fears of subversion that began in the earliest years of the nation. The first scare was during the administration of John Adams, exemplified by the passing and signing of the Alien and Sedition acts. The Sedition Act punished people with fines or jail time for 'malicious writing' against the President or Congress. It was the first example of the power of the federal government using power to limit speech and association. Those who verbally opposed the acts were criticized too. Anti-immigrant campaigns of the antebellum period included the famed NINA (No Irish Need Apply) signs. The populist movement of the 1880s had a nativist element as well. The Chinese Exclusion Act of 1882, following political pressure from the far west, stopped the immigration of Chinese. Both Chinese and Irish workers had laboured on the Transcontinental Railroad, from the west coast and mid-west, respectively. The xenophobia was not, however, rooted in fear of subversion, but in qualms about changes in culture and challenges to labour.

The entry of the USA into the First World War brought new anti-sedition and anti-espionage laws in 1917 and 1918. The new laws not only fined subversives, but allowed for prison terms of up to 20 years, reflecting the Wilson administration's perception of the seriousness of the threat. The entry of the USA into the war was opposed by many groups, including

Research skills

How did the US policy of containment affect your country between 1945 and 1953?

This is a research project in which you will write a one-page summary (single space, Times New Roman 12-point font) to be distributed to your class for their information. It should include proper referencing and there should be a source list that is in a commonly accepted form.

the International Workers of the World. Opposition to the draft brought federal prosecution for Eugene V Debs, a union leader and prominent socialist. Numerous people were prosecuted and thousands were jailed during the war, including many resident aliens of German ancestry.

The Russian Revolution brought fears of Bolshevism and the wary eye of the government. When President Wilson selected A Mitchell Palmer to become attorney general in late winter of 1919, the stage was set for the first 'Red Scare' of the 20th century. Palmer did not start by pursuing communists, in fact he released many of those placed in custody during the First World War soon after entering office. But a wave of bombings in spring 1919 by anarchists, one exploding in the attorney general's front yard, and the discovery of dozens of bomb-containing packages in a post office provoked a strong response from the federal government. A young attorney, J Edgar Hoover, was hired to head investigations targeting anarchists, radicals, and communists. The quickly constructed lists of potential suspects numbered in the hundreds of thousands, and tens of thousands were to be watched closely. Civil liberties were routinely violated and scores of people were held in custody for days without any permitted contact with families or attorneys. Those visiting jailed suspects were often arrested themselves: simply being an acquaintance was sufficient grounds for detention. The 'Red Scare' spread to beatings, and sometimes shootings, of individuals who did not show proper respect to the US flag or the national anthem, while crowds cheered the assaults. Palmer accelerated his raids, eventually arresting 249 resident aliens and putting them on board a ship, *The Buford*, heading for the Soviet Union. By the end of the Wilson presidency, Palmer's excessive actions lost popular and political support and the 'Red Scare' wound down. Palmer's head of the investigative branch, Hoover, stayed on though, starting a career in the Justice Department that would last half a century. He was director of the FBI from 1924 to his death in 1972, maintaining a constant focus on hunting suspected communists both outside and inside the government.

Following the Great Depression, the New Deal, and the Second World War, the year 1947 marked the intensification of the actions of the House Un-American Activities Committee (HUAC) and the creation and activities of the Federal Loyalty Programme. In the heated political environment, after more than a decade of Democratic Party control of the presidency and the legislative branch, the Republican Party representatives in Congress activated the HUAC, which had been created in 1938. Historians Alan Brinkley and Frank Friedel argue that an instrumental reason for the sudden escalation of investigations into subversive, essentially communist, activities was an attempt by the GOP (Republican Party) to weaken Democrats before the 1948 election. HUAC, began investigating the movie industry, with California Congressman Richard Nixon taking a prominent role. Hollywood producers, directors, writers and actors were accused of embedding Soviet propaganda in popular films. Hollywood personalities were called to testify publicly before the committee and were asked, 'Are you now or have you ever been a member of the Communist Party?' Among those compelled to testify were screenwriters Ring Lardner Jr and Dalton Trumbo, part of the famous Hollywood Ten declared criminally

in contempt of Congress for their defiant responses to questions from members of the committee. Witnesses before HUAC often 'took the 5th', meaning they chose to remain silent under rights enumerated in the fifth amendment to the US Constitution. While legally permissible and not supposed to imply any guilt, under repeated questions from committee members and attorneys the witnesses often seemed guilty. Many were tainted by the hearings, but not tried or convicted of subversion. Others chose to cooperate, some because they felt that communism was a real threat to the USA, naming Hollywood colleagues as communists. Well-known director Elia Kazan, a member of the American Communist Party in the 1930s, identified several members of the Hollywood community as communists, engendering the long-term wrath of many fellow actors and directors, hard feelings that remained even when Kazan received the Oscar for lifetime achievement in 1999. The hearings intimidated many in the industry as hundreds of movie studio employees and contractors were 'blacklisted', meaning studio owners fired and refused to hire anyone so designated.

HUAC did not limit its investigations to Hollywood. Perhaps the most famous case involved Alger Hiss, a mid-level staffer in the State Department. The controversial prosecution and conviction of Hiss would be debated into the 21st century. In 1948, a self-identified former communist, Whitaker Chambers, accused Hiss of providing him with classified government documents during the 1930s, knowing that the destination was Moscow. It was not possible, due to the time between the alleged crime of espionage and the charges, to prosecute Hiss, but eventually he was charged with perjury for his testimony. The case riveted the nation with testimony of microfilm hidden inside hollowed-out pumpkins in Chambers' garden and a typewriter of Hiss's tested and confirmed to be the origin of several documents. GOP Congressman Richard Nixon took a special interest in the case; his role in pursuing Hiss solidified his credibility as a fierce anti-communist, making him a national political figure, but also led many people, especially Democrats, to regard Nixon as, at best, unprincipled. The conviction of Hiss damaged the Democratic Party establishment, as many, including Illinois governor and future presidential candidate Adlai Stevenson and Secretary of State Dean Acheson, made forceful public statements in Hiss's defence. In fear of being labelled soft on communism or dupes, Democrats learned to speak and act with caution.

Concurrent with this round of HUAC investigations was the Truman administration's persistent prosecution of leaders of the American Communist Party under the Smith Act, resulting in more than 200 jail terms, and the formation and actions of the Federal Loyalty Programme, launched by President Truman in March 1947. The programme established 'loyalty boards' to investigate the influence and infiltration of communists and communist sympathizers in the executive branch. The programme authorized the investigation of both applicants to and employees of the federal government to guarantee loyalty because, in the words of the 21 March Executive Order 9835, 'it is of vital importance that persons employed in the Federal service be of complete and unswerving loyalty to the United States; and ... the presence within the Government service of any disloyal or subversive person constitutes a threat to our democratic processes …'.

Historian Alan Brinkley attributes Truman's desire to counter Republican attacks and to build support for his foreign policies as the reason for the Federal Loyalty Programme, but it is also quite reasonable to take Truman at his stated purpose. The order followed the 12 March speech that established the Truman Doctrine and made the fight against communism, one form of subversion, an essential part of both domestic and foreign policy. Although the programme did not specify what constituted disloyalty, within four years 200 hundred employees were fired and an additional 2000 resigned. Furthermore, the Federal Loyalty Programme was an impetus for other investigations by the Justice Department. It gave additional leeway for FBI Director Hoover to undertake his own inquiries, and use the power of the agency to harm the reputations of many US citizens, including, but not limited to, those suspected of being subversives.

The combination of HUAC and the Truman administration actively and publicly pursuing disloyal citizens increased the fever of the 'Red Scare'. In 1950 it led to the passage of the McCurran Internal Security Act, which became law over the veto of the President. The Act, among other provisions, required the registration of all communist groups with the federal government and determined that their internal documents were not private. The act furthered the intimidation of those who had been involved in legal, but unpopular, political activities. VENONA, a top-secret programme that deciphered Soviet communications, provided information that revealed spies within the Manhattan Project. While the source of the information remained secret until 1995, British scientist Karl Fuchs was exposed as having given atomic secrets to the Soviet Union. The uncovering of Fuchs began a trail that eventually led to Ethel and Julius Rosenberg, who were accused of being spies by Ethel's brother David Greenglass.

Greenglass had been exposed as a spy by Harry Gold, who was revealed by Fuchs. Greenglass confessed, turning in his wife Ruth, as well. In exchange for a sentence reduction and his wife's freedom, Greenglass provided testimony to investigators and prosecutors that played a major part in the conviction of the Rosenbergs. The Rosenbergs insisted they were innocent of turning over nuclear secrets to the Soviets, but in 1953 became the only Americans to be executed for espionage during the Cold War. Decades later, in 1996, David Greenglass revealed that he had lied about his sister Ethel in order to spare his wife, but continued to insist that Julius Rosenberg was a Soviet spy, a belief, while disputed, that was corroborated by intelligence records and other testimonies. The revelation that allies and US citizens had freely given atomic secrets to Stalin's Soviet Union served to further intensify fears of communist infiltration.

Additionally, the victory of Mao Zedong's communists over Chiang Kai-shek's nationalists in China in 1949 seemed to project a rising and threatening communist tide. To the citizens of the USA, only a few years after an Allied victory that was, to them, a triumph of democracy and freedom over totalitarianism, the 'loss of China' exacerbated fears of communism.

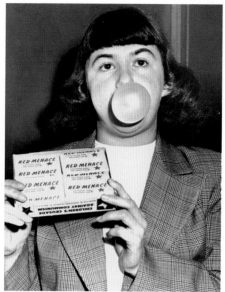

▲ Left: Members of the movie industry including prominent actors Lauren Bacall (left) and Humphrey Board (right) demonstrated against HUAC in Washington DC in this 1947 protest march

Right: A woman posing with a box of anti-communist chewing gum

Senator Joseph McCarthy and McCarthyism

By New Year's Eve 1950, the federal government's pursuit of domestic communists was well under way. Liberal organizations, including the American Civil Liberties Union (ACLU) and the National Association for the Advancement of Colored People (NAACP), had purged or were actively expelling communists from their ranks. A month later, on 9 February, in Wheeling, West Virginia, Wisconsin Senator Joe McCarthy announced 'I have here in my hand a list of 205 … a list of names that were made known to the Secretary of State as being members of the Communist Party and who, nevertheless, are still working and shaping policy in the State Department …'. It was on that date that the hunt for subversives began to reach a level of alarm that seemed to consume much of the USA for the next four years.

The first-term Republican senator's anti-communism came not from conviction, but rather from the desire for political gain. He faced an election in 1952 and found anti-communism to be a compelling issue for voters. McCarthy had created his own persona as 'Tail Gunner' Joe, but had never flown a mission. He was also known to be an alcoholic. Historian James Patterson writes that McCarthy was lazy to the point that he knew little about Joseph Stalin or even the American Communist Party, the membership of which had diminished significantly by 1950. Over the next few years, most Republican politicians chose to support McCarthy or remain silent about his wild accusations because it was to their advantage. Even General Dwight D Eisenhower demurred from defending General George C Marshall when McCarthy accused him of betraying the USA. For the most part, Democrats, often the objects of McCarthy's attacks, stayed silent, fearing being identified with hated communists. Senators who stood up to McCarthy faced withering personal counter-attacks and accusations. McCarthy struck fear into much of Washington.

McCarthy's accusations were loud but inconsistent. Two days after the Wheeling address, he sent a letter to President Truman claiming to know the identity of 57 communists in the State Department, and demanding that the President hand over evidence to his senate committee to investigate. Truman refused: the dossiers were often assembled records of uncorroborated testimony and hearsay. Ever the opportunist, McCarthy used Truman's refusal to turn over executive branch files as an excuse for not revealing the names of those he accused. McCarthy continued to change the alleged number of subversives in the State Department (the next time to 81), and also changed his charge to 'loyalty risks'. A few weeks after his initial speech, McCarthy began using his committee to investigate many areas of the federal government. Assisted by David Schine and Roy Cohn, who even travelled to overseas offices to investigate, and with information provided by FBI Director Hoover, McCarthy used the Senate Permanent Subcommittee on Investigations to publicly intimidate and often destroy the reputation of government officials. In committee hearings McCarthy could not be pinned to any specific accusation. When asked to produce a list he claimed secrecy, when challenged on a specific charge he altered his language so that his accusations were moving targets. When challenged to produce one name, in March McCarthy gave the name Owen Lattimore, a college professor of Asian Studies, who McCarthy stated was a 'top Russian agent'. Lattimore was not a public figure, and the charges were not supported by solid evidence. Lattimore's closest tie to communism seemed to be a lack of criticism of either the Soviet or Chinese leadership. Lattimore was to be the last person McCarthy accused by name. The failure of the example of Lattimore did not appear to affect McCarthy, who tied the names of Illinois Governor Adlai Stevenson (Democratic nominee for president in 1952 and 1956), and Secretary of State Dean Acheson to communists, and accused General George C Marshall of losing China. In Senator McCarthy's words the entire Democratic Party was responsible for '20 years of treason' and the Truman administration had through its own weaknesses encouraged communist subversion.

North Korea's invasion of South Korea on 25 June 1950 further justified McCarthy's claims and added to the fear of communist encirclement. When communist Chinese 'volunteers' came to the aid of North Korean forces that winter and overran US troops, the threat from Beijing and Moscow appeared greater, coinciding as this did with relentless charges from McCarthy.

Truman responded to McCarthy, stating that the charges were untrue, and that McCarthy and his followers were the 'greatest asset the Kremlin had'. Truman, however, was not running for re-election. In 1952 several incumbent Democratic senators who had vigorously stood up to McCarthy were defeated at the polls. Few newspapers openly opposed him and most reports accurately detailed his speeches, but few attempted further investigation. This is not surprising in that the kind of investigative journalism made famous by the Woodward and Bernstein exposure of Watergate in *The Washington Post* was foreign to journalism in the 1950s. Haynes Johnson wrote in *The Age of Anxiety: From McCarthyism to terrorism* that part of McCarthy's success came from the maintenance of good relationships with reporters. Johnson credits a number of periodicals and several reporters including Mary McGrory, I F Stone, Drew Pearson, Edward R Murrow, cartoonist Herblock (nee Herbert Lawrence Block), and several others with repeatedly trying 'admirably

to hold him accountable for his falsehoods'. However, that was a small minority of the press. According to Johnson, the failure of the press to hold McCarthy accountable was a major contributor to the damage and longevity of McCarthyism.

McCarthy's campaign began to falter in the Eisenhower era. Anti-communism was an important cause, but a 1954 poll revealed that only 3% of Americans had ever known a single communist. McCarthy's downfall came suddenly. Accusations by the army against McCarthy's assistant Roy Cohn for attempting to get special treatment for fellow assistant David Schine, who was drafted into the army, followed by McCarthy's own counter-charges, resulted in the Army–McCarthy hearings from 22 April to 17 June 1954. The hearings, among the first to be nationally televised, revealed an abusive, rude and evasive Joseph McCarthy to the nation. Many people mimicked his 'point of order' cry with derision. A key moment in the hearings came on 9 June when McCarthy accused a young attorney at the law firm of Special Counsel Joseph Welch of being a communist sympathizer. Welch, who had been hired by the army to represent them in the hearings, responded, 'Until this moment, senator, I think I never gauged your cruelty or recklessness. ... Have you no sense of decency, sir, at long last? Have you left no sense of decency?' Applause filled the hearing room as Welch ignored another McCarthy interruption. It was the beginning of a quick end to Joseph McCarthy. Nearing the close of the hearings, Senator Stuart Symington of Missouri told the Wisconsin Senator, 'The American people have had a look at you for six weeks. You are not fooling anyone'. In September a Senate committee charged with investigating McCarthy's conduct concluded that he was not only 'vulgar', but that his behaviour as Chairman of the Senate Permanent Subcommittee on Investigations was reprehensible and inexcusable. In December, the full Senate voted 67 to 22 to condemn him for abuse of power. McCarthyism lost its star protagonist. After the Senate action, McCarthy's drinking increased and health problems from heavy alcohol consumption eventually developed into acute hepatitis. McCarthy died on 2 May 1957. While the boorish, shrill and shifting tactics of McCarthyism faded when its demagogue was exposed, the government's hunt for subversives continued well into the 1950s.

▲ Senator Joseph McCarthy testifies against the US army during the Army-McCarthy Hearings, Washington DC, June 9, 1954. He is standing in front of a map that allegedly charts communist activity in the USA.

The Lavender Scare and its security implications

When asked who were the traitors dismissed from the US State Department, in February 1950 Undersecretary John Peurifoy answered, 'homosexuals', launching a wholescale search for and persecution of homosexuals in the employ of the US government. In June 1950 the Hoey Subcommittee was charged with investigating the employment of 'sexual deviants' and the report it released in December of that year came to the conclusions that homosexuality had a negative effect on government agencies and that gay men in particular were susceptible to espionage because they were blackmail risks. As a result, Eisenhower issued Executive Order 10450 (May 1953) which did not explicitly target homosexuals but instead allowed the FBI to investigate those whom the FBI felt could be security risks, not just employees whose loyalty was questioned.

For the gay and lesbian community it meant that their sexual orientation was sufficient grounds for dismissal. By 1955, 800 homosexuals had either been removed from their positions or resigned for fear of dismissal even though there was not one known instance of a homosexual participating in espionage due to blackmail. More lost their jobs from the Lavender Scare than the 'Red Scare' that precipitated these actions. In Canada, the **Royal Canadian Mounted Police (RCMP)** undertook a similar initiative, establishing 'anti-queer' squads and intimidating suspects to give names of other homosexuals. The RCMP even attempted to design a chair to detect suspects' responses to various stimuli along the lines of a lie detector test. The most high profile case was that of Canadian ambassador to the Soviet Union John Watkins. While the Soviets had attempted to blackmail him, he had rebuffed them yet he was still detained by the RCMP and died while in its custody.

The effect on gays and lesbians in the USA was far-reaching as the popular culture of the time began to focus heavily on the idea of traditional family values and homosexuality was actively portrayed as an assault on, and threat to, the US way of life. Homosexual communities in the USA reacted by forming a number of organizations that they felt would demonstrate that homosexuals were respectable members of society who contributed as much as others. In doing so, they ousted known communists from their ranks and the **Mattachine Society** even denounced communism. In trying to resist oppression, gay organizations became more conservative and mainstream and with the loss of communist members, the most progressive voices were gone. They also focused more on the middle- and upper-class members of their ranks, alienating working-class, non-white individuals from their organizations. It would take the Stonewall Riots of 1969 for the issue of gay rights to re-emerge in the USA.

Royal Canadian Mounted Police (RCMP)
The RCMP, or Mounties as they are commonly called, serve as a national police force throughout the entire country with the exceptions of Ontario and Quebec.

Mattachine Society
Founded in 1950 it was one of the first groups to advocate for the rights of homosexuals.

Salami tactics
Also called a piecemeal strategy. This is the elimination of opposition by slicing away all of its strengths.

Anti-communism and McCarthyism: an assessment

There are many reasons why people in the USA supported the hunt for subversives and McCarthyism. First, post-war events served to illustrate the strength and aggression of the Soviet Union. **Salami tactics** in Poland, the Berlin Blockade, the exploding of atomic and later thermonuclear bombs, along with the communist victory in the Chinese Civil War and its support for North Korea's invasion of South Korea all contributed to the US public's opinion of communism.

Internal developments, such as the theft of atomic secrets by Klaus Fuchs and the exposure of Julius Rosenberg, also provided reason for fears of subversion. Additionally, the fact that President Truman and Congressman Nixon both used the levers of government to attack communism at home provided a bipartisan affirmation. Politically, McCarthyism proved valuable to Republican attempting to become the majority party after two decades of Democrat control of the White House. Top GOP officials, including Senator Robert Taft and President Eisenhower, maintained public silence about Joseph McCarthy when he attacked democrats. Democrats, for their part, were often timid in opposition. Fears of communism dated back to the second decade of the century and fears of subversion to the beginning of the nation, as demonstrated by Benedict Arnold's defection to the British during the War of Independence. Lastly, there was the charismatic demagogue McCarthy himself. None of these factors alone explain the frenetic nature of the era of McCarthyism. Even when taken as a whole, the relative effects of circumstances and personalities remain difficult to quantify.

Social and cultural impact of the Cold War in the Truman era

The Cold War and anti-communist hysteria of the late 1940s and 1950s created a society in which, according to historian Howard Zinn, 'The whole culture was permeated with anti-Communism.' Still, much of life in the post-war USA centred around suburbia, the quest for material goods, family, and entertainment of every kind. To assume that North Americans thought about the Cold War constantly is to exaggerate its influence, but to a significant extent it did steer many of the cultural elements of the period. Film, television, education, music, literature, theatre and the role of religion both influenced and reflected the anti-communist mood.

The film industry was affected significantly by the blacklisting of writers and actors. Fame and popularity did not deter the HUAC or the State Department: even film great Charlie Chaplin, a British citizen who had worked in the USA for four decades, was refused re-entry into the USA for his alleged sexual immorality and sympathy toward the Popular Front, even though he had never been a member of any communist or associated organization. Many writers could no longer work, or used a front to present scripts. Producers were careful not to present any theme that remotely endorsed communism or even a challenge to the existing social order. Films such as *The Grapes of Wrath* (1940), originally a Steinbeck novel, challenged the principles and main components of capitalism were not made in the USA during the 1950s. Victor Navasky, author of *Naming Names* (1980), observes that social-themed films that were common in the 1930s and early 1940s almost completely disappeared in the initial Cold War period and were replaced by either pure entertainment or anti-communist themes. Evil communists were the antagonists of more than 40 Hollywood films, productions of all but one Hollywood studio, during the late 1940s to the fall of Joseph McCarthy in 1954. Titles included *I Married a Communist* (1949), *I was a Communist for the FBI* (1951), *Invasion, U.S.A.* (1952), and the films *My Son John* (1952), and *Big Jim McLain* (1952). *My Son John* featured a communist son and a mother who exposed him. *Big Jim McLain* starred John Wayne and James Arness, both well-known actors in westerns. In the film, federal agent Jim McLain (John Wayne) hunts down murdering communists and finds romance in Hawaii. The opening scene shows disgust and anger by McLain and his hot-headed partner Mal Baxter as alleged communists refusing to testify are released without punishment. Revealingly, John Wayne expressed particular disdain for the western *High Noon* (1952). The film, scripted by soon-to-be-blacklisted Carl Foreman, features a reluctant sheriff, played by Gary Cooper, who is forced to stand alone against bandits because of the cowardice of the townspeople. Wayne, who in a *Playboy Magazine* interview decades later called the movie 'the most un-American thing I've ever seen,' interpreted *High Noon* as criticism of HUAC's methods and those who cooperated. Films defending the free speech of defenders of leftist political views were few. Instead, Elia Kazan's *On the Waterfront* (1954), a story about mob informers, allegorically defended Kazan for naming names in his HUAC testimony. Taking the opposite point of view, Arthur Miller wrote the play *The Crucible* (1953) as a Broadway theatre production (the theatre was not attacked by HUAC the way Hollywood was and remained mostly free of blacklisting). *The Crucible* addressed the mass hysteria of the Salem witch trials in the 1690s to examine and criticize the anti-communist witch hunts in which people were attacked and their lives ruined for being acquainted with a suspected communist, or refusing to name people. Conversely, confronting the issues of superpower war, films depicting the dangers of nuclear war were also popular and included *The Day the Earth Stood Still* (1951).

Although movies attracted significant attention from government officials, by the end of the 1950s film was no longer the dominant entertainment medium. Movie-goers declined by 50% over the decade. Television was on the rise. The penetration of television grew from under 10% of US households in 1950 to 90% of US households by 1960. According to Stephen J Whitfield, author of *Culture of the Cold War* (1996), television also coincided with the decline of radio listenership and magazine readership. As a trustworthy news source, the public rated television equal to newspapers. Entering US homes at a faster pace than any previous technological device, it was only surpassed by the advent of the personal computer.

In the 1950s television programming was dominated by comedies, variety shows, theatre and dramas and, as the decade wore on, westerns and game shows. The Cold War's influence was not absent from the small screen but its day-to-day appearance was often subtle. Edward R Murrow, famed for his 1954 denunciation of McCarthy, commented: 'Television in the main is being used to distract, delude, amuse and insulate us.' Whitfield argues that the primary motivation for avoiding controversial content was due to the desire of programme sponsors to attract the largest audience possible. Television was at the same time used to promote anti-Soviet passions and support for

ATL Communication skills

Entertainers were targeted in the HUAC hearings of the 1940s and were often pressured to 'name names' of colleagues or friends who were known communists. Why were the arts seen as a potential den for communists? Why would artists of all types be disposed to the idea of communism?

US defence and foreign policy. There were live broadcasts of nuclear explosions. News coverage followed administration policy leaders, but rarely examined their statements for accuracy. Murrow's own public affairs show *See It Now* owed its independence to its reliance on a single sponsor, Alcoa. The Colombia Broadcasting System (CBS) did not support the programme, alerting FBI Director Hoover to its dangers before the famous exposé of Senator McCarthy. Inquisitive television journalists threatened the profits of broadcasting companies and sponsors, and were therefore not encouraged.

In the USA public education has often been viewed as an important way for poorer members of society (usually, the most recent immigrants) to climb the social and economic ladder. The systems have also served to teach all students the norms of citizenship, US history, and the thought-to-be common values of the society. For example, school children around the country recited the Pledge of Allegiance daily. Until 1943, schools had the right to compel students to say the Pledge regardless of religion or citizenship. After the Supreme Court decision, most public schools conducted a daily flag salute, with pressure to participate from fellow classmates and school staff commonplace.

With the threat of Soviet 'godless communism' came an increased effort by some religious groups to emphasize the importance of God in the lives of Americans. In 1954, the Catholic organization the Knights of Columbus lobbied to modify the Pledge of Allegiance to include the words 'under God'. The US Congress passed a law, and with President Eisenhower's signature the Pledge included a government-mandated acknowledgment of a supreme being as protection against the menace of communism.

The federal government did not just concern itself with educating children, but also in educating the general public of the dangers of the atomic age. In 1951 the Federal Civil Defense Administration (FCDA) was created. Its mission was to assure Americans that steps could be taken to survive nuclear war. The agency contracted with private film-makers to create a series of instructional movies, some of which are featured and satirized in *Atomic Café*, a 1982 documentary collection of 1940s and 1950s Cold War government-produced or contracted instructional films. The most famous of the films was *Duck and Cover*, featuring a turtle named Bert. Produced specifically for school children, the nine-minute film taught students across the USA to fall to their knees under their desks and to lower their heads while covering their necks whenever the teacher shouted 'Drop'. Part of the logic for the 'drop drills' was to make students feel that in the event of nuclear war they were not helpless. Survivability was a significant theme for many other FCDA films for all age groups, designed to convert fear into a sense of calm.

Popular music of the 1950s seems to be mostly about romance – failed, flawed or all-consuming, but some pop artists recorded songs directly related to the Cold War or nuclear disaster. Musicians recorded songs such as 'When They Drop the Atomic Bomb', 'I'm Gonna Dig Myself a Hole', 'I'm No Communist','Your Atom Bomb Heart' and 'Guided Missiles', a love song by the group the Cuff Links. Music from country to blues to jazz commented on, and reflected the influence of, the Cold War.

Perhaps the best-known song in this genre was recorded by Bill Haley, one of the first rock 'n' roll artists, famous for 'Rock Around the Clock' and 'See You Later Alligator'. He recorded 'Thirteen Women (and Only One Man in Town)' about his multiple romances and the domestic benefits of being a man surrounded by women, all due to a nuclear war that eliminated all other men. The song was later recorded by Dinah Shore and actress Ann-Margret as 'Thirteen Men', showing the popularity and allure of this theme.

The Cold War had an impact on literature. Modern art was accused of being communist-influenced. The atomic bomb led to what Dr Alan Filreis of the University of Pennsylvania called 'nuclear holocaust literature', beginning with John Hersey's *Hiroshima* (1946) first published in the magazine, *The New Yorker,* and including British author Nevil Shute's *On the Beach* (1957). In the mystery genre, writer Mickey Spillane's hard-bitten detective Mike Hammer bragged in *One Lonely Night* (1951), 'I killed more people tonight than I have fingers on my hands. I shot them in cold blood and enjoyed every minute of it. ... They were Commies'. Novelist Allan Drury published *Advise and Consent* in 1959, a book of political intrigue over a nominee for secretary of state, who is strongly supported by liberals and the intellectual elite. To some critics, the character appeared to be modelled on Alger Hiss, uniting fiction with McCarthyism. Literature that was openly critical of US society and culture was not subject to the same restraints as films or television, leaving avenues of dissent open, but in a time when increasing numbers of people were getting their information from television programmes and sponsors' advertisements, social criticism in book form had limited audience reach.

The culture and society of the late 1940s and 1950s were greatly affected by the Cold War. Society reflected a desire for national unity and fear of communism and nuclear war. The arts, especially film and television, were constrained by the political mood and outright or manipulative governmental pressure of the period. Popular culture, with some exceptions, played to popular themes and did not challenge the prevailing conventional wisdom, as challenges to the establishment were commonly viewed as un-American.

TOK discussion

Choose one piece of US art (visual, musical, cinema, dance, literature) from the 1940s or early 1950s and answer the following questions.

1 Does it reflect rejection or support for Cold War ideology? Why or why not?

2 If it seems neutral, what does that suggest about the arts during the Cold War?

3 Is that any different from the art in previous eras?

4 Is this work still relevant today? Why or why not?

Key questions

→ To what extent was US involvement in the Korean War consistent with the US policy of containment?

→ How did the Korean War affect the US presidency of Harry Truman?

→ What was the impact of the Korean War on the Cold War?

Key concepts

→ Continuity

→ Consequence

On 25 June 1950, 100 000 North Korean soldiers equipped with Soviet battle tanks, artillery and fighter planes crossed the 38th parallel and invaded South Korea, announcing a new phase in the Cold War: proxy wars between the superpowers. This form of indirect warfare in which at least one state was not directly involved would later be repeated in Vietnam, Afghanistan and a dozen other locations throughout the world.

The North Korean objective was to reunite Korea under the communist government of Kim Il-Sung. They planned for a two-month war. The United Nations (UN) declared the invasion illegal and authorized the USA to take command of a UN force and restore the borders. Fifteen UN nations committed their military and the Korean War became the first real test of the UN's concept of collective security. Intended to be a limited war, it would drag on for three years, ravaging the Korean peninsula. During its course the Chinese intervened, the USA contemplated using nuclear weapons and millions of Korean civilians became casualties and refugees. The war would end where it started, with no changes to the borders and the lessons learned would dictate US foreign policy and that of other nations in the Americas until the Cold War ended in 1989.

From civil war to UN police action

Korea is a long peninsula which borders China to the north and Japan to the south-east. The Japanese had occupied Korea since 1910. At the end of the Second World War, after Japan had surrendered in August 1945, the Soviet Union and USA divided Korea at the 38th parallel with the Soviets occupying the north and the USA the southern half of the country. The respective populations numbered 9 million and 21 million. The occupation was assumed to be temporary but by 1947 the USA, eager to withdraw its forces and send its soldiers home, handed the administration of South Korea over to the UN in the hopes of changing the status quo. The Soviets suggested that both powers withdraw and let the Koreans determine their own future but the Americans rejected this solution, concerned about the build-up of Soviet forces in the North. On 14 August 1947 the UN created the United Nations Temporary Commission on Korea (UNTCOK) to oversee withdrawal of occupation forces and to supervise elections that would reunify Korea. The North Koreans denied UNTCOK entry. On 10 May 1948 the UN supervised elections in the South and Syngman Rhee was elected president. In the north the reins of power were firmly held by Soviet-backed leader Kim Il-Sung, who refused to hold elections.

The Soviets played the next move skillfully and announced the withdrawal of their forces from North Korea, forcing the USA to do the same in South Korea. Meanwhile, the Soviets equipped the North Korean army with heavy artillery, tanks and armoured vehicles and provided experienced Soviet instructors and technical advisers. The USA and South Korea were unaware of the build-up: the USA had equipped the South Korean security forces with rifles and small calibre artillery (cannons) and a few armoured vehicles but no tanks, heavy artillery or fighter aircraft. If war came, South Korea would be incapable of defending itself. Both sides claimed they were Korea's legitimate government and North Korean armed incursions into the south became common. UNTCOK warned of a possible civil war.

Kim appealed to Mao Zedong to assist him in reunifying Korea but Mao was reluctant, having just emerged from a lengthy civil war. Kim also approached Stalin who was initially unenthusiastic but changed his mind in the spring of 1950 upon hearing the text of what came to be known as the Pacific Perimeter speech. Secretary of Defense Dean Acheson addressed the Washington Press Club on 12 January 1950 to explain US interests in eastern Asia and listed the countries which the USA was committed to protect. His list did not include Korea and therefore Stalin believed that the USA did not see Korea as part of its sphere of influence. Upon learning this, he counseled Kim to proceed.

The North Koreans crossed the border at 4 a.m. on 25 June 1950. The South Koreans fought bravely but were overwhelmed. Roads became clogged with soldiers and refugees fleeing the communist juggernaut, impeding attempts to move reinforcements north to stop the invasion.

In the USA, President Harry S Truman was determined to respond quickly and was willing to act unilaterally but wanted UN authorization. Truman asked the Security Council to pass a resolution condemning the North Koreans' invasion and giving the US command of the UN military response. On 27 June the UN Security Council passed a resolution that the invasion constituted a 'breach of the peace'. The Soviet delegate was boycotting proceedings in protest of the UN's refusal to grant China's seat to the People's Republic of China instead of to the Nationalist Republic of China, or Taiwan. A Soviet veto would have prevented the resolution from passing. On 8 July Truman appointed General Douglas MacArthur as commander of the UN forces, and 15 other UN nations pledged support.

Truman was determined to limit the war to Korea and prevent it going global for several reasons. First, he wanted to keep the Soviets out and avoid a direct confrontation: the Soviets had successfully tested an A-bomb in August 1949 and the nuclear stand-off made direct

confrontation extremely risky and dangerous. Second, there was a general fear among NATO allies that Korea might be a diversion to distract the USA and allow the Soviets to expand further into Europe. They also saw Korea as another Soviet test of US resolve that was previously seen in Greece and Turkey (1947), Czechoslovakia (1948) and Berlin (1948–49). Finally, Truman had to consider public opinion. Americans had sacrificed much during the Second World War and it was unlikely they would support another major conflict on the other side of the world, yet he had been charged with being soft on communism and was determined to change that perception.

Truman was convinced that the USA and its allies had to fight to contain communism and the regional conflict to the Korean peninsula. He was also sensitive to accusations by the Republican-controlled Congress that he had lost China in 1949 through inaction. To counter these insinuations he decided to take a hard line against the Korean communists, hoping to improve his image and silence his critics. The executive was convinced Stalin was probing the West's defences but this time he had gone too far and Truman was determined that no one would level charges of appeasement against him.

It was a volatile situation. Truman had to act carefully to keep the confidence and support of the citizens of the USA, as well as the UN, while keeping the conflict localized to Korea. His next move was designed to meet all of these objectives: rather than ask Congress for a declaration of war he instead declared the Korean conflict a 'police action' under the aegis of the UN. The tactic worked: the military mobilized, the UN gave the USA command and other countries volunteered their services.

Military developments

Stage 1: Invasion and Inchon – June to September 1950

On 29 June, four days after the invasion started North Korea captured Seoul, South Korea's capital. The South Korean army had been routed and was in headlong retreat to Pusan in the far south of the peninsula. US units arrived from Japan but were unprepared, relatively small in number and too lightly armed to make much difference. The roads were clogged with refugees making reinforcement all but impossible. US air power, however, was able to slow the North Korean advance and by late August the invasion had run out of steam. As more US ground forces arrived, the front stabilized around the port of Pusan called the Pusan Perimeter.

On September 15, in a bold and decisive manoeuvre, General MacArthur decided to circumvent the army that occupied most of the peninsula by sailing up the Sea of Japan. Two divisions (about 25 000 men) were landed at Inchon on the west coast near Seoul and moved inland. At the same time the allied forces broke out of the Pusan Perimeter and began to advance northwards. Faced with being cut off and surrounded, the North Korean army fled, retracing their July victory march, this time in retreat. MacArthur's forces quickly recaptured Seoul and crossed the 38th parallel.

Stage 2: Chinese intervention

The temptation to reunite Korea was balanced against the likelihood of Chinese intervention. Flushed with victory, MacArthur charged into North Korea and captured the capital of Pyongyang. By November the North Korean army was all but finished. In late November, as US and South Korean forces neared the Yalu River (the border between China and Korea), MacArthur received warnings that the Chinese were coming. He scoffed, believing the Chinese would never dare to fight the US army, and if they did he felt his forces were vastly superior and would easily defeat the Chinese. When MacArthur and Truman met in October he told the President that the Chinese threat was overblown and that they did not pose a serious threat. Truman supported his general, not knowing that MacArthur downplayed several brushes with Chinese units.

On 27 November US troops awoke to the sound of bugles announcing the arrival of 300 000 Chinese soldiers. Taken by surprise, the USA suffered one of the worst defeats in its military history. The 1st Marine Division was cut off and barely escaped annihilation, saved by the US and Canadian navies' evacuation at Cochin. Within weeks the Chinese had pushed the UN forces back across the border and recaptured Seoul. Meanwhile, tensions between President Truman and General MacArthur, which had been simmering behind the scenes since the war began, were about to become public.

Stage 3: Stalemate and peace talks

On 20 March 1951 Truman issued a statement that his policy was to continue to fight a limited war and seek a negotiated peace. This seemed wise considering recent Chinese peace feelers. The day after the President's announcement MacArthur publicly stated his opposition to the policy, chastised the Chinese and threatened to use atomic weapons. This was clear and blatant insubordination. Truman met with his chiefs of staff and on 11 April 1951 fired MacArthur, following which the US military's most famous general came home to a hero's welcome. General Matthew Ridgway took command and quickly mounted a counter-offensive that recaptured Seoul (the fourth time it changed hands during the war) and stopped the advance north at the border.

The war became a stalemate: trench warfare like the First World War, stretched across the hills and valleys of the 38th parallel, from coast to coast. Battles became small engagements to straighten the line here and capture a hill there. The focus shifted to the negotiations. Kaesong, the ancient capital of Korea, was the first venue. Talks began on 10 July l951, but broke down in late August when no progress was made. In late October 1951, following bitter fighting in September and October, talks resumed and shifted to Panmunjom, on the border in Gyeonggi Province.

The main point of contention concerned the repatriation of prisoners of war: the Chinese and North Koreans insisted that their men be repatriated. However many of their prisoners of war expressed an unwillingness to return home, and so the UN and South Korean delegations refused to agree to this concession. Negotiations dragged on for another two years; fighting continued amidst a series of ceasefires that broke down.

During the stalemate both the USA and the Soviet Union had changes in leadership. Dwight D Eisenhower was elected President of the USA in November 1952 and in March 1953 Josef Stalin died, leading to a power struggle that kept Communist Party leadership focused on internal affairs and eager to end the Korean conflict.

The final ceasefire was signed on 27 July 1953. A demilitarized zone roughly along the 38th parallel divided the belligerents. Although the fighting stopped, these negotiations continued and in 1954 a permanent armistices was agreed upon without a treaty. Technically, North Korea and South Korea remained at war.

The war lasted three years and two days. The casualties of war included Koreans on both sides of the border, with civilian losses estimated at 2 to 2.5 million. North Korea lost 215 000 soldiers and South Korea lost 137 000. Chinese casualty figures are controversial, depending on the source. Officially the Chinese report about half a million casualties but US sources contend it was over a million. The USA came next with 36 000 battlefield deaths and the UN forces lost 3600 soldiers. The limited war had proved costly, totalling over 3 million lives on all sides.

Truman was heavily criticized for his handling of the war, particularly his firing of MacArthur and inability to negotiate an end to the fighting. The war was the main reason that he decided not to run for a second term. Dwight D Eisenhower came home from his NATO command, accepted the Republican nomination and defeated Adlai Stevenson with the slogan 'I will go to Korea.' He fulfilled this objective in 1953 when he went to Korea and shortly thereafter signed a negotiated settlement. The war ended without a clear victory but with a sense of relief. In the eyes of the USA it was a nasty little war, in a faraway place that cost the lives of too many US soldiers.

Canada and Colombia in the Korean War

Canadian Prime Minister Louis St Laurent cautiously brought Canada into the war. He and his cabinet were determined to support the UN and initially offered a token force of three light cruisers and an airforce transport squadron but no ground forces. Following the Chinese intervention, and pressured by the Defence Minister and Secretary of State, the Prime Minister authorized the recruitment of a special volunteer force comprising an infantry brigade, tanks and artillery. He decided against using existing standby forces, fearing a Soviet move into Europe. Canada eventually sent 27 000 soldiers, sailors and aircrew to Korea, the third largest UN contingent after the USA and the UK. Over 500 Canadians were killed and 1500 wounded.

Colombia also sent roughly 6200 soldiers, many of whom notably participated in the Battle of Pork Chop Hill, the bloodiest battle of the war, from March to July 1953. A regiment of 1000 men fought with the US forces and suffered heavy losses; almost half of the contingent were killed or wounded. Colombia also sent six warships to assist in the amphibious landings. This was the lone Latin American participant in the war; in a sign of hemispheric solidarity, this force was dispatched and the last Colombian troops did not leave the peninsula until 1955.

Political and diplomatic outcomes of the Korean War

Canadian historian David Bercuson contends that to view the war as a futile is incorrect. Korea was the first effort by a communist state to take over a non-communist neighbour. 'In a very real sense, the first real victory of the West in the Cold War was won in the bloody hills of central Korea.' US historian John Gaddis offers a different lesson (2005):

> 'The only decisive outcome of the war was the precedent it set: that there could be a bloody and protracted conflict involving the nations armed with nuclear weapons and they could chose not to use them. The lesson was not lost and Vietnam would be next, only this time the ending would be very different.'

In Canada, the government's response to Korea was to initiate the most massive and costly peacetime rearmament in the nation's history. By the middle of the 1950s, 45% of the annual budget went to defence and Canada's NATO contribution in Europe was 10 000 soldiers, sailors and aircrew – a big commitment for a small nation. The contingent was reduced during the 1970s but Canadians stood on guard in Europe for four decades until the Cold War ended.

For Latin Americans the Korean War signalled an increased sense of marginalization. After the optimism of the 1940s they realized the USA was more interested in containing communism than assisting in economic development and democratization in the region. The era of hemispheric solidarity was entering a new phase as the spirit of egalitarianism among states gave way to US dominance over the region and military assistance to authoritarian regimes that preached anti-communism.

In the USA, the Korean War further strained relations with the Soviet bloc. After Truman, President Eisenhower had continued to support containment, although he worried about the defence budget's rising costs. He supported the French in Vietnam against Ho Chi Minh's Viet Minh forces. He had little choice: since 1945, the USA was becoming increasingly committed to regime protection against communist forces in South Asia, with the commitment to support and supply the nationalist Chinese army of Chiang Kai-shek against Mao's revolutionary army, and later its support to Taiwan. After three bloody years in Korea, the USA remained committed to protecting the fledgling Republic of South Korea, stationing thousands of troops along the 38th parallel. They would not be caught off guard again.

The political consequence of Korea in the USA was a commitment to containment by every US President up to the 1990s. In decades to come, this allegiance restricted the freedom of presidents to consider other policy options and alternatives. This monopoly was supported by US public opinion that expected presidents to be tough administration until the end of the Cold War

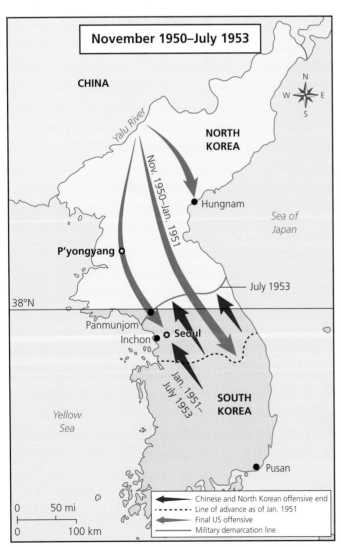

▲ Map of the Korean conflict with changes of fronts, 1950–53

on communism. Vietnam would begin to change all that. In the short term, Korea helped bring an end to 20 years of Democratic control of the White House, paving the way for Eisenhower. Kennedy, a Democrat would take a harder line against communism than Eisenhower's Republican. Johnson would follow Kennedy's lead and the result was the escalation in Vietnam.

▲ Left: Korean civilians fell the fighting, 1950.

Right: US trucks crossing the 38th parallel. The Korean War stopped where it started.

Source skills

The Korean War

Political cartoon of three men in a tub.

The description of this cartoon from the Library of Congress is as follows: The GOP elephant sits in a tub in the sea labeled "Korean War", angrily pointing an accusatory finger at the democratic donkey, who balances "US Foreign Policy". Each blames the other, while John Q Public, caught between them, peers from the wooden tub.

Questions

1 What is the intended message of this cartoon?

2 How does this reflect the outcome of the 1952 presidential election?

Conceptual understanding

Key questions

→ How important were covert operations in US foreign policies under Eisenhower?

→ What were the motivating factors in US foreign policy in the Americas in the 1950s?

Key concepts

→ Change

→ Consequence

After expecting Eisenhower's foreign policies would be dominated by the Korean War, that conflict abruptly, if ambiguously, ended by June 1953. Instead, Eisenhower's administration focused on implementing containment elsewhere and the USA returned to its interest in the Americas. The Arbenz administration in Guatemala was seen as one of the biggest threats; the policies of that democratically elected president were perceived of as socialist and pro-Soviet. It was one among many countries in the region deemed vulnerable to the communist threat in this period. The USA used the skills of the recently created Central Intelligence Agency (CIA) to engage in operations that would undermine those regimes it felt threatened regional stability through socialist policies or communist governments.

The core question that arose repeatedly, especially with regard to the so-called "banana republics" of Central America, is how the Cold War advanced the aims of certain key elites within the USA. For example, it is impossible to address Central America without looking at the debilitating effect that the American-owned United Fruit Company (UFCO) had on the politics, economies and societies in these countries. The Soviet Union argued that it was not containment, but the capitalist interests of US elites that provoked the policies used in the region. In South America the issues were the same, although the USA did not always dominate as completely. In many areas, the wartime policies of the USA had meant that US economic and military dominance replaced the British. In some cases US influence was welcomed by the elites but was increasingly questioned by an emerging intellectual, middle class.

The USA increasingly supported military regimes that were previously considered anathema to US ideals but were now tolerated due to the anti-communist positions taken up by such dictators and the economic interests of American elites. This pattern, which began under Truman, was clearly supported by Eisenhower and in full force until the late 1970s. The emphasis on human rights under President Jimmy Carter brought about some changes, but these changes in policy were not uniform across the region.

The New Look: Characteristics and reasons for the policy

Dwight D Eisenhower won the 1952 election, taking the presidency away from the Democrats for the first time since 1933. As a retired general who had led the invasion at Normandy and took command of NATO forces, and a Republican, it was unlikely that he would be considered soft on communism (a charge consistently levelled at democrats), and with John Foster Dulles as his Secretary of State, the two were formidable anti-communists. Their policies were an extension of the containment policies of Truman but Dulles's virulent diatribes against communism and potential communist threats made the administration seem much harsher in its approach. On the other hand, the USA was facing an economic downturn and Eisenhower was looking for ways to curb US expenditures, especially those overseas. Republican economic policy in the 1950s reflected a free market, laissez-faire (see page 298) approach. In foreign policy, this meant limited economic assistance, including the end of a number of low-interest loans. These policies were specific to the Americas:

- Commodities proposals made during the Truman administration were put on hold, leaving the cacao and coffee producers particularly vulnerable to market fluctuations.

- The creation of an Intra-American Development Bank was halted.

- Latin American states were advised that, in the interest of regional stability and cooperation, they should not discourage private foreign investment (US interests).

The national security policy was called the New Look as it was supposed to reflect a coming change in military orientation. Developed out of **NSC-162/2** (1953), it was a re-evaluation of US military priorities, committing the USA to a smaller army and navy while building up nuclear weapons reserves and expanding the air force which would be required in the event of nuclear strikes. From his position as a military man, Eisenhower viewed nuclear weapons tactically or strategically. Complementing the military shift, Dulles formulated a rhetoric that stated that the USA was on a moral crusade against communism and it would prevent the spread of communism through the use of all force necessary, including nuclear, to combat aggression. This led to the strategy of **brinkmanship**: the idea was that through the threat of massive retaliation, the USA could contain communism by forcing the Soviet (or Chinese) opposition to back down. Brinkmanship led to an increase in the number of nuclear weapons the USA possessed. During the Eisenhower administration, the US stockpile grew from 1200 to 22 229.

Despite his endorsement of this pro-nuclear shift, Eisenhower recognized the danger of nuclear weapons; the USA could not simply stockpile weapons and the Soviet Union would stand idly by – it, too, was increasing its cache of nuclear weapons. Indeed, the quest for new forms of weaponry (hydrogen bombs, missiles in outer space) fuelled a growing defence industry. Eisenhower recognized that technology brought about the idea of Mutual Assured Destruction (MAD), which theorized that massive retaliation from one side would produce the same on the other; this, in turn, led to two US–Soviet summits in 1955 and 1959 to address the threat of nuclear weapons.

NSC-162/2
A National Security Document issued in October 1953 which addressed the Soviet nuclear threat and US determination to maintain nuclear superiority.

brinkmanship
The practice of allowing events to escalate to dangerous levels in the hope that the opposition will back down, fearful of the consequences. During the Cold War this meant pushing events to the edge of direct conflict between the US and USSR.

Yet another way of combating communism was developed in the Eisenhower era: covert operations and the use of the CIA. Born out of the Office of Strategic Services (OSS) from the Second World War, the CIA was created in 1947 as a data-gathering organization to assist policymakers in their decisions. During the Second World War the USA discovered, largely due to its work in South America, that its espionage was not well developed and the OSS floundered. However, its potential was soon recognized by Dulles and Eisenhower; it was an agency that worked mostly overseas, gaining information on those considered enemies of the USA. Headed by Allan Dulles (brother to the Secretary of State), the CIA was soon involved in subversive tactics and paramilitary actions as well as information acquisition. To perform its functions, CIA actions included:

- having foreign leaders on its payroll
- subsidizing anti-communist labour unions, newspapers and political parties overseas
- hiring US journalists and academics to make contact with foreign student leaders
- co-opting business executives who worked overseas to report back on economic circumstances and vulnerabilities
- creating the US Information Agency to spread US culture, including the funding and programming for the Voice of America and Radio Liberty
- funding Radio Free Europe
- training foreign military officers in counter-revolutionary methods
- conducting covert operations to overthrow regimes hostile to the USA.

A core principle of the CIA is that the US President is removed from its decision-making. According to the principle of **plausible deniability**, the President could arrange for certain actions to take place but the links would be so well concealed that he could later deny knowledge of these actions. This allowed Eisenhower (and subsequent presidents) to disavow US involvement in a number of activities conducted to destabilize, overthrow or even assassinate leaders of hostile regimes. The deniability of such actions was reduced over time, but during Eisenhower's tenure he used this to his advantage in places such as Iran and Guatemala.

plausible deniability
The practice of withholding information from government officials to protect them from being implicated in possibly illegal actions.

Application of the New Look and its repercussions in the Americas

Under the New Look policy, defence of the USA was a prime concern and the US military community argued strongly that there needed to be a continental defence policy, not simply a protection of US borders. Canadian politicians were understandably concerned; although they shared US fears of Soviet expansion and understood the destructive potential embedded in massive retaliation, they also feared US encroachment on Canadian territory. Negotiations began in 1953 and finally, in 1958, they reached an agreement, and the North American Aerospace Defense Command (NORAD) was created. NORAD is a binational defence organization that provides advance warning of missile and air attacks on the USA and Canada and protects the sovereignty of airspace in North America. It also maintains an airborne force to be used in the event of attack.

Dulles constantly stated that communism was on the rise in Latin America and that it remained the largest threat to US security. In his nomination hearings he argued that the conditions there were similar to those of China in the 1930s and that if the USA remained non-interventionist, Latin America would meet a similar fate. Added to this was the idea of the **domino theory**. Although formulated to address the fear of communism in South East Asia, the same argument was made for the western hemisphere: if one country fell to communism, others were sure to follow, especially in the Central American countries which were geographically contiguous. Dulles raised suspicions about the governments in Costa Rica and Guatemala. Their governments were democratically elected but their economic and social policies, and the existence of known communists in their governments, alarmed him. The reasons for this are not simply founded in anti-communism; US involvement in the region was also clearly based on its economic interests in Central America.

While Marxist thought in Latin America had a long history among intellectuals, the communist parties that had grown in the 1930s had largely been discredited by the 1950s. Until its dissolution in 1956, the Cominform had directed communist party activities outside of the Soviet Union. As the atrocities of the purges, Five Year Plans and the Soviet army's treatment of civilian populations emerged, these parties were identified as Stalinist and moved to the fringes in most Latin American countries. While socialist ideals were present in many countries, they did not usually appear through a communist party. Nonetheless, links with communism were almost always established.

In reality, many Latin American elites were embracing new models of economic development that more accurately represented their histories and resources. These models did not always complement US ideas of the free market; at the same time that Eisenhower entreated Latin America to keep itself open to foreign investment many countries were adopting **Import Substitution Industrialization (ISI)** as a way to create their own local industries. This was seen as a threat to US economic interests that had dominated the region, especially after the Second World War.

The New Look's focus on minimizing costs was reflected in the support of the military in the Americas and the use of covert operations. To support its ideology and policy decisions, Latin American military men were armed and/or trained by US forces, most notoriously through the Latin American Training Center for US Ground Forces (later known as the Western Hemisphere Institute for Security Cooperation or School of the Americas) based in Panama before relocating to Georgia in 1984. The training centre was a US Department of Defense military academy for Latin American officers to be instructed in the fields of leadership, infantry and counter-insurgency. The New Look's policy was illustrated by US actions in Guatemala in 1954.

US covert operations in Guatemala

The most evident source of the US administration's discontent with Latin American governments was the situation in Guatemala. Guatemala had suffered under the brutal dictatorship of Jorge Ubico until a 1944 coup d'etat ousted him. Like his predecessors, Ubico endorsed pro-US policies and supported the United Fruit Company (UFCO) in its monopoly over banana production. UFCO not only controlled the main crop but also

> **domino theory**
> The idea that if one country in a region became communist the others would inevitably follow suit.

> **Import Substitution Industrialization (ISI)**
> An economic policy which encouraged domestic production of goods that are usually imported to create a favorable balance of trade and stimulate domestic industry.

owned most of the country's infrastructure, including railways, ports and utilities. Ubico was replaced briefly by a military junta until elections were held in December 1944. In 1945 Juan José Arévalo Bermejo became the first democratically elected President of Guatemala, and a new constitution was written that included provisions for land and labour reform. Arévalo was succeeded in 1951 by Jacobo Arbenz Guzmán, a centre-leftist who pledged social and economic reforms for the country. By all accounts, his election was free, fair and devoid of corruption.

In his inaugural speech, Arbenz articulated three objectives for his people: economic independence; the establishment of a modern, capitalist state; and an increased standard of living for the population. He and his followers felt that the key to achieving these objectives was through agrarian reform. To this end, in June 1952, the Arbenz administration enacted the Agrarian Reform Bill (or Decree 900) that allowed the Guatemalan government to expropriate uncultivated lands from large plantations. The landowners would be compensated through 25-year bonds with 3% interest on the value of the land determined by the taxable worth of the land as of May 1952. After June 1952, 1.5 million acres were distributed to 100 000 families; this included 1700 acres owned by Arbenz himself.

Much of the expropriated land was owned by UFCO; 85% of this land was unused. Based on the official tax value of the land, the Guatemalan government offered UFCO $627 572 in compensation. But over the years, UFCO had deliberately undervalued its holdings to avoid paying tax and it now complained to the US government that it was not being compensated fairly for the loss of land. As a counter offer, the US State Department demanded $15 854 849. There was an additional conflict of interest in these negotiations: not only was UFCO a US company, but John Foster Dulles worked for the law firm that represented it and Allan Dulles had been president of the UFCO board.

In this case, the interrelationship of US political and economic interests in the region became very clear. The statements that came out of the State Department clearly charged Arbenz with communism or, at the very least, of not stopping a communist insurgency in the country, yet they were coupled with a demand for more money to go to UFCO for the land expropriated. On the issue of UFCO undervaluing its land the State Department was silent.

Once again, the domino theory was applied; the US position was that, if Arbenz could not be stopped, all of Central America and possibly even the USA itself could fall to communism. In particular, it was argued that the Panama Canal could become Soviet controlled, thereby limiting global free trade. Therefore, it was the duty of the USA to act on behalf of all countries that supported free trade.

Despite such accusations, Arbenz continued with his land reforms and refused to oust the four communists in the legislature (of 56). The USA responded by appealing to the Organization of American States (OAS) for assistance, hoping that the group would act collectively against Guatemalan actions. Although a measure for action against Arbenz was passed it did not allow for direct OAS intervention and the USA could not act under its auspices to force a policy or regime change. In addition, while most Latin American countries subscribed to the Caracas Declaration of March 1954 which rejected Marxism, there was not much force behind such declarations. The US government resorted to both

embargoes and covert operations to oppose Arbenz. The USA refused to sell military equipment to Guatemala, forcing Arbenz, fearful of invasion, to approach Eastern Europe for military support.

The arms shipment from Poland that arrived on 17 May 1954 gave the USA the pretext it needed in support of its claims that Arbenz was communist, and in neighbouring Honduras the USA assisted exiled Colonel Carlos Castillo Armas to lead a group of exiles in an armed insurrection against the Guatemalan government. On 18 June 1954 Castillo and an army of approximately 150 crossed into Guatemala. They were assisted by CIA operatives who provided news reports from the jungles that over-reported the strength of the opposition to Arbenz. At the same time, US pilots strafed the capital, causing minimal physical damage but producing the image of a city under siege. The army refused to support the government, fearing the outbreak of a bloody battle, and Arbenz was forced to resign and go into exile. The US ambassador assisted in the transition of power to Castillo who ruled the country for three years without holding elections. Castillo reversed Decree 900, and his rule was marked by a return to the brutality of dictatorship and the dominance of local and foreign elites.

After successfully overthrowing the Arbenz regime, the situation in Latin America seemed to quieten down and throughout 1957 and 1958 the Dulles brothers argued that the threat of communism had been seriously diminished through US actions in the region. The US State Department policies in the area reflected a diminished fear of communism while crediting and maintaining containment policies. Vice President Richard Nixon's visit to South America in May 1958 would shift the administration's view yet again.

Nixon's visit to South America

In May 1958 Nixon was dispatched to Latin America to congratulate Argentine President Arturo Frondizi on his recent election. Nixon decided to extend his tour throughout Latin America to evaluate the situation for himself and was surprised by the anti-Americanism he encountered in city after city. In most cases, he found himself engaged in debates with students and intellectuals who challenged US dominance in the region, and in general the opposition he encountered was respectful. However, in the cities of Lima and Caracas, he met with angry crowds that threatened to turn violent; in Caracas, he was first stoned and then the crowds attempted to pull him from his car.

The State Department and press portrayed the protestors as angry mobs of communists; their opposition to the USA and its policies towards South America was not communicated to the US public. Nonetheless, upon his return, a shaken Nixon reported to Eisenhower that the USA had to change its policy directions in Latin America. Eisenhower called in a number of experts and, ultimately, it was agreed that to keep the region stable and prevent the Leftists from coming to power the USA needed to endorse and commit to economic aid. Through the Intra-American Development Bank, Eisenhower's administration provided money for social and economic programmes in the region. The problem for the USA was that a downturn in the US economy made it difficult to justify foreign aid when the USA itself was struggling. State Department officials also cautioned that economic aid sent to Latin America would remain in the hands of the oligarchs and dictators, so the implementation of the revised policies was tenuous at best. In the end, the USA committed $500 million to a new programme, rather than the $20–30 billion initially envisaged, and the commitment to economic aid lost momentum when Fidel Castro came to power in 1959.

ATL Communication and research skills

To what extent did the US pursue a consistent policy in Central America?

Chooses a country in Central America other than Guatemala: Panama, Costa Rica, El Salvador, Nicaragua or Honduras. Carry out research on your chosen country in which you determine the form of government and US influence in that government; and the economy of the country and the influence the USA has on it.

Discuss with others who have researched other countries to find similarities and differences in US policies, including those relating to Guatemala.

Produce a Venn diagram of your research and subsequent discussion.

Eisenhower and the Cuban Revolution

On 1 January 1959, with former dictator Fulgencio Batista in exile in the Dominican Republic, Cuba's government shifted decisively to the Left. Fidel Castro and his followers made a victory tour from one side of the island to the other and, upon reaching Havana, Castro made a victory speech that ushered in a new era. He promised free and fair elections once the situation in Cuba had stabilized, and he promised to implement economic and social reforms. The USA viewed the Cuban Revolution with trepidation given Cuba's location, 90 miles from the US border. Castro was clearly pursuing socialist policies and, while he did not initiate nationalization or relations with the Soviet Union immediately, his government had ambitious social policies that the Cuban government could not afford without finding new sources of revenue.

In April 1959 Castro went on a press tour of the USA where he engaged journalists, but Eisenhower refused to meet with him. Instead, he was received by Nixon, a snub that ended any potential collaboration between the two countries. Shortly thereafter, Eisenhower authorized a CIA plan to train Cuban exiles to overthrow Castro's regime. The programme floundered in late 1960 when Vice President Nixon lost the presidential election to John F Kennedy, but the course of Eisenhower and Dulles remained steady throughout; to the end, they used the New Look policies in an attempt to prevent communism from taking root in the Americas.

▲ Left: A man carries a stem of bananas over his shoulder at a United Fruit Company plantation, Tiguisate, Guatemala, 1945

Center: Sign showing the organization of unions anathema to United Fruit Company in Guatemala

Right: Demonstrators attack Vice President Nixon's car on May 13, 1958, in Venezuela

7.4 US involvement in Vietnam

Conceptual understanding

Key questions

→ Why did the USA remain in Vietnam until the 1970s?

→ How did US involvement in Vietnam have an impact on domestic affairs in the USA?

→ To what extent did countries in the Americas oppose US involvement in Vietnam?

Key concept

→ Continuity and change

→ Significance

US involvement in Vietnam can be divided into three stages. The first from 1945 to 1964 was one of assistance, first to France and then to South Vietnam, consistent with the policy of containment. The second stage lasted from 1964 to 1968, under President Lyndon B Johnson, and was a period of escalation in which US military involvement went from 15 000 military advisers to 500 000 soldiers. The final stage, known as Vietnamization, was Richard Nixon's attempt to withdraw from Vietnam and achieve 'peace with honour'. US involvement led to a protracted civil war in Vietnam and profound social changes in the USA itself.

US involvement in Indochina, 1945–64

The war in Indochina began immediately after the Second World War. The French wanted to regain control over the Indochinese peninsula (Vietnam, Laos, Cambodia and Thailand) – their colonies since the 1880s. During the Second World War, the French ceded control to the Japanese. The USA had supplied weapons to Ho Chi Minh, the leader of the tenacious and skilled Viet Minh guerrillas who made life difficult for the Japanese. At the war's end, Ho declared Vietnam independent from France. The French, assisted by the British, sent in a joint military force to re-establish French control.

Truman was initially sympathetic to the Viet Minh and was not supportive of the return of French colonial rule. When resistance to the forces of the Viet Minh proved more difficult than they had expected, the French approached the USA to assist them financially but President Truman refused this first request. By 1947 everything had changed due to Soviet expansion westward into Europe and the development of the policy of containment. In 1949 Mao Zedong's Chinese communist forces defeated the nationalist Chinese, and Asia was seen as just as vulnerable to communism as Europe. In July 1949 the US perception of Vietnam began to change; the USA labelled the Viet Minh a communist regime taking orders from Moscow. Initially, US interest in supporting the French had more to do with securing the situation in Europe than helping to defeat Ho, but that changed in July 1950 at the onset of the Korean War. US soldiers were fighting in the Far East against an aggressive communist regime with the full backing and support of the Soviet Union.

The Truman administration concluded that the situation in Indochina, China and Korea marked a new phase in Soviet expansionism and that nowhere in the world was safe from communism. That same year, Truman gave the French $40 million in economic assistance and military equipment – and so began US involvement in Vietnam. Between 1950 and 1954 the USA gave 2.6 billion dollars to the French accounting for half the total cost of the war. In 1954, the French had sent 400 000 troops into Vietnam but were losing the war. The knockout blow came in the spring of 1954 at the Battle of Dien Bien Phu where 10 000 French troops were surrounded, cut off and captured by the Viet Minh. The French government pleaded with Eisenhower to send US ground forces to save the situation. Eisenhower stood firm against the advice of Vice President Nixon and his military commanders and refused the request. The defeat ended the French regime. The Geneva Conference was convened to restore peace and unify Vietnam.

In April of 1954 President Eisenhower articulated his version of containment for South East Asia. He claimed that if one nation in the region fell, it was only a matter of time until its neighbours were brought under the control of creeping communism. They would fall like dominoes. Eisenhower prophesied that if the Viet Minh won, the remaining countries in South East Asia would be menaced by a greater flanking movement, explaining the domino theory of a communist takeover.

The Geneva Accords were signed in July 1954. South Vietnam and the USA did not sign, but acquiesced to the division of north and south at the 17th parallel. The UN would supervise the terms of the ceasefire; Viet Minh forces below the 17th parallel went north and French forces went south. About 450 000 refugees fled to the south, mainly Roman Catholics who feared a communist government, and about 50 000 refugees crossed into the north. The accords created the independent states of Cambodia and Laos and called for UN-supervised elections in 1956 to form a single government for Vietnam, an election that Ho was certain to win. The USA reluctantly got involved, at this stage covertly. The CIA supported the fledgling government in the south of Ngo Dinh Diem. In 1955 Diem cancelled the elections. Meanwhile eight nations, including the USA, Great Britain, France and Australia, signed the Southeast Asia Treaty Organization (SEATO) that insured collective security of the region against aggression and included specific mention of Cambodia, Laos and South Vietnam.

When the elections were cancelled, Ho's guerrilla units, called the Viet Cong (VC), began infiltrating into the south. Diem became President of South Vietnam (the Republic of Vietnam). The Eisenhower administration continued to support the Diem regime and provided equipment, weapons and 1000 US military soldiers as advisers to arm, train and mentor the Army of the Republic of Vietnam (ARVN). The direct involvement of the US military in Vietnam had begun. By 1957 the Viet Minh began active VC operations in South Vietnam, employing the same tactics they used against the French: controlling the jungle and attacking towns, cities and ARVN military bases then melting back into the jungle. By 1959 the VC had killed 2600 government officials and controlled large portions of the countryside. The US military had little confidence in the ARVN's fighting ability and sent more advisers (about 8000 by the time President Kennedy took office in 1961) without success. The majority of ARVN units were poorly led, badly trained and unmotivated. It was increasingly evident to senior US commanders that without the insertion of US ground forces, the south would lose the war.

President Kennedy's first year in office was a foreign policy nightmare. Despite his guarantee that he would act rather than react to the threat of communism, events undermined his bravado. In 1961 the Bay of Pigs fiasco (see page 46), the building of the Berlin Wall and a reprimand from Soviet leader Khrushchev in Vienna had made him appear weak. He needed to change his approach or lose the support of the US public. In November 1961 he committed more forces to Vietnam and sent Vice President Johnson on a fact-finding mission. The result was US covert involvement in the overthrow and murder of the corrupt, authoritarian leader of the south, Diem, who they had originally supported due to his firm anti-communist stance. From this point on, Kennedy had no other choice but to support the south and start the escalation of US involvement in Vietnam. The course was set. Then Kennedy went to Dallas.

On 22 November 1963, just hours after Kennedy's assassination, Vice President Lyndon Baines Johnson was sworn in as US President. Shrouded under the pall of the Kennedy tragedy, a little-known war in a South East Asian country smaller than Johnson's native Texas was about to take centre stage in a drama that would prove the most divisive event in US history since the civil war and destroy his presidency.

Johnson and escalation, 1964–68

On 2 August 1964 the *USS Maddox*, a US destroyer, was attacked by three North Vietnamese torpedo boats. It was joined by carrier-based aircraft and the three torpedo boats were hit and damaged. On 4 August the *Maddox* was joined by another destroyer and returned to the same area. During the night, the *Maddox* believed it was under attack and fired on radar contacts but never made visual contact. It was likely there was no attack, no North Vietnamese boats in the area, and the radar had malfunctioned and given false contacts. Nonetheless, when President Johnson and his advisers learned of the incident, he was determined to take strong action. He asked Congress to pass a resolution that provided the President with broad powers to assist any member of the Southeast Asia Collective Defense Treaty, namely Vietnam, with whatever support he deemed necessary. The resolution was approved by Congress virtually without debate or dissenting votes. The fateful step had been taken.

Following the Gulf of Tonkin Resolution, the USA went from advising South Vietnam to taking control of the war. Like the war in Korea, it was a limited conflict for the USA. There was no formal declaration of war. The USA made a concerted effort to keep the conflict localized to Vietnam. Johnson asserted that his decision to escalate the war was based on the argument that it was the logical outgrowth of two decades of incremental decisions by his presidential predecessors and it required resolution.

▲ *USS Maddox* was the ship responsible for the Gulf of Tonkin Resolution

Immediately following the Tonkin resolution the military began 'Operation Rolling Thunder', an air campaign to bomb North Vietnam into submission. US bombers flew thousands of missions attacking key North Vietnamese installations, and dropping thousands of tons of bombs. Simultaneously, the USA escalated its land war. The USA employed helicopters to lift ground forces into remote jungle regions and attack enemy strongholds. The Viet Cong countered by attacking US fire bases and ambushing US patrols. US casualties increased and the US public began to question the cost of the war.

Johnson questioned the war as well. He wanted to create a 'Great Society' that would eliminate racism and poverty and had no desire to drag the USA into a war that could undermine his domestic agenda. He hoped to get the USA out of the war quickly to focus on his plans for a better America. He lamented, 'I can't get out, I can't finish with what I've got, so what the hell do I do?'

His own answer was to try to win the war before the 1968 presidential election. He hoped that the air war would force North Vietnam to negotiate before he committed large numbers of ground troops. By June 1965 the air force was flying 3600 bombing missions a month and ground forces were increasing incrementally; by the end of 1966 the number was set at 450 000 soldiers. It was evident that the air campaign would not win the war alone. The White House told the US people they were winning the war and that the sacrifices would soon bring victory but they had to send more ground troops. Johnson was determined to win and refused to be the first US President to lose a war against the communists.

The Tet Offensive of January 1968 proved to be the turning point in the Vietnam War. General Westmoreland had told the US public that North Vietnam's forces were being systematically ground down, and it was unlikely they would be capable of launching major attacks against US forces. The reports were more than propaganda; the north *was* being worn down in a war of attrition and the heavy losses could not be sustained. However, the USA needed a major victory. Johnson's popularity was fragile and the anti-war movement was gaining momentum.

"Tet" is the Vietnamese New Year and the two sides typically observed a temporary ceasefire at that time. During the lull in the fighting, about 85 000 Viet Cong and North Vietnamese soldiers infiltrated the major cities of South Vietnam. On 31 January, the first day of the lunar New Year, they attacked and seized control of important government institutions including the US embassy in Saigon (present day Ho Chi Minh City). It took several weeks of heavy fighting to clear out the attackers. Losses on both sides were heavy and in the end the Tet Offensive was decisively defeated on the battlefield. However, in the living rooms of the USA, the early evening news television

broadcast showed uncensored combat footage of desperate fighting and a determined enemy that did not appear on the verge of defeat. Westmoreland asked for another 200 000 soldiers to end the war once and for all. Middle America, the heartland of the USA that had opposed the anti-war movement and staunchly supported the President, now began to question US involvement.

The Tet Offensive was a huge gamble for the North Vietnamese that turned the tide of the war, but not due to the military outcome of the battle. General Vo Nguyen Giap, Supreme Commander of the North Vietnamese army, said, 'The war was fought on many fronts. At that time [Tet] the most important one was American public opinion.' The USA had established a number of large military installations called fire bases in remote jungle locations close to the North Vietnamese supply routes. Khe Sanh was one such base in Quang Tri province, near the Laotian border, garrisoned by 6000 US marines and ARVN soldiers. During the Tet Offensive, the base was surrounded and besieged by approximately 15 000–20 000 North Vietnamese soldiers for 77 days. The US military feared another Dien Bien Phu but Khe Sanh was supplied from the air and a relief column eventually broke through to relieve the embattled marines and the siege ended. The garrison suffered about 4400 casualties, and the North Vietnamese casualties were estimated at double that number.

In reality, the Tet Offensive was a success for the US military and the North Vietnamese army was significantly weakened by its assault. It would never regain its former power, but in the end this proved less important than the propaganda that resulted from the offensive in the USA. Rather than focusing on the speed with which the USA and ARVN re-established control, the US public saw the losses – television cameras made them witness to emotionally charged but ultimately short-lived Vietnamese successes. While it was true that the US embassy was taken, it was re-secured by the US military less than eight hours later. However, back in the USA, people wondered how a guerrilla army that was on the verge of collapse could mount a siege of such magnitude and nearly overrun a major US military installation such as Khe Sanh.

On 31 March 1968 President Johnson went on national television and announced he would not run for a second term. He had achieved considerable milestones, notably the passage of civil rights legislation, but the escalation of the war had short-changed his domestic ambitions gobbling up a quarter of every tax dollar spent on the Great Society programmes. Johnson had tried and failed to fight a war on two fronts. He did, however, suspend the bombing campaign which opened the door to negotiations. Republican candidate Richard Nixon won the November 1968 election, promising to restore order on the streets, listen to the silent majority and bring peace with honour and an end to the war.

▲ Troops fighting during the Tet Offensive

Nixon and Vietnamization, 1969–75

Nixon's policy to turn the war over to the South Vietnamese army was called Vietnamization. To concurrently increase the ARVN's role in the war and gradually withdraw US ground forces, he sent his chief adviser Henry Kissinger to negotiate a peace treaty that would recognize a permanent division between North Vietnam and South Vietnam. Nixon visited communist China and supported China's admission to the UN. He also negotiated an arms control treaty with the Soviets. As with the situation in Korea, the talks dragged on and the USA escalated the war when that happened. The heaviest bombing raids of the war, including the capital of Hanoi and the mining of Haiphong harbour to stop shipping, leveraged the North Vietnamese back to the table. In 1970 President Nixon authorized secret operations sending ground forces and bombing raids to disrupt North Vietnamese supply routes (the Ho Chi Minh trail) in Cambodia and Laos. These tactics worked and North Vietnam came back to the negotiation table. Troop withdrawals took place between 1969 and 1972. The last US bombing raid was in August 1972, the Paris Peace Accords were signed in January 1973 and the war was over for the USA. Nixon had been re-elected to a second term in November 1972 hoping to pursue a domestic agenda once the war ended but the Watergate scandal erupted and ended in his resignation on 4 August 1974.

After a brief pause, the fighting began again in 1975. In early March the North Vietnamese began a full scale invasion of South Vietnam. ARVN forces fought bravely at first, but then collapsed and Saigon was captured on 30 April. Vietnam had been reunited under the Hanoi government 20 years after the Geneva Accords had split the country.

Social effects of the Vietnam War on the US public

The 1960s was a chaotic decade in the USA. The rise of the middle class, the civil rights movement, the women's movement, government initiatives in social reform and a baby boomer generation announced a changing political climate.

The war accelerated some of these changes but more than that, it made the USA reconsider its global image and status. By 1968, the US consensus regarding the containment of communism was weakening and support for the Vietnam War in particular was crumbling. A counter-culture had emerged that challenged the status quo and demanded social and political reform. The youth movement took their disquiet to the streets and protests, sit-ins and music festivals became the gatherings that defined this new generation. Universities became centres for dissent. Young men burned their draft cards, and as many as 60 000 draft dodgers went to Canada. Muhammad Ali, the heavyweight boxing champion and Olympic gold medalist declared himself a conscientious objector and was jailed. He became a martyr for the anti-war movement and symbolized injustice for millions of young people who opposed the war, also drawing attention to the high proportion of African Americans who were drafted. Then, to make matters worse, the two men who had captured the imagination of young Americans of all races and promised a brighter future were assassinated: on 4 April Martin Luther King and, a few months later, presidential candidate Robert Kennedy.

The 1968 Democratic National Convention in Chicago turned into a pitched battle between the police and anti-war protestors. Television coverage showed policemen beating young people with batons. There were thousands of marches, sit-ins and rallies across the country. Nevertheless, a significant majority of middle- and working-class Americans considered the youth movement an aberration. They did not like hippies, loud music and tie-dyed clothing. Middle class Americans paid their taxes, voted in elections and supported President Johnson and the war.

The CBS newsreader Walter Cronkite was Middle class America incarnate, always ending his early evening news programme with the statement, 'And that's the way it is'. So, when he voiced criticism of the war, in an uncharacteristic departure from his standard objective non-partisan role as newsreader, his comments rocked the nation. Cronkite had been in Vietnam during the Tet Offensive and on 27 February 1968 he hosted a television documentary on the war, closing with the words:

> 'It seems now more certain than ever that the bloody experience of Vietnam is to end in a stalemate. ... But it is increasingly clear to this reporter that the only rational way out then will be to negotiate, not as victors, but as honorable people who lived up to their pledge to defend democracy, and did the best they could.'

Cronkite's disenchantment with the war, made public that February night, was a turning point further galvanizing US public opinion against the war. When President Johnson heard Cronkite's comment he lamented, 'That's it. If I've lost Cronkite, I've lost middle America'.

The situation worsened for Johnson. On 16 March 1968, a company of US soldiers deliberately massacred 350–400 villagers in the tiny hamlet of My Lai. The military tried to cover it up, but one of the soldiers went to the press. How could this happen? Who was to blame? In the USA the belief was that the US military did not murder unarmed civilians. The reputation of the US army was in tatters. The company commander Lieutenant William Calley and several of his men were charged and faced court martial but the stain of the massacre was permanent. My Lai provided fresh fodder for the anti-war movement. In October and November hundreds of thousands of protestors gathered in Washington to demand an end to the war, reminiscent of the freedom march of 1963. The rallies were coordinated with similar events across the country. Some radicals called for a general strike. Nixon vowed not to be swayed by the protests.

A more radical movement emerged, the most important group being the Weathermen whose slogan was 'You don't need a weatherman to tell you which way the wind is blowing'. In October 1969 the group launched a campaign against US imperialism and advocated mass violence. The call for violence was unpopular and did not reflect the growing anti-establishment mantra of the youth counter-culture.

▲ Walter Cronkite in Vietnam during the Tet Offensive

Kent State

On 30 April 1970 President Nixon announced the invasion and bombings of Cambodia by US forces. Nixon had been previously

▲ Kent State shooting, May 4, 1970. Mary Ann Vecchio kneeling over Jeffry Miller. John Filo, a student, took the picture.

quoted as saying that he would never consider this course of action. Kent State University in Ohio had been a hotbed of student protest during the war. On the heels of Nixon's announcement the students began four days of protest, starting on 1 May. During the first three days some property was vandalized and a handful of protesters were arrested. A rally was planned for 4 May which university officials tried to cancel. The Ohio National Guard was on campus to keep the peace. About 2000 protestors gathered and taunted the guardsmen but were dispersed with tear gas. The crowd reformed and a company of guardsmen wearing tear gas masks and with fixed bayonets advanced on the crowd in a line. Without warning, and for reasons still not known, they then opened fire. Out of 77 soldiers, 29 fired 67 rounds at the students. Nine students were wounded and four were killed. The country was thrown into a state of civil unrest. Five days after the shooting over 100 000 protestors descended on Washington.

A student strike closed over 900 university campuses. Then on 14 May two students were killed by police at Jackson State University (Mississippi) under similar circumstances. Nixon blamed communist radicals inciting the students, but his comments sounded hollow.

New York Mayor John Lindsay denounced Nixon and claimed the country was on the edge of a spiritual and physical breakdown. Nixon responded by organizing a pro-war march by New York construction workers. His defensive attitude only added fuel to the anti-war movement and criticism of the government. No guardsmen were ever convicted for the shootings. Two weeks after the Kent State shooting, songwriter Neil Young's hit song 'Ohio' hit the air waves and captured the mood of the times. The real enemy to freedom was the President.

Conclusion

Between 7 August 1964 (Gulf of Tonkin Resolution) and 29 March 1973, when the last troops pulled out, over 2 million Americans served in Vietnam: more than 58 000 US citizens had lost their lives and 153 000 were wounded including 5000 amputees. Over 500 000 had resisted the draft. The effect of the war on the USA was divisive. The country's belief in itself as the protector of freedom and democracy was shattered. No longer was the nation the unquestioned leader of the free world. After the war, the US people tried to make sense of it but the nation was bitterly divided to find meaning. Historians have struggled to determine the war's legacy and a historical consensus has yet to emerge on that critical question.

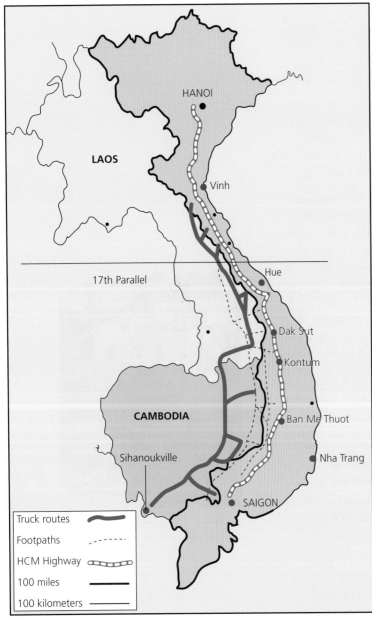

HANOI

LAOS

Vinh

17th Parallel

Hue

Dak Sut

Kontum

CAMBODIA

Ban Me Thuot

Sihanoukville

Nha Trang

SAIGON

Truck routes	
Footpaths	
HCM Highway	
100 miles	
100 kilometres	

▲ Map of Indochina/Vietnam War

Canada's opposition to the Vietnam War

Canada's position regarding Vietnam is more complicated than is often portrayed. In the first Indochina War Canada supported France, providing modest assistance, and after the Battle of Dien Bien Phu Canadians participated in the Geneva peace talks that created the new borders. In line with its position as a middle power with a developing military, Canada was one of a group of countries responsible for implementing the accords as part of the International Commission for Supervision and Control of Vietnam – later called the ICSC. With Indian and Polish troops, Canadian forces remained in Indochina to report on any ceasefire violations.

Its position on the ICSC gave Canada an official pretext to remain neutral when the Vietnam War began but its actions were often contradictory. Canadian members of the ICSC often cooperated with the USA and even provided intelligence information to the US military stationed in Vietnam, and at the start of the war most Canadians supported the US position as the North Vietnamese were seen as clear aggressors. The Canadian government provided humanitarian assistance to South Vietnam through the Red Cross but remained steadfastly neutral, developing new prerequisites for engaging in war or joining new alliances. These were as follows:

- There were to be no dedicated military alliances – there had to be economic and social components.

- Canadian initiatives had to be supported by the people in the countries involved.

- Other countries in the region had to support the actions, either directly or in principle.

- Canada would not be involved in re-establishing colonialism in any form.

- Any multilateral action had to conform to the UN Charter.

These guidelines guaranteed that Canada would not be involved in Indochina.

As the war progressed the Canadian public was increasingly anti-war and protests against US actions in Vietnam took place throughout Canada. In April 1965, on a visit to the USA, Prime Minister Pearson gave a speech at a US university which began with him saying, 'The government and great majority of people of my country have supported wholeheartedly the US peacekeeping and peacemaking policies in Vietnam' but ended with a call for the USA to cease its bombing campaign of North Vietnam. An infuriated President Johnson summoned Pearson to a private meeting and it was later reported, perhaps apocryphally, that Johnson grabbed Pearson and chastised him for criticizing US policy on US soil. Pearson later said that they parted amicably, and relations between Canada and the USA actually improved under Pearson.

However, Canada supported the US anti-war movement through its acceptance of US draft dodgers and deserters. In 1969 the Canadian government announced that it would no longer ask men about their military status as they entered the country. This attitude and proximity to the USA made Canada the main destination for those seeking to avoid military service in Vietnam. US citizens were the largest contingent of immigrants to Canada during the Vietnam War era as an estimated 40 000 men moved to Canada to avoid serving in the US military.

At the same time that there was general protest against the Vietnam War, there were some Canadians quietly in favour of US actions. The Canadian government's official designation as non-belligerent meant that Canada agreed it would not trade in war materials with either side, but Canadian companies continued to supply the US military. Some of this trade could be considered beyond the scope of war materials – food and boots are usually cited – but also included Napalm and **Agent Orange**, both of which were tested in Canada during the war, and raw materials such as lead and copper. And as US men crossed the border to avoid fighting in Vietnam, approximately 30 000 Canadians volunteered for the US army in the Vietnam War era.

Canadians were relieved when the war drew to a close and willingly accepted refugees from the wars in Indochina. These 'boat people' led to a spike in the South East Asian population in Canada, especially in Vancouver, Toronto and Montreal in the 1970s. Canada's position in the Vietnam War is seen as critical in the development of the Canadian national identity and came during a time when the nature of identity was being questioned and reformulated.

Agent Orange
A chemical that removes the leaves from plants, first used by the US in the Vietnam War.

Source skills

US involvement in Vietnam

The image below shows an American cartoonist's perspective on the meeting between US President Johnson and Canadian Prime Minister Pearson after the latter's criticism of US involvement in Vietnam at Drexel University in Philadelphia.

Questions

1   What is the intended message of this cartoon?

2   Do you think that the cartoon was published in a newspaper in Canada or the USA? Why?

Latin American views of the war

There is no one view of the Vietnam War in Latin America. On the far left, Castro and the Cuban government supported the North Vietnamese and there are even reports that Cubans participated in the interrogation and torture of US soldiers in Vietnam. On the far right, the authoritarian regimes that were supported by the USA took the US line of anti-communism. However, most Latin Americans endorsed a middle position that at times supported South Vietnam's right to be defended from northern aggression and at other times opposed US actions.

As in the USA and Canada there was a protest movement led largely by university students. In the case of Latin America the students identified with both the communist and anti-US (or more broadly, anti-imperialist) aims of the North Vietnamese. This was especially true in Mexico where students went so far as to establish pro-Viet Cong societies, and in the most extreme case the Costa Rican government reported that students there actually travelled to Vietnam to join the North Vietnamese army.

As the war drew to a close in the 1970s these movements died down and the students turned their attention to other actions of US domination, focusing mostly on the region. The message they took from the Vietnam War was that armed insurgency could be successful against the USA. Not surprisingly, revolutionary movements that supported socialist or leftist ideals gained support and momentum in the 1970s.

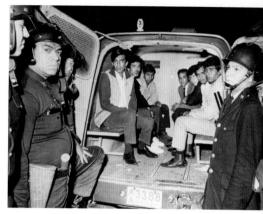
▲ Captured student rioters in a police van in Mexico City, 1968

TOK discussion

Historian Douglas Brinkley concurs with the common perception of Walter Cronkite's commentary on Vietnam when he writes that the anchorman's report of 27 February 1968 was 'immediately seen as a catalyst by pundits in the Monday newspapers… Cronkite turned dove, and the hawk Johnson lost his talons'.

In the 1960s the role of anchorman in the USA was intended to report the news. Walter Cronkite was considered one of the most respectable newsmen in the USA at the time.

By giving his opinion that the war in Vietnam could not be won, was Cronkite acting in a principled or ethical manner?

Write an outline to this question as follows:

1 Respond to the question.

2 Present the evidence for a position.

3 Present a counterclaim which also has support, but then explain why it is flawed.

4 Give your explicit answer to the question.

The characteristics of and reasons for policies; implications for the region

> ## Conceptual understanding
>
> ### Key questions
>
> → Why did the Alliance for Progress fail?
>
> → What is the significance of the Cuban Missile Crisis?
>
> → Why did the USA intervene in Chile in the 1970s?
>
> → How did Carter's policies in the region differ from his predecessors?
>
> ### Key concepts
>
> → Continuity and change
>
> → Significance

Kennedy's administration

John F Kennedy served as US President for less than three years but his foreign policy legacy was immense. In Vietnam, he began the escalation of US troop involvement; in Berlin, he defused a looming crisis over the sovereignty of West Berlin. His administration is best known for the resolution of the Cuban Missile Crisis though: 13 days of intense negotiation and ultimatums designed to end a stand-off between the USA and the Soviet Union that, it is argued, brought the world to the brink of nuclear war.

Although the Missile Crisis dominates his administration's political legacy, Kennedy was determined to change the world view of other countries through a series of programmes to assist them in economic and social change rather than through military intimidation or direct assistance to military regimes. For the Americas he created the Alliance for Progress, a programme that aimed for the same political stability as other Cold War policies but attempted to achieve it through assistance rather than coercion. Nonetheless, Kennedy's foreign policy concentrated on the US–Soviet rivalry and his presidency was marked by the arrival of a strong Soviet presence in the region.

When Kennedy assumed the presidency in January 1961 he reiterated the US commitment to contain communism that had marked the Truman and Eisenhower administrations before him. He clearly stated his intention to expand upon both containment and the New Look. Addressing the former, and arguably restating the Monroe Doctrine, the Kennedy Doctrine warned the Soviet Union to stay out of the Americas and pledged to reverse any Soviet incursions into the region that had already occurred. Due to Castro's ascension in 1959 a key focus of his policy in the Americas would be based on ousting Soviet influence from Cuba.

The New Look and its core concept of massive retaliation was transformed into the idea of flexible response. This policy did not preclude nuclear war as an option but considered it the choice of last resort. Other options included: negotiation with the Soviets; economic assistance to developing nations; continuation of covert operations; and expansion of conventional forces. These policies were articulated in the inaugural address he delivered on 20 January 1961. In this speech he laid out his global objectives but also those specific to the region. The Kennedy Doctrine showed US commitment to the Americas even before the events of the early 1960s revealed the necessity of a specific policy towards the rest of the region.

The Alliance for Progress

Both Nixon's trip to Latin American in 1958 and Castro's success in Cuba showed the previous administration that there was a need to change US policies in the region. It was left to Kennedy, however, to implement such changes. Returning to the Act of Bogotá, Kennedy fulfilled a pledge to distribute $500 million in assistance to Latin American countries and established a 10-year plan that had 6 objectives:

- increase per capita income
- diversify trade
- industrialize and increase employment
- bring about price stability
- eliminate adult illiteracy
- bring about social reform.

Kennedy argued that only through prosperity in the region would there be stability, and these two conditions would eliminate the appeal of Marxism and nurture democracy. Participating countries had to develop plans that included redistributive reforms: in most Latin American countries, 5–10% of the population controlled 70–80% of the land. He recognized that US economic assistance was very limited and could do little to change the situation, nor would a short-term fix be possible. The USA – and its Latin American partners – would have to commit to a long-term programme for there to be success.

Prior administrations had contributed very little to the economic development of Latin America. Truman had only allocated 3% of US foreign aid, and while Eisenhower increased that amount to 9% there was some question as to how it was allocated. For his part, Kennedy (and Johnson after him) increased assistance to Latin America to 18% of all US overseas aid; this amounted to $22.3 billion throughout the 1960s. Ultimately, however, the Alliance for Progress failed. Despite its ambitions, all of that money only amounted to $10 per person per year in the affected countries. Furthermore, planning and allocation of funds was based on a system with a strong middle class, and the reality was that the middle classes in the countries in question were relatively small and tended to support dictatorships rather than progressive ideas. Latin America began the 1960s with a very limited democratic base that only got smaller throughout the decade.

In Kennedy's last year as president there were six coups in Latin America, forcing him to soften his stance towards dictatorships in the region. Rather than supporting democracies, the change of course supported dictatorships to try to bring about change. Unfortunately, this often strengthened and perpetuated these regimes and the economic development monies rarely reached their intended recipients. By the end of the decade dictatorships prevailed in the region, and while these may have assuaged US fears of Marxist regimes they did little to end the discontent that most Latin Americans experienced.

Cuba: The Bay of Pigs and the Missile Crisis

Of all countries in the region, Cuba consumed the most of President Kennedy's time. From Eisenhower he inherited an unresolved situation in the Caribbean: Cuban exiles were being trained to overthrow the regime of Castro. Kennedy's decision-making led to a foreign policy debacle that had farther-reaching consequences than anyone could have imagined. During the 1960 election campaign, Kennedy took a hard stance against Castro and accused the Eisenhower government of not doing enough to combat Castro. He promised Cuban exiles in the USA that he would take every opportunity to combat communism in the region and restore Cuba as a democracy.

Kennedy was ambivalent about the CIA-directed plan that had been created by Eisenhower and Dulles. According to the plan, the exiles would launch an amphibious invasion of Cuba that would lead to an uprising on the island as it was assumed that many Cubans rejected Castro's rule. With US air support, the exiles would take a beach head, and a government-in-arms would ask for further assistance from the USA. The USA would recognize this government and assist it in stabilizing the country and overthrowing Castro.

The plan relied on stealth, a bit of luck and the support of the Cuban population. The exiles had been planning the invasion for over a year, and it is estimated that the US government spent close to $5 million on the project. However, intelligence gathered by the CIA revealed that, despite the propaganda levelled against the Castro regime, most Cubans would not support an armed insurrection. The exiles were largely hated enemies of the Cubans who remained and it was foolhardy to expect them to support the return of those who had exploited the previous system.

Kennedy himself was unsure how to proceed. He promised to be hard on communism and to support the exiles yet the plan was highly flawed. A State Department memo argued for the cancellation of the invasion on legal grounds, stating that such an action would violate US commitments to the Organization of American States (OAS) and the obligations incurred by signing the Act of Bogotá. Congressmen further argued that this was an immoral action that exaggerated Castro's threat to the region and was an invitation for Soviet actions. At a press conference on 12 April 1961 Kennedy said, 'I want to say that there will not be, under any conditions, an intervention in Cuba by the United States Armed Forces. This government will do everything it possibly can … I think it can meet its responsibilities, to make sure that there are no Americans involved in any actions inside Cuba … The basic issue in Cuba is not one between the United States and Cuba. It is between the Cubans themselves.'

Despite the internal debates on the morality and legality of US support for an invasion, the Bay of Pigs invasion took place on 17 April. This action was a disaster; at the last moment, Kennedy decided that the USA would not provide air support to the invading force, leaving them vulnerable to the Cuban air force, and the exiles lacked supplies. This resulted in the death of 200 rebel forces and a further 1197 were captured by the Cuban army. The Cuban people did not rise. For the USA it was a public relations disaster. US involvement was not covert and thus the administration was guilty not only of violating international law, but also of failing in its attempted coup. Castro, for his part, claimed the success of his revolution over the US operation. However, Castro was also shaken by the attempt and went so far as to request assistance from the Soviets in the defence of Cuba. This, in turn, led to the Cuban Missile Crisis.

In the summer of 1962, US intelligence began to report heavy Soviet activity in and around the island of Cuba. CIA agents in Cuba dispatched reports of Soviet trucks hauling machinery into the countryside and U-2 spy planes photographed images of cruise-missile launch sites. On the strength of these reports, the USA stepped up surveillance and Kennedy warned both the Cubans and the Soviets in speeches that the USA would defend itself and its neighbours from hostile attacks.

On 16 October 1962 President Kennedy was informed that a U-2 spy plane had taken photographs of medium-range ballistic missile sites in Cuba. For nearly a week Kennedy deliberated with his advisers on possible courses of actions before making any concrete decisions. On 22 October Kennedy gave a televised address to the US public informing them of the installations and announced that a quarantine was placed on Cuba and that any violation of the quarantine would be seen as a hostile action that would force the USA to retaliate. On the following day the OAS approved the quarantine. This reified the policy of brinkmanship in an instant, and the ideas of massive retaliation and Mutual Assured Destruction became potential realities. At the same time, the Soviets dispatched a ship heading to Cuba; the USA would consider this an act of war. Subsequent negotiations and compromises, however, resulted in Khrushchev ordering the ship to turn around, and the crisis was averted. The Soviets agreed to dismantle and remove the weapons under UN supervision. For his part, Kennedy promised that the USA would not try another invasion on Cuba; it also secretly agreed to dismantle and remove nuclear weapons it had in Turkey.

The implications for the Cold War were immense as many citizens were confronted with the possibility of nuclear war. While Castro was left out of much of the decision-making process, his regime remained unharmed and able to develop. In the future, Cuba would become a centre for revolutionary and guerrilla activity in the region and around the globe. This did not end US activities in Cuba; the USA continued its boycott on Cuban goods, not allowing trade or travel with Cuba. Additionally, it kept its embassy closed although there were unofficial US advisers in Cuba. Covert operations also continued. It was later revealed that the CIA had made several failed assassination attempts on Castro that have passed into legend: exploding cigars and poison-infused shaving cream were two reported methods used to try to kill Castro.

US relations with Cuba during Kennedy's administration show how many aspects of the flexible response policy were used, and the commitment to the Kennedy Doctrine that was articulated so early in his presidency.

▲ President and Mrs Kennedy visited Colombia in December 1961. Here they visit the dedication of a housing project to be built using Alliance for Progress funds.

MEDIUM RANGE BALLISTIC MISSILE BASE IN CUBA
SAN CRISTOBAL

LAUNCH POSITION
MISSILE-READY TENTS
MISSILE ERECTORS
LATE OCTOBER

▲ A US spy photo taken in October, 1962, of a medium-range ballistic missile base in San Cristobal, Cuba

Kennedy's covert operations in Guyana

British Guiana, which became the independent country of Guyana in 1966, was one of the first targets of US covert operations. This was a multiracial, multicultural colonial possession that was important due to its geographical location and possession of bauxite mines. Cheddi Jagan, the son of Indian immigrants, emerged as the leader of the People's Progressive Party (PPP) and was elected Chief Minister of the colony in 1953 in elections overseen by the British government. Both the UK and the USA identified Jagan as a Marxist, but the UK was in a better position to remove him from power. The UK government suspended constitutional rule and after 133 days in power, Jagan was ousted and the colony was once again occupied by the British.

When elections were held in 1961 Jagan was once again elected Chief Minister and this time it was the USA that tried to remove him from power. During the Kennedy administration the CIA chose several tactics – including the use of US labour unions that trained Guyanese labour unions. A key CIA operative who was also an AFL-CIO officer was involved in organizing anti-Jagan strikes and advocated the use of violent protest. Guyana was racially divided and US labour took advantage of this by supporting the largely Afro-Caribbean People's National Congress against the PPP. These were so successful that Jagan lost much of his support, and when Guyana became independent in 1966 it was governed by the dictatorial regime of Forbes Burnham for 20 years, a regime that received support from the US government on the strength of its anti-communism.

The undermining of the Jagan regime was seen as a CIA success that was similar to the overthrow of Arbenz in Guatemala and allowed the CIA to regain some of its confidence after the botched Bay of Pigs disaster. The Kennedy administration pursued the policies not for economic gain (as in Guatemala) but due to fear of the spread of communism in the Caribbean.

The Johnson administration: The continuation of Kennedy's policies in the Americas

If the Cuban Missile Crisis was emblematic of Kennedy's presidency, President Lyndon Johnson's legacy was Vietnam. Assuming the presidency because of Kennedy's assassination, Johnson maintained his commitment to Kennedy's policies until he could run for election himself. In the Americas, then, he was committed to continuing the Alliance for Progress and containing and eliminating communism. To assist him in Latin America, he enlisted an old friend from Texas, Thomas Mann, who had been the key adviser to Eisenhower in his regional policies. Mann was named Alliance for Progress administrator and Assistant Secretary of State for Inter-American affairs, and he developed a new line in regional affairs. The Mann Doctrine, revealed in March 1964, attempted to resolve the conflicting US interests in the region. It stated that US policies towards Latin American and the Caribbean should focus on: economic growth with a neutral stance towards social reform; protection of US private investments; opposition to communism; and non-intervention. It also affirmed that the USA should have no moral reservations about cooperating with military generals to achieve its policy goals; there should be no preference for democratic states or institutions. The Mann Doctrine promoted stability over democracy and protected US private investments in the region. Few distinctions were made between anti-US politicians and groups and pro-communist forces.

In April 1964 the USA had the first opportunity to implement this new course. The Brazilian President João Goulart was overthrown in a coup that installed a military dictatorship. The USA offered assistance to the regime in the form of $1.5 billion in economic and military assistance (25% of all money that went to Latin America) and, in return, Brazil adopted a pro-US, anti-communist policy.

Taking the policies even further, in spring 1965 the USA sent 22 000 troops to the Dominican Republic to maintain the pro-US government there. Johnson and Mann also went on to give support to Duvalier (Haiti), Somoza (Nicaragua), Stroessner (Paraguay) and numerous other dictatorships that were anti-communist, despite being led by brutal dictators.

The war in Vietnam was taking a substantial toll on Alliance for Progress assistance. As US military commitments in South East Asia grew, there was a need to cut funding elsewhere. As a result, Johnson cut funds for economic assistance – but not military assistance. Even where economic assistance continued, the money rarely reached its intended destination.

El Salvador and Nicaragua

El Salvador was dominated by dictatorships that early on recognized the value of claiming anti-communism. When a group of moderate officers tried to take power in 1960, the USA withheld recognition and forced the junta's collapse. It was subsequently replaced by a right-wing regime. Upon reviewing Alliance for Progress statistics, El Salvador seemed to be a model of success: it had high growth rates and its exports increased, however, alliance monies were usually diverted to the landowning oligarchy, and the peasants who were supposed to benefit from the economic assistance remained impoverished and uneducated. The food grown in the country was exported, rather than used for feeding the hunger-stricken peasants. Resistance to the regime was growing, although the CIA reported that there were few revolutionary threats to the regime.

In Nicaragua, the Somoza family ruled the country from 1937. When the patriarch Anastasio Somoza was assassinated in 1956, his sons assumed control over the country. They had the support of US Presidents, including Lyndon Johnson, and they seemed to have undisputed control over the country, a situation that benefited US investors in the country and conformed to the Mann Doctrine. Change was afoot though. In 1961, opposition insurrectionists formed the National Sandinista Liberation Front (FSLN) or Sandinistas, a guerrilla group committed to overthrowing the Somozas. Although the CIA reported that the group was no real threat, it began urban warfare in 1966, and by 1967 the USA began to commit military advisers to assist Nicaragua's National Guard, and provided military training to officers through the School of the Americas. Despite such measures, support for the FSLN continued to grow, and would lead to revolution in future decades.

The Nixon administration

Johnson's decision to step down from the presidency led to the election of Richard Nixon, previously the vice president who had witnessed anti-American protests in 1958. At the end of his vice presidency he had counselled a change in course regarding Latin America, and had in some respects sown the seeds for the Alliance for Progress. However, it was his administration that would discontinue the alliance. Evaluating the aims and outcomes, he determined that the alliance had not fulfilled its goals, and that it had actually fuelled discontent in some areas. While this was an astute observation, he did little to try to remedy the problems and often continued the same policies that had been in place. Like Johnson before him, foreign policy was dominated by Asia – first Vietnam and the promises he made for the withdrawal of US forces, and later by opening the People's Republic of China to the west.

US operations in Chile

Latin America came to the forefront of US foreign relations when Nixon had to contend with a democratically elected Marxist President in Chile. In 1970, upon the election of Salvador Allende of the Unidad Popular (UP) party, it was made clear that the US objective was to keep him from taking office; or, in the worst case scenario, to remove him from power as quickly as possible.

US companies had over $1 billion invested in Chile. International Telephone and Telegraph as well as the copper conglomerates Anaconda and Kennecott all feared that an Allende presidency would mean nationalization of their companies and the collapse of revenue streams. The USA had intelligence stations in Chile that monitored

Soviet submarine fleets and there was fear of a domino effect in South America. Kissinger felt that Chile posed a more serious threat than Cuba as the Marxists in place had been democratically elected in free and fair elections, and ratified by the Chilean Congress.

The USA used both covert operations and economic measures to try to oust Allende. From 1970 to 1973, an estimated $10 million was spent in trying to bring about his downfall. To do so, the USA:

- cut off all economic assistance to Chile, amounting to $70 million

- discouraged foreign private investment

- opposed international credits and loans from the IMF, World Bank and Inter-American Development Bank

- tried to disrupt the international copper market (critical to the Chilean economy)

- put diplomatic pressure on other Latin American countries to oppose Allende

- gave money to the opposition

- used the CIA to bring about a strike of truckers

- organized a break-in of the Chilean embassy in Washington DC.

In reality, the popularity of Allende and his UP had begun to wane. The Chilean military and middle classes strongly opposed his programmes for social reform and were willing to take action themselves. The country was in chaos with reforms that were costly and a lack of income to pay for ambitious social programmes. In August 1973, Augusto Pinochet was named commander-in-chief of the Chilean military, sealing the fate of Allende's administration. On 11 September the navy seized the port of Valparaiso and by 4 p.m. armed forces that stormed the Presidential Palace announced that Allende had committed suicide.

▲ President Salvador Allende

With the benefit of hindsight it seems that Chile was headed towards political change with or without US intervention and in that light the covert operations seem like money unnecessarily spent. However, it is significant that the USA was willing to go to such lengths to overthrow a democratically elected government. The USA embraced the Pinochet regime and enthusiastically supported it as it brutally repressed the opposition and removed all social reforms that had been put in place to assist the poor. However, the Nixon administration was soon embroiled in its own affairs, and while covert actions might have been acceptable overseas, they were not only immoral but illegal at home. Nixon resigned, facing impeachment, and leaving the affairs of Latin America to Gerald Ford until the 1976 elections.

The Rockefeller report of August 1969 addressed Latin America and assessed that there was potential for political upheaval and a strong Marxist presence in the region; it therefore made sense to collaborate with military rulers to prevent the spread of communism in the region.

Carter's foreign policy

The presidency of Jimmy Carter marked an initial shift away from what had become traditional Cold War foreign policy. When he took office in 1977 Carter asked the US public to put aside their 'inordinate fear of communism' and embrace a new programme. He promised to: reduce the US military presence overseas and exhort other NATO members to pay more for their own defence; cut back on arms sales that had reached $10 billion per year under Nixon; and slow the arms race with a new round of nuclear weapons talks. Instead, he wanted to address environmental issues and improve human rights abroad through US assistance and pressure. Even in the aftermath of Vietnam Carter found the US public resistant to his ideas. Part of the problem was a division in his own government: National Security Council head Zbigniew Brzezinski was an anti-communist hardliner who was suspicious of Soviet motives; Secretary of State Cyrus Vance, on the other hand, advocated a policy of 'quiet diplomacy' and rapprochement. Carter's main foreign policy advisers were often in opposition with one another.

The other problems that Carter faced came towards the end of his presidency from events in central Asia. In late 1978 the Soviets began to step up their involvement in Afghanistan, and they eventually invoked the Brezhnev Doctrine and invaded the neighbouring country. This led to the deterioration of détente and the arms talks stalled; a US boycott of the 1980 Moscow Olympics further hurt US–Soviet relations. At the same time revolution engulfed Iran and led to a foreign policy crisis wherein US citizens were held hostage by an incoherent government angered by the sanctuary the USA provided the deposed Shah. As a result of the international instability, the defence budget ballooned to over $15 billion.

The Panama Canal Treaties

In the Americas Carter's policies were focused on human rights and the Panama Canal. In November 1903, the Hay–Bunau-Varilla Treaty gave the USA the right to build a canal in Panama that would connect the Atlantic and Pacific Oceans. Additionally, the USA would lease the land from Panama in perpetuity for $250 000 per year plus $10 million and would reserve the right to use military force if necessary to protect the canal. Under President Ford, and with the assistance of Secretary of State Henry Kissinger, negotiations regarding the canal began but a number of politicians, particularly southern Republicans, opposed returning the land and the canal to the Panamanians. In a statement that reflected this view, future president Ronald Reagan said, 'We built it, we paid for it and we are going to keep it.'

Panama was struggling economically in the 1970s and the financial returns of the canal seemed crucial to keeping the country in the US sphere. Even though Panama had joined the Non-Aligned Movement, Carter used the argument about Panama's economy to gain support from conservatives who did not want the USA to lose the canal. Carter made Panama Canal negotiations a priority, seeing it as a constructive approach to improving hemispheric relations and promoting economic stability for the region. Like Ford before him, Carter faced a very vocal opposition that mobilized US public opinion against the treaty. In the aftermath of Vietnam, it was easy to appeal to US pride as a reason for maintaining the canal even though few Americans would benefit from this decision. Interestingly, the administration was supported by the conservative William F Buckley who wrote, 'the United States, by signing these treaties, is better off militarily, is better off financially, and is better off spiritually'. Despite strong opposition, Carter persevered and treaty discussions continued into 1977.

In September 1977 Jimmy Carter and Panamanian President Omar Torrijos signed two treaties that returned the land and the canal to Panama. According to the terms of one treaty, Panama took control of the Panama Canal on 31 December 1999, with joint protection, management and defence in the interim period. The second treaty emphasized the neutrality of the canal in times of peace and war, requiring that it remain open to all vessels of all countries. To gain acceptance a clause was introduced into the treaty stating that the USA would maintain a military presence in Panama but would not intervene in Panama's internal affairs. Carter was successful in achieving his primary foreign policy goal with these treaties.

▲ The Panama Canal

Human rights

In an unprecedented move, military and economic assistance could be denied to countries that were seen as obvious human rights abusers. Under this, Guatemala, Chile and Argentina lost their US funding, and support of the Somoza regime in Nicaragua was also withdrawn as the Sandinistas were gaining momentum. It appeared as if, at least in the Americas, US policies were moving away from Cold War domination, that is, until the impact of events in Central Asia reversed this development.

In 1979 the new government of Nicaragua was recognized, given $8 million in emergency relief and promised a further $75 million. However, an October 1979 coup in El Salvador prompted US fears that Central America was mirroring South East Asia and soon the whole region would collapse into communism. After fueling support against the right-wing regime, the USA soon withdrew support for the younger, more moderate officers and their coalition fell apart. They were replaced by yet another vicious military-backed government that oversaw, among other things, the assassination of Archbishop Oscar Romero in March 1980 and the murder of three North American nuns and a lay worker in December 1980. The USA continued to provide military assistance through atrocities in which 10 000 political murders were committed in 1980 alone.

▲ Jimmy Carter and Daniel Ortega, leader of Nicaragua, in 1979

The promises of Carter's inauguration were unfulfilled due to inconsistencies in his administration's policies and events beyond US borders. The events in Central America, the Soviet Union and Iran all led to a reversion to Cold War policies of containment and a fear of the domino effect – policies that had been in place since the onset of the Cold War. In the end, little changed in the outlook of the USA, and its attitudes in Latin America were stirring up revolutions that would soon be unleashed.

Reasons for foreign and domestic policies and implementation

Conceptual understanding

Key questions

→ How was Canada's Cold War foreign policy similar to that of the USA?

→ Why did Cuba engage in revolutionary warfare throughout the world?

Key concept

→ Continuity

Canada

Canada's role in the Cold War is often oversimplified. Canada's focus was on self-protection through a series of strategic alliances centred on the USA. Many cite its NATO membership, participation in the Korean War and agreement to the North American Aerospace Defense Command (NORAD) as clear indicators of Canada as little more than a follower of US policy. However, this view of Canadian foreign policy ignores its ambivalent relationship with the USA, Commonwealth membership and commitment to the UN and humanitarian efforts. It is true that the USA was Canada's most important ally due to geographical proximity and economic cooperation, but Canada did not blindly follow the USA. There were periods of significant disagreement between the two countries, especially regarding Cuba and Vietnam. Between 1945 and 1981 Canada had six prime ministers with very different agendas and the country had an evolving sense of national identity. It also went through a number of profound social changes that affected the Canadian public, partly due to the Cold War and the public's perception of Canada's role in this struggle.

The Gouzenko affair and the origins of the Cold War

There are a number of historians who argue that the Cold War began on 5 September 1945 in Ottowa. It was on this night that a Soviet embassy employee, Igor Gouzenko, smuggled 109 documents out of the embassy and, in an attempt to defect to Canada, tried to present them to the Royal Canadian Mounted Police (RCMP), Department of Justice and the *Ottowa Journal*. Unsuccessful in his first try, he and his family were hidden by neighbours as Soviet agents searched for him and the Canadian government tried to decide what to do. Finally, on 7 September, the government placed him and his family in protective custody and began to evaluate the documents. Extraordinarily, the documents showed evidence of a Soviet spy ring in Canada that demonstrated a Soviet expansionistic, pro-communist group that had

infiltrated the Canadian Civil Service, the military, the British High Commission, atomic researchers and even the Canadian parliament.

The Canadian government was opposed to outlawing the Communist Party but it began investigations that centred on the Canadian Civil Service and trade union members. This led to a series of arrests and 20 trials of individuals charged with treason; 11 were convicted of spying for the Soviet Union and served terms between five and 10 years. When Gouzenko's accusations were borne out, he became a very valuable source of information that eventually led to the arrest of Ethel and Julius Rosenberg in the USA.

As Canadian historian Jack Granatstein notes, the Gouzenko affair signalled that Canada was an important player in international relations and could no longer be ignored or bypassed by its more powerful allies, especially due to its military strength at the end of the war. Along with the UK and the USA, Canadian pilots participated in the Berlin Airlift, providing much needed food and fuel to a blockaded West Berlin.

It also led to a change in Canadian public opinion against the Soviet Union. During the war, the Soviets were seen as fierce and determined allies worthy of admiration. Gouzenko's revelations changed this and led to a 'Red Scare'. For its part the government established an extensive system of security checks for Canadian citizens (conducting 70 000 in the year 1951 alone) and the Padlock Law of 1937 was used by local law officials to close down any site suspected of spreading subversive or anti-government material. Canadian anti-communist hysteria never reached the level of that in the USA and died down the middle of the 1950s but, as in the USA, it had an effect on popular culture and society. After the Soviets successfully detonated a nuclear weapon of their own, women specifically were enlisted by the government to help defend the home front by stocking emergency pantries full of canned goods and learning basic first aid to treat the injured. The threat of nuclear war increased the importance of women as a line of defence in the Cold War.

With a focus on national defence, Canada joined a number of international organizations that it saw as important to preventing future global conflicts and its economic development. Canada was an active and engaged member of the UN from the beginning; upholding the UN Charter was seen as a fundamental duty. Its position as a middle power was both an asset and a liability. It was often seen as an appropriate mediator; in this capacity Canada sent observers to India in 1947 and Palestine in 1948 to oversee UN operations there. However, while its opinions were solicited by its allies it was often ignored by the permanent members of the Security Council – the only states more powerful than Canada in the post-war period.

Canada was also a founding member of NATO, seeing collective security as both a deterrent for Soviet aggression and a means of national defence if war did occur. Some argue that Ottawa was responsible for gaining US membership and preventing the USA from retreating into isolation again, but this is highly debatable given the Brussels Pact and the events in central Europe up to its creation in April 1949. As a member, Canada was primarily responsible for patrolling the North Atlantic, and it used its navy and air force for NATO operations. With the UK and USA both as members, Canadians hoped that NATO would grow into an economic and social union, but this never came to fruition.

Canada also became a member of the British Commonwealth upon its formation. However, Canada was judicious in its choices, refusing to join the OAS. The USA urged Canada to join but it steadfastly refused, arguing that its relations with the rest of the hemisphere were limited and that it saw no constructive reason for participation.

The Korean War as a UN action was consistent with Canada's foreign policy and Canada willingly sent troops to defend South Korea against North Korean aggression. However, Canadians questioned MacArthur's decision to cross the 38th parallel. They were wondering whether Canada should reconsider its participation and were considering recognizing the Beijing government as legitimate when the Chinese invaded in November. Not only was there fear of communist aggression but there was also the spectre of nuclear war. Canada did not just provide support but it professionalized its military. Defence spending increased from $493 million in 1950 to $1.16 billion in 1951, and increased the size of Canada's military to 118 000. By the end of the Korean War, Canada had a well-equipped, effectively trained military that cost 7.6% of its GDP and it had over 30 000 troops serving abroad.

The Canadian commitment to the UN was further evidenced by its response to the Suez Crisis. In 1956 the Egyptian military seized the Suez Canal and nationalized it, effectively ending 80 years of European control over it. Angered by this, British and French politicians enlisted the help of the Israelis in retaking the Suez Canal, launching an international crisis: the UK and France opposed the USA, and the Soviet Union threatened to assist the Egyptians if necessary. Canadian diplomats wanted to restore peace to the region while repairing relations among its allies and Pearson proposed the creation of an international force of peacekeepers under the aegis of the UN that would serve as a buffer between the belligerents. This solution was quickly adopted by the UN and led to a ceasefire. UN forces took up residence in the Sinai. There were international accolades for Pearson, who received the Nobel Peace Prize, but Canadians were unhappy with the government's unwillingness to support the UK and France and demonstrated this by voting the Liberal Party government out of power.

St Laurent was replaced by John Diefenbaker, a progressive Conservative whose policies were staunchly anti-communist and pro-NATO but who also wanted to demonstrate Canadian autonomy from the USA. In 1957 he agreed to the creation of the North American Aerospace Defense Command (NORAD), a binational agreement between Canada and the USA. It provided defence of North American airspace from the Arctic to the Tropics against Soviet nuclear weapons. This was readily accepted but Diefenbaker made a much more controversial decision by accepting US-made surface-to-air missiles. Although the Bomarcs did not have nuclear weapons, that was the only way in which they were effective and the Canadian public was clearly opposed to having nuclear weapons on Canadian soil, fearing that the USA – through NORAD – could make a decision to launch these weapons without Canadian agreement. Thus, the Bomarcs were in Canada without nuclear warheads.

Another component of NORAD was three sets of radar stations, most of which were located in Canada. From south to north, the stations were called Pinetree, Mid-Canada and Distant Early Warning (DEW) above the Arctic Circle. This network was set up to detect incoming Soviet bombers and provide early warning for a land-based invasion.

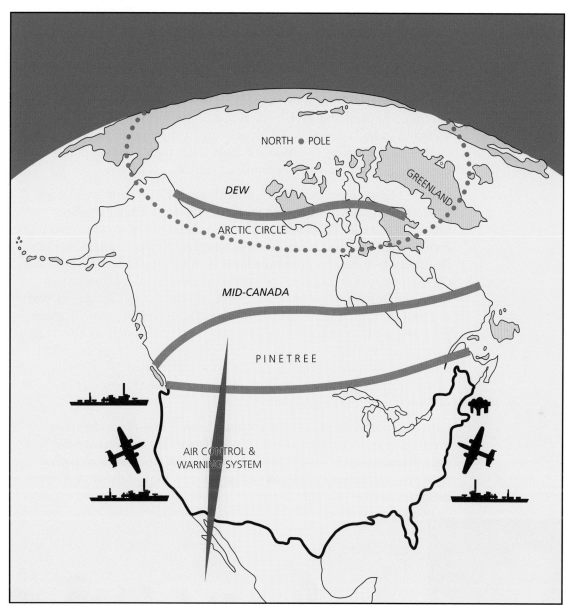

▲ Map of DEW network

In 1959 Castro came to power in Cuba and rather than following the US embargo, Canada took advantage of US trade withdrawal to make its own agreements that would be beneficial to Canadian companies. When the Missile Crisis occurred in 1962 the Canadian Parliament was required to debate and vote on whether or not to go on alert. Like the general public, the parliament was split on whether or not to agree to the US request and feared angering the Soviets. They were also determined to act independently of the USA. In the end, they voted in favour of the US request and put their forces on alert; however, they still refused to join the OAS despite US pressure to do so. It was later revealed the Canadian Defense Minister Harkness put Canadian forces on alert without informing Diefenbaker or parliament, leading to the collapse of the government and new elections.

The former UN ambassador and Secretary of State Lester B Pearson became the new prime minister, and one of his first orders of business was to accept nuclear weapons from the USA in an attempt to stabilize relations with the USA once again. However, Pearson – like most Canadians – was opposed to US actions in Vietnam. In 1954 Canada dispatched both diplomats and military officers to Indochina to serve on the International Control Commission that oversaw the implementation of the Geneva Accords. Work on the International Commission for Supervision and Control of Vietnam (ICSC) officially obliged Canada to remain neutral and gave it the rationale for not joining the USA in Vietnam. Canada developed a list of prerequisites for engaging in war or joining new alliances to insulate it from what the Canadian public as an increasingly irrational anti-communist stance.

Canada's relaxed policy towards draft dodgers came with the election of a Liberal Party government led by Pierre Trudeau. Unlike Pearson, he sought to distance Canada from the USA and wanted to be seen as more independent. This was clear in 1970 when he recognized the People's Republic of China and dismantled the Bomarc missile site. Trudeau also cut the national defence budget and reduced Canada's commitment to NATO. Despite these moves the USA still remained Canada's closest ally and continued to participate in both NATO and NORAD. Trudeau tried to improve Canada's international position through accentuating its status as a middle power and a bridge between the developed and developing worlds. However, Canada stood with the USA in the boycott of the Moscow Olympics in 1980, in protest against the Soviet invasion of Afghanistan in the previous year.

Canadian policy throughout the Cold War was one of loyalty to its Western allies as a means of protection. Once that protection was established, Canada sought to establish itself as a power in its own right with an independent policy aligned with that of the USA, but not determined solely by the USA.

▲ Igor Gouzenko in an interview in 1954

▲ Despite tensions over the Vietnam War, the relationship between Pearson and Johnson was warm and cordial

Cuba

Cuban Cold War policies are a direct reflection of the governments in power and their relations with the USA at that point in time. From 1945 to 1958, under the regime of Fulgencio Batista, Cuba was inextricably tied to the USA and its policies were closely aligned with those of the USA in the region. Batista even severed relations with the Soviet Union in 1952 in a show of clear anti-communism. During the revolutionary period of the 1950s the USA grew uncomfortable with Batista's brutality but did little to stop it, as any change to the regime could have negatively affected US economic and political interests in the country. In 1958 the USA withdrew its military aid to Batista and, shortly after this, Castro and his supporters took power in the country.

Castro's ascension to power changed Cuba's foreign policy position dramatically. For the duration of the Cold War, there were two facets: relations with the Soviet Union and export of revolution. The former began in February 1960 with an economic agreement centred on the Soviet purchase of Cuban sugar in exchange for Cuban purchase of Soviet oil. Additionally, Cuba had nationalized US-owned refineries and the Soviets sent specialists to run the refineries and train Cubans to operate them. The agreement kept the Cuban economy dependent upon sugar for the duration of the Cold War but allowed Cuban social programmes to develop and flourish.

Although the Cuban Missile Crisis tends to dominate most narratives of Cuba in the Cold War, Cuba itself was not a major player in the negotiations, much to Castro's chagrin. After the weapons were dismantled and removed, tension between the Soviets and Cubans remained, largely regarding the idea of revolution. The Cubans, led by Che Guevara, advocated for revolutionary groups in the developing world, feeling that it was the obligation of established socialist states to help nascent socialist movements. In the 1960s and 1970s, the Soviets took the position of supporting socialist parties and helping them come to power legally (as they would in Chile in 1970). In 1968, however, Castro publicly criticized the Prague Spring and endorsed the Brezhnev Doctrine as a means of keeping socialist governments in power. There is some debate on the sincerity of this statement, and Castro's belief in what he said has been questioned by analysts ever since.

Guevara left Cuba in 1965 to assist revolutionary movements in the Americas and Africa. Cubans trained guerrilla revolutionaries to engage in warfare against the corrupt, capitalist regimes in power, and provided weapons and troops to assist these groups. Cubans also helped socialists spread their message, especially on the radio. Since many of the supporters of such groups were illiterate, Cubans helped them spread their messages using the radio in local languages. In the Andes, Guaraní and Aymará were more commonly spoken than Spanish, so Cubans helped groups enlist locals to translate and disseminate information. Cubans also provided social assistance – doctors and nurses were sent to the front lines to provide public health instruction and care for the ill – and infrastructure development by providing engineers and architects. These movements took Cubans to Panama, Angola, Venezuela, the Congo and Bolivia, before Guevara was killed in 1967. After that, revolutionary work continued in Vietnam, Nicaragua, El Salvador, Grenada, Ethiopia and Mozambique, and Cubans assisted the Irish Republican Army and Palestine Liberation Organization.

In the Americas, Cuba was expelled from the OAS in 1962 for having a government that was seen as incompatible with the goals of the OAS and in 1964 a number of OAS countries applied sanctions to Cuba for its revolutionary activities in the region. Only Chile, Mexico and Uruguay broke with this decision and continued to engage in trade and diplomacy with Cuba. In the 1970s there was a change in attitude towards Cuba and in 1973 the OAS voted to allow countries to decide whether or not to re-establish ties with Cuba. This signalled a shift in hemispheric relations that went against the dominant, anti-communist stance of the USA.

Cuba was an inaugural member of the Non-Aligned Movement. At first, Castro seemed uninterested and while he sent representatives to the initial meetings, little was done to advance the cause. In the 1970s, however, Castro began to endorse globalism and assistance to developing nations, all the while maintaining its relationship with the Soviet Union. From 1979 to 1983 Cuba held the chair of the movement, highlighting its commitment. Cuba also restored relations with a number of its neighbour states – those that broke off relations due to pressure from the USA. Nonetheless, the USA remained hostile to Cuba and refused to end its embargo.

▲ Castro and Nasser, leaders of the Non-Aligned Movement

Jamaica and the Cold War

Due to the presence of bauxite (aluminium) in Jamaica and the country's proximity to Cuba, the USA wanted to ensure that it had friendly relations with Jamaica during the Cold War, but sometimes relied on covert operations to ensure that Jamaica's government was aligned with the USA after its independence in 1962. From then until 1972 the USA had little to fear but in 1972 the democratic socialist Michael Manley became the country's fourth prime minister and changed diplomatic course to suit the needs of the population.

Jamaicans were among the poorest in the British Commonwealth and Manley's programme involved socio-economic reforms that were similar to those of other newly decolonized countries that included land reform, literacy programmes and gender equality legislation. In foreign policy Manley was much less inclined to follow US policies and instead engaged in relations with Cuba, which he saw as a positive model for developing countries to follow, and strengthened Jamaica's connection to the Non-Aligned Movement.

This led the USA to increase its covert actions in the region. While there is little evidence of the methods employed, US operatives were active in Jamaica, especially after Manley began the process to establish government majority ownership over the bauxite mines. While there were no overt assassination attempts, it has been suggested that Jamaican gangs were funded by the US government to increase the political violence during Manley's government. When he was voted out of office in 1980 he remained the opposition leader, and the country returned to a foreign policy that was more acceptable to the USA and consistent with its Cold War objectives.

ATL Communication and research skills

Choose a country in the Americas other than Canada, Cuba or the USA and research the impact of the Cold War on its foreign and domestic policies, 1945–1981. You will present this material to your class in a 10-minute presentation that includes up to 10 visual aids. You may not use video and while key words or important quotations can be presented, visually you cannot put extended text on any visual aid. Be sure to include:

- a map that situates your country of choice

- the form of government and important leader(s)

- the official position the country took in the Cold War (i.e. pro-west, pro-Soviet or non-aligned)

- the actual position it took (which can differ depending on the time or government in power)

- the impact that the Cold War had on its government

- the impact that the Cold War had on its economy

- the impact that the Cold War had on its society.

You should also be prepared to answer questions from your classmates.

Conclusion

The USA clearly dominated the Cold War foreign policies of the region, but not always with the impact they hoped for. In the case of Cuba, the USA had to co-exist with a socialist country 145 kilometres off its coast, and fears of a domino effect in the region persisted throughout the Cold War. This in turn put the USA in a series of uncomfortable alliances with brutal dictatorships that were funded by the USA in the name of anti-communism. The OAS became what Argentina had feared in the 1930s: an organization dominated by US interests. It was only in the 1970s that countries began to vote against US hegemony in the organization.

Canada was the US's closest ally both geographically and ideologically but there were times when they disagreed on the course of international relations. Canada used its position as a middle power to negotiate between rival groups and it was a Canadian suggestion that led to the creation of the UN peacekeeping forces. It maintained links to the UK through its monarchy and the Commonwealth but these were cultural and economic rather than political links. By the 1980s Canada had its own identity that grew out of a foreign policy that was designed to achieve Canadian desires of security, economic growth and international development. Its policies were usually aligned with the USA's, but distinct from them.

Exam-style questions

1 Examine the effects of McCarthyism on society and culture in the USA from the late 1940s to the late 1950s.

2 Analyse the reasons for the participation of **one** country in the Americas in the Korean War.

3 Examine the features of Eisenhower's New Look foreign policy and evaluate its impact on the region of the Americas.

4 Compare and contrast the nature of the USA's involvement in Vietnam during **two** presidencies from 1954 to 1973.

5 Analyse the successes and failures of President Kennedy's foreign policies towards Latin America between 1961 and 1963.

6 Evaluate the impact of the Nixon administration's covert operations on the government of Chile in the early 1970s.

7 'Jimmy Carter was the first president since John F Kennedy to actively pursue improved relations with Latin America.' To what extent do you agree with this statement?

8 'The containment policy of the USA had a negative effect on the other countries in the Americas.' To what extent do you agree with this statement?

9 With reference to **one** country in the region (excluding the USA), analyse the impact of the Cold War on the development and implementation of that nation's foreign policy.

Using different perspectives

Markbands in Paper 3

In the 10–12 and 13–15 markbands there is mention of different perspectives. This means not limiting your essays to historiography; that is, mentioning only historians who have different views on historical events. People can have different viewpoints based on their nationality, gender, social class, or ideological framework. Your level of awareness of these differences will be reflected in the markband you achieve.

For markbands 10–12 you need to show "some awareness and evaluation of different perspectives".

For markbands 13–15 you need to show "evaluation of different perspectives … integrated effectively into the answer".

It is not enough just to state what these different perspectives are; you also need to look at their validity and put them into the essay in an effective manner.

Evaluating different perspectives

An example of gratuitous use of a historian's perspective that does nothing to advance an argument would be:

"According to Alperovitz, Truman decided to use the atom bomb against Japan to end the war."

However, if you were to extend the reference and evaluate it, this will help you advance an argument about the timing of the origins of the Cold War:

"Although Alperovitz argued that Truman stated that the use of the atom bomb against Japan would hasten the end of the war, he also saw it as an opportunity to demonstrate its military superiority against an aggressive Soviet Union. This supports the idea that by late 1945 the US saw the Soviets as a potential enemy …"

Perspectives on policies can be strengthened when particular leaders are referenced:

"It is difficult to argue that Arbenz was a communist sympathizer when one of his stated campaign goals for Guatemala was to create a viable, capitalist economy."

Another perspective is that of public opinion:

"Although the US government attributed Cuban anti-Americanism to communist sympathizers, many moderate Cubans were opposed to the US dominance of Cuba's political and economic systems."

Class practice

Below are several examples where students show awareness of perspectives but do not go beyond that. Choose one example and either rewrite the statement or augment it so that it is integrated into a larger argument.

On the origins of Cold War politics:

"In <u>Diplomacy</u>, Henry Kissinger argues that, at Potsdam, the US State Department was opposed to dividing Eastern Europe into spheres of influence because it was seen as a threat to world peace."

On the reasons for installing missiles in Cuba:

"According to Gaddis, Khrushchev wanted to place missiles in Cuba to advance the cause of revolution in Latin America."

On American interests in Chile under Allende:

"Richard Nixon wanted to make the Chilean economy 'scream'."

On American involvement in Vietnam:

"According to famed newscaster Walter Cronkite, after the Tet Offensive, US and North Vietnamese armed forces were at a stalemate."

Internal Assessment skills: reflection

After you have completed your historical investigation, the final component of the IA is a reflection on the process and what you accomplished. To do this effectively, consider:

- how you conducted your research
- what was successful or unsuccessful
- how you made any corrections.

You should also consider the quality and number of sources you used.

- Were there enough?
- Was there a good range of perspectives in the works you consulted?
- Could you find sufficient primary sources?
- What did you learn as a historian in the process?

In answering these questions, you will have good idea of what worked well, where more assistance or time would have been helpful, and what you will do differently in the future.

Question

Was the US responsible for undermining the Allende regime in Chile between 1970 and 1973?

Analysis

The following table is a sample reflection on the question that has been annotated to show how it addressed all the necessary elements.

The question of the US involvement in Allende is very interesting to consider, especially as one of its architects, Henry Kissinger, is still alive and commented extensively on it over the years.	This shows a direct link between the reflection and the investigation.
With many events, the problem is that there is not a lot of information available; in some respects, I had difficulties because there were too many sources. In addition to Kissinger's White House Years, there are also transcripts from the Nixon administration and information from the so-called Chicago Boys who had a vested interest in supporting the Pinon example of chet regime.	Methods used by historians are understood and explained.
These sources are all supportive of US involvement, and it was difficult for me to find primary sources that looked at other, opposing views. Some of the analytical works used primary sources to support their arguments, but most of them were in Spanish, a language I don't speak and thus cannot authenticate. They seemed reasonable and supported but I could not always be certain; Chileans on both sides are very emotional and it is difficult to see their views as rational.	Here is an awareness of the challenges that face historians.
I found that writing this investigation instructed me on how many factors historians must consider when making judgments and producing analysis. It is not always easy to determine the correct answer to a research question, and having more information doesn't always make it easier. Knowing that many of my sources were anti-Allende helped me be critical of them, but I wish I had seen more pro-Allende sources to balance the information I had.	This is a solid, if a bit repetitive, synthesis of conducting research. It acknowledges what the student gained from the investigation but is not focused on the investigation itself.

Although this reflection has its weaknesses and is a bit formulaic, it has addressed all the necessary elements and would thus receive full marks.

8 CIVIL RIGHTS AND SOCIAL MOVEMENTS IN THE AMERICAS POST-1945

Global context

In his "Letter from Birmingham Jail", Dr Martin Luther King wrote: "freedom is never voluntarily given by the oppressor; it must be demanded by the oppressed." After the Second World War, groups increasingly demanded political, economic and social rights. Women, indigenous peoples, African Americans and Hispanic Americans in the United States faced powerful institutions, including governments, that worked to maintain the status quo. The groups' methods and degree of success varied. This post-war civil rights generation was motivated to form other protest and cultural movements, too. They focused on tangible issues such as the Vietnam War and many rejected their parents' culture in favour of alternative lifestyles.

In this chapter we will examine the Americas' post-war movements, including the background and causes, phases and methods, key events, important leaders and organizations, opposition characteristics and methods, as well as the results.

Timeline

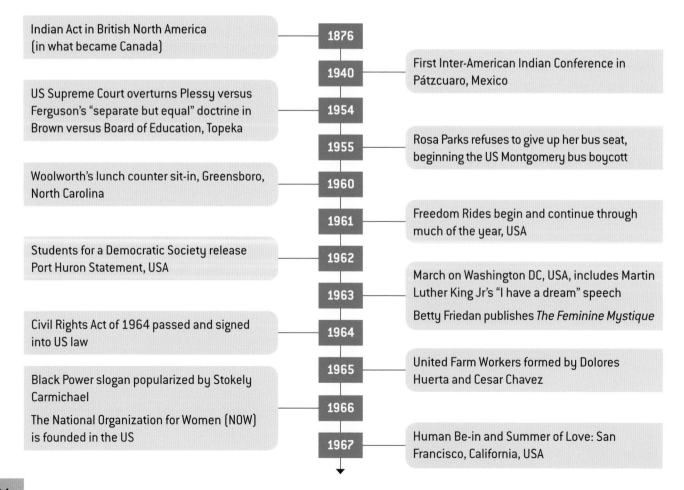

Indian Act in British North America (in what became Canada)	1876
	1940 — First Inter-American Indian Conference in Pátzcuaro, Mexico
US Supreme Court overturns Plessy versus Ferguson's "separate but equal" doctrine in Brown versus Board of Education, Topeka	1954
	1955 — Rosa Parks refuses to give up her bus seat, beginning the US Montgomery bus boycott
Woolworth's lunch counter sit-in, Greensboro, North Carolina	1960
	1961 — Freedom Rides begin and continue through much of the year, USA
Students for a Democratic Society release Port Huron Statement, USA	1962
	1963 — March on Washington DC, USA, includes Martin Luther King Jr's "I have a dream" speech; Betty Friedan publishes *The Feminine Mystique*
Civil Rights Act of 1964 passed and signed into US law	1964
	1965 — United Farm Workers formed by Dolores Huerta and Cesar Chavez
Black Power slogan popularized by Stokely Carmichael; The National Organization for Women (NOW) is founded in the US	1966
	1967 — Human Be-in and Summer of Love: San Francisco, California, USA

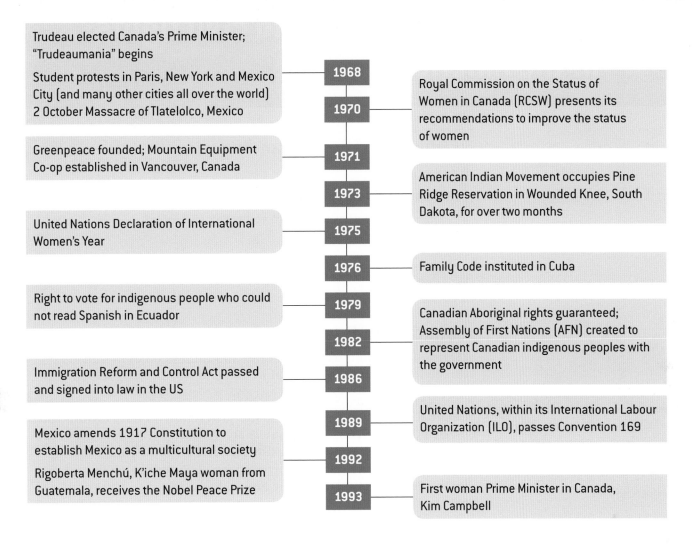

Trudeau elected Canada's Prime Minister; "Trudeaumania" begins

Student protests in Paris, New York and Mexico City (and many other cities all over the world) 2 October Massacre of Tlatelolco, Mexico

1968

1970 — Royal Commission on the Status of Women in Canada (RCSW) presents its recommendations to improve the status of women

Greenpeace founded; Mountain Equipment Co-op established in Vancouver, Canada

1971

1973 — American Indian Movement occupies Pine Ridge Reservation in Wounded Knee, South Dakota, for over two months

United Nations Declaration of International Women's Year

1975

1976 — Family Code instituted in Cuba

Right to vote for indigenous people who could not read Spanish in Ecuador

1979

1982 — Canadian Aboriginal rights guaranteed; Assembly of First Nations (AFN) created to represent Canadian indigenous peoples with the government

Immigration Reform and Control Act passed and signed into law in the US

1986

1989 — United Nations, within its International Labour Organization (ILO), passes Convention 169

Mexico amends 1917 Constitution to establish Mexico as a multicultural society

Rigoberta Menchú, K'iche Maya woman from Guatemala, receives the Nobel Peace Prize

1992

1993 — First woman Prime Minister in Canada, Kim Campbell

8.1 Indigenous peoples and civil rights in the Americas

Conceptual understanding

Key questions

→ What were the conditions that spurred indigenous people to demand civil rights?

→ How successful have they been in obtaining civil rights?

Key concept

→ Causation

→ Change

Canadian indigenous peoples

(Maps of First Nations communities and Inuit peoples in Canada can be found on the Aboriginal Affairs and Northern Development Canada website.)

First Nations
Canadian Aboriginal peoples who are neither Métis (an ethnic group descended from European and Indian parents) nor Inuit (an ethnic group of people who live in the north of Canada).

Before the arrival of Europeans in the 11th century, **First Nations** tribes divided the land. They were hunters and gatherers who were dependent on the natural world for their existence. In the 1500s, European explorers established relations by exchanging European goods for furs. By the 1600s the British and the French had established bases and alliances with different First Nations groups.

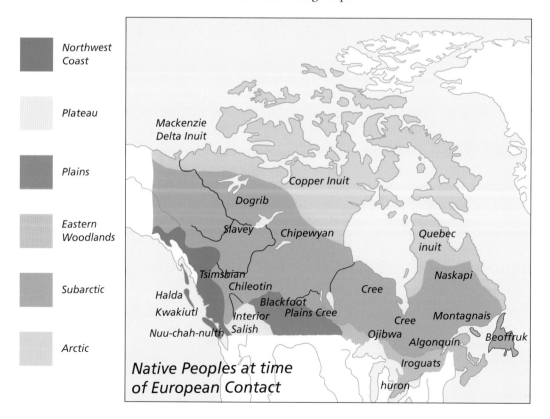

Northwest Coast

Plateau

Plains

Eastern Woodlands

Subarctic

Arctic

Mackenzie Delta Inuit

Copper Inuit

Dogrib

Slavey

Chipewyan

Quebec inuit

Tsimshian

Chileotin

Cree

Naskapi

Halda

Kwakiutl

Blackfoot
Plains Cree

Interior Salish

Cree

Montagnais

Nuu-chah-nulth

Ojibwa

Algonquin

Beoffruk

Native Peoples at time of European Contact

Iroguats

huron

426

As the British and French began to compete more actively for control of North America, strong alliances with the First Nations people became essential. Just before the final British clash with the French in North America, known as the **Seven Years War** (1756–1763), the British created the Indian Department in 1755 to, amongst other jobs, coordinate alliances. With the British victory in the war, all French land was ceded to the British, and the British established the first treaties with many First Nations bands. The Royal Proclamation of 1763 specified how the area was to be administered, and the Indian Department was in charge of Indian affairs. Most crucially, as only the government could purchase land, the Proclamation became the first public recognition of First Nations' rights to **land titles**; however, the First Nations people were not adequately compensated in the process.

To accommodate the United Empire Loyalists and their Indian allies who fled the American Revolution, land was acquired from the First Nations bands, and the first **reserves** were established. The British alliance with the First Nations bands was essential during the War of 1812. Afterwards, there was no longer a need for alliances with the First Nations bands, and there was more pressure to obtain land for European settlement. By the 1830s most land in eastern Canada had been seized with treaties, so many First Nations tribes lost the ability to live as they had before.

In addition to the British control of land in the east, the Hudson's Bay Company (HBC) continued to expand its influence as it pushed west in search of resources such as fur. A unique ethnic group, the Métis, emerged in the plains areas of Canada as a result of the intermarriage between First Nations bands and Europeans. The Europeans altered the nature of First Nations society: as they became part of "fort" society, they also began to drink European alcohol and were infected by European diseases to which they had no immunity. This situation had a devastating long-term impact on First Nations communities throughout Canada.

Indian Act 1876–1971

Ten years after Canada was created, in 1876 the new government passed one of its most controversial acts: the Indian Act. The Act gave immense power to the Department of Indian Affairs, particularly in deciding who was an Indian and what rights they had. Due to this Act, most First Nations people were not integrated into mainstream Canadian society: most lived in rural areas, with over 60% employed in trapping, fishing, logging and other seasonal, low paid jobs. However, the Second World War had a significant impact on the status of minorities as their rights began to be reconsidered in Canada. Due to the important role Canadian indigenous people played in the First and Second World Wars, the Canadian government amended the Indian Act:

- In 1946 the government reviewed the management of the Indian Act and allowed First Nations leaders to express their desires for autonomy.

- In 1951 a Land Claims Commission was created.

- In 1960 the right to vote was given.

Seven Years War
A war between Great Britain and France for territory overseas. Great Britain defeated France in 1763 which led to massive territorial gains in North America.

land title
The innate indigenous right to ancestral lands due to historical occupation and a continued socio-political relationship with it.

reserve
An area of land set aside for indigenous people to inhabit, but the legal title is still held by the government.

Class discussion

Watch *The Agenda with Steve Paikin: Who Really Won the War of 1812?* on the TVO.org website.

To what extent do you agree that the First Nations people "lost"?

residential schools
Starting in 1883 First Nations people were forcibly assimilated through the use of residential schools. Run by various Christian organizations, aboriginal students were only allowed to speak in English or French, and were banned from wearing traditional clothes or practising their customs.

Regardless of improvements, however, the living conditions in First Nations communities were much lower than in the rest of Canada. In addition, in 1969 PM Trudeau moved to repeal the Indian Act with its White Paper, which stated that all Canadians should be equal with no special privileges. The First Nations overwhelmingly rejected the White Paper. Even though there were many discriminatory provisions in the Indian Act, the few protections and benefits it provided, such as preferential taxation and **residential schools**, were seen as essential to sustain their communities. Massive demonstrations led the government to withdraw the White Paper in 1971.

Challenges and achievements
Enfranchisement
Status Indians have such benefits as being exempt from paying income tax and some other taxes, and getting special health care coverage, access to special funds to build structures such as homes and schools. Status Indians are not just those of "Indian" ancestry. For example, it was initially only given to men, who could pass it along their blood line, and to women whose father or husband was Indian. If a woman married a "non-status" man, she would become "enfranchised." This led to greater discrimination of First Nations women. *Bill C-31* amended the *Indian Act* of 1985 and abolished enfranchisement and restored status to those who had had status removed through enfranchisement.

Indigenous nationalism and organization
Post-war changes in the Indian Act created a new form of indigenous nationalism. First Nations leaders from across the country created new associations to protect and promote their rights. The Indian Association of Alberta produced a paper in 1970 entitled Citizens Plus that stated that indigenous peoples had unique rights and benefits. This became known as the Red Paper. Inspired by the Red Paper and the AIM movement in the US, a new Red Power movement emerged with a new tactic of direct action versus lobbying. A turning point in the Red Power movement came in July 1974 when an Ojibway group stated that a park in Kenora, Ontario had been wrongfully taken from them by the city in 1959; a 39 day stand off with police ensued. A division occurred in the Red Power movement between those who advocated the use of violence (most famously in the Oka Crisis of 1990) versus those who preferred non-violence – a debate that continues today.

patriate
To legally transfer the authority over certain legislation from the original colonial power to a sovereign state; in Canada's case, to transfer their Constitution from the UK to Canada from May 1980 to Nov 1981.

Constitution Express 1980–1981
Arthur Manuel, President of the Union of BC Chiefs, chartered two trains from Vancouver that transported a thousand people to Ottawa, with the goal to publicize concern that aboriginal rights would be abolished in the new 1982 Constitution. When this massive peaceful demonstration did not initially change Prime Minister Trudeau's position, delegations went to the United Nations in New York and Europe to garner support, and Trudeau acquiesced.

By 1978, First Nations communities felt that they needed direct political representation, particularly regarding PM Trudeau's desire to **patriate** the Canadian Constitution. Hundreds of chiefs met in Ottawa in 1980 and created a manifesto entitled the Declaration of First Nations. One of the most famous demonstrations was the **Constitution Express** 1980–1981, an action that organizer Arthur Manuel described as "the most effective direct action in Canadian history", because Section 35 was added to the Constitution, guaranteeing indigenous rights. In 1982 the Assembly of First Nations (AFN) was officially founded with a goal to make First Nations chiefs the formal representatives of aboriginal people regarding provincial and federal negotiations for aboriginal claims, and to create a national governing assembly.

In reference to its origin and purpose, analyze the value and limitations of the *Declaration of First Nations* in regards to promoting First Nations rights.

A Declaration of First Nations

We the Original Peoples of this land know the Creator put us here.

The Creator gave us laws that govern all our relationships to live in harmony with nature and mankind.

The Laws of the Creator defined our rights and responsibilities.

The Creator gave us our spiritual beliefs, our languages, our culture, and a place on Mother Earth which provided us with all our needs.

We have maintained our Freedom, our Languages, and our Traditions from time immemorial.

We continue to exercise the rights and fulfill the responsibilities and obligations given to us by the Creator for the land upon which we were placed.

The Creator has given us the right to govern ourselves and the right to self-determination.

The rights and responsibilities given to us by the creator cannot be altered or taken away by any other Nation.

Source: www.afn.ca/index.php/en/about-afn/a-declaration-of-first-nations

Self-government

Once indigenous rights were codified in the Constitution, groups began to advocate for autonomous self-government within Canada. As there was disagreement regarding how it should be achieved, the government established the Penner Committee in 1983. The Committee resolved that the First Nations "right for self-government" needed to be entrenched in the Constitution in Section 35. There have been many self-government negotiations, but only one has been enacted. On 1 April 1999, the new self-governing Inuit territory of **Nunavut** was created.

Land claims settlements

The most visible aboriginal issue in Canadian society regards land claims. The 1839 Crown Lands Protection Act made the government the guardian of all Crown and reserve lands. However, due to the way Canada was settled, treaty negotiations widely varied depending on the province or territory. From 1871 to 1921, the Canadian government signed land surrender Numbered Treaties to secure land for Canadian settlers, and provide some benefits for the First Nations bands, such as creating reserves, schools and allowing for hunting, fishing and farming rights. Despite the loss of land title, many First Nations people welcomed these treaties as their communities were ravaged by disease and famine, particularly in the west as the buffalo were becoming extinct, and trade with HBC was ending as the company downsized.

The first major successful land claim was the James Bay hydroelectric project in Quebec in 1971. Cree and Inuit bands protested that treaties had not been signed regarding the lands of Northern Quebec; as they still held the land, they filed an injunction to halt the dam construction. In 1973 the Superior Court of Quebec ruled in favour of the tribes that led to the 1975 James Bay and Northern Quebec Hydropower Agreement. This set an important precedent for how governments could negotiate, not just impose, settlements regarding land claims. The British Columbia government chose to engage with the First Nations peoples in a more confrontational way. After decades of persistence, the Nisga'a people succeeded in bringing their case to the Supreme Court of Canada,

Nunavut

A term for "our land", Nunavut comprises of 20% of Canada's land coverage and was taken from the Northwest Territories. The Inuit, 85% of the area's population, gained self-rule over their ancestral lands.

arguing for 15,000 sq km in the Nass Valley. In their 1973 decision, the Court ruled in favor of the Nisga'a, confirming the legality of Aboriginal title, but it was not until the Nisga'a Final Agreement of 2000 that the first modern land claims treaty in British Columbia was created, which became an important precedent for future land claims. From 1975 to 2009, 22 comprehensive land claims agreements, or modern treaties, were concluded throughout Canada.

Conclusion

There has continued to be a difference between the law and its implementation and enforcement regarding Canadian aboriginal policy. In November 2012 the **"Idle No More"** movement was founded with a mission of calling "on all people to join in a revolution that honours and fulfills Indigenous sovereignty that protects the land and water". It is clear that there will continue to be assertive aboriginal demands for control of their ancestral lands, and an active promotion and celebration of their traditional ways of living.

Idle No More
A movement founded in 2012 in response to the Canadian government passing law C-45 that once again changed the Indian Act to give the federal government more power to negotiate land usage. As a grassroots organization, "Idle No More" has been compared to the Occupy Movement; even though it's not formally associated with the AFN, the AFN has supported it as it has encouraged more discussions of, and interest in, indigenous issues in the national media.

Source skills

In 2014 Bob Rae wrote an opinion article for The Globe and Mail:

Some First Nations are moving successfully to claim jurisdiction and assert responsibility, but in the numbered treaties this is not happening, and the gap in status, well-being and power between and among indigenous people in Canada has to be better understood so it can be remedied...

But the issues will not go away, or get any easier, as time goes on. The indigenous population is the fastest growing in the country, and will become an increasing factor in urban life, where most Canadians live. And resource development is now extending deep into the traditional territory of people who have strong views about their own jurisdiction, rights, and needs.

Governments and companies ignore these realities at their peril.

Some governments and premiers understand this, and some not so much. But if the insistence of our constitutional law that accommodations must be reached is not matched by serious political action, the result will not be a trail of tears. It will be a series of confrontations, large and small, which in themselves will require a response. It has been said that good public policy is what happens when all the alternatives have been exhausted. Enough already.

Question

With the knowledge you have acquired by reading this section, as well as conducting further research, debate the merits and deficiencies of Rae's assertions.

Indigenous peoples in the United States

Indigenous peoples were subjected to a seemingly never-ending procession of occupations, actions and laws that resulted in a lack of property rights, civil rights, political sovereignty, and often inferior legal status within the United States.

In the late 1950s and into the 1970s American Indians living and legal circumstances lagged behind every other group in the United States: they were the least prosperous and least healthy ethnic group. On South Dakota indigenous reservations the average lifespan was 44 years, infant mortality three times the national average, and unemployment ranged up to 70%. In Minneapolis, Minnesota, Indigenous people comprised 70% of the jail population while making up only a tenth of the total population. These figures were reflected across the United States, as indigenous unemployment was ten times the national rate,

Research skills

A by-product of mandated assimilation was forcing children of North American indigenous peoples to attend residential boarding schools. Research the Indian boarding schools for information on language and culture policies as well as travel and visitation.

life expectancy was 20 years less than other Americans, and the suicide rate among indigenous youths was one hundred times that of white youths. Even with, or despite, a federal government agency The Bureau of Indian Affairs (BIA) dedicated to them, the indigenous population of a little more than half a million had little political power in a nation of 179 million citizens.

What government policies led to a indigenous civil rights movement?

Three important policy initiatives of the United States government were the Dawes Act of 1887, the Wheeler-Howard Act of 1934 and the Termination Acts beginning in 1953.

The Dawes Act was officially titled The General Allotment Act. The purpose was to eliminate **traditional tribal landholding** in favour of the ideal of the small-plot individual farmer by assigning small allotments of land, causing assimilation. Surplus land was sold by the United States government, first to Indians, but after 1891 to non-Indians as well. Due to the small size of allotments and the lack of credit to purchase supplies, many farms failed and farmers had to sell their land. The result was a massive reduction in total land holdings and increased poverty.

By the 1920s numerous white Americans became aware of the disastrous results of the Dawes Act. Commissioner of Indian Affairs, John Collier pushed forward the Indian Reorganization Act (Wheeler-Howard Act of 1934) in an "Indian New Deal". The purpose was to restore indigenous communal life, preserve culture, and improve health and welfare. It stopped allotments, restored unsold surplus land to tribes and enabled tribes to purchase more land. Tribes were encouraged to form democratic governments and organize themselves as corporate entities for economic development. Despite Collier's best intentions, the Act failed. Most tribes were not economically viable without government support. A number of tribal governments were corrupt.

By the 1940s several congressmen and senators saw the reversion to tribal entities and culture as harmful to American Indians. Their belief in the benefits of American culture, political structure and capitalism in light of the Second World War and the escalating Cold War meant that a return to assimilation was seen as the best path for indigenous peoples. House Resolution 108 (1953) called for the termination of federal responsibility for American Indians and the end of all tribes' legal status as quickly as possible. Public Law 280 (1953) stated the right to assume legal jurisdiction over tribes without permission or even consultation. To encourage American Indians to leave reservations, the BIA provided one-way bus fare and the promise of employment assistance: an estimated 200,000 indigenous peoples left their homes for urban areas by 1962. The effectiveness of the relocation policy is reflected in the rise in the percentage of indigenous peoples living in urban areas, from 13% in 1940 to over 50% in 1980.

traditional tribal landholding
The right to land had been provided by treaty with individual tribes. In Article 1, Section 8 (enumerating the powers of the legislature) of the United States Constitution, Indian tribes were classified with foreign nations and the states "to regulate commerce with foreign nations, and among the several states, and with the Indian tribes".

ATL Thinking skills

1 Write a short summary of each government policy, include the purpose and methods of each.

2 Write one paragraph comparing the different policies.

3 Write one paragraph contrasting the different policies.

How did indigenous peoples organize themselves to change government policies?

Article I Section 8 of the United States Constitution acknowledges the sovereignty of indigenous tribes in the words "To regulate commerce with foreign nations, and among the several states, and with the Indian tribes". But almost all treaties between the various tribes and the federal government were violated by federal, state and local government entities. Indigenous people organized to reclaim self-determination and compel the United States to fulfill its responsibilities.

The first national organization, the National Council of American Indians (NCAI), formed in 1944. Membership was limited to indigenous. Charter members included the 80 representatives of approximately 50 tribal governments formed under Wheeler, along with some employees of the Indian Office (it became the BIA in 1947). The NCAI focused on reservation and tribal issues, along with voting rights. The NCAI worked throughout the 1950s to end forced termination, and proposed an assistance programme with the goal of economic self-sufficiency and tribal self-determination.

Further NCAI legislative successes include the 1965 Indian Self-Determination and Education Act, the 1968 Indian Civil Rights Act, the 1975 Indian Self-Determination and Education Assistance Act, the 1976 Indian Health Care Improvement Act and the American Indian Religious Freedom Act. The NCAI expanded to issues of environmental and resource management in the 1980s. During the 1990s NCAI worked to pass legislation that guaranteed tribes' control of criminal jurisdiction of indigenous peoples on their land as an inherent right. The NCAI made significant progress in its goal of tribal self-determination, but problems remained, especially for indigenous peoples living in urban areas.

How did the movement become more militant?

One effect of the termination policy previously mentioned was the movement of hundreds of thousands of indigenous people to urban areas. California's indigenous population was over 80% urban by 1960, with most residing in San Jose, Oakland, San Francisco and Los Angeles. An unexpected result was political activism.

The first urban indigenous activism began in November 1969, when a group called the Indians of All Tribes, initially led by Richard Oakes and LaNada Boyer-Means, occupied **Alcatraz Island** in San Francisco Bay. Students from California colleges began constructing facilities for a long occupation. The name "Indians of All Tribes" symbolized pan-Indianism, the idea that all indigenous peoples of the United States – and the Americas – should work together to achieve important political and economic goals.

The students explained the purpose of the siege with a sense of humour. They pointed out that like many reservations the island had no electricity, no fresh water, no schools, not enough land to support

Alcatraz Island
Alcatraz had been a high security federal prison, but had closed in 1963.

its population, and few jobs. They issued a proclamation to the "Great White Father" that:

- claimed Alcatraz Island by right of discovery

- offered $1.50 an acre or $24 total to purchase the island, citing increased land costs compared to the purchase of Manhattan Island

- promised to give white inhabitants a portion of the island for their own use "to be held in trust by the Bureau of Caucasian Affairs" and teach them Indian religion and traditions to advance their civilization.

The occupation grew as the local and state government, as well as federal authorities, hesitated to use force. More indigenous people joined and the population of Alcatraz grew beyond 200. Thousands came for short stays during the 19-month occupation. Time and poor living conditions took a toll on morale and participation. The occupation ended on 11 June as law enforcement officers arrested the remaining 15 occupants.

Alcatraz began a wave of more than 200 occupations and protests over the next few years. The American Indian Movement (AIM) was involved in several important actions in the early 1970s.

AIM began in Minneapolis, Minnesota in 1968, founded by Ojibwas Dennis Banks, Clyde Bellecourt and George Mitchell to openly confront injustice against American Indians. The urban underclass indigenous people comprised the majority of AIM. Its original complaint, voiced at the Minneapolis office of the BIA, was that the agency was only interested in "reservation Indians". Modelled after the Black Panthers to monitor police harassment and "**preventative detention**" of indigenous people, members followed police, resulting in reduced arrests. On 4 July 1971 AIM occupied Mount Rushmore to protest employment discrimination. The protest included hanging a large banner made of bed sheets reading "Sioux Indian Power" from George Washington's head. Following the publicity, AIM chapters opened in cities across the United States and Canada. "Red Power" had spread from its West Coast origins.

AIM sought to make a larger statement and in autumn 1972 conducted the Trail of Broken Treaties. A caravan of hundreds of cars and more than 500 indigenous people travelled from the West Coast to Washington, DC to present a list of 20 demands, including the abolition of the BIA. Elected officials refused to meet with them – it was a few days before the national general election and politicians were busy campaigning – and the group was left miles from home with little money and no plan. They occupied the main auditorium of the BIA. Federal law enforcement made attempts to force their way in and AIM responded by arming themselves with chair legs as well as dropping several standard typewriters from upper floor windows in front of police as a warning. The Nixon White House negotiated with AIM, and on 8 November negotiators reached a settlement by providing $66,000 for transportation of the entire group back to their homes. AIM left behind more than $2 million in damage, including the theft and destruction of files that included property titles, water rights and treaties. Among the seized documents were papers detailing the sterilization of indigenous women, often without their informed consent.

ATL Communication skills

Achieving change often requires persuasion. How did the activists on Alcatraz use language to communicate and satirize?

preventative detention

When police place an individual or group in custody (usually jail) to provide protection from harm from others or themselves. No criminal charges are made against those held.

TOK discussion

1 To what extent are leaders responsible for the actions of their followers?

2 Analyse the actions of AIM through the lenses of Immanuel Kant's reasoned approach to Categorical Imperatives and Jeremy Bentham's Utilitarianism. Do you arrive at the same conclusion?

The BIA occupation achieved fame, and a greater interest in indigenous people's affairs by the White House, but lacked concrete results. AIM continued to press indigenous people's rights, especially against what they saw as unjust actions by government officials and law enforcement. On 6 February 1973 a demonstration in Custer, South Dakota to protest at the lack of a murder charge for the killing of Wesley Bad Heart Bull turned violent. For reasons that are unclear demonstrators pushed their way through the courthouse doors and fought with police. Police fired tear gas to clear the courthouse. Demonstrators set fire to the courthouse and the Chamber of Commerce building. Firefighters were hit with bottles and rocks. Twenty-five people were eventually charged with felonious rioting and other crimes. The violence had not been planned, but as in Washington, DC, it occurred during the event.

The most famous AIM action was the 71-day occupation of the town of **Wounded Knee**, South Dakota, beginning on 27 February 1973. Dick Wilson, chairman of the Oglala Lakota, had his own private militia that was accused of violence against opponents, including murder, and selling grazing rights to whites and mineral rights to private companies. After an attempt by the Oglala Sioux Civil Rights Organization (OSCRO) to impeach Wilson failed, OSCRO requested AIM's help. AIM occupied Wounded Knee with a force of two to three hundred members. Heavily armed federal law enforcement officers surrounded the area. Shooting occurred almost daily during the 71-day occupation and siege, resulting in the deaths of two AIM members and leaving a US marshall paralysed. Media coverage was extensive. In May Banks and Means, among others, were arrested, although charges were dropped. It was the last large-scale AIM militant act.

While AIM procured nationwide attention, local protests were also significant. In Washington State, fish-ins began in 1964 to protest state policy restricting treaty rights that guaranteed the unrestricted use of natural resources. Poverty was high among indigenous people in the area, and fish constituted a significant portion of their diet. Native Americans who fished off reservation land were arrested despite the guarantees of the 1854 Medicine Creek Treaty. After a decade of protests that included violent reprisals by white vigilantes, and Internal Revenue Service Agents being escorted off reservations by armed (usually female) indigenous people, Federal District Judge George Hugo Boldt decided in favour of tribal fishing rights.

The indigenous people civil rights movement proceeded in several ways, from lobbying to violent protest. The movement gained a great deal of attention and obtained significant legal victories that did improve the lives of many indigenous people, but also left many impoverished and with a multitude of unsolved problems. The movement led to a formal apology from US Assistant Secretary for Indian Affairs Kevin Gover in 2000, and a joint Resolution of Apology to Native Peoples of the United States from the House and Senate in 2009.

Indigenous peoples in Latin America and the Caribbean

Latin Americans share a past in which there has been a mix of indigenous peoples and Europeans for 500 years but they experienced this past in different ways. Although some indigenous groups, especially

Wounded Knee
The site of the 1890 massacre of about 300 Lakota men, women and children, on the Pine Ridge Reservation.

▲ Russell Means and Clyde Bellecourt of AIM after being arraigned in Federal Court for AIM's occupation of Wounded Knee, 16 April 1973

sedentary and semi-sedentary groups, lived free in small tribes or bands, the largest populations in Mesoamerica and in the Andean highlands were dominated by empires. European domination was therefore partly superimposed over Inca and Aztec domination. Disease and war characterized the contact between indigenous and European cultures.

There was no real plan of contact and conquest. Indigenous cultures were absorbed into colonial hierarchies of power. This inclusion, however, included lack of equity, mistreatment and, for the first 200 years, slavery. In some areas, African slaves were forcibly brought to replace indigenous slaves. In the 19th century, the newly independent nations of Latin America tried to redress injustices by including indigenous people as citizens with civil rights. In practice, however, exclusion and in some cases, outright extermination was the case. The white elite remained in control of land and wealth.

The 20th century has shown how durable the cultural and racial legacies of this shared past are. The centuries-long mix of indigenous, European and African peoples in Latin America have made **mestizos** and **mulattoes** the majority. Yet there are indigenous communities that have survived in large numbers and many began to claim civil rights after 1945. The table below shows the percentage of indigenous populations in 11 Latin American countries:

mestizos
Term used in Latin America to denominate persons of European and indigenous ancestry and culture.

mulattoes
Term used in Latin America to denominate persons of European and African ancestry and culture.

ATL Self-management and research skills

Countries (with census dates)	% of indigenous population
Bolivia (2001)	62.5
Brazil (2000)	0.4
Chile (2002)	4.7
Costa Rica (2000)	1.8
Ecuador (2001)	6.7
Guatemala (2002)	41.2
Honduras (2001)	7.1
Mexico (2000)	6.5
Panama (2000)	10.2
Paraguay (2002)	1.8
Venezuela, Rep. Bol. de (2001)	2.3

Source: Economic Commission for Latin America and the Caribbean (ECLAC).

The Economic Commission for Latin America and the Caribbean (ECLAC) in Santiago, Chile was established by the United Nations in 1948 with the purpose of contributing to the economic development of Latin America and the Caribbean, and coordinating actions directed towards this end. Source: http://celade.cepal.org/redatam/PRYESP/SISPPI/ Accessed 12 August 2014.

Look at the statistics above and determine the countries with the largest indigenous populations. What were their original pre-Columbian indigenous empires and geographical areas?

Throughout the 20th century, movements for civil rights emerged in the Americas. Some social movements were organized by groups based on race or ethnicity to promote equity, particularly starting in the 1980s. From the 1940s others were imposed by governments to improve the lives of indigenous populations. One such movement was Indigenismo.

Indigenismo

By the 1940s, Latin American countries were mainly run by politicians who represented the mestizo ascendancy. The prevalent culture of the 1940s, admittedly racist from a 21st century perspective, celebrated the advent of the mestizo culture as having mixed the best qualities of the Europeans and the indigenous populations.

In 1940, the First Inter-American Indian Conference was held in Pátzcuaro, Mexico. Representatives from Latin American nations coordinated efforts to promote the development of indigenous peoples by integrating them into each nation. The framework of the agreement was one of respect for the "positive aspects" of indigenous culture, promotion of equal rights as citizens of each particular country and, above all, the advancement and assimilation of indigenous groups through education and modern technology. After the formation of the Organization of American States (OAS) in 1948, conferences were held under its auspices until the end of the 20th century. Nowhere was the idea of indigenismo more assiduously promoted at the state level than in Mexico.

Case study: Mexico

After the Mexican Revolution that started in 1910, and particularly during the presidency of Lázaro Cárdenas, the inclusion of Mexico's indigenous peoples became paramount. To this end, the government set up the Independent Department of Native Affairs in 1946 under the aegis of the Ministry of Education. At the time, Mexico's indigenous population spoke over 60 different languages and the state sought to teach them Spanish, so that they could participate in modern post-revolutionary Mexico. The idea was that only through acculturation could Mexico's indigenous population become assimilated to the Mexican national project. This idea did not emanate from the indigenous people themselves, but from the educated mestizo middle classes of post-revolutionary Mexico in the 1940s. In fact, most indigenistas were not indigenous people.

Mexican social scientists and anthropologists were convinced that only through education could the indigenous population become modern, productive Mexican citizens. The mestizo mix was mythologized. The government built museums and preserved archaeological remains of the ancient Mesoamerican cultures of the Aztecs and the Mayas, but stressed that these cultures were dead and the modern Mexican Indian needed to be assimilated into the prevalent mestizo culture. Only then could they overcome their social and economic "backwardness".

In 1948, the National Indigenist Institute (Instituto Nacional Indigenista, INI) was created. Coordinating centres were established for social scientists to evaluate indigenous communities. Then policies were formulated regarding the indigenous population's education, health and agricultural practices. The INI also sought to integrate the indigenous population into the Mexican political system established after the revolution, specifically, working in community groups with the Institutional Revolutionary Party (Partido Revolucionario Institucionalizado, PRI).

The results of the state policy of indigenismo were mixed. Boarding schools were established to forcibly promote the Spanish language among children. In addition, fully bilingual students were later trained as teachers for future schools. Not all children attended school to learn Spanish, and many left in grade school to work in farming. State experts went to the Indian communities to promote new cash crops and moneymaking crafts to incorporate indigenous peoples into a market economy. Yet despite these concerted efforts, by the late 1970s the Indian communities, languages and culture had remained impervious to full assimilation, and social and economic conditions had not improved. The INI was criticized as rigid and culturally oppressive by the left and members of the educated indigenous communities.

At the same time, international jurisprudence on the subject of human rights became more prevalent in the 1970s. It helped to end many military dictatorships in Latin America in the 1980s that abused human rights. It also created a new awareness in indigenous groups. Non-governmental organizations (NGOs) became increasingly powerful in channelling indigenous rights. In fact, in the last decades of the 20th century, Mexican indigenous organizations would join other indigenous groups throughout Latin America, who demanded the human right to remain ethnically distinct.

In addition, the economic crisis starting in 1982 in Mexico led to budgetary cuts imposed by international lenders like the International Monetary Fund (IMF). The INI was drastically reduced to a small educational role, setting up committees to train community leaders to campaign for the human rights of indigenous Mexicans.

These circumstances in the world and Mexico led to an amendment to the 1917 Mexican Constitution in 1992. This amendment established Mexico as a multicultural society and for the first time recognized that a person could be both indigenous and Mexican. In other words, indigenous Mexicans were respected for who they were and not treated as being in a process of assimilation into a Mexican mestizo culture.

This major change in government social policy has led to much discussion among indigenous people on how to channel Mexican government and private resources aimed at indigenous groups. It also has led to discussions on how to remain true to their ethnic roots. An example of this is the Wixaritari (language: Huichol) of northern Jalisco, a western state of Mexico. They received financial support from a local association set up by the INI called the Jalisco Union of Huichol Indigenous Communities (UCIHJ) – an association accepted by the Wixaritari and set up on their own terms, with tribal leaders running it. The UCIHJ has supported local initiatives, such as a new high school in San Andrés Cohamiata with Huichol teachers of the Wixaritari's culture, as well as the Spanish language national curriculum. University students from the Wixaritari studying in the city of Guadalajara have organized a cultural centre to support communication between the two cultures they live in. The purpose is to build respect for the diverse Mexicans who study at the university, acknowledging their multi-ethnicity, multiculturalism and multilingualism.

Source skills

▲ *La Patria (The Motherland)*, 1962, by Mexican painter Jorge González Camarena, was on the cover of free Ministry of Education textbooks.

Question

Look at this illustration. What do you think is the message it conveys to indigenous and mestizo children who used these textbooks in the 1960s and 1970s in Mexico? Notice the symbols.

Indigenous rights in Latin America in the 21st century

Few countries in Latin America developed similar government programmes to Mexico's indigenismo. Others have made changes prompted by international jurisprudence regarding human rights and the general awareness created in indigenous communities. Constitutional reforms have included the right to vote for indigenous people who could not read Spanish. These laws were enacted in Ecuador in 1979 and in Peru in 1980.

An event that created awareness in Latin American indigenous communities was the notoriety of a K'iche Maya woman from Guatemala, Rigoberta Menchú. In 1992 she was the recipient of the Nobel Peace Prize "in recognition of her work for social justice and ethno-cultural reconciliation based on respect for the rights of indigenous peoples". The Maya in Guatemala were more than half of the population. They lived in poverty and provided a source of cheap labour for the Guatemalan elites and *ladino* (mestizo) population. During the civil war that started in 1960, the military engaged in genocide against many Maya communities; Menchú lost her father, brother and mother in the civil war. When she began to organize indigenous associations, she was persecuted and had to flee to Mexico in 1981. Her Nobel Peace Prize brought attention to the plight of the Guatemalan indigenous population in the bloody Guatemalan Civil War. A total of 83% of those killed by the counter-insurgency troops of the Guatemalan military dictatorship were indigenous Maya. The war finally ended in 1996 with mediation from the UN, Spain and Norway between the government and the guerrilla groups. In 1999 US President Clinton regretted that the US had supported the Guatemalan army in the brutal civilian killings.

> ## Self-management and thinking skills
>
> Watch the docudrama *When the Mountains Tremble* produced by US documentary film-maker Peter Kinoy and directed by Pamela Yates in 2004. How did the Maya Indians become involved in the Cold War polarization that characterized the Guatemalan Civil War (1960–1996)?

Source skills

At an international level, the United Nations, within its International Labour Organization (ILO), passed Convention 169 in 1989, the first to refer specifically to indigenous peoples. Part of the preamble reads as follows:

Considering that the developments which have taken place in international law since 1957, as well as developments in the situation of indigenous and tribal peoples in all regions of the world, have made it appropriate to adopt new international standards on the subject with a view to removing the assimilationist orientation of the earlier standards, and recognising the aspirations of these peoples to exercise control over their own institutions, ways of life and economic development and to maintain and develop their identities, languages and religions, within the framework of the States in which they live, and noting that in many parts of the world these peoples are unable to enjoy their fundamental human rights to the same degree as the rest of the population of the States within which they live, and that their laws, values, customs and perspectives have often been eroded.

Source: International Labour Organization (ILO)

Question

How does the wording of this UN Convention reflect the historical changes in attitude towards indigenous peoples?

As countries around the world have ratified this convention, it has become a part of a nation's legal system. This has caused countries to make amendments to their constitutions to accommodate this view of indigenous populations. This was done by Colombia (1991), Mexico (1992), Paraguay (1992), Peru (1993), Bolivia (1994), Ecuador, (1998) and Venezuela (1999).

These changes have led to much debate in individual countries as to the ramifications of respecting these previously abused rights. It has led to discussions on differentiated citizenship (recognition of difference on the basis of equality), autonomy, self-determination, self-government, self-development and territorial control for indigenous communities and areas. This has become a contentious issue, especially regarding ownership of natural resources. A case in point is in the forests of southern Chile, where the Mapuche reject the exploitation of the privately owned forests in ancestral lands. Another case is in Cochabamba, Bolivia where traditional water rights are claimed by indigenous communities. This case was illustrated in the following film.

▲ President of Bolivia Evo Morales (left) and the Guatemalan Nobel Peace Prize winner, Rigoberta Menchú (right) during the G77 Summit in Santa Cruz, Bolivia, 14 June 2014

ATL Thinking and communication skills

Watch the 2010 film *Even the Rain*, by Spanish director Icíar Bollaín. She tells the story of Columbus' takeover in the Caribbean filmed by a modern film-maker in Bolivia. Do you see parallels in European "discovery" and modern indigenous rights, and exploitation of natural resources by foreigners? Discuss.

As countries began to ratify and apply UN ILO Convention 169, special representatives from indigenous groups have been included in governing bodies. This has created political clout for indigenous leaders, as they have formed part of government reform committees. Bolivia is an example, where Evo Morales became the first Aymará to be elected president.

Only from the vantage point of the 21st century can we see that with these objective advancements of indigenous rights, a cultural change may be in store for Latin America and the Caribbean nations.

8.2 African American civil rights movement

Conceptual understanding

Key questions

→ What tactics and to what effect did African Americans seek to achieve equal rights?

→ How, and for what reasons did government officials on local, state and federal levels react to efforts by civil rights activists?

Key concept

→ Causation

→ Consequence

→ Change

→ Perspective

Origins of the civil rights movement

The phrase "civil rights movement" is most often associated with the quest for African Americans to achieve the same legal rights, economic opportunities and social standing as white Americans, or as historian Charles Payne writes, "…the struggle against white supremacy". Following the end of the Reconstruction, any gains African Americans had made, were effectively removed and Black Codes were put in place in the states of the former Confederacy. The effective enforcement of these state and local laws became known as "Jim Crow". With the support of several United States Supreme Court rulings narrowing the interpretation of the 14th Amendment, including the "Slaughterhouse cases" (1873) and Plessy versus Ferguson (1896), the Jim Crow system solidified by the end of the 19th century.

Jim Crow, believed to be named after a 19th century vaudeville character, was the racial cast system that existed mostly in the American South, but also existed to some degree in northern states as well. Supported by laws, pseudo-scientific studies, and religious justification that legitimized white supremacy, Jim Crow was an entire social system enabled by constant threats and violence against African Americans.

Jim Crow ensured that daily humiliation of African Americans was an integral part of southern life. Laws included banning whites and African Americans from using the same recreational facilities; there were separate phone booths, taxis, elevators, drinking fountains, sections of theatres, toilets, even different bibles were used for taking an oath in court. Preventing close contact was the foundation for Jim Crow.

Violence and economic control supported the system. Lynching, the mob killing of people through "**frontier justice**", became a common way of keeping African Americans from achieving legal, social or economic equality. In the 11 states that had formed the Confederacy, African

TOK discussion

What were the underlying beliefs and assumptions of white society that justified Jim Crow?

frontier justice

Imprisonment for the crime of vagrancy, the offence of not having a job, was not only a system designed to use government power to prevent African Americans from seeking economic, legal or social advancement, it was a labour system that reintroduced slavery, if not in name, to the South.

Americans comprised 86% of the 3,521 people lynched. Economic reprisals, while not as dramatic, involved such actions as banks refusing credit, stores refusing to sell supplies so that spring planting could not occur, the seizing of land from sharecroppers, and firing from jobs, sometimes followed by imprisonment for vagrancy.

The experience of African Americans in the First World War led to new or enhanced perspectives on Jim Crow. Charles Hamilton Houston, the first African-American editor of the Harvard Law Review, and the future spearhead of the NAACP's legal fight to destroy Jim Crow, volunteered to serve in the Great War. As quoted in the documentary *Road to Brown*, "The hate and scorn showered on us Negro officers by our fellow Americans convinced me there was no sense in my dying for a world ruled by them… I made up my mind… that if I got through this war, I would study law and use my time fighting for men who could not strike back".

The Second World War impacted the quest "to make America be America for all its citizens" by creating greater awareness of the inconsistency of fighting Nazism in Europe while enduring racism at home. African Americans served in a still-segregated army. The contributions of African Americans to the war effort provided impetus to demand equality. Following the war, many veterans, including Medgar Evers, Robert Williams and Floyd McKissick, returned to a Jim Crow South, but began to assert their rights and became active in the civil rights movement.

Important precursors to the African American civil rights movement of the last half of the 20th century began with the 1905 **Niagara Movement** and the 1909 formation of the NAACP. The New Deal began the movement of African Americans into the Democratic Party, providing a growing balance to southern segregationist white party members. This coincided with the tremendous growth of what are now known as historically African American colleges and universities (**HBCUs**). By 1927 there were 77 such schools, with approximately 14,000 students. HBCUs and enrollment in them increased over the next decades, leading to a rising African American professional class. Additionally, industrial unions under such leaders as Walter Reuther and John L Lewis spoke out against Jim Crow, arguably because it inhibited the organizing of unions. African American and white union members working together saw improvements to working conditions and pay. Consequently, the African American middle class grew significantly, median income doubled from 1940 to 1960, and economic success contributed to increased political involvement.

Some historians explain part of the rise of the civil rights movement that began with the Montgomery Bus Boycott to change in the social atmosphere of the United States. The awakening of much of America to the injustices and humiliations endured by African Americans created additional space for civil rights leaders. In 1944, as the Second World War still raged, Swedish sociologist Gunnar Myrdal published a 1,483-page report entitled *An American Dilemma* that made plain the reality of segregation and the vast chasm between American ideals and the reality of Jim Crow. Religious leaders of various faiths addressed the problem as one for Americans not just one for African Americans. The increasing tension of the Cold War caused reflection on the ideal of freedom for every American citizen and a realization that discrimination and segregation

---

Research skills

Write a list of civil rights leaders, beginning with Charles Houston. Along with columns for organization, actions, and effects, add a column for learner profile attributes demonstrated. Identify characteristics and create a learner profile for leaders of your choice. You may also want to create learner profiles for opponents to civil rights for discussion and analysis.

Niagara Movement

The Niagara Movement grew from a meeting in Niagara Falls, New York, led by WEB DuBois.

HBCUs

HBCUs located from Washington, DC and throughout the South provided higher level education to African Americans where colleges or universities were white only. While Alcorn State was the first established HBCU, the Morrill Land–Grant Act of 1890 required states to either admit African Americans or establish colleges and universities for African Americans.

Source skills

Read Truman's speech, *Special Message to the Congress on Civil Rights*, on the Internet.

Questions

1 What is the main message of the speech?

2 With reference to origin, purpose, and content, what are the values and limitations of this speech for a student researching the Truman administration's civil rights programmes?

betrayed those ideals. The treatment of African Americans allowed the USSR to repeatedly point out the hypocrisy of the United States.

In February 1948 President Harry Truman gave a speech dedicated to civil rights, stating that: "the Federal Government has a clear duty to see that Constitutional guarantees of individual liberties and of equal protection under the laws are not denied…". Truman continued, recommending 10 objectives that were echoed in the Democratic Party platform later that year, causing the defection of southern Democrats and the formation of the short-lived States' Rights Democratic Party (Dixiecrats) whose ideology included white supremacy and racial segregation (see page 294). Truman gained 70% of the African American vote and survived the loss of defectors to win re-election. This was one example of rising African American political influence. While voter registration was minimized in the South due to legal obstacles, economic reprisals, and violence, African American voter registration in the northern states grew to over two million, creating a significant motivation for change in the political status quo.

Into the 1950s African Americans faced discrimination throughout the United States. Certainly it was much worse in the South, but throughout the country African Americans faced economic, education, legal and social obstacles. Two events that historians often point to that set the stage for the civil rights mass movement that began with the Montgomery bus boycott were the 1954 Supreme Court decision of Brown versus Board of Education, Topeka, and the murder of Emmett Till the following year. Brown, while dealing only with public school segregation, destroyed the legal basis for Jim Crow by overturning the 1896 Plessy decision. The court was seen to have evolved from that of a century before that had ruled in Dred Scott versus Sanford "that they (African-Americans) had no rights which the white man was bound to respect". The year after Brown, 14-year-old Till was murdered for speaking to a 21-year-old white woman while visiting his cousin in Mississippi. Mamie Till Bradley, Emmett's mother, insisted that the casket remain open at the memorial service in Chicago and photos of his mutilated corpse were printed in the *Chicago Defender* and *Jet* magazine. The shocking images immediately made international news. The accused murderers were acquitted, but later admitted to shooting Till in an interview published in *Look* magazine. The fury over the killing and the acquittal, combined with a view that the federal government was moving in the direction of equal rights, set the stage for the first big event of the modern civil rights movement: the Montgomery bus boycott.

Tactics

To secure their rights African Americans used a variety of strategies and tactics during the 20th century. These included boycotts, sit-ins and federal lawsuits as well as lobbying lawmakers and organizing rallies, where speeches were made advocating everything from non-violence to threatening armed resistance. The most well-known strategy was that of non-violent resistance. The methods had varying degrees of success. This section will explore the legal strategy to remove the legal foundations for Jim Crow, the Civil Rights Acts of 1957, 1960, and 1964 and 1968, the use of economic boycotts in Montgomery and Birmingham, Alabama, sit-ins at lunch counters and Freedom Rides, the efforts to overcome obstacles to voting focusing on Freedom Summer, and the 1963 March on Washington.

ATL Research skills

Investigate the main legal principle of the following important Supreme Court decisions leading to Brown:

1 Murray versus Maryland

2 State of Missouri ex rel. Gaines versus Canada, Alston et al. versus School Board of City of Norfolk et al.

3 Sipuel versus Board of Regents of University of Oklahoma, Sweatt versus Painter.

▲ Thurgood Marshall (1908–1993), Chief Counsel for the National Association for the Advancement of Colored People, talking to newsmen in New York City, 1955

TOK discussion

One important principle that many legal systems follow is that of precedent. Following precedent can be considered legal continuity. What are the benefits and problems to legal systems and society caused by following or breaking precedent?

How was segregation and inequality in education challenged legally?

Jim Crow was not only based on the social mores of the white majority, but also on a multitude of state and local laws that were supported by the 1896 Plessy versus Ferguson decision. The case established a precedent that segregation was legal, provided that equal facilities existed. In the three decades following the 1896 Plessy decision, the court confirmed the constitutionality of segregation and disproportionate funding of public schools and colleges.

Almost since its inception in 1909, the NAACP had pursued civil rights through legal channels regarding voting rights, residential discrimination, and due process in criminal cases.

The legal journey to make the equal protection clause of the 14th Amendment apply to government-enforced racial segregation was led by the NAACP with a legal strategy initiated by Nathan Ross Margold. The approach was incremental and involved schools: Margold was convinced that the justices did not want to enshrine school segregation as part of the US Constitution. He recommended selecting cases that would be appealed to the Supreme Court to chip away at precedents. The report was to inspire many key attorneys, including Thurgood Marshall (see page 296), who referred to Margold's work as the bible of the NAACP legal campaign.

It was not until Charles Houston was appointed the NAACP Special Counsel in 1934 that the drive began. Houston modified Margold's approach. His team would first assault the "equal" part of Plessy to make equality so costly that public institutions would desegregate and to set up a series of progressive precedents that would be used to overturn Plessy.

Less challenging, but still difficult, was recruiting graduate school applicants to sue universities. Only when precedents were built up with those cases, would desegregation of public schools be pursued; after all by 1935, in all 44 cases where school segregation was challenged directly courts ruled that segregated schools were constitutional. The Second World War years saw the new leader of the NAACP legal arm, Thurgood Marshall, travel through much of the country arguing numerous cases of various types, while all the while building support for the NAACP's efforts.

Brown versus Board of Education 1954

The NAACP had helped African American plaintiffs bring desegregation lawsuits against school districts in a number of states. Brown was a consolidation of Briggs versus Elliot (South Carolina), Davis versus County Board of Education of Prince Edward County (Virginia), Bolling versus Sharpe (District of Columbia) and Gebhart versus Belton (Delaware). The Supreme Court heard the case twice, once under Chief Justice Vinson and, after he died, under new Chief Justice, Earl Warren. It was under Warren that the Court issued a unanimous verdict on 17 May 1954, declaring that racial segregation in public schools violated the Equal Protection Clause of the 14th Amendment. A critical issue in Brown was remedy: how critical issue in Brown was remedy: how de jure (by law) segregated schools were to be desegregated. Discussions were delayed until 1955 when the Court concluded vaguely that desegregation should occur with "all deliberate speed". The phrasing created space for school districts throughout the South and various states to delay desegregation.

How did states, schools, and communities react to Brown?

Many school districts began to desegregate in the wake of Brown. However, the South was almost united in its opposition. On 12 March 1956 the South spoke as a unit when 77 members of the House of Representatives and 19 senators signed the "Southern Manifesto" – a resolution condemning the Brown decision and openly encouraged states to defy the ruling. Several state legislatures created laws that imposed sanctions on any school district that complied with the court ruling.

In Virginia, a group of white local government officials formed the Defenders of State Sovereignty and Individual Liberties with the purpose of maintaining segregation. Direct disobedience to Brown became known as Massive Resistance, a term created by Democrat Senator Harry F Byrd, Sr, a former governor of the state. The strategy was replicated in various ways throughout the South. Under Massive Resistance, the state government could close any school district that attempted to desegregate. Massive Resistance was challenged in both state and federal court and lost. In response some districts closed all schools, allowing white-only private academies to be opened, leaving African Americans with no schools to attend. The closing of schools displaced many white students too, causing significant white opposition to Virginia's policy. Some prominent businessmen pressured the governor and legislators to relent. In 1959 Virginia Governor Lindsay Almond declared resistance was over, and with his prompting the legislature repealed the segregation statutes. Still, a few counties resisted, closing their schools. It was not until 1968 with the Supreme Court decision Green versus County School Board of New Kent County, Virginia, that large-scale desegregation took place in the state. Still, many schools could not be substantially desegregated due to the accelerated development of segregated suburbs and the establishment of numerous white-only private academies.

The popular President, Dwight Eisenhower, provided at best weak support for Brown stating, "I think it makes no difference whether or not I endorse it". Historian Richard Kluger argued that Eisenhower's lack of support gave resisters strength, making desegregation more difficult and traumatic. The President did act when local and state governments defied the federal government openly. When nine African American students attempted to enroll at Central High School in Little Rock, Arkansas, Governor Orval Faubus used Arkansas National Guard soldiers to block the students from entering. The NAACP obtained a federal court order preventing Faubus from blocking entry and the students entered the school on 23 September 1957 escorted by police. The threat of violence from a growing mob caused the police to take the students home. It was only after that incident, and with Little Rock becoming a national and international news story, that Eisenhower ordered troops from the US Army's 101st Airborne Division to protect the students. For the entire year each student was assigned a soldier as a personal escort, and troops, along with the Arkansas National Guard, maintained security in and around Central High School. The following year Governor Faubus closed all four Little Rock High Schools in line with actions in other southern states.

When John Kennedy became president in 1961, civil rights were not a priority. However, the Justice Department, under his younger brother Robert's orders, brought lawsuits against resisting school districts. Some progress occurred: 31 districts desegregated in 1961, 46 in 1962, and 166 districts in 1963.

The issue of remedy continued to be problematic into the 1970s. In 1971 (Swann versus Charlotte-Mecklenburg) the United States Supreme Court established that use of quotas was a legitimate starting point, remediation was to be judged by effectiveness, close scrutiny would be applied to predominantly African American schools, and **busing** could be used to achieve desegregation. The use of forced busing was limited in 1974 (Milliken versus Bradley) to situations of proven de jure segregation only within school district lines, not across. This decision paved the way for white flight (a phrase describing whites moving to suburban school districts to attend white-only schools) in cities throughout the country from Los Angeles to Boston where forced busing saw opposition that sometimes led to rioting. By the 1990s many districts were resegregated.

busing
Desegregation busing refers to transporting students to schools assigned to them. Students could be assigned to a school that was not near their home in order to get a mix of races in a school.

How were boycotts used to promote civil rights?

Lasting a year, the Montgomery bus boycott (December 1955 to December 1956) was the first community action that brought nationwide attention to the civil rights struggle.

In the latter part of 1953, Jo Ann Robinson, an English teacher at Alabama State College, formed the Women's Political Council (WPC) with several other African American leaders in Montgomery, Alabama. The WPC met with Montgomery City officials to discuss racial bus policies. On 2 March 1955, a 15-year-old young African American woman was arrested for refusing to give up her seat to a white woman. Later that month ED Nixon, Jo Ann Robinson, Rosa Parks, Rufus A Lewis and Martin Luther King met with city officials to discuss city bus seating policies. Another African American woman, Mary Louise Smith, was arrested in October for refusing to give up her seat. By the time Rosa Parks was arrested for the same crime on 1 December 1955, a series of civil disobedient acts had occurred.

ATL Communication skills

Assess the language and the content of WPC's leaflets. In light of the time period, how persuasive was it. What is the role of communication in mass action?

> This is for Monday, December 5, 1955
>
> Another Negro woman has been arrested and thrown into jail because she refused to get up out of her seat on the bus for a white person to sit down.
>
> It is the second time since the Claudette Colbert case that a Negro woman has been arrested for the same thing This has to be stopped.
>
> Negroes have rights, too, for if Negroes did not ride the buses, they could not operate. Three-fourths of the riders are Negroes, yet we are arrested, or have to stand over empty seats. If we do not do something to stop these arrests, they will continue. The next time it may be you, or your daughter, or mother.
>
> This woman's case will come up on Monday. We are, therefore, asking every Negro to stay off the buses Monday in protest of the arrest and trial. Don't ride the buses to work, to town, to school, or anywhere on Monday.
>
> You can afford to stay out of school for one day if you have no other way to go except by bus.
> You can also afford to stay out of town for one day. If you work, take a cab, or walk. But please, children and grown-ups, don't ride the bus at all on Monday. Please stay off of all buses ~~Monday~~.

▲ WPC leaflet printed 2 December 1955

What was different about this event were the actions of local activists. It is important to understand that the boycott was a grass roots movement. The main protagonist, Rosa Parks, had been a civil rights activist since 1932. In 1943, more than a decade before the bus boycott, Parks had an encounter with a white bus driver. African Americans had to pay up front, exit the bus and re-enter through the rear door. Parks refused. She was forced to exit the bus and the driver, James F Blake, drove off before Parks could re-board. It was after that incident that she joined the NAACP and was elected the Montgomery chapter secretary – a dangerous job that required her to document violent acts and investigate murders, voter intimidation and rape. Rosa Parks was not an accidental activist.

It was the same driver who was driving the bus on 1 December 1955. Parks and three other African Americans were ordered by Blake to give up their seats and move to the back. The other three agreed, but Parks refused, was arrested and taken to jail. The following day the Montgomery civil rights leaders formed the Montgomery Improvement Association. Later that day the Women's Political Council, led by Jo Ann Robinson, printed over 50,000 leaflets calling for a one-day boycott and distributed them in less than 24 hours.

The one-day boycott was successful. A leadership meeting of the Montgomery Improvement Association was held that morning at which Martin Luther King Jr, was elected president. That evening a mass meeting of the Montgomery Improvement Association at Holt Street Baptist Church attracted thousands from Montgomery's African American community. Covered by press and television, the meeting opened with hymns and prayer, followed by a speech by King.

> …there comes a time when people get tired of being trampled over by the iron feet of oppression. There comes a time, my friends, when people get tired of being flung across the abyss of humiliation…
>
> …And we are not wrong, we are not wrong in what we are doing. If we are wrong, the Supreme Court of this nation is wrong. If we are wrong, the Constitution of the United States is wrong.

The speech was the beginning of King's national prominence as a civil rights leader.

Most African Americans and some whites walked or got rides through an organized transportation operation, including car pools. The boycott continued into January. On the 30 January King's home was bombed. Two days later a lawsuit (Aurelia S Browder, et al. versus WA Gayle et al.) challenging the constitutionality of segregated buses was filed in the federal court. The boycott continued and city officials tried to break it, including bringing conspiracy charges against scores of boycott leaders. The trial and conviction of King brought national attention to the cause in March. On 5 June the federal court in Montgomery ruled that Alabama's bus segregation laws violated the 14th Amendment. The defendants appealed while the boycott continued. The United States Supreme Court affirmed the lower court ruling on 13 November. MIA members voted to continue the boycott until city leaders agreed to implement the Supreme Court

▲ Martin Luther King Jr, speaking at a meeting of the Montgomery Improvement Association, the organization formed after Rosa Park was arrested for not moving to the back of the bus

order and on 20 December, a year after the boycott began, city leaders ended the policy of segregated buses.

Source skills

Ella Baker remarked that,

My basic sense of it has always been to get people to understand that in the long run they themselves are the only protection they have against violence or injustice. ... People have to be made to understand that they cannot look for salvation anywhere but to themselves.

Question

Evaluate the validity of Ella Baker's view of the importance of grass roots, rather than leader-focused movements when reading about the methods and results of the Montgomery bus boycott.

Montgomery City buses desegregated with little violence. The Jim Crow caste system remained in the city, with buses being the sole exception. However, it can be argued that the success transformed the attitudes of southern African Americans from one of fear of whites, especially the Ku Klux Klan, to a growing defiance in the face of threats and brutality. Montgomery showed that a united African American community could successfully challenge Jim Crow and spawned movements in numerous other southern cities. It elevated Martin Luther King Jr, into a national figure as well as promoting non-violent resistance as a method to achieve racial equality. Lastly, Montgomery served as a spark for the creation of the Southern Christian Leadership Conference (SCLC) by King, Bayard Rustin, Ella Baker, Joseph Lowery, Fred Shuttlesworth, Ralph Abernathy and numerous African American ministers in 1957.

Why and how did the disruption of business through sit-ins evolve as a tactic, and to what effects?

Sit-ins had been tried as early as 1943, but did not result in mass mobilization as the 1960 sit-ins that began in Greensboro, North Carolina did. The grass roots movement led by the Congress of Racial Equality (CORE) used the tactic of the sit-in which was grounded in non-violent direct action. The idea was to demonstrate the unfairness of racial segregation in businesses by preventing regular business from occurring by demanding to be served just as whites were. In 1960 sit-ins took hold, gained nationwide publicity, and in numerous cities achieved levels of desegregation in retail businesses.

The initial sit-in at the white-only lunch counter in Woolworth's department store in Greensboro began on 1 February 1960. Joseph McNeil, Ezell Blair, Franklin McCain and David Richmond, students at North Carolina A&T College, sat down at the lunch counter after purchasing several items at the store. As expected, they were denied service. The students returned the next morning and the group swelled to more than 20 students. By the end of the second day, the sit-in

▲ African Americans sit in protest at a whites-only lunch counter in Nashville, Tennessee in 1960.

acquired media coverage, along with groups of whites who harassed the students. The sit-in continued for five days before the students agreed to a mayoral request to halt the protests while the city worked toward resolution. CORE and newly formed organizations such as the Committee on Appeal for Human Rights used Greensboro to launch sit-ins in other cities. By the end of February similar demonstrations had occurred in more than 30 locations in seven different states. By the end of the year more than 70,000 people had demonstrated or marched in support of the desegregation of public facilities and retail establishments.

Nashville, Tennessee, was the location of particularly well-organized and successful student demonstrations. Students from Fisk University including John Lewis, Diane Nash and Marion Barry, and James Lawson from Vanderbilt University, all of whom became significant figures in the southern civil rights movement, organized and led thousands of students from traditional African American colleges in the Nashville area. At first, just as in Greensboro, demonstrators encountered only threats and verbal abuse. On 17 February, a group of white teenagers attacked participants. When police arrived they let the assailants go, but arrested the demonstrators. As planned, more students took their place; they were arrested and replaced as the protests spread to other locations. In April the home of Z Alexander Looby, lead lawyer for the demonstrators, was bombed and substantially destroyed, but the Loobys were unhurt. In the aftermath several thousand people marched to City Hall to confront Mayor Ben West. West agreed that discrimination on the basis of race was wrong. By mid-May Nashville lunch counters were desegregated, which was followed by the integration of lunch counters in San Antonio, Texas. Greensboro followed on 25 July, and the regionwide department store chains of Woolworth, Grant, Kress and McCrory-McClellan integrated their lunch counters as well.

The sit-ins had long-lasting effects beyond successfully desegregating some facilities. A new student organization grew from the movement. With leadership from Ella Baker, at the time the NAACP's executive director, students from 12 states, including Lewis, Nash, Lawson and Berry, formed a new student-headed organization: the Student Non-violent Coordinating Committee (SNCC). SNCC became an independent force in the southern civil rights movement. The sit-ins also demonstrated the effectiveness of non-violence and opened a new front on the battle for racial equality.

What strategy did activists use to get the federal government to support civil rights and desegregation?

In 1947 CORE had conducted an interracial bus ride through the upper South, but the effort gained almost no media coverage. In early 1961 CORE Director James Farmer, a follower and advocate of Gandian non-violent philosophy, thought the time had arrived to take action again. CORE had two goals. The first was to force the federal government to actively protect the civil rights of African Americans. Farmer explained the methodology: "We put on pressure and create a crisis (for federal leaders) and then they react." The second equally important goal was to insure that the Supreme Court decisions that made segregated interstate transportation and related facilities unconstitutional were obeyed. These two goals would be achieved by interracial groups of men and women sitting together in buses and terminals and knowingly countering the Jim Crow traditions of the Deep South. Two interracial groups were to ride Greyhound and Trailways buses from Washington, DC to New Orleans, Louisiana. The Freedom Riders expected threats, arrests, and possibly severe violence.

Direct confrontation was risky to those involved and possibly to the communities along the way, but in his view the cautious ways of the 1950s had not garnered nationwide support, especially from the political leaders of the country.

Thirteen Freedom Riders, six white and seven African American, began their trip on 4 May. On 14 May incidents made the rides into a national news story. As the first bus pulled up to the bus terminal in Anniston, Alabama, 30–50 men armed with sticks and metal bars surrounded the bus. Police were not in sight because Anniston officials had given the Ku Klux Klan permission to attack. Rocks were thrown through bus windows and two tires were slit.

▲ A Freedom Rider's bus was destroyed by a mob of whites opposing their efforts to integrate public transportation facilities in Alabama, 1961.

As the bus drove off, forty cars followed. When the two slashed tyres went flat the driver stopped on the side of the highway; the mob surrounded and tried to storm the bus. An incendiary bomb was thrown into the bus, causing a fire and the bus filled with smoke. As the passengers streamed out, they were attacked and beaten. When the violence ended, the young daughter of the owner of the local store who had witnessed the attack came out with water and towels, wiping the faces of victims. Others invited them inside.

The second bus was attacked and threatened in Anniston as well, but continued on to Birmingham, Alabama, where a mob of 30 men armed with baseball bats, chains and pipes beat the Freedom Riders, several bystanders, and reporters and news photographers. After 15 minutes the mob melted away as the police showed up. Photos of the beaten riders and stories of the Klan's mob attack were featured in major newspapers.

Before the rides began the FBI and the Attorney General were aware of potential violence. The FBI also knew that Sheriff Bull Connor had given the Ku Klux Klan time to assault the riders, but did nothing other than alert Attorney General Robert Kennedy. Kennedy notified the local police, ignorant of the complicity of local law enforcement.

The Freedom Riders wanted to continue, but drivers refused to drive buses with the Freedom Riders on board, so the group was stranded in the Birmingham bus terminal. With the assistance of Robert Kennedy's aide John Seigenthaler, the group was taken to the airport and flown to New Orleans, ending the first Freedom Ride.

The Kennedy administration was unhappy with the Freedom Riders, the Ku Klux Klan, Governor Patterson and the local police. Civil rights was a low priority for the four-month-old administration that was focused on the Cold War. The President called for calm, but did not publicly blame anyone for the attacks. James Farmer had expected the administration to defend the civil rights activists and allow them to continue with their federally protected interstate trip, but the administration did not act.

The Freedom Rides did not end, although CORE no longer directed them, having been replaced by SNCC. John Lewis, Diane Nash and fellow students from Nashville immediately organized a second trip of 10 riders, making the President furious, ignoring the President's request to cancel the ride. Nevertheless, the administration ordered Greyhound to supply a bus or be in violation of federal law. In Montgomery, Freedom Riders and Robert Kennedy's representative John Seigenthaler were beaten. That night there was a rally headed by Martin Luther King at Ralph Abernathy's church. A mob surrounded the church, yelling and tossing tear gas through a church window. The Attorney General called in 500 unarmed federal marshals who kept the mob at bay until being relieved by the Alabama National Guard. President Kennedy called for a "cooling off period", but the riders would have none of it. The following day the Freedom Riders were set to continue into Mississippi and invited King to join them. The most nationally recognized face of the movement declined, citing a need not to violate probation, but several riders stated that they, too, were on probation. King lost significant respect, some riders believing he was afraid and began to refer to him disrespectfully as "De Lawd".

The Kennedy administration, fearing more violence, made a deal with Mississippi Senator James Eastland that in exchange for a guarantee of protection from physical violence the state could arrest them for disturbing the peace and like violations. They both kept their word and the riders were arrested, spending time in the notorious Parchman Prison. On 29 May the administration announced a ban on segregation on interstate buses (beginning 1 November). Many facilities were desegregated with little publicity in the succeeding months. CORE reported that by the end of 1962, segregation of interstate travel had ended.

The rides achieved the specific goal of integrating interstate travel. They did not, however, achieve James Farmer's overall objective of obtaining overt, active and continued support for civil rights from the Kennedy administration. The combination of the 1960 sit-ins and 1961 Freedom Rides brought about a split within the civil rights movement itself.

Mass demonstrations evolve

With the completion of the sit-ins and Freedom Rides, the movement broadened its approach with varying degrees of success. In the next two years, three major demonstrations would take place in Albany, Georgia, Birmingham, Alabama and Washington, DC. They ranged in length from eleven months to one day. By the close of the August 1963 March on Washington, the southern civil rights movement had become a critical component of American political, civil and social discourse.

In fall of 1961, riding on the wave of publicity and hard-won success of the Freedom Rides, SNCC went to Albany, Georgia to organize a prolonged protest campaign to eliminate all forms of racial segregation in the city. Police Chief Laurie Pritichett had studied police and white supremacist reactions to the protests; creating a strategy of gentle arrests and jailing beyond city limits, thus out of sight of press cameras.

Despite the added publicity from the arrival of Martin Luther King Jr. in December, Pritchett was able to diffuse confrontations. One example, when King and Ralph Abernathy were arrested, an anonymous person posted bail, thus avoiding news coverage of imprisonment of the famed civil rights leaders. King left in July after his third arrest, but the demonstrations and arrests continued into late summer, 1962, and Albany's civic leaders granted no concessions. The Albany movement had shown that an organized African American community could conduct long-term protests without wavering, but King's image within the movement suffered as 10 months of non-violent confrontation yielded no progress. Civil rights activists learned an important lesson; targets must be chosen to provoke violent confrontations or they would not command attention from national media and federal officials.

Birmingham: April and May 1963

Civil rights activists believed that they had to create a crisis. They needed more action from the federal government. They chose Birmingham, Alabama, a city known as the most segregated city in the United States, nicknamed "Bombingham" for the constant level of extreme violence segregationists employed to protect Jim Crow. With lessons learned from Albany, the Alabama Christian Movement for Human Rights, led by Fred Shuttlesworth, and the SCLC, led by Martin Luther King Jr, plotted a direct action campaign of mass meetings, sit-ins, marches on city hall, a boycott of downtown stores and voter registration attempts. Local activists were recruited beforehand to train demonstrators in non-violent philosophy and tactics. The campaign began on 2 April after a mayoral run-off election that resulted in moderate Alfred Boutwell defeating Public Safety Commissioner Bull Connor, an extreme segregationist. Connor remained in charge of Birmingham's police and fire departments.

Within days hundreds of protesters were arrested. On 10 April, a state circuit court issued an injunction banning the protests. Shuttlesworth, King and the rest of the leadership discussed whether to obey the court order as they had in Albany. Instead, they chose to continue the campaign with King declaring that the court's ruling was "unjust, undemocratic, and unconstitutional". Hundreds more were arrested and King was jailed on 12 April, then placed in solitary confinement.

It was in jail that King wrote what became known as the "Letter from Birmingham Jail". Writing with a smuggled pen on the margins of a newspaper, King responded to an appeal by local clergy to halt the protests as untimely and to wait for the new city administration to implement new policies. King's response explained that "one has a moral responsibility to disobey unjust laws", and captured the moral and practical reasons, not only for the Birmingham campaign but for the entire movement.

I am in Birmingham because injustice is here … Injustice anywhere is a threat to justice everywhere…

We know through painful experience that freedom is never voluntarily given by the oppressor; it must be demanded by the oppressed… For years now I have heard the word "Wait!" It rings in the ear of every Negro with piercing familiarity. This "Wait" has almost always meant "Never." …

But when you have seen vicious mobs lynch your mothers and fathers at will and drown your sisters and brothers at whim; when you have seen hate filled policemen curse, kick and even kill your black brothers and sisters; when you see the vast majority of your twenty million Negro brothers smothering in an airtight cage of poverty in the midst of an affluent society; when you suddenly find your tongue twisted and your speech stammering as you seek to explain to your six year old daughter why she can't go to the public amusement park that has just been advertised on television… There comes a time when the cup of endurance runs over, and men are no longer willing to be plunged into the abyss of despair.

King was released after eight days. The movement was running out of adults who were willing to go to jail. James Bevel of the SCLC suggested that high school students be used in demonstrations. Some movement leaders questioned the morality of using children, but Bevel's idea was implemented. On 2 May the Children's Crusade began with more than a thousand students marching towards downtown. Hundreds were arrested and jailed. On 3 May another march was attempted, but as soon as the youths left the church Bull Connor ordered the police and fire departments to halt the protest forcefully using high pressure water hoses so powerful they tore bark off trees and clothing off demonstrators. They also sent police dogs trained to bite and officers with clubs. Photos and film of the city's violent response to children peacefully protesting appeared in newspapers and on nightly television news, creating outrage around the United States and beyond its borders.

The turmoil alarmed Birmingham's whites, most of whom supported Jim Crow but were repulsed by Connor's tactics. In the chaos of sit-ins, violent police responses and arrests almost no one was shopping downtown. The Kennedy administration sent Burke Marshall to mediate. At first the city's power elite, the Senior Citizen's Council, refused, but after seeing downtown still occupied by demonstrators singing freedom songs an agreement was reached that called for an immediate halt to the protests in exchange for desegregation as demanded and downtown merchants integrating the workforce. The hospitalized Shuttlesworth was furious and accused King of settling for promises. Hardline segregationists including Governor George Wallace simply ignored the settlement, and took actions to reinforce Jim Crow. In the next weeks bombs exploded at the home of King's brother and at the Gaston Motel, where King and SCLC staff had stayed during the protests. Violence grew as some African Americans threw rocks at police, who, along with state troopers, responded by randomly beating African Americans.

President Kennedy finally took action on 12 May, moving 3,000 army troops to Birmingham's city limits. He warned that he would not allow extremists to undermine the agreement. The violence lessened; downtown merchants began to remove racial signs and began hiring a few African Americans. The city's segregation laws were repealed. By employing non-violent confrontation against an appropriate target the civil rights movement achieved a major victory: awakening an entire nation to the reality of segregation, racial violence, and the need for a federal government commitment of support. Birmingham was still the home to extreme violent acts from hardline segregationists, and a church was bombed in September, killing four young girls; the city known nationally for its adherence to Jim Crow, African Americans gained important ground for racial equality.

TOK discussion

Many works of literature have a protagonist who struggles with a powerful antagonist. How important was antagonist Bull Connor to the success of the Birmingham Civil Rights movement's protagonists? If Conner would have reacted as the officials in Albany did, would Birmingham have garnered the attention of the nation as well as the President? Explain.

TOK discussion

The civil rights leaders in Birmingham used children with full knowledge that some would be jailed and some would probably be injured. What ethical responsibilities do leaders have to protect those who are not responsible for their own actions? When is a cause more important than the present welfare of children?

Birmingham forced the President to re-examine his position. Civil rights was not something to be pushed aside in favour of the Cold War. On 24 May at a meeting with civil rights leaders, Attorney General Robert Kennedy was jolted from complacency by 24-year-old Freedom Rider, Jerome Smith, who told the Attorney General that it was obvious the Kennedys did not care about the demonstrators and that it made him nauseous to be in the same room as the Attorney General. Others joined in to vehemently criticize the administration's lack of policy and action. Kennedy took a verbal barrage that Kenneth Clark, the sociologist integral to Brown, described as "one of the most violent, emotional, verbal assaults that I had ever witnessed before or since". At first angered, in the following days and weeks a reflective Robert Kennedy realized that African Americans had a multitude of legitimate grievances. According to historian Robert Schlesinger, "Racial justice was no longer an issue in the middle distance. Robert Kennedy now saw it face to face, and he was on fire". John and Robert Kennedy watched as protests and demonstrations grew into hundreds of thousands of participants in the wake of Birmingham and tried to come up with policies to correct the injustices exposed in the previous two years and hold what seemed to be a fraying nation together. One result was President Kennedy's 11 June 1963 civil rights speech in which he declared, "We are confronted primarily with a moral issue", and that the United States "will not be fully free until all its citizens are free". It was in that speech that he proposed the civil rights bill that would become the Civil Rights Act of 1964.

March on Washington for jobs and freedom

A famous image of the civil rights struggle is of Martin Luther King Jr, standing on the steps of the Lincoln Memorial in Washington, DC on 28 August 1963. King's "I Have a dream" speech was an important part of the March on Washington for Jobs and Freedom; it was the culmination of a day-long event that sought a comprehensive civil rights bill that would outlaw segregation of all public facilities, ensure voting rights, provide training for workers and a public works programme, ban discrimination in all employment public and private, reduce congressional representation for states that disenfranchised voters, would provide for enforcement of those aims. The March had been years in the making and months in planning. It became a massive one-day demonstration with estimates of the numbers taking part ranging from 250,000 to over a half million people. The march dramatically increased the pressure on the President and Congress to take up and pass the new civil rights bill.

Biographer Taylor Branch writes that the thought of hundreds of thousands of African Americans on the streets of Washington, DC caused apprehension among "authorities from all sectors" as well as much of the public. The White House prepared emergency declarations that would bring in 19,000 soldiers to suppress rioting, all liquor stores were closed, courts prepared for all-night hearings. Hospitals cancelled scheduled elective surgery. Major League Baseball cancelled two Washington Senator home games.

The morning of the march, packed trains and buses poured into Washington terminals. Of the more than a quarter of a million arriving, approximately 60,000 were whites who joined the march

---

Class discussion

Framing a historical debate, James T Patterson poses this question:

"How much importance should we attach to 'top-down' actors – presidents, the Supreme Court justices, leaders such as King – as contrasted to the doings of unsung activists, including women, sharecroppers, blue-collar workers, and young people at the grass roots?"

Reflecting on the boycotts, Freedom Rides and demonstrations, how much credit do you give leadership versus grass roots activists?

as well. Crowds surrounded the Reflecting Pool before the largest rally in the capital's history officially began. Singers Bob Dylan, Joan Baez, Odetta and the folk group Peter, Paul and Mary performed. The programme started with several impromptu short speeches by Fred Shuttlesworth, Ralph David Abernathy and Dick Gregory, among others. The event was covered by more than 1,700 reporters – more than covered Kennedy's inauguration.

Randolph gave the first scheduled speech, which framed the rest of the day's speakers. John Lewis, the Freedom Rider and SNCC activist, gave toned-down remarks after pressure from the White House and the march's organizers. Lewis called out both major political parties for hypocrisy, declaring that African Americans would not stop marching until meaningful legislation became law. James Farmer was the next scheduled speaker, but was in jail and his forceful statement was read.

Martin Luther King was the final speaker. He began a little after 3.30 pm with the speech that contained many memorable phrases, "Now is the time to make real the promises of democracy". He repeated the phrase, "We can never be satisfied as long as", and listed affronts against African American people that included police violence, African American children being robbed of their dignity by Jim Crow, voting rights being denied in the South while in the North there was "nothing for which to vote". King had worked on a conclusion, but abandoned the text in favour of his more familiar Sunday sermon rhythm with the encouragement of Mahalia Jackson. The famous conclusion began with the phrase, "I have a dream," which captured his vision of a more just America, "…when all God's children, African American men and white men, Jews and Gentiles, Protestants and Catholics, will be able to join hands and sing in the words of the old Negro spiritual, 'Free at last! Free at Last! Thank God Almighty, we are free at last!'" King left the podium immediately. After a benediction and the singing of "We Shall Overcome" the crowd made their way to the terminals.

▲ Singer Odetta at the 1963 Civil Rights March on Washington. Aug. 28, 1963.

The effects of the March on Washington for Jobs and Freedom are difficult to quantify. The President, who had warily viewed the preparations, was so impressed by the demonstration that he invited 10 of the main organizers to a White House reception, connecting his administration to the movement. Dr King became an even more important public figure and voice for civil rights. Conversely, Malcolm X called it the "Farce on Washington" and a circus.

For much of white America the peaceful march removed a level of uncertainty and brought some support, especially middle class, to the movement. But, Senator Hubert Humphrey, a liberal and consistent supporter of civil rights who had placed a proposal to end racial segregation in the 1948 Democratic Party platform, doubted that the event had changed the minds of many in the House or Senate. Violence, but not from participants, occurred in the aftermath as buses leaving the city were pelted with rocks. Two weeks later the Birmingham church

Class discussion

Malcom X argues that the March on Washington effectively accomplished nothing. What were the consequences of the March? What progress can be tied to King's words and acts? How certain can historians be when assigning causes and consequences?

bombing killed four young girls took place.
The President condemned the violence and travelled to the South to speak in favour of the need for significant legislation.

How did groups work for voting rights in rural areas and fight for political influence?

Seeing other civil rights organizations focused on southern cities, SNCC decided to undertake voter registration drives in rural areas of the Deep South, specifically Mississippi. Of the 50 states, Mississippi had the highest population percentage of African Americans, but the white upper class held tightly to the caste system that had changed little since the 1800s. In 1956 the state legislature established the Mississippi State Sovereignty Commission (MSSC) to maintain Jim Crow after Brown by using almost unlimited "necessary" methods. Under Governor JP Coleman, the state-run body functioned as a propaganda machine and spied on African American activists and civil rights organizations, providing intelligence to local police. However, the MSSC became significantly more active when Ross Barnett became governor in 1960. Intelligence activities increased significantly and the MSSC directed funds to the Citizens Councils (white supremacist organizations that originated in Mississippi). Citizens Councils claimed they pursued only political and economic retribution, but often advocated violence for African Americans who sought to exercise their political and civil rights. Numerous African Americans had been murdered for registering or attempting to register to vote.

Despite the violence and the multiple means by which white Mississippians maintained Jim Crow, Robert (Bob) Moses, a former high school teacher with a Masters Degree in Philosophy from Harvard, came to Mississippi in 1961 to encourage voter registration. The constant violence and economic intimidation, greatly curtailed the success of SNCC's work. In 1962 Robert Kennedy, helped organizations working on voter registration projects to acquire funds, but offered no protection from violence. The efforts bore fruit in cities where approximately 500,000 African Americans were registered by 1964. Mississippi was not part of the success, due to obstacles including literacy tests, violence and intimidation by segregationist groups such as the Ku Klux Klan and police: only one per cent of the 400,000 potential African American voters were registered. SNCC leaders decided to flood Mississippi with volunteers in 1964 to change the status quo. Freedom Summer was to combine voter education, registration and political activism, as well as to conduct Freedom Schools to teach literacy and civics to adults and children.

Freedom Summer was to be a fully integrated project, bringing in middle and upper class white student volunteers from across the nation. A number of African American activists preferred an all-African American campaign, reasoning that whites working with African Americans might further enrage segregationists and that college-educated white students would usurp leadership positions. Bob Moses acknowledged their concerns, but firmly rejected the premise in favour of the "**Beloved Community**" ideal. Beyond the Beloved Community was a reason that could only be shared privately among the COFO leadership: only if middle and upper class whites were threatened or victims of violence

Class discussion

1 Think about the qualities of the Freedom Summer volunteers. What attributes of the learner profile were required to participate? What attributes are necessary? Are there any attributes that might be detrimental to success?

2 Read Dave Dennis' explanation of the effect of the death of a white college student on the next page. What learner profile attributes did he exhibit?

Beloved Community
A term popularized by Martin Luther King Jr, that comes from love and a commitment to non-violence. The Beloved Community would not tolerate any form of discrimination, poverty, hunger or homelessness. Disputes, whether local or international, would be resolved through the process of conflict resolution with the dual goals of peace and justice.

would the federal government provide protection. Dave Dennis of COFO explained that the "death of a white college student would bring on more attention…" while also acknowledging the "cold" calculation of inviting those students to Mississippi. Thousands of applications arrived; ultimately 900, mostly white, applicants were accepted. The training emphasized the likelihood of violence and gave volunteers the opportunity to drop out, leaving a force ready to go into African American communities for their summer vacation.

The first major setback to Freedom Summer occurred during the training period. Three civil rights workers were reported missing in, Mississippi. James Chaney, a African American Mississippian from Meridian, and white-Jewish New Yorkers Mickey Schwerner (veteran CORE activist) and Andrew Goodman had come to investigate the burning of Mt Zion Methodist Church which had committed to hold voter education and registration sessions. The volunteers headed south despite the uncertainty over what had happened to the missing civil rights activists.

The project went forward: 41 Freedom Schools were established and more than 3,000 African American youths attended. Voter registration efforts went forward: potential voters were tutored in interpreting the Mississippi Constitution. Thousands came to classes and 17,000 applied for the right to vote, but only 1,600 were accepted. Freedom Summer leaders had anticipated the resistance of white Mississippians, and worked with local African American Mississippians to promote an alternative political party: the Mississippi Freedom Democratic Party (MFDP) that formed in April to challenge the all-white Democrat Party of Mississippi.

The Democratic Party national convention began on 24 August. The MFDP selected its own delegates to be seated in Atlantic City. Before the convention began, a credentials hearing took place in which several MFDP delegates presented their case. Fannie Lou Hamer, who had grown up a delta sharecropper and had been beaten by police and prison guards for attempting to register to vote, argued forcefully that MFDP delegates should be seated instead of the Mississippi Democratic Party regulars. As Hamer began, President Johnson, fearing that his forces would lose control of the convention and lose the support of southern white Democrats, held a press conference causing network television to shift away from Hamer's speech to the president. Hamer's testimony was filmed and excerpts were shown later, including her powerful conclusion.

> *All of this is on account of we want to register, to become first-class citizens. And if the Freedom Democratic Party is not seated now, I question America. Is this America, the land of the free and the home of the brave, where we have to sleep with our telephones off the hooks because our lives be threatened daily, because we want to live as decent human beings, in America?*

A compromise giving the MFDP two delegates while seating all regular Democratic Party ones was rejected by the MFDP. All but three of the regular delegates left the convention because they would not support the slate of candidates. A number of MFDP members obtained credentials from sympathetic delegates from other states and sat in the vacant Mississippi delegation seats.

Class discussion

You may want to write or outline the answers to the following questions:

1   "Birmingham was only successful because of the arrogant and violent actions of the police." Evaluate.

2   James Farmer stated, "We put on pressure and create a crisis and then they (federal government) react." How successful was the civil rights movement in provoking the President to act?

TOK discussion

Discuss the potential ethical differences and similarities between the use of children in Birmingham and the use of adult white college students in Mississippi.

▲ Fannie Lou Hamer (1917–1977), African American civil rights leader and vice-chairperson of the Mississippi Freedom Democratic Party (MFDP), challenged the legitimacy of the all-white Mississippi Democratic Party at the Democratic National Convention Atlantic City, New Jersey, in August 1964.

Freedom Summer was a series of setbacks with few successes. However, the lack of registered voters demonstrated the need for federal enforcement of voting rights, thus paving the way for the 1965 Voting Rights Act. Efforts to enfranchise African Americans continued in the South and were usually met with substantial resistance, sometimes violence. The efforts included the 1965 five-day march from Selma, Alabama, to the capital, Montgomery. The controversy in Atlantic City spurred the Democratic Party to change its rules. In 1968 the MFDP delegation was seated to represent Mississippi at the Democratic National Convention.

What was the effect of Black Nationalism and Black Power on civil rights and economic power?

The integrationist philosophy of the major civil rights groups during the 1950s and first half of the 1960s was not universal. Many African Americans had sought equality but did not have faith that whites would ever accept complete racial equality in social settings, business and employment, and recreational activities, not to mention the educational and political realms. The alternative paths of Malcolm X, SNCC's Stokely Carmichael and the Black Panthers are a sharp contrast to the major thrust of the Beloved Community of Dr Martin Luther King Jr, James Farmer and other civil rights leaders.

Seeking separate routes to equality and prosperity for the African American community can be traced back to the 19th century. The first decades of the 20th century saw the rise of Marcus Garvey, founder of the Universal Negro Improvement Association (UNIA). Garvey voiced the concepts that became known as Pan Africanism, the uniting of African peoples in Africa, the Americas and Europe, and Black Nationalism, the concept of racially defined national identity that was necessary to build racial pride and strong institutions to benefit African Americans in societies that had systematically used race to oppress African Americans. Garvey's promotion of African American economic and political independence led to thousands of followers in the United States, including Earl Little, the head of UNIA's local branch, and the father of Malcolm X.

Malcolm X's childhood experience of racism, threats, violence against his family, as well as the break-up of the family with the children sent to different homes, contributed to his views of American society. His entrance into the Nation of Islam (NOI) followed the well-known narrative of his prison experience. The NOI did not strive for equality through integration; instead Elijah Muhammad preached racial solidarity and racial superiority. Reflecting arguments used by white racists who claimed Bible stories illustrated God's condemnation of Africans to slavery, Muhammad preached that whites were created by the evil black Yacub, and that African American were God's chosen people who would triumph with the help of Allah. Muhammad taught that discipline and economic self-reliance was critical. Along with prayer and observing the faith, NOI adherents were to abstain from alcohol, drugs, gambling, adultery and other sins. African Americans should become more highly educated and practise small-scale community capitalism, meaning owning local businesses and patronizing only African American-owned stores. It was a message that appealed to many in the northern urban ghettos including those of Detroit, Chicago and New York, where the civil rights movement, with most of its focus on

desegregation in southern states, had not resulted in significant change. Unemployment was high and housing was dilapidated, often as the result of **redlining**. African American communities could exert little pressure on local or state politicians, resulting in run-down schools, abusive police and a lack of city services, often to the point of no garbage collection. The conditions led to despair, along with high rates of drug abuse and crime compared with the new suburbs.

Malcolm X changed his name from the "slave name" Little to "X" as representative of an unknown African name taken from his ancestors. Out of prison in 1952, he became the leading spokesperson for NOI and the editor of its publication *The Messenger*. Articulate and witty, Malcolm X appealed to the desperation of urban African Americans. Beginning in Chicago then moving to Harlem in 1954, he attracted thousands to the NOI mosque No 7. Malcolm X's charisma and speeches expanded NOI's membership to more than 50,000, making the NOI a household name in the United States, and one feared by many whites and some middle and upper class blacks. Mainstream periodicals including *Time Magazine* and *The New York Times* wrote detailed stories about him. Malcolm X belittled established civil rights leaders' goal of integration as fantasy saying, "These Negroes aren't asking for any nation—they're trying to crawl back on the plantation". Black Nationalism was the correct path. White society corrupted everything it touched. African Americans should follow the strict lifestyle of NOI, separate from whites, and should establish a land of their own. In a 1963 speech Malcom X stated that land itself was the "basis of freedom justice and equality… A revolutionary wants land so he can set up his own nation, an independent nation."

By the late 1950s the NOI had achieved notoriety. An example of the impact of Malcolm X and NOI is illustrated in the provocative 1959 five-part documentary, "The Hate that Hate Produced", broadcast twice in the span of two weeks on a New York City television station. The series began with narrator **Mike Wallace's** introduction:

> *While city officials, state agencies, white liberals, and sober-minded Negroes stand idly by, a group of Negro dissenters is taking to street-corner step ladders, church pulpits, sports arenas, and ballroom platforms across the United States, to preach a gospel of hate that would set off a federal investigation if it were preached by Southern whites.*

The documentary immediately switched to the voice of Louis X (Farrakan) preaching to a crowd of African Americans, carrying the following words:

> *I charge the white man with being the greatest liar on earth! … I charge the white man, ladies and gentlemen of the jury, with being the greatest murderer on earth. I charge the white man with being the greatest peace-breaker on earth. … I charge the white man with being the greatest deceiver on earth. I charge the white man with being the greatest troublemaker on earth. So therefore, ladies and gentlemen of the jury, I ask you, bring back a verdict of guilty as charged!*

Wallace then told the audience, "The indictment you just heard is being delivered over and over again in most of the major cities across

redlining
The practice of denying or limiting banking and insurance services to entire neighbourhoods because of race and/or poverty was practised by financial institutions during the early 1900s. The term comes from the New Deal Home Owners' Loan Corporation practice of drawing maps with red lines around neighbourhoods deemed risky. Private financial institutions also relied on the HOLC maps.

▲ Malcolm X, speaking to an outdoor rally in Harlem in 1963.

Mike Wallace
A television journalist for CBS and lead reporter for the CBS television news magazine *60 minutes*.

the country." The message was different from King's, Abernathy's and mainstream civil rights organizations', repelled many white liberals.

The opposition of Malcolm X from within the civil rights movement was substantial. Leadership complained that the NOI minister and spokesman attracted disproportionate media coverage, diverting the nation's attention from critical issues. Malcolm X was aware that NOI brought out pride in African Americans in their heritage as it advocated solidarity in a society that worked to keep them weak and fragmented. But, he also knew that unlike SNCC, the SCLC, the NAACP and others, NOI had no active programme or plan to effect change.

By 1964 Malcolm X came to the conclusion that moral righteousness was insufficient and searched for a programme to replace his disillusionment with the NOI's narrow focus. He went on a pilgrimage to Mecca and came back to the United States no longer espousing the inherent evilness of whites, while still strongly discussing racism within the United States. He spoke in favour of Pan Africanism while admitting its limits, criticized capitalism, but also praised African American entrepreneurship. Constant was his dismissal of non-violence as a way to achieve human rights for African Americans, but he favoured violence only in response to violence. In perhaps his most famous speech "The Ballot or the Bullet" of 3 April 1964, Malcolm X explained that Black Nationalism "only means that the African American man should control the politics and the politicians in his own community… that we will have to carry on a program, a political program of re-education… make us more politically conscious, politically mature…". He further argued African Americans were justified in using any means necessary to defend themselves if the government was incapable of protecting them or if it chose not to. That year millions of African Americans would attempt to vote. If they were not allowed to do so, or the process rendered their votes useless, the bullet was the alternative. "…[T]his country can become involved in a revolution that won't take bloodshed. All she's got to do is give the African American man in this country everything that's due him, everything."

Malcolm X spent much of the rest of the year trying to establish deeper ties with civil rights leaders. He formed the Organization of African American Unity. He evoked both cooperation and militancy in voicing support for any action by any group that worked. In an act of support for the jailed Martin Luther King Jr. Malcolm X privately met with King's wife Coretta Scott King, explaining, "If white people realize what the alternative is, perhaps they will be more willing to hear Dr. King". Weeks later Malcolm X was assassinated by members of the NOI, leaving a legacy that both united and divided the civil rights movement, but also brought significantly greater awareness of the grievances and frustrations of African Americans to all of the United States, as well as pride in African identity that lasted decades beyond his death.

In what ways and with what effects did Black Power develop and evolve?

The Black Power Era is often viewed as beginning in 1966 and continuing into the mid-1970s as frustration over the slow and piecemeal progress of the civil rights movement grew within the African American community, especially with younger civil rights activists. However, an increasing

---

Class discussion

Malcolm X and Martin Luther King Jr. are often regarded as opposites.

1 Create three Venn diagrams labeled *views*, *goals* and *methods*.

2 Write an essay comparing and contrasting the two leaders.

Then conduct a debate organized around the three themes. "Proposed: (my leader) was a more successful civil rights leader because…"

number of historians, including Peniel E Joseph, argue that Black Power was more faceted and has deeper roots, emerging within post-Second World War America in various philosophies and forms. Concepts of African American political and economic self-determination, control of educational curriculum, cultivation and celebration of African and African American arts, Pan Africanism, African American pride and African American self-defence grew concurrently with the mainstream civil rights movement. Additionally, "violent self-defense" as it was called by the NAACP leader Rob Williams of Monroe, North Carolina, was common among African Americans in the rural South. Williams carried a gun and formed the Black Guard in the late 1950s, an armed group whose purpose was to protect Monroe's African American citizens. After a white man was acquitted of attempted rape of a African American woman, Williams stood on the courthouse steps to advocate for African American self-defence, "…it is time for Negro men to stand up and be men and if it is necessary for us to die we must be willing to die. If it is necessary for us to kill we must be willing to kill." Thus, all main elements that would characterize the Black Power Era were already a part of the wide quest in the "struggle against white supremacy".

The established narrative of the Black Power Era from 1966 to 1975 is set in the turmoil of the period. Large-scale urban riots began in 1965 in Watts (a section of Los Angeles), continuing in scores of cities in 1966 and 1967 and occurring again on 4 April 1968, following Dr Martin Luther King's assassination. City streets seemed to be battlegrounds and to many in the movement the civil rights establishment's solutions were ineffective. Violence against African Americans, including police brutality, was all too commonplace. The Black Power Era can be said to begin with national recognition of the phrase "Black Power" on the James Meredith March Against Fear in 1966.

On 5 June 1966 James Meredith, who had integrated the University of Mississippi in 1962, began a solo "March Against Fear" from Memphis, Tennessee to Jackson, Mississippi to publicize racism in the South and to promote voter registration in rural Mississippi. A member of the Ku Klux Klan shot Meredith on the second morning of the march. As Meredith recovered in the hospital, three major civil rights figures, Floyd McKissick of CORE, Stokely Carmichael, who had replaced civil rights hero John Lewis as president of SNCC, and Martin Luther King Jr, met with Meredith and asked if they could continue the march. The protest became the "James Meredith March Against Fear", growing to thousands by the time it reached Jackson, Mississippi. The march widened fissures between the strands of the movement. Younger activists disavowed both non-violence and an integrated civil rights movement. McKissick told King that non-violence was no longer a viable tactic while Carmichael pushed for a "Black only" civil rights movement and added that African Americans should seize power where they were in the majority. A group of African Americans called the Deacons for Defense from Louisiana joined the march at SNCC's request, carrying pistols and semi-automatic rifles.

On 16 June Carmichael was arrested as the marchers entered the grounds of an elementary school to set up camp for the night. He was only held briefly, but when released the SNCC leader proclaimed, "This is the

ATL Communication skills

What is the importance of labels in communicating a message? Consider the "March Against Fear", "Black Power", "Freedom Summer", "Black Pride" and "Beloved Community". What do these terms denote? What messages are contained within the phrases? Can they mean different things to different people and to what effect?

▲ Stokely Carmichael speaking at the University of California at Berkeley

▲ Black Panthers in Bobby Hutton Park, 1967.

twenty-seventh time I have been arrested and I ain't going to jail no more! The only way we gonna stop them white men from whuppin' us is to take over. What we gonna start sayin' now is Black Power." The crowd shouted "Black Power" back, then Willie Ricks, who had lobbied Carmichael to use the phrase, led the crowd in a cheer, "What do you want?" with the crowd again responding "Black Power". The march continued with national press coverage of the shouting matches of "Freedom Now" alternating with "Black Power". The divisions were accentuated by an attack by police in Canton that bloodied scores of marchers, making the dedication to non-violence more difficult and justifying the abandonment of that philosophy in the eyes of many demonstrators.

Stokely Carmichael promoted African American pride and solidarity with the African American community as necessary for any significant gains, reasoning that America had systematically sapped the self-respect of African Americans. The idea took hold in African American communities as "Afro" hair styles, clothing featuring traditional African colour schemes, and the phrase "Black is beautiful" became popular, reflecting a positive racial consciousness. The use of the word "Black" was promoted to replace Negro. Kwanzaa, an African American and Pan African holiday celebrating family, community and culture, was created by Maulana Karenga. James Brown, the soul singer, sang "Say it loud, I'm black and I'm proud!" Black Studies programmes at colleges and high schools proliferated.

Concurrent with the rise of African American pride was the establishment of the Black Panther Party for Self Defense in Oakland, California in 1966. The co-founders, Huey Newton and Bobby Seale, who had been students at Merritt College in Oakland, formed the Black Panthers to record incidents of police violence directed at African Americans and to provide a vehicle for increased political activity. During college they became disillusioned with what they perceived as inherent racism in capitalism and were also influenced by the writings of Afro-French philosopher Franz Fanon, who defended the moral rights of colonized people to use violence. The philosophy of the Black Panther Party (BPP) became a combination of Marxist-Leninism, Pan Africanism, and Black Nationalism, but aligned more with the radical left than African American separatists. Newton and Seale saw benefits to working with all races to achieve their goals.

Historian Clayborn Carson attributes much of the popularity of the Black Panthers with young African Americans to its willingness to openly arm itself to challenge policy power. The Panthers spoke openly about armed revolt. Photos of armed Black Panthers dressed in leather jackets and berets emphasized their image. On 2 May 1967 more than a dozen armed Black Panthers entered the California State Assembly in Sacramento while others waited just outside. They were ushered out of the building and arrested. Bobby Seale stated that the demonstration

was for the purpose of defending their right to carry weapons. The incident gained the group national attention for its militancy.

But the BPP offered more than image or a threatening stance. It enumerated a set of demands in a Ten Point Plan that included the freedom by African Americans and "all oppressed people" to determine the destiny of their communities, to own land, and a right to full employment, housing, education and free health care, an end to police brutality, retrials by a jury of their peers for all African American and oppressed peoples in prison, and an end to wars of aggression. The programme was in line with many of the demands of Malcolm X and other Black Power leaders.

As its popularity and notoriety grew, the BPP ran into obstacles. The combination of socialist leanings and Black Power incited J Edgar Hoover and his FBI to infiltrate its ranks, provide misinformation, and accelerate rivalries with other African American organizations. In October 1967 Huey Newton was arrested for the murder of a policeman (he was imprisoned for voluntary manslaughter and freed on reversal two years later). This resulted in leadership being shared by Bobby Seale and Eldridge Cleaver, then being led by Stokely Carmichael who became the group's Prime Minister, merging the BPP with SNCC. Multiple police raids in a number of cities resulted in the deaths of an estimated 28 party members, including Mark Clark and the charismatic 21-year-old Fred Hampton; Elridge Cleaver left the United States rather than return to prison for a parole violation. Stokely Carmichael became the main voice of the BPP, but his advocacy of African American solidarity conflicted with the Marxist-Leninist belief of the BPP that welcomed like-minded activists of all races.

The party attempted to recast its image and focus on positive programmes. After being freed in 1970, Huey Newton promoted political participation in elections and is given some credit for the victories of African American officials in cities such as Gary, Indiana. The BPP began a series of what it called "survival programmes" that included shoe giveaways, coat giveaways, educational programmes and a programme to give free breakfast to children. But, plagued by internal rivalries resulting in expulsion and desertion, external factors that included continued FBI and police harassment, the decline of the party accelerated. By the mid-1970s the BPP had lost most of its leadership and were left with only 27 members by the end of the decade.

TOK discussion

Many civil rights histories virtually ignore the study of gender roles within the movement. Investigate the roles of women in the CRM, including Ella Baker, Rosa Parks, Bernice Johnson Reagon and Fannie Lou Hamer. Also investigate the male-female dynamics of the NAACP, SNCC and the Black Panthers. A starting point could be Rhonda Williams' essay "Black Women and Black Power".

How did federal civil rights bills become law, and what effects did they have?

ATL Research skills

Create a table with a row for each civil rights bill. Include at least the following:

Name of bill	Date of passage	Key provisions	Effects	Reactions

While much of the history of the civil rights movement focuses on persons and groups, legislative activity was also critical. Every year from 1945 to 1956 at least one civil rights bill was introduced in either the House of Representatives or the Senate, but failed because of opposition by southern Democrats or conservative Republicans. From 1957 to 1970 a number of attempts to write and pass federal legislation were attempted, with six becoming law: the Civil Rights Act of 1957, Civil Rights Act of 1960, Civil Rights Act of 1964, the 24th Amendment to the United States Constitution, Voting Rights Act of 1965 and the Civil Rights Act of 1968.

Civil Rights Act of 1957

The Civil Rights Act of 1957 was the first federal civil rights law since Reconstruction. The bill was the subject of the longest filibuster in the history of the United States Senate at 24 hours, 18 minutes by Strom Thurmond of South Carolina, with significant opposition from southern legislators. The bill, a weakened version of President Dwight Eisenhower's original proposal, passed with bipartisan support by a 62–15 vote in the Senate. The law added a Civil Rights Division to the Department of Justice (DOJ) which was tasked to investigate voting rights violations and bring limited lawsuits for voting discrimination before a judge rather than a jury (all-white juries were the overwhelming norm in the South and were not receptive to attempts by African Americans to gain voting rights). It also added a Civil Rights Commission to supervise voting practices. The bill was mostly viewed as weak by civil rights leaders. John Doar, who served in high positions in the DOJ's Civil Rights Division from 1960 to 1967, reported that by February of 1960 the division had taken no effective actions on voting rights. However, there was some progress. One lawsuit came before Judge Frank Johnson in Alabama. Johnson, who had previously ordered the release of voting registration records in Montgomery, Alabama in 1958, ordered "freezing relief" – all applicants who were as qualified as the least qualified registered white to be added to voting rolls. As Jack Bass shows in his book *Unlikely Heroes*, Federal District Court and Circuit Appeals Court judges served a critical function in the rollback of racial discrimination in the South.

Civil Rights Act of 1960

Three years later the Civil Rights Act of 1960 was passed with the purpose of strengthening the 1957 law. The new law, while lacking significant enforcement mechanisms, did show that the United States government stood behind voting rights. Although short of manpower, the DOJ investigated violations and brought cases to court. Under the Kennedy administration some FBI resources were also added. However, as previously noted, the new administration did not provide sufficient personnel to stop violence and retaliation against African Americans or the activists who helped them.

The 24th Amendment

The 24th Amendment which made the poll tax unconstitutional in all federal elections was ratified on 23 January 1964. This tax had been used to prevent poor African Americans from voting. Only one state outright rejected the amendment, Mississippi, but only Florida and Tennessee of the former Confederacy voted to ratify. The amendment did not outlaw poll taxes for state and local elections. The Supreme

Court, citing the equal protection clause of the 14th Amendment, wrote that "Voter qualifications have no relation to wealth".

Civil Rights Act of 1964

The Civil Rights Act of 1964 is the most famous of all civil rights legislation. Author Clay Risen calls it "The Bill of the Century". Relying on the 14th and 15th Amendments as well as the Commerce Clause in Article 1 Section 8 of the Constitution, the law encompassed voting rights, public accommodations, desegregation of public facilities, limits on discrimination within federally funded programmes and employment discrimination, and authorized higher court review of district court referrals to state courts. It also expanded the Civil Rights Commission. While the bill did not resolve many problems of racial discrimination, it was a significant step in federal responsibility and power in equal rights enforcement.

After the events in Birmingham in 1963, pressure increased significantly on President John Kennedy to act. During the first two years of his presidency, Kennedy proposed no civil rights legislation and thought Freedom Riders were disrupting efforts to respond to Soviet aggression. However, by many accounts, the rising tide of violence against civil rights activists, both African American and white, disgusted and shocked the president. From May to July there were approximately 1,000 demonstrations in 209 different cities and towns. In a televised address on 11 June 1963, President Kennedy proposed a comprehensive bill covering discrimination in public accommodations and employment, as well as strengthening voting rights enforcement mechanisms. Violence continued unabated. The murder of Medgar Evers in his front yard the evening after Kennedy's speech and the September church bombing that killed four girls reinforced the president's message.

▲ President Lyndon Johnson meets with civil rights leaders in the second month of his presidency, 1964 (Left to right: Martin Luther King Jr, President Johnson, Whitney Young and James Farmer)

Kennedy's assassination placed Lyndon Baines Johnson (LBJ) in the White House. Johnson biographer Robert Caro writes that until 1957, LBJ had a perfect record in the House and Senate opposing civil rights legislation. As slow as Kennedy had been to reach an understanding of the need for action on civil rights, most mainstream civil rights leaders had considered him a friend to the freedom fight and had little confidence in the new president. However, Johnson used the full force of his office to push the civil rights bill.

Over the next several months the bill went through numerous rewritings. A surprise amendment by Virginia Senator Howard Smith added the word "sex" to Title VII, making gender a protected class, along with race, ethnicity and religion. Historians cannot agree whether Smith was serious about women's rights, or if he added the word to make it politically unattractive to enough senators to cause the bill to fail. The amendment stayed. With pressure from lobbying groups, churches, some of whose members sat in legislators' offices day after day, exhaustive work by Senator Dirksen, President Johnson's engagement and political

Class discussion

Consider the following essay questions.

1 "Congress and the President were prodded into action primarily because of the actions of civil rights leaders and groups." Assess.

2 In what ways and with what effects did civil rights legislation increase the power of the Federal Government?

hardball, the bill passed in the Senate by a vote of 73–27, and the House 289–126 on 2 July. President Johnson signed the bill the same day, surrounded by an audience that included Dr Martin Luther King Jr.

The Voting Rights Act

In January 1965 the SCLC, led by Martin Luther King Jr, opened a voting rights campaign in Selma, Alabama previously an area of work focused on by the SNCC. On 7 March, what was to become known as "Bloody Sunday", Selma police and Alabama patrolmen responded to a planned protest march from Selma to Montgomery with tear gas and billy clubs, injuring more than 50 people. The campaign showed once again the extent to which white supremacists had gone and would go to prevent African Americans from voting. The heightened pressure motivated Lyndon Johnson and Congress to act. The result was the Voting Rights Act of 1965.

The Voting Rights Act of 1965 gave the Attorney General the power to assign federal examiners to observe and direct voter registration where less than half of the eligible residents were registered to vote. This was a major change from the costly and slow lawsuit remedy provided for in previous voting acts: now the Justice Department could work actively to guarantee voting rights.

The Fair Housing Act

Segregated neighbourhoods were still the norm in hundreds of towns and cities. Obstacles to minorities moving in to all-white communities included restrictive covenants, redlining and real estate agents who steered minorities away from white neighbourhoods. In 1966, at the invitation of the Coordinating Council of Community Organizations, Dr Martin Luther King Jr, led protests against housing discrimination in Chicago. At times white neighbourhoods reacted by throwing bottles, bricks and rocks, one of which hit King in the head. The Chicago actions ended with an agreement from the city to put a height limit on public housing and by the Mortgage Bankers Association to provide home loans regardless of race. By March the next year, seeing the lack of progress, King called it another unfulfilled promise. The Chicago example pointed again to the need for federal involvement. After Dr King's assassination in Memphis on 4 April 1968 and the civil unrest that followed, President Johnson pressed for immediate action. In just one week the bill was on the president's desk.

The Fair Housing Act (Title VIII of the Civil Rights Act of 1968) provided for federal enforcement of housing laws. It barred discrimination in the sale or rental of housing based on race, ethnicity, religion or national origin, and prohibited steering, the setting of different financial terms, and false claims that a property was unavailable. The law also made it illegal "to induce… to sell or rent" by indicating that people of a certain "race, color, religion, or national origin" were coming into the neighbourhood, thus lowering the purchase price. The law was expanded in 1974 to include sex. Investigatory and enforcement powers for the Department of Housing and Urban Development (HUD) were enhanced as well as increased involvement of the Department of Justice in court proceedings.

Additionally, federal agencies were required to work with HUD to insure that financial institutions complied with the law. The 1968 law significantly increased federal government action to reducing housing discrimination.

Source skills

Read the following historical perspectives on the African American civil rights movement. The first two are extracts from Adam Fairclough's article. The third is from Philip Klinker's book *The Unsteady March*, and the fourth is by Steven F Lawson from James Patterson's *Debating the Civil Rights Movement*.

1 Clayborne Carson has challenged the notion that "The civil rights movement died during the mid-1960s" to be displaced by a Black Power movement with dissimilar goals. In reality, argues Carson, local activists made no such distinction: the earlier movement to attain political rights evolved into a movement to exercise those rights; both comprised a larger "African American freedom struggle seeking a broad range of goals."

2 The community study, if properly handled, overcomes a major weakness of much civil rights historiography: the tendency to segregate history by race. Most histories have examined either white actions or African American actions… only rarely have the twain met. Studies of Massive Resistance and southern politics have little to say about the civil rights movement. The only whites to appear in most histories of the civil rights movement are the Bull Connors and Jim Clarks. We need to marry the two perspectives: the civil rights movement involved a dialectic between African American and whites. Neither side, moreover, was monolithic, and a study of this dialectic enables us to escape from the stereotypes that have too often reduced history to a simple-minded morality play.

Source: Fairclough, Adam. Dec. 1990. "Historians and the Civil Rights Movement". *Journal of American Studies*. Vol. 24, No. 3. Pp. 387–398. Cambridge University Press on behalf of the British Association for American Studies www.jstor.org/stable/27555365

3 …our answer is that at least so far in American history, substantial progress toward greater (never yet full) racial equality has come only when three factors have concurred. Progress has come only:

1 in the wake of a large-scale war requiring extensive economic and military mobilization of African Americans for success;

2 when the nature of America's enemies has prompted American leaders to justify such wars and their attendant sacrifices by emphasizing the nation's inclusive, egalitarian, and democratic traditions, and

3 when the nation has possessed domestic political protest movements willing and able to bring pressure upon national leaders to live up to that justificatory rhetoric by instituting domestic reforms.

Source: Klinker, Philip A with Smith, Rogers M. 1999. *The Unsteady March: The Rise and Decline of Racial Equality in America.* Chicago, IL, USA. University of Chicago Press. Pp 3–4.

4 The federal government played an indispensable role in shaping the fortunes of the civil rights revolution. It is impossible to understand how African Americans achieved first-class citizenship rights in the South without concentrating on what national leaders in Washington, D.C., did to influence the course of events leading to the extension of racial equality. Powerful presidents, congressional lawmakers, and members of the Supreme Court provided the legal instruments to challenge racial segregation and disfranchisement. Without their crucial support, the struggle against white supremacy in the South still would have taken place but would have lacked the power and authority to defeat state governments intent on keeping African Americans in subservient positions.

Source: Lawson, Steven F, Payne, Charles; Patterson, James T. *Debating the Civil Rights Movement, 1945–1968* (Debating Twentieth-Century America). Kindle Edition. Kindle Locations 48–52.

Question

Which approach provides the clearest window into the goals, methods, personalities and accomplishments of the movement?

8.3 Feminist movements in the Americas

Conceptual understanding

Key questions

→ What were the conditions that prompted women to demand equal rights in the Americas?

→ How successful have they been in obtaining them?

Key concepts

→ Significance

→ Change

→ Consequence

Since 1945, women's movements arose all over the Americas. They organized to redress entrenched injustices, to obtain legal and political rights, and for the power to make choices previously denied. The injustices that led to women's movements and feminism after 1945 stemmed from economic, political and social causes.

Definition of feminism

The standard dictionary definition of the word "feminism" is a movement that seeks to obtain the social, political and economic equality of men and women. Few people in the Americas would disagree with equality for all, men and women. Yet the word "feminism" causes the most varied reactions among people.

One reason for the varied perceptions of the word "feminism" is that women have organized movements that comprise a variety of issues, not all of them pertaining exclusively to women. These may include civil rights, equal employment opportunities, equal pay for equal work, political representation and participation, legal rights, acceptance into the armed forces and educational opportunities. They also may include reproductive rights, domestic violence, rape, sexual harassment, sexual orientation freedom and abortion. At times women's movements have organized themselves under just one of these causes; others have been more general and included several causes at once. This is one reason why academics at present prefer the term "feminisms", because each issue above deals with a different aspect of feminism: it is not just one movement that seeks to obtain the social, political, and economic equality of men and women, but it comprises very different movements. As we will see in the following pages, sometimes these movements are even at odds with each other. Some movements receive a great deal of notoriety from the media, while others work quietly behind the scenes.

TOK discussion

We examine what we know using knowledge frameworks, like specific terminology and concepts. Ask people what they understand by the term "feminism". Ask them "how do they know" and note the ways of knowing (WOKs) mentioned. Discuss the prevalent WOKs cited. Which are used more? How does this inform the difficulty in defining the aims of women's movements and feminism?

Finally, there are so many feminisms because any movement that promotes rights for half of humanity cannot possibly be monolithic. It is bound to have different, sometimes even antagonistic, splinter groups. That's where political orientation, race, class, religion, sexual orientation and national origin come in to divide women. Then the media takes care to augment these differences by focusing on the flashier, more militant splinter groups that give the more understated movements a "bad press". These groups naturally resent this and divisions ensue.

Background pre-1945

Much of the activism of feminist groups in the early 20th century focused on obtaining the vote for women. Male political and church leaders felt that men and women had different spheres of influence in life, with women in the private realm of the family, motherhood and the home and men in the public realm of the world outside the home. Church leaders, whether Protestant in the US and parts of Canada or Roman Catholic in Latin America and Quebec in Canada, often added to this argument by citing traditional religious values and writings.

Feminist groups, sometimes emanating from women's literary or philanthropic clubs in the case of middle and upper class women, began to organize to propose changes in the laws. Lower class women who worked in factories, began to organize as feminists within labour unions. Women used many different tactics to persuade men in power to grant them the vote. They signed petitions; they enlisted supportive legislators; they worked towards obtaining the vote in their province, state or municipality; they marched and picketed; they used the judicial system to challenge the voting exclusion; they participated in silent vigils and hunger strikes.

Ecuador's constitution had eliminated the word "male" from its citizenship requirements in the Constitution of 1896. When Dr Matilde Hidalgo wanted to sign up to vote in 1922 and was denied for being a woman, she contested this. She met the requirements for citizenship by being over 21 and being able to read and write. The Council of State decreed that there was no impediment, and she voted in 1925. It took until 1929 for the female vote to be incorporated into the new Constitution of 1929, after a military dictatorship took over.

In Argentina (see page 258) the populist president Juan Perón, at the insistence of his wife Eva Perón, gave women the vote in the hopes that they would vote for him in the next election. They did. Authoritarian regimes in Brazil, Cuba and El Salvador did the same. In these countries, although there were small groups of feminists seeking the female vote, they did not have to fight for it as hard as other countries.

At times success was achieved piecemeal. An example of this is in Canada, where the province of Manitoba voted to allow women to vote and run for provincial office in 1916, but the province of Quebec did not allow this until 1940. Canada as a nation gave women the vote in national elections in 1918. In 1919 women could run for office in the House of Commons, but the Senate remained off limits until 1929. In addition, indigenous Canadian women (and men) had to wait until 1960

Timeline of Women's Suffrage in the Americas	
Canada	1918
United States	1920
Ecuador	1929
Brazil	1932
Uruguay	1932
Puerto Rico	1932
Cuba	1934
El Salvador	1939
Dominican Republic	1942
Jamaica	1944
Panama	1945
Guatemala	1945
Costa Rica	1945
Venezuela	1947
Argentina	1947
Chile	1949
Haiti	1950
Bolivia	1952
Mexico	1953
Honduras	1955
Nicaragua	1955
Peru	1955
Colombia	1957
Paraguay	1961

to vote without giving up their indigenous treaty status. The case of the United States was more contentious and took decades to come through. Nine states in the West of the country had adopted voting rights for women by 1912. Finally in 1920 the necessary three-quarters of the states voted to amend the Constitution, and the Nineteenth Amendment giving US women the vote was passed. Indigenous women (and men), however, were only able to vote after 1924.

The table to the right shows that 13 countries in the Americas had given women the vote by 1945, while 11 had not. The following sub-sections will deal with the causes feminists fought for in the Americas post-1945. In some countries the fight for the vote continued until the 1960s. All over the Americas, women realized that obtaining the vote still did not mean equality with men. There were still many laws and traditions that kept women from obtaining full political, economic and social equality.

The general trends in the Americas show more variations than similarities. Easy generalizations escape the careful historian. At times feminists took up causes that were very divisive, such as abortion. The right to divorce was less divisive in the US and Canada than it was in Chile, where divorce was finally allowed in 2006. In long-lasting democracies, women fought for equality under the law through feminist movements, to be on a par with men.

United States and Canada

Although US and Canadian women were needed and active in the war effort before 1945, for tasks ranging from piloting aircraft, soldering cables and riveting plane parts in factories to nursing and clerical duties, after the war they were again relegated to the domestic sphere. In Canada, the "baby boom", as it has become known, increased the population by 15%, or 8.2 million babies. In the US, it was 76 million babies.

Given the deeply entrenched tradition of patriarchy, the majority of women gave up or did not start careers, in order to raise these babies. The term "patriarchy" refers to societies where power is held by males; women are excluded from power and are subordinate to men. In addition, after the war the expectation for most middle and upper class women was that they did not have to work because men earned a good salary to support the family. Housework and child rearing was not considered work, but rather, the prevalent expectation within women's domestic role. Lower class women often did have to work outside the home, in factory and domestic service jobs, especially African American women. This was in addition to the expectations of domestic work in the home, leading to a double day of work.

The media, especially television and magazines, took care to record an image of 1950s America, creating an almost mythical world of white middle class prosperity. In this view of life, women were happy housewives whose only purpose in life was to care for their homes and families. They had no ambitions other than finding a husband, getting married and having children. In hindsight, the historical record has shown that although this myth reflected the lives of many white middle and upper class women, it certainly did not speak for all of them.

ATL

Thinking and communication skills

Does the media create or reflect public opinion? How does journalism present a challenge to historians? Discuss with reference to women's roles in US and Canadian societies.

Political work continued as women's groups in the late 1950s, such as the Women's Peace Party and the Women's Joint Congressional Committee, protested against Cold War policies, such as the arms race and brinkmanship. Women also joined civil rights movements. Many women began to criticize not being allowed leadership roles and realized that although women had obtained the vote in 1920, equality with men had not been achieved. The women's movement was born (see page 312).

US President John Kennedy created the President's Commission on the Status of Women, headed by Eleanor Roosevelt, in 1961. This aided the cause of eliminating discrimination against women government employees. When the Civil Rights Act was proposed to Congress in 1964 a women's organization called the National Woman's Party, active since the suffrage movement, successfully lobbied to incorporate a ban on sex discrimination in employment.

In 1963 Betty Friedan published *The Feminine Mystique*. This book exposed the myth of happy housewives and revealed the discontent of upper and middle class women in the US. By 1966, many of these women, in conjunction with younger women, founded the National Organization for Women (NOW) to advance women's rights. This group was founded as a reaction to the Civil Rights Act, passed by Congress in 1964. When advocating for the application of this act against sex discrimination in employment, they were denied a voice. They decided to become more militant and began to demonstrate. Betty Friedan became its first President.

ATL Thinking and communication skills

Betty Friedan, President of the National Organization for Women (NOW), gave an interview to the press during a march in New York City on 26 August – the 50th anniversary of the passing of the Nineteenth Amendment which granted American women full suffrage. That day, NOW called upon women nationwide to strike for equality.

Observe the above image carefully. What are some of the grievances expressed in the placards? What areas of US life remained unequal between men and women in 1970? Discuss.

▲ Betty Friedan, President of the National Organization for Women (NOW), giving an interview to the press

Some feminists felt that NOW was too conservative in its constituency and methods, using committees, lobbying, petitions and demonstrations. More radical women felt that women needed to be freed from their subordinate position in the traditional patriarchy. The more radical feminists organized across the US in 1967 and 1968 and were more varied in their make-up, with members from diverse groups, including sister organizations like the National Black Feminist Organization and Asian Sisters in Action. This radicalization had an important impact in feminism in the US, as well as in Canada.

Certainly, the rest of the world was watching and reading about feminists in the US. In Canada, the militancy of women's movements was more subdued than in the US, but Canadian women organized in movements such as the Vancouver Women's Caucus in 1968, followed by the Montréal Women's Liberation Movement in 1969. In 1967 the federal government had set up the Royal Commission on the Status of Women to study the state of affairs regarding women's rights. By 1970 the Commission was able to make 167 recommendations for greater equality for women. In 1968, 37% of Canadian women worked for pay outside the home, but by 1971 they were just under 39%, dealing with the double day of housework and child-rearing as well. Many women's movements concentrated on obtaining equality in the workplace.

In the 1970s, the women's movements in the US split further along many different fracture lines, including class, ethnicities, and increasingly, sexual orientation. The Cold War also had an effect in splitting some groups that favoured a more leftist ideology. Feminist theory evolved; Kate Millett was instrumental in articulating feminist theory in her 1970 book *Sexual Politics*. In the province of Quebec in Canada the Centre des femmes (Women's centre) edited the first French-language radical feminist periodical, *Québécoises deboutte!* (Quebec Women Stand Up!) between 1971 and 1975. In other Canadian provinces women's groups formed, some more radical than others, preferring the formation of women's theatre groups, reproductive rights clinics and shelters for victims of domestic violence and rape, rather than massive demonstrations. In the US, some radical demonstrations captured media attention. One such demonstration was led by the Redstockings group in 1969, against the Miss America (US) Pageant.

After the creation of Ms. Magazine, feminist theory and controversial issues like reproductive rights, birth control and abortion found a media outlet. As more women became aware of the lack of equality in the workplace and a double standard for men and women in society, they joined the women's movements. Despite the many splinter groups, NOW was able to organize a massive march on Washington, DC as a strike for equality. The aim was to promote the Equal Rights Amendment (ERA) as a constitutional guarantee. Although Congress passed the ERA in 1972, the struggle to have it ratified failed by 1982, three states short of the two-thirds requirement. One reason for this was the massive organization of conservative opposition groups, made up of both men and women. A strong activist for these groups was the constitutional lawyer and conservative activist Phyllis Schlafly.

Although the ERA did not pass, many of the feminists' goals were significant. In 1973, the landmark case of Roe versus Wade gave women reproductive rights in this US Supreme Court decision that allowed abortion within the first three months of pregnancy. This continues to be a strongly contentious issue in the US, with opposition still being led by conservative and religious groups.

A boon to feminism in the US was the United Nations Declaration of 1975 as International Women's Year. As a signatory, the US government organized a conference with women delegates from all states, to discuss women's issues regarding equality with men. It gave the movement a national agenda, so that in the following decades, there would be state action in the US on equality in education, employment, political representation and sports, in addition to childcare, health and reproductive issues, and violence against women.

In Canada, a contrasting reality emerged in women's movements. The preferred form for seeking redress for women's inequality began with forming a committee to study and document discrimination and injustice, for example, in the workplace. The committee would then elaborate solutions, propose them to the federal government and continue to keep up the pressure until they were implemented. Working women organized in unions, such as Nova Scotia fish-processing plant workers, who were mostly women. Exhausted by the double day, they demanded and eventually received daycare, safety and workday flexibility, but not equal pay. In 1971, Canadian women doing the same job earned 60% of what men earned. Trying to amend this inequality has been a long, arduous fight. By 1993, this percentage had only increased to 66.7%. This has proven just as difficult a hurdle for feminists when seeking equal pay for equal work in the US, where women still earn 77% of what men earn, a statistic that has remained constant since 2002.

The 1980s brought an anti-feminist backlash in the US that stalled many reforms leading to equality between men and women. They portrayed the feminist agenda as seeking to destroy the traditional family made up of a heterosexual married couple, in which the husband went out into the world to work and provide for his family, and the wife stayed home to raise children and keep house. Women's groups like Concerned Women for America and the National Pro-Family Movement, spearheaded these efforts. The advent of the conservative administration of President Ronald Reagan ensured that government appointees would put a brake on the feminist agenda starting in 1981. The media, which had created the myth of the happy housewives of the 1950s and sensationalized the women's liberation movement of the 1960s and 1970s, lambasted feminists or ignored them entirely in the 1980s. Even the word "feminism" began to be replaced by terms like "women's issues", as the focus shifted to easing the work and family double day of the working mother.

Women's organizations in the 1990s, however, persevered in both the US and Canada, and continued to work for equality and the end of women's subordinate role to men. Some retained a focus on special issues, like employment or equal pay, or on ethnicities, like women of colour in the National Political Congress of Black Women. Daughters of Bilitis became a group to organize lesbians. The National Women's Political Caucus continued to lobby for increasing the number of female politicians. They supported the nomination of Geraldine Ferraro for vice-president in 1984.

During the Liberal Party government of Prime Minister Pierre Trudeau, the Canadian Charter of Rights and Freedoms ended sex discrimination

Self-management and thinking skills

Read the CNN short article "Five Things Women Couldn't Do in the 1960s."

Do you think the feminist agenda in the US has been successful? Why or why not?

Class discussion

Investigate the writings of Betty Friedan, Kate Millett, Germaine Greer, Gloria Steinem and Shulamith Firestone. Write a research question, such as a comparison/contrast of their different ideas regarding feminism, or the methods they advocated.

Research and communication skills

Another important international influence on Latin American and Caribbean feminists, as it has been on other worldwide signatories, has been the United Nations.

Search the UN website on women's conferences to find out what the twelve major areas of concerns in advancing gender equality were at the Beijing conference in 1995.

Research what various countries in Latin America and the Caribbean have done to advance gender equality since signing the 1995 pledge in Beijing.

in 1982. In Canada, the North America Free Trade Agreement (NAFTA) in 1994 brought Canadian women that work in agriculture and food processing together in groups like Women for the Survival of Agriculture and Concerned Farm Women of Ontario to deal with the consequences of globalization for these working women, and to deal with international and environmental issues in agriculture.

The 1990s would bring more feminist grievances to light: sexual harassment and sexual violence against women. On the other hand, some advances within the traditional patriarchal system also occurred, like the Family and Medical Leave Act of 1993, which permitted unpaid, job-protected leave for specified family and medical reasons, like childbirth. The feminist agenda has endured, sometimes brashly, sometimes behind the scenes. It remains the movement that seeks to obtain the social, political and economic equality of men and women.

Latin America and the Caribbean

Feminism and women's movements in Latin America and the Caribbean followed similar trends to their American and Canadian counterparts. Some issues, such as obtaining women's suffrage, were considered in at least 11 nations between 1947 and 1961: Venezuela, Argentina, Chile, Haiti, Bolivia, Mexico, Honduras, Nicaragua, Peru, Colombia and Paraguay.

The women's liberation movements in the US and later in Canada reached very few countries in Latin America, although feminist ideas slowly permeated women's groups and found their way into legislation. This was for cultural reasons, such as a strong Roman Catholic tradition and Iberian colonial roots, but feminism and its manifestations were also very different from the US and Canada for structural reasons. Many Latin American and Caribbean countries, especially after the 1950s, had government systems that were not based on grass roots democracy and freedom of expression. Many were authoritarian, conservative governments, including military dictatorships that suppressed change and reform in all areas, including women's role in society. Women continued to enter the professions, but were not involved in decision-making and did not have leadership roles in them, or in business and politics.

Women who believed in feminism, with the goal of obtaining the social, political and economic equality of men and women, organized themselves in a muted form, sometimes under the aegis of political parties, when these were allowed. In the 1980s, a new form of women's organization was created under authoritarian governments: women mobilized and formed social movements in Argentina, Chile and Brazil during military dictatorships, to seek answers to their loved ones' disappearances.

Latin American feminists organized Encuentros (Encounters), starting in 1981, to develop a regional feminist agenda to confront authoritarian governments in Latin America. By 2000, participation of indigenous and Afro-descendent women, and lesbians had increased the diversity of these encounters. As democracy returned to most countries by the late 1980s, their experiences in organizing in their communities served them well in seeking demands for women. They gained more representation in political parties and legislatures, and special interest groups formed to advance the rights of temporary female agricultural workers, labour unions and lesbians.

Feminists in Latin America and the Caribbean have had unique circumstances that differentiate them from the US and Canada. Popular women's movements have tended to be involved in bettering conditions for their families without recognizing themselves as feminists.

For three case studies on feminism in Chile, Cuba and Mexico, please visit www.oxfordsecondary.com/ibhistory-resources.

ATL Thinking and communication skills

Watch the interview with the Director of UN Women in 2011, Michelle Bachelet (currently President of Chile) called *Bachelet: Empowering women country by country*.

In view of what you have learned about feminisms in the Americas, discuss how Bachelet reflect the lessons learned by women's movements since 1945.

Conclusion

Feminism continues in the 21st century, not only in the Americas. The strongest impetus is now coming from international pressure on individual countries through the United Nations, as countries commit to empowering women to reach gender equality in social, political and economic areas of society.

8.4 Hispanic civil rights movement in the United States

Thinking skills

As you read this section, create a graphic organizer of your choice that allows for the comparison and contrast of the experiences of indigenous people African Americans and Hispanic Americans in terms of legal, social, political and economic status in the years prior to the civil rights movement.

Bracero Program
The Bracero Program recruited Mexican labourers to take the place of men drafted into the armed forces. The program continued until 1964.

The characteristics and results of the Hispanic civil rights movement are both different and similar to other United States civil rights movements. A significant difference is that Hispanics were and are not racially homogenous. There were also national identifications: American, Mexican, Puerto Rican, Cuban, and more. Segments of the movement focused on different issues: economic/labour, land restoration, education, identity and nationalism. Just as other movements had different groups with different ideas within them, strategies and tactics ranged from non-violent demonstrations to economic boycotts to walkouts to political power acquisition to brandishing weapons. This examination of the post-1945 period will look at agricultural workers, Puerto Rican inner city activism, the Chicano student movement, and militant nationalism.

Hispanics from different regions of the Americas came to live in the United States for a variety of reasons. Mexicans living in what is now the southwestern United States became Mexican Americans following the United States–Mexican War of 1846–1848, when the United States obtained (through the Treaty of Guadalupe Hidalgo and the Gadsden Purchase) approximately half of Mexico's land. Migration of Mexicans into the Southwest increased in the 1890s due to railway construction, restriction of Asian labourers, and increased agricultural and mining activities. Uncertainty following the Mexican Revolution (1917) sparked more migration, and this time destinations included the central part of the United States. However, the economic downturn of the Great Depression resulted in Mexican repatriation: an estimated 500,000 to two million Mexicans and Mexican Americans were expelled from the United States during the decade. It is estimated that more than half were American citizens. The United States reversed its policy with the onset of the Second World War with the **Bracero Program**, recruiting Mexicans to perform agricultural labour. The program brought in approximately 50,000 workers each year. Beginning in 1951, at the behest of the growers, the numbers quadrupled and by the late 1950s over 400,000 per year entered.

Latino migration extended to the Caribbean and Central American regions. Political and economic unrest led several thousand Puerto Ricans to immigrate to the United States in the 1800s. The Spanish American War (1898) brought Puerto Rico into the growing empire of the United States, and Puerto Rican workers and families were recruited to labour in Hawaii, Arizona, New Mexico, Missouri, New York City, as well as other areas with labour shortages. In 1917, with entry into the First World War, the Jones Act made all Puerto Ricans US citizens, to make it easier to provide unskilled and semi-skilled labour to industry in the north-east and agriculture in the south. The 1924 National Origins Act produced a shortage in cheap labour. Puerto Ricans, having no restriction on moving from the island to the mainland due to citizenship, migrated by the tens of thousands. By 1950 Il Barrio in East Harlem, New York City, swelled to over 300,000 people. Cubans immigrated to Florida just before as well as immediately after the Cuban Revolution, changing the tourist town of Miami into a major commerce centre. Many of the approximately 200,000 immigrants were upper and professional class. The Central American Wars of the 1970s and 1980s, often made larger by Cold War powers, created tens of thousands of displaced Guatemalans, Nicaraguans and Salvadorians, who came to live in communities across the United States, causing, as with each wave of immigrants, a backlash from many United States citizens and legislators who felt their culture and economy threatened.

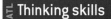

Thinking skills

Add the Latino civil rights organizations to the table you've been keeping during this chapter.

How did the farm workers' movement develop and what impact did it have?

Perhaps the most well known Latino rights movements are the agricultural strikes and boycotts of the late 1960s, starting in the San Joaquin Valley of California, one of the most productive agricultural areas in the world. The farm workers of the region had made unsuccessful attempts to organize in the decades before. Agricultural workers were not covered by the Fair Labor Standards Act (1938). In 1962 Dolores Huerta, Cesar Chavez and others formed the National Farm Worker Association (NFWA) in Delano, California. In 1965 Filipino farm workers near Delano went on strike for higher pay and better working conditions in the grape fields. Workers were overcharged for substandard housing and rarely provided with fresh water during farm work. The NFWA joined the Filipinos' strike. Growers countered them by busing in strike-breakers and using physical intimidation, including spraying protesters with pesticides. Chavez felt more action was needed. An admirer of Dr King and Mahatma Gandhi, he decided that a march to California's capital, Sacramento, arriving Easter Sunday, was needed to gain attention for the workers' struggle. A religious man and aware of the importance of symbolism, the march became a pilgrimage, *La Causa*. The scheduled march received the desired attention, including that of Senator Robert Kennedy who conducted an open investigatory hearing at which he grilled a town sheriff for unconstitutional arrests of strikers. The 300-mile march began in March 1966. A grower, Schenley, in the face of bad publicity and pressure from politicians and union figures including Walter Reuther, began negotiations with the farm workers, led by Delores Huerta. A labour contract between the NFWA and Schenley resulted, but labour difficulties in the fields continued with other growers.

▲ Cesar Chavez ended his hunger strike with Senator Robert Kennedy. The leader of the United Farm Workers Organizing Committee (UFWOC) ate his first solid food in 23 days in support of non-violence in the strike against grape growers in Delano California in the San Joaquin Valley, 10 March 1968.

Alianza Federal de Pueblos Libres

Alianza was first called Alianza Federal de Mercedes or the Federal Land Grant Alliance.

Rodolfo Gonzales

Coloradan Rodolfo Gonzales was a featherweight boxer who became involved with politics after retiring from the ring. He founded the Crusade for Justice, opened a summer school for Chicano children and even helped found the Ballet Chicano de Atlan.

In mid-1966 the NFWA and AWOC united to become the United Farm Workers Organizing Committee (UFW), affiliated with the American Federation of Labor and Congress of Industrial Organizations (AFL-CIO). Strikes against various growers expanded, but, getting no positive results, the UFW promoted a nationwide boycott of table grapes that lasted more than three years, finally ending with a union contract with the growers in July 1970. A lettuce boycott followed, then another grape boycott. Strikes and boycotts continued as UFW membership reached 70,000 by 1972. In 1975 California enacted legislation designed to protect agricultural unions. As years passed, many of the gains evaporated as contracts expired. Cesar Chavez, who had also fasted and maintained his dedication to non-violence became a national figure in the late 1960s.

Militancy

Most Mexican Americans were not farm workers and were angered by mistreatment, lack of economic opportunity, substandard education and, to some, the injustice of Mexican land taken by Anglos following 1848. The period of militant activity began with the **Alianza Federal de Pueblos Libres**, the movement to reclaim lost land as their rightful heritage. Led by the charismatic Reies López Tijerina, who, unlike Chavez, was not averse to violence, Alianza both used the courts and engaged in forceful actions that included a 1966 occupation of a campground in Kit Carson National Forest, claiming the land as theirs. In 1967 Alianza raided the Rio Arriba County Courthouse in New Mexico. Tijerina was captured and later imprisoned on federal charges, but the event brought the issue of land ownership to the attention of the general public.

Brown pride, student walkouts and political power

At the same time Alianza was organizing, a student movement was forming in Los Angeles. The movement was part of a Mexican American identity and political power *movimiento* that coincided with the rise of pan Africanism and the Free Speech Movement. Activists traced their heritage to the Aztecs, taking the word for Aztec which sounds like Chicano to use for themselves. The concept of Chicano, not Mexican American, began to take hold. Literary inspiration came in the words of **Rodolfo Gonzales**' poem "Yo Soy Joaquin", which evoked confusion, history, identity and a call to action.

Murals reflecting Mexican heritage appeared in East Los Angeles during the 1960s, but at the same times the Los Angeles public schools failed to serve the 130,000 Mexican and Mexican American children who attended. Far less than half graduated from high school and only one in a thousand went on to earn a college degree. Latino students were usually placed in vocational and low level courses, sometimes in what are now termed special education classes. At Belmont High School, teacher Sal Castro was ignored when he complained to the administration that there were no Mexican Americans in academic courses or in student government. College-educated Chicanos had tried to change the school system through established channels: PTA meetings, principal conferences, school board meetings, and even electing Julian Nava, an Angeleno and a college professor, to the school board, but little changed.

The combined organizing efforts of Brown Berets (formerly the Young Citizens for Community Action), United Mexican American Students (UMAS), Sal Castro, and two community newspapers led to the first of two weeks of school walkouts on 6 March 1968. Police countered with several beatings, but demonstrators carried signs that read "Walk Out Now or Drop Out Tomorrow", "Viva La Revolucion" and "Chicano Power" bringing national media attention. The students published 39 demands of LA Unified School District, including bicultural education, the teaching of Mexican contributions to the United States, student rights, and facility improvements. The daily walkouts of approximately 15,000 students became known as the Blowout. The school board agreed to most of the demands, but eventually reneged on most of them. Castro lost his job and 13 organizers were arrested, but charges were dropped three years later, and with pressure from the community the school board reinstated Castro.

Political power was an important objective for part of the Chicano movement. While Chavez and Huerta had pursued economic issues, Castro, educational, the Brown Berets, Mexican nationalism, and Alianza, land, the pursuit of political power and self-determination was the main goal of La Raza Unida Party (LRUP). LRUP was founded in January 1970 in Crystal City, Texas, and soon spread to other Southwestern states. Spearheaded by José Angel Gutiérrez, Rudolfo Gonzalez and Mario Compean, LRUP was founded to focus on issues such as economic power, social equality and elimination of violence against Mexican Americans by law enforcement. LRUP was to compete in local elections where Hispanics comprised a significant part of the electorate. Gutiérrez rejected the concept of the melting pot, blaming "gringos" (whites) for most problems facing Texas's Latino community. In April elections LRUP candidates won majorities in two city councils, two school boards and to mayoral elections. Gutiérrez was elected president of the Crystal City School Board and later was elected to a county judgeship. LRUP's electoral success was fleeting, however. In October 1971 at its Texas state convention, members voted to organize at the state level, including run a candidate for governor. LRUP ran candidates for a total of 11 state offices, winning none. Instead of refocusing on local politics, Rudolfo Gonzalez and José Angel Gutiérrez attempted to transform LRUP into a national party. Approximately 300 delegates from 40 states met in El Paso, Texas in the first week of September 1972. Critical issues including unemployment, education, farm labour and political self-determination were discussed. In the months after the convention rivalries between leaders and branches caused a lack of cohesion and LRUP ceased to effectively exist as a national party. The local successes of LRUP illustrated the power of a Mexican American focused party, but it collapsed from a combination of ambition and the coopting of issues by the Democratic Party.

Puerto Rican civil rights

The Puerto Rican communities of northern American cities, especially Chicago, Illinois and New York, New York, expanded as people left the island for economic opportunities and family on the mainland. Puerto Ricans competed with other ethnic groups for space, acceptance and economic opportunity. Unlike the other civil rights movements discussed

Class discussion

Compare and contrast the circumstances, goals, methods and consequences of the Mississippi Freedom Democratic Party with the La Raza Unida Party. Decide which was more successful and why.

in this chapter, the Puerto Rican movement was almost entirely urban and attempted to alter the urban political, social, economic and educational structures. The Puerto Rican movement had a strong nationalistic flavour, promoting independence for Puerto Rico, as well as Puerto Rican pride and power. An important part of the movement was the Young Lords Organization, which began in Chicago and quickly spread to other north-eastern cities.

The Young Lords began in 1959 as a gang to protect territory in the Puerto Rican ghetto in the Lincoln Park neighbourhood of Chicago. One member, Cha Cha Jiménez, was arrested multiple times as a boy and as a young man. While in jail, similar to Malcolm X, Jiménez reflected on the economic, political, and legal injustice experienced daily by Puerto Ricans. He also read a great deal: subjects included Martin Luther King Jr, Malcolm X and Puerto Rican nationalist Albizu Campos. His thinking became revolutionary as he no longer blamed rival gangs for Lincoln Park's problems, but rather the political structure of Chicago, headed by "Boss" Richard Daley, the last of the big machine mayors, and the white-dominated US government. After his release, Jiménez came to know Chicago Black Panther leader Fred Hampton, motivating Jiménez to work to transform the Young Lords from a gang into a revolutionary-nationalist organization in 1967. The gang became the Young Lords Organization, followed quickly by a chapter opening in "El Bario", the East Harlem section of New York City. Soon Young Lords chapters operated in half a dozen East Coast cities.

The Young Lord Organization chapters published several newspapers, including the *YLO*, *El Young Lord Latin Liberation News Service*, *Palante* and *Ramparts*. An important part of the YLO programme was instilling a sense of ethnic and national pride in the entire community. Over the next few years, the YLO operated a free children's breakfast programme, a day-care centre, and other community services. In New York the Young Lords Party (a name change to reflect political focus) conducted Garbage Offensive in the summer of 1969 to clear the streets of uncollected refuse, an effort that included using stolen New York City brooms. The YLP conducted tuberculosis and lead poisoning tests. But the YLP also acted to gain publicity in attempts to force government action. It piled up garbage in the street and set it on fire, occupied a church and even "liberated" a mobile chest X-ray vehicle to use in El Bario. The YLP and the Puerto Rican Student Union organized "Free Puerto Rico Now" conferences in high schools and colleges. In Chicago, the YLO focused on attempts by the city government to displace Puerto Ricans in favour of urban renewal and seized the McCormick Theological Seminary for days to demand the Daley administration provide a children's centre, low income housing and a Latin American cultural centre.

Despite, and partially because of, the YLO's community work, but also because of its militant and confrontational stance and actions, the Daley administration targeted members via Chicago Police's Gang Intelligence Unit a unit of 200 officers. He was just one of several YLO members to be harassed in this way. Additionally, the FBI's Counterintelligence Program (COINTEL) targeted the YLO through disinformation, sowing internal discord and disruption, causing the Young Lords to weaken substantially

by late 1972. As it declined, the YLO increasingly focused on socialistic and nationalistic ideological purity, alienating some members and community supporters. Still, historian Judson Jeffries argues that the YLO "laid the groundwork for a new kind of Puerto Rican—a less passive generation ...".

How did immigration reform evolve and with what results?

While the United States is often referred to as "a nation of immigrants", the United States Congress has passed a variety of bills to control entrance into the country. Legislation resulted in immigration quotas to maintain the cultural and ethnic make up of the United States. The McCarran-Walter Act (1952) removed specified quotas by national origin, but used ethnic and links to communism in the early Cold War period, resulting in a modified quota system. In 1965 the Hart-Cellar Act saw the complete elimination of national or ethnic quotas, but limited entry visas to 170,000 per year, with some exceptions. In the following 20 years, laws were passed to provide preferential treatment for immigrants from Indo-china as a result of the Vietnam War. With few exceptions, in the 20th century the United States limited immigration, and for the majority of the time controlled for national origin, race and ethnicity.

However, many people, mostly Mexican and Central American, entered the country during the latter half of the century without legal documents to work and to join family members. The agricultural and garment industries of the Southwest thrived on the cheap labour during the 1960s and 1970s, leading to millions of workers without employment visas. Additionally, refugees from wars in Nicaragua and El Salvador came to the United States, arriving in places from Los Angeles to Washington, DC.

By the early 1980s, the Border Patrol apprehended over one million immigrants without visas each year. The influx of immigrants created a political crisis. A substantial number of American citizens called for a slowdown of immigration via upgraded border protection and the deportation of all undocumented (illegal) aliens, arguing that they posed economic and cultural threats. Several attempts at legislation were made. Attempts to pass bills in 1982, 1983 and 1985 failed to become law after significant lobbying from Hispanic Americans, the United States Chamber of Commerce, and a variety of other interest groups. In 1986, large agricultural businesses and other employers dropped some objections to employer sanctions in favour of temporary worker permits. The majority of congressmen and senators saw the deportation of millions as impractical as well as undesirable. Importantly, the conservative president, Ronald Reagan, was against mass deportation and worked with the legislature to craft a bill. The included employer sanctions for hiring undocumented workers, expanded border control, used language that prohibited discrimination in hiring by national origin and offered amnesty for undocumented aliens who could prove that they were residents by 1982. It both houses and was signed by President Reagan in November 1986.

ATL Self-management and research skills

1 Identify the goals of the groups supporting, writing and passing the Simpson-Mazzoli Bill.

2 List the main provisions of the bill and the mechanisms enacted to carry out the goals.

3 Assess the successes, failures and uncertain results.

4 Considering the mechanisms and the results, analyse the reasons for the legal, social, political and economic effects of the 1986 law.

The purpose of the various provisions was to provide enforceable disincentives for hiring unauthorized aliens, and to make working and living conditions better for those aliens legally working in the United States. Despite provisions barring discrimination, documented workers, especially Hispanics, were denied jobs in the late 1980s as employers sought to avoid penalties. The legislation did allow many newly legalized immigrants to come out of the shadows. Thousands left seasonal agricultural work for jobs in construction, factories, or trades such as plumbing, pursue an education and purchase a home. But the exit from the fields created a demand for new undocumented workers. When funding shifted primarily to border security, unauthorized immigration increased because employer sanctions were rarely enforced. A majority of California voters felt federal government immigration measures were ineffective and passed **Proposition 187** in 1994 to prohibit undocumented aliens from accessing public services. A 1996 United States Appeals Court ruling negated the law as an attempt by California to pre-empt federal jurisdiction.

After the terrorist attacks of 11 September 2001, even more resources were devoted to border security. As a result, once immigrants crossed the border or overstayed temporary visas undetected, it was relatively easy to stay. As increased border security made crossing riskier, undocumented aliens stopped returning to their countries in the off season, mostly ending the circular migration pattern and increasing immigrants by hundreds of thousands each year. By 2005 the number of estimated undocumented aliens topped 10 million, leading to efforts to revisit immigration policy. Even the support of President George W Bush could not sway enough votes within his party (Republican) to move legislation forward. Immigration policy remained unsettled as many legislators sought tighter controls and harsher penalties. The proposal of such legislation led to massive protests in 2006 from Los Angeles to Washington, DC, with millions protesting against the bill and in 102 cities across the country on 10 April. The immigration debate continued into the 21st century.

Proposition 187
In California citizens, after gathering sufficient signatures of registered voters, can place a proposition on the ballot for the next election that, if passed, becomes law. The process, which grew out of good government reforms at the turn of the 20th century, provides a path to legislation outside of the state legislature.

8.5 Youth culture and protests of the 1960s and 1970s

Conceptual understanding

Key questions

→ What were the circumstances that prompted the youth cultures and protests of the 1960s and 1970s?

→ How did young people manifest their discontent?

Key concepts

→ Perspectives

→ Change

→ Consequence

Youth culture and protests of the 1960s and 1970s in the US

The post-Second World War "**baby boom**" generation grew up in the United States during a period of Cold War tension, unprecedented affluence that prompted an eightfold increase in college enrollment over two decades, and the first dramatic years of the African American civil rights movement. It was then that the seeds of the counterculture were planted. The nuclear arms race, spy scandals in the United Kingdom and the United States, including the trial of **Julius and Ethel Rosenberg**, bus boycotts and protests, emerging sexual freedom and the rise of Jack Kerouac and the Beat Generation combined to create a small but significant minority of middle and upper class youths, mostly white, who became dissatisfied with the political and economic structure of the US.

The youth and counterculture movements manifested themselves in a variety of ways: free speech, political activism, alternative lifestyles, admiration for Marxist revolutionaries such as Che Guevara but rejection by others of the same, the attempted creation of a parallel society to the two main economic-governmental systems of communism and democratic capitalism, and the use of targeted violence. All these movements had significant doubts about the equity of society. Those doubts led to efforts focused not only on causes such as civil rights, economic fairness, free speech and the Vietnam War, but also on the destruction of the old order. This section will examine some of the major participants in that era: Students for a Democratic Society, the Free Speech Movement and the counterculture.

baby boom
By 1960 close to half of all citizens of the United States were under 18 years old.

Julius and Ethel Rosenberg
The Rosenbergs were tried and convicted of spying for the Soviet Union. They were both executed. The trial and death sentences were controversial. Evidence declassified in 1995 exonerated Ethel, but confirmed the guilt of Julius Rosenberg.

▲ Students for a Democratic Society (SDS) put on a parody of the Columbia administration's suspension of students who took part in the previous spring's disorder, in front of Columbia University's Alma Mater statue on the first day of registration for the fall semester, 1968

Students for a Democratic Society

Students for a Democratic Society (SDS) was founded in 1960, beginning what has been called "a decade of defiance". It was an outgrowth of left-wing organizations. Based on college campuses, the SDS attempted to create a community of political and educational factions that brought together liberals and radicals, scholars and students, and activists. The vision was enunciated in the Port Huron Statement (1962) that introduced members' disappointment with the actions of the United States government, racial injustice, uncontrolled technology that degraded the importance of man, the threat of nuclear holocaust, an anarchic world order and rampant unprincipled exploitation of natural resources. The SDS "would replace power rooted in possession, privilege, or circumstance by power and uniqueness rooted in love, reflectiveness, reason, and creativity".

Initially headed by founding President Tom Hayden and headquartered in New York City, the SDS would try to reach its goals via "a new left". The SDS made attempts to move beyond campuses into impoverished inner-city neighbourhoods, with little effect, but on campus membership continued to grow. In 1965 the group gained impetus with an anti-war "teach-in" at the University of Michigan, followed quickly on other university campuses, and organized a sizeable protest escalation of the Vietnam War in Washington DC. The anti-war movement brought the SDS increased influence. Increased membership brought organizational problems. Factions, ranging from Maoists to anarchists to old guard sympathizers who focused the ambitions of the Port Huron Statement, competed for influence. Still, membership in SDS increased into the late 1960s with the largest national student strike in history led by the SDS in 1968. The SDS joined with the Worker-Student Alliance (SDS-WSA) and expanded its efforts to helping striking workers while continuing to actively oppose the Vietnam War. A separate dual organization, the SDS-Revolutionary Youth Movement (SDS-RYM) also formed in 1969, with a much more radical focus than the SDS-WSA; several members later formed the Weathermen Underground, a group that advocated violence against the government and corporations as a legitimate method to reverse what they saw as immoral actions.

The Free Speech Movement (FSM)

While the SDS operated across the United States, another student political movement took flight in the San Francisco Bay area: the Free Speech Movement. The seeds of the FSM began in San Francisco in May 1960. Organized by SLATE, a campus political party, several hundred University of California, Berkeley students protested HUAC hearings and were barred from the hearing room. Police used fire hoses to clear the crowd from inside the building, with some students falling down the marble steps. A total of 31 students were arrested and the next day 5,000 people protested the hearings. In the next three years SLATE contested speech restrictions by the UC Berkeley administration concerning issues such as housing discrimination, HUAC and compulsory Reserve Officers' Training Corps (ROTC) training. SLATE continued to work for an independent student government at UC Berkeley, and in 1964, after the commencement of the Free Speech Movement, SLATE candidates won an election to run student government.

Class discussion

Many of the groups and movements largely consisted of and were led by youths: SDS, SNCC, Young Lords Organization, the Free Speech Movement and the Los Angeles student walkout.

1 Why were youths such a major force in groups that challenged established political, social, cultural and economic structures?

2 In what ways can the many civil rights movements be viewed through the lens of change versus continuity?

In September 1964 UC Berkeley expanded restrictions on speech and political activity. The ban brought together radical, liberal and conservative students to protest. The first protest was small, consisting of five tables with a student sitting at each one. Upon refusing to leave when ordered to do so, university officials took their names. The citing of the students prompted a protest led by Freedom Summer veteran Mario Savio. He led 500 students to the administration building, all demanding to be punished as well. Eight students were suspended, creating an even larger demonstration that involved groups such as SNCC and SDS setting up information tables in banned locations.

▲ Mario Savio and other student protestors march through Sather Gate on the UC Berkeley campus, heading for a meeting of the UC Regents

When a police officer arrested civil rights veteran Jack Weinberg, hundreds of students surrounded the police car. Led by Mario Savio, who removed his shoes before climbing on the patrol car to avoid damage, numerous students spoke to a growing crowd over the next day and a half, despite harassment, including being targeted with raw eggs by fraternity brothers. The standoff ended peacefully, but led to the formation of the Free Speech Movement: its purpose to making Supreme Court established boundaries on the 1st Amendment the only limits to political activity on university grounds. The FSM was joined by teacher's assistants, strengthening the ability of the FSM to violate campus political activity regulations. As the UC Regents proceeded to punish participants, the protests grew until on 2 December 4,000–5,000 students gathered in front of the administration building to hear Savio speak. The speech invoked the principles of the civil rights movement, but with a new vocabulary:

There's a time when the operations of the machine becomes so odious, makes you so sick at heart, that you can't take part; you can't even passively take part. And you've got to put your bodies upon the gears and upon the wheels, upon the levers, upon all the apparatus, and you've got to indicate to the people who own it that unless you're free, the machines will be prevented from working at all.

Still, the Governor of California, Edmund "Pat" Brown ordered police to end the demonstrations. Instead of ending the protests, a one-day strike that included many members of the faculty followed. In 1965 the Regents appointed a new university Chancellor, Martin Meyerson, who reversed restrictions on student on-campus political activity.

How did students contribute to the anti-Vietnam war movement?

The SDS and the FSM contributed significantly to student political involvement in the anti-war movement. Many students supported Johnson over Barry Goldwater in the 1964 election and felt betrayed by Johnson's escalation of the war. Along with SDS's teach-ins, protests took place in Washington, DC. Demonstrations grew in response to the draft and Operation Rolling Thunder (large-scale bombing of North Vietnam). The Tet Offensive in January 1968 provided more impetus for the anti-war movement. From 1966 onwards students demonstrated and sometimes halted the operation of draft centres, as well as protesting against companies including Dow Chemical, the manufacturer of napalm. Some protests spurred violent reactions by authorities; the most well known took place in May 1970 when a peaceful protest at Kent State University in Ohio resulted in National Guard troops firing on unarmed students, killing four and wounding nine. In Vietnam, American troops invaded Cambodia in pursuit of Viet Cong in the same time period, bringing about massive anti-war protests at about 1,300 college campuses.

The protests spawned a pro-war backlash with increased membership in organizations such as Young Americans for Freedom and American Friends of Vietnam, but these groups never reached the size of anti-war organizations. Conservative legislators at the state and national levels condemned the protests. The election of Ronald Reagan as California's governor in 1966, who vowed to "clean up the mess at Berkeley" which was "a haven for communist sympathizers", and the victorious Republican team of Richard Nixon and Spiro Agnew, who called for patriotism, law and order, to the presidency and vice-presidency in 1968, illustrated that the majority of American voters disapproved of the unrest.

Counterculture in lifestyle

The 1960s and 1970s were not just political in nature, but featured a large and influential counterculture typified by Timothy Leary's advice to "turn on, tune in, and drop out". Commonly called **hippies**, these youths grew out of the Beat Generation and the quest to find an alternative to the mainstream culture that they saw as empty, materialistic, hypocritical and technologically amok. Rather than try to change society, choices were made to live in an alternative one that dismissed traditional values, in favour of a closer relationship with the environment and basic human desires. Scholars have discussed the period as one that embraced the fulfillment of the self as the highest goal. Lifestyle choices included non-western religions, rural communes, cults, sexual freedom, and often the use of drugs, especially hallucinogens, that were thought to open the door to a more enlightened way of interacting with the world. Music reflected and influenced the lifestyle: groups such as the Grateful Dead, The Jimi Hendrix Experience, and Jefferson Airplane provided musical narratives and commentaries to the era. While hippies ranged across the country, the most famous gathering of this counterculture was the Haight-Ashbury district of San Francisco.

Haight-Ashbury, with inexpensive apartments and hospitable weather, attracted thousands of hippies in the late 1960s. Typically long-haired (both men and women), dressed in decoratively patched jeans, flowing skirts, peasant blouses, hats and derivatives of British "mod" style, the hippies also passed out flowers. The streets became crowded with singers and street corner philosophers who spoke on everything from eastern religions to the benefits of altered consciousness to free love. Music, especially a new form of LSD-influenced songs called Psychedelic Pop, could be heard as well. Newcomers were often offered free clothes, food and shelter.

▲ Timothy Leary (1920–1996), American psychologist, at the "Summer of Love" 1967.

One such food-distributing group was the Diggers, named for the Utopian English Diggers of the 17th century. The Diggers' goal was to create a city in which every service and need was free: the Free City. They performed street theatre, but they also gathered excess food from restaurants and supermarkets, prepared it in a communal kitchen and distributed it every day in a park, as well as running a free medical clinic. From 1967–1968 the Diggers Free City Collective operated in several Bay Area neighbourhoods.

In 1967 the San Francisco Bay Area attracted approximately 100,000 youths from across the nation to share in the hippy lifestyle in what became known as the Summer of Love. It began with national media stories about city leaders' pleas to stop an influx of more hippies during the spring. The stories prompted more young people to travel to the Bay Area. At the end of the summer, most of the new flower children returned to their communities, bringing the hippy culture back home.

At the beginning of the summer, the City of Monterey, a picturesque town on the Pacific Ocean, about a hundred miles south of San Francisco, was the setting for a free three-day music festival organized by John Philips of the music group the Mamas and the Papas and their producer Lou Adler. To promote the festival John Philips wrote the song "San Francisco (Be Sure to Wear Flowers in your Hair)". Sung by Scott McKenzie, the song became an instant hit. Monterey was already known for its jazz and folk festivals; the organizers hoped the festival would elevate the cultural status of rock music. Monterey Pop took place in June 1967, with performances that included Jefferson Airplane, Janis Joplin, the Mamas and the Papas, Otis Redding, and introduced Jimi Hendrix and sitar artist Ravi Shankar to American audiences. Jimi Hendrix setting his guitar on fire and The Who's Pete Townsend smashing his on stage projected a rebellious image. Monterey Pop began the era of large rock music festivals that peaked with Woodstock in 1969.

Municipal and state officials were unhappy with the influx of young people living according to their own rules. Long-time residents of Haight-Ashbury and other communities demanded help from police and local government to restore their communities to the previous state. Local police made arrests, but were often overwhelmed by the numbers of people who roamed the public streets and parks. California's Governor Ronald Regan spoke out against the counterculture repeatedly and used force against those whom he believed had exceeded legal limits. People's Park is an example of government reaction.

People's Park was created from land owned by the University of California but was littered with garbage. At a meeting in April 1969, local merchants and residents decided to build a park on the land without consulting UC officials. More than a thousand volunteers cleared the lot and built the park with donated plants and construction materials in weeks.

The building of People's Park infuriated Governor Reagan. He directed his Chief of Staff Ed Meese to clear the park. In the early morning on 15 May hundreds of law enforcement officers, destroyed most of the recent work, and constructed a fence around the lot. Word spread quickly and by the afternoon thousands of demonstrators neared the park. The confrontation escalated quickly and hundreds more police officers were sent in to break up the demonstration. Police used tear gas, shields and billy clubs, but also fired shotguns into the crowd and at surrounding buildings. One bystander, James Rector, died after being shot. Hundreds of people were injured, both demonstrators and police officers. The violent break-up of the protest and the response prompted Reagan to deploy several thousand National Guardsmen. The protests continued. The National Guard responded by spraying tear gas from a helicopter over the Berkeley campus neighbourhoods. The Park remained contested space for a decade; protests and confrontations were commonplace until a permanent park was constructed in the 1980s.

Canadian youth culture and protests

The 1960s to early 1970s are known as the "Liberation" decade in Canada. Young people had the time and ability to be able to advocate for more personal liberty and freedom. Youth culture was seen as nonconformist, and various youth movements were essential in changing Canada into a more multicultural and progressive society.

Youth culture: characteristics and manifestations

Young people in Canada in the 1960s and 70s sought their own unique identity, but there was substantial influence from the US **counterculture** due to Canada's **special relationship** with the country. As Canadian Prime Minister Trudeau said in 1969, "Living next to you [the United States] is in some ways like sleeping with an elephant; no matter how friendly and even-tempered is the beast, if I may call it that, one is affected by every twitch and grunt."

counterculture
Term first associated with "hippies" in the 1960s to describe beliefs which differ from the prevailing norm. This movement grew to include other anti-establishment groups.

special relationship
US presidents since Franklin Delano Roosevelt have publicly spoken of this connection. However, in 1972 Nixon declared the "special relationship" dead after Canadian Prime Minister Trudeau introduced his "Third Option" policy, trying to stop Canadian dependence on US markets. Despite what Nixon said, this relationship continues.

▲ Police beat up hippies during Yorkville sit-in, *The Globe and Mail*, 21 August 1967

The San Francisco Bay Area modelled an attractive counterculture and influenced the way many Canadian youths lived. Different areas of Canada's biggest cities, such as in Vancouver's Kitsilano ("Canada's answer to Haight-Ashbury"), Montreal's Plateau, and Toronto's Yorkville were reorganized. The people who frequented these areas believed in pacifism and direct protest in favour of a more equal, liberal society. Some of the leaders were members of the **New Left**. One of their central tenets was that social and political relations should be based on consensus. Consequently, they established urban and rural communes in which to live, collectives that published literature and art that was not motivated by a profit, and cooperatives whose profits were shared equally. Not everyone embraced the counterculture, however. In 1969, when Richard Nixon appeared on television asking the "silent majority" for their support to help end the Vietnam War,

New Left
A movement that began in the 1960s, led by German-American Herbert Marcuse, whose radical goal was to break with the "old" Democratic Party left, and fight for greater social justice and against the military-industrial complex. In Canada, this group was also anti-American, against the three main Canadian political parties (Tories, Liberals and NDP), and in favour of Quebec independence.

Katimavik

Founded in 1977, Katimavik (which means "meeting place" in Inuktitut) had a goal to engage youth through community service focused on multiculturalism and environmental protection. Starting with 1,000 volunteers who worked to improve 80 communities in their six-month stints, it has since involved 35,000 Canadians. Katimavik has been a member of the UN Economic and Social Council (ECOSOC) since 2008.

it became clear that some chose not to "drop out/be-in". In Canada the majority did not embrace the counterculture lifestyle – it was almost solely an urban phenomenon in the largest cities. Regardless of this, the counterculture, through its provocative actions, still had a significant cultural impact on Canada.

The Canadian government wanted to harness the energy of the youth movement, so it created the Company of Young Canadians (CYC). In 1964, the CYC sent young Canadians across Canada to work on social and public programmes. It had some difficulties, for example, government officials protested against CYC members encouraging the Metis to advocate for more sovereignty, so it was eventually disbanded. However, one of its successful legacies was **Katimavik.**

Communes, collectives and cooperatives

In the 1960s communes were created in wilderness areas such as the Slocan Valley in BC, where deserted farms were reclaimed to create "utopian" communities. They were also established in "squats", like those on Wreck Beach in Vancouver or on Denman Island, by those who didn't believe in public property rights.

One of the most famous collectives came from the theatre movement called "collective creation". With a goal to democratize the creative process, theatre groups like Theatre Passe Muraille in English Canada, and Le Grand Cirque Ordinaire in Quebec, staged productions with the goal "of implied left-wing populism, a critique of artistic hierarchy and a commitment to local culture". Some Yippies, members of the Youth International Party, were

inspired by this movement, and combined theatre with protest: they helped to build People's Parks in many cities across Canada, which later inspired the Occupy Movement in 2011–2012.

One of the most successful examples of a cooperative is Mountain Equipment Co-op (MEC). Started in Vancouver in 1971, its philosophy is to sell outdoor gear at a low mark up, equally share the profits with its "members" (which is every patron), and integrate sustainable development into its business practices. Their consumer cooperative business model has helped MEC to be one of the most successful outdoor recreation gear and clothing companies in Canada.

Class discussion

Scroll through the images of Prime Minister Trudeau in the retrospective, "What the heck is Pierre Trudeau doing?" on the Huffington Post website (Canadian edition).

Which image do you think most exemplifies the liberation decade and why? Do politicians act similarly or differently today? Discuss.

Trudeaumania

The immense popularity Trudeau experienced when he first entered the House of Commons due to his youthfulness and promise of change.

Young people also expressed themselves through their appearance and behaviour. Canadians were influenced by American fashions, such as jeans, dresses and blouses with flowery prints, and long hair. Similar to President Kennedy in the US, Canada's Prime Minister Pierre Elliott Trudeau had a tremendous cultural impact on society. He epitomized the "Liberation" decade's individualism as a youthful, bilingual francophone from Montreal, propagating the importance of individual liberty. As Minister of Justice, he declared that "the state has no business in the bedrooms of the nation," and created laws that made divorce easier and ended the criminal prosecution of homosexual acts. This won him support among liberals. During his 1968 campaign to become the leader of the Liberal Party, his anti-establishment, youthful image inspired a phenomenon called **"Trudeaumania."** Not all Canadians agreed with Trudeau's "liberation" style, particularly those in rural areas, and many of the older generation of Canadians preferred stability and tradition after decades of instability and war. Liberation also had negative consequences such as an escalating divorce rate, an increased permissiveness regarding sex, alcohol and drugs that led to irreversible damage for many.

One of the most famous expressions of Canadian youth culture was its music. Canadian protest music galvanized many to seek more peaceful ways to resolve conflict. A group of four folk artists who used to hang around coffee houses in Yorkville, Toronto and Greenwich Village,

NYC became particularly famous: Leonard Cohen, Neil Young, Buffy Sainte-Marie and Joni Mitchell. Initially, their songs were covered by more famous artists, and they spent so much time in the US that many thought they were American. However, Canadians proudly claimed these uncompromising musicians as their own. Despite their impact, some of the more famous and popular Canadian singers of the 1960s and 1970s were not politically active and produced more escapist fare, such as Anne Murray's "Snowbird" (1969) and BTO's "Taking Care of Business" (1973).

Class discussion

Read this excerpt from the *Toronto Star*, "Where has the protest music gone?"

Protest songs — at least the kind that galvanized thousands at a time during the labour struggles of the 1920s and '30s, anti-nuclear and civil rights marches in the 1950s, the anti-Vietnam war rallies in the 1960s …— seem to have disappeared from the landscape. 'They haven't disappeared, we just have to hunt them down,' argues singer Bruce Cockburn. Protest songs are alive and well, he says. They are just hiding in plain sight. 'We just don't hear them. We don't hear anything worthwhile these days unless we go looking for it.'

Source: Quill, Greg. *Where have all the protest songs gone?* 2010. www.thestar.com

Listen to the four songs listed below. Research the cultural impact of one of them.

- "Universal Soldier," Buffy Sainte Marie (1963)
- "Story of Isaac", Leonard Cohen (1969)
- "Ohio", Neil Young (1970)
- "Big Yellow Taxi", Joni Mitchell (1970)

Compare and contrast them to more recent protest music, for example, linked to the Occupy movement or anti-Bush foreign policy.

How and why has protest music changed?

New multimedia technologies allowed for the immediate transmission of ideas, which influenced the Canadian youth movement. Americans dominated the new broadcast culture, and it was a Canadian professor in the US, **Marshall McLuhan**, who coined the term, "The medium is the message". Due to the pervasive influence of American culture, there was a move in Canada to promote its distinctiveness. The **National Film Board of Canada (NFB)** created films that portrayed the counterculture, and helped propagate their ideals. The impact of television on Canadian society was massive: since the vast majority of Canadians lived close to the American border, they tended to watch American TV, some of which had anti-war and liberation themes, such as MASH and All in the Family. The Canadian and Radio Telecommunications Commission (CRTC) in 1968 imposed Canadian content quotas on movies, television programmes and broadcast radio that created a more conservative, home grown Canadian cultural identity.

The overall impact of the youth counterculture movement on Canadian society is debatable. As historian Desmond Morton pointed out, "Most Canadians avoided drugs, stayed married, and never voted for Pierre Elliott Trudeau. As a fashion, liberation was more conspicuous in BC, big cities, and among the middle class than in Newfoundland, small towns, and among the poor. The unfashionable majority might have wondered

Marshall McLuhan
A Professor of Communications Theory from Edmonton. In his seminal 1964 work *Understanding Media*, he identified and analysed the vast influence that new telecommunications were having on popular culture.

The National Film Board of Canada (NFB)
In 1939 the Canadian government created the NFB which produced a wide variety of films (documentaries, animation, feature-length fiction) that examined various aspects of the Canadian identity. Despite the fact that some called it a "colonial institution" with too small a budget, its award-winning work has had a profound impact on Canadian culture.

mutually assured destruction

A central tenet of the defence policy of US President Kennedy's Secretary of Defense Robert McNamara. In essence it stated that both sides in the Cold War had so many nuclear weapons that one side could survive a first attack and launch its own: the resulting response would be so massive that the enemy would suffer "assured destruction". This was the essence of nuclear deterrence: it would be irrational for one side to launch a nuclear strike as they would know that they themselves would also be annihilated.

Greenpeace

Founded in Vancouver, Greenpeace's first action occurred on 15 September 1971, when it sent a chartered ship, the Phyllis Cormack, which was renamed Greenpeace, to oppose US testing of nuclear devices in Alaska.

Pollution Probe

An environmental organization whose goal, through letter-writing campaigns, inquiries, stunts (such as a funeral for the Don River) and packing community meetings, was to try to improve Toronto's urban pollution crisis. Pollution Probe campaigns inspired organizations across the country.

Royal Commission on the Status of Women in Canada (RCSW)

The RCSW was launched as a direct response to a six-month campaign mounted by a coalition of 32 women's organizations led by Ontario activist Laura Sabia, president of the Canadian Federation of University Women. The RCSW, under Florence Bird's leadership, conducted three years of studies and hearings, and made 167 recommendations for reforms such as equal pay for equal work of equal value, maternity leave, and birth control. The Trudeau government responded in 1971 by creating the Office of the Status of Women, a cabinet position of Minister Responsible for the Status of Women, and procedures to deal with women's rights.

why priests were urging secularism in education, or why governments financed the counter-culture through the Company of Young Canadians." Regardless, the counterculture had a resounding influence as it is recognized as a distinct historical era in Canadian history.

Youth protests: characteristics and manifestations

Civil rights movements around the world inspired Canadian young people to protest, often on university campuses. In the 1960s, the percentage of Canadian youth attending university was higher than any other country apart from the US and Sweden, and the level of women at universities reached 47% in 1980. Students, through strikes, sit-ins and other demonstrations, fought for a more equitable society.

One of the topics of protest was nuclear proliferation. The concept of **"mutually assured destruction"** had an important impact on Canada. Although Canada had not detonated a nuclear device, it maintained them as a part of a North American defensive shield with the US called NORAD (North American Aerospace Defense Command), and the DEW Line stations (Distant Early Warning) were in Canada's Arctic. In 1960 the Canadian Voice of Women for Peace was created to call for action against the threat of nuclear war. Another famous "direct action" organization that came out of the anti-nuclear movement was **Greenpeace**.

The modern environmental movement evolved out of the youth movements of the 1960s. Canadians had the leisure time to appreciate Canada's vast wilderness, and some realized there was a need to protect it from the detrimental impact of resource extraction. An article entitled, "Pollution: Is there a future for our generation?" in *The Varsity* (February 1969) from the University of Toronto sparked the youth-led modern environmental movement, and led to the establishment of **Pollution Probe**, Canada's first major environmental organization. The international hit song "Big Yellow Taxi", released by Joni Mitchell in 1970, symbolized the cultural outrage at increased urbanization and pollution. In response to the galvanized environmental movement, Trudeau established the Department of the Environment in 1971, and other agencies to help regulate society's impact on the environment.

The protests in favour of equal rights for women followed American ones in favour of the Equal Rights Amendment (ERA). However, there were also those that were innately Canadian. In 1960 when *Toronto Star* journalist Lotta Dempsey spoke out about the increasing danger of nuclear war and the role of women to protest against it, hundreds of women rallied with her. From this the Voice of Women was created, which eventually led to the establishment of the 1967 **Royal Commission on the Status of Women in Canada (RCSW)**. When the government failed to concretely act on the commission's recommendations, the National Action Committee for the Equality of Women (NAC) transformed itself, so that by 1972 it was Canada's largest feminist lobby of three hundred groups representing three million women. Unlike the ERA in the US, in Canada a version was adopted as Article 15 of the Charter of Rights and Freedoms in the 1981 Constitution.

Red Power protests

In the 1960s there were protests fighting for Canadian indigenous peoples, some of which were organized by the **Red Power movement**. In 1968 activists at Simon Fraser University attempted to change the name of their newly established university to "Louis Riel" University. These activists argued that rather than being a "Loyalist, fur-trader and explorer", Simon Fraser had actually been a "member of the vanguard of pirates, thieves, and carpet-baggers which dispossessed and usurped the native Indians of Canada from their rightful heritage". They advocated that the university be re-named Louis Riel University "in order to honour the single man who, by his actions to gain justice and freedom for Canadians of Indian ancestry, courageously wrote the single page of the history of the Canadian West of which we can be thoroughly proud, and who, by his cruel murder, revealed clearly the means by which our ancestors (non-Indian) gained control of this land." Although this campaign was ultimately unsuccessful, it was indicative of many protests that occurred on university campuses in favour of indigenous rights.

Protests against the Vietnam War

Even though Canada did not send military forces to the Vietnam War it impacted Canada culture. The Vietnam War, according to University of Regina student activist Don Mitchell, had "a broad influence in disillusioning people about ... super power politics and raised awareness about … conditions in third world countries". Thousands of Americans came to Canada to avoid the draft, impacting the demographics of many communities. The Canadian government was criticized for providing the US with military and political support, and activists demanded that the government prevent Canadian companies from exporting war materials for use in Vietnam. On 20 November 1967, 80 University of Toronto students and faculty held a sit-in as parts of the campus were associated with Dow, the producer of Agent Orange and Napalm. Some engineering students who Dow was recruiting vehemently disagreed with the protests, causing minor discord. Although a majority of students did not get involved in the protests, the mood on university campuses across Canada was deeply affected by the protests against the war.

Red Power movement

This was created in the US in the late 1960s as a way of trying to advocate for aboriginal interests. Inspired by the movements of other minority groups to fight oppression around the world, the Canadian Red Power movement advocated for the rights of a half million aboriginal people who had been exploited for centuries, particularly by the changes to the Indian Act in the 1950/1960s.

TOK discussion

Should Simon Fraser University have been renamed?

Conduct brief research on Simon Fraser and Louis Riel. Then read the excerpt on the demonstration from *Radical Campus: Making Simon Fraser University* by Hugh Johnston.

How can one gauge the extent to which a history is told from a particular cultural or national perspective?

▲ Anglo and French Canadians protesting against the Canadian government's stance on the Vietnam War

Quebec independence: "Vive le Québec Libre!" and the FLQ

For many young people in Quebec, the most important youth movement was one for Quebec independence. The Liberal Party victory in Quebec in 1960 was the beginning of the **Quiet Revolution**, a period when French Canadians strove to modernize their province in a uniquely Québécois way. When the President of France Charles de Gaulle proclaimed the rallying cry of Quebec separatists at Expo '67 in Montreal, "Vive le Québec Libre!" the phrase became the resolution of the League for Socialist Action (Ligue Socialiste Ouvrière) in July 1968. This Ligue, among others, led many peaceful protests in favour of a sovereign Quebec. However, there were those who felt the changes were not radical enough and became violent. The Front de liberation du Québec (FLQ), a separatist paramilitary group, was formed in 1963 with the goal of creating an independent, francophone Marxist Quebec state. It targeted the government, English speakers and businesses, and the Catholic church. In October 1970, the October Crisis began which was the only purposefully violent political protest in Canadian history. After the October Crisis ended and the FLQ was disbanded, there was decreased support for the Quebec separatist movement and a 1980 sovereignty referendum failed.

The Liberation decade ended at the end of the 1970s. Trudeau continued to lead Canada until 1982, but he evolved from being the symbol of "liberation" to advocating greater federal power, economic autarky and the repatriation of the Constitution. The more radical 1960/1970s youth movements gave way to a more conservative era in the 1980s; although protests continued, particularly against nuclear proliferation and advocating for the disenfranchised in Latin America and South Africa, their counterculture character had changed.

Youth culture and protests in Latin America

Young people in Latin America and the Caribbean in the 1960s and 1970s used various methods to express their different ways of thinking, such as through clothing and appearance. There was some imitation of the US and European youth culture seen on television, in films and heard on the radio. Long hair, especially for males, became fashionable and a source of friction with older generations. As blue jeans in the US were increasingly worn by middle class youths rather than by cowboys and factory workers, they became a symbol of class solidarity and the subculture of rebellion. Latin Americans even coined a Spanglish term for blue jeans: *bluyine*s ("blue jeans" pronounced and written in Spanish). Hippie-style dressing also became prevalent, with long, flowing skirts and miniskirts for women, and bell-bottomed jeans for both females and males. Hippie communes, where young people lived together advocating free love and drug use, were another manifestation of this youth culture. Young artists and craftsmen specializing in leather and woollen handicrafts sold to live in a community. Examples of these were the Horcón group in central Chile, Veracruz in eastern Mexico and the El Bolsón community in southern Argentina.

Quiet Revolution

The Quiet Revolution included governmental steps to assert greater sovereignty over Quebec's political, social and economic institutions. It was a decade of great societal change carried out through peaceful means.

ATL Research and communication skills

After reading this section on Canadian youth and doing some additional research, do you think that the period of the 1960s and 1970s was one of more change or continuity?

▲ Poster for the International Protest Song Encounter in Cuba

The most enduring manifestation of youth culture was music. In 1967, Cuba held the International Protest Song Encounter (Encuentro Internacional de la Canción Protesta) in Havana. Musicians from 18 countries shared discussions on singing for a cause, especially to protest and change unfair social conditions. There was also imitation rock and roll, and protest music, with festivals such as Woodstock in upstate New York, US in 1969, and the Piedra Roja Festival in Santiago, Chile in 1970. Soon national bands flourished, taking up their own forms of protest and sometimes including traditional instruments and folklore.

Youth protests: characteristics and manifestations

The Cold War context also played a role in the background of youth demonstrations, especially when protesting against the US and its role in the Vietnam War. Demonstrations reflected the lines of the Cold War bipolar split, as students demonstrated against traditional, conservative politics, which they perceived as responsible for the world's ills.

Communications, including television, radio and news services, allowed people to be almost immediately aware of events everywhere. Young people in Latin America and the Caribbean saw the demonstrations in the US South, Martin Luther King's assassination, Vietnam War coverage, student demonstrations in Paris and New York, and peace marches and riots all over the world. They identified with some of the issues dealing with social justice, freedom and having a voice in their own national government.

Youths demonstrated against national conditions that they perceived to be unfair or corrupt. Through the media, students all over the world, as well as in Latin America and the Caribbean, observed and sympathized with students at Columbia University in New York in April 1968. In France in May 1968, when students protested against what they considered old-fashioned rules at two Paris universities, they were brutally dispersed by the police. The demonstrations turned into three weeks of riots, as hundreds of thousands of students and most of France's labour unions joined in a sympathy strike and countered violence with violence. Young people in the Americas sympathized with New York and Parisian students and took a hard look at conditions in their own universities and countries.

Tlatelolco massacre

In August 1968, Mexican students at the Universidad Autónoma de Mexico, UNAM (Mexico National Autonomous University), held a demonstration in downtown Mexico City, on the eve of Mexico's hosting of the Olympics. Thousands of students, carrying banners from the various departments, such as law, medicine, humanities, and others, gathered in the Tlatelolco plaza to protest against the corruption of the single-party state of the PRI. They had been holding strikes and demonstrations since 1966, but this time they were joined by workers, high school students, neighbours and common citizens. They demanded: the right to strike and not be disbanded by the military; an end to the holding of political prisoners by the government; and the dismissal of the

Thinking and communication skills

In class watch the documentary *Massacre at Tlatelolco* by Robert Latorre, Alan Tomlinson-De Onis Productions; Discovery Channel. This was originally produced in the US and Mexico as a television programme and was broadcast in 2010 in Spanish with English subtitles. Discuss the methods used by both student demonstrators and the government forces that led to the massacre.

Class discussion

To what extent can we say that youths act as an agent of change in society?

chief of police. The government continued to take a hard line, sending thousands of troops to seize university campuses, jailing demonstrators and refusing to get drawn into any discussion. The showdown occurred 2 October 1968 at the demonstration held at Tlatelolco Square in Mexico City. The government, embarrassed by the attention of the world with the upcoming Olympics, dealt with the students severely. Police, army units and tanks surrounded the square. The troops opened fire with automatic weapons and thousands were wounded. Snipers on buildings surrounded the square and killed at least a hundred students, although the exact number is unknown: the government admitted to fewer than 50 deaths; most believe there were up to 400.

University students all over the Americas were affected by this display of violence, and the continuing harsh treatment of student demonstrators, including the Kent State shootings in Ohio, US, by the National Guard. Some disgruntled youths chose to go underground and follow the teachings of Che Guevara, the Argentine revolutionary who had joined Fidel Castro in the Cuban Revolution in 1959. They joined guerrilla movements that were later to surface in Bolivia, Guatemala, Nicaragua, Colombia, Venezuela, Peru, Mexico and Argentina. Some formed urban underground movements like the Black Panthers in the US, the FMLN in El Salvador, the MIR in Chile, the MR-80 in Brazil and many others. These groups believed in responding to government violence with violence. In the 1980s some groups led by youths would change their countries forever, like the Sandinistas in Nicaragua. Others would remain local, like the Zapatistas in Chiapas, Mexico. Later, counterinsurgency escalated the violence, leading to civil war or military takeovers in some countries. Youth protest groups had a profound effect on political events in Latin America and the Caribbean, far beyond the 1960s and 1970s.

Exam-style questions

1 To what extent have indigenous peoples been successful in achieving their goals?

2 Compare and contrast the ways that indigenous peoples have fought for their rights in the Americas.

3 To what extent did post-war civil rights legislation successfully address the nation's race-based issues?

4 "The African-American Freedom Struggle achieved significant success in achieving equal treatment." Evaluate this statement.

5 Analyze the role of leadership in results of two of the following: the Montgomery bus boycott, lunch counter sit-ins, Freedom Rides, Birmingham, Freedom Summer and the Mississippi Freedom Democratic Party.

6 Compare and contrast the methods of the SCLC, SNCC, Black Muslims and Black Panthers.

7 Compare and contrast the evolution of militancy in the civil rights movements of American Indians, African Americans and Hispanic Americans.

8 In what ways and with what effects has immigration been a critical civil rights issue in the Americas? How have immigration legislation and government actions been both a progressive and reactionary response to the growth of the Hispanic American communities?

9 To what extent were young people in the Americas affected by the counterculture movement?

10 Compare and contrast the methods used by young protesters.

11 Evaluate the success of one youth-led movement.

12 Did societal change in the Americas occur more due to government actions or the independent work of individuals? Discuss.

Writing effective conclusions

Question

"The rise of radical African-American activism (1965–8) damaged the efforts of Dr Martin Luther King to achieve racial equality in the United States." To what extent do you agree with this statement?

Analysis

Perhaps the least practised and least appreciated part of a history essay is the conclusion. However, ending your essay with a concise, well-written concluding paragraph will make your response to the question more effective and help the examiner appreciate your historical argument.

For the two highest Paper 3 mark bands, there is a requirement for a conclusion:

For mark bands 10–12 you need to show that your response "argues to a consistent conclusion".

For mark bands 13–15 you need to show that your response "argues to a reasoned conclusion".

Consequently, to achieve high marks, you should produce a well-constructed conclusion to each response. Your conclusion should a) be consistent with your essay and b) logically synthesize your argument. A well-written conclusion offers one additional feature: it points out the significance of your response. After the examiner reads your conclusion, she will know your reasons and your strongest evidence for your response.

Writing an effective conclusion will help your essay earn the marks it deserves. By preparing and organizing your response, and then reviewing the prompt and what you have written, you will be able to write a complete conclusion that effectively unites your response and this will have an impact on the mark you achieve.

Concluding your essay step by step

Constructing your effective conclusion should not be a difficult task. Before writing it, reread the exam question to remind yourself of exactly what the question is asking and what the examiner will be looking for. Consider the command term used (see the list of these and what they mean in Topic 10 on page 00). Then read your thesis paragraph to remind yourself of your response, and if you have time, scan your body paragraphs to remind yourself of your strongest evidence and key arguments. Then do the following:

1   Write the first sentence as a direct response to the question.

2   Select the two to four most critical pieces of argument and evidence to add as additional sentences to support your stated conclusion. Construct your sentences specifically to support your initial sentence.

3 Once you have added the sentences, reread your conclusion to ensure that it is consistent (i.e. there are no arguments or evidence that conflict).

4 Now write a final sentence that indicates the significance of your response to the prompt.

5 Lastly, reread your conclusion to ensure that it is cohesive and responds to the question without deviation.

Now look at a sample student conclusion in response to the above question:

Dr Martin Luther King did not achieve his goals of racial equality in the United Sates, but, as he said, he had "been to the mountain top". He ran into obstacles, including the government of the United States and opposition from segregationist groups. Additionally, racial inequality had been in the United States for centuries and it would take longer to reverse all the racist institutions and practices. Those are the main reasons why racial equality was not achieved in his lifetime.

This conclusion begins by addressing part of the question, but immediately loses focus with King's "mountain top" phrase, which is not relevant to the question. The candidate has failed to address the issue of radical African-American activism and its effects. Thus, assuming there was a discussion of this issue in the main body of the essay itself, the conclusion is not consistent or appropriate. The candidate has attempted to write a reasoned conclusion with the last sentence but brings in material not asked for ("racial inequality…for centuries") and makes a knowledge claim regarding how long change takes, but without support. Consequently, it is not a "reasoned conclusion." This conclusion reveals a candidate who does not stay focused on the requirements of the question.

What if I've used different perspectives within my essay?

Since the higher mark bands require an "evaluation of different perspectives", you may have included historical perspectives in your body paragraphs. It is important that your conclusion does not confirm an alternative perspective and that the evidence and arguments you have used support your thesis and your conclusion. Introducing another perspective into your concluding paragraph will add confusion and weaken your paper.

If I forgot an important point, can I include it in the conclusion?

You should not include any element not previously discussed in your conclusion. Introducing new material at this point will violate two points in the mark bands:

- Your conclusion will not be consistent with the rest of the essay.

- Your conclusion will not be a reasoned summary of the essay.

Instead, find the body paragraph where your point belongs, write the sentence(s) on a separate page in your exam booklet and indicate next to the body paragraph that there is an addition.

Further reading

Chapter 1

Albert, Bill and Henderson, Paul. 1988. *South America and the First World War: The Impact of the War on Brazil, Argentina, Peru and Chile*. Cambridge: Cambridge University Press.

Carnegie, Andrew. 1901 'Distant Possessions: The Parting of the Ways.' *The Gospel of Wealth*. New York: The Century Co

Finlay, JL and DN Sprague, 1984. *The Structure of Canadian History*. Scarborough: Prentice Hall.

Kennedy, Paul. 1988. *Rise and Fall of the Great Powers: Economic and Military Conflict from 1500 to 2000*. London: Fontana Press.

Mitchell, Nancy. 1999. *The Danger of Dreams: German and American Imperialism in Latin America*. University of North Carolina Press.

Morris, Edmund. "'A matter of extreme urgency': Theodore Roosevelt, Wilhelm II, and the Venezuela Crisis of 1902." *Naval War College Review*. Spring 2002.

Ramsay Tompkins, Stuart. 1989. *A Canadian's Road to Russia: Letters from the Great War Decade*. Doris H Pieroth (ed.) Edmonton: University of Alberta Press.

Rusling, General James. 'Interview with President William McKinley.' *The Christian Advocate*. 22 January 1903. P. 17. Reprinted in Schirmer, Daniel and Rosskamm Shalom, Stephen. (eds.) 1987. *The Philippines Reader*. Boston: South End Press.

Trueman, John et al. 1979. *Modern Perspectives*. 2nd edn. Toronto: McGraw, Hill, Ryerson.

Online sites

Beveridge, Albert J. 'The March of the Flag.' 1898. *History Tools.org: Resources for the Study of American History*. http://www.historytools.org/sources/beveridge.html.

Henry Cabot Lodge on the League of Nations. 12 August 1919. http://www.firstworldwar.com/source/lodge_leagueofnations.htm.

President Woodrow Wilson's Address in Favour of the League of Nations. 25 September 1919. http://www.firstworldwar.com/source/wilsonspeech_league.htm

Chapter 2

Beezley, William H and Maclachlan, Colin M. 2009. *Mexicans in Revolution 1910–1946*. University of Nebraska Press, USA.

Buchenau, Jurgen. 2007. *Plutarco Elias Calles and the Mexican Revolution*. Rowman & Littlefield Publishers, Inc., USA.

Buchenau, Jurgen. 2011. *The Last Caudillo: Álvaro Obregón and the Mexican Revolution*. Blackwell Publishing, UK.

Drinot, Paul and Knight, Alan (eds.). 2014. *The Great Depression in Latin America*. Duke University Press, USA.

Camin, Hector Aguilar and Meyer, Lorenzo. Translated by Fierro, Luis Alberto. 1994. *In the Shadow of the Mexican Revolution*. University of Texas Press, USA.

Eisenhower, John D. 1993. *Intervention: the United States and the Mexican Revolution, 1913–1917*. W.W. Norton & Company, USA.

Garner, Paul. 2001. *Porfirio Díaz, Profiles in Power*. Pearson Education Limited, UK.

Gonzales, Michael J. 2002. *The Mexican Revolution 1910–1940*. University of New Mexico Press, USA.

Hall, Linda B. 1981. *Álvaro Obregón Power and Revolution in Mexico, 1911–1920*. Texas A&M University Press, USA.

Katz, Friedrich (ed.). 1988. *Riot, rebellion, and revolution – rural social conflict in Mexico*. Princeton University Press, USA.

Kiddle, Amelia M and Munoz, Maria LO (eds.). 2010. *Populism in 20th Century Mexico – the presidencies of Lazaro Cárdenas and Luis Echeverria*. The University of Arizona Press, USA.

Knight, Alan. 1986. "Counter-revolution and reconstruction", *The Mexican Revolution*, volume 2. Cambridge University Press, USA.

Knight, Alan. 1986. "Porfirians, Liberals and Peasants", *The Mexican Revolution*, volume 1. Cambridge University Press, USA.

McLynn, Frank. 2000. *Villa and Zapata – A History of the Mexican Revolution*. Basic Books Publishing, UK.

Poniatowska, Elena. 1999. *Women of the Mexican Revolution*. Cinco Puntos Press, USA.

Schuler, Friedrich E. 1998. *Mexico between Hitler and Roosevelt – Mexican foreign relations in the age of Lazaro Cárdenas 1934–1940*. University of New Mexico Press, USA.

Vaughan, Mary Kay and Lewis, Stephen E. 2006. *The Eagle and the Virgin Nation and Cultural Revolution in Mexico, 1920–1940*. Duke University Press, USA.

Womack, John. 1986. *Zapata and the Mexican Revolution*. Random House, USA.

Online sites

Trailer for the film *The Storm that Swept Mexico*, and videos related to the revolution. www.pbs.org/itvs/storm-that-swept-mexico/the-revolution/

Chapter 3

Egan, T. 2006. *The Worst Hard Time*. Mariner Books. New York, USA.

Freidel F and Brinkley, A. 1982. *America in the Twentieth Century*. (5th edition). McGraw Hill, Inc. New York, USA.

Galbraith, JK. 1954 (reprint 2009). *The Great Crash 1929*. Mariner Books. New York, USA.

Leuchtenburg, WE. 1963 (reprint 2009). *Franklin D Roosevelt and the New Deal: 1932–1940*. Harper Perennial. New York, USA.

Levine, R. 1998. *Father of the Poor? Vargas and his Era*. Cambridge University Press. Cambridge, UK.

Skidmore, TE. 1967. *Politics in Brazil 1930–1964: An Experiment in Democracy*. Oxford University Press. Oxford, UK.

Wandersee Bolin, WD. 'The economics of middle-income family life: working women during the Great Depression.' *The Journal of American History*, volume 65, number 1. June 1978. Pp. 60–74.

Online sites

America in the 1930s. http://xroads.virginia.edu/~1930s/front.html

Herbert Hoover presidential library. http://www.hoover.archives.gov/

New Deal Cultural Programs, Experiments in Cultural Democracy. http://www.wwcd.org/policy/US/newdeal.html

New Deal Network. http://newdeal.feri.org

Franklin Delano Roosevelt presidential library. www.fdrlibrary.marist.edu

Chapter 4

Commission on Wartime Relocation and Internment of Civilians. 1981. *Personal Justice Denied*. Page 18. Government Printing Office. Washington, DC, USA.

Donald, H. 2008. *We were not the enemy: remembering the Latin American civilian internment program of World War II*. iUniverse Inc. New York, USA.

Leonard, T., and Brazel, J., eds. *Latin America during World War II*. 2007. Rowmand and Littlefield Publishers. Lanham, Maryland, USA.

Morton, D. 1999. *A military history of Canada from Champlain to Kosovo*. McClelland and Stewart. Toronto, Canada.

Ogelsby, J. 1976. *Gringos from the Far North: Essays in the history of Canadian-Latin American relations 1866–1968*. Macmillan. Toronto, Canada.

Prange, G., Goldstein, D. and Dillon K. 1981. *At Dawn We Slept: the untold story of Pearl Harbor*. Penguin Publisher. New York, USA.

Reeves, R. 2015. *Infamy: the shocking story of the Japanese American internment in World War II*. Henry Holt and Company. New York, USA.

Rock, D. 1994. *Latin America in the 1940s: war and postwar transitions*. University of California Press. Berkely, California, USA.

Russell, J. 2015. *The Train to Crystal City: FDR's secret prisoner exchange program and America's only family internment camp during World War II*. Scribner. New York, USA.

Sadlier, D. 2012. *Americans All: Good Neighbor cultural diplomacy in World War II*. University of Texas Press. Austin, Texas, USA.

Chapter 5

Baer, W. 1972. 'Import Substitution and Industrialization in Latin America: experiences and interpretations'. *Latin American Research Review*. Vol 7, number 1. Spring issue. Pp 95–122. Published by The Latin American Studies Association: http://www.jstor.org/stable/2502457. Accessed 19 June 2013.

Berryman, P. 1987. *Liberation Theology Essential Facts about the Revolutionary Religious Movement in Latin America and Beyond*. Temple University Press. Philadelphia, PA, USA.

Blum, W. 2008. *Killing Hope: U.S. Military and C.I.A. Interventions Since World War II*. Common Courage Press. Monroe, ME, USA.

Boff, L and Boff, C. 1987. *Introducing Liberation Theology*. Orbis Books. Maryknoll, NY, USA.

Cerna, L and Ignoff, MJ. 2014. *La Verdad: A witness to the Salvadoran martyrs*. Orbis Books. Maryknoll, NY, USA.

Chomsky, A. 2003. *The Cuba Reader*. Duke University Press. Durham, NC, USA.

DeFronzo, J. 2011. *Revolutions and Revolutionary Movements*. Westview Press. Boulder, CO, USA.

Groppo, A, et al. 2013. *The Two Princes. Juan D. Perón and Getulio Vargas. A comparative study of Latin America populism*. Poliedros – Serie Ernesto Laclau (Kindle edition).

Gutiérrez, Gustavo. *A Theology of Liberation: History, Politics, and Salvation*. Orbis Books. Maryknoll, NY, USA.

Halperín-Donghi, T. 1997. 'The Peronist revolution and its ambiguous legacy'. Paper given at the University of London Institute of Latin American Studies. http://sas-space.sas.ac.uk/4564/1/B73_-_The_Peronist_Revolutionand_Its_Ambiguous_Legacy.pdf. Accessed 7 August 2014.

LaFeber, W. 1993. *Inevitable Revolutions: The United States in Central America*. WW Norton & Company. New York, USA.

Milanesio, N. 2006. 'The guardian angels of the domestic economy: housewives' responsible consumption in Peronist Argentina.' *Journal of Women's History*. Vol 18, number 3. Fall issue. Pp 91–117.

Pérez-Stable, M. 1998. *The Cuban Revolution: Origins, Course, and Legacy*. 2nd edition. Oxford University Press. Oxford, UK.

Rogoziński, J. 1994. *A Brief History of the Caribbean: From the Arawak and the Carib to the present*. Plume (Penguin Group). New York, USA.

Rose, RS. 2000. *One of the Forgotten Things: Gétulio Vargas and social control 1930–1954*. Greenwood Press. Westport, CN, USA.

Skidmore, Thomas, et al. 2005. *Modern Latin America*. 6th edition, Oxford University Press. Oxford, UK.

Weitz, R. 1986. 'Insurgency and counterinsurgency in Latin America, 1960–1980'. *Political Science Quarterly*. Vol 101, number 3. Pp 397–413 Published by The Academy of Political Science: http://www.jstor.org/stable/2151622.

Winn, Peter. 1992. *Americas: The changing face of Latin America and the Caribbean*. Pantheon Books. New York, USA.

Wood, E. 2003. *Insurgent Collective Action and Civil War in El Salvador* (Cambridge Studies in Comparative Politics).Cambridge University Press. Cambridge, UK.

Chapter 6

Abernathy, M. Glenn, ed. 1984. *The Carter Years: The President and Policy Making*. St. Martin's Press, USA.

Abramson, Jill. October 2013. Kennedy, The Elusive President. *New York Times*.

Ambrose, Stephen. 1989. *Nixon: The Triumph of a Politician 1962–1972*. Simon and Schuster, New York, USA.

Bailyn, Bernard, et al. 1985. *The Great Republic: A History of the American People*. D.C. Heath and Company, Toronto.

Brinkley, Alan and Dyer, Davis, eds. 2004. *The American Presidency*. Houghton Mifflin Company, New York, USA.

Caro, Robert. 2012. *The Passage of Power: The Years of Lyndon Johnson, Vol. IV*. Vintage Books, New York, USA.

Carter, James Earl. 1975. *Why Not the Best?* Broadman Press, Nashville, USA.

Carter, Jimmy. 2010. *White House Diary*. Farrar, Straus, and Giroux, New York, USA.

Cayton, Andrew, Perry, Elisabeth Israels and Winkler, Allan M. 1995. *America: Pathways to the Present*. Needham, Mass: Prentice Hall.

Dallek, Robert. 2003. *An Unfinished Life: John F. Kennedy, 1917–1963*. Little, Brown and Company, New York, USA.

Dallek, Robert. 2003. *An Unfinished Life: John F Kennedy 1917–63*. Back Bay Books, New York, USA.

English, John. 2009. *Just Watch Me: The Life of Pierre Elliot Trudeau, Volume 2: 1968–2000*. Vintage Canada, Toronto, Canada.

Garrison, Lora D. 2006. *Bracing for Armageddon: Why Civil Defense Never Works*. Oxford University Press, New York, USA.

Greene, John Robert. 1995. *The Presidency of Gerald R Ford*. University Press of Kansas Lawrence, Kansas, USA.

Harrington, Michael. 1962. *The Other America*. Touchstone, New York, USA.

Isinger, Russell and Donald C. Story. 1998. *The Plane Truth: The Avro Canada CF-105 Arrow Program*. In *The Diefenbaker Legacy: Canadian Politics, Law, and Society since 1957*, edited by Donald C Story and R Bruce Sheppard. Canadian Plains Research Center, Regina, Canada.

Johnson, Lyndon B. 1964. *State of the Union Address*. Washington, DC, USA.

McCullough, David. 1993. *Truman*. Simon & Schuster, New York, USA.

Nadar, Ralph. 1965. *Unsafe at Any Speed: The Designed-in Dangers of the American Automobile*. Grossman Publishers, New York, USA.

Newton, Jim. 2011. *Eisenhower: the White House Years*. Random House of Canada, Toronto, Canada

Nixon, Richard. 2013. *RN: The Memoirs of Richard Nixon*. Simon & Schuster, New York, USA.

Nixon, Richard. 1962. *Six Crises*. Doubleday, New York, USA.

Osnos, Peter. April 2014. How Pop Culture Is Re-evaluating Lyndon B. Johnson's Legacy. *The Atlantic*.

Romanow, Roy, Whyte, John and Leeson, Howard. 2007. *Canada . . . Notwithstanding: The Making of the Constitution, 1976-1982, 25th Anniversary Edition*. Carswell, Toronto, Canada.

Saywell, John. 1971. *Quebec 70 A Documentary Narrative*. University of Toronto Press, Toronto, Canada.

Smith, Denis. 1995. *Rogue Tory: The life and Legend of John G. Diefenbaker*. McClelland and Stewart, Toronto, Canada.

Tetley, William. 2010. *The October Crisis, 1970: An Insider's View*. McGill Queen's Press, Kingston, Canada.

Weil, Martin and Brown, Emma. 2010. Ted Sorensen, JFK's speechwriter and defender, dies at 82. *The Washington Post*.

Whitman, Alden. 1972. Truman obituary. *New York Times*.

Weil, Martin and Brown, Emma. 2010. Ted Sorensen, JFK's speechwriter and defender, dies at 82. *The Washington Post*.

Online site

Bélanger, Claude. 1999. *Documents on the October Crisis*. Marianopolis College, Quebec, Canada. http://faculty.marianopolis.edu/c.Belanger/quebechistory/docs/october/flqreact.htm

Chapter 7

Bercuson, D. 1999. *Blood in the Hills: The Canadian army in the Korean War*. University of Toronto Press. Toronto, Canada.

Brands, H. 2010. *Latin America's Cold War*. Harvard University Press. Cambridge, MA, USA.

Gaddis, J. 2005. *Cold War: A New History*, page 50. Penguin. London, UK.

Gaddis, JL. 2005. *The Cold War: A New History*. Penguin Books. New York, USA.

Grandin, G. 2004. *The Last Colonial Massacre: Latin America in the Cold War*. University of Chicago Press. Chicago, IL, USA.

Morton, DA. 1999. *Military History of Canada*. 4th edition. McClelland and Stewart, Inc. Toronto, Canada.

Rabe, SG. 2012. *The Killing Zone: the United States wages Cold War in Latin America*. Oxford University Press. Oxford, UK.

Reid, M. 2009. *Forgotten Continent: The battle for Latin America's soul*. Yale University Press. New Haven, CT, USA.

Schoultz, L. 1998. *Beneath the United States: A history of US policy toward Latin America*. Harvard University Press. Cambridge, MA, USA.

Smith, PH. 1996. *Talons of the Eagle: Dynamics of US-Latin American relations*. Oxford University Press. Oxford, UK.

Whitaker, R and Hewitt, S. 2003. *Canada and the Cold War*. James Lorimer and Company. Toronto, Canada.

Winn, P. 2006. *Americas: The Changing face of Latin America and the Caribbean*. 3rd edition. University of California Press. Berkley, CA, USA.

Wright, TC. 2001. *Latin America in the Era of the Cuban Revolution*. Praeger Publishers. Westport, CT, USA.

Chapter 8

Alvarez, Sonia, Friedman, Elisabeth, Beckman, Ericka, Blackwell, Maylei, Chinchilla, Norma Stoltz, Lebon, Nathalie, Navarro, Marysa and Tobar, Marcela. "Encountering Latin American and Caribbean Feminisms." *Signs: Journal of Women in Culture and Society*, Vol. 28 (2), Pp 537–579.

Basu, Amrita, editor. 1995. *The Challenge of Local Feminisms, Women's Movements in Global Perspectives*. Boulder, San Francisco, Oxford. Westview Press.

Bourque, Susan C. "Gender and the State Perspectives from Latin America," in *Women, the State and Development*, Sue Ellen Charlton, Jana Everett, Kathleen Staudt, editors. 1989. NY, USA. State University of New York Press.

Branch, Taylor. 2013. *The King Years: Historic Moments in the Civil Rights Movement*. New York, NY, USA. Simon & Schuster.

Cardinal, Tantoo, Highway, Tomson and King, Thomas. 2005. *Our Story: Aboriginal Voices on Canada's Past*. Toronto, Canada. Random House Canada.

Cohen, Marjorie Griffin and Pierson, Ruth Roachs. 1995. *Canadian Women's Issues: Volume II: Bold Visions*. Toronto, Canada. James Lorimer & Company.

Goyette, Linda. 2003. *Disinherited Generations: Our Struggle to Reclaim Treaty Rights for First Nations Women and Their Descendants*. Edmonton: University of Alberta Press.

Hallowell, Gerald ed. 2006. *The Oxford Companion to Canadian History*. Toronto, Canada. Oxford University Press.

Lawson, Steven F, Payne, Charles, James and Patterson, T. 2006. *Debating the Civil Rights Movement, 1945–1968 (Debating Twentieth-Century America)*. Lanham. Rowman & Littlefield Publishers.

Lee, Jennifer. *Feminist: Stories From Women's Liberation*. Trailer from YouTube.

Morton, Desmond. 2006. *A Short History of Canada (6th Edition)*. Toronto, Canada. McClelland & Stewart.

Navarro, Marysa, and Sánchez Korrol, Virginia. 1999. *Women in Latin America and the Caribbean*. Indiana University Press.

Packard, Jerrold M. 2001. *American Nightmare: The History of Jim Crow*. New York, NY, USA. St. Martin's Press.

Risen, Clay. 2014. *The Bill of the Century: The Epic Battle for the Civil Rights Act*. New York, NY, USA. Bloomsbury Press.

Rosales, F. Arturo. 1997. *Chicano!: The History of the Mexican American Civil Rights Movement*. Houston, TX, USA. Arte Público Press (University of Houston).

Weisbrot, Robert. 1990. *Freedom Bound: A History of America's Civil Rights Movement*. New York, NY, USA. Penguin Books.

Index